Authorized Self-Study Guide
Building Scalable Cisco Internetworks (BSCI)
Third Edition

Diane Teare
Catherine Paquet

Cisco Press

800 East 96th Street
Indianapolis, Indiana 46240 USA

Authorized Self-Study Guide: Building Scalable Cisco Internetworks (BSCI), Third Edition

Diane Teare

Catherine Paquet

Copyright © 2007 Cisco Systems, Inc.

Published by:
Cisco Press
800 East 96th Street
Indianapolis, IN 46240 USA

Printed in the United States of America 1 2 3 4 5 6 7 8 9 0

First Printing December 2006

Library of Congress Number: 2004114556

ISBN: 1-58705-223-7

Warning and Disclaimer

This book is designed to provide information about building scalable Cisco internetworks. Every effort has been made to make this book as complete and as accurate as possible, but no warranty or fitness is implied.

The information is provided on an "as is" basis. The authors, Cisco Press, and Cisco Systems, Inc. shall have neither liability nor responsibility to any person or entity with respect to any loss or damages arising from the information contained in this book or from the use of the discs or programs that may accompany it.

The opinions expressed in this book belong to the author and are not necessarily those of Cisco Systems, Inc.

Corporate and Government Sales

Cisco Press offers excellent discounts on this book when ordered in quantity for bulk purchases or special sales.

For more information, please contact: **U.S. Corporate and Government Sales** 1-800-382-3419 corpsales@pearsontechgroup.com

For sales outside of the U.S. please contact: **International Sales** 1-317-581-3793 international@pearsontechgroup.com

Trademark Acknowledgments

All terms mentioned in this book that are known to be trademarks or service marks have been appropriately capitalized. Cisco Press or Cisco Systems, Inc. cannot attest to the accuracy of this information. Use of a term in this book should not be regarded as affecting the validity of any trademark or service mark.

Feedback Information

At Cisco Press, our goal is to create in-depth technical books of the highest quality and value. Each book is crafted with care and precision, undergoing rigorous development that involves the unique expertise of members from the professional technical community.

Readers' feedback is a natural continuation of this process. If you have any comments regarding how we could improve the quality of this book, or otherwise alter it to better suit your needs, you can contact us through e-mail at feedback@ciscopress.com. Please make sure to include the book title and ISBN in your message.

We greatly appreciate your assistance.

Publisher: Paul Boger

Cisco Representative: Anthony Wolfenden

Cisco Press Program Manager: Jeff Brady

Executive Editor: Mary Beth Ray

Managing Editor: Patrick Kanouse

Development Editor: Andrew Cupp

Project Editor: Seth Kerney

Copy Editor: Keith Cline

Technical Editors: Mark Gallo, Joe Harris

Publishing Coordinator: Vanessa Evans

Book and Cover Designer: Louisa Adair

Composition: ICC Macmillan Inc.

Indexer: Tim Wright

Americas Headquarters
Cisco Systems, Inc.
170 West Tasman Drive
San Jose, CA 95134-1706
USA
www.cisco.com
Tel: 408 526-4000
800 553-NETS (6387)
Fax: 408 527-0883

Asia Pacific Headquarters
Cisco Systems, Inc.
168 Robinson Road
#28-01 Capital Tower
Singapore 068912
www.cisco.com
Tel: +65 6317 7777
Fax: +65 6317 7799

Europe Headquarters
Cisco Systems International BV
Haarlerbergpark
Haarlerbergweg 13-19
1101 CH Amsterdam
The Netherlands
www-europe.cisco.com
Tel: +31 0 800 020 0791
Fax: +31 0 20 357 1100

Cisco has more than 200 offices worldwide. Addresses, phone numbers, and fax numbers are listed on the Cisco Website at **www.cisco.com/go/offices.**

©2006 Cisco Systems, Inc. All rights reserved. CCVP, the Cisco logo, and the Cisco Square Bridge logo are trademarks of Cisco Systems, Inc.; Changing the Way We Work, Live, Play, and Learn is a service mark of Cisco Systems, Inc.; and Access Registrar, Aironet, BPX, Catalyst, CCDA, CCDP, CCIE, CCIP, CCNA, CCNP, CCSP, Cisco, the Cisco Certified Internetwork Expert logo, Cisco IOS, Cisco Press, Cisco Systems, Cisco Systems Capital, the Cisco Systems logo, Cisco Unity, Enterprise/Solver, EtherChannel, EtherFast, EtherSwitch, Fast Step, Follow Me Browsing, FormShare, GigaDrive, GigaStack, HomeLink, Internet Quotient, IOS, IP/TV, iQ Expertise, the iQ logo, iQ Net Readiness Scorecard, iQuick Study, LightStream, Linksys, MeetingPlace, MGX, Networking Academy, Network Registrar, Packet, PIX, ProConnect, RateMUX, ScriptShare, SlideCast, SMARTnet, StackWise, The Fastest Way to Increase Your Internet Quotient, and TransPath are registered trademarks of Cisco Systems, Inc. and/or its affiliates in the United States and certain other countries.

All other trademarks mentioned in this document or Website are the property of their respective owners. The use of the word partner does not imply a partnership relationship between Cisco and any other company. (0609R)

About the Authors

Diane Teare is a professional in the networking, training, and e-learning fields. She has more than 20 years of experience in designing, implementing, and troubleshooting network hardware and software and has also been involved in teaching, course design, and project management. She has extensive knowledge of network design and routing technologies and is an instructor with one of the largest authorized Cisco Learning Partners. She was recently the director of e-learning for the same company, where she was responsible for planning and supporting all the company's e-learning offerings in Canada, including Cisco courses. Diane was part of the team that developed the latest version of the BSCI course. She has a bachelor's degree in applied science in electrical engineering (BASc) and a master's degree in applied science in management science (MASc). She is a certified Cisco Systems instructor and currently holds her CCNP and CCDP certifications. She coauthored the Cisco Press titles *Campus Network Design Fundamentals* and the first two editions of this book; and edited *CCDA Self-Study: Designing for Cisco Internetwork Solutions (DESGN)* and *Designing Cisco Networks*.

Catherine Paquet has in-depth knowledge of security systems, remote access, and routing technology. She is a CCSP, a CCNP, and a CCSI with one of the largest Cisco Learning Partners. She started her internetworking career as a LAN manager, moved to MAN manager, and eventually became the nationwide WAN manager with a federal agency. Prior to starting Netrisec Inc., a network security consultancy, Catherine was the director of technical resources for a Cisco Learning Partner. Catherine currently works on network design and implementation projects and lectures on topics related to security frameworks, regulations, and return on security investments. In 2002 and 2003, she volunteered with the U.N. mission in Kabul, Afghanistan, to train Afghan public servants in the area of networking. Catherine has a master's degree in business administration with a major in management information systems (MBA [MIS]). She coauthored the Cisco Press titles *Campus Network Design Fundamentals*, *The Business Case for Network Security: Advocacy, Governance, and ROI*, and the first two editions of this book, and edited *Building Cisco Remote Access Networks*.

About the Technical Reviewers

Mark Gallo is a Systems Engineering Manager at Cisco within the Channels organization. He has led several engineering groups responsible for positioning and delivering Cisco end-to-end systems, and for designing and implementing enterprise LANs and international IP networks. He has a bachelor of science degree in electrical engineering from the University of Pittsburgh and holds Cisco CCNP and CCDP certifications. Mark resides in northern Virginia with his wife, Betsy, and son, Paul.

Joe Harris, CCIE No. 6200, has both CCIE Security and Routing and Switching certifications and is a Commercial Systems Engineer with Cisco specializing in advanced routing and security. He has more than 12 years of experience in the field of designing and implementing Cisco network solutions. Joe holds a bachelor of science degree from Louisiana Tech University and resides with his wife and two children in Frisco, Texas.

Dedications

If a man empties his purse into his head, no man can take it away from him. An investment in knowledge always pays the best interest.
—Benjamin Franklin

From Diane:

This book is dedicated to my loving husband, Allan Mertin, who again has encouraged, supported, and "held the fort" during this project; to our charming son, Nicholas, whose inquisitive mind, knowledge, and antics are both entertaining us and making sure that we will be life-long learners; and to my parents, Syd and Beryl, for their continuous caring and support.

From Catherine:

To my parents and sister—Maurice, Florence, and Hélène Paquet—for your continuous support: Thank you. To my children, Laurence and Simon: "Develop a passion for learning. If you do, you will never cease to grow" (Anthony J. D'Angelor). And, finally, to Pierre Rivard, my soul mate, husband, and an eternal learner: Your enthusiasm is contagious. Thanks for sharing it with us.

Acknowledgments

We would like to thank many people for helping us put this book together:

The Cisco Press team: Mary Beth Ray, the executive editor, coordinated the entire team and ensured that everything was lined up for the successful completion of the book. Drew Cupp, the development editor, has once again been invaluable with his eye for detail and speedy responses to our many queries. We also want to thank Seth Kerney, the project editor, and Keith Cline, the copy editor, for their excellent work in steering this book through the editorial process. Finally, we want to thank Brett Bartow, the executive editor on the previous editions to this book (and our other books), for sticking with us all these years!

The Global Knowledge and Cisco Systems team: Many other people were involved in the development of the latest version of the BSCI course, and we want to extend our thanks to them—our apologies if we have forgotten someone! The Global Knowledge team included Ray Dooley and his team—Carol Kavalla, Bill Treneer, and Norma Douthit—Patti Hedgspeth, Kimberly Ferguson, Ammarah Abbasi, Karie Krueger, Joy Rau, Richard Chapin, and Margaret Prince. The Cisco team included Ray Garra, Bob Martinez, Roger Beatty, Cynthia Barnette, Peter Wood, Dennis Keirnan, Brenda Nichols, Glenn Tapley, Drew Blair, Mike Bevan, James Cagney, Kathy Yankton, Ray Viscaina, Andy Esponsa, Eric De Jesus, Christy Faria, Jeremy Creech, Lee Rogers, Adriana Vascan, and Charles Newby. Thanks also to the other members of the development teams of the original BSCN and BSCI courses, including Patrick Lao, Kip Peterson, Keith Serrao, Kevin Calkins, Won Lee, and Imran Quershi.

The technical reviewers: We want to thank the technical reviewers of this book—Mark Gallo and Joe Harris—for their thorough, detailed review and very valuable input.

Our families: Of course, this book would not have been possible without the constant understanding and patience of our families. They have always been there to motivate and inspire us. We thank you all.

Each other: Last, but not least, this book is a product of work by two friends, which made it even more of a pleasure to complete.

This Book Is Safari Enabled

The Safari® Enabled icon on the cover of your favorite technology book means the book is available through Safari Bookshelf. When you buy this book, you get free access to the online edition for 45 days.

Safari Bookshelf is an electronic reference library that lets you easily search thousands of technical books, find code samples, download chapters, and access technical information whenever and wherever you need it.

To gain 45-day Safari Enabled access to this book:

- Go to http://www.ciscopress.com/safarienabled
- Complete the brief registration form
- Enter the coupon code EXKH-6PHI-YW2V-ULJL-ER8V

If you have difficulty registering on Safari Bookshelf or accessing the online edition, please e-mail customer-service@safaribooksonline.com.

Contents at a Glance

x

Contents

Icons Used in This Book

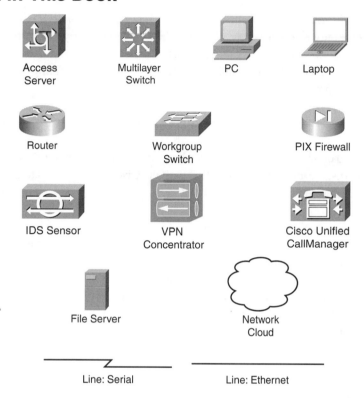

Command Syntax Conventions

The conventions used to present command syntax in this book are the same conventions used in the IOS Command Reference. The Command Reference describes these conventions as follows:

- **Boldface** indicates commands and keywords that are entered literally as shown. In actual configuration examples and output (not general command syntax), boldface indicates commands that are manually input by the user (such as a **show** command).

- *Italics* indicate arguments for which you supply actual values.

- Vertical bars (|) separate alternative, mutually exclusive elements.

- Square brackets [ ] indicate optional elements.

- Braces { } indicate a required choice.

- Braces within brackets [{ }] indicate a required choice within an optional element.

Foreword

Authorized Self-Study Guide: Building Scalable Cisco Internetworks (BSCI), Third Edition, is an excellent self-study resource for the CCNP BSCI exam. Whether you are studying to become CCNP certified or are just seeking to gain a better understanding of switching technology, implementation and operation, planning and design, and troubleshooting, you will benefit from the information presented in this book.

Cisco Press Self-Study Guide titles are designed to help educate, develop, and grow the community of Cisco networking professionals. As an early-stage exam-preparation product, this book presents a detailed and comprehensive introduction to the technologies used to build scalable routed networks. Developed in conjunction with the Cisco certifications team, Cisco Press books are the only self-study books authorized by Cisco Systems.

Most networking professionals use a variety of learning methods to gain necessary skills. Cisco Press Self-Study Guide titles are a prime source of content for some individuals and can also serve as an excellent supplement to other forms of learning. Training classes, whether delivered in a classroom or on the Internet, are a great way to quickly acquire new understanding. Hands-on practice is essential for anyone seeking to build, or hone, new skills. Authorized Cisco training classes, labs, and simulations are available exclusively from Cisco Learning Solutions Partners worldwide. Please visit http://www.cisco.com/go/training to learn more about Cisco Learning Solutions Partners.

I hope and expect that you will find this guide to be an essential part of your exam preparation and a valuable addition to your personal library.

Don Field
Director, Certifications
Cisco System, Inc.
December 2006

Introduction

Internetworks are growing at a fast pace to support more protocols and users and are becoming more complex. As the premier designer and provider of internetworking devices, Cisco Systems is committed to supporting these growing networks.

This book teaches you how to design, configure, maintain, and scale a routed network. It focuses on using Cisco routers connected in LANs and WANs typically found at medium-to-large network sites. After completing this book, you will be able to select and implement the appropriate Cisco IOS services required to build a scalable, routed network.

In this book, you study a broad range of technical details on topics related to routing. Routing protocol principles are examined in detail before the following routing protocols are explored: Enhanced Interior Gateway Routing Protocol (EIGRP), Open Shortest Path First (OSPF), Intermediate System-to-Intermediate System (IS-IS), and Border Gateway Protocol (BGP). Running multiple routing protocols and controlling the information passed between them are examined, and IP multicast and IP version 6 (IPv6) are explored.

Configuration examples and sample verification outputs demonstrate troubleshooting techniques and illustrate critical issues surrounding network operation. Chapter-ending Configuration Exercises and Review Questions illustrate and help solidify the concepts presented in this book.

This book starts you down the path toward attaining your CCNP, CCIP, or CCDP certification, because it provides in-depth information to help you prepare for the BSCI exam.

The commands and configuration examples presented in this book are based on Cisco IOS Release 12.4.

Who Should Read This Book

This book is intended for network architects, network designers, systems engineers, network managers, and network administrators who are responsible for implementing and troubleshooting growing routed networks.

If you are planning to take the BSCI exam toward your CCNP, CCIP, or CCDP certification, this book provides you with in-depth study material. To fully benefit from this book, you should be CCNA certified or should possess the following knowledge:

- A working knowledge of the OSI reference model
- An understanding of internetworking fundamentals, including commonly used networking terms, numbering schemes, topologies, distance vector routing protocol operation, and when to use static and default routes

■ The ability to operate and configure a Cisco router, including displaying and interpreting a router's routing table, configuring static and default routes, enabling a WAN serial connection using High-Level Data Link Control (HDLC) or PPP, configuring Frame Relay permanent virtual circuits (PVC) on interfaces and subinterfaces, configuring IP standard and extended access lists, and verifying router configurations with available tools, such as **show** and **debug** commands

■ Working knowledge of the TCP/IP stack, and configuring IP addresses and the Routing Information Protocol (RIP)

If you lack this knowledge and these skills, you can gain them by completing the Cisco Introduction to Cisco Networking Technologies (INTRO) and Interconnecting Cisco Network Devices (ICND) courses or by reading the related Cisco Press books.

What's New in This Edition

This book is an update to *CCNP Self-Study: Building Scalable Cisco Internetworks (BSCI),* Second Edition (ISBN 1-58705-146-X). This third edition addresses changes to the BSCI course. The following are the major changes between books:

■ Each topic has been rewritten. Any items that were removed from the main portion of the previous edition because of course changes have been put in an appendix or sidebar, as appropriate. The appendixes have been modified and updated to reflect the content of the book.

■ New chapters on network architecture framework and design models, IP multicast, and IPv6 are included.

■ Route authentication is included for EIGRP, OSPF, and BGP.

■ Examples and Configuration Exercises now use Cisco IOS Release 12.4 on Cisco 2811 routers; outputs have been redone using this new release on these routers.

■ The "Advanced IP Addressing" chapter was removed; much of the information from this chapter has been included in Appendix C, "IPv4 Supplement."

Objectives of This Book

When you complete the readings and exercises in this book, you will be able to describe the converged network requirements of various networked applications within the Cisco architectures. You will also be able to describe advanced IP routing principles, including static and dynamic routing characteristics and the concepts of classful and classless routing and address summarization. You will be able to implement and verify EIGRP, OSPF, and Integrated IS-IS for scalable multiarea networks, and BGP for enterprise Internet service provider (ISP) connectivity.

You will also be able to manipulate routing updates and packet flow. You will be able to implement and verify IP multicast forwarding using Protocol Independent Multicast (PIM) and related protocols, and describe how IPv6 functions to satisfy the increasingly complex requirements of hierarchical addressing.

Summary of Contents

The chapters and appendixes in this book are as follows:

- Chapter 1, "Network Architecture Framework and Design Models," introduces converged networks and the variety of traffic within them. Some strategies, frameworks, and models used in the network design process are presented.

- Chapter 2, "Routing Principles," covers the principles of routing, including static and dynamic routing characteristics, classful and classless routing, and the differences between distance vector, link-state, and hybrid routing protocol behavior.

- Chapter 3, "Configuring the Enhanced Interior Gateway Routing Protocol," introduces EIGRP. Topics include EIGRP terminology and concepts, EIGRP configuration, verification, and troubleshooting. EIGRP authentication is also included.

- Chapter 4, "Configuring the Open Shortest Path First Protocol," introduces the OSPF routing protocol. Basic configuration of OSPF, in both single and multiple areas is described. OSPF configuration over specific network types is also explored.

- Chapter 5, "Advanced Open Shortest Path First Protocol Configuration," covers advanced operation, configuration, and verification of the OSPF protocol. The different types of OSPF routers and link-state advertisements (LSAs) are introduced. OSPF route summarization configuration is covered and default routes are introduced. Stub areas, virtual links, and OSPF authentication configuration are explored.

- Chapter 6, "Configuring the Integrated Intermediate System-to-Intermediate System Protocol," provides an overview of the Integrated IS-IS protocol, including its operation and configuration (and basic configuration examples).

- Chapter 7, "Manipulating Routing Updates," discusses different ways to control routing update information. Route redistribution to interconnect networks that use multiple routing protocols is explained. Information between the protocols can be controlled by using distribute lists and route maps and by changing the administrative distance; the chapter discusses the configuration of each of these techniques. The chapter concludes with a discussion of the Dynamic Host Configuration Protocol (DHCP) and how to enable DHCP server functionality on a Cisco IOS device.

- Chapter 8, "Configuring the Border Gateway Protocol," introduces BGP, including terminology and the fundamentals of BGP operation, configuration, and troubleshooting techniques. BGP authentication and the use of route maps for manipulating BGP path attributes are also introduced.

- Chapter 9, "Implementing IP Multicast," provides an introduction to IP multicast, multicast addressing and protocols, and the implementation of IP multicast on Cisco devices.

- Chapter 10, "Implementing IPv6," introduces IPv6 and the IPv6 addressing scheme. Routing protocols that support IPv6 are explored, and the details of OSPF for IPv6 configuration are presented. The chapter also discusses how IPv4 networks can be transitioned to IPv6.

- "Acronyms and Abbreviations" identifies abbreviations, acronyms, and initialisms used in this book and in the internetworking industry.

- Appendix A, "Answers to Review Questions," contains the answers to the review questions that appear at the end of each chapter.

- Appendix B, "Configuration Exercise Equipment Requirements and Backbone Configurations," contains information on the equipment requirements for the Configuration Exercises, along with the initial configuration commands for the backbone routers.

In addition to the material in the printed book, you can also find the following appendixes at ciscopress.com on your My Registered Books page after you register your book (see the next section, "Online Material," for details):

- Appendix C, "IPv4 Supplement," provides job aids and supplementary information that are intended for your use when working with IPv4 addresses. Topics include subnetting job aid, decimal-to-binary conversion chart, IPv4 addressing review, IPv4 access lists, IP address planning, hierarchical addressing using variable-length subnet masks (VLSMs), route summarization, and classless interdomain routing (CIDR).

- Appendix D, "Manipulating Routing Updates Supplement," provides supplementary information about the features and configuration of policy-based routing (PBR).

- Appendix E, "BGP Supplement," provides supplementary information on BGP covering the following topics: BGP route summarization, redistribution with interior gateway protocols (IGPs), policy control and prefix lists, communities, and route reflectors.

- Appendix F, "Summary of BSCI Router Commands," lists some of the Cisco router IOS commands you might find in this book, organized in various categories.

- Appendix G, "Open System Interconnection (OSI) Reference Model," is a brief overview of the OSI seven-layer model.

Online Material

After you register your book on the Cisco Press website, you can find helpful material related to this book.

To register this book, go to http://www.ciscopress.com/bookstore/register.asp and enter the book's ISBN located on the back cover. You'll then be prompted to log in or join ciscopress.com to continue registration.

After you register the book, a link to the supplemental content will be listed on your My Registered Books page. There you can find the supplemental material in Appendixes C through G. You can also download three configuration files for use in the book's Configuration Exercises, as well as a copy of the network diagram used for the Configuration Exercises.

The printed book does contain helpful references to the online appendixes to guide you in making the best use of this supplemental and background material.

Configuration Exercises and Review Questions

Configuration Exercises at the end of the chapters let you practice configuring routers with the commands and topics presented. If you have access to real hardware, you can try these exercises on your routers; refer to Appendix B for a list of recommended equipment and initial configuration commands for the backbone routers. However, even if you do not have access to any routers, you can go through the exercises and keep a log of your own running configurations. Commands used and solutions to the Configuration Exercises are provided within the exercise sections.

At the end of each chapter, you can test your knowledge by answering Review Questions on the subjects covered in that chapter. You can compare your answers to the answers provided in Appendix A to find out how you did and what material you might need to study further.

Author's Notes, Key Points, Sidebars, and Cautions

The notes, sidebars, and cautions found in this book provide extra information on a subject. The key points highlight specific points of interest.

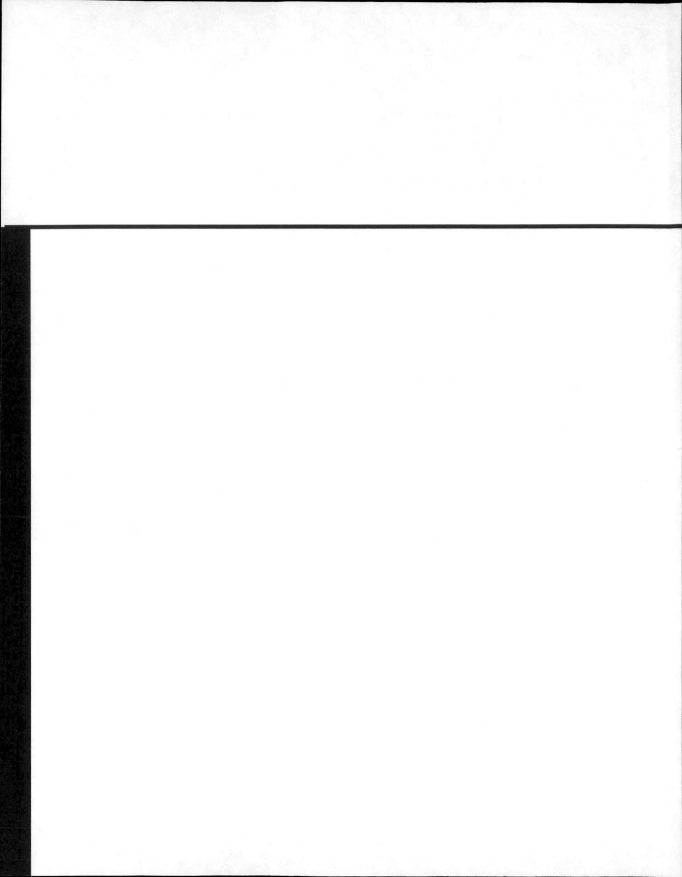

Part I: Network Architecture and Design

This chapter discusses network architecture framework and design models. It covers the following topics:

- Converged Networks

- Cisco Intelligent Information Network

- Cisco Service-Oriented Network Architecture Framework

- Cisco Enterprise Architecture

- Cisco Hierarchical Network Model

- Cisco Enterprise Composite Network Model

- Routing and Routing Protocols Within the Enterprise Composite Network Model

CHAPTER 1

Network Architecture Framework and Design Models

This chapter introduces converged networks and the variety of traffic within them. To accommodate the requirements of such networks, Cisco has introduced the Intelligent Information Network (IIN) strategy along with the Service-Oriented Network Architecture (SONA) framework that guides the evolution of enterprise networks toward an IIN, both of which this chapter describes.

The components of the Cisco enterprise-wide systems architecture are introduced. Two network design models—the traditional hierarchical network model and the Enterprise Composite Network Model are described. The chapter concludes with a discussion of how routing protocols fit within the Enterprise Composite Network Model.

Converged Networks

A converged network is one in which data, voice, and video traffic coexists on a single network. When voice and video are transported across a network, the voice and video are seen by the network as being just like any other application data.

Converged networks contain a variety of different types of traffic, including the following:

- **Voice and video traffic**—Examples include IP telephony, involving applications such as contact centers, and video broadcast and conferencing.

- **Mission-critical traffic**—This data is generated by applications critical to an organization (for example, information generated by a stock exchange application at a finance company, patient records at a hospital, and so forth).

- **Transactional traffic**—This information is generated by applications such as those for e-commerce.

- **Routing protocol traffic**—Data from whichever routing protocols are running in the network, such as the Routing Information Protocol (RIP), Open Shortest Path First Protocol (OSPF), Enhanced Interior Gateway Routing Protocol (EIGRP), Intermediate System-to-Intermediate System Protocol (IS-IS), and Border Gateway Protocol (BGP).

- **Network management traffic**—Including information about the status of the network and its devices.

The requirements on the network differ significantly depending on the mix of traffic types, especially in terms of security and performance.

For example, voice and video performance requirements include low delay and jitter (variation in delay), whereas transactional traffic requires high reliability and security with relatively low bandwidth. Voice applications, such as IP telephony, also require high reliability and availability because user expectations for "dial tone" in an IP network are exactly the same as in the traditional telephone network. Video traffic is frequently carried as IP multicast traffic, requiring multicast features to be enabled on the network. To meet these traffic requirements, converged networks use quality of service (QoS) mechanisms so that, for example, voice and video traffic are given priority over web-based traffic.

Several security strategies, such as device hardening with strict access control and authentication, intrusion protection, intrusion detection, and traffic protection with encryption, can minimize or possibly eliminate network security threats. Security is a key issue in all networks and becomes even more important in wireless networks where access is possible virtually anywhere.

Cisco Intelligent Information Network

To accommodate today's and tomorrow's network requirements, the Cisco vision of the future includes the IIN, a strategy that addresses how the network is integrated with businesses and business priorities. The IIN encompasses the following features:

- **Integration of networked resources and information assets that have been largely unlinked**—The modern converged networks with integrated voice, video, and data require that IT departments (and other departments that were traditionally responsible for other technologies) more closely link the IT infrastructure with the network.

- **Intelligence across multiple products and infrastructure layers**—The intelligence built in to each component of the network is extended network-wide and applies end to end.

- **Active participation of the network in the delivery of services and applications**—With added intelligence, the IIN makes it possible for the network to actively manage, monitor, and optimize service and application delivery across the entire IT environment.

The IIN offers much more than basic connectivity, bandwidth for users, and access to applications—it offers an end-to-end functionality and centralized, unified control that promotes true business transparency and agility.

With the IIN, Cisco is helping organizations to address new IT challenges, such as the deployment of service-oriented architectures, web services, and virtualization (as described in the upcoming "Phase 2" bullet). The IIN technology vision offers an evolutionary approach that consists of three phases in which functionality can be added to the infrastructure as required. The three phases are as follows:

- **Phase 1: Integrated transport**—Everything (data, voice, and video) consolidates onto an IP network for secure network convergence. By integrating data, voice, and video transport into a single, standards-based, modular network, organizations can simplify network management and generate enterprise-wide efficiencies. Network convergence also lays the foundation for a new class of IP-enabled applications, now known as Cisco Unified Communications solutions.

NOTE   *Cisco Unified Communications* is the name, launched in March 2006, for the entire range of what were previously known as *Cisco IP communications* products. These include all call control, conferencing, voicemail and messaging, customer contact, IP phone, video telephony, videoconferencing, rich media clients, and voice application products.

- **Phase 2: Integrated services**—When the network infrastructure is converged, IT resources can be pooled and shared, or *virtualized*, to flexibly address the changing needs of the organization. By extending this virtualization concept to encompass server, storage, and network elements, an organization can transparently use all of its resources more efficiently. Business continuity is also enhanced because in the event of a local systems failure, shared resources across the IIN can provide needed services.

- **Phase 3: Integrated applications**—This phase focuses on making the network *application aware* so that it can optimize application performance and more efficiently deliver networked applications to users. With Application-Oriented Networking (AON) technology, Cisco has entered this third IIN phase. In addition to capabilities such as content caching, load balancing, and application-level security, the Cisco AON makes it possible for the network to simplify the application infrastructure by integrating intelligent application message handling, optimization, and security into the existing network.

NOTE   You can access the IIN home page at http://www.cisco.com/go/iin.

Cisco Service-Oriented Network Architecture Framework

The Cisco SONA is an architectural framework that illustrates how to build integrated systems and guides the evolution of enterprise networks toward an IIN. Using the SONA framework, enterprises can improve flexibility and increase efficiency by optimizing applications, business processes, and resources to enable IT to have a greater impact on business.

The SONA framework leverages the extensive product-line services, proven architectures, and experience of Cisco and its partners to help enterprises achieve their business goals.

The SONA framework, shown in Figure 1-1, shows how integrated systems can allow a dynamic, flexible architecture and provide for operational efficiency through standardization and virtualization. In this framework, the network is the common element that connects and enables all components of the IT infrastructure.

Figure 1-1   *Cisco SONA Framework*

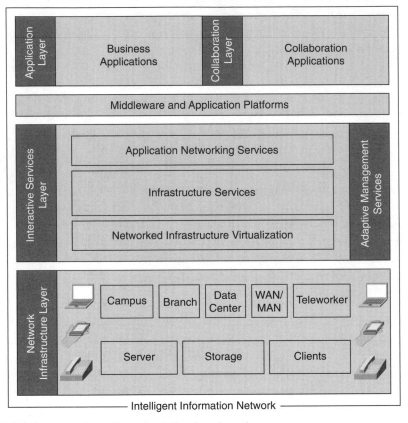

The SONA framework outlines the following three layers:

■ **Networked infrastructure layer**—Where all the IT resources are interconnected across a converged network foundation. The IT resources include servers, storage, and clients. The network infrastructure layer represents how these resources exist in different places in the network, including the campus, branch, data center, wide-area network (WAN), metropolitan-area network (MAN), and with the teleworker. The objective of this layer is to provide connectivity, anywhere and anytime.

■ **Interactive services layer**—Enables efficient allocation of resources to applications and business processes delivered through the networked infrastructure. This layer comprises these services:

— Voice and collaboration services

— Mobility services

— Security and identity services

— Storage services

— Computer services

— Application networking services

— Network infrastructure virtualization

— Services management

— Adaptive management services

■ **Application layer**—This layer includes business applications and collaboration applications. The objective of this layer is to meet business requirements and achieve efficiencies by leveraging the interactive services layer.

NOTE   You can access the SONA home page at http://www.cisco.com/go/sona.

Cisco Enterprise Architecture

Cisco provides an enterprise-wide systems architecture that helps companies to protect, optimize, and grow the infrastructure that supports their business processes. As illustrated in Figure 1-2, the architecture provides for integration of the entire network—campus, data center, branches, teleworkers, and WAN—offering staff secure access to the tools, processes, and services they require.

Figure 1-2   *Cisco Enterprise Architecture*

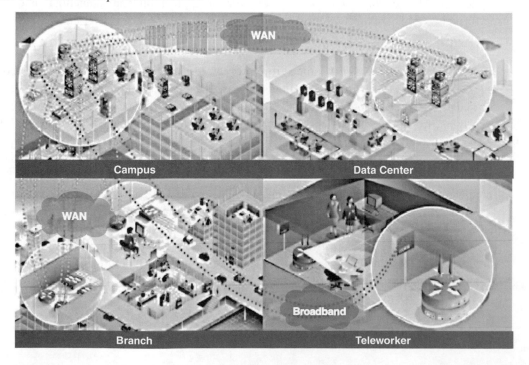

The Cisco Enterprise *Campus* Architecture combines a core infrastructure of intelligent switching and routing with tightly integrated productivity-enhancing technologies, including IP communications, mobility, and advanced security. The architecture provides the enterprise with high availability through a resilient multilayer design, redundant hardware and software features, and automatic procedures for reconfiguring network paths when failures occur. IP multicast capabilities provide optimized bandwidth consumption, and QoS features ensure that real-time traffic (such as voice, video, or critical data) is not dropped or delayed. Integrated security protects against and mitigates the impact of worms, viruses, and other attacks on the network, including at the switch port level. For example, the Cisco enterprise-wide architecture extends support for security standards, such as the Institute for Electrical and Electronic Engineers (IEEE) 802.1x port-based network access control standard and the Extensible Authentication Protocol (EAP). It also provides the flexibility to add IPsec and Multiprotocol Label Switching virtual private networks (MPLS VPNs), identity and access management, and virtual local-area networks (VLANs) to compartmentalize access. These features help improve performance and security while decreasing costs.

The Cisco Enterprise *Data Center* Architecture is a cohesive, adaptive network architecture that supports requirements for consolidation, business continuance, and security while enabling emerging service-oriented architectures, virtualization, and on-demand computing. Staff, suppliers, or customers can be provided with secure access to applications and resources, simplifying and streamlining management and significantly reducing overhead. Redundant data centers provide backup using synchronous and asynchronous data and application replication. The network and devices offer server and application load balancing to maximize performance. This architecture allows the enterprise to scale without major changes to the infrastructure.

The Cisco Enterprise *Branch* Architecture allows enterprises to extend head-office applications and services (such as security, IP communications, and advanced application performance) to thousands of remote locations and users or to a small group of branches. Cisco integrates security, switching, network analysis, caching, and converged voice and video services into a series of integrated services routers (ISRs) in the branch so that the enterprises can deploy new services without buying new routers. This architecture provides secure access to voice, mission-critical data, and video applications—anywhere, anytime. Advanced routing, VPNs, redundant WAN links, application content caching, and local IP telephony call processing features are available with high levels of resilience for all the branch offices. An optimized network leverages the WAN and LAN to reduce traffic and save bandwidth and operational expenses. The enterprise can easily support branch offices with the ability to centrally configure, monitor, and manage devices located at remote sites, including tools, such as AutoQoS, which configures devices to handle congestion and bandwidth issues before they affect network performance.

The Cisco Enterprise *Teleworker* Architecture allows enterprises to securely deliver voice and data services to remote small or home offices over a standard broadband access service, providing a business-resiliency solution for the enterprise and a flexible work environment for employees. Centralized management minimizes the IT support costs. Integrated security and identity-based networking services enable the enterprise to extend campus security policies to the teleworker. Staff can securely log in to the network over an *always-on* VPN and gain access to authorized applications and services from a single cost-effective platform. Productivity can further be enhanced by adding an IP phone, thereby providing cost-effective access to a centralized IP communications system with voice and unified messaging services.

The Cisco Enterprise *WAN* Architecture offers the convergence of voice, video, and data services over a single Cisco Unified Communications network, which enables the enterprise to cost-effectively span large geographic areas. QoS, granular service levels, and comprehensive encryption options help ensure the secure delivery of high-quality corporate voice, video, and data resources to all corporate sites, enabling staff to work productively and efficiently wherever they are located. Security is provided with multiservice VPNs (IPsec and MPLS) over Layer 2 or Layer 3 WANs, hub-and-spoke, or full-mesh topologies.

Cisco Hierarchical Network Model

Traditionally, the three-layer hierarchical model has been used in network design, providing a modular framework that allows design flexibility and facilitates implementation and trouble-shooting. The hierarchical model divides networks or modular blocks within a network into the access, distribution, and core layers, as illustrated in Figure 1-3. The features of the hierarchical layers are as follows:

- **Access layer**—This layer is used to grant users access to network devices. In a network campus, the access layer generally incorporates switched LAN devices with ports that provide connectivity to workstations and servers. In the WAN environment, the access layer at remote sites or at teleworkers' homes provides access to the corporate network across various WAN technologies.

- **Distribution layer**—This layer aggregates the wiring closets and uses switches to segment workgroups and isolate network problems in a campus environment. Similarly, the distribution layer aggregates WAN connections at the edge of the campus and provides policy-based connectivity (in other words, it implements the organization's policies).

- **Core layer (also referred to as the backbone)**—The core layer is a high-speed backbone and is designed to switch packets as fast as possible. Because the core is critical for connectivity, it must provide a high level of availability and adapt to changes quickly.

Figure 1-3 *Cisco Hierarchical Network Model*

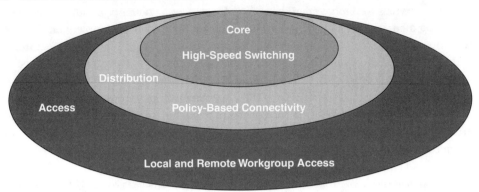

The hierarchical model can be applied to networks that include any type of connectivity, such as LANs, WANs, wireless LANs (WLANs), MANs, and VPNs. For example, Figure 1-4 demonstrates the hierarchical model applied to a WAN environment.

Figure 1-4 *Hierarchical Model Applied to a WAN*

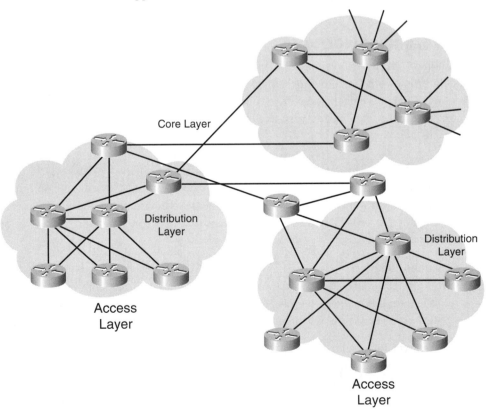

The hierarchical model is useful for smaller networks, but does not scale well to today's larger, more complex networks. The Enterprise Composite Network Model, introduced in the following section, provides additional modularity and functionality.

Cisco Enterprise Composite Network Model

Cisco has developed a set of best practices for security, comprising a blueprint for network designers and administrators for the proper deployment of security solutions to support network applications and the existing network infrastructure. This blueprint is called "SAFE." SAFE includes the Enterprise Composite Network Model, which network professionals can use to describe and analyze any modern enterprise network. This model supports larger networks than those designed with only the hierarchical model and clarifies the functional boundaries within the network.

> **NOTE** You can access the SAFE blueprint home page at http://www.cisco.com/go/safe.

The Enterprise Composite Network Model first divides the network into three functional areas, as illustrated in Figure 1-5 and described as follows:

- **Enterprise Campus**—This functional area contains the modules required to build a hierarchical, highly robust campus network. Access, distribution, and core principles are applied to these modules appropriately.

- **Enterprise Edge**—This functional area aggregates connectivity from the various elements at the edge of the enterprise network, including to remote locations, the Internet, and remote users.

- **Service Provider Edge**—This area is not implemented by the organization; instead, it is included to represent connectivity to service providers such as Internet service providers (ISPs), WAN providers, and the public switched telephone network (PSTN).

Figure 1-5 *Enterprise Composite Network Model Functional Areas*

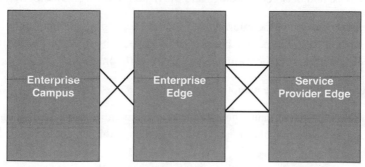

As illustrated in Figure 1-6, each of these functional areas contains various network modules. These modules can in turn include hierarchical core, distribution, and access layer functionality.

Figure 1-6 *Modules Within the Enterprise Composite Network Model*

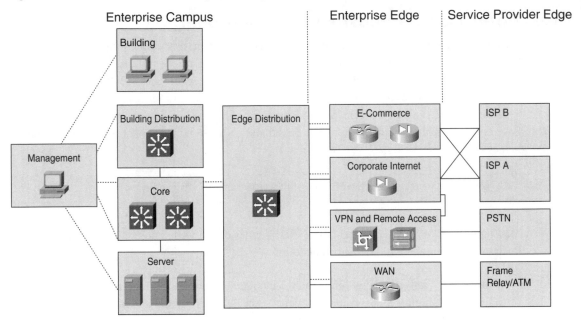

The Enterprise Campus functional area comprises the following modules:

■ **Building**—Containing access switches and end-user devices (including PCs and IP phones).

■ **Building Distribution**—Includes distribution multilayer switches to provide access between workgroups and to the Core.

■ **Core**—Also called the backbone, provides a high-speed connection between buildings themselves, and between buildings and the Server and Edge Distribution modules.

■ **Edge Distribution**—The interface between the Enterprise Campus and the Enterprise Edge functional areas. This module concentrates connectivity to and from all branches and teleworkers accessing the campus via a WAN or the Internet.

■ **Server**—Represents the campus's data center.

■ **Management**—Represents the network management functionality, including monitoring, logging, security, and other management features within an enterprise.

Figure 1-7 illustrates how the Building, Building Distribution, and Core modules map directly onto the hierarchical model's access, distribution, and core layers. The figure also shows how multiple buildings can be represented by multiple sets of a Building and a Building Distribution module, with each connected to the Core.

Figure 1-7 *Multiple Buildings Represented Within the Enterprise Campus*

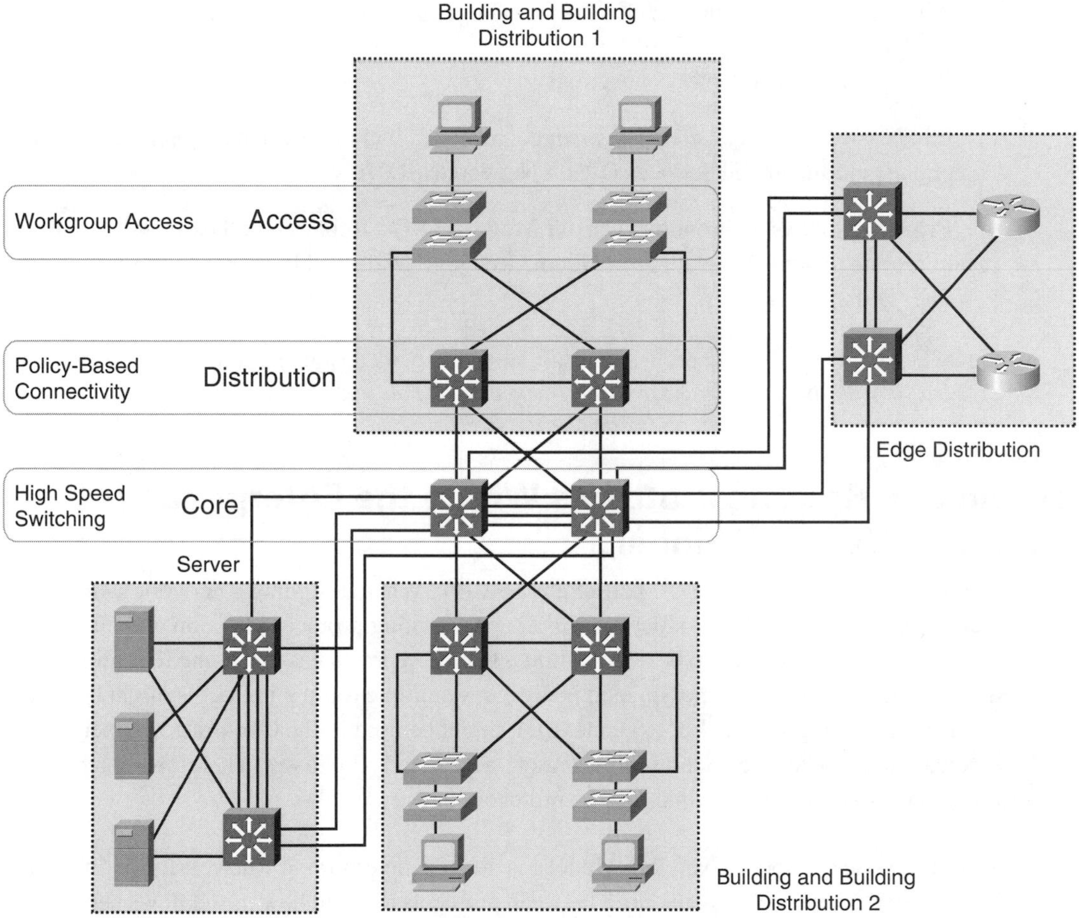

The Enterprise Edge functional area is the interface between the Enterprise Campus functional area (through the Edge Distribution module) and the Service Provider Edge functional area. It is composed of the following four modules:

- **E-commerce**—Includes the servers, network devices, and so forth necessary for an organization to provide e-commerce functionality, such as online ordering

- **Corporate Internet**—Provides Internet access for the organization, and passes VPN traffic from external users to the VPN and Remote Access module

- **VPN and Remote Access**—Terminates VPN traffic and dial-in connections from external users

- **WAN**—Provides connectivity from remote sites using various WAN technologies

The three modules within the Service Provider Edge functional area are as follows:

- **ISP**—Represents Internet connections

- **PSTN**—Represents all *nonpermanent* connections, including via analog phone, cellular phone, and Integrated Services Digital Network (ISDN)

- **Frame Relay/Asynchronous Transfer Mode (ATM)**—Represents all *permanent* connections to remote locations, including via Frame Relay, ATM, leased lines, cable, digital subscriber line (DSL), and wireless

> **NOTE** For further information and details about network design, refer to the Cisco Press book *CCDA Self-Study: Designing for Cisco Internetwork Solutions (DESGN)*.

Routing and Routing Protocols Within the Enterprise Composite Network Model

Routing protocols are an integral part of any network. When designing a network using the architectures and models introduced in this chapter, routing protocol selection and planning are among the design decisions to be made. Although the best practice is to use one IP routing protocol throughout the enterprise if possible, in many cases multiple routing protocols might be required, as illustrated in Figure 1-8. For example, BGP might be used in the Corporate Internet module, whereas static routes are often used for remote-access and VPN users. Therefore, enterprises might have to deal with multiple routing protocols.

The Enterprise Composite Network Model can assist in determining where each routing protocol is implemented, where the boundaries between protocols are, and how traffic flows between them will be managed.

Figure 1-8 *Multiple Routing Protocols May Be Used Within a Network*

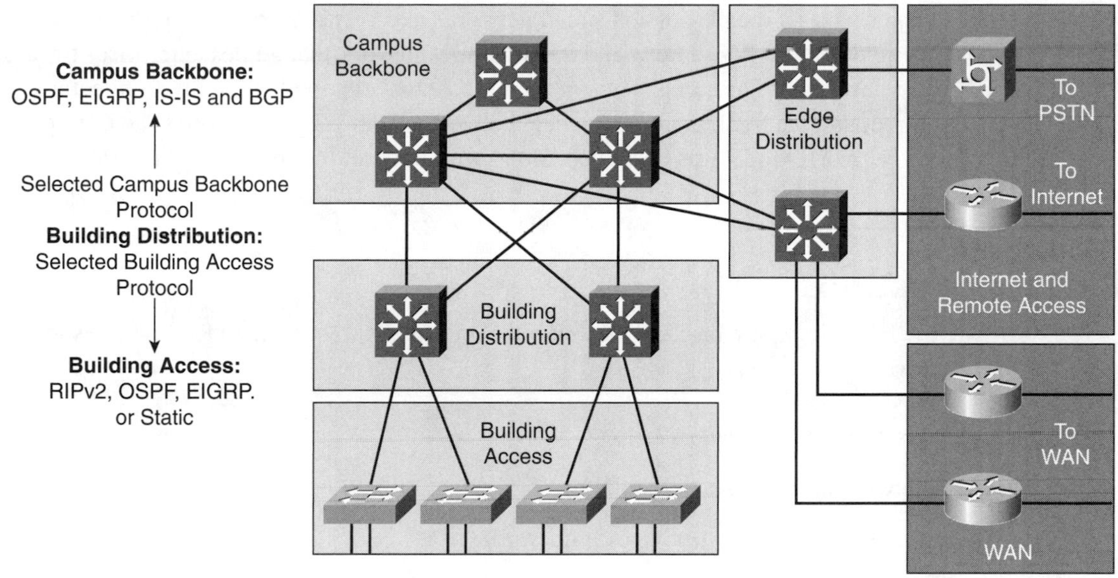
Campus Backbone:
OSPF, EIGRP, IS-IS and BGP
Selected Campus Backbone Protocol
Building Distribution:
Selected Building Access Protocol
Building Access:
RIPv2, OSPF, EIGRP.
or Static
Campus Backbone
Edge Distribution
To PSTN
To Internet
Internet and Remote Access
Building Distribution
Building Access
To WAN
WAN

Each routing protocol has its own unique characteristics, some of which Table 1-1 identifies. The next part of this book, Part II, focuses on the characteristics, operation, and configuration of IP routing protocols.

Table 1-1 *Routing Protocol Comparison*

Parameters	EIGRP	OSPF	IS-IS
Size of network (small-medium-large-very large)	Large	Large	Very large
Speed of convergence (very high-high-medium-low)	Very high	High	High
Use of VLSM (yes-no)	Yes	Yes	Yes
Support for mixed-vendor devices (yes-no)	No	Yes	Yes
Network support staff knowledge (good, fair, poor)	Good	Good	Fair

Summary

In this chapter, you learned about converged networks and network architecture frameworks and design models. The IIN strategy and the SONA framework that guides enterprises toward an IIN were described. The components of the Cisco enterprise-wide systems architecture were explored, and the traditional hierarchical network model was introduced. The Enterprise Composite Network Model was described, along with how routing protocols fit within this model.

Review Questions

Answer the following questions, and then refer to Appendix A, "Answers to Review Questions," for the answers.

1. What is a converged network?

2. What are the three phases of the IIN?

3. Which are layers within the SONA framework?

   a. Access

   b. Network Infrastructure

   c. Interactive Services

   d. Enterprise Edge

   e. Application

   f. Edge Distribution

4. What are the components of the Cisco Enterprise Architecture?

5. Which are the layers within the hierarchical network model?

   a. Access

   b. Network Infrastructure

   c. Core

    d. Distribution

    e. Application

    f. Edge Distribution

    g. Network Management

6. Describe each of the functional areas of the Enterprise Composite Network Model.

7. Which modules are within the Enterprise Campus functional area?

8. Why might a network need to have more than one routing protocol running?

Part II: IP Routing Protocols

This chapter discusses IP routing principles. It covers the following topics:

- IP Routing Overview

- Characteristics of Routing Protocols

- RIP

- IP Routing Protocol Comparisons

CHAPTER 2

Routing Principles

This chapter covers IP routing principles, including static and dynamic routing characteristics, classful and classless routing, and manual and automatic route summarization across network boundaries. It explains the difference between distance vector, link-state, and hybrid routing protocols; and includes comparisons of IP routing protocols. Characteristics and configuration of the Routing Information Protocol (RIP) are described.

> **NOTE** The online Appendix C, "IPv4 Supplement," includes job aids and supplementary information related to IPv4 addresses that you should understand before reading the rest of the book. Therefore, you are encouraged to review any of the material in Appendix C that you are not familiar with before reading the rest of this chapter.

IP Routing Overview

Routers forward packets toward destination networks. To forward the packets, routers must know about these remote networks and determine the best way to reach them. This section addresses the ways in which routers learn about networks and how routers can incorporate static and dynamic routes.

Routers must be aware of destination networks to be able to forward packets to them. A router knows about the networks directly attached to its interfaces; it calculates the subnet or network number of an interface by using the address and subnet mask configured on that interface. For networks not directly connected to one of its interfaces, however, the router must rely on outside information. A router can be made aware of remote networks in two ways: An administrator can manually configure the information (static routing), or a router can learn from other routers (dynamic routing). A routing table can contain both static and dynamically recognized routes.

Network administrators can use static routing, dynamic routing, or a combination of both.

Principles of Static Routing

This section explains the situations in which static routes are the most appropriate to use.

A static route can be used in the following circumstances:

■ When it is undesirable to have dynamic routing updates forwarded across slow bandwidth links, such as a dialup link.

■ When the administrator needs total control over the routes used by the router.

■ When a backup to a dynamically recognized route is necessary.

■ When it is necessary to reach a network accessible by only one path (a stub network). For example, in Figure 2-1, there is only one way for router A to reach the 10.2.0.0/16 network on router B. The administrator can configure a static route on router A to reach the 10.2.0.0/16 network via 10.1.1.1.

Figure 2-1 *Configuring Static Routing*

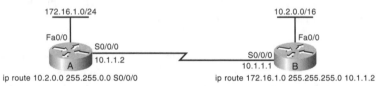

■ When a router is underpowered and does not have the CPU or memory resources necessary to handle a dynamic routing protocol.

■ When a route should appear to the router as a directly connected network.

A perfect use for static routing is a hub-and-spoke design, with all remote sites defaulting back to the central site and the one or two routers at the central site having a static route for all subnets at each remote site. However, without proper design, as the network grows into hundreds of routers, with each router having numerous subnets, the number of static routes on each router also increases. Each time a new subnet or router is added, an administrator must add a static route to the new networks on a number of routers. The administrative burden to maintain this network can become excessive, making dynamic routing a better choice.

Another drawback of static routing is that when a topology change occurs on the internetwork, an administrator might have to reroute traffic by configuring new static routes around the problem area. In contrast, with dynamic routing, the routers must learn the new topology. The routers share information with each other and their routing processes automatically discover whether any alternative routes exist and reroute without administrator intervention. Because the routers mutually develop an independent agreement of what the new topology is, they are said to *converge* on what the new routes should be. Dynamic routing provides faster convergence.

KEY POINT

Convergence

A network is converged when routing tables on all routers in the network are synchronized and contain a route to all destination networks. Convergence time is the time it takes for all routers in a network to agree on the new topology.

Configuring a Static Route

The following command, explained in Table 2-1, is used to create static routes:

```
RouterA(config)#ip route prefix mask {address | interface} [distance]
    [permanent] [tag tag]
```

Table 2-1 **ip route** *Command*

ip route Command	Description
prefix mask	The IP network and subnet mask for the remote network to be entered into the IP routing table.
address	The IP address of the next hop that can be used to reach the destination network.
interface	The local router outbound interface to be used to reach the destination network.
distance	(Optional) The administrative distance to be assigned to this route.
permanent	(Optional) Specifies that the route will not be removed from the routing table even if the interface associated with the route goes down.
tag *tag*	(Optional) A value that can be used as a match value in route maps.

NOTE Use static routes pointing to an interface on point-to-point interfaces only, because on multiaccess interfaces the router will not know the specific address to which to send the information. On point-to-point interfaces, the information is sent to the only other device on the network.

If no dynamic routing protocol is used on a link connecting two routers, such as in Figure 2-1, a static route must be configured on the routers on both sides of the link. Otherwise, the remote router will not know how to return the packet to its originator located on the other network; there will be only one-way communication.

While configuring a static route, you must specify either a next-hop IP address or an exit interface to notify the router which direction to send traffic. Figure 2-1 shows both configurations. Router A recognizes the directly connected networks 172.16.1.0 and 10.1.1.0. It needs a route to the remote network 10.2.0.0. Router B knows about the directly connected networks 10.2.0.0 and 10.1.1.0; it needs a route to the remote network 172.16.1.0. Notice that on router B, the next-hop IP address of the router A serial interface has been used. On router A, however, the **ip route** command specifies its own Serial 0/0/0 interface as the exit interface. If a next-hop IP address is used, it should be the IP address of the interface of the router on the other end of the link. If an exit interface is used, the local router sends data to the router on the other end of its attached link. When an exit interface is specified, the router considers this a directly connected route.

Configuring a Static Default Route

In some circumstances, a router does not need to recognize the details of remote networks. The router is configured to send all traffic, or all traffic for which there is no entry in the routing table, in a particular direction, known as a default route. Default routes are either dynamically advertised using routing protocols or statically configured.

To create a static default route, use the normal **ip route** command, but with the destination network (the *prefix* in the command syntax) and its subnet mask (the *mask* in the command syntax) both set at 0.0.0.0. This address is a type of wildcard designation; any destination network will match. Because the router tries to match the longest common bit pattern, a network listed in the routing table is used before the default route. If the destination network is not listed in the routing table, the default route is used.

In Figure 2-2, on router A, the static route to the 10.2.0.0 network has been replaced with a static default route pointing to router B. On router B, a static default route has been added, pointing to its Internet service provider (ISP). Traffic from a device on the router A 172.16.1.0 network bound for a network on the Internet is sent to router B. Router B recognizes that the destination network does not match any specific entries in its routing table and sends that traffic to the ISP. It is then the ISP's responsibility to route that traffic to its destination.

Figure 2-2 *Configuring the Static Default Route*

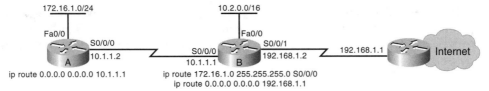

In Figure 2-2, to reach the 172.16.1.0/24 network, router B still needs a static route pointing out its S0/0/0 interface.

Entering the **show ip route** command on router A in Figure 2-2 returns the information shown in Example 2-1.

Example 2-1   show ip route *Command*

```
RouterA#show ip route
<output omitted>
Gateway of last resort is not set
C    172.16.1.0 is directly connected, FastEthernet0/0
C    10.1.1.0 is directly connected, Serial0/0/0
S*   0.0.0.0/0 [1/0] via 10.1.1.1
```

Principles of Dynamic Routing

Dynamic routing allows the network to adjust to changes in the topology automatically, without administrator involvement. This section describes dynamic routing principles.

A static route cannot respond dynamically to changes in the network. If a link fails, the static route is no longer valid if it is configured to use that failed link, so a new static route must be configured. If a new router or new link is added, that information must also be configured on every router in the network. In a very large or unstable network, these changes can lead to considerable work for network administrators. It can also take a long time for every router in the network to receive the correct information. In situations such as these, it might be better to have the routers receive information about networks and links from each other using a dynamic routing protocol.

When using a dynamic routing protocol, the administrator configures the routing protocol on each router, as shown in Figure 2-3. The routers then exchange information about the reachable networks and the state of each network. Routers exchange information only with other routers running the same routing protocol. When the network topology changes, the new information is dynamically propagated throughout the network, and each router updates its routing table to reflect the changes. The following are some examples of dynamic routing protocols:

■ RIP

■ Enhanced Interior Gateway Routing Protocol (EIGRP)

■ Intermediate System-to-Intermediate System (IS-IS)

■ Open Shortest Path First (OSPF)

■ Border Gateway Protocol (BGP)

Figure 2-3 *Routers Running a Dynamic Routing Protocol Exchange Routing Information*

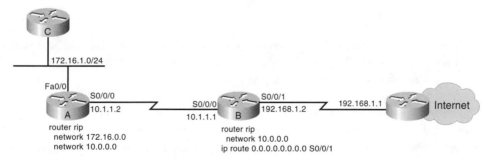

The information exchanged by routers includes the metric or cost to each destination (this value is sometimes called the distance).

KEY POINT

Metric

A *metric* is a value (such as path length) that routing protocols use to measure paths to a destination.

Different routing protocols base their metric on different measurements, including hop count, interface speed, or more-complex metrics. Most routing protocols maintain databases containing all the networks that the routing protocol recognizes and all the paths to each network. If a routing protocol recognizes more than one way to reach a network, it compares the metric for each different path and chooses the path with the lowest metric. If multiple paths have the same metric, a maximum of 16 can be installed in the routing table, and the router can perform load balancing between them. EIGRP can also perform load balancing between unequal-cost paths.

> **NOTE**   Prior to Cisco IOS Release 12.3(2)T, the maximum number of parallel routes (equal-cost paths) supported by IP routing protocols was 6; in Cisco IOS Release 12.3(2)T that maximum was changed to 16.

To configure an IP dynamic routing protocol, use the **router** *protocol* command. Protocols other than RIP also require specification of either an autonomous system or a process number. You also need the **network** command under the router configuration mode of all routing protocols except IS-IS and BGP.

For RIP, EIGRP, and OSPF, the **network** command tells the router which interfaces are participating in that routing protocol. Any interface that has an IP address that falls within the range specified in the **network** statement is considered active for that protocol. In other words, the router sends updates from the specified interfaces and expects to receive updates from the same interfaces. Some protocols look for neighbors by sending hello packets out those interfaces. Thus, because a **network** statement identifies interfaces on the local router, it is configured only for directly connected networks. A router also originates advertisements for the networks connected to the specified interfaces.

RIP allows only major network numbers (Class A, B, or C network numbers) to be specified in the **network** command. EIGRP and OSPF permit exact specification of interfaces with a combination of a subnet or interface address and a wildcard mask.

The **network** statement functions differently in BGP. BGP requires its neighbors to be statically configured. The **network** statement in BGP tells the router to originate an advertisement for that network. Without a **network** statement, BGP passes along advertisements it receives from other routers, but it does not originate any network advertisements itself. In BGP, the network listed in the **network** statement does not have to be directly connected, because it does not identify interfaces on the router as it does in other protocols (this process is explained in detail in Chapter 8, "Configuring the Border Gateway Protocol").

Integrated IS-IS does not use the **network** statement. Instead, interfaces participating in the IS-IS routing process are identified under interface configuration mode. (OSPF also permits the interfaces to be specified this way, as an alternative to using the **network** command.)

Example 2-2 shows the configuration of the routers in Figure 2-3. Both routers A and B are configured with RIP. Router A has two directly attached networks and RIP is used to advertise to neighbors on both of those interfaces. Therefore, **network** statements are configured for both the 172.16.1.0 network and the 10.1.1.0 network. Router A sends RIP packets out interfaces Fa0/0 and S0/0/0, advertising the networks that are attached to those interfaces.

Example 2-2 *Configuring RIP*

```
routerA(config)#router rip
routerA(config-router)#network 172.16.0.0
routerA(config-router)#network 10.0.0.0

routerB(config)#ip route 0.0.0.0 0.0.0.0 Serial0/0/1
routerB(config)#router rip
routerB(config-router)#network 10.0.0.0
```

Router B also has two directly attached networks. However, router B wants only the network it shares with router A to participate in RIP. Therefore, a **network** statement is configured only for the 10.1.1.0 network. As explained earlier, with RIP, only the major network number is actually used in the **network** command. Router B also has a static default route pointing toward its ISP to reach other networks. Router B sends RIP packets out its interface S0/0/0, but not out its interface S0/0/1. It does not advertise the 192.168.1.0 network attached to S0/0/1 or the static default route unless specifically configured to do so.

Principles of On-Demand Routing

A drawback of static routes is that they must be manually configured and updated when the network topology changes. A drawback of dynamic routing protocols is that they use network bandwidth and router resources. In a hub-and-spoke network with hundreds of spokes, both the configuration needed for static routes and the resource usage of dynamic routing can be considerable.

There is a third option: on-demand routing (ODR). ODR uses the Cisco Discovery Protocol (CDP) to carry network information between spoke (stub) routers and the hub router. ODR provides IP routing information with minimal overhead compared to a dynamic routing protocol and requires less manual configuration than static routes.

ODR is applicable in a hub-and-spoke topology only. In this type of topology, each spoke router is adjacent only to the hub. Another name for a spoke router is stub router. The stub router may have some LAN networks connected to it and typically has a WAN connection to the hub router. The hub router needs to recognize the networks connected to each spoke, but the spokes need only a default route pointing to the hub.

When ODR is configured, the stub routers use CDP to send IP prefix information to the hub router. Stub routers send prefix information for all their directly connected networks. ODR reports the subnet mask, so it allows different subnets within the same major network to have different subnet masks. This is known as variable-length subnet masking (VLSM) and is described in detail in Appendix C.

The hub router, in turn, sends a default route to the spokes that points back to itself. It installs the stub networks reported by ODR in its routing table and can be configured to redistribute these routes into a dynamic routing protocol. For a next-hop address, the hub router uses the IP address of the spoke routers as reported to it by CDP.

ODR is not a true routing protocol because the information exchanged is limited to IP prefixes and a default route. ODR reports no metric information; the hub router uses a hop count of 1 as the metric for all routes reported via ODR. However, by using ODR, routing information for stub networks can be obtained dynamically without the overhead of a dynamic routing protocol, and default routes can be provided to the stub routers without manual configuration.

Configuring ODR

ODR is configured on the hub router using the **router odr** global configuration command.

On the stub router, there must be no IP routing protocol configured. In fact, from the standpoint of ODR, a router is automatically considered a stub when no IP routing protocols have been configured. Figure 2-4 shows a hub-and-spoke topology.

Figure 2-4 *Hub-and-Spoke Topology: Configuring ODR*

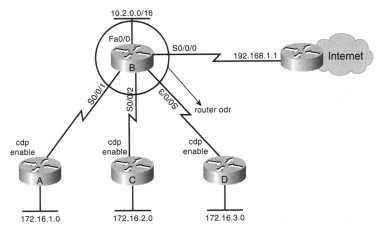

ODR can also be tuned with optional commands, including using a distribute list to control the network information that is recognized through ODR, and adjusting the ODR timers with the **timers basic** router configuration command.

ODR relies on the CDP to carry the information between the hub router and the spoke routers. Therefore, CDP must be enabled on the links between the hub router and spokes. Cisco routers by default have CDP enabled both globally and per interface. However, on some WAN links, such as ATM, CDP must be explicitly enabled.

The CDP updates are sent as multicasts. On WAN links that require mappings, such as dialer links and Frame Relay, it is important to use the **broadcast** keyword in the mapping statements; allowing broadcasts also allows multicasts across the link. CDP uses Subnetwork Access Protocol (SNAP) frames, so it runs on all media that support SNAP.

CDP updates are sent every 60 seconds by default. This setting might be too infrequent in rapidly changing networks or too often in stable ones. You can adjust the timers with the **cdp timer** global configuration command. You can verify CDP settings by using the **show cdp interface** command.

As soon as ODR is configured and running, routes from the stub routers are identified in the hub router's routing table with an o character, as shown in Example 2-3. Notice in the example that the metric is 1, and the administrative distance for ODR is 160. (Administrative distance is described in the "Administrative Distance" section later in this chapter.) Also, do not confuse the o character of ODR routes with the O character of OSPF routes.

Example 2-3 *Routing Table with ODR Routes*

```
RouterB#show ip route
<output omitted>
172.16.0.0/16 is subnetted, 4 subnets
o   172.16.1.0/24 [160/1] via 10.1.1.2, 00:00:23, Serial0/0/1
o   172.16.2.0/24 [160/1] via 10.2.2.2, 00:00:03, Serial0/0/2
o   172.16.3.0/24 [160/1] via 10.3.3.2, 00:00:16, Serial0/0/3
<output omitted>
```

The routing table for each spoke router contains only its connected networks and a static default route injected by ODR from the hub router.

Characteristics of Routing Protocols

Routing protocols can be classified into different categories such as distance vector, link-state, or a hybrid of these two. IP routing protocols can also be classified as either classful or classless. These characteristics are explored in this section.

Distance Vector, Link-State, and Hybrid Routing Protocols

When a network is using a distance vector routing protocol, all the routers send their routing tables (or a portion of their tables) to only their neighboring routers. The routers then use the received information to determine whether any changes need to be made to their own routing table (for example, if a better way to a specific network is now available). This process repeats periodically.

In contrast, when a network is using a link-state routing protocol, each of the routers sends the state of its own interfaces (its links) to all other routers (or to all routers in a part of the network, known as an area) only when there is a change. Each router uses the received information to recalculate the best path to each network and then saves this information in its routing table.

As its name suggests, a hybrid protocol has characteristics of both distance vector and link-state protocols. Hybrid protocols send only changed information (similar to link-state protocols) but only to neighboring routers (similar to distance vector protocols).

Classful Routing Protocol Concepts

IP routing protocols can be categorized as classful or classless.

KEY POINT

Classless and Classful Routing Protocols

Routing updates sent by a classful routing protocol do not include the subnet mask. RIP Version 1 (RIPv1) is a classful routing protocol.

Routing updates sent by a classless routing protocol include the subnet mask. RIP Version 2 (RIPv2), EIGRP, OSPF, IS-IS, and BGP are classless routing protocols.

Classful Routing Protocol Behavior

When classful protocols were originally developed, networks were very different from those used now. The best modem speed was 300 bps, the largest WAN line was 56 kbps, router memory was less than 640 KB, and processors were running in the kHz range. Routing updates had to be small enough not to monopolize the WAN link bandwidth. In addition, routers did not have the resources to maintain current information about every subnet.

A classful routing protocol does not include subnet mask information in its routing updates. Because no subnet mask information is known, when a classful router sends or receives routing updates, the router makes assumptions about the subnet mask being used by the networks listed in the update, based on IP address class.

Routers send update packets from their interfaces to other connected routers. A router sends the entire subnet address when an update packet involves a subnet of the same classful network as the IP address of the transmitting interface. The receiving router then assumes that the subnet in the update and the interface use the same subnet mask.

If that route is using a different subnet mask, the receiving router will have incorrect information in its routing table. Thus, when using a classful routing protocol, it is important to use the same subnet mask on all subnets belonging to the same classful network.

When a router using a classful routing protocol needs to send an update about a subnet of a network across an interface belonging to a different network, the router assumes that the remote router will use the default subnet mask for that class of IP address. Therefore, when the router sends the update, it does not include the subnet information. The update packet contains only the classful network information. This process is called *autosummarization across the network boundary*; the router sends a summary of all the subnets in that network by sending only the major network information. Classful routing protocols automatically create a classful summary route at major network boundaries. Classful routing protocols do not allow summarization at other points within the major network address space.

The router that receives the update behaves in a similar fashion. When an update contains information about a different classful network than the one in use on its interface, the router applies the default classful mask to that update. The router must assume what the subnet mask is because the update does not contain subnet mask information.

In Figure 2-5, router A advertises the 10.1.0.0 subnet to router B because the interface connecting them belongs to the same major classful 10.0.0.0 network. When router B receives the update packet, it assumes that the 10.1.0.0 subnet uses the same 16-bit mask as the one used on its 10.2.0.0 subnet.

Figure 2-5 *Network Summarization in Classful Routing*

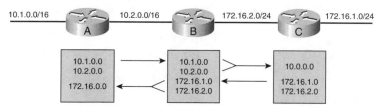

Router C advertises the 172.16.1.0 subnet to router B because the interface connecting them belongs to the same major classful 172.16.0.0 network. Therefore, router B's routing table has information about all the subnets that are in use in the network.

However, router B summarizes the 172.16.1.0 and 172.16.2.0 subnets to 172.16.0.0 before sending them to router A. Therefore, router A's routing table contains summary information about only the 172.16.0.0 network.

Similarly, router B summarizes the 10.1.0.0 and 10.2.0.0 subnets to 10.0.0.0 before sending the routing information to router C. This summarization occurs because the update crosses a major network boundary. The update goes from a subnet of network 10.0.0.0, subnet 10.2.0.0, to a subnet of another major network, network 172.16.0.0. Router C's routing table contains summary information about only the 10.0.0.0 network.

Summarizing Routes in a Discontiguous Network

Discontiguous subnets are subnets of the same major network that are separated by a different major network.

Classful protocols summarize automatically at network boundaries, which means that

- Subnets are not advertised to a different major network.

- Discontiguous subnets are not visible to each other.

In the example shown in Figure 2-6, routers A and B do not advertise the 172.16.5.0 255.255.255.0 and 172.16.6.0 255.255.255.0 subnets, because RIPv1 cannot advertise subnets across a different major network; both router A and router B advertise 172.16.0.0. This leads to confusion when routing across network 192.168.14.16/28. Router C, for example, receives routes about 172.16.0.0 from two different directions; it therefore might make an incorrect routing decision.

Figure 2-6 *Classful Routing Protocols Do Not Support Discontiguous Subnets*

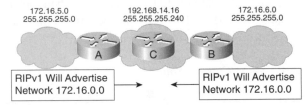

You can resolve this situation by using RIPv2, OSPF, IS-IS, or EIGRP and not using summarization, because the subnet routes will be advertised with their actual subnet masks.

The ip classless Command

The behavior of a classful routing protocol changes when the **ip classless** global configuration command is used.

> **NOTE**   The **ip classless** command is enabled by default in Release 12.0 and later of the Cisco IOS Software; in earlier releases it is disabled by default.

When running a classful protocol (RIPv1), **ip classless** must be enabled if you want the router to select a default route when it must route to an unknown subnet of a network for which it knows some subnets. For example, consider a router's routing table that has entries for subnets 10.5.0.0/16 and 10.6.0.0/16 and a default route of 0.0.0.0. If a packet arrives for a destination on the 10.7.0.0/16 subnet and **ip classless** is not enabled, the packet is dropped. Classful protocols assume that if they know some of the subnets of network 10.0.0.0, they must know all that network's existing subnets. Enabling **ip classless** tells the router that it should follow the best supernet route or the default route for unknown subnets of known networks, and for unknown networks.

The Routing Table Acts Classfully

It is actually the routing table itself that acts classfully by default without the **ip classless** command, and will do so even if no routing protocols are running. For example, if you have only static routes and no routing protocols, you still would not be able to reach a subnet of a known major network using a default route unless the **ip classless** command is enabled.

A CCIE technical reviewer of an earlier edition of this book performed the following test using two Cisco 2520 routers running Cisco IOS c2500-i-l.122-8.T5.bin. The two routers, R1 and R2, were connected via interface E0, and no routing protocols were enabled on either router.

Router R1 configuration:

```
!
interface Loopback 0
 ip address 10.1.0.1 255.255.0.0
interface Loopback 1
 ip address 10.2.0.1 255.255.0.0
interface Ethernet 0
 ip address 10.3.0.1 255.255.0.0
!
ip route 0.0.0.0 0.0.0.0 10.3.0.2
!
no ip classless
```

Router R2 configuration:

```
!
interface Loopback 0
 ip address 10.4.0.1 255.255.0.0
interface Ethernet 0
 ip address 10.3.0.2 255.255.0.0
!
```

Test 1:

R1 has a default route pointing to R2 and has the **no ip classless** command configured. A ping from R1 to R2's loopback0 fails. When the **ip classless** command is entered on R1, the ping from R1 to R2's loopback0, via the default route, succeeds. This test proves that even though no routing protocols are used, the routing table acts classfully.

Test 2:

The second step is to test the classful nature of the routing table using a classless routing protocol, OSPF. OSPF is turned on for all interfaces on R1 but is activated only on R2's Ethernet link.

R2's OSPF is configured to inject a default route into R1 using the **default-information originate always** command (which is covered in detail in Chapter 5, "Advanced Open Shortest Path First Protocol Configuration"). R1 therefore has a default route pointing to R2 that is introduced via OSPF. The pings from R1 to R2's loopback0 succeed regardless of the **ip classless** command. Therefore, turning on OSPF, a classless protocol, overrides the routing table's classful nature.

Classless Routing Protocol Concepts

Classless routing protocols can be considered second-generation protocols because they are designed to address some of the limitations of the earlier classful routing protocols. One of the most serious limitations in a classful network environment is that the subnet mask is not exchanged during the routing update process, and therefore, the same subnet mask must be used on all subnetworks within the same major network.

With classless routing protocols, different subnets within the same major network can have different subnet masks; in other words, they support VLSM. If more than one entry in the routing table matches a particular destination, the longest prefix match in the routing table is used. For example, if a routing table has different paths to 172.16.0.0/16 and to 172.16.5.0/24, packets addressed to 172.16.5.99 are routed through the 172.16.5.0/24 path, because that address has the longest match with the destination network.

Another limitation of the classful approach is the need to automatically summarize to the classful network boundary at major network boundaries. In a classless environment, the route summarization process can be controlled manually and can usually be invoked at any bit position within the address. Because subnet routes might be propagated throughout the routing domain, manual route summarization might be required to keep the size of the routing tables manageable.

RIPv2 and EIGRP Automatic Network-Boundary Summarization

By default, RIPv2 and EIGRP perform automatic network summarization at classful boundaries, just like a classful protocol does. Automatic summarization lets RIPv2 and EIGRP be backward compatible with their predecessors, RIPv1 and Interior Gateway Routing Protocol (IGRP).

NOTE   IGRP is no longer supported, as of Cisco IOS Release 12.3.

The difference between these protocols and their predecessors is that you can manually turn off automatic summarization, using the **no auto-summary** router configuration command. You do not need this command when you are using OSPF or IS-IS, because neither protocol performs automatic network summarization by default.

The autosummarization behavior can cause problems in a network that has discontiguous subnets or if some of the summarized subnets cannot be reached via the advertising router. If a summarized route indicates that certain subnets can be reached via a router, when in fact those subnets are discontiguous or unreachable via that router, the network might have problems similar to those caused by a classful protocol. For example, in Figure 2-7, both router A and router B are advertising a summarized route to 172.16.0.0/16. Router C therefore receives two routes to 172.16.0.0/16 and cannot identify which subnets are attached to which router.

Figure 2-7   *Automatic Network-Boundary Summarization*

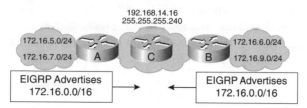

You can resolve this problem by disabling automatic summarization when running RIPv2 or EIGRP. Classless routers use the longest prefix match when selecting a route from the routing table; therefore, if one of the routers advertises without summarizing, the other routers see subnet routes and the summary route. The other routers can then select the longest prefix match and follow the correct path. For example, in Figure 2-7, if router A continues to summarize to 172.16.0.0/16 and router B is configured not to summarize, router C receives explicit routes for 172.16.6.0/24 and 172.16.9.0/24, along with the summarized route to 172.16.0.0/16. All traffic for router B subnets is sent to router B, and all other traffic for the 172.16.0.0 network is sent to router A.

Another example is shown in Figures 2-8 and 2-9. In the RIPv2 network illustrated in Figure 2-8, notice how router C, which is attached to router B via the 192.168.5.0/24 network, handles routing information about network 172.16.0.0. Router B automatically summarizes the 172.16.1.0/24 and 172.16.2.0/24 subnets to 172.16.0.0/16 before sending the route to router C, because it is sent over an interface in a different network. Instead of using the subnet mask known to router B (/24), router C uses this default classful mask for a Class B address (/16) when it stores the 172.16.0.0 information in its routing table.

Figure 2-8   *RIPv2 Summarizes By Default; OSPF Does Not*

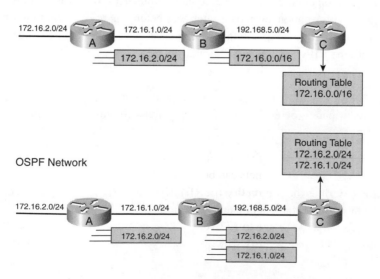

In the OSPF network shown in Figure 2-9, router B passes the subnet and subnet mask information to router C, and router C puts the subnet details in its routing table. Router C does not need to use default classful masks for the received routing information because the subnet mask is included in the routing update, and OSPF does not automatically summarize networks.

Figure 2-9 *Effect of the* **no auto-summary** *Command for RIPv2*

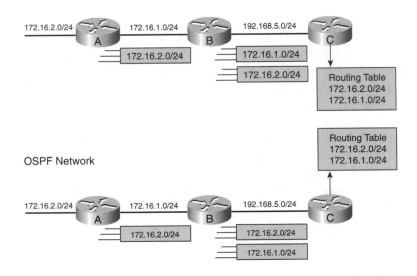

You can disable automatic summarization for RIPv2 and EIGRP with the **no auto-summary** router configuration command. When automatic summarization is disabled, RIPv2 and EIGRP forward subnet information, even over interfaces belonging to different major networks. In Figure 2-9, automatic summarization has been disabled. Notice that now the routing table is the same for both the RIPv2 and the OSPF routers.

> **NOTE** The BGP **auto-summary** router configuration command determines how BGP handles redistributed routes; Chapter 8 describes this command in detail.

RIP

This section describes the two versions of RIP, RIPv1 and RIPv2, and how to configure them; later chapters in this book detail the other routing protocols.

Characteristics of RIPv1

RIPv1 is described in RFC 1058, *Routing Information Protocol*. Its key characteristics include the following:

- Hop count is used as the metric for path selection.

- The maximum allowable hop count is 15.

- Routing updates are broadcast every 30 seconds by default. Because it is a distance vector routing protocol, updates are sent even if no change has occurred.

- RIP can load balance over as many as 16 equal-cost paths (4 paths by default).

- It has no authentication support.

> **NOTE**   RFCs are available at http://www.rfc-editor.org/rfcsearch.html.

RIPv1 is a classful distance vector routing protocol that does not send the subnet mask in its updates. Therefore, RIPv1 does not support VLSM.

Characteristics of RIPv2

RIPv2 is a classless distance vector routing protocol defined in RFC 1721, *RIP Version 2 Protocol Analysis*; RFC 1722, *RIP Version 2 Protocol Applicability Statement*; and RFC 2453, *RIP Version 2*. The most significant addition to RIPv2 is the inclusion of the mask in the RIPv2 routing update packet, allowing RIPv2 to support VLSM. RIPv2 automatically summarizes routes on classful network boundaries; but as described earlier, you can disable this behavior.

In addition, RIPv2 uses multicast addressing for more-efficient periodic updating on each interface. RIPv2 uses the 224.0.0.9 multicast address to advertise to other RIPv2 routers. This approach is more efficient than RIPv1's approach. RIPv1 uses a 255.255.255.255 broadcast address, so all devices, including PCs and servers, must process the update packet. They perform the checksum on the Layer 2 packet and pass it up their IP stack. IP sends the packet to the User Datagram Protocol (UDP) process, and UDP checks to see whether RIP port 520 is available. Most PCs and servers do not have any process running on this port and discard the packet. RIP can fit up to 25 networks and subnets in each update, and updates are dispatched every 30 seconds. For example, if the routing table has 1000 subnets, 40 packets are dispatched every 30 seconds (80 packets a minute). With each packet being a broadcast, all devices must look at it; most of the devices discard the packet.

The IP multicast address for RIPv2 has its own multicast MAC address. Devices that can distinguish between a multicast and a broadcast at the MAC layer read the start of the Layer 2 frame and determine that the destination MAC address is not for them. They can then discard all these packets at the interface level and not use CPU resources or buffer memory for these unwanted packets. Even on devices that cannot distinguish between broadcast and multicast at Layer 2, the worst that will happen is that the RIP updates will be discarded at the IP layer instead of being passed to UDP, because those devices are not using the 224.0.0.9 multicast address.

RIPv2 also supports security between RIP routers using message-digest or clear-text authentication. (RIPv2 security features are not covered in this book.)

RIP Configuration Commands

To activate the RIP process (Version 1 by default), use the following command:

```
Router(config)#router rip
```

By default, the Cisco IOS software receives both RIPv1 and RIPv2 packets; however, it sends only Version 1 packets. To configure the software to send and receive packets from only one version, use the **version** {**1** | **2**} router configuration command.

To select participating attached networks, use the following command, specifying the major classful network number:

```
Router(config-router)#network network-number
```

Regardless of the RIP version, a **network** command using the classful network number is required under the RIP routing process.

Although the RIP **version** command controls RIP's overall default behavior, you might need to control the version of RIP on a per-interface basis. To control the version of RIP on each interface, use the **ip rip send version** and **ip rip receive version** interface configuration commands. Version control per interface might be required when you are connecting legacy RIP networks to newer networks. The command syntax is as follows:

```
Router(config-if)#ip rip {send | receive} version {1 | 2 | 1 2}
```

By default, automatic summarization across network boundaries is activated for all networks in both versions of RIP. Manually summarizing routes in RIPv2 improves scalability and efficiency in large networks because the more-specific routes are not advertised. Only the summary routes are advertised, thus reducing the size of the IP routing table and allowing the router to handle more routes.

Manual summarization is done at the interface. One limitation of RIPv2 is that routes can be summarized only up to the classful network boundary; RIPv2 does not support classless interdomain routing (CIDR)-type summarization to the left of the classful boundary.

NOTE   CIDR is described in Appendix C.

To summarize RIP routes on nonclassful boundaries, do the following:

- Turn off autosummarization using the **no auto-summary** command under the RIP process.

- Use the **ip summary-address rip** *network-number mask* interface configuration command to define a network number and mask that meet the particular requirement.

Figure 2-10 illustrates how RIPv1 and RIPv2 may coexist in the same network. Router A is running RIPv2, and router C is running RIPv1. Router B runs both versions of RIP. Notice that the **ip rip send version 1** and **ip rip receive version 1** commands are required only on interface Serial 0/0/3 of router B, because RIPv2 is configured as the primary version for all interfaces. The Serial 0/0/3 interface has to be manually configured to support RIPv1 so that it can connect correctly with router C.

Figure 2-10   *RIPv2 Configuration Example*

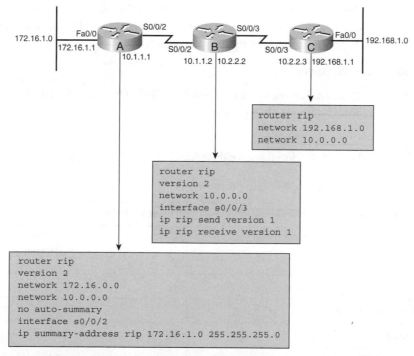

An **ip summary-address rip** command is configured on router A along with the **no auto-summary** command. The combination of these two commands allows router A to send the 172.16.1.0 subnet detail to router B. Because router B is in a different network (10.0.0.0), the default behavior for router A is to send only the classful summarization (172.16.0.0) to router B.

> **NOTE**   In Figure 2-10, the **ip summary-address rip 172.16.1.0 255.255.255.0** command is actually unnecessary because the **no auto-summary** command is also applied. The moment that the **no auto-summary** command is used, the subnet 172.16.1.0 is advertised as such because it uses a 24-bit mask.

IP Routing Protocol Comparisons

This section compares and contrasts the various IP routing protocols. It also discusses some IP routing protocol characteristics, such as administrative distance, and describes floating static routes.

Administrative Distance

Most routing protocols have metric structures and algorithms that are incompatible with other protocols. It is critical that a network using multiple routing protocols be able to seamlessly exchange route information and be able to select the best path across multiple protocols. Cisco routers use a value called administrative distance to select the best path when they learn of two or more routes to the same destination from different routing protocols.

Administrative distance rates a routing protocol's believability. Cisco has assigned a default administrative distance value to each routing protocol supported on its routers. Each routing protocol is prioritized in the order of most to least believable.

KEY POINT | **Administrative Distance**

The administrative distance is a value between 0 and 255. The lower the administrative distance value, the higher the protocol's believability.

Table 2-2 lists the default administrative distance of the protocols supported by Cisco routers.

Table 2-2   *Administrative Distance of Routing Protocols*

Route Source	Default Distance
Connected interface	0
Static route out an interface	0
Static route to a next-hop address	1
EIGRP summary route	5
External BGP	20
Internal EIGRP	90
IGRP[1]	100
OSPF	110
IS-IS	115
RIPv1, RIPv2	120
Exterior Gateway Protocol (EGP)	140
ODR	160
External EIGRP	170
Internal BGP	200
Unknown	255

[1] IGRP is no longer supported, as of Cisco IOS Release 12.3. It is included in this table for completeness.

> **NOTE**   Static routes are configured with the **ip route** *prefix mask* {*address | interface*} [*distance*] [**permanent**] [**tag** *tag*] global configuration command, described in the "Principles of Static Routing" section earlier in this chapter. If the *address* parameter is used in this command, specifying the address of the next-hop router to use to reach the destination network, the default administrative distance is 1. If the *interface* parameter is used instead, specifying the local router outbound interface to use to reach the destination network, the router considers this a directly connected route, and the default administrative distance is 0.

For example, in Figure 2-11, if router A receives a route to network 10.0.0.0 from RIP and also receives a route to the same network from OSPF, the router compares RIP's administrative distance, 120, with OSPF's administrative distance, 110, and determines that OSPF is more believable. The router therefore adds the OSPF version of the route to the routing table.

Figure 2-11 *Route Selection and Administrative Distance*

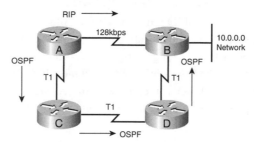

Floating Static Routes

Based on default administrative distances, routers believe static routes over any dynamically learned route. There might be times when this default behavior is not the desired behavior. For example, when you configure a static route as a backup to a dynamically learned route, you do not want the static route to be used as long as the dynamic route is available. In this case, you can manipulate the optional *distance* parameter in the **ip route** command to make the static route appear less desirable than another static or dynamic route.

KEY POINT

Floating Static Route

A static route that appears in the routing table only when the primary route goes away is called a floating static route.

The administrative distance of the static route is configured to be higher than the administrative distance of the primary route and it "floats" above the primary route, until the primary route is no longer available.

In Figure 2-12, routers A and B have two connections: a point-to-point serial connection that is the primary link, and an ISDN link to be used if the other line goes down. Both routers use EIGRP, but do not use a routing protocol on the ISDN 172.16.1.0 network link.

Figure 2-12 *Floating Static Routes*

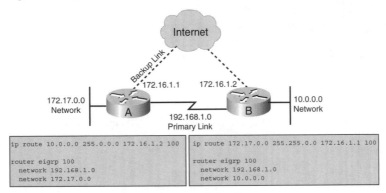

A static route that points to the ISDN interface of the other router has been created on each router. Because EIGRP has an administrative distance of 90, the static route has been given an administrative distance of 100. As long as router A has an EIGRP route to the 10.0.0.0 network, it appears more believable than the static route, and the EIGRP route is used. If the serial link goes down and disables the EIGRP route, router A inserts the static route into the routing table. A similar process happens on router B with its route to the 172.17.0.0 network.

Criteria for Inserting Routes in the IP Routing Table

A Cisco router chooses the best route for a specific destination among those presented by routing protocols, manual configuration, and various other means by considering the following four criteria:

- **Valid next-hop IP address**—As each routing process receives updates and other information, the router first verifies that the route has a valid next-hop IP address.

- **Metric**—If the next hop is valid, the routing protocol chooses the best path to any given destination based on the lowest metric. The routing protocol offers this path to the routing table. For example, if EIGRP learns of a path to 10.1.1.0/24 and decides that this particular path is the best EIGRP path to this destination, the routing protocol offers the learned path to the routing table.

- **Administrative distance**—The next consideration is administrative distance. If more than one route exists for the same network (with the same prefix), the router decides which route to install based on the administrative distance of the route's source. If the routing protocol that is presenting the path to a particular destination has the lowest administrative distance compared to the other ways the router has learned about this network, the router installs the route in the routing table. If that route does not have the best administrative distance, it is rejected.

■ **Prefix**—The router looks at the prefix being advertised. If there is no exact match to that prefix in the routing table, the route is installed. For example, suppose the router has three routing processes running on it, and each process has received the following routes:

— RIPv2: 192.168.32.0/26

— OSPF: 192.168.32.0/24

— EIGRP: 192.168.32.0/19

Because each route has a different prefix length (different subnet mask), the routes are considered different destinations and are all installed in the routing table. As discussed in the "Classless Routing Protocol Concepts" section earlier in this chapter, if more than one entry in the routing table matches a particular destination, the longest prefix match in the routing table is used. Therefore, in this example, if a packet arrives for the address 192.168.32.5, the router will use the 192.168.32.0/26 subnet, advertised by RIPv2, because it is the longest match for this address.

Comparing Routing Protocols

This section provides comparative summaries of routing protocols.

IGRP, EIGRP, and OSPF are transport layer protocols that run directly over IP, whereas RIP and BGP both reside at the application layer. RIP uses UDP as its transport protocol; its updates are sent unreliably with best-effort delivery. BGP uses the Transmission Control Protocol (TCP) as its transport protocol; it takes advantage of TCP's reliability mechanisms and windowing. Table 2-3 lists the protocol numbers, port numbers, and how reliability is handled for the various routing protocols.

Table 2-3   *Protocols, Ports, and Reliability of Routing Protocols*

Routing Protocol	Protocol Number	Port Number	Update Reliability
IGRP[1]	9	—	Best-effort delivery
EIGRP	88	—	1-to-1 window
OSPF	89	—	1-to-1 window
RIP	—	UDP 520	Best-effort delivery
BGP	—	TCP 179	Uses TCP windowing

[1] IGRP is no longer supported, as of Cisco IOS Release 12.3. It is mentioned in this table for completeness.

> **NOTE** IS-IS is a network layer protocol and does not use the services of IP to carry its routing information. IS-IS packets are encapsulated directly into a data link layer frame. Chapter 6, "Configuring the Integrated Intermediate System-to-Intermediate System Protocol," describes IS-IS in detail.

Table 2-4 compares some of the characteristics of the different routing protocols.

Table 2-4 *Routing Protocol Comparison*

Characteristic	RIPv2	EIGRP[1]	IS-IS	OSPF	BGP[2]
Distance vector	✓	✓			✓
Link-state			✓	✓	
Hierarchical topology required			✓	✓	
Automatic route summarization	✓	✓			✓
Manual route summarization	✓	✓	✓	✓	✓
VLSM support	✓	✓	✓	✓	✓
Classless	✓	✓	✓	✓	✓
Metric	Hops	Composite metric	Metric	Cost	Path attributes
Convergence time	Slow	Very fast	Fast	Fast	Slow

[1]EIGRP is an advanced distance vector protocol with some characteristics also found in link-state protocols.

[2]BGP is a path vector policy-based protocol.

RIPv2 is described in an earlier section in this chapter. Subsequent chapters in this book detail EIGRP, OSPF, IS-IS, and BGP operation and configuration.

Summary

In this chapter, you learned about IP routing principles, including static, default, dynamic, and on-demand routing. Routing protocol characteristics such as distance vector, link-state, hybrid, classful, and classless were explored. Characteristics and configuration of RIP were described, and comparisons between various IP routing protocols were presented.

Configuration Exercise: Basic Configuration and Migrating to a Classless Routing Protocol

In this exercise, you give the routers in your pod a basic configuration and set up RIPv2.

Introduction to the Configuration Exercises

This book uses Configuration Exercises to help you practice configuring routers with the commands and topics presented. If you have access to real hardware, you can try these exercises on your routers. See Appendix B, "Configuration Exercise Equipment Requirements and Backbone Configurations," for a list of recommended equipment and configuration commands for the backbone routers. However, even if you do not have access to any routers, you can go through the exercises and keep a log of your own running configurations or just read through the solution. Commands used and solutions to the Configuration Exercises are provided within the exercises.

In the Configuration Exercises, the network is assumed to consist of two pods, each with four routers. The pods are interconnected to a backbone. You configure one of the pods, pod 1. No interaction between the two pods is required, but you might see some routes from the other pod in your routing tables in some exercises if you have it configured. In most of the exercises, the backbone has only one router; in some cases, another router is added to the backbone. Each Configuration Exercise assumes that you have completed the previous chapters' Configuration Exercises on your pod.

NOTE   Throughout the exercise, the pod number is referred to as x, and the router number is referred to as y. Substitute the appropriate numbers as needed.

Objectives

The objectives of this exercise are to:

- Put a basic configuration on your pod devices and verify connectivity with directly connected devices.

- Configure RIPv1 as a routing protocol and explore its shortcomings.

- Configure RIPv2 and examine its behavior.

Visual Objective

Figure 2-13 illustrates the topology used in this exercise.

NOTE   Backbone router 2 (BBR2), shown in Figure 2-13, is not used until a later Configuration Exercise.

Figure 2-13 *Configuration Exercise Topology*

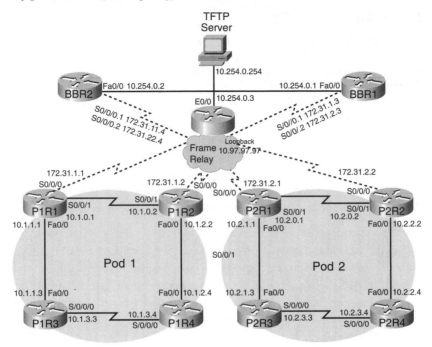

Command List

In this exercise, you use the commands in Table 2-5, listed in logical order. Refer to this list if you need configuration command assistance during the exercise.

> **CAUTION** Although the command syntax is shown in this table, the addresses shown are typically for the P*x*R1 and P*x*R3 routers. Be careful when addressing your routers! Refer to the exercise instructions and the appropriate visual objective diagram for addressing details.

Table 2-5 *Configuration Exercise Command List*

Command	Description
(config)#**hostname** *PxRy*	Assigns a hostname
(config)#**enable secret cisco**	Specifies *cisco* as the secret password
(config)#**line vty 0 4**	Enters configuration mode for vty lines
(config-line)#**login**	Specifies that a password is required to log in when telnetting
(config-line)#**password sanfran**	Specifies *sanfran* as the password required to log in when telnetting
(config)#**line con 0**	Enters configuration mode for console port

Table 2-5   *Configuration Exercise Command List (Continued)*

Command	Description
(config-line)#**logging synchronous**	Synchronizes output on the configured line
(config-line)#**exec-timeout 0 0**	Specifies no timeout on the configured line
(config)#**no ip domain lookup**	Disables Domain Name System (DNS) lookup
(config-if)#**ip address 10.*x*.1.*y* 255.255.255.0**	Assigns an IP address to an interface
(config-if)#**no shutdown**	Enables an interface
(config-if)#**encapsulation frame-relay**	Enables Frame Relay encapsulation on an interface
(config-if)#**no frame-relay inverse-arp**	Turns off Inverse ARP on a Frame Relay interface
(config-if)#**frame-relay map ip 172.31.*x*.3 1*xy* broadcast**	Maps a next-hop IP address to a permanent virtual circuit (PVC)
(config-if)#**clock rate 64000**	Assigns a clock rate on a data circuit-terminating equipment (DCE) interface
#**ping 10.*x*.0.*y***	Pings an address
#**copy run start**	Copies the running configuration file (in RAM) into the startup configuration file (in NVRAM)
(config)#**no ip classless**	Instructs the router to behave classfully
(config)#**router rip**	Turns on RIP
(config-router)#**version 1**	Runs RIPv1
(config-router)#**network 172.31.0.0**	Specifies a classful network that RIP should run within
#**show ip protocols**	Displays information about the IP routing protocols running on the router
#**debug ip rip**	Starts the console display of the IP RIP-related events on the router
#**show ip route**	Displays the IP routing table
(config-router)#**default-information originate**	Advertises the default route through RIP
(config)#**ip classless**	Instructs the router to behave classlessly
(config-router)#**version 2**	Runs RIPv2
(config-router)#**no auto-summary**	Instructs the router to not automatically summarize routes at classful boundaries

> **NOTE**   This book assumes that you are familiar with basic Cisco IOS router configuration commands, some of which are required in this Configuration Exercise but are not explicitly covered in this chapter. If you are not familiar with these commands, you might want to refer to another source, such as the Cisco Press book *CCNA Self-Study: Interconnecting Cisco Network Devices (ICND) 640-811, 640-801, 2nd Edition* (ISBN: 1587051427).

> **NOTE**   The exercise tasks include answers and solutions. Some answers cover multiple steps; the answers are given after the last step to which that answer applies.

Task 1: Setting Up the Edge Routers

In this task, you use a terminal utility to establish a console connection to the equipment. You establish connectivity between the edge routers in your pod (P*x*R1 and P*x*R2) and the BBR1 router. Complete the following steps:

Step 1   Connect to each of your pod edge routers (P*x*R1 and P*x*R2); they should not have configurations on them. If a router does have a configuration, delete the configuration using the **erase start** command, and then use the **reload** command to reboot.

Step 2   Do not use the initial configuration mode to configure your routers; instead, use the Cisco IOS command line. Configure the hostname of your router (P*x*R1 and P*x*R2). Configure the enable secret password to be cisco, and the vty password to be sanfran. Configure the **logging synchronous** command and the **exec-timeout 0 0** command on the console line. What do these two commands do? Configure the **no ip domain lookup** command; what does this command do?

Step 3   On P*x*R1, assign an IP address of 10.*x*.1.*y*/24 to the FastEthernet 0/0 interface, where *x* is your pod number and *y* is your router number. Enable the interface.

Step 4   On P*x*R2, assign an IP address of 10.*x*.2.*y*/24 to the FastEthernet 0/0 interface, where *x* is your pod number and *y* is your router number. Enable the interface.

Step 5   Configure the Serial 0/0/0 interface for Frame Relay by turning on Frame Relay encapsulation.

Step 6   Assign an IP address to your Serial 0/0/0 interface. Your IP address is 172.31.*x*.*y*/24, where *x* is your pod number and *y* is your router number.

Step 7   Inverse ARP has been turned off in the core Frame Relay network; turn off **inverse arp** on your Frame Relay interface. Manually map a data-link connection identifier (DLCI) to BBR1 (172.31.*x*.3). The DLCI number is in the form 1*xy*, where *x* is your pod number, and *y* is your router number. For instance, P2R1 will use DLCI 121.

> **NOTE** Remember to specify the **broadcast** keyword so that the Frame Relay mapping supports broadcasts and multicasts, such as routing protocol traffic.

Step 8   Enable the S0/0/0 interface.

Step 9   Assign an IP address to your Serial 0/0/1 interface. Your IP address is 10.*x*.0.*y*/24, where *x* is your pod number, and *y* is your router number.

Step 10   The Serial 0/0/1 interface on your P*x*R1 router is DCE; configure a clock rate of 64 kbps on this interface.

Step 11   Enable the S0/0/1 interface.

> **NOTE** Remember to configure both of your edge routers, P*x*R1 and P*x*R2.

Solution:

The following shows how to perform the required steps on the P1R1 router:

```
Router (config)#hostname P1R1
P1R1(config)#enable secret cisco
P1R1(config)#line vty 0 4
P1R1(config-line)#login
% Login disabled on line 322, until 'password' is set
% Login disabled on line 323, until 'password' is set
% Login disabled on line 324, until 'password' is set
% Login disabled on line 325, until 'password' is set
% Login disabled on line 326, until 'password' is set
P1R1(config-line)#password sanfran
P1R1(config-line)#line con 0
P1R1(config-line)#logging synchronous
P1R1(config-line)#exec-timeout 0 0
P1R1(config-line)#no ip domain lookup
P1R1(config)#int fa0/0
P1R1(config-if)#ip address 10.1.1.1 255.255.255.0
P1R1(config-if)#no shutdown
P1R1(config-if)#int s0/0/0
P1R1(config-if)#encapsulation frame-relay
P1R1(config-if)#ip address 172.31.1.1 255.255.255.0
P1R1(config-if)#no frame-relay inverse-arp
P1R1(config-if)#frame map ip 172.31.1.3 111 broadcast
P1R1(config-if)#no shutdown
P1R1(config-if)#int s0/0/1
P1R1(config-if)#ip address 10.1.0.1 255.255.255.0
P1R1(config-if)#clock rate  64000
P1R1(config-if)#no shutdown
```

The **logging synchronous** command synchronizes the terminal output on configured line. For example, if you are in the middle of typing a command and the router outputs a message to the terminal, your text will be repeated on the screen when the output is complete.

The **exec-timeout 0 0** command specifies no timeout on the configured line, so that the EXEC session will not time out.

The **no ip domain lookup** command disables DNS lookups; this command proves useful when you do not have a DNS server in your network, such as in a lab environment.

Step 12   Verify successful connectivity between your P*x*R1 and P*x*R2 routers using the **ping** command.

Step 13   Verify successful connectivity from your P*x*R1 and P*x*R2 routers to the core BBR1 router (172.31.*x*.3) using the **ping** command.

Step 14   Save your configurations to NVRAM.

Solution:

The following shows how to perform the required steps on the P1R1 router:

```
P1R1#ping 10.1.0.2

Type escape sequence to abort.
Sending 5, 100-byte ICMP Echos to 10.1.0.2, timeout is 2 seconds:
!!!!!
Success rate is 100 percent (5/5), round-trip min/avg/max = 28/28/32 ms
P1R1#ping 172.31.1.3

Type escape sequence to abort.
Sending 5, 100-byte ICMP Echos to 172.31.1.3, timeout is 2 seconds:
!!!!!
Success rate is 100 percent (5/5), round-trip min/avg/max = 28/46/108 ms
P1R1#copy run start
Destination filename [startup-config]?
Building configuration...
[OK]
P1R1#
```

Task 2: Setting Up the Internal Routers

In this task, you use a terminal utility to establish a console connection to the equipment. You establish connectivity between the internal routers (P*x*R3 and P*x*R4) and the edge routers in your pod (P*x*R1 and P*x*R2). Complete the following steps:

Step 1   Connect to each of your pod internal routers (P*x*R3 and P*x*R4); they should not have configurations on them. If a router does have a configuration, delete the configuration using the **erase start** command, and then use the **reload** command to reboot.

Step 2   Do not use the initial configuration mode to configure your routers; instead, use the Cisco IOS command line. Configure the hostname of your router (P*x*R3 and P*x*R4). Configure the enable secret password to be cisco, and the vty password to be sanfran. Configure the **logging synchronous** command and the **exec-timeout 0 0** command on the console line. Configure the **no ip domain lookup** command.

Step 3   On P*x*R3, assign an IP address of 10.*x*.1.*y*/24 to the FastEthernet 0/0 interface, where *x* is your pod number, and *y* is your router number. Enable the interface.

Step 4   On P*x*R4, assign an IP address of 10.*x*.2.*y*/24 to the FastEthernet 0/0 interface, where *x* is your pod number, and *y* is your router number. Enable the interface.

Step 5   Assign an IP address to your Serial 0/0/0 interface. Your IP address is 10.*x*.3.*y*/24, where *x* is your pod number, and *y* is your router number.

Step 6   The Serial 0/0/0 interface on your P*x*R3 router is DCE; configure a clock of 64 kbps on this interface.

Step 7   Enable the S0/0/0 interface.

Solution:

The following shows how to perform the required steps on the P1R3 router:

```
Router(config)#hostname P1R3
P1R3(config)#enable secret cisco
P1R3(config)#line vty 0 4
P1R3(config-line)#login
% Login disabled on line 322, until 'password' is set
% Login disabled on line 323, until 'password' is set
% Login disabled on line 324, until 'password' is set
% Login disabled on line 325, until 'password' is set
% Login disabled on line 326, until 'password' is set
P1R3(config-line)#pass sanfran
P1R3(config-line)#line con 0
P1R3(config-line)#logging synchronous
P1R3(config-line)#exec-timeout 0 0
P1R3(config-line)#exit
P1R3(oonfig)#no ip domain-lookup
P1R3(config)#int fa0/0
P1R3(config-if)#ip address 10.1.1.3 255.255.255.0
P1R3(config-if)#no shutdown
P1R3(config-if)#int s0/0/0
P1R3(config-if)#ip address 10.1.3.3 255.255.255.0
P1R3(config-if)#clock rate 64000
P1R3(config-if)#no shutdown
```

Step 8   Verify successful connectivity between your P*x*R3 and P*x*R4 routers using the **ping** command.

Step 9   Verify successful connectivity between your edge routers (P*x*R1 and P*x*R2) and your internal routers (P*x*R3 and P*x*R4) using the **ping** command.

Step 10   Save your configurations to NVRAM.

Solution:

The following shows how to perform the required steps on the P1R3 router:

```
P1R3#ping 10.1.3.4

Type escape sequence to abort.
Sending 5, 100-byte ICMP Echos to 10.1.3.4, timeout is 2 seconds:
!!!!!
```

```
Success rate is 100 percent (5/5), round-trip min/avg/max = 28/28/32 ms
P1R3#ping 10.1.1.1

Type escape sequence to abort.
Sending 5, 100-byte ICMP Echos to 10.1.1.1, timeout is 2 seconds:
.!!!!
Success rate is 80 percent (4/5), round-trip min/avg/max = 1/1/4 ms
P1R3#
P1R3#copy run start
Destination filename [startup-config]?
Building configuration...
[OK]
P1R3#
```

Task 3: Exploring Classful Routing

In this task, you explore classful routing. Follow these steps:

Step 1   On all the routers within your assigned pod, enter the **no ip classless** global
configuration command.

> **NOTE**   The **no ip classless** command forces your router to behave classfully; recall that in
> Cisco IOS 12.0 and later the default is the **ip classless** command. You return the routers to the
> default behavior later in this exercise.

Step 2   On all the routers within your assigned pod, configure RIPv1 for the pod
network 10.0.0.0. Include the 172.31.0.0 Frame Relay network in the edge
routers' configurations.

Step 3   By default, RIP sends Version 1 advertisements and can receive Versions 1
and 2. Explicitly specify RIPv1 using the **version 1** command.

Solution:

The following configuration is for the pod 1 routers:

```
P1R1(config)#no ip classless
P1R1(config)#router rip
P1R1(config-router)#version 1
P1R1(config-router)#network 10.0.0.0
P1R1(config-router)#network 172.31.0.0

P1R2(config)#no ip classless
P1R2(config)#router rip
P1R2(config-router)#version 1
P1R2(config-router)#network 10.0.0.0
P1R2(config-router)#network 172.31.0.0

P1R3(config)#no ip classless
P1R3(config)#router rip
P1R3(config-router)#version 1
P1R3(config-router)#network 10.0.0.0
```

```
P1R4(config)#no ip classless
P1R4(config)#router rip
P1R4(config-router)#version 1
P1R4(config-router)#network 10.0.0.0
```

Step 4   Verify that your routers accept only Version 1 advertisements using the
                  show ip protocols command.

Solution:

The following sample output is from the P1R1 router. Note that under the Recv column, only
Version 1 is displayed:

```
P1R1#show ip protocols
Routing Protocol is "rip"
  Sending updates every 30 seconds, next due in 14 seconds
  Invalid after 180 seconds, hold down 180, flushed after 240
  Outgoing update filter list for all interfaces is not set
  Incoming update filter list for all interfaces is not set
  Redistributing: rip
  Default version control: send version 1, receive version 1
    Interface           Send  Recv  Triggered RIP  Key-chain
    FastEthernet0/0      1     1
    Serial0/0/0          1     1
    Serial0/0/1          1     1
  Automatic network summarization is in effect
  Maximum path: 4
  Routing for Networks:
    10.0.0.0
    172.31.0.0
  Routing Information Sources:
    Gateway         Distance      Last Update
    10.1.1.3             120      00:00:18
    10.1.0.2             120      00:00:15
    172.31.1.3           120      00:00:07
  Distance: (default is 120)
```

Step 5   Test connectivity to the Trivial File Transfer Protocol (TFTP) server
                  (10.254.0.254) from the internal routers using the **ping** command. Do the
                  pings work?

Solution:

The following sample output is from the P1R3 router. The ping did not work:

```
P1R3#ping 10.254.0.254
Type escape sequence to abort.
Sending 5, 100-byte ICMP Echos to 10.254.0.254, timeout is 2 seconds:
.....
Success rate is 0
percent (0/5) P1R3#
```

Step 6   To investigate the results of the previous step, use the **debug ip rip** and
                  show ip route commands to examine the routers' behavior.

                  Can your internal router reach the core router? Why or why not?

Solution:

The internal router cannot reach the core because it does not have a route for the 10.254.0.0 subnet in its routing table. Classful routing protocols such as RIPv1 do not exchange subnet mask information and either assume a constant mask throughout the classful network or advertise the entire classful network. Advertisements between the pod edge routers and BBR1 go across the 172.31.0.0 network. Therefore, all three routers summarize the subnets of network 10.0.0.0 and advertise network 10.0.0.0 to each other. Each router ignores this advertisement, because it already has a route to the 10.0.0.0 network. Classful routing behavior is to look for known routes within the connected classful network (10.0.0.0 in this case) and to not consider less-specific routes. You can verify this behavior with the **debug ip rip** command and by displaying the routing table on the internal router, looking for a route to the 10.254.0.0 network. The following output is from the P1R1 and P1R3 routers:

```
P1R1#debug ip rip
RIP protocol debugging is on
P1R1#
*Apr 28 19:19:07 EST: RIP: received v1 update from 10.1.0.2 on Serial0/0/1
*Apr 28 19:19:07 EST:      10.1.2.0 in 1 hops
*Apr 28 19:19:07 EST:      10.1.3.0 in 2 hops
*Apr 28 19:19:07 EST:      172.31.0.0 in 1 hops
P1R1#
*Apr 28 19:19:15 EST: RIP: sending v1 update to 255.255.255.255 via FastEthernet0/0
   (10.1.1.1)
*Apr 28 19:19:15 EST: RIP: build update entries
*Apr 28 19:19:15 EST:      subnet 10.1.0.0 metric 1
*Apr 28 19:19:15 EST:      subnet 10.1.2.0 metric 2
*Apr 28 19:19:15 EST:      network 172.31.0.0 metric 1
*Apr 28 19:19:15 EST: RIP: sending v1 update to 255.255.255.255 via Serial0/0/0
   (172.31.1.1)
*Apr 28 19:19:15 EST: RIP: build update entries
*Apr 28 19:19:15 EST:      network 10.0.0.0 metric 1
*Apr 28 19:19:15 EST:      subnet 172.31.1.0 metric 1
*Apr 28 19:19:15 EST:      subnet 172.31.2.0 metric 2
*Apr 28 19:19:15 EST: RIP: sending v1 update to 255.255.255.255 via Serial0/0/1
   (10.1.0.1)
P1R1#
*Apr 28 19:19:15 EST: RIP: build update entries
*Apr 28 19:19:15 EST:      subnet 10.1.1.0 metric 1
*Apr 28 19:19:15 EST:      subnet 10.1.3.0 metric 2
*Apr 28 19:19:15 EST:      network 172.31.0.0 metric 1
P1R1#
*Apr 28 19:19:19 EST: RIP: received v1 update from 172.31.1.3 on Serial0/0/0
*Apr 28 19:19:19 EST:      10.0.0.0 in 1 hops
*Apr 28 19:19:19 EST:      172.31.2.0 in 1 hops
*Apr 28 19:19:19 EST: RIP: ignored v2 packet from 172.31.1.3 (illegal version)
P1R1#

P1R1#show ip route
<output omitted>
     172.31.0.0/24 is subnetted, 2 subnets
R       172.31.2.0 [120/1] via 172.31.1.3, 00:00:26, Serial0/0/0
C       172.31.1.0 is directly connected, Serial0/0/0
     10.0.0.0/24 is subnetted, 4 subnets
R       10.1.3.0 [120/1] via 10.1.1.3, 00:00:14, FastEthernet0/0
R       10.1.2.0 [120/1] via 10.1.0.2, 00:00:11, Serial0/0/1
C       10.1.1.0 is directly connected, FastEthernet0/0
C       10.1.0.0 is directly connected, Serial0/0/1
P1R1#
```

```
P1R3#
P1R3#show ip route
<output omitted>
R    172.31.0.0/16 [120/1] via 10.1.1.1, 00:00:16, FastEthernet0/0
     10.0.0.0/24 is subnetted, 4 subnets
C       10.1.3.0 is directly connected, Serial0/0/0
R       10.1.2.0 [120/1] via 10.1.3.4, 00:00:04, Serial0/0/0
C       10.1.1.0 is directly connected, FastEthernet0/0
R       10.1.0.0 [120/1] via 10.1.1.1, 00:00:16, FastEthernet0/0
P1R3#
```

Step 7   To try to allow the internal routers to reach the core, advertise a default route from the edge routers through RIP using the **default-information originate** router configuration command.

Solution:

The following illustrates how to configure the edge routers in pod 1:

```
P1R1(config)#router rip
P1R1(config-router)#default-information originate

P1R2(config)#router rip
P1R2(config-router)#default-information originate
```

Step 8   Look at the routing table on the internal routers. Is there a path now? Remember that RIP is slow to converge. You might need to wait up to a minute, even in this small network, before the default route appears on the internal router. To force convergence, you can issue the **clear ip route *** command.

Solution:

The following sample output is from P1R3:

```
P1R3#show ip route
<output omitted>
Gateway of last resort is 10.1.1.1 to network 0.0.0.0

R    172.31.0.0/16 [120/1] via 10.1.1.1, 00:00:26, FastEthernet0/0
     10.0.0.0/24 is subnetted, 4 subnets
C       10.1.3.0 is directly connected, Serial0/0/0
R       10.1.2.0 [120/1] via 10.1.3.4, 00:00:14, Serial0/0/0
C       10.1.1.0 is directly connected, FastEthernet0/0
R       10.1.0.0 [120/1] via 10.1.1.1, 00:00:26, FastEthernet0/0
R*   0.0.0.0/0 [120/1] via 10.1.1.1, 00:00:26, FastEthernet0/0
```

The following sample output is from P1R4:

```
P1R4#show ip route
<output omitted>
Gateway of last resort is 10.1.3.3 to network 0.0.0.0

R    172.31.0.0/16 [120/1] via 10.1.2.2, 00:00:17, FastEthernet0/0
     10.0.0.0/24 is subnetted, 4 subnets
C       10.1.3.0 is directly connected, Serial0/0/0
C       10.1.2.0 is directly connected, FastEthernet0/0
R       10.1.1.0 [120/1] via 10.1.3.3, 00:00:14, Serial0/0/0
```

```
R        10.1.0.0 [120/1] via 10.1.2.2, 00:00:17, FastEthernet0/0
R*   0.0.0.0/0 [120/2] via 10.1.3.3, 00:00:14, Serial0/0/0
                    [120/2] via 10.1.2.2, 00:00:17, FastEthernet0/0
```

Notice a default route in the P*x*R3 and P*x*R4 routing tables. This default route is the result of the pod's edge routers, P*x*R1 and P*x*R2, advertising themselves as default with the **default-information originate** command. Notice that only one route to the 0.0.0.0 default route appears in the routing table for P1R3, whereas P1R4 has two equal-cost routes to 0.0.0.0. This is because P1R3 advertises its default route to P1R4 first (because P1R1 was the first to be configured and it sends its route to P1R3); because of split horizon, P1R4 does not advertise the default route back to P1R3. The routing table for P1R2 also has the default route, learned from P1R1; P1R1 does not have the default route from P1R2, again because of split horizon.

Step 9   Again, test connectivity from the internal routers to the TFTP server using **ping**. Do the pings work now?

Solution:

The following sample output is from the P1R3 and P1R4 routers. The pings still do not work. (The reasoning behind this is examined in the next task.)

```
P1R3#ping 10.254.0.254
Type escape sequence to abort.
Sending 5, 100-byte ICMP Echos to 10.254.0.254, timeout is 2 seconds:
.....
Success rate is 0 percent (0/5)

P1R3#
P1R4#ping 10.254.0.254
Type escape sequence to abort.
Sending 5, 100-byte ICMP Echos to 10.254.0.254, timeout is 2 seconds:
.....
Success rate is 0 percent (0/5)
P1R4#
```

Task 4: Exploring Classless Forwarding

The ping to the TFTP server in the preceding task did not work because the behavior of classful routing is to look for known routes within the connected classful network (10.0.0.0 in this case) and to not consider less-specific routes, such as a default route. Given that classful behavior is the cause of the problem, this task explores classless behavior. Follow these steps:

Step 1   The TFTP server cannot be reached because the router has been instructed to route classfully with the **no ip classless** command. Enable classless IP on each router in your pod to explore classless behavior.

Solution:

The following sample configuration is on the P1R1 router:

```
P1R1(config)#ip classless
```

Step 2   Test connectivity from the internal routers to the TFTP server. Do the pings work now?

Solution:

The following outputs are from the P1R3 and P1R4 routers. The pings still do not work:

```
P1R3#ping 10.254.0.254
Type escape sequence to abort.
Sending 5, 100-byte ICMP Echos to 10.254.0.254, timeout is 2 seconds:
U.U.U
Success rate is 0 percent (0/5)

P1R4#ping 10.254.0.254
Type escape sequence to abort.
Sending 5, 100-byte ICMP Echos to 10.254.0.254, timeout is 2 seconds:
UU.UU
Success rate is 0 percent (0/5)
```

The U result for the pings indicates that this router has a valid route in its routing table (the default route), but the echo reply still was not received. Although you changed the router behavior, RIPv1 still is a classful routing protocol and still is autosummarizing across the Frame Relay link. The BBR1 router does not have a route back to the 10.x.1.0/24 or 10.x.2.0/24 subnets, so the ping does not work.

Step 3   To fix the connectivity problem, change to the classless version of RIP, RIPv2, and turn off RIP automatic route summarization on the edge routers.

Solution:

The following sample configuration is on the pod 1 routers:

```
P1R1(config)#router rip
P1R1(config-router)#version 2
P1R1(config-router)#no auto-summary

P1R2(config)#router rip
P1R2(config-router)#version 2
P1R2(config-router)#no auto-summary

P1R3(config)#router rip
P1R3(config-router)#version 2

P1R4(config)#router rip
P1R4(config-router)#version 2
```

Step 4   One more time, test connectivity from the internal routers to the TFTP server. Do the pings work now?

Solution:

The following sample output is from the P1R3 and P1R4 routers. The pings now work:

```
P1R3#ping 10.254.0.254
Type escape sequence to abort.
```

```
Sending 5, 100-byte ICMP Echos to 10.254.0.254, timeout is 2 seconds:
!!!!!
Success rate is 100 percent (5/5), round-trip min/avg/max = 32/33/36 ms
P1R3#

P1R4#ping 10.254.0.254
Type escape sequence to abort.
Sending 5, 100-byte ICMP Echos to 10.254.0.254, timeout is 2 seconds:
!!!!!
Success rate is 100 percent (5/5), round-trip min/avg/max = 36/36/40 ms
P1R4#
```

Task 5: Optimizing Classless Routes for Scalability

As the network grows, large routing tables are inefficient because of the memory required to store them. Any routing event (such as a flapping line) must be propagated throughout the network for each route in the routing table. Summarization limits the update traffic and minimizes the size of the routing tables of all routers. In this task, you configure summarization on your edge routers. Follow these steps:

Step 1   From an internal router, use Telnet to connect to BBR1 (172.31.x.0); the password is cisco. Notice that all of your pod's networks are listed in BBR1's routing table.

Solution:

The following sample output is from the BBR1 router, showing the relevant portion of the routing table:

```
BBR1>show ip route
<output omitted>
     10.0.0.0/24 is subnetted, 6 subnets
R       10.1.3.0 [120/2] via 172.31.1.2, 00:00:09, Serial0/0.1
                 [120/2] via 172.31.1.1, 00:00:13, Serial0/0.1
R       10.1.2.0 [120/1] via 172.31.1.2, 00:00:09, Serial0/0.1
R       10.1.1.0 [120/1] via 172.31.1.1, 00:00:13, Serial0/0.1
B       10.97.97.0 [20/0] via 10.254.0.3, 00:00:13
R       10.1.0.0 [120/1] via 172.31.1.2, 00:00:09, Serial0/0.1
                 [120/1] via 172.31.1.1, 00:00:13, Serial0/0.1
C       10.254.0.0 is directly connected, FastEthernet0/0
```

> **NOTE**   The 10.97.97.0 subnet is a loopback address, configured on the Frame Relay switch router, for use in a later configuration exercise.

Step 2   Configure the edge routers to announce a summary route of 10.x.0.0 255.255.0.0 to BBR1. Where should you place the appropriate command?

Solution:

The following sample configuration is on the P1R1 and P1R2 routers. The summarization commands are placed on the S0/0/0 interfaces that connect to the BBR1 router:

```
P1R1(config)#int s0/0/0
P1R1(config-if)#ip summary-address rip 10.1.0.0 255.255.0.0

P1R2(config)#int s0/0/0
P1R2(config-if)#ip summary-address rip 10.1.0.0 255.255.0.0
```

Step 3   Review the routing table on BBR1 again. What is the difference now?
Remember that RIP is slow to converge, so you might need to wait up to a
minute, even in this small network, before the summaries appear on BBR1.

Solution:

The following sample output is from the BBR1 router, showing the relevant portion of the
routing table:

```
BBR1>show ip route
<output omitted>
     10.0.0.0/8 is variably subnetted, 3 subnets, 2 masks
B       10.97.97.0/24 [20/0] via 10.254.0.3, 00:00:08
R       10.1.0.0/16 [120/1] via 172.31.1.2, 00:00:08, Serial0/0.1
                    [120/1] via 172.31.1.1, 00:00:00, Serial0/0.1
C       10.254.0.0/24 is directly connected, FastEthernet0/0
```

Step 4   Examine the output from the **show ip protocols** command for details about
the operation of RIP.

Solution:

The following sample output is from the P1R2 router. It shows that RIPv2 is running for network
10.0.0.0, that autosummarization is off, and that manual summarization to 10.1.0.0/16 is on
Serial 0/0/0:

```
P1R2#show ip protocols
Routing Protocol is "rip"
  Sending updates every 30 seconds, next due in 16 seconds
  Invalid after 180 seconds, hold down 180, flushed after 240
  Outgoing update filter list for all interfaces is not set
  Incoming update filter list for all interfaces is not set
  Redistributing: rip
  Default version control: send version 2, receive version 2
    Interface          Send  Recv  Triggered RIP  Key-chain
    FastEthernet0/0     2     2
    Serial0/0/0         2     2
    Serial0/0/1         2     2
  Automatic network summarization is not in effect
  Address Summarization:
    10.1.0.0/16 for Serial0/0/0
  Maximum path: 4
  Routing for Networks:
    10.0.0.0
    172.31.0.0
  Routing Information Sources:
    Gateway         Distance      Last Update
    10.1.0.1             120      00:00:22
    10.1.2.4             120      00:00:06
    172.31.1.3           120      00:00:08
  Distance: (default is 120) P1R2#
```

Exercise Verification

You have successfully completed this exercise when you achieve the following results:

■   You have put a basic configuration on your pod devices, and verified connectivity with directly connected devices.

■   You have configured RIPv1 as a routing protocol and explored its shortcomings.

■   You have configured RIPv2 and examined its behavior.

Review Questions

Answer the following questions, and then refer to Appendix A, "Answers to Review Questions," for the answers.

1. Which of the following is not a scenario in which static routes would be used?

    a. When the administrator needs total control over the routes used by the router

    b. When a backup to a dynamically recognized route is necessary

    c. When rapid convergence is needed

    d. When a route should appear to the router as a directly connected network

2. What are two drawbacks of static routes?

    a. Reconfiguring to reflect topology changes

    b. Complex metrics

    c. Involved convergence

    d. Absence of dynamic route discovery

3. What is used by traffic for which the destination network is not specifically listed in the routing table?

    a. Dynamic area

    b. Default route

    c. Border gateway

    d. Black hole

4. The **show ip route** command usually provides information on which of the following two items?

  a. Next hop

  b. Metric

  c. CDP

  d. Hostname

5. When using dynamic routing protocols, what does the administrator configure the routing protocol on?

  a. Each area

  b. Each intermediate system

  c. Each router

  d. Each gateway of last resort

6. Which of the following is not a dynamic routing protocol?

  a. IS-IS

  b. CDP

  c. EIGRP

  d. BGP

  e. RIPv2

7. What is a metric?

  a. A standard of measurement used by routing algorithms

  b. The set of techniques used to manage network resources

  c. Interdomain routing in TCP/IP networks

  d. Services limit the input or output transmission rate

8. Which routing protocol uses only major classful networks to determine the interfaces participating in the protocol?

  a. EIGRP

  b. RIPv1

  c. IS-IS

  d. BGP

  e. OSPF

9. ODR uses what to carry network information between spoke (stub) routers and the hub?

   a. Metric

   b. BGP

   c. Convergence

   d. CDP

10. Which of the following is not a classification of routing protocols?

    a. Link-state

    b. Default

    c. Hybrid

    d. Distance vector

11. What do you call the process when a router, using a classful routing protocol, sends an update about a subnet of a classful network across an interface belonging to a different classful network and assumes that the remote router will use the default subnet mask for that class of IP address?

    a. Autosummarization

    b. Default routing

    c. Classful switching

    d. Tunneling

12. True or false: Discontiguous subnets are subnets of the same major network that are separated by a different major network.

13. Classless routing protocols allow _____.

    a. QoS

    b. VLSM

    c. VPN

    d. RIP

14. What is the command to turn off autosummarization?

    a. **no auto-summarization**

    b. **enable classless**

    c. **ip route**

    d. **no auto-summary**

15. What is the OSPF default administrative distance value?

    a. 90

    b. 100

    c. 110

    d. 120

16. When a static route's administrative distance is manually configured to be higher than the default administrative distance of dynamic routing protocols, that static route is called what?

    a. Semistatic route

    b. Floating static route

    c. Semidynamic route

    d. Manual route

17. Which variables can be used to calculate metrics?

    a. Hops

    b. Convergence time

    c. Administrative distance

    d. Path attributes

    e. Cost

This chapter introduces you to Enhanced Interior Gateway Routing Protocol (EIGRP). This chapter covers the following topics:

- EIGRP Overview

- EIGRP Terminology and Operation

- Configuring and Verifying EIGRP

- Configuring EIGRP Authentication

- Using EIGRP in an Enterprise Network

- Verifying EIGRP Operation

CHAPTER 3

Configuring the Enhanced Interior Gateway Routing Protocol

In present-day and future routing environments, Enhanced Interior Gateway Routing Protocol (EIGRP) offers benefits and features over historic distance vector routing protocols, such as Routing Information Protocol Version 1 (RIPv1) and Interior Gateway Routing Protocol (IGRP). These benefits include rapid convergence, lower bandwidth utilization, and multiple-routed protocol support.

> **NOTE** As of Cisco IOS Software Release 12.3, IGRP is no longer supported.

This chapter introduces EIGRP terminology and concepts and EIGRP configuration, verification, and troubleshooting. The chapter also explores topics such as route summarization, load balancing, bandwidth usage, and authentication. The chapter concludes with a discussion of EIGRP design and configuration techniques to implement an effective enterprise network.

EIGRP Overview

This section introduces EIGRP and describes its four underlying technologies.

EIGRP Capabilities and Attributes

EIGRP is a Cisco-proprietary protocol that combines the advantages of link-state and distance vector routing protocols. EIGRP has its roots as a distance vector routing protocol and is predictable in its behavior. Like its predecessor IGRP, EIGRP is easy to configure and is adaptable to a wide variety of network topologies. What makes EIGRP an *advanced* distance vector protocol is the addition of several link-state features, such as dynamic neighbor discovery. EIGRP is an *enhanced* IGRP because of its rapid convergence and the guarantee of a loop-free topology at all times. Features of this hybrid protocol include the following:

- **Fast convergence**—EIGRP uses the Diffusing Update Algorithm (DUAL) to achieve rapid convergence. A router running EIGRP stores its neighbors' routing tables so that it can quickly adapt to changes in the network. If no appropriate route or backup route exists in the local routing table, EIGRP queries its neighbors to discover an alternative route. These queries are propagated until an alternative route is found, or it is determined that no alternative route exists.

- **Variable-length subnet masking (VLSM) support**—EIGRP is a classless routing protocol, which means that it advertises a subnet mask for each destination network; this enables EIGRP to support discontinuous subnetworks and VLSM.

- **Partial updates**—EIGRP sends partial triggered updates instead of periodic updates. These updates are sent only when the path or the metric for a route changes; they contain information about only that changed link rather than the entire routing table. Propagation of these partial updates is automatically bounded so that only those routers that require the information are updated. As a result, EIGRP consumes significantly less bandwidth than IGRP. This behavior is also different than link-state protocol operation, which sends a change update to *all* routers within an area.

- **Multiple network layer support**—EIGRP supports IP, AppleTalk, and Novell NetWare Internetwork Packet Exchange (IPX) using protocol-dependent modules that are responsible for protocol requirements specific to the network layer. EIGRP's rapid convergence and sophisticated metric offer superior performance and stability when implemented in IP, IPX, and AppleTalk networks.

NOTE Only the IP implementation of EIGRP is thoroughly covered in this book. Refer to the Cisco IOS technical documentation at http://www.cisco.com for information about how EIGRP operates, and how to configure it, for AppleTalk and IPX.

Other EIGRP features include the following:

- **Seamless connectivity across all data link layer protocols and topologies**—EIGRP does not require special configuration to work across any Layer 2 protocols. Other routing protocols, such as Open Shortest Path First (OSPF), require different configurations for different Layer 2 protocols, such as Ethernet and Frame Relay (as you will see in Chapter 4, "Configuring the Open Shortest Path First Protocol"). EIGRP was designed to operate effectively in both local-area network (LAN) and wide-area network (WAN) environments. In multiaccess topologies, such as Ethernet, neighbor relationships are formed and maintained using reliable multicasting. EIGRP supports all WAN topologies: dedicated links, point-to-point links, and nonbroadcast multiaccess (NBMA) topologies. EIGRP accommodates differences in media types and speeds when neighbor adjacencies form across WAN links. The amount of bandwidth that EIGRP uses on WAN links can be limited.

- **Sophisticated metric**—EIGRP uses the same algorithm for metric calculation as IGRP, but represents values in a 32-bit format, rather than IGRP's 24-bit format, to give additional granularity (thus, the EIGRP metric is the IGRP metric multiplied by 256). A significant advantage of EIGRP (and IGRP) over other protocols is its support for unequal metric load balancing that allows administrators to better distribute traffic flow in their networks.

■ **Use of multicast and unicast**—EIGRP uses multicast and unicast for communication between routers, rather than broadcast. As a result, end stations are unaffected by routing updates or queries. The multicast address used for EIGRP is 224.0.0.10.

Like most IP routing protocols, EIGRP relies on IP packets to deliver routing information (Integrated Intermediate System-to-Intermediate System [IS-IS] is the exception, as you will see in Chapter 6, "Configuring the Integrated Intermediate System-to-Intermediate System Protocol"). The EIGRP routing process is a transport layer function of the Open System Interconnection (OSI) reference model. IP packets carrying EIGRP information have protocol number 88 in their IP header, as illustrated in Figure 3-1.

Figure 3-1 *EIGRP Is a Transport Layer Function*

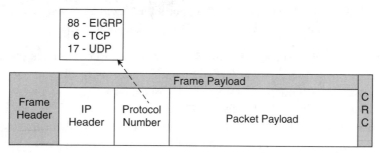

Figure 3-2 illustrates how EIGRP performs automatic route summarization at major network boundaries. Administrators can also configure manual summarization on arbitrary bit boundaries on any router interface (as long as a more-specific route exists in the routing table) to shrink the size of the routing table. EIGRP also supports the creation of supernets or aggregated blocks of addresses (networks).

Figure 3-2 *EIGRP Performs Route Summarization by Default*

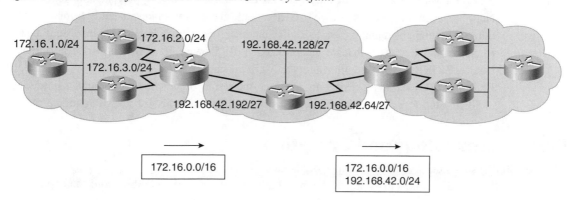

EIGRP supports both hierarchical and nonhierarchical IP addressing.

Underlying Processes and Technologies

EIGRP uses the following four key technologies that combine to differentiate it from other routing technologies:

■ **Neighbor discovery/recovery mechanism**—EIGRP's neighbor discovery mechanism enables routers to dynamically learn about other routers on their directly attached networks. Routers also must discover when their neighbors become unreachable or inoperative. This process is achieved with low overhead by periodically sending small hello packets. As long as a router receives hello packets from a neighboring router, it assumes that the neighbor is functioning, and the two can exchange routing information.

■ **Reliable Transport Protocol (RTP)**—RTP is responsible for guaranteed, ordered delivery of EIGRP packets to all neighbors. RTP supports intermixed transmission of multicast or unicast packets. For efficiency, only certain EIGRP packets are transmitted reliably.

For example, on a multiaccess network that has multicast capabilities, such as Ethernet, it is not necessary to send hello packets reliably to all neighbors individually, so EIGRP sends a single multicast hello packet containing an indicator that informs the receivers that the packet need not be acknowledged. Other types of packets, such as updates, indicate in the packet that acknowledgment is required. RTP contains a provision for sending multicast packets quickly even when unacknowledged packets are pending, which helps ensure that convergence time remains low in the presence of varying speed links.

■ **DUAL finite-state machine**—DUAL embodies the decision process for all route computations. DUAL tracks all routes advertised by all neighbors and uses distance information, known as a *metric* or *cost*, to select efficient, loop-free paths to all destinations.

■ **Protocol-dependent modules**—EIGRP's protocol-dependent modules are responsible for network layer protocol-specific requirements. EIGRP supports IP, AppleTalk, and Novell NetWare; each protocol has its own EIGRP module and operates independently from any of the others that might be running. The IP-EIGRP module, for example, is responsible for sending and receiving EIGRP packets that are encapsulated in IP. Likewise, IP-EIGRP is also responsible for parsing EIGRP packets and informing DUAL of the new information that has been received. IP-EIGRP asks DUAL to make routing decisions, the results of which are stored in the IP routing table. IP-EIGRP is also responsible for redistributing routes learned by other IP routing protocols.

EIGRP Terminology and Operation

EIGRP sends out five different types of packets—hello, update, query, reply, and acknowledge (ACK)—that are used to establish the initial adjacency between neighbors and to keep the topology and routing tables current. When troubleshooting an EIGRP network, network administrators must understand what EIGRP packets are used for and how they are exchanged. For example, if routers running EIGRP do not form neighbor relationships, those routers cannot exchange EIGRP updates with each other. Without EIGRP routing updates, users cannot connect to services across the internetwork. This section explains EIGRP terminology, followed by an explanation of the mechanisms for creating the various EIGRP tables and a discussion about the five types of EIGRP packets. This section also explores how EIGRP routers become neighbors, initial route discovery, route selection, and how the DUAL algorithm functions.

EIGRP Terminology

The following terms are related to EIGRP and are used throughout the rest of this chapter:

- **Neighbor table**—EIGRP routers use hello packets to discover neighbors. When a router discovers and forms an adjacency with a new neighbor, it includes the neighbor's address and the interface through which it can be reached in an entry in the neighbor table. This table is comparable to the neighborship (adjacency) database used by link-state routing protocols (as described in Chapter 4). It serves the same purpose—ensuring bidirectional communication between each of the directly connected neighbors. EIGRP keeps a neighbor table for each network protocol supported; in other words, the following tables could exist: an IP neighbor table, an IPX neighbor table, and an AppleTalk neighbor table.

- **Topology table**—When the router dynamically discovers a new neighbor, it sends an update about the routes it knows to its new neighbor and receives the same from the new neighbor. These updates populate the topology table. The topology table contains all destinations advertised by neighboring routers; in other words, each router stores its neighbors' routing tables in its EIGRP topology table. If a neighbor is advertising a destination, it must be using that route to forward packets; this rule must be strictly followed by all distance vector protocols. An EIGRP router maintains a topology table for each network protocol configured (IP, IPX, and AppleTalk).

- **Advertised distance (AD) and feasible distance (FD)**—DUAL uses distance information, known as a *metric* or *cost*, to select efficient, loop-free paths. The lowest-cost route is calculated by adding the cost between the next-hop router and the destination—referred to as the *advertised distance*—to the cost between the local router and the next-hop router. The sum of these costs is referred to as the *feasible distance*.

- **Successor**—A successor, also called a current successor, is a neighboring router that has a least-cost path to a destination (the lowest FD) that is guaranteed not to be part of a routing loop; successors are offered to the routing table to be used for forwarding packets. Multiple successors can exist if they have the same FD.

- **Routing table**—The routing table holds the best routes to each destination and is used for forwarding packets. Successor routes are offered to the routing table. As discussed in Chapter 2, "Routing Principles," if a router learns more than one route to exactly the same destination from different routing sources, it uses the administrative distance to determine which route to keep in the routing table. By default, up to 4 routes to the same destination with the same metric can be added to the routing table (recall that the router can be configured to accept up to 16 per destination). The router maintains one routing table for each network protocol configured.

■ **Feasible successor (FS)**—Along with keeping least-cost paths, DUAL keeps backup paths to each destination. The next-hop router for a backup path is called the feasible successor. To qualify as a feasible successor, a next-hop router must have an AD less than the FD of the current successor route; in other words, a feasible successor is a neighbor that is closer to the destination, but it is not the least-cost path and, thus, is not used to forward data. Feasible successors are selected at the same time as successors but are kept only in the topology table. The topology table can maintain multiple feasible successors for a destination.

If the route via the successor becomes invalid (because of a topology change) or if a neighbor changes the metric, DUAL checks for feasible successors to the destination. If a feasible successor is found, DUAL uses it, thereby avoiding recomputing the route. If no suitable feasible successor exists, a recomputation must occur to determine the new successor. Although recomputation is not processor-intensive, it does affect convergence time, so it is advantageous to avoid unnecessary recomputations.

Populating EIGRP Tables

Figure 3-3 illustrates the three tables that EIGRP uses in its operation:

■ The neighbor table lists adjacent routers

■ The topology table lists all the learned routes to each destination

■ The routing table contains the best route (the successor route) to each destination.

Figure 3-3 *EIGRP Maintains a Neighbor Table, a Topology Table, and a Routing Table*

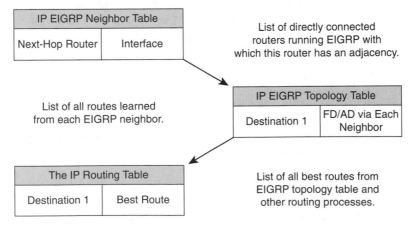

The neighbor table includes the address of each neighbor and the interface through which it can be reached.

The neighbor-table entry also includes information required by RTP. Sequence numbers are employed to match acknowledgments with data packets, and the last sequence number received from the neighbor is recorded, to detect out-of-order packets. A transmission list is used to queue packets for possible retransmission on a per-neighbor basis. Round-trip timers are kept in the neighbor-table entry to estimate an optimal retransmission interval.

Each router forwards a copy of its IP routing table to all its adjacent EIGRP neighbors, as specified in its EIGRP neighbor table. Each router then stores the routing tables of the adjacent neighbors in its EIGRP topology table (database). The topology table also maintains the metric that each neighbor advertises for each destination (the AD) and the metric that this router would use to reach the destination via that neighbor (the FD). The **show ip eigrp topology all-links** command displays all the IP entries in the topology table, while the **show ip eigrp topology** command displays only the successor(s) and feasible successor(s) for IP routes.

The topology table is updated when a directly connected route or interface changes or when a neighboring router reports a change to a route.

A topology-table entry for a destination can exist in one of two states: active or passive.

KEY POINT

Passive Versus Active Routes

A route is considered *passive* when the router is not performing recomputation on that route. A route is *active* when it is undergoing recomputation (in other words, when it is looking for a new successor).

Note that *passive* is the operational, stable state.

If feasible successors are always available, a destination never has to go into the active state, thereby avoiding a recomputation.

A recomputation occurs when the current route to a destination, the successor, goes down and there are no feasible successors for the destination. The router initiates the recomputation by sending a query packet to each of its neighboring routers. If the neighboring router has a route for the destination, it will send a reply packet; if it does not have a route, it sends a query packet to its neighbors. In this case, the route is also in the active state in the neighboring router. While a destination is in the active state, a router cannot change the routing table information for the destination. After a router has received a reply from each neighboring router, the topology table entry for the destination returns to the passive state.

Each router then examines its EIGRP topology table and determines the best route and other feasible routes to every destination network. A router compares all FDs to reach a specific network and then selects the route with the lowest FD and places it in the IP routing table; this is the successor route. The FD for the chosen successor route becomes the EIGRP routing metric to reach that network in the routing table.

EIGRP Packets

EIGRP uses the following five types of packets:

- **Hello**—Hello packets are used for neighbor discovery. They are sent as multicasts and do not require an acknowledgment. (They carry an acknowledgment number of 0.)

- **Update**—Update packets contain route change information. An update is sent to communicate the routes that a particular router has used to converge; an update is sent only to affected routers. These updates are sent as multicasts when a new route is discovered, and when convergence is completed (when the route becomes passive). To synchronize topology tables, updates are sent as unicasts to neighbors during their EIGRP startup sequence. Updates are sent reliably.

- **Query**—When a router is performing route computation and does not have a feasible successor, it sends a query packet to its neighbors, asking if they have a successor to the destination. Queries are normally multicast but can be retransmitted as unicast packets in certain cases; they are sent reliably.

- **Reply**—A reply packet is sent in response to a query packet. Replies are unicast to the originator of the query and are sent reliably.

- **ACK**—The ACK is used to acknowledge updates, queries, and replies. ACK packets are unicast hello packets and contain a nonzero acknowledgment number. (Note that hello and ACK packets do not require acknowledgment.)

The hello packet is the first type exchanged by EIGRP routers. The following section provides details of the hello protocol and how hello packets are used. The details of how the other packet types are used are provided throughout the rest of the chapter.

EIGRP Hello Packets

Through the hello protocol, an EIGRP router dynamically discovers other EIGRP routers directly connected to it. The router sends hello packets out of interfaces configured for EIGRP using the EIGRP multicast address 224.0.0.10. When an EIGRP router receives a hello packet from a router belonging to the same autonomous system (AS), it establishes a neighbor relationship (adjacency).

> **NOTE**   The term *autonomous system* as used by EIGRP (and OSPF) is not the same as a Border Gateway Protocol (BGP) autonomous system. For EIGRP, consider the autonomous system to be a group of routers all running the same protocol. You may have more than one EIGRP autonomous system (group) within your network, in which case you might want to redistribute (share) routes between them; redistribution is detailed in Chapter 7, "Manipulating Routing Updates."

The time interval of hello packets varies depending on the medium. Hello packets are released every 5 seconds on a LAN link such as Ethernet, Token Ring, and FDDI. The default interval is also set to 5 seconds for point-to-point links such as PPP, High-Level Data Link Control (HDLC), point-to-point Frame Relay, and Asynchronous Transfer Mode (ATM) subinterfaces, and for multipoint circuits with bandwidth greater than T1, including Integrated Digital Services Network (ISDN) Primary Rate Interface (PRI), ATM, and Frame Relay. Hello packets are sent out less frequently on lower-speed links, such as multipoint circuits with a bandwidth less than or equal to T1, including ISDN Basic Rate Interface (BRI), Frame Relay, ATM, and X.25. Hellos are generated at 60-second intervals on these types of interfaces.

**KEY
POINT**

Hello Packets

By default, hello packets are sent every 60 seconds on T1 or slower multipoint interfaces and every 5 seconds on other serial interfaces and on LANs.

You can adjust the rate at which hello packets are sent, called the *hello interval*, on a per-interface basis with the **ip hello-interval eigrp** *as-number seconds* interface configuration command.

Hello packets include the hold time.

The hold-time interval is set by default to 3 times the hello interval. Therefore, the default hold-time value is 15 seconds on LAN and fast WAN interfaces and 180 seconds on slower WAN interfaces. You can adjust the hold time with the **ip hold-time eigrp** *as-number seconds* interface configuration command.

**KEY
POINT**

Hold Time

The hold time is the amount of time a router considers a neighbor up without receiving a hello or some other EIGRP packet from that neighbor.

NOTE   The hold time is not automatically adjusted after a hello interval change. If you change the hello interval, you must manually adjust the hold time to reflect the configured hello interval.

If a packet is not received before the expiration of the hold time, the neighbor adjacency is deleted, and all topology table entries learned from that neighbor are removed, as if the neighbor had sent an update stating that all the routes are unreachable. If the neighbor is a successor for any destination networks, those networks are removed from the routing table, and alternative paths, if available, are computed. This lets the routes quickly reconverge if an alternative feasible route is available.

EIGRP Neighbors

The possibility exists for two routers to become EIGRP neighbors even though the hello and hold time values do not match; this means that the hello interval and hold-time values can be set independently on different routers.

Secondary addresses can be applied to interfaces to solve particular addressing issues, although all routing overhead traffic is generated through the primary interface address. EIGRP will not build peer relationships over secondary addresses, because all EIGRP traffic uses the interface's primary address. To form an EIGRP adjacency, all neighbors use their primary address as the source IP address of their EIGRP packets. Adjacency between EIGRP routers takes place if the primary address of each neighbor is part of the same IP subnet. In addition, peer relationships are not formed if the neighbor resides in a different autonomous system or if the metric-calculation mechanism constants (the K values) are misaligned on that link. (K values are discussed in the "EIGRP Metric Calculation" section later in this chapter.)

Neighbor Table

An EIGRP router multicasts hello packets to discover neighbors; it forms an adjacency with these neighbors so that it can exchange route updates. Only adjacent routers exchange routing information. Each router builds a neighbor table from the hello packets it receives from adjacent EIGRP routers running the same network layer protocol. EIGRP maintains a neighbor table for each configured network-layer protocol. You can display the IP neighbor table with the **show ip eigrp neighbors** command, as shown in Example 3-1.

Example 3-1 *Sample Output for the* **show ip eigrp neighbors** *Command*

```
R1#show ip eigrp neighbors
IP-EIGRP neighbors for process 100
H    Address         Interface    Hold  Uptime    SRTT    RTO  Q   Seq
                                  (sec)           (ms)         Cnt Num
0    192.168.1.102   Se0/0/1      10    00:07:22  10      2280 0   5
R1#
```

This table includes the following key elements:

- **H (handle)**—A number used internally by the Cisco IOS to track a neighbor.

- **Address**—The neighbor's network-layer address.

- **Interface**—The interface on this router through which the neighbor can be reached.

- **Hold Time**—The maximum time, in seconds, that the router waits to hear from the neighbor without receiving anything from a neighbor before considering the link unavailable. Originally, the expected packet was a hello packet, but in current Cisco IOS software releases, any EIGRP packets received after the first hello from that neighbor resets the timer.

- **Uptime**—The elapsed time, in hours, minutes, and seconds since the local router first heard from this neighbor.

- **Smooth Round Trip Timer (SRTT)**—The average number of milliseconds it takes for an EIGRP packet to be sent to this neighbor and for the local router to receive an acknowledgment of that packet. This timer is used to determine the retransmit interval, also known as the retransmit timeout (RTO).

- **RTO**—The amount of time, in milliseconds, that the router waits for an acknowledgment before retransmitting a reliable packet from the retransmission queue to a neighbor.

- **Queue count**—The number of packets waiting in the queue to be sent out. If this value is constantly higher than 0, a congestion problem might exist. A 0 indicates that no EIGRP packets are in the queue.

- **Seq Num**—The sequence number of the last update, query, or reply packet that was received from this neighbor.

EIGRP Reliability

EIGRP's reliability mechanism ensures delivery of critical route information to neighboring routers. This information is required to allow EIGRP to maintain a loop-free topology. For efficiency, only certain EIGRP packets are transmitted reliably.

KEY POINT

Reliable Packets

All packets carrying routing information (update, query, and reply) are sent reliably (because they are not sent periodically), which means that a sequence number is assigned to each reliable packet and an explicit acknowledgment is required for that sequence number.

Recall that RTP is responsible for guaranteed, ordered delivery of EIGRP packets to all neighbors. RTP supports an intermixed transmission of multicast and unicast packets.

RTP ensures that ongoing communication is maintained between neighboring routers. As such, a retransmission list is maintained for each neighbor. This list indicates packets not yet acknowledged by a neighbor within the RTO. It is used to track all the reliable packets that were sent but not acknowledged.

KEY POINT

RTO Timer

If the RTO expires before an ACK packet is received, the EIGRP process transmits another copy of the reliable packet, up to a maximum of 16 times or until the hold time expires.

The use of reliable multicast packets is efficient. However, a potential delay exists on multiaccess media where multiple neighbors reside. The next reliable multicast packet cannot be transmitted until all peers have acknowledged the previous multicast. If one or more peers are slow to respond, this adversely affects all peers by delaying the next transmission. RTP is designed to handle such exceptions: Neighbors that are slow to respond to multicasts have the unacknowledged multicast packets retransmitted as unicasts. This allows the reliable multicast operation to proceed without delaying communication with other peers, helping to ensure that convergence time remains low in the presence of variable-speed links.

The multicast flow timer determines how long to wait for an ACK packet before switching from multicast to unicast. The RTO determines how long to wait between the subsequent unicasts. The

EIGRP process for each neighbor calculates both the multicast flow timer and RTO, based on the SRTT. The formulas for the SRTT, RTO, and multicast flow timer are Cisco-proprietary. In a steady-state network where no routes are flapping, EIGRP waits the specified hold-time interval before it determines that an EIGRP neighbor adjacency is down. Therefore, by default, EIGRP waits up to 15 seconds on high-speed links and up to 180 seconds on low-speed, multipoint links. When EIGRP determines that a neighbor is down and the router cannot reestablish the adjacency, the routing table removes all networks that could be reached through that neighbor. The router attempts to find alternative routes to those networks so that convergence can occur. The 180-second hold time on low-speed links can seem excessive, but it accommodates the slowest-speed multipoint links, which are generally connected to less-critical remote sites. In some networks with mission-critical or time-sensitive applications (such as IP telephony), even on high-speed links, 15 seconds is too long. The point to remember is that other conditions can override the hold time and allow the network to converge quickly.

For example, if the network is unstable and routes are flapping elsewhere because a remote site is timing out on its adjacency, EIGRP hold timers begin counting down from 180 seconds. When the upstream site sends the remote site an update, and the remote site does not acknowledge the update, the upstream site attempts 16 times to retransmit the update. The retransmission occurs each time the RTO expires. After 16 retries, the router resets the neighbor relationship. This causes the network to converge faster than waiting for the hold time to expire.

Initial Route Discovery

EIGRP combines the process of discovering neighbors and learning routes. Figure 3-4 illustrates the initial route discovery process.

Figure 3-4 *Initial Route Discovery*

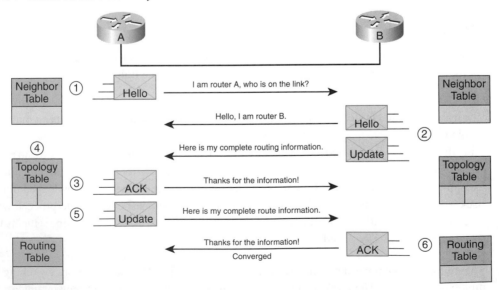

The following describes the initial route discovery process:

1. A new router (Router A) comes up on the link and sends out a hello packet through all of its EIGRP-configured interfaces.

2. Routers receiving the hello packet on one interface (Router B in Figure 3-4) reply with update packets that contain all the routes they have in their routing table, except those learned through that interface (because of the split horizon rule). Router B sends an update packet to Router A, but a neighbor relationship is not established until Router B sends a hello packet to Router A. The update packet from Router B has the initial bit set, indicating that this is the initialization process. The update packet contains information about the routes that the neighbor (Router B) is aware of, including the metric that the neighbor is advertising for each destination.

3. After both routers have exchanged hellos and the neighbor adjacency is established, Router A replies to Router B with an ACK packet, indicating that it received the update information.

4. Router A inserts the update packet information in its topology table. The topology table includes all destinations advertised by neighboring (adjacent) routers. It is organized so that each destination is listed, along with all the neighbors that can get to the destination and their associated metrics.

5. Router A then sends an update packet to Router B.

6. Upon receiving the update packet, Router B sends an ACK packet to Router A.

After Router A and Router B successfully receive the update packets from each other, they are ready to chose the successor (best) and feasible successor (backup) routes in the topology table, and offer the successor routes to the routing table.

Split Horizon

Split horizon controls the sending of IP EIGRP update and query packets. When split horizon is enabled on an interface, no update or query packets for destinations for which this interface is the next-hop are sent out of this interface. This reduces the possibility of routing loops. By default, split horizon is enabled on all interfaces.

Split horizon blocks information about a destination from being advertised by a router out of any interface that the router uses to route to that destination. This behavior usually optimizes communications among multiple routers, particularly when links are broken.

When a router changes its topology table in such a way that the interface through which the router reaches a network changes, it turns off split horizon and poison reverses the old route out of all interfaces indicating that the route is unreachable. This ensures that other routers will not try to use the now invalid route.

Route Selection

The EIGRP route selection process is perhaps what most distinguishes it from other routing protocols. EIGRP selects primary (successor) and backup (feasible successor) routes and injects those into the topology table. The primary (successor) routes are then moved to the routing table.

EIGRP supports several types of routes: internal, external, and summary. Internal routes originate within the EIGRP autonomous system. External routes are learned from another routing protocol or another EIGRP autonomous system. Summary routes are routes encompassing multiple subnets.

EIGRP uses DUAL to calculate the best route to a destination. DUAL selects routes based on the composite metric and ensures that the selected routes are loop-free. DUAL also calculates backup routes (feasible successor routes) to a destination that are loop-free. If the best route fails, EIGRP immediately uses a backup route without any need for holddown, because the feasible successor route (if one exists) is loop-free; this results in fast convergence.

EIGRP Metric Calculation

The EIGRP metric calculation can use five variables, but EIGRP uses only two by default:

- **Bandwidth**—The smallest (slowest) bandwidth between the source and destination

- **Delay**—The cumulative interface delay along the path

The following criteria, although available, are not commonly used, because they typically result in frequent recalculation of the topology table:

- **Reliability**—The worst reliability between the source and destination, based on keepalives.

- **Loading**—The worst load on a link between the source and destination based on the packet rate and the interface's configured bandwidth.

- **Maximum transmission unit (MTU)**—The smallest MTU in the path. (MTU is included in the EIGRP update but is actually not used in the metric calculation.)

EIGRP calculates the metric by adding together weighted values of different variables of the path to the network in question. The default constant weight values are K1 = K3 = 1, and K2 = K4 = K5 = 0.

In EIGRP metric calculations, when K5 is 0 (the default), variables (bandwidth, bandwidth divided by load, and delay) are weighted with the constants K1, K2, and K3. The following is the formula used:

$$\text{metric} = (K1 * \text{bandwidth}) + [(K2 * \text{bandwidth}) / (256 - \text{load})] + (K3 * \text{delay})$$

If these K values are equal to their defaults, the formula becomes

$$\text{metric} = (1 * \text{bandwidth}) + [(0 * \text{bandwidth}) / (256 - \text{load})] + (1 * \text{delay})$$
$$\text{metric} = \text{bandwidth} + [0] + \text{delay}$$
$$\text{metric} = \text{bandwidth} + \text{delay}$$

If K5 is not equal to 0, the following additional operation is performed:

$$\text{metric} = \text{metric} * [K5 / (\text{reliability} + K4)]$$

K values are carried in EIGRP hello packets. Mismatched K values can cause a neighbor to be reset (only K1 and K3 are used, by default, in metric compilation). These K values should be modified only after careful planning; changing these values can prevent your network from converging and is generally not recommended.

KEY POINT

Delay and Bandwidth Values

The format of the delay and bandwidth values is different from those displayed by the **show interfaces** command.

The EIGRP delay value is the sum of the delays in the path, in tens of microseconds, multiplied by 256. The **show interfaces** command displays delay in microseconds.

The EIGRP bandwidth is calculated using the minimum bandwidth link along the path, represented in kilobits per second (kbps). 10^7 is divided by this value, and then the result is multiplied by 256.

EIGRP uses the same metric formula as IGRP, but EIGRP represents its metrics in a 32-bit format instead of the 24-bit representation used by IGRP. This representation allows a more granular decision to be made when determining the successor and feasible successor.

The EIGRP metric value ranges from 1 to 4,294,967,296. The IGRP metric value ranges from 1 to 16,777,216. EIGRP metrics are backward compatible with IGRP, as illustrated in Figure 3-5. When integrating IGRP routes into an EIGRP domain using redistribution, the router multiplies the IGRP metric by 256 to compute the EIGRP-equivalent metric. When sending EIGRP routes to an IGRP routing domain, the router divides each EIGRP metric by 256 to achieve the proper 24-bit metric.

Figure 3-5 *Initial Route Discovery*

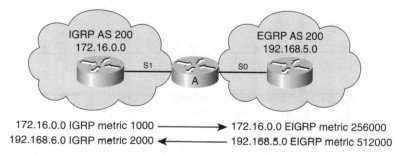

EIGRP Metric Calculation Example

In Figure 3-6, Router A has two paths to reach Router D (and thus any networks behind Router D). The bandwidths (in kbps) and the delays (in tens of microseconds) of the various links are also shown.

Figure 3-6 *EIGRP Metric Calculation Example*

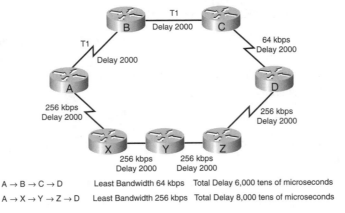

A → B → C → D   Least Bandwidth 64 kbps   Total Delay 6,000 tens of microseconds
A → X → Y → Z → D   Least Bandwidth 256 kbps   Total Delay 8,000 tens of microseconds

The least bandwidth along the top path (A → B → C → D) is 64 kbps. The EIGRP bandwidth calculation for this path is as follows:

bandwidth = $(10^7$ / least bandwidth in kbps) * 256
bandwidth = (10,000,000 / 64) * 256 = 156,250 * 256 = 40,000,000

The delay through the top path is as follows:

delay = [(delay A → B) + (delay B → C) + (delay C → D)] * 256
delay = [2000 + 2000 + 2000] * 256
delay = 1,536,000

Therefore, the EIGRP metric calculation for the top path is as follows:

metric = bandwidth + delay
metric = 40,000,000 + 1,536,000
metric = 41,536,000

The least bandwidth along the lower path (A → X → Y → Z → D) is 256 kbps. The EIGRP bandwidth calculation for this path is as follows:

bandwidth = $(10^7$ / least bandwidth in kbps) * 256
bandwidth = (10,000,000 / 256) * 256 = 10,000,000

The delay through the lower path is as follows:

$$delay = [(delay\ A \to X) + (delay\ X \to Y) + (delay\ Y \to Z) + (delay\ Z \to D)] * 256$$
$$delay = [2000 + 2000 + 2000 + 2000] * 256$$
$$delay = 2,048,000$$

Therefore, the EIGRP metric calculation for the lower path is as follows:

$$metric = bandwidth + delay$$
$$metric = 10,000,000 + 2,048,000$$
$$metric = 12,048,000$$

Router A therefore chooses the lower path, with a metric of 12,048,000, over the top path, with a metric of 41,536,000. Router A installs the lower path with a next-hop router of X and a metric of 12,048,000 in the IP routing table.

The bottleneck along the top path, the 64-kbps link, can explain why the router takes the lower path. This slow link means that the rate of transfer to Router D would be at a maximum of 64 kbps. Along the lower path, the lowest speed is 256 kbps, making the throughput rate up to that speed. Therefore, the lower path represents a better choice, such as to move large files quickly.

Routing Table and EIGRP DUAL

DUAL is the finite-state machine that selects which information is stored in the topology and routing tables. As such, DUAL embodies the decision process for all EIGRP route computations. It tracks all routes advertised by all neighbors; uses the metric to select an efficient, loop-free path to each destination; and inserts that choice in the routing table.

Advertised Distance and Feasible Distance

KEY POINT

> **Advertised Distance Versus Feasible Distance**
>
> The AD is the EIGRP metric for an EIGRP *neighbor router* to reach a particular network. This is the metric between the next-hop neighbor router and the destination network.
>
> The FD is the EIGRP metric for *this router* to reach a particular network. This is the sum of the AD for the particular network learned from an EIGRP neighbor, plus the EIGRP metric to reach that neighbor (the cost between this router and the next-hop router).

A router compares all FDs to reach a specific network in its topology table. The route with the lowest FD is placed in its IP routing table; this is the successor route. The FD for the chosen route becomes the EIGRP routing metric to reach that network in the routing table.

For example, in Figure 3-7, Routers A and B send their routing tables to Router C, whose tables are shown in the figure. Both Routers A and B have paths to network 10.1.1.0/24 (among many others that are not shown).

Figure 3-7 *EIGRP Chooses the Route with the Lowest Feasible Distance*

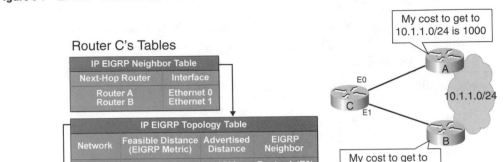

The routing table on Router A has an EIGRP metric of 1000 for 10.1.1.0/24. Therefore, Router A advertises 10.1.1.0/24 to Router C with a metric of 1000. Router C installs 10.1.1.0/24 from Router A in its EIGRP topology table with an AD of 1000. Router B has network 10.1.1.0/24 with a metric of 1500 in its IP routing table. Therefore, Router B advertises 10.1.1.0/24 to Router C with an AD of 1500. Router C places the 10.1.1.0/24 network from Router B in the EIGRP topology table with an AD of 1500.

Router C in Figure 3-7 has two entries to reach 10.1.1.0/24 in its topology table. The EIGRP metric for Router C to reach either Router A or B is 1000. This cost (1000) is added to the respective AD from each router, and the results represent the FDs that Router C must travel to reach network 10.1.1.0/24. Router C chooses the least-cost FD (2000) and installs it in its IP routing table as the best route to reach 10.1.1.0/24. The EIGRP metric in the routing table is the best FD from the EIGRP topology table.

Successor and Feasible Successor

KEY POINT

Successor

A successor is a neighboring router used for packet forwarding that has a least-cost path to a destination that is guaranteed not to be part of a routing loop.

A router is chosen as a successor because it has the lowest FD of all possible paths to that destination network. The successor is the next router in line to reach that destination. In other words, it is the router with the best path to reach that destination network.

An EIGRP router selects the best path to reach a given network and then installs the destination network, the metric to reach that network, the outbound interface to reach the next-hop router, and the IP address of the next-hop router into the IP routing table. If the EIGRP topology table has many entries that have an equal-cost FD to a given destination network, all successors (up to four by default) for that destination network are installed in the routing table.

KEY POINT

FD and AD

Note that it is the FD, not the AD, that affects the selection of the best routes for incorporation in the routing table; the AD is used only to calculate the FD.

All routing protocols can install only the next-hop router information in the routing table; information about the subsequent routers in the path is not put in the routing table. Each router relies on the next-hop router to make a reliable decision to reach a specific destination network. The hop-by-hop path through a network goes from one router to the next. Each router makes a path selection to reach a given network and installs the best next-hop address along the path to reach that destination network. A router trusts a route's successor (the best next-hop router) to send traffic toward that destination address.

The routing table is essentially a subset of the topology table; the topology table contains more detailed information about each route, any backup routes, and information used exclusively by DUAL.

KEY POINT

Feasible Successor

A feasible successor is a router providing a backup route. The route through the feasible successor must be loop free; in other words, it must not loop back to the current successor.

FSs are selected at the same time the successors are identified. These FS routes are kept in the topology table; the topology table can retain multiple FS routes for a destination.

KEY POINT

Feasible Successor Requirements

An FS must be mathematically proven. To qualify as an FS, a next-hop router must have an AD less than the FD of the current successor route for the particular network.

This requirement ensures that the FS cannot use a route through the local router (which would be a routing loop), because the AD through the FS is less than the best route through the local router. For example, as shown in Figure 3-8, Router B is an FS, because the AD through Router B (1500) is less than the FD of the current successor, Router A (2000).

Figure 3-8   *Feasible Successor's AD Must Be Less Than the Successor's FD*

EIGRP Topology Table			
Network	FD (EIGRP Metric)	AD	EIGRP Neighbor
10.1.1.0/24	2000-Successor	1000	Router A (E0)
10.1.1.0/24	2500	1500 Feasible Successor	Router B (E1)

When a router loses a route, it looks at the topology table for an FS. If one is available, the route does not go into an active state; rather, the best FS is promoted as the successor and is installed in the routing table. The FS can be used immediately, without any recalculation. If there are no FSs, a route goes into active state, and route computation occurs. Through this process, a new successor is determined (if there is one). The amount of time it takes to recalculate the route affects the convergence time.

Figure 3-9 illustrates another example. Router C's initial topology table is shown at the top of the figure. Router B is the successor for network 10.1.1.0/24, and Router D is the FS.

Figure 3-9   *With a Feasible Successor, EIGRP Can Recover Immediately from Network Failures*

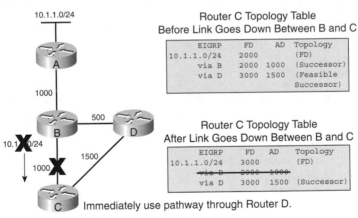

In Figure 3-9, the link between Router B and Router C fails. Router C removes the route 10.1.1.0/24 through Router B from its routing table and searches the EIGRP topology table for an FS; Router D is an FS. Because Router D can still reach the network and does not send an update or query packet to inform Router C of the lost route, Router C immediately uses the path through Router D. Router C chooses this path because the AD through Router D (1500) is less than the FD of the best route, through Router B (2000); this path is guaranteed to be loop free.

DUAL Example

The mathematical formula to ensure that the FS is loop free requires that the AD of the backup route be *less than* the FD of the successor. When the AD of the second-best route is greater than or equal to the FD of the successor, an FS cannot be chosen. In this case, a discovery process that uses EIGRP queries and replies must be used to find any alternative paths to the lost networks.

The following example examines partial entries for network 10.1.1.0/24 in the topology tables for Routers C, D, and E in Figure 3-10, to give you a better understanding of EIGRP behavior. The partial topology tables shown in Figure 3-10 indicate the following:

■ **AD**—The advertised distance is equal to the cost of the path to network 10.1.1.0/24 as advertised by neighboring routers.

■ **FD**—The feasible distance is equal to the sum of the AD for a neighbor to reach 10.1.1.0/24, plus the metric to reach that neighbor.

■ **Successor**—The successor is the forwarding path used to reach network 10.1.1.0/24. The cost of this path is equal to the FD.

■ **FS**—The feasible successor is an alternative loop-free path to reach network 10.1.1.0/24.

Figure 3-10 *DUAL Example, Step 1*

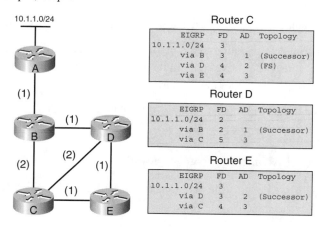

The network shown in Figure 3-10 is stable and converged.

NOTE   As mentioned earlier, EIGRP implements split horizon. For example, Router E does not pass its route for network 10.1.1.0/24 to Router D, because Router E uses Router D as its next hop to network 10.1.1.0/24.

In Figure 3-11, Routers B and D detect a link failure. After being notified of the link failure, DUAL does the following, as shown in Figure 3-11:

■ At Router D, it marks the path to network 10.1.1.0/24 through Router B as unusable.

Figure 3-11 *DUAL Example, Step 2*

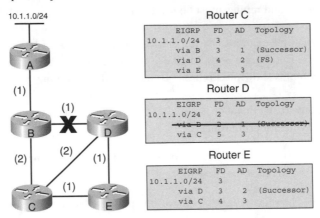

The following steps then occur, as shown in Figure 3-12:

■ At Router D, there is no FS to network 10.1.1.0/24, because the AD via Router C (3) is greater than the FD via Router B (2). Therefore, DUAL does the following:

— Sets the metric to network 10.1.1.0/24 as unreachable (–1 is unreachable).

— Because an FS cannot be found in the topology table, the route changes from the passive state to the active state. In the active state, the router sends out queries to neighboring routers looking for a new successor.

— Sends a query to Routers C and E for an alternative path to network 10.1.1.0/24.

— Marks Routers C and E as having a query pending (q).

■ At Router E, DUAL marks the path to network 10.1.1.0/24 through Router D as unusable.

■ At Router C, DUAL marks the path to network 10.1.1.0/24 through Router D as unusable.

Figure 3-12 *DUAL Example, Step 3*

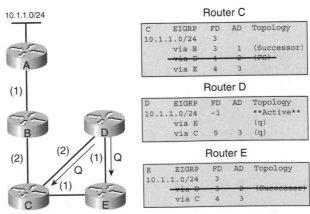

The following steps then occur, as shown in Figure 3-13:

- At Router D:

    — DUAL receives a reply from Router C that indicates no change to the path to network 10.1.1.0/24.

    — DUAL removes the query flag from Router C.

    — DUAL stays active on network 10.1.1.0/24, awaiting a reply from Router E to its query (q).

- At Router E, there is no FS to network 10.1.1.0/24, because the AD from Router C (3) is not less than the original FD (also 3).

    — DUAL generates a query to Router C.

    — DUAL marks Router C as query pending (q).

- At Router C, DUAL marks the path to network 10.1.1.0/24 through Router E as unusable.

Figure 3-13 *DUAL Example, Step 4*

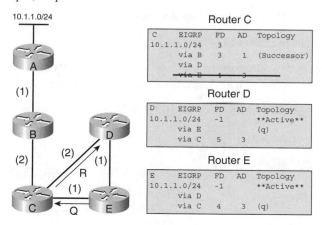

The following steps then occur, as shown in Figure 3-14:

- At Router D, DUAL stays active on network 10.1.1.0/24, awaiting a reply from Router E (q).

- At Router E:

    — DUAL receives a reply from Router C indicating no change.

    — It removes the query flag from Router C.

    — It calculates a new FD and installs a new successor route in the topology table.

    — It changes the route to network 10.1.1.0/24 from active to passive (converged).

Figure 3-14   *DUAL Example, Step 5*

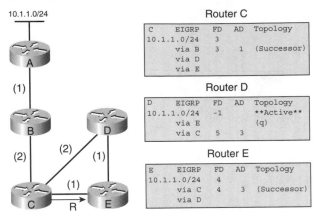

The following steps then occur, as shown in Figure 3-15:

■ At Router D

— DUAL receives a reply from Router E.

— It removes the query flag from Router E.

— It calculates a new FD.

— It installs new successor routes in the topology table. Two routes (through Routers C and E) have the same FD, and both are marked as successors.

— It changes the route to network 10.1.1.0/24 from active to passive (converged).

Figure 3-15   *DUAL Example, Step 6*

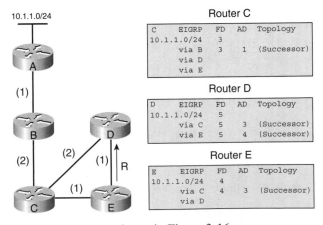

The following steps then occur, as shown in Figure 3-16:

■ At Router D, two successor routes are in the topology table for network 10.1.1.0/24. Both successor routes are listed in the routing table, and equal-cost load balancing is in effect.

- The network is stable and converged.

Figure 3-16 *DUAL Example, Step 7*

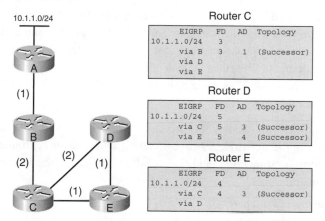

Figure 3-10, the original topology before the link failure, shows traffic from Router E passing through Routers D and B. In Figure 3-16, the new topology shows traffic from Routers D and E going through Routers C and B. Notice that throughout the entire convergence process, routes to network 10.1.1.0/24 become active only on Routers D and E. The route to network 10.1.1.0/24 on Router C remains passive because the link failure between Routers B and D does not affect the successor route from Router C to network 10.1.1.0/24.

> **NOTE** When DUAL decides that a packet needs to be transmitted to a neighbor, the packets are not actually generated until the moment of transmission. Instead, the transmit queues contain small, fixed-size structures that indicate which parts of the topology table to include in the packet when it is finally transmitted. This means that the queues do not consume large amounts of memory. It also means that only the latest information is transmitted in each packet. If a route changes state several times, only the last state is transmitted in the packet, thus reducing link utilization.

Configuring and Verifying EIGRP

This section covers the commands used to configure EIGRP features. The following topics are discussed:

- Basic EIGRP configuration

- Configuring the **ip default-network** command for EIGRP

- Route summarization

- EIGRP load balancing

- EIGRP and WAN links

Basic EIGRP Configuration

Follow these steps to configure basic EIGRP for IP:

Step 1   Enable EIGRP and define the autonomous system using the **router eigrp** *autonomous-system-number* global configuration command. In this command, the *autonomous-system-number* identifies the autonomous system and is used to indicate all routers that belong within the internetwork. This value must match on all routers within the internetwork.

Step 2   Indicate which networks are part of the EIGRP autonomous system using the **network** *network-number* [*wildcard-mask*] router configuration command. Table 3-1 summarizes the parameters of this command.

Table 3-1 **network** *Command Parameters*

Parameter	Description
network-number	This parameter can be a network, a subnet, or the address of an interface. It determines which links on the router to advertise to, which links to listen to advertisements on, and which networks are advertised.
wildcard-mask	(Optional) An inverse mask used to determine how to interpret the *network-number*. The mask has wildcard bits, where 0 is a match and 1 is do not care. For example, 0.0.255.255 indicates a match in the first 2 octets.

If you do not use the optional wildcard mask, the EIGRP process assumes that all directly connected networks that are part of the major network will participate in the EIGRP routing process, and EIGRP will attempt to establish EIGRP neighbor relationships from each interface that is part of the overall Class A, B, or C network.

Use the optional wildcard mask to identify a specific IP address, subnet, or network. The router interprets the network number using the wildcard mask to determine which connected networks will participate in the EIGRP routing process. If you want to specify an interface address, use the mask 0.0.0.0 to match all 4 octets of the address. An address and wildcard mask combination of 0.0.0.0 255.255.255.255 matches all interfaces on the router.

Step 3   For serial links, define the link's bandwidth for the purposes of sending routing update traffic on the link. If you do not define the bandwidth value for these interfaces, EIGRP assumes that the bandwidth on the link is the default, which varies with interface type. Recall that EIGRP uses bandwidth as part of its metric calculation. If the link is actually slower than the default, the router might not be able to converge, or routing updates might become lost. The percent of the interface's bandwidth that EIGRP uses can also be limited, as described in the section "EIGRP and WAN Links" later in this chapter. To define the bandwidth, use the **bandwidth** *kilobits* interface configuration command. In this command, *kilobits* indicates the intended bandwidth in kbps.

For generic serial interfaces such as PPP and HDLC, set the bandwidth to match the line speed. For Frame Relay point-to-point interfaces, set the bandwidth to the committed information rate (CIR). For Frame Relay multipoint connections, set the bandwidth to the sum of all CIRs, or if the permanent virtual circuits (PVCs) have different CIRs, set the bandwidth to the lowest CIR multiplied by the number of PVCs on the multipoint connection.

Basic EIGRP Configuration Example

Figure 3-17 shows a sample network, including the configuration of Router A for EIGRP.

All routers in the network are part of autonomous system 109. (For EIGRP to establish a neighbor relationship, all neighbors must be in the same autonomous system.)

Figure 3-17 *Basic EIGRP Configuration Sample Network*

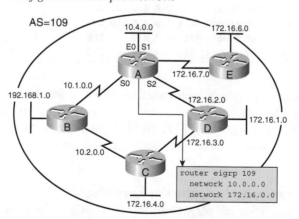

Because the wildcard mask is not used in Router A's configuration, all interfaces on Router A that are part of network 10.0.0.0/8 and network 172.16.0.0/16 participate in the EIGRP routing process. In this case, this includes all four interfaces. Note that network 192.168.1.0 is not configured in the EIGRP configuration on Router A, because Router A does not have any interfaces in that network.

Instead, suppose that the configuration in Example 3-2 was entered onto Router A.

Example 3-2 *Alternative Configuration of Router A in Figure 3-17*

```
routerA(config)#router eigrp 109
routerA(config-router)#network 10.1.0.0
routerA(config-router)#network 10.4.0.0
routerA(config-router)#network 172.16.7.0
routerA(config-router)#network 172.16.2.0
```

Because no wildcard mask was specified, Router A would automatically change the **network** commands to have classful networks, and the resulting configuration would be as shown in Example 3-3.

Example 3-3 *Router A's Interpretation of the Configuration in Example 3-2*

```
router eigrp 109
 network 10.0.0.0
network 172.16.0.0
```

Alternatively, consider what would happen if the configuration shown in Example 3-4 was entered for Router A.

Example 3-4 *Another Alternative Configuration of Router A in Figure 3-17*

```
routerA(config)#router eigrp 109
routerA(config-router)#network 10.1.0.0 0.0.255.255
routerA(config-router)#network 10.4.0.0 0.0.255.255
routerA(config-router)#network 172.16.2.0 0.0.0.255
routerA(config-router)#network 172.16.7.0 0.0.0.255
```

In this case, Router A uses the wildcard mask to determine which directly connected interfaces participate in the EIGRP routing process for autonomous system 109. All interfaces that are part of networks 10.1.0.0/16, 10.4.0.0/16, 172.16.2.0/24, and 172.16.7.0/24 participate in the EIGRP routing process for autonomous system 109; in this case, all four interfaces participate.

EIGRP Configuration Example Using the Wildcard Mask

Figure 3-18 shows another sample network that runs EIGRP in autonomous system 100. The configuration for Router C uses the wildcard mask, because Router C has subnets of Class B network 172.16.0.0 on all interfaces. Router C connects to a router external to autonomous system 100 on its serial interface, and the administrator does not want to run EIGRP with the same autonomous system number there. Without using the wildcard mask, Router C would send EIGRP packets to the external network. This would waste bandwidth and CPU cycles and would provide unnecessary information to the external network. The wildcard mask tells EIGRP to establish a relationship with EIGRP routers from interfaces that are part of network 172.16.3.0/24 or 172.16.4.0/24, but not 172.16.5.0/24.

Figure 3-18 *EIGRP Configuration with Wildcard Mask Example*

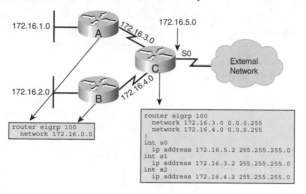

Configuring the ip default-network Command for EIGRP

The EIGRP default route can be created with the **ip default-network** *network-number* global configuration command. A router configured with this command considers the *network-number* the last-resort gateway that it will announce to other routers. The network must be reachable by the router that uses this command before it announces it as a candidate default route to other EIGRP routers. The network number in this command must also be passed to other EIGRP routers so that those routers can use this network as their default network and set their gateway of last resort to this default network. This means that the network must either be an EIGRP-derived network in the routing table, or be generated with a static route and redistributed into EIGRP.

Multiple default networks can be configured; downstream routers then use the EIGRP metric to determine the best default route.

For example, in Figure 3-19, Router A is directly attached to external network 172.31.0.0/16. Router A is configured with the 172.31.0.0 network as a candidate default network using the **ip default-network 172.31.0.0** command. Router A also has that network listed in a **network** command under the EIGRP process and, therefore, passes it to Router B. On Router B, the EIGRP-learned 172.31.0.0 network is flagged as a candidate default network (indicated by the * in the routing table). Router B also sets the gateway of last resort as10.5.1.1 (Router A) to reach the default network of 172.31.0.0.

> **NOTE**   In earlier versions of the IOS software, the router on which the **ip default-network** command was configured would not set the gateway of last resort. Figure 3-19 illustrates that it now does set the gateway of last resort to 0.0.0.0, to the network specified in the **ip default-network** command.

> **NOTE** When you configure the **ip default-network** command and specify a subnet, a static route (the **ip route** command) is generated in the router's configuration; however, the IOS does not display a message to indicate that this has been done. The entry appears as a static route in the routing table of the router where the command is configured. This can be confusing when you want to remove the default network; the configuration must be removed with the **no ip route** command, not with the **no ip default-network** command.

Figure 3-19 *EIGRP* **ip default-network** *Sample Network*

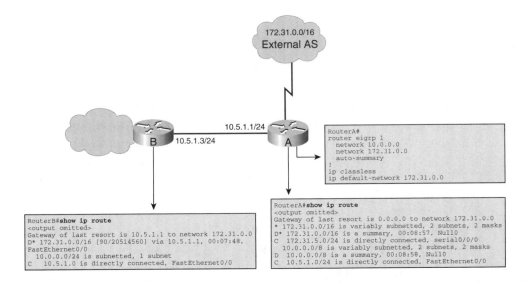

> **NOTE** EIGRP (and IGRP) behave differently than RIP when using the **ip route 0.0.0.0 0.0.0.0** command. For example, EIGRP does not redistribute the 0.0.0.0 0.0.0.0 default route by default. However, if the **network 0.0.0.0** command is added to the EIGRP configuration, it redistributes a default route as a result of the **ip route 0.0.0.0 0.0.0.0** *interface* command (but not as a result of the **ip route 0.0.0.0 0.0.0.0** *address* or **ip default-network** command). For example, the partial configuration shown in Example 3-5 illustrates a router with the 0.0.0.0 route passed to the router's EIGRP neighbors.

Example 3-5 *EIGRP Passes a Default Route Only if It Is Configured to Do So*

```
Router#show run
<output omitted>
interface serial 0/0/0
  ip address 10.1.1.1 255.255.255.0
!
```

Example 3-5 *EIGRP Passes a Default Route Only if It Is Configured to Do So (Continued)*

```
ip route 0.0.0.0 0.0.0.0 serial 0/0/0
!
router eigrp 100
  network 0.0.0.0
<output omitted>
```

Route Summarization

Some EIGRP features, such as automatically summarizing routes at a major network boundary, have distance vector characteristics. Traditional distance vector protocols, which are classful routing protocols, must summarize at network boundaries. They cannot presume the mask for networks that are not directly connected, because masks are not exchanged in the routing updates.

KEY POINT

EIGRP Summarization

EIGRP automatically summarizes on the major network boundary by default; this feature can be turned off. In addition, EIGRP summary routes can be configured on any bit boundary within the network as long as a more specific route exists in the routing table.

Summarizing routes at classful major network boundaries creates smaller routing tables. Smaller routing tables, in turn, make the routing update process less bandwidth intensive. Cisco distance vector routing protocols have autosummarization enabled by default. As mentioned earlier, EIGRP has its roots in IGRP and, therefore, summarizes at the network boundary by default. For EIGRP, this feature can be turned off.

The inability to create summary routes at arbitrary boundaries with a major network has been a drawback of distance vector protocols since their inception. EIGRP has added functionality to allow administrators to create one or more summary routes within a network on any bit boundary (as long as a more specific route exists in the routing table). When the last specific route of the summary goes away, the summary route is deleted from the routing table. The minimum metric of the specific routes is used as the metric of the summary route.

When summarization is configured on a router's interface, a summary route is added to that router's routing table, with the route's next-hop interface set to null0—a directly connected, software-only interface. The use of the null0 interface prevents the router from trying to forward traffic to other routers in search of a more precise, longer match, thus preventing traffic from looping within the network. For example, if the summarizing router receives a packet to an unknown subnet that is part of the summarized range, the packet matches the summary route based on the longest match. The packet is forwarded to the null0 interface (in other words, it is dropped or sent to the *bit bucket*). This prevents the router from forwarding the packet to a default route and possibly creating a loop.

For effective summarization, blocks of contiguous addresses (subnets) should funnel back to a common router so that a single summary route can be created and then advertised. The number of subnets that can be represented by a summary route is directly related to the difference in the number of bits between the subnet mask and the summary mask. The formula 2^n, where n equals the difference in the number of bits between the summary and subnet masks, indicates how many subnets can be represented by a single summary route. For example, if the summary mask contains 3 fewer bits than the subnet mask, eight ($2^3 = 8$) subnets can be aggregated into one advertisement.

For example, if network 10.0.0.0 is divided into /24 subnets and some of these subnets are summarized to the summarization block 10.1.8.0/21, the difference between the /24 networks and the /21 summarizations is 3 bits; therefore, $2^3 = 8$ subnets can be aggregated. The summarized subnets range from 10.1.8.0/24 through 10.1.15.0/24.

When creating summary routes, the administrator needs to specify the IP address of the summary route and the summary mask. Cisco IOS handles the details of proper implementation, such as metrics, loop prevention, and removal of the summary route from the routing table if none of the more specific routes are valid.

Configuring Manual Route Summarization

EIGRP automatically summarizes routes at the classful boundary, but, as discussed, in some cases you might want to turn off this feature. For example, if you have discontiguous subnets, you need to disable autosummarization. Note that an EIGRP router does not perform automatic summarization of networks in which it does not participate.

To turn off automatic summarization, use the **no auto-summary** router configuration command. Use the **ip summary-address eigrp** *as-number address mask* [*admin-distance*] interface configuration command to manually create a summary route at an arbitrary bit boundary, as long as a more specific route exists in the routing table. Table 3-2 summarizes the parameters for this command.

Table 3-2 **ip summary-address eigrp** *Command Parameters*

Parameter	Description
as-number	EIGRP autonomous system number.
address	The IP address being advertised as the summary address. This address does not need to be aligned on Class A, B, or C boundaries.
mask	The IP subnet mask being used to create the summary address.
admin-distance	(Optional) Administrative distance. A value from 0 to 255.

For example, Figure 3-20 shows a discontiguous network 172.16.0.0. By default, both Routers A and B summarize routes at the classful boundary; as a result, Router C would have two equally good routes to network 172.16.0.0 and would perform load balancing between Router A and Router B. This would not be correct routing behavior.

Figure 3-20 *Summarizing EIGRP Routes*

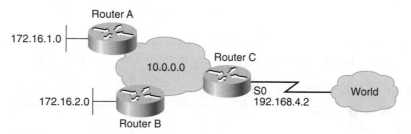

As shown in Example 3-6, you can disable the automatic route summarization on Router A; the same configuration would be done on Router B. With this configuration, Router C knows precisely that 172.16.1.0 is reached via Router A and that 172.16.2.0 is reached only via Router B. The routing tables of the routers in the 10.0.0.0 network, including Router C, now include these discontiguous subnets.

Example 3-6 *Turning Off EIGRP Autosummarization on Router A (and Router B) in Figure 3-20*

```
RouterA(config)#router eigrp 1
RouterA(config-router)#network 10.0.0.0
RouterA(config-router)#network 172.16.0.0
RouterA(config-router)#no auto-summary
```

An EIGRP router autosummarizes routes for only networks to which it is attached. If a network was not autosummarized at the major network boundary, as is the case in this example on Routers A and B because autosummarization is turned off, all the subnet routes are carried into Router C's routing table. Router C will not autosummarize the 172.16.1.0 and 172.16.2.0 subnets because it does not own the 172.16.0.0 network. Therefore, Router C would send routing information about the 172.16.1.0 subnet and the 172.16.2.0 subnet to the WAN.

Forcing a summary route out Router C's interface s0/0/0, as shown in Example 3-7, helps reduce route advertisements about network 172.16.0.0 to the world.

Example 3-7 *Forcing Summarization on Router C in Figure 3-20*

```
RouterC#show run
<output omitted>
router eigrp 1
  network 10.0.0.0
  network 192.168.4.0
```

continues

Example 3-7   *Forcing Summarization on Router C in Figure 3-20 (Continued)*

```
!
<output omitted>
int s0/0/0
  ip address 192.168.4.2 255.255.255.0
  ip summary-address eigrp 1 172.16.0.0 255.255.0.0
<output omitted>
```

Example 3-8 illustrates Router C's routing table. Router C has both 172.16.1.0 and 172.16.2.0, the discontiguous subnets, in its routing table, and the summary route to null 0.

Example 3-8   *Routing Table of Router C in Figure 3-20*

```
RouterC#show ip route
<output omitted>
Gateway of last resort is not set
     172.16.0.0/16 is variably subnetted, 3 subnets, 2 masks
D       172.16.0.0/16 is a summary, 00:00:04, Null0
D       172.16.1.0/24 [90/156160] via 10.1.1.2, 00:00:04, FastEthernet0/0
D       172.16.2.0/24 [90/20640000] via 10.2.2.2, 00:00:04, Serial0/0/1
C    192.168.4.0/24 is directly connected, Serial0/0/0
     10.0.0.0/8 is variably subnetted, 3 subnets, 2 masks
C       10.2.2.0/24 is directly connected, Serial0/0/1
C       10.1.1.0/24 is directly connected, FastEthernet0/0
D       10.0.0.0/8 is a summary, 00:00:05, Null0
RouterC#
```

KEY POINT

Summary Route

For manual summarization, the summary is advertised only if a component (a more specific entry that is represented in the summary) of the summary route is present in the routing table.

NOTE   IP EIGRP summary routes are given an administrative distance value of 5. Standard EIGRP routes receive an administrative distance of 90, and external EIGRP routes receive an administrative distance of 170.

You will notice the EIGRP summary route with an administrative distance of 5 only on the local router that is performing the summarization (with the **ip summary-address eigrp** command), by using the **show ip route** *network* command, where *network* is the specified summarized route.

EIGRP Load Balancing

KEY POINT

Load Balancing

Load balancing is a router's capability to distribute traffic over all of its network ports that are the same metric from the destination address.

Load balancing increases the utilization of network segments, thus increasing effective network bandwidth.

By default, the Cisco IOS balances between a maximum of four equal-cost paths for IP. Using the **maximum-paths** *maximum-path* router configuration command, you can request that up to 16 equally good routes be kept in the routing table (set *maximum-path* to 1 to disable load balancing). When a packet is process-switched, load balancing over equal-cost paths occurs on a per-packet basis. When packets are fast-switched, load balancing over equal-cost paths is on a per-destination basis.

> **NOTE**   If you are testing load balancing, do not ping to or from the routers with the fast-switching interfaces, because these locally router-generated packets are process-switched rather than fast-switched and might produce confusing results.

> **NOTE**   Load balancing is performed only on traffic that passes *through* the router, not traffic generated by the router.

EIGRP can also balance traffic across multiple routes that have different metrics; this is called unequal-cost load balancing. The degree to which EIGRP performs load balancing is controlled by the **variance** *multiplier* router configuration command. The multiplier is a variance value, between 1 and 128, used for load balancing. The default is 1, which means equal-cost load balancing. The multiplier defines the range of metric values that are accepted for load balancing. For example, in Figure 3-21, a variance of 2 is configured, and the range of the metric values (the FDs) for Router E to get to Network Z is 20 to 45. This range of values is used in the procedure to determine the feasibility of a potential route.

KEY POINT | **Feasible Route with Variance**

A route is feasible if the next router in the path is closer to the destination than the current router and if the metric for the entire alternate path is within the variance.

Figure 3-21   *EIGRP Load Balancing with a Variance of 2*

Network	Neighbor	FD	AD
Z	B	30	10
	C	20	10
	D	45	25

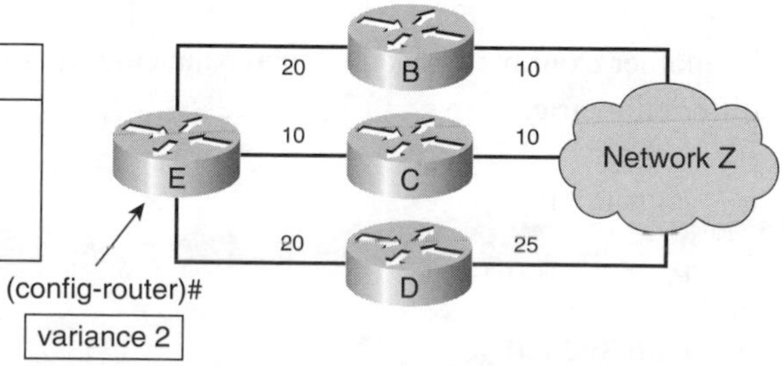

Only paths that are feasible can be used for load balancing; the routing table indicates only feasible paths. The two feasibility conditions are as follows:

- The local best metric (the current FD) must be greater than the best metric (the AD) learned from the next router. In other words, the next router in the path must be closer to the destination than the current router; this prevents routing loops.

- The variance multiplied by the local best metric (the current FD) must be greater than the metric through the next router (the alternative FD).

If both of these conditions are met, the route is called feasible and can be added to the routing table.

To control how traffic is distributed among routes when multiple routes exist for the same destination network and they have different metrics, use the **traffic-share [balanced | min across-interfaces]** router configuration command. With the keyword **balanced**, the router distributes traffic proportionately to the ratios of the metrics associated with the different routes. With the **min across-interfaces** option, the router uses only routes that have minimum costs. (In other words, all routes that are feasible and within the variance are kept in the routing table, but only those with the minimum cost are used.)

In Figure 3-21, Router E has three paths to Network Z, with the following metrics:

- Path 1: 30 (via B)

- Path 2: 20 (via C)

- Path 3: 45 (via D)

Router E uses Router C as the successor because its FD is lowest (20). With the **variance 2** command applied to Router E, the path through Router B meets the criteria for load balancing. In this case, the FD through Router B is less than twice the FD for the successor (Router C). Router D is not considered for load balancing because the FD through Router D is greater than twice the FD for the successor (Router C). In this example, however, Router D would never be a feasible successor, no matter what the variance is. Router D is not a feasible successor because its AD of 25 is greater than Router E's FD of 20; therefore, to avoid a potential routing loop, Router D is not considered closer to the destination than Router E and cannot be a feasible successor.

In another example of unequal load balancing, four paths to a destination have the following different metrics:

- Path 1: 1100

- Path 2: 1100

- Path 3: 2000

- Path 4: 4000

By default, the router routes to the destination using both Paths 1 and 2. Assuming no potential routing loops exist, you would use the **variance 2** command to load balance over Paths 1, 2, and 3, because $1100 * 2 = 2200$, which is greater than the metric through Path 3. Similarly, to also include Path 4, you would issue the **variance 4** command.

EIGRP and WAN Links

EIGRP operates efficiently in WAN environments and is scalable on both point-to-point links and NBMA multipoint and point-to-point links. Because of the inherent differences in links' operational characteristics, default configuration of WAN connections might not be optimal. A solid understanding of EIGRP operation coupled with knowledge of link speeds can yield an efficient, reliable, scalable router configuration.

EIGRP Link Utilization

KEY POINT

EIGRP Bandwidth on an Interface

By default, EIGRP uses up to 50 percent of the bandwidth declared on an interface or subinterface. EIGRP uses the bandwidth of the link set by the **bandwidth** command, or the link's default bandwidth if none is configured, when calculating how much bandwidth to use.

You can adjust this percentage on an interface or subinterface with the **ip bandwidth-percent eigrp** *as-number percent* interface configuration command. The *as-number* is the EIGRP autonomous system number. The *percent* parameter is the percentage of the configured bandwidth that EIGRP can use. You can set the percentage to a value greater than 100, which might be useful if the bandwidth is configured artificially low for routing policy reasons. Example 3-9 shows a configuration that allows EIGRP to use 40 kbps (200 percent of the configured bandwidth, 20 kbps) on the interface. It is essential to make sure that the line is provisioned to handle the configured capacity. (The next section, "Examples of EIGRP on WANs," provides more examples of when this command is useful.)

Example 3-9 *Adjusting the EIGRP Link Utilization*

```
Router(config)#interface serial0/0/0
Router(config-if)#bandwidth 20
Router(config-if)#ip bandwidth-percent eigrp 1 200
```

Cisco IOS assumes that point-to-point Frame Relay subinterfaces are operating at the default speed of the interface. In many implementations, however, only fractional T1 speeds are available. Therefore, when configuring these subinterfaces, set the bandwidth to match the contracted CIR.

When configuring multipoint interfaces (especially for Frame Relay, but also for ATM and ISDN PRI), remember that the bandwidth is shared equally by all neighbors. That is, EIGRP uses the **bandwidth** command on the physical interface divided by the number of Frame Relay neighbors connected on that physical interface to get the bandwidth attributed to each neighbor. EIGRP configuration should reflect the correct percentage of the actual available bandwidth on the line.

Each installation has a unique topology, and with that comes unique configurations. Differing CIR values often require a hybrid configuration that blends the characteristics of point-to-point circuits with multipoint circuits. When configuring multipoint interfaces, configure the bandwidth to represent the minimum CIR times the number of circuits. This approach might not fully use the higher-speed circuits, but it ensures that the circuits with the lowest CIR will not be overdriven. If the topology has a small number of very low-speed circuits, these interfaces are typically defined as point-to-point so that their bandwidth can be set to match the provisioned CIR.

Examples of EIGRP on WANs

In Figure 3-22, Router C's interface has been configured for a bandwidth of 224 kbps. Four neighbors exist in this pure multipoint topology, so each circuit is allocated one-quarter of the configured bandwidth on the interface, and this 56-kbps allocation matches the provisioned CIR of each circuit.

Figure 3-22 *Frame Relay Multipoint in Which All VCs Share the Bandwidth Evenly*

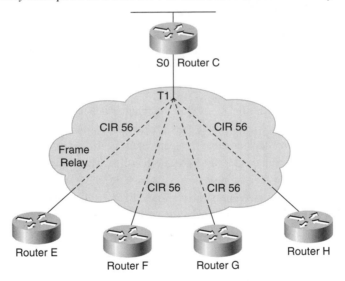

• All VCs share bandwidth evenly: 4 x 56 = 224

Example 3-10 shows the configuration for Router C's Serial 0 interface.

Example 3-10 *Adjusting the* **bandwidth** *Command on an Interface on Router C in Figure 3-22*

```
RouterC(config)#interface serial 0
RouterC(config-if)#encapsulation frame-relay
RouterC(config-if)#bandwidth 224
```

In Figure 3-23, one of the circuits has been provisioned for a 56-kbps CIR, and the other circuits have a higher CIR. This interface has been configured for a bandwidth that represents the lowest CIR multiplied by the number of circuits being supported (56 * 4 = 224). This configuration protects against overwhelming the slowest-speed circuit in the topology.

Figure 3-23 *Frame Relay Multipoint in Which VCs Have Different CIRs*

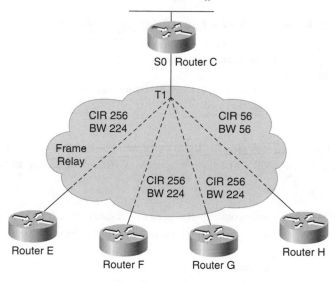

• Lowest CIR x # of VC: 56 x 4 = 224

Figure 3-24 presents a hybrid solution. There is only one low-speed circuit, and other VCs are provisioned for a higher CIR.

Figure 3-24 *Frame Relay Multipoint and Point-to-Point*

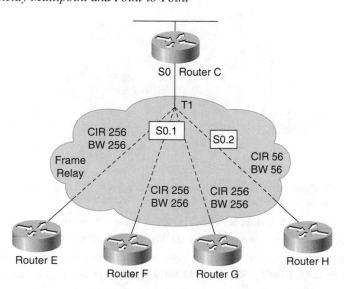

• Configure lowest CIR VC as point-to-point, specify BW = CIR
• Configure higher CIR VCs as multipoint, combine CIRs

Example 3-11 shows the configuration applied to Router C in Figure 3-24.

Example 3-11 *Adjusting the Bandwidth for a Frame Relay Subinterface on Router C in Figure 3-24*

```
RouterC(config)#interface serial 0.1 multipoint
RouterC(config-subif)#bandwidth 768
RouterC(config-subif)#exit
RouterC(config)#interface serial 0.2 point-to-point
RouterC(config-subif)#bandwidth 56
```

Example 3-11 shows the low-speed circuit configured as point-to-point. The remaining circuits are designated as multipoint, and their respective CIRs are added up to set the interface's bandwidth.

Figure 3-25 illustrates a common hub-and-spoke oversubscribed topology with 10 VCs to the remote sites. (Only 4 of the 10 remote sites are shown in the figure.)

Figure 3-25 *Frame Relay Hub-and-Spoke Topology*

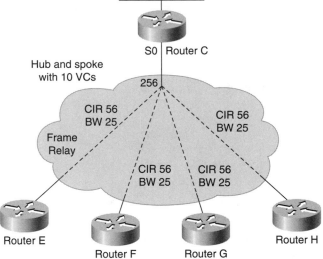

• Configure each VC as point-to-point, specify BW = 1/10 of link capacity
• Increase EIGRP utilization to 50% of actual VC capacity

The circuits are provisioned as 56-kbps links, but there is insufficient bandwidth at the interface to support the allocation. For example, if the hub tries to communicate to all remote sites at the same time, the bandwidth that is required exceeds the available link speed of 256 kbps for the hub—10 times the CIR of 56 kbps equals 560 kbps. In a point-to-point topology, all VCs are treated equally and are therefore configured for exactly one-tenth of the available link speed (25 kbps).

Example 3-12 shows the configuration used on Routers C and G of Figure 3-25.

Example 3-12   *EIGRP WAN Configuration: Point-to-Point Links on Routers C and G in Figure 3-25*

```
RouterC(config)#interface serial 0.1 point-to-point
RouterC(config-subif)#bandwidth 25
RouterC(config-subif)#ip bandwidth-percent eigrp 63 110
<output omitted>
RouterC(config)#interface serial 0.10 point-to-point
RouterC(config-subif)#bandwidth 25
RouterC(config-subif)#ip bandwidth-percent eigrp 63 110

RouterG(config)#interface serial 0
RouterG(config-if)#bandwidth 25
RouterG(config-if)#ip bandwidth-percent eigrp 63 110
```

By default, EIGRP uses 50 percent of a circuit's configured bandwidth. As mentioned, EIGRP configuration should reflect the correct percentage of the actual available bandwidth on the line. Therefore, in an attempt to ensure that EIGRP packets are delivered through the Frame Relay network in Figure 3-25, each subinterface has the EIGRP allocation percentage raised to 110 percent of the specified bandwidth. This adjustment causes EIGRP packets to receive approximately 28 kbps of the provisioned 56 kbps on each circuit. This extra configuration restores the 50-50 ratio that was tampered with when the bandwidth was set to an artificially low value.

NOTE   Suppressing ACKs also saves bandwidth. An ACK is not sent if a unicast data packet is ready for transmission. The ACK field in any reliable unicast packet (RTP packet) is sufficient to acknowledge the neighbor's packet, so the ACK packet is suppressed to save bandwidth. This is a significant feature for point-to-point links and NBMA networks, because on those media, all data packets are sent as unicasts and, thus, can carry an acknowledgment themselves (this is also known as a piggyback ACK). In that instance, there is no need for an ACK packet.

Configuring EIGRP Authentication

You can prevent your router from receiving fraudulent route updates by configuring neighbor router authentication. You can configure EIGRP neighbor authentication (also called *neighbor router authentication* or *route authentication*) such that routers can participate in routing based on predefined passwords.

This section first describes router authentication in general, followed by a discussion of how to configure and troubleshoot EIGRP Message Digest 5 (MD5) authentication.

Router Authentication

Neighbor router authentication can be configured such that routers only participate in routing based on predefined passwords.

By default, no authentication is used for routing protocol packets. When neighbor router authentication has been configured on a router, the router authenticates the source of each routing update packet that it receives. This is accomplished by the exchange of an authentication key (also called a *password*) that is known to both the sending and the receiving router.

The router uses two types of authentication:

■ **Simple password authentication (also called plain text authentication)**—Supported by Integrated System-Integrated System (IS-IS), Open Shortest Path First (OSPF), and Routing Information Protocol Version 2 (RIPv2)

■ **MD5 authentication**—Supported by OSPF, RIPv2, BGP, and EIGRP

NOTE This book covers authentication for EIGRP, OSPF, and BGP.

Both forms of authentication work in the same way, with the exception that MD5 sends a message digest instead of the authenticating key itself. The message digest is created using the key (and a key ID with some protocols) and a message, but the key itself is not sent, preventing it from being read while it is being transmitted. Simple password authentication sends the authenticating key itself over the wire.

NOTE Simple password authentication is not recommended for use as part of your security strategy because it is vulnerable to passive attacks. Anybody with a link analyzer could easily view the password on the wire. The primary use of simple password authentication is to avoid accidental changes to the routing infrastructure. Using MD5 authentication, however, is a recommended security practice.

CAUTION As with all keys, passwords, and other security secrets, it is imperative that you closely guard the keys used in neighbor authentication. The security benefits of this feature are reliant upon keeping all authenticating keys confidential. Also, when performing router management tasks via Simple Network Management Protocol (SNMP), do not ignore the risk associated with sending keys using nonencrypted SNMP.

With simple password authentication, a password (key) is configured on a router; each participating neighbor router must be configured with the same key.

MD5 authentication is a cryptographic authentication. A key (password) and key ID are configured on each router. The router uses an algorithm based on the routing protocol packet, the key, and the key ID to generate a message digest (also called a *hash*) that is appended to the packet. Unlike the simple authentication, the key is not exchanged over the wire—the message digest is sent instead of the key, which ensures that nobody can eavesdrop on the line and learn keys during transmission.

EIGRP MD5 Authentication

By default, no authentication is used for EIGRP packets. You can configure EIGRP to use MD5 authentication.

When EIGRP neighbor authentication has been configured on a router, the router authenticates the source of each routing update packet that it receives. The MD5 keyed digest in each EIGRP packet prevents the introduction of unauthorized or false routing messages from unapproved sources.

For EIGRP MD5 authentication, you must configure an authenticating *key* and a *key ID* on both the sending router and the receiving router. Each key has its own key ID, which is stored locally. The combination of the key ID and the interface associated with the message uniquely identifies the authentication algorithm and MD5 authentication key in use.

EIGRP allows keys to be managed using *key chains*. Each key definition within the key chain can specify a time interval for which that key will be activated (known as its lifetime). Then, during a given key's lifetime, routing update packets are sent with this activated key. Only one authentication packet is sent, regardless of how many valid keys exist. The software examines the key numbers in order from lowest to highest, and it uses the first valid key it encounters.

KEY POINT

EIGRP Keys

When configuring EIGRP authentication, you specify the key ID (number), the key (password), and the lifetime of the key. The first (by key ID), valid (by lifetime), key is used.

Keys cannot be used during time periods for which they are not activated. Therefore, it is recommended that for a given key chain, key activation times overlap to avoid any period of time for which no key is activated. If a time period occurs during which no key is activated, neighbor authentication cannot occur, and therefore routing updates will fail.

> **NOTE** The router needs to know the time to be able to rotate through keys in synchronization with the other participating routers, so that all routers are using the same key at the same moment. Refer to the Network Time Protocol (NTP) and calendar commands in the "Performing Basic System Management" chapter of the *Cisco IOS Configuration Fundamentals Configuration Guide* for information about configuring time on your router.

Configuring MD5 Authentication

To configure MD5 authentication for EIGRP, complete the following steps:

Step 1   Enter configuration mode for the interface on which you want to enable authentication.

Step 2   Specify MD5 authentication for EIGRP packets using the **ip authentication mode eigrp** *autonomous-system* **md5** interface configuration command. The *autonomous-system* is the EIGRP autonomous system number in which authentication is to be used.

Step 3   Enable the authentication of EIGRP packets with a key specified in a key chain by using the **ip authentication key-chain eigrp** *autonomous-system name-of-chain* interface configuration command. The *autonomous-system* parameter specifies the EIGRP autonomous system number in which authentication is to be used. The *name-of-chain* parameter specifies the name of the authentication key chain from which a key is to be obtained for this interface.

Step 4   Enter the configuration mode for the key chain using the **key chain** *name-of-chain* global configuration command.

Step 5   Identify a key ID to use and enter configuration mode for that key using the **key** *key-id* key-chain configuration command. The *key-id* is the ID number of an authentication key on a key chain. The range of keys is from 0 to 2147483647; the key ID numbers need not be consecutive.

Step 6   Identify the key string (password) for this key using the **key-string** *key* key-chain-key configuration command. The *key* is the authentication key-string that is to be used to authenticate sent and received EIGRP packets. The key string can contain from 1 to 80 uppercase and lowercase alphanumeric characters, except that the first character cannot be a number.

Step 7   Optionally specify the time period during which this key will be accepted for use on received packets using the **accept-lifetime** *start-time* {**infinite** | *end-time* | **duration** *seconds*} key-chain-key configuration command. Table 3-3 describes the parameters for this command.

Table 3-3   **accept-lifetime** *Command Parameters*

Parameter	Description
start-time	Beginning time that the key specified by the **key** command is valid for use on received packets. The syntax can be either of the following: ```\nhh:mm:ss month date year\nhh:mm:ss date month year\n hh — hours\n mm — minutes\n ss — seconds\n month — first three letters of the month\n date — date (1-31)\n year — year (four digits)\n``` The default start time and the earliest acceptable date is January 1, 1993.
infinite	Indicates the key is valid for use on received packets from the *start-time* value on.
end-time	Indicates the key is valid for use on received packets from the *start-time* value until the *end-time* value. The syntax is the same as that for the *start-time* value. The *end-time* value must be after the *start-time* value. The default end time is an infinite time period.
seconds	Length of time (in seconds) that the key is valid for use on received packets. The range is from 1 to 2147483646.

Step 8   Optionally specify the time period during which this key can be used for sending packets using the **send-lifetime** *start-time* {**infinite** | *end-time* | **duration** *seconds*} key-chain-key configuration command. Table 3-4 describes the parameters for this command.

Table 3-4   **send-lifetime** *Command Parameters*

Parameter	Description

start-time	Beginning time that the key specified by the **key** command is valid to be used for sending packets. The syntax can be either of the following:
	
	`hh:mm:ss month date year`
	`hh:mm:ss date month year`
	`hh — hours`
	`mm — minutes`
	`ss — seconds`
	`month — first three letters of the month`
	`date — date (1-31)`
	`year — year (four digits)`
	
	The default start time and the earliest acceptable date is January 1, 1993.

infinite	Indicates the key is valid to be used for sending packets from the *start-time* value on.
end-time	Indicates the key is valid to be used for sending packets from the *start-time* value until the *end-time* value. The syntax is the same as that for the *start-time* value. The *end-time* value must be after the *start-time* value. The default end time is an infinite time period.
seconds	Length of time (in seconds) that the key is valid to be used for sending packets. The range is from 1 to 2147483646.

NOTE   If the **service password-encryption** command is not used when implementing EIGRP authentication, the key-string will be stored as plain text in the router configuration. If you configure the **service password-encryption** command, the key-string will be stored and displayed in an encrypted form; when it is displayed, there will be an *encryption-type* of 7 specified before the encrypted key-string.

MD5 Authentication Configuration Example

Figure 3-26 shows the network used to illustrate the configuration, verification, and troubleshooting of MD5 authentication.

Figure 3-26   *Network for EIGRP Authentication Configuration Example*

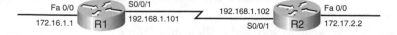

Example 3-13 shows the configuration of the R1 router.

Example 3-13 *Configuration of Router R1 in Figure 3-26*

```
R1#show running-config
<output omitted>
key chain R1chain
 key 1
  key-string firstkey
  accept-lifetime 04:00:00 Jan 1 2006 infinite
  send-lifetime 04:00:00 Jan 1 2006 04:01:00 Jan 1 2006
 key 2
  key-string secondkey
  accept-lifetime 04:00:00 Jan 1 2006 infinite
  send-lifetime 04:00:00 Jan 1 2006 infinite
<output omitted>
interface FastEthernet0/0
 ip address 172.16.1.1 255.255.255.0
!
interface Serial0/0/1
 bandwidth 64
 ip address 192.168.1.101 255.255.255.224
 ip authentication mode eigrp 100 md5
 ip authentication key-chain eigrp 100 R1chain
!
router eigrp 100
 network 172.16.1.0 0.0.0.255
 network 192.168.1.0
 auto-summary
```

MD5 authentication is configured on the serial 0/0/1 interface with the **ip authentication mode eigrp 100 md5** command. The **ip authentication key-chain eigrp 100 R1chain** command specifies that the key chain *R1chain* is to be used.

The **key chain R1chain** command enters configuration mode for the *R1chain* key chain. Two keys are defined. Key 1 is set to *firstkey* with the **key-string firstkey** command. This key is acceptable for use on packets received by R1 from January 1, 2006 onward, as specified in the **accept-lifetime 04:00:00 Jan 1 2006 infinite** command. However, the **send-lifetime 04:00:00 Jan 1 2006 04:01:00 Jan 1 2006** command specifies that this key was only valid for use when sending packets for 1 minute on January 1, 2006; it is no longer valid for use in sending packets.

Key 2 is set to *secondkey* with the **key-string secondkey** command. This key is acceptable for use on packets received by R1 from January 1, 2006 onward, as specified in the **accept-lifetime 04:00:00 Jan 1 2006 infinite** command. This key can also be used when sending packets from January 1, 2006 onward, as specified in the **send-lifetime 04:00:00 Jan 1 2006 infinite** command.

R1 will therefore accept and attempt to verify the MD5 digest of any EIGRP packets with a key ID equal to 1 or 2. All other MD5 packets will be dropped. R1 will send all EIGRP packets using key 2, because key 1 is no longer valid for use when sending packets.

Example 3-14 shows the configuration of the R2 router.

Example 3-14   *Configuration of Router R2 in Figure 3-26*

```
R2#show running-config
<output omitted>
key chain R2chain
 key 1
  key-string firstkey
  accept-lifetime 04:00:00 Jan 1 2006 infinite
  send-lifetime 04:00:00 Jan 1 2006 infinite
 key 2
  key-string secondkey
  accept-lifetime 04:00:00 Jan 1 2006 infinite
  send-lifetime 04:00:00 Jan 1 2006 infinite
<output omitted>
interface FastEthernet0/0
 ip address 172.17.2.2 255.255.255.0
!
interface Serial0/0/1
 bandwidth 64
 ip address 192.168.1.102 255.255.255.224
 ip authentication mode eigrp 100 md5
 ip authentication key-chain eigrp 100 R2chain
!
router eigrp 100
 network 172.17.2.0 0.0.0.255
 network 192.168.1.0
auto-summary
```

MD5 authentication is configured on the serial 0/0/1 interface with the **ip authentication mode eigrp 100 md5** command. The **ip authentication key-chain eigrp 100 R2chain** command specifies that the key chain *R2chain* is to be used.

The **key chain R2chain** command enters configuration mode for the *R2chain* key chain. Two keys are defined. Key 1 is set to *firstkey* with the **key-string firstkey** command. This key is acceptable for use on packets received by R2 from January 1, 2006 onward, as specified in the **accept-lifetime 04:00:00 Jan 1 2006 infinite** command. This key can also be used when sending packets from January 1, 2006 onward, as specified in the **send-lifetime 04:00:00 Jan 1 2006 infinite** command.

Key 2 is set to *secondkey* with the **key-string secondkey** command. This key is acceptable for use on packets received by R2 from January 1, 2006 onward, as specified in the **accept-lifetime**

04:00:00 Jan 1 2006 infinite command. This key can also be used when sending packets from January 1, 2006 onward, as specified in the **send-lifetime 04:00:00 Jan 1 2006 infinite** command.

R2 will therefore accept and attempt to verify the MD5 digest of any EIGRP packets with a key ID equal to 1 or 2. R2 will send all EIGRP packets using key 1, because it is the first valid key in the key chain.

Verifying MD5 Authentication

Example 3-15 provides the output of the **show ip eigrp neighbors** and **show ip route** commands on the R1 router depicted in the network in Figure 3-26. The neighbor table indicates that the two routers have successfully formed an EIGRP adjacency. The routing table verifies that the 172.17.0.0 network has been learned via EIGRP over the serial connection. Example 3-15 also shows the results of a **ping** to the R2 Fast Ethernet interface address to illustrate that the link is working.

Example 3-15 *Output on Router R1 in Figure 3-26*

```
R1#
*Apr 21 16:23:30.517: %DUAL-5-NBRCHANGE: IP-EIGRP(0) 100: Neighbor 192.168.1.102 (Serial0/
  0/1) is up: new adjacency

R1#show ip eigrp neighbors
IP-EIGRP neighbors for process 100
H   Address                 Interface       Hold Uptime    SRTT    RTO  Q  Seq
                                            (sec)          (ms)        Cnt Num
0   192.168.1.102           Se0/0/1          12 00:03:10    17   2280  0  14
R1#show ip route
<output omitted>
Gateway of last resort is not set
D    172.17.0.0/16 [90/40514560] via 192.168.1.102, 00:02:22, Serial0/0/1
     172.16.0.0/16 is variably subnetted, 2 subnets, 2 masks
D        172.16.0.0/16 is a summary, 00:31:31, Null0
C        172.16.1.0/24 is directly connected, FastEthernet0/0
     192.168.1.0/24 is variably subnetted, 2 subnets, 2 masks
C        192.168.1.96/27 is directly connected, Serial0/0/1
D        192.168.1.0/24 is a summary, 00:31:31, Null0
R1#ping 172.17.2.2
Type escape sequence to abort.
Sending 5, 100-byte ICMP Echos to 172.17.2.2, timeout is 2 seconds:
!!!!!
Success rate is 100 percent (5/5), round-trip min/avg/max = 12/15/16 ms
```

Troubleshooting MD5 Authentication

This section provides some examples of how to troubleshoot EIGRP MD5 authentication.

Example of Successful MD5 Authentication

Example 3-16 shows output from the **debug eigrp packets** command on R1, which displays that R1 is receiving EIGRP packets with MD5 authentication, with a key ID equal to 1, from R2.

Example 3-16 **debug eigrp packets** *Command Output on Router R1 in Figure 3-26*

```
R1#debug eigrp packets
EIGRP Packets debugging is on
    (UPDATE, REQUEST, QUERY, REPLY, HELLO, IPXSAP, PROBE, ACK, STUB, SIAQUERY, SIAREPLY)
*Apr 21 16:38:51.745: EIGRP: received packet with MD5 authentication, key id = 1
*Apr 21 16:38:51.745: EIGRP: Received HELLO on Serial0/0/1 nbr 192.168.1.102
*Apr 21 16:38:51.745:   AS 100, Flags 0x0, Seq 0/0 idbQ 0/0 iidbQ un/rely 0/0 peerQ un/
  rely 0/0
```

Similarly, the output of the **debug eigrp packets** command on R2 shown Example 3-17 illustrates that R2 is receiving EIGRP packets with MD5 authentication, with a key ID equal to 2, from R1.

Example 3-17 **debug eigrp packets** *Command Output on Router R2 in Figure 3-26*

```
R2#debug eigrp packets
EIGRP Packets debugging is on
    (UPDATE, REQUEST, QUERY, REPLY, HELLO, IPXSAP, PROBE, ACK, STUB, SIAQUERY, SIAREPLY)
R2#
*Apr 21 16:38:38.321: EIGRP: received packet with MD5 authentication, key id = 2
*Apr 21 16:38:38.321: EIGRP: Received HELLO on Serial0/0/1 nbr 192.168.1.101
*Apr 21 16:38:38.321:   AS 100, Flags 0x0, Seq 0/0 idbQ 0/0 iidbQ un/rely 0/0 peerQ un/
  rely 0/0
```

Example of Troubleshooting MD5 Authentication Problems

For this example, the key string for router R1's key 2, the one that it uses when sending EIGRP packets, is changed to be different from the key string that router R2 is expecting. Example 3-18 shows the changes to the configuration for R1.

Example 3-18 *Changes to the Configuration of Router R1 in Figure 3-26*

```
R1(config-if)#key chain R1chain
R1(config-keychain)#key 2
R1(config-keychain-key)#key-string wrongkey
```

The output of the **debug eigrp packets** command on R2 shown in Example 3-19 illustrates that R2 is receiving EIGRP packets with MD5 authentication, with a key ID equal to 2, from R1, but that there is an authentication mismatch. The EIGRP packets from R1 are ignored, and the neighbor relationship is declared to be down. The output of the **show ip eigrp neighbors** command confirms that R2 does not have any EIGRP neighbors.

Example 3-19 *Output on Router R2 in Figure 3-26*

```
R2#debug eigrp packets
EIGRP Packets debugging is on
    (UPDATE, REQUEST, QUERY, REPLY, HELLO, IPXSAP, PROBE, ACK, STUB, SIAQUERY, SIAREPLY)
R2#
*Apr 21 16:50:18.749: EIGRP: pkt key id = 2, authentication mismatch
*Apr 21 16:50:18.749: EIGRP: Serial0/0/1: ignored packet from 192.168.1.101, opcode = 5
 (invalid authentication)
*Apr 21 16:50:18.749: EIGRP: Dropping peer, invalid authentication
*Apr 21 16:50:18.749: EIGRP: Sending HELLO on Serial0/0/1
*Apr 21 16:50:18.749:   AS 100, Flags 0x0, Seq 0/0 idbQ 0/0 iidbQ un/rely 0/0
*Apr 21 16:50:18.753: %DUAL-5-NBRCHANGE: IP-EIGRP(0) 100: Neighbor 192.168.1.101
 (Serial0/0/1) is down: Auth failure

R2#show ip eigrp neighbors
IP-EIGRP neighbors for process 100
R2#
```

The two routers keep trying to reestablish their neighbor relationship. Because of the different keys used by each router in this scenario, R1 will authenticate hello messages sent by R2 using key 1. When R1 sends a hello message back to R2 using key 2, however, an authentication mismatch exists. From R1's perspective, the relationship appears to be up for a while, but then it times out, as illustrated by the messages received on R1 shown in Example 3-20. The output of the **show ip eigrp neighbors** command on R1 also illustrates that R1 does have R2 in its neighbor table for a short time.

Example 3-20 *Output on Router R1 in Figure 3-26*

```
R1#
*Apr 21 16:54:09.821: %DUAL-5-NBRCHANGE: IP-EIGRP(0) 100: Neighbor 192.168.1.102 (Serial0/
 0/1) is down: retry limit exceeded
*Apr 21 16:54:11.745: %DUAL-5-NBRCHANGE: IP-EIGRP(0) 100: Neighbor 192.168.1.102 (Serial0/
 0/1) is up: new adjacency
R1#show ip eigrp neighbors
H   Address         Interface    Hold Uptime    SRTT   RTO  Q  Seq
                                 (sec)          (ms)        Cnt Num
0   192.168.1.102   Se0/0/1       13 00:00:38    1     5000  1  0
```

Using EIGRP in an Enterprise Network

EIGRP is a scalable routing protocol that ensures that as a network grows larger, it operates efficiently and adjusts rapidly to changes. This section describes practical EIGRP-specific design and configuration techniques to implement an effective, scalable enterprise network.

EIGRP Scalability

The following are some of the many variables that affect network scalability:

- **The amount of information exchanged between neighbors**—If more information than necessary for routing to function correctly is exchanged between EIGRP neighbors, unnecessary work during routing startup and topology changes results.

- **Number of routers**—When a topology change occurs, the amount of resources consumed by EIGRP is directly related to the number of routers that must be involved in the change.

- **The topology's depth**—The topology's depth can affect the convergence time. Depth refers to the number of hops that information must travel to reach all routers. For example, a multinational network without route summarization has a large depth and therefore increased convergence time.

    A three-tiered network design (as described in Chapter 1, "Network Architecture Framework and Design Models") is highly recommended for all IP routing environments. There should never be more than seven hops between any two routing devices on an enterprise internetwork. The propagation delay and the query process across multiple hops when changes occur can slow down the convergence of the network when routes are lost.

- **The number of alternative paths through the network**—A network should provide alternative paths to avoid single points of failure. However, too many alternative paths can create problems with EIGRP convergence, because the EIGRP routing process, using queries, needs to explore all possible paths for lost routes. This complexity creates an ideal condition for a router to become stuck-in-active (described in the later "EIGRP Queries and Stuck-in-Active" section) as it awaits a response to queries that are being propagated through these many alternative paths.

For proper EIGRP operation, you should follow some common design principles. For example, routers located at convergence points within the network need sufficient memory to buffer a large number of packets and to support numerous processes related to routing large volumes of traffic.

On WAN links, and especially with the hub-and-spoke topology, enough bandwidth should be provided to prevent router overhead traffic from interfering with normal user-generated traffic. In this respect, the impact of EIGRP packets being lost because of contention for bandwidth might be greater than application delays experienced by some users.

EIGRP Route Summarization

Route summarization is most effective with a sound address allocation. Having a two- or three-layer hierarchical network design, with routers positioned by function rather than by geography, greatly assists traffic flow and route distribution.

> **NOTE**   For a full discussion of internetwork design, refer to *Designing for Cisco Internetwork Solutions (DESGN)* (Cisco Press, 2003).

Figure 3-27 shows the topology of a nonscalable internetwork in which addresses (subnets) are either randomly assigned or assigned by historical requirements. In this example, multiple subnets from different major networks are located in each cloud, requiring many subnet routes to be injected into the core. In addition, because of the random assignment of addresses, query traffic cannot be localized to any portion of the network, thus increasing convergence time. Administration and troubleshooting are also more complex in this scenario.

Figure 3-27   *Nonscalable Internetwork*

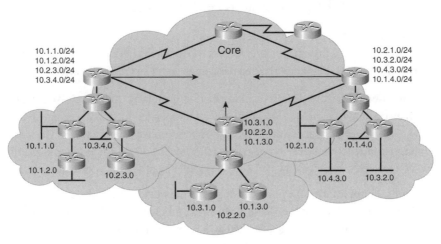

Figure 3-28 illustrates a better-designed network. Subnet addresses from individual major networks are localized within each cloud. This allows summary routes to be injected into the core. As an added benefit, the summary routes act as a boundary for the queries generated by a topology change.

Figure 3-28   *Scalable Internetwork*

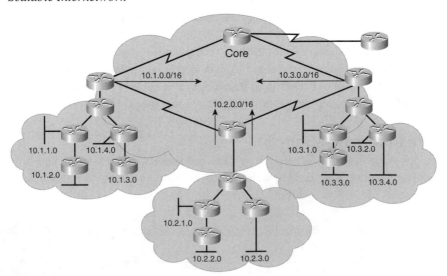

EIGRP Queries and Stuck-in-Active

As an advanced distance vector routing protocol, EIGRP relies on its neighbors to provide routing information. If a route is lost and no FS is available, EIGRP queries its neighbors about the lost route.

Recall that when a router loses a route and does not have an FS in its topology table, it looks for an alternative path to the destination. This is known as *going active* on a route. (A route is considered passive when a router is not recomputing that route.) Recomputing a route involves sending query packets to all neighbors on interfaces other than the one used to reach the previous successor (split horizon), inquiring whether they have a route to the given destination. If a router has an alternative route, it answers the query with a reply packet and does not propagate the query further; the reply includes the alternate route. If a neighbor does not have an alternative route, it queries each of its own neighbors for an alternative path. The queries then propagate through the network, thus creating an expanding tree of queries. When a router answers a query, it stops the spread of the query through that branch of the network; however, the query can still spread through other portions of the network as other routers attempt to find alternative paths, which might not exist.

Because of the reliable multicast approach used by EIGRP when searching for an alternative to a lost route, it is imperative that a reply be received for each query generated in the network. In other words, when a route goes active and queries are initiated, the only way this route can come out of the active state and transition to passive state is by receiving a reply for every generated query.

KEY POINT

| **Stuck-in-Active**

If the router does not receive a reply to all the outstanding queries within 3 minutes (the default time), the route goes to the stuck-in-active (SIA) state.

> **NOTE** You can change the active-state time limit from its default of 3 minutes using the **timers active-time** [*time-limit* | **disabled**] router configuration command. The *time-limit* is in minutes.

When a route goes to SIA state, the router resets the neighbor relationships for the neighbors that failed to reply. This causes the router to recompute all routes known through that neighbor and to re-advertise all the routes it knows about to that neighbor.

The most common reasons for SIA routes are as follows:

- The router is too busy to answer the query—generally as a result of high CPU usage or memory problems—and cannot allocate memory to process the query or build the reply packet.

- The link between the two routers is not good, so some packets are lost between the routers. The router receives an adequate number of packets to maintain the neighbor relationship, but the router does not receive all queries or replies.

- A failure causes traffic on a link to flow in only one direction. This is called a *unidirectional link*.

> **NOTE**   Use the **eigrp log-neighbor-changes** command to enable the logging of neighbor adjacency changes to monitor the routing system's stability and to help detect problems related to SIA.

One erroneous approach for decreasing the chances of a stuck-in-active route is to use multiple EIGRP autonomous systems to bound the query range. Many networks have been implemented using multiple EIGRP autonomous systems (to somewhat simulate OSPF areas), with mutual redistribution between the different autonomous systems. Although this approach changes how the network behaves, it does not always achieve the results intended. If a query reaches the edge of the autonomous system (where routes are redistributed into another autonomous system), the original query is answered. However, then the edge router initiates a new query in the other autonomous system. Therefore, the query process has not been stopped; the querying continues in the other autonomous system, where the route can potentially go in SIA.

Another misconception about autonomous system boundaries is that implementing multiple autonomous systems protects one autonomous system from route flaps in another autonomous system. If routes are redistributed between autonomous systems, route transitions from one autonomous system are detected in the other autonomous systems.

Preventing SIA Connections

SIA-Query and SIA-Reply are two new additions to the Type, Length, Value (TLV) triplets in the EIGRP packet header. These packets are generated automatically with no configuration required, from Cisco IOS Software Release 12.1(5) and later, with the *Active Process Enhancement* feature. This feature enables an EIGRP router to monitor the progression of the search for a successor route and ensure that the neighbor is still reachable. The result is improved network reliability by reducing the unintended termination of neighbor adjacency.

The diagram on the left in Figure 3-29 illustrates what would happen before this feature was introduced. Router A sends a query for network 10.1.1.0/24 to Router B. Router B has no entry for this network, so it queries Router C. If problems exist between Router B and C, the reply packet from Router C to Router B might be delayed or lost. Router A has no visibility of downstream progress and assumes that no response indicates problems with Router B. After Router A's 3-minute active timer expires, the neighbor relationship with Router B is reset, along with all known routes from Router B.

In contrast, with the Active Process Enhancement feature, as illustrated in the diagram on the right in Figure 3-29, Router A queries downstream Router B (with an SIA-Query) at the midway point of the active timer (one and a half minutes by default) about the status of the route. Router B responds (with an SIA-Reply) that it is searching for a replacement route. Upon receiving this SIA-Reply response packet, Router A validates the status of Router B and does not terminate the neighbor relationship.

Figure 3-29 *Cisco IOS Active Process Enhancement*

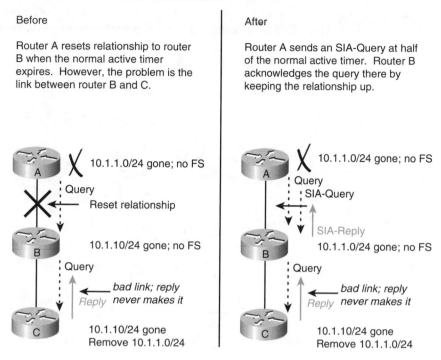

Before

Router A resets relationship to router B when the normal active timer expires. However, the problem is the link between router B and C.

After

Router A sends an SIA-Query at half of the normal active timer. Router B acknowledges the query there by keeping the relationship up.

Meanwhile, Router B will send up to three SIA-Queries to Router C. If they go unanswered, Router B will terminate the neighbor relationship with Router C. Router B will then update Router A with an SIA-Reply indicating that the network 10.1.1.0/24 is unreachable. Routers A and B will remove the active route from their topology tables. The neighbor relationship between Routers A and B remains intact.

EIGRP Query Range

Limiting the scope of query propagation through the network (the query range), also known as *query scoping*, helps reduce incidences of SIA. Keeping the query packets close to the source reduces the chance that an isolated failure in another part of the network will restrict the convergence (query/reply) process. This section introduces an example that examines how to manage the query range.

Remote routers rarely need to know all the routes advertised in an entire network. Therefore, it is the network manager's responsibility to look at what information is necessary to properly route user traffic and to consider the use of a default route.

For example, in Figure 3-30, Router B notices the loss of network 10.1.8.0 and sends a query to Routers A, C, D, and E. In turn, these routers send queries to their neighbors, requesting an FS for 10.1.8.0. When the query process starts, each path receives duplicate queries because of the redundant topology. Therefore, not only are the remote routers required to respond to queries from the regional offices, but they also continue the search by reflecting the queries back toward the other regional office's router. This significantly complicates the convergence process on the network.

Figure 3-30 *Effect of the EIGRP Update and Query Process*

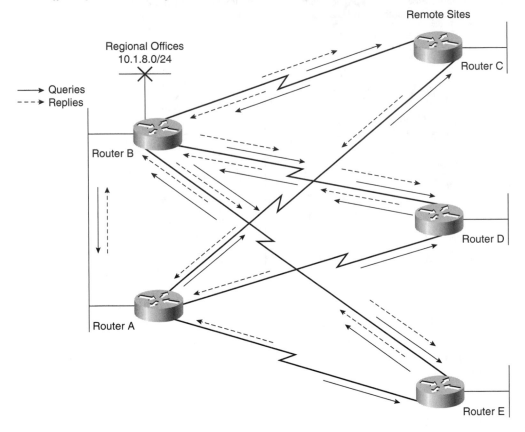

In this sample network with only two regional and three remote routers, the problem might not be very significant. In a network with hundreds of remote offices, the problem can be severe.

Examine the query process for the 10.1.8.0/24 subnet. Router B advertises 10.1.8.0/24 to all other routers. The best path for Router A to reach 10.1.8.0/24 is over the Ethernet link to Router B. The remote routers (C, D, and E) use the serial link to B as their preferred path to reach 10.1.8.0/24 but still learn about an alternative path through Router A. For this example, assume that the EIGRP metric for Ethernet is 1000 and the metric for a serial link is 100,000.

Table 3-5 shows the content of the IP EIGRP topology table on Routers C, D, and E for network 10.1.8.0/24. Table 3-6 shows the content of the IP EIGRP topology table on Router A for network 10.1.8.0/24.

Table 3-5   *IP EIGRP Topology Table for 10.1.8.0/24 on Routers C, D, and E in Figure 3-30*

Neighbor	FD	AD
Router A	102,000	2000
Router B	101,000	1000

Table 3-6   *IP EIGRP Topology Table for 10.1.8.0/24 on Router A in Figure 3-30*

Neighbor	FD	AD
Router B	2000	1000
Router C	201,000	101,000
Router D	201,000	101,000
Router E	201,000	101,000

Note that Routers C, D, and E determine that for network 10.1.8.0/24, Router B is the successor and Router A is an FS (because the AD is 2000 through Router A, which is less than the FD through Router B). Also, note that Router A does not have an FS, because all paths through the remote routers have an AD larger than the FD through Router B.

When Router B loses the path to network 10.1.8.0/24, it queries all four of its neighbors. When the remote sites receive this query, they automatically install the path through Router A in their routing tables and respond to Router B with their supposedly good path through Router A. They also remove the bad path through Router B from their topology tables.

Router B now has responses to three of its four queries, but it must wait until Router A responds as well.

When Router A receives the query from Router B for network 10.1.8.0/24, Router A creates a query and sends it to Routers C, D, and E, because Router A does not have an FS but knows that a path exists through each remote site to reach 10.1.8.0/24.

Routers C, D, and E receive the query from Router A; they now know that their path through Router A is not good, so they check their topology tables for alternative paths. However, none of these routers currently has another path, because Router B has just informed them that it does not have a path to this network. Because the remote routers do not have an answer to the query from Router A, Routers C, D, and E create a query and send it to all neighbors except the neighbor (interface) that these routers received the original query from. In this case, the remote routers send the query only to Router B.

Router B learns from these queries that none of the remote routers has a path to network 10.1.8.0/24, but it cannot respond that it does not know of a path, because Router B is waiting for Router A to reply to a query. Router A is waiting for either Router C, D, or E to reply to its query, and these remote sites are waiting for Router B to reply to their queries. Because Router B sent out the first query, its SIA timer expires first, and Router B reaches the SIA state for network 10.1.8.0/24 first (in 3 minutes by default). Router B resets its neighbor relationship with Router A. As soon as the neighbor relationship goes down, Router B can respond to Routers C, D, and E immediately, saying that Router B does not have a path to 10.1.8.0/24. Routers C, D, and E can then respond to Router A that they do not have a path.

After the EIGRP neighbor relationship between Routers A and B is reestablished (just after the adjacency is reset), Router B, which no longer has a path to 10.1.8.0/24, does not pass the 10.1.8.0/24 network to Router A. Router A learns that the remote sites do not have a path to 10.1.8.0/24, and the new relationship with Router B does not include a path to 10.1.8.0/24, so Router A removes the 10.1.8.0 network from its IP EIGRP topology table.

In Figure 3-30, the network architect provides redundancy with dual links from the regional offices to the remote sites. The architect does not intend for the traffic to go from a regional office to a remote office and back to a regional office, but unfortunately this is the situation. The design of the network shown in Figure 3-30 is sound, but because of EIGRP behavior, remote routers are involved in the convergence process.

If the remote sites are not acting as transit sites between the regional sites, the regional routers can be configured to announce only a default route to the remote routers, and the remote routers can be configured to announce only their directly connected stub network to the regional routers to reduce the complexity and the EIGRP topology table and routing table size.

The following section describes other solutions for limiting the EIGRP query range.

Limiting the EIGRP Query Range

The network manager must determine the information necessary to properly route user traffic to the appropriate destination. The amount of information needed by the remote routers to achieve the desired level of path selection must be balanced against the bandwidth used to propagate this information. To achieve maximum stability and scalability, the remote routers can use a default route to reach the core. If some specific networks need knowledge of more routes to ensure optimum path selection, a business decision is necessary to determine whether the benefits of propagating the additional routing information outweigh the additional bandwidth required to achieve this goal.

In a properly designed network, each remote site has redundant WAN links to separate distribution sites. If both distribution sites pass a default route to the remote sites, the remote sites load balance to all networks behind the distribution site routers. This maximizes bandwidth utilization and allows the remote router to use less CPU and memory, which means that a smaller and less expensive remote router can be used at that site.

If the remote site can see all routes, the router can select a path that is best to reach a given network. However, depending on the number of routes in the internetwork and the amount of bandwidth connecting the remote site to the distribution sites, this approach can mean that higher-bandwidth links or large routers are needed to handle the additional overhead.

After you determine the minimum routing requirements, you can make EIGRP more scalable. Two of the best options are the following:

■ Configure route summarization using the **ip summary-address eigrp** command on the outbound interfaces of the appropriate routers.

■ Configure the remote routers as stub EIGRP routers.

Other methods to limit query range include route filtering and interface packet filtering. For example, if specific EIGRP routing updates are filtered to a router and that router receives a query about those filtered (blocked) networks, the router indicates that the network is unreachable and does not extend the query any further.

Limiting Query Range with Summarization

One solution to limit the EIGRP query range is to use route summarization.

For example, in Figure 3-31, Router B sends a summary route of 172.30.0.0/16 to Router A. When network 172.30.1.0/24 goes down, Router A receives a query from Router B about that network. Because Router A has received only a summary route, that specific network is not in the routing table. Router A replies to the query with a "network 172.30.1.0/24 unreachable" message and does not extend the query any further.

Figure 3-31   *EIGRP Summarization Can Limit Query Range*

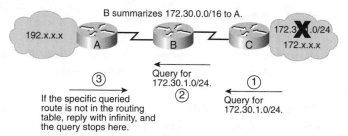

Summarization minimizes the size of the routing table, which means less CPU and memory usage to manage it and less bandwidth to transmit the information. Summarization reduces the chance of networks becoming SIA, because it reduces the number of routers that see each query, so the chance of a query encountering one of these issues is also reduced.

KEY POINT	Query Range
	A remote router extends the query about a network only if it has an exact match in the routing table.

Figure 3-32 illustrates how route summarization can affect the network shown in Figure 3-30. The **ip summary-address eigrp** command is configured on the outbound interfaces of Routers A and B so that Routers A and B advertise the 10.0.0.0/8 summary route to the remote Routers C, D, and E.

Figure 3-32 *Limiting Updates and Queries Using Summarization*

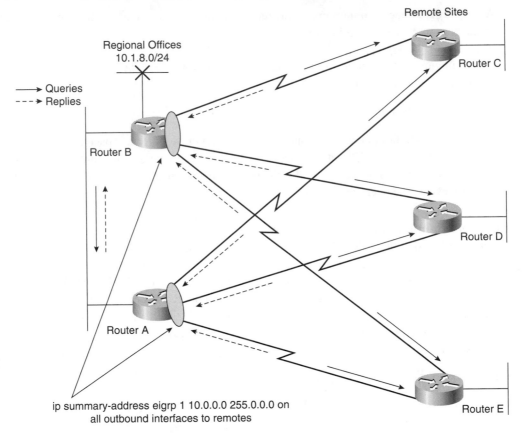

The 10.1.8.0/24 network is not advertised to the remote routers. Therefore, the remote routers (C, D, and E) do not extend the queries about the 10.1.8.0/24 network back to the regional routers (A and B), reducing the convergence traffic (queries and replies) caused by the redundant topology. When Routers A and B send the query for 10.1.8.0/24 to Routers C, D, and E, these routers immediately reply to Routers A and B that the destination is unreachable. Queries for the lost 10.1.8.0/24 networks are not propagated beyond the remote sites, preventing Routers A and B from becoming SIA waiting for the query process to receive all the replies.

Limiting Query Range Using a Stub

Hub-and-spoke network topologies commonly use stub routing. In this topology, the remote router forwards all traffic that is not local to a hub router; the remote router does not need to retain a complete routing table. Generally, the hub router needs to send only a default route to the remote routers.

In a hub-and-spoke topology, having a full routing table on the remote routers serves no functional purpose, because the path to the corporate network and the Internet is always through the hub router. Additionally, having a full routing table at the spoke routers increases the amount of memory required. Route summarization and route filtering can also be used to conserve bandwidth and memory requirements on the spoke routers.

Traffic from a hub router should not use a remote router as a transit path. A typical connection from a hub router to a remote router has significantly less bandwidth than a connection at the network core; attempting to use the connection to a remote router as a transit path typically results in excessive congestion. The EIGRP stub routing feature can prevent this problem by restricting the remote router from advertising the hub router's routes back to other hub routers. For example, routes recognized by the remote router from hub Router A are not advertised to hub Router B. Because the remote router does not advertise the hub routes back to the hub routers, the hub routers do not use the remote routers as a transit path. Using the EIGRP stub routing feature improves network stability, reduces resource utilization, and simplifies stub router configuration.

KEY POINT

EIGRP Stub

Only the remote routers are configured as stubs. The stub feature does not prevent routes from being advertised to the remote router.

The EIGRP stub feature was first introduced in Cisco IOS Release 12.0(7)T.

A stub router indicates in the hello packet to all neighboring routers its status as a stub router. Any neighbor that receives a packet informing it of the stub status does not query the stub router for any routes. Therefore, a router that has a stub peer does not query that peer.

KEY POINT

EIGRP Stub Routers Are Not Queried

Stub routers are not queried. Instead, hub routers connected to the stub router answer the query on behalf of the stub router.

The EIGRP stub routing feature also simplifies the configuration and maintenance of hub-and-spoke networks. When stub routing is enabled in dual-homed remote configurations, you do not have to configure filtering on remote routers to prevent them from appearing as transit paths to the hub routers.

CAUTION   EIGRP stub routing should be used on stub routers only. A stub router is defined as a router connected to the network core or hub layer, and through which core transit traffic should not flow. A stub router should have only hub routers for EIGRP neighbors. Ignoring this restriction causes undesirable behavior.

To configure a router as an EIGRP stub, use the **eigrp stub** [**receive-only** | **connected** | **static** | **summary**] router configuration command. A router configured as a stub with this command shares information about connected and summary routes with all neighbor routers by default. Table 3-7 describes the four optional keywords that can be used with the **eigrp stub** command to modify this behavior.

Table 3-7 **eigrp stub** *Command Parameters*

Parameter	Description
receive-only	The **receive-only** keyword restricts the router from sharing any of its routes with any other router within an EIGRP autonomous system. This keyword does not permit any other keyword to be specified, because it prevents any type of route from being sent. Use this option if there is a single interface on the router.
connected	The **connected** keyword permits the EIGRP stub routing feature to send connected routes. If a **network** command does not include the connected routes, it might be necessary to redistribute connected routes with the **redistribute connected** command under the EIGRP process. This option is enabled by default and is the most widely practical stub option.
static	The **static** keyword permits the EIGRP stub routing feature to send static routes. Redistributing static routes with the **redistribute static** command is still necessary.
summary	The **summary** keyword permits the EIGRP stub routing feature to send summary routes. You can create summary routes manually with the **ip summary-address eigrp** command or automatically at a major network border router with the **auto-summary** command enabled. This option is enabled by default.

The optional parameters in this command can be used in any combination, with the exception of the **receive-only** keyword. If any of the keywords (except **receive-only**) is used individually, the connected and summary routes are not sent automatically.

In Example 3-21, the **eigrp stub** command is used to configure the router as a stub that advertises connected and summary routes.

Example 3-21 **eigrp stub** *Command to Advertise Connected and Summary Routes*

```
Router(config)#router eigrp 1
Router(config-router)#network 10.0.0.0
Router(config-router)#eigrp stub
```

In Example 3-22, the **eigrp stub receive-only** command is used to configure the router as a stub. Connected, summary, or static routes are not sent.

Example 3-22 **eigrp stub** *Command to Receive Only Routes*

```
Router(config)#router eigrp 1
Router(config-router)#network 10.0.0.0 eigrp
Router(config-router)#eigrp stub receive-only
```

The EIGRP stub feature does not automatically enable route summarization on the hub router. The network administrator should configure route summarization on the hub routers if desired,

If a true stub network is required, the hub router can be configured to send a default route to the spoke routers. This approach is the most simple and conserves the most bandwidth and memory on the spoke routers.

> **NOTE** Although EIGRP is a classless routing protocol, it has classful behavior by default, such as having automatic summarization on by default. When you configure the hub router to send a default route to the remote router, ensure that the **ip classless** command on the remote router. By default, the **ip classless** command is enabled in all Cisco IOS images that support the EIGRP stub routing feature.

Without the stub feature, EIGRP sends a query to the spoke routers if a route is lost somewhere in the network. If there is a communication problem over a WAN link between the hub router and a spoke router, an EIGRP SIA condition can occur and cause instability elsewhere in the network. The EIGRP stub routing feature allows a network administrator to prevent sending queries to the spoke router under any condition. Cisco highly recommends using both EIGRP route summarization and EIGRP stub features to provide the best scalability.

Figure 3-33 illustrates how using the EIGRP stub feature affects the network shown in Figure 3-30. Each of the remote routers is configured as a stub. Queries for network 10.1.8.0/24 are not sent to Routers C, D, or E, thus reducing the bandwidth used and the chance of the routes being stuck-in-active.

Figure 3-33 *Limiting Updates and Queries Using the EIGRP Stub Feature*

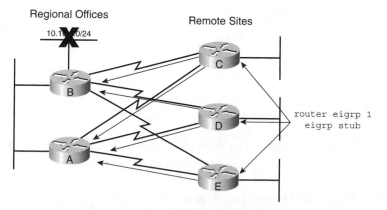

Using the EIGRP stub feature at the remote sites allows the hub (regional offices) sites to immediately answer queries without propagating the queries to the remote sites, saving CPU cycles and bandwidth, and lessening convergence time even when the remote sites are dual-homed to two or more hub sites.

Figure 3-34 illustrates another example network; Example 3-23 shows part of the configuration for Router B.

Figure 3-34   *Network for* **eigrp stub** *Command Example*

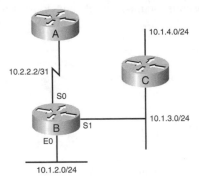

Example 3-23   *Configuration for Router B in Figure 3-34*

```
RouterB#show running-config
<output omitted>
ip route 10.1.4.0 255.255.255.0 10.1.3.10
!
interface ethernet 0
 ip address 10.1.2.1 255.255.255.0
!
interface serial 0
 ip address 10.2.2.3 255.255.255.254
 ip summary-address eigrp 100 10.1.2.0 255.255.254.0
!
interface serial 1
 ip address 10.1.3.1 255.255.255.0
!
router eigrp 100
 redistribute static 1000 1 255 1 1500
 network 10.2.2.2 0.0.0.1
 network 10.1.2.0 0.0.0.255
<output omitted>
```

Using this example network and configuration, consider which networks will be advertised when the various options of the **eigrp stub** command are also configured on Router B:

■   With the **eigrp stub connected** command, Router B will advertise only 10.1.2.0/24 to Router A. Notice that although 10.1.3.0/24 is also a connected network, it is not advertised to Router A because it is not advertised in a **network** command, and connected routes are not redistributed.

- With the **eigrp stub summary** command, Router B will advertise only 10.1.2.0/23, the summary route that is configured on the router, to Router A.

- With the **eigrp stub static** command, router B will advertise only 10.1.4.0/24, the static route that is configured on the router, to Router A.

- With the **eigrp stub receive-only** command, Router B will not advertise anything to Router A.

Graceful Shutdown

Graceful shutdown, implemented with the *goodbye message* feature, is designed to improve EIGRP network convergence.

In Figure 3-35, Router A is using Router B as the successor for a number of routes; Router C is the feasible successor for the same routes. Router B normally would not tell Router A if the EIGRP process on Router B was going down, for example, if Router B was being reconfigured. Router A would have to wait for its hold timer to expire before it would discover the change and react to it. Packets sent during this time would be lost.

Figure 3-35 *Graceful Shutdown Causes Router to Say Goodbye*

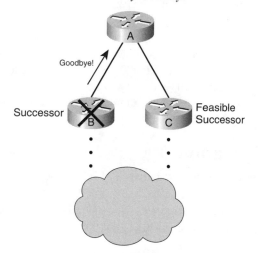

With graceful shutdown, a goodbye message is broadcast when an EIGRP routing process is shut down, to inform adjacent peers about the impending topology change. This feature allows supporting EIGRP peers to synchronize and recalculate neighbor relationships more efficiently than would occur if the peers discovered the topology change after the hold timer expired.

The goodbye message is supported in Cisco IOS Software Release 12.3(2), 12.3(3)B, and 12.3(2)T and later.

<table>
<tr><td>KEY
POINT</td><td>

Goodbye Messages

Goodbye messages are sent in hello packets.

EIGRP sends an interface goodbye message with all K values set to 255 when taking down all peers on an interface.

</td></tr>
</table>

The following message is displayed by routers that support goodbye messages when one is received:

```
*Apr 26 13:48:42.523: %DUAL-5-NBRCHANGE: IP-EIGRP(0) 1: Neighbor 10.1.1.1 (Ethernet0/0)
   is down: Interface Goodbye received
```

A Cisco router that runs a software release that does not support the goodbye message will misinterpret the message as a K-value mismatch and therefore display the following message:

```
*Apr 26 13:48:41.811: %DUAL-5-NBRCHANGE: IP-EIGRP(0) 1: Neighbor 10.1.1.1 (Ethernet0/0)
   is down: K-value mismatch
```

NOTE   The receipt of a goodbye message by a nonsupporting peer does not disrupt normal network operation. The nonsupporting peer will terminate the session when the hold timer expires. The sending and receiving routers will reconverge normally after the sender reloads.

NOTE   An EIGRP router will send a goodbye message on an interface if the **network** command (under the EIGRP process) that encompasses the network on that interface is removed (with the **no network** command). An EIGRP router sends a goodbye message on all interfaces if the EIGRP process is shut down (with the **no router eigrp** command). An EIGRP router will not, however, send a goodbye message if an interface is shut down or the router is reloaded.

Verifying EIGRP Operation

This section discusses commands used to verify EIGRP operation.

Table 3-8 describes some **show** commands used to verify EIGRP operation. Other options might be available with these commands; use the Cisco IOS integrated help feature to see the full-command syntax.

Table 3-8   *EIGRP* **show** *Commands*

Command	Description
show ip eigrp neighbors	Displays neighbors discovered by EIGRP.
show ip route	Displays the current entries in the IP routing table for all configured routing protocols.
show ip route eigrp	Displays the current EIGRP entries in the IP routing table.

Table 3-8   *EIGRP* **show** *Commands (Continued)*

Command	Description
show ip protocols	Displays the parameters and current state of the active routing protocol processes. For EIGRP, this command shows the EIGRP autonomous system number, filtering and redistribution numbers, and neighbors and distance information.
show ip eigrp interfaces	Displays information about interfaces configured for EIGRP.
show ip eigrp topology	Displays the EIGRP topology table. This command shows the topology table, the active or passive state of routes, the number of successors, and the FD to the destination. Note that only successor and feasible successor routes are displayed; add the **all-links** keyword to display all routes, including those not eligible to be successor or feasible successor routes.
show ip eigrp traffic	Displays the number of EIGRP packets sent and received. This command displays statistics on hello packets, updates, queries, replies, and acknowledgments.

Table 3-9 describes **debug** commands used to verify EIGRP operation. Other options might be available with these commands; use the Cisco IOS integrated help feature to see the full command syntax.

Table 3-9   *EIGRP* **debug** *Commands*

Command	Description
debug eigrp packets	Displays the types of EIGRP packets sent and received. A maximum of 11 packet types can be selected for individual or group display.
debug ip eigrp	Displays packets that are sent and received on an interface. Because this command generates large amounts of output, use it only when traffic on the network is light.
debug ip eigrp summary	Displays a summarized version of EIGRP activity. It also displays filtering and redistribution numbers and neighbors and distance information.
debug eigrp neighbors	Displays neighbors discovered by EIGRP and the contents of the hello packets.

The following sections provide sample output from some of these commands, using the network in Figure 3-36 to illustrate the configuration, verification, and troubleshooting of EIGRP. Example 3-24 shows the configuration of the R1 router.

Figure 3-36   *Example Network for EIGRP Verification*

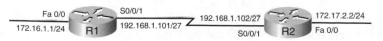

Example 3-24   *Configuration for Router R1 in Figure 3-36*

```
R1#show running-config
<output omitted>
interface FastEthernet0/0
  ip address 172.16.1.1 255.255.255.0

<output omitted>
interface Serial0/0/1
 bandwidth 64
 ip address 192.168.1.101 255.255.255.224

<output omitted>
router eigrp 100
 network 172.16.1.0 0.0.0.255
 network 192.168.1.0
```

On the R1 router, EIGRP is enabled in autonomous system 100. The **network 172.16.1.0 0.0.0.255** command starts EIGRP on the Fast Ethernet 0/0 interface and allows router R1 to advertise this network. With the wildcard mask used, this command specifies that only interfaces on the 172.16.1.0/24 subnet will participate in EIGRP. Note, however, the full Class B network 172.16.0.0 will be advertised, because EIGRP automatically summarizes routes on the major network boundary by default. The **network 192.168.1.0** command starts EIGRP on the serial 0/0/1 interface, and allows router R1 to advertise this network.

Example 3-25 shows the configuration of the R2 router.

Example 3-25   *Configuration for Router R2 in Figure 3-36*

```
R2#show running-config
<output omitted>
interface FastEthernet0/0
  ip address 172.17.2.2 255.255.255.0

<output omitted>
interface Serial0/0/1
 bandwidth 64
 ip address 192.168.1.102 255.255.255.224

<output omitted>
router eigrp 100
 network 172.17.2.0 0.0.0.255
 network 192.168.1.0
```

EIGRP is also enabled in autonomous system 100 on the R2 router. The **network 172.17.2.0 0.0.0.255** command starts EIGRP on the Fast Ethernet 0/0 interface and allows router R2 to advertise this network. With the wildcard mask used, this command specifies that only interfaces on the 172.17.2.0/24 subnet will participate in EIGRP. Note, however, the full Class B network 172.17.0.0 will be advertised, because EIGRP automatically summarizes routes on the major network boundary by default. The **network 192.168.1.0** command starts EIGRP on the serial 0/0/1 interface and allows router R2 to advertise this network.

> **NOTE**   The "EIGRP Neighbors" section, earlier in this chapter, provides output from the **show ip eigrp neighbors** command and a description of the output.

show ip route and show ip route eigrp for EIGRP Examples

To verify that the router recognizes EIGRP routes for any neighbors, use the **show ip route eigrp** command, as shown in Example 3-26. Example 3-27 exhibits the **show ip route** command, which displays the full IP routing table, including the EIGRP routes.

Example 3-26   **show ip route eigrp** *Command Output*

```
R1#show ip route eigrp
D    172.17.0.0/16 [90/40514560] via 192.168.1.102, 00:07:01, Serial0/0/1
     172.16.0.0/16 is variably subnetted, 2 subnets, 2 masks
D       172.16.0.0/16 is a summary, 00:05:13, Null0
     192.168.1.0/24 is variably subnetted, 2 subnets, 2 masks
D       192.168.1.0/24 is a summary, 00:05:13, Null0
```

Example 3-27   **show ip route** *Command Output*

```
R1#show ip route
<output omitted>
Gateway of last resort is not set
D    172.17.0.0/16 [90/40514560] via 192.168.1.102, 00:06:55, Serial0/0/1
     172.16.0.0/16 is variably subnetted, 2 subnets, 2 masks
D       172.16.0.0/16 is a summary, 00:05:07, Null0
C       172.16.1.0/24 is directly connected, FastEthernet0/0
     192.168.1.0/24 is variably subnetted, 2 subnets, 2 masks
C       192.168.1.96/27 is directly connected, Serial0/0/1
D       192.168.1.0/24 is a summary, 00:05:07, Null0
```

Using the highlighted line in Example 3-26 as an example, the fields in the routing table are interpreted as follows:

- Internal EIGRP routes are identified with a D in the leftmost column. (External EIGRP routes, not shown in this example, are identified with a D EX in the leftmost column.)

- The next column is the network number (172.17.0.0/16 in this example).

- After each network number is a field in brackets (90/40514560 in this example). The second number in brackets is the EIGRP metric. As discussed in the "EIGRP Metric Calculation" section earlier in this chapter, the default EIGRP metric is the least-cost bandwidth plus the accumulated delays. The EIGRP metric for a network is the same as its FD in the EIGRP topology table.

The first number, 90 in this case, is the administrative distance. Recall from Chapter 2 that administrative distance is used to select the best path when a router learns two or more routes to exactly the same destination from different routing sources. For example, consider that this router uses RIP and EIGRP and that RIP has a route to network 172.17.0.0 that is three hops away. The router, without the administrative distance, cannot compare three hops to an EIGRP metric of 40,514,560. The router does not know the bandwidth associated with hops, and EIGRP does not use hop count as a metric.

To correct this problem, Cisco established an administrative distance for each routing protocol: the lower the value, the more preferred the route is. By default, EIGRP internal routes have an administrative distance of 90, and RIP has an administrative distance of 120. Because EIGRP has a metric based on bandwidth and delays, it is preferred over RIP's hop count metric. As a result, in this example, the EIGRP route would be installed in the routing table.

NOTE   Remember that routers use the administrative distance only if the two routes are to the exact same destination (address and mask); for example, a router will choose a RIP route over an EIGRP route if the RIP route is a more specific route than the EIGRP route.

- The next field, via 192.168.1.102 in this example, is the address of the next-hop router to which this router passes packets destined for 172.17.0.0/16. The next-hop address in the routing table is the same as the successor in the EIGRP topology table.

- The route also has a time associated with it (00:07:01 in this example); this is the length of time since EIGRP last advertised this network to this router. EIGRP does not refresh routes periodically; it resends the routing table only when neighbor adjacencies change.

- The interface, serial 0/0/1 in this case, indicates the interface out which packets for 172.17.0.0 are sent.

Notice that the routing table includes routes, to null0, for the advertised (summarized) routes. Cisco IOS Software automatically puts these routes in the table; they are called *summary routes*. Null 0 is a directly connected, software-only interface. The use of the null0 interface prevents the router from trying to forward traffic to other routers in search of a more precise, longer match. For example, if the R1 router in Figure 3-36 receives a packet to an unknown subnet that is part of the summarized range—172.16.3.5 for example—the packet matches the summary route based on the longest match. The packet is forwarded to the null0 interface (in other words, it is dropped, or sent to the *bit bucket*), which prevents the router from forwarding the packet to a default route and possibly creating a routing loop.

show ip protocols Example

Use the **show ip protocols** command to provide information about any and all dynamic routing protocols running on the router.

As shown in Example 3-28, the command output displays any route filtering occurring on EIGRP outbound or inbound updates. It also identifies whether EIGRP is generating a default network or receiving a default network in EIGRP updates and provides information about additional settings for EIGRP, such as default K values, hop count, and variance.

Example 3-28 **show ip protocols** *Command Output*

```
R1#show ip protocols
Routing Protocol is "eigrp 100"
  Outgoing update filter list for all interfaces is not set
  Incoming update filter list for all interfaces is not set
  Default networks flagged in outgoing updates
  Default networks accepted from incoming updates
  EIGRP metric weight K1=1, K2=0, K3=1, K4=0, K5=0
  EIGRP maximum hopcount 100
  EIGRP maximum metric variance 1
  Redistributing: eigrp 100
  EIGRP NSF-aware route hold timer is 240s
  Automatic network summarization is in effect
  Automatic address summarization:
    192.168.1.0/24 for FastEthernet0/0
      Summarizing with metric 40512000
    172.16.0.0/16 for Serial0/0/1
      Summarizing with metric 28160
  Maximum path: 4
  Routing for Networks:
    172.16.1.0/24
    192.168.1.0
  Routing Information Sources:
    Gateway         Distance      Last Update
    (this router)         90      00:09:38
    Gateway         Distance      Last Update
    192.168.1.102         90      00:09:40
Distance: internal 90 external 170
```

> **NOTE**   Because the routers must have identical K values for EIGRP to establish an adjacency, the **show ip protocols** command helps determine the current K-value setting before an adjacency is attempted.

The output in Example 3-28 also indicates that automatic summarization is enabled (this is the default) and that the router is allowed to load-balance over a maximum of four paths. Cisco IOS

Software allows configuration of up to 16 paths for equal-cost load balancing, using the **maximum-paths** router configuration command.

The networks for which the router is routing are also displayed. As shown in Example 3-28, the format of the output varies, depending on the use of the wildcard mask in the **network** command. If a wildcard mask is used, the network address is displayed with a prefix length. If a wildcard mask is not used, the Class A, B, or C major network is displayed.

The routing information source portion of this command output identifies all other routers that have an EIGRP neighbor relationship with this router. The **show ip eigrp neighbors** command provides a detailed display of EIGRP neighbors.

The **show ip protocols** command output also provides the two administrative distances for EIGRP. An administrative distance of 90 applies to networks from other routers inside the same autonomous system number; these are considered internal networks. An administrative distance of 170 applies to networks introduced to EIGRP for this autonomous system through redistribution; these are called external networks.

show ip eigrp interfaces Example

Example 3-29 demonstrates **show ip eigrp interfaces** command output.

Example 3-29 **show ip eigrp interfaces** *Command Output*

```
R1#show ip eigrp interfaces
IP-EIGRP interfaces for process 100
                    Xmit Queue    Mean   Pacing Time   Multicast    Pending
Interface    Peers  Un/Reliable   SRTT   Un/Reliable   Flow Timer   Routes
Fa0/0        0        0/0          0        0/10          0           0
Se0/0/1      1        0/0          10       10/380        424         0
```

The **show ip eigrp interfaces** command displays information about interfaces configured for EIGRP. This output includes the following key elements:

- **Interface**—Interface over which EIGRP is configured

- **Peers**—Number of directly connected EIGRP neighbors

- **Xmit Queue Un/Reliable**—Number of packets remaining in the Unreliable and Reliable transmit queues

- **Mean SRTT**—Mean SRTT interval, in milliseconds

- **Pacing Time Un/Reliable**—Pacing time used to determine when EIGRP packets should be sent out the interface (for unreliable and reliable packets)

- **Multicast Flow Timer**—Maximum number of seconds that the router will wait for an ACK packet after sending a multicast EIGRP packet, before switching from multicast to unicast

- **Pending Routes**—Number of routes in the packets in the transmit queue waiting to be sent

show ip eigrp topology Example

Another command used to verify EIGRP operations is the **show ip eigrp topology** command; Example 3-30 demonstrates output generated from this command.

Example 3-30   **show ip eigrp topology** *Command Output*

```
R1#show ip eigrp topology
IP-EIGRP Topology Table for AS(100)/ID(192.168.1.101)
Codes: P - Passive, A - Active, U - Update, Q - Query, R - Reply,
       r - reply Status, s - sia Status
P 192.168.1.96/27, 1 successors, FD is 40512000
        via Connected, Serial0/0/1
P 192.168.1.0/24, 1 successors, FD is 40512000
        via Summary (40512000/0), Null0
P 172.16.0.0/16, 1 successors, FD is 28160
        via Summary (28160/0), Null0
P 172.16.1.0/24, 1 successors, FD is 28160
        via Connected, FastEthernet0/0
P 172.17.0.0/16, 1 successors, FD is 40514560
        via 192.168.1.102 (40514560/28160), Serial0/0/1
```

The command output illustrates that router R1 has an ID of 192.168.1.101 and is in autonomous system 100. The EIGRP ID is the highest IP address on an active interface for this router.

The command output also lists the networks known by this router through the EIGRP routing process. The codes used in the first column of this output are as follows:

- **Passive (P)**—This network is available, and installation can occur in the routing table. Passive is the correct state for a stable network.

- **Active (A)**—This network is currently unavailable, and installation cannot occur in the routing table. Being active means that outstanding queries exist for this network.

- **Update (U)**—This network is being updated (placed in an update packet). This code also applies if the router is waiting for an acknowledgment for this update packet.

- **Query (Q)**—There is an outstanding query packet for this network other than being in the active state. This code also applies if the router is waiting for an acknowledgment for a query packet.

- **Reply (R)**—The router is generating a reply for this network or is waiting for an acknowledgment for the reply packet.

- **Stuck-in-active (S)**—There is an EIGRP convergence problem for this network.

The number of successors available for a route is indicated in the command output. The number of successors corresponds to the number of best routes with equal cost; all networks in Example 3-30 have one successor.

For each network, the FD is listed next, followed by an indication of how the route was learned, such as the next-hop address if the route was learned via another router. Next is a field in brackets. The first number in the brackets is the FD for that network through the next-hop router, and the second number in the brackets is the AD from the next-hop router to the destination network.

show ip eigrp traffic Example

To display the number of various EIGRP packets sent and received, use the **show ip eigrp traffic** command, as illustrated in Example 3-31. For example, in this network, router R1 has sent 429 hello messages and received 192 hello messages.

Example 3-31 **show ip eigrp traffic** *Command Output*

```
R1#show ip eigrp traffic
IP-EIGRP Traffic Statistics for AS 100
  Hellos sent/received: 429/192
  Updates sent/received: 4/4
  Queries sent/received: 1/0
  Replies sent/received: 0/1
  Acks sent/received: 4/3
  Input queue high water mark 1, 0 drops
  SIA-Queries sent/received: 0/0
  SIA-Replies sent/received: 0/0
  Hello Process ID: 113
PDM Process ID: 73
```

debug eigrp packets Examples

You can use the **debug eigrp packets** command to verify EIGRP connectivity. This command displays the types of EIGRP packets sent and received by the router that this command is executed on. Different packet types can be selected for individual or group display. Example 3-32 shows some output from this command on R2, when an interface on R1 comes up.

Example 3-32 **debug eigrp packets** *Command Output on R2 When a Neighbor's Interface Comes Up*

```
R2#debug eigrp packets
EIGRP Packets debugging is on
    (UPDATE, REQUEST, QUERY, REPLY, HELLO, IPXSAP, PROBE, ACK, STUB, SIAQUERY, SIAREPLY)
*May 11 04:02:55.821: EIGRP: Sending HELLO on Serial0/0/1
*May 11 04:02:55.821:   AS 100, Flags 0x0, Seq 0/0 idbQ 0/0 iidbQ un/rely 0/0
R2#
*May 11 04:02:58.309: EIGRP: Received HELLO on Serial0/0/1 nbr 192.168.1.101
```

Example 3-32 **debug eigrp packets** *Command Output on R2 When a Neighbor's Interface Comes Up (Continued)*

```
*May 11 04:02:58.309:   AS 100, Flags 0x0, Seq 0/0 idbQ 0/0 iidbQ un/rely 0/0 peerQ un/
  rely 0/0
*May 11 04:02:58.585: EIGRP: Sending HELLO on FastEthernet0/0
*May 11 04:02:58.585:   AS 100, Flags 0x0, Seq 0/0 idbQ 0/0 iidbQ un/rely 0/0
*May 11 04:02:59.093: EIGRP: Received UPDATE on Serial0/0/1 nbr 192.168.1.101
*May 11 04:02:59.093:   AS 100, Flags 0x0, Seq 5/4 idbQ 0/0 iidbQ un/rely 0/0 peerQ un/
  rely 0/0
*May 11 04:02:59.093: EIGRP: Enqueueing ACK on Serial0/0/1 nbr 192.168.1.101
*May 11 04:02:59.093:   Ack seq 5 iidbQ un/rely 0/0 peerQ un/rely 1/0
*May 11 04:02:59.097: EIGRP: Sending ACK on Serial0/0/1 nbr 192.168.1.101
*May 11 04:02:59.097:   AS 100, Flags 0x0, Seq 0/5 idbQ 0/0 iidbQ un/rely 0/0 peerQ un/
  rely 1/0
*May 11 04:02:59.109: EIGRP: Enqueueing UPDATE on Serial0/0/1 iidbQ un/rely 0/1 serno 9-9
*May 11 04:02:59.113: EIGRP: Enqueueing UPDATE on Serial0/0/1 nbr 192.168.1.101 iidbQ un/
  rely 0/0 peerQ un/rely 0/0 serno 9-9
*May 11 04:02:59.113: EIGRP: Sending UPDATE on Serial0/0/1 nbr 192.168.1.101
*May 11 04:02:59.113:   AS 100, Flags 0x0, Seq 5/5 idbQ 0/0 iidbQ un/rely 0/0 peerQ un/
  rely 0/1 serno 9-9
*May 11 04:02:59.133: EIGRP: Received ACK on Serial0/0/1 nbr 192.168.1.101
*May 11 04:02:59.133:   AS 100, Flags 0x0, Seq 0/5 idbQ 0/0 iidbQ un/rely 0/0 peerQ un/
  rely 0/1
*May 11 04:02:59.133: EIGRP: Serial0/0/1 multicast flow blocking cleared
R2#
*May 11 04:03:00.441: EIGRP: Sending HELLO on Serial0/0/1
*May 11 04:03:00.441:   AS 100, Flags 0x0, Seq 0/0 idbQ 0/0 iidbQ un/rely 0/0
R2#
*May 11 04:03:03.209: EIGRP: Received HELLO on Serial0/0/1 nbr 192.168.1.101
*May 11 04:03:03.209:   AS 100, Flags 0x0, Seq 0/0 idbQ 0/0 iidbQ un/rely 0/0 peerQ un/
  rely 0/0
```

The **debug eigrp packets** command traces transmission and receipt of EIGRP packets. The output in Example 3-32 shows normal transmission and receipt of EIGRP packets. The serial link is an HDLC point-to-point link; therefore, the default hello time interval is 5 seconds. Hello packets are sent unreliably, so the sequence number (Seq) does not increment.

In this sample output, when R2 receives an update from R1, values appear in the sequence number field. Seq 5/4 indicates that 192.168.1.101 is sending this packet as sequence number 5 to R2 and that sequence number 4 has been received from R2 by neighbor 192.168.1.101. 192.168.1.101 is expecting to receive sequence number 5 in the next reliable packet from R2.

R2 returns an ACK packet with Seq 0/5. The acknowledgment is sent as an unreliable packet, but the neighbor unreliable/reliable flag (un/rel 1/0) is set. This means that the acknowledgment was sent in response to a reliable packet.

The serial number (serno 9-9) reflects the number of changes that the two neighbors register in their EIGRP topology tables. A single update can contain more than 100 networks that all produce an update, because all are now unavailable.

<table>
<tr><td>KEY
POINT</td><td>

Sequence Number Versus Serial Number

The sequence number increments each time a query, update, or reply packet is sent, whereas the serial number increments each time the topology table changes. Therefore, if the topology table has more than 100 changes, the serial number increases substantially, but the sequence number may only increase by 1.

</td></tr>
</table>

When an interface on R1 (R2's EIGRP neighbor 192.168.1.101) is shut down, the resulting output on R2 is shown in Example 3-33. R1 sends a query packet to R2 to determine whether R2 knows a path to the lost network. R2 responds with an ACK packet to acknowledge the query packet; a reliable packet must be explicitly acknowledged with an ACK packet. R2 also responds to the query with a reply packet. The serial number reference (10-12) represents the number of changes to the topology table since the start of the neighbor relationship between these two EIGRP neighbors.

Example 3-33 **debug eigrp packets** *Command Output on R2 When a Neighbor's Interface Is Shut Down*

```
R2#debug eigrp packets
*May 11 04:20:43.361: EIGRP: Received QUERY on Serial0/0/1 nbr 192.168.1.101
*May 11 04:20:43.361:   AS 100, Flags 0x0, Seq 6/5 idbQ 0/0 iidbQ un/rely 0/0 peerQ un/
  rely 0/0
*May 11 04:20:43.361: EIGRP: Enqueueing ACK on Serial0/0/1 nbr 192.168.1.101
*May 11 04:20:43.361:   Ack seq 6 iidbQ un/rely 0/0 peerQ un/rely 1/0
*May 11 04:20:43.365: EIGRP: Sending ACK on Serial0/0/1 nbr 192.168.1.101
*May 11 04:20:43.365:   AS 100, Flags 0x0, Seq 0/6 idbQ 0/0 iidbQ un/rely 0/0 peerQ un/
  rely 1/0
*May 11 04:20:43.373: EIGRP: Enqueueing REPLY on Serial0/0/1 nbr 192.168.1.101 iidbQ un/
  rely 0/1 peerQ un/rely 0/0 serno 10-12
*May 11 04:20:43.377: EIGRP: Requeued unicast on Serial0/0/1
R2#
*May 11 04:20:43.381: EIGRP: Sending REPLY on Serial0/0/1 nbr 192.168.1.101
*May 11 04:20:43.381:   AS 100, Flags 0x0, Seq 6/6 idbQ 0/0 iidbQ un/rely 0/0 peerQ un/
  rely 0/1 serno 10-12
*May 11 04:20:43.405: EIGRP: Received ACK on Serial0/0/1 nbr 192.168.1.101
*May 11 04:20:43.405:   AS 100, Flags 0x0, Seq 0/6 idbQ 0/0 iidbQ un/rely 0/0 peerQ un/
  rely 0/1
```

debug ip eigrp Examples

You can use the **debug ip eigrp** command to verify EIGRP operation. This command displays EIGRP packets that this router sends and receives. Example 3-34 shows the contents of the updates that are reported when you use the **debug ip eigrp** command on R2 to monitor when an interface on R1 comes up.

Example 3-34 **debug ip eigrp** *Command Output on R2 When a Neighbor's Interface Comes Up*

```
R2#debug ip eigrp
IP-EIGRP Route Events debugging is on
R2#
*May 11 04:24:05.261: IP-EIGRP(Default-IP-Routing-Table:100): Processing incoming UPDATE
  packet
```

Example 3-34   **debug ip eigrp** *Command Output on R2 When a Neighbor's Interface Comes Up (Continued)*

```
*May 11 04:24:05.261: IP-EIGRP(Default-IP-Routing-Table:100): Int 192.168.1.0/24
 M 4294967295 - 40000000 4294967295 SM 4294967295 - 40000000 4294967295
*May 11 04:24:05.261: IP-EIGRP(Default-IP-Routing-Table:100): Int 172.16.0.0/16
M 40514560 - 40000000 514560 SM 28160 - 25600 2560
*May 11 04:24:05.261: IP-EIGRP(Default-IP-Routing-Table:100): route installed for
172.16.0.0  ()
*May 11 04:24:05.277: IP-EIGRP(Default-IP-Routing-Table:100): Int 172.16.0.0/16 metric
40514560 - 40000000 514560
```

In this example, an internal route (indicated by Int) for 172.16.0.0/16 is advertised to R2.

Recall that by default the EIGRP metric is equal to the bandwidth plus the delay. The EIGRP process uses the source metric (SM) information in the update to calculate the AD and place it in the EIGRP topology table. In this example, the SM information is SM 28160 – 25600 2560, which means the source metric (the AD) = 28160 = 25600 (the bandwidth) + 2560 (the delay).

The EIGRP metric calculation for the total delay uses the metric (M) information in the update. In this example, the M information is M 40514560 – 40000000 514560, which means the metric (the FD) = 40514560 = 40000000 (the bandwidth) + 514560 (the delay).

The EIGRP metric for this route is equal to the FD and, therefore, is 40,514,560.

Example 3-35 illustrates what occurs when R2 processes an incoming query packet for network 172.16.0.0/16 when the interface on the neighboring router (R1) that leads to that network is shut down. Note that comments (preceded by an exclamation point [!]) have been added to this output for easier understanding.

Example 3-35   **debug ip eigrp** *Command Output*

```
R2#debug ip eigrp
IP-EIGRP Route Events debugging is on
R2#
! An interface on EIGRP neighbor R1 was shutdown
! R2 receives a query looking for a lost path from R1
*May 11 04:35:44.281: IP-EIGRP(Default-IP-Routing-Table:100): Processing incoming QUERY
  packet
*May 11 04:35:44.281: IP-EIGRP(Default-IP-Routing-Table:100): Int 172.16.1.0/24
M 4294967295 - 0 4294967295 SM 4294967295 - 0 4294967295
*May 11 04:35:44.281: IP-EIGRP(Default-IP-Routing-Table:100): Int 192.168.1.0/24
 M 4294967295 - 0 4294967295 SM 4294967295 - 0 4294967295
*May 11 04:35:44.281: IP-EIGRP(Default-IP-Routing-Table:100): Int 172.16.0.0/16
M 4294967295 - 0 4294967295 SM 4294967295 - 0 4294967295
! R2 realizes that if it cannot use R1 for this network then
! it does not have an entry in the routing table for this network
```

continues

Example 3-35 **debug ip eigrp** *Command Output (Continued)*

```
*May 11 04:35:44.281: IP-EIGRP(Default-IP-Routing-Table:100): 172.16.0.0/16 routing table
  not updated thru 192.168.1.101
R2#
*May 11 04:35:44.301: IP-EIGRP(Default-IP-Routing-Table:100): 172.16.1.0/24 - not in IP
  routing table
*May 11 04:35:44.301: IP-EIGRP(Default-IP-Routing-Table:100): Int 172.16.1.0/24 metric
  4294967295 - 0 4294967295
*May 11 04:35:44.301: IP-EIGRP(Default-IP-Routing-Table:100): 192.168.1.0/24 - poison
  advertise out Serial0/0/1
*May 11 04:35:44.301: IP-EIGRP(Default-IP-Routing-Table:100): Int 192.168.1.0/24 metric
  40512000 - 40000000 512000
*May 11 04:35:44.301: IP-EIGRP(Default-IP-Routing-Table:100): 172.16.0.0/16 - not in IP
  routing table
! R2 sends an update to R1 saying it does not know how to reach that network either
*May 11 04:35:44.301: IP-EIGRP(Default-IP-Routing-Table:100): Int 172.16.0.0/16 metric
  4294967295 - 40000000 4294967295
R2#
```

The neighbor previously advertised 172.16.0.0/16 to this router. The query performs the following two functions:

- R2 discovers that its neighbor no longer knows how to get to network 172.16.0.0/16. The metric value (4,294,967,295) is the highest possible value; it indicates that the route is unreachable. R2 removes this entry from the EIGRP topology table and looks for alternative EIGRP routes.

- The debug output indicates that the routing table is not updated; this means that EIGRP did not find an alternative route to the network. The next statement verifies that the EIGRP process has removed the old route and that the route is not in the IP routing table. R2 then informs the neighbor that it does not have a path to this network either.

Summary

In this chapter, you learned about Cisco's own EIGRP, an advanced distance vector routing protocol. The chapter presented the following topics:

- Features of EIGRP, including fast convergence, VLSM support, use of partial updates, multiple network layer support, seamless connectivity across all data link layer protocols and topologies, sophisticated metric, and use of multicast and unicast.

- EIGRP's underlying processes and technologies—neighbor discovery/recovery mechanism, RTP, DUAL finite state machine, and protocol-dependent modules.

- EIGRP terminology, including EIGRP's tables—neighbor table, topology table, and routing table; the advertised distance and the feasible distance; and the successor and feasible successor.

- The five EIGRP packet types: hello, update, query, reply, and acknowledgment.

- Passive and active routes.

- The EIGRP metric calculation, which defaults to bandwidth + delay.

- Basic EIGRP configuration commands.

- EIGRP summarization, EIGRP equal-cost and unequal-cost load balancing, and EIGRP operation in WAN environments.

- Configuring, verifying, and troubleshooting EIGRP MD5 authentication.

- EIGRP scalability factors and EIGRP use in an enterprise network.

- Verifying and troubleshooting EIGRP.

References

For additional information, refer to the following resources:

- The EIGRP protocol home page, http://www.cisco.com/go/eigrp

- The "IGRP Metric" document at http://www.cisco.com/en/US/tech/tk365/technologies_tech _note09186a008009405c.shtml (a good reference for the "EIGRP Metric Calculation" section)

Configuration Exercise: Configuring and Tuning EIGRP

In this exercise, you first configure EIGRP and investigate its default behavior. You next configure EIGRP summarization, a stub, and a default route.

Introduction to the Configuration Exercises

This book uses Configuration Exercises to help you practice configuring routers with the commands and topics presented. If you have access to real hardware, you can try these exercises on your routers. See Appendix B, "Configuration Exercise Equipment Requirements and Backbone Configurations," for a list of recommended equipment and initial configuration commands for the backbone routers. However, even if you do not have access to any routers, you can go through the exercises, and keep a log of your own running configurations, or just read through the solution. Commands used and solutions to the Configuration Exercises are provided within the exercises.

In the Configuration Exercises, the network is assumed to consist of two pods, each with four routers. The pods are interconnected to a backbone. You configure pod 1. No interaction between the two pods is required, but you might see some routes from the other pod in your routing tables in some exercises if you have it configured. In most of the exercises, the backbone has only one router; in some cases, another router is added to the backbone. Each Configuration Exercise assumes that you have completed the previous chapters' Configuration Exercises on your pod.

> **NOTE** Throughout this exercise, the pod number is referred to as *x*, and the router number is referred to as *y*. Substitute the appropriate numbers as needed.

Exercise Objectives

The objectives of this exercise are as follows:

- Set up EIGRP

- Investigate the default behavior of EIGRP

- Optimize the EIGRP configuration

Visual Objective

Figure 3-37 illustrates the topology used and what you will accomplish in this exercise.

Figure 3-37 *EIGRP Configuration Exercise Topology*

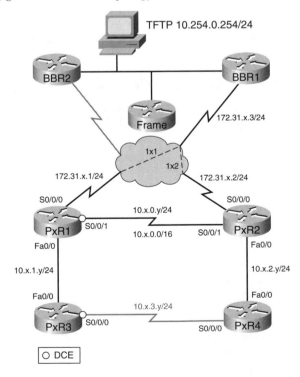

Command List

In this exercise, you use the commands in Table 3-10, listed in logical order. Refer to this list if you need configuration command assistance during the exercise.

CAUTION   Although the command syntax is shown in this table, the addresses shown are typically for the P*x*R1 and P*x*R3 routers. Be careful when addressing your routers! Refer to the exercise instructions and the appropriate visual objective diagram for addressing details.

Table 3-10 *EIGRP Configuration Exercise Commands*

Command	Description
(config)#**router eigrp 1**	Enters configuration mode for EIGRP in autonomous system 1
(config-router)#**network 10.*x*.0.0 0.0.255.255**	Specifies that EIGRP should run within network 10.*x*.0.0/16
(config-router)#**no auto-summary**	Turns off automatic summarization at classful network boundaries
#show ip protocols	Displays the parameters and current state of all the active routing protocol processes
#debug ip eigrp	Displays EIGRP updates
(config-if)#**ip summary-address eigrp 1 10.*x*.0.0 255.255.0.0**	Creates and advertises a summary route 10.*x*.0.0/16 for EIGRP autonomous system 1 out of this interface
(config-router)#**eigrp stub**	Specifies that this router should behave as an EIGRP stub router
#show ip eigrp neighbors detail	Displays detailed EIGRP neighbor information
(config-if)#**ip summary-address eigrp 1 0.0.0.0 0.0.0.0**	Creates and advertises a default route for EIGRP autonomous system 1 out of this interface and suppresses all other specific routes
#show ip eigrp topology	Displays the EIGRP topology table
#show ip eigrp traffic	Displays EIGRP traffic statistics
#show ip eigrp interfaces	Displays information about interfaces configured for EIGRP
#show ip eigrp neighbors	Displays EIGRP neighbor information

NOTE   The exercise tasks include answers and solutions. Some answers cover multiple steps; the answers are given after the last step to which that answer applies.

Task 1: Configuring Basic EIGRP

In this task, you configure EIGRP on each router in your pod so that there are EIGRP routes from the core, between edge routers, and between the edge and the internal routers. Follow these steps:

Step 1   Shut down the serial interface between the internal routers (s0/0/0 on PxR3 and PxR4); this link is not used in this exercise.

Solution:

The following shows the required step on the P1R3 router:

```
P1R3(config)#int s0/0/0
P1R3(config-if)#shutdown
```

Step 2   Configure EIGRP on each router in your pod in autonomous system 1, using the appropriate network and wildcard values to include all interfaces in the EIGRP routing process. Disable autosummarization on the edge routers.

Solution:

The following shows the required steps on the P1R1 and P1R3 routers:

```
P1R1(config)#router eigrp 1
P1R1(config-router)#network 10.1.0.0 0.0.255.255
P1R1(config-router)#network 172.31.1.0 0.0.0.255
P1R1(config-router)#no auto-summary

P1R3(config-if)#router eigrp 1
P1R3(config-router)#network 10.1.0.0 0.0.255.255
```

Step 3   Verify that the routing protocols are set up correctly using the **show ip protocols** command. Make sure that the autonomous system number is correct and that all neighbors are exchanging routes.

Solution:

The following shows example output on the P1R1 router:

```
P1R1#show ip protocols
Routing Protocol is "eigrp 1"
  Outgoing update filter list for all interfaces is not set
  Incoming update filter list for all interfaces is not set
  Default networks flagged in outgoing updates
  Default networks accepted from incoming updates
  EIGRP metric weight K1=1, K2=0, K3=1, K4=0, K5=0
  EIGRP maximum hopcount 100
  EIGRP maximum metric variance 1
  Redistributing: eigrp 1
  EIGRP NSF-aware route hold timer is 240s
  Automatic network summarization is not in effect
  Maximum path: 4
```

```
Routing for Networks:
  10.1.0.0/16
  172.31.1.0/24
Routing Information Sources:
  Gateway         Distance      Last Update
  10.1.1.3              90      00:00:37
  10.1.0.2              90      00:00:35
  172.31.1.3            90      00:00:35
Distance: internal 90 external 170

P1R1#
```

Step 4   Verify that routes from other routers in your pod and from the backbone
router BBR1 are being recognized via EIGRP on each router.

Solution:

The following shows example output on the P1R1 router:

```
P1R1#show ip route
<output omitted>
Gateway of last resort is not set

      172.31.0.0/24 is subnetted, 2 subnets
D        172.31.2.0 [90/21024000] via 172.31.1.3, 00:04:41, Serial0/0/0
C        172.31.1.0 is directly connected, Serial0/0/0
      10.0.0.0/24 is subnetted, 4 subnets
D        10.1.2.0 [90/20514560] via 10.1.0.2, 00:10:08, Serial0/0/1
C        10.1.1.0 is directly connected, FastEthernet0/0
C        10.1.0.0 is directly connected, Serial0/0/1
D        10.254.0.0 [90/20514560] via 172.31.1.3, 00:04:42, Serial0/0/0
P1R1#
```

The highlighted routes are being learned by EIGRP.

Step 5   Use **debug ip eigrp** on the internal routers in your pod to monitor the
EIGRP queries.

Step 6   Shut down the serial interface between the edge routers (the S0/0/1
interface on P*x*R1 and P*x*R2).

Step 7   View the EIGRP queries sent to the internal routers.

Solution:

The following shows the required command on the P1R3 router, the configuration on the P1R1
router, and example output on the P1R3 router:

```
P1R3#debug ip eigrp
IP-EIGRP Route Events debugging is on
P1R3#

P1R1(config)#int s0/0/1
P1R1(config-if)#shutdown

P1R3#
*Mar  6 02:19:11.363: IP-EIGRP(Default-IP-Routing-Table:1): Processing incoming QUERY
    packet
```

```
*Mar  6 02:19:11.367: IP-EIGRP(Default-IP-Routing-Table:1): Int 10.1.0.0/24 M
   4294967295 - 0 4294967295 SM 4294967295 - 0 4294967295
*Mar  6 02:19:11.367: IP-EIGRP(Default-IP-Routing-Table:1): 10.1.0.0/24 routing table
   not updated thru 10.1.1.1
*Mar  6 02:19:11.367: IP-EIGRP(Default-IP-Routing-Table:1): Int 10.1.2.0/24 M
   4294967295 - 20000000 4294967295 SM 4294967295 - 20000000 4294967295
*Mar  6 02:19:11.367: IP-EIGRP(Default-IP-Routing-Table:1): 10.1.2.0/24 routing table
   not updated thru 10.1.1.1
*Mar  6 02:19:11.387: IP-EIGRP(Default-IP-Routing-Table:1): 10.1.0.0/24- not in IP
   routing table
*Mar  6 02:19:11.387: IP-EIGRP(Default-IP-Routing-Table:1): Int 10.1.0.0/24 metric
   4294967295 - 20000000 4294967295
*Mar  6 02:19:11.387: IP-EIGRP(Default-IP-Routing-Table:1): 10.1.2.0/24 - not in IP
   routing table
*Mar  6 02:19:11.387: IP-EIGRP(Default-IP-Routing-Table:1): Int 10.1.2.0/24 metric
   4294967295 - 20000000 4294967295
P1R3#
```

P1R3 receives a query for network 10.1.0.0/24 from P1R1; 10.1.0.0/24 is unreachable, as indicated by the infinite metric 4294967295. P1R3 replies to the query, indicating that 10.1.0.0/24 is unreachable (using the same infinite metric).

Step 8   Turn off all debugging.

Solution:

The following shows the required command on the P1R3 router:

```
P1R3#no debug all
All possible debugging has been turned off
P1R3#
```

Step 9   Reenable the serial interface between the edge routers (the S0/0/1 interface on P*x*R1 and P*x*R2).

Solution:

The following shows the required configuration on the P1R1 router:

```
P1R1(config)#int s0/0/1
P1R1(config-if)#no shutdown
```

Task 2: Configuring EIGRP Summarization

In this task, you configure EIGRP route summarization. This will add stability and speed convergence of the network by controlling the scope of queries, minimizing update traffic, and minimizing routing table size. Follow these steps:

Step 1   Telnet to BBR1 (172.31.*x*.3) and verify that you see the specific subnet routes from your pod.

Solution:

The following shows sample output on the BBR1 router:

```
BBR1>show ip route eigrp
      10.0.0.0/24 is subnetted, 7 subnets
D        10.1.2.0 [90/20514560] via 172.31.1.2, 00:00:28, Serial0/0/0.1
D        10.1.1.0 [90/20514560] via 172.31.1.1, 00:00:29, Serial0/0/0.1
D        10.1.0.0 [90/21024000] via 172.31.1.2, 00:00:32, Serial0/0/0.1
                  [90/21024000] via 172.31.1.1, 00:00:32, Serial0/0/0.1
BBR1>
```

Step 2   Manually configure the edge routers (PxR1 and PxR2) to summarize the pod EIGRP routes to BBR1 into a single 10.x.0.0/16 advertisement (where x is your pod number).

Solution:

The following shows the required configuration on the P1R1 router:

```
P1R1(config)#int s0/0/0
P1R1(config-if)#ip summary-address eigrp 1 10.1.0.0 255.255.0.0
P1R1(config-if)#
```

Both edge routers require the same summarization configuration.

Step 3   Telnet to BBR1 (172.31.x.3) and verify that you see only the summary route and not the more specific routes from your pod. If both edge routers are configured correctly, you should see two equal-cost paths available to BBR1.

Solution:

The following shows sample output on the BBR1 router:

```
BBR1>show ip route eigrp
      10.0.0.0/8 is variably subnetted, 5 subnets, 2 masks
D        10.1.0.0/16 [90/20514560] via 172.31.1.2, 00:00:33, Serial0/0/0.1
                     [90/20514560] via 172.31.1.1, 00:00:33, Serial0/0/0.1
BBR1>
```

Only the summarized 10.1.0.0/16 route is displayed; there are two equal-cost routes to this network, via P1R1 and P1R2.

Task 3: Configuring the EIGRP Stub

Having optimized BBR1's routing table by summarizing the routes from the pod's edge routers to the core BBR1 router, you now limit the query traffic from the pod's edge routers to its internal routers. Follow these steps:

Step 1   Configure the internal routers (PxR3 and PxR4) as EIGRP stubs. Remember that this bounds queries but does not affect the routing table.

Solution:

The following shows the required configuration on the P1R3 router:

```
P1R3(config)#router eigrp 1
P1R3(config-router)#eigrp stub
```

Step 2   Verify that the edge router recognizes its internal EIGRP neighbor as a stub.

Solution:

The following shows sample output on the P1R1 router. The highlighted lines indicate that P1R1 sees P1R3 (10.1.1.3) as a stub:

```
P1R1#show ip eigrp neighbors detail
IP-EIGRP neighbors for process 1
H   Address                    Interface       Hold Uptime   SRTT   RTO  Q  Seq
                                               (sec)         (ms)       Cnt Num
1   10.1.1.3                   Fa0/0           10 00:02:05   12     200  0  12
    Version 12.4/1.2, Retrans: 0, Retries: 0
    Stub Peer Advertising ( CONNECTED SUMMARY ) Routes
    Suppressing queries
0   10.1.0.2                   Se0/0/1         12 00:06:46   25     1140 0  40
    Version 12.4/1.2, Retrans: 0, Retries: 0, Prefixes: 8
2   172.31.1.3                 Se0/0/0         159 00:18:03  225    1350 0  4340
    Restart time 00:04:37
    Version 12.4/1.2, Retrans: 0, Retries: 0, Prefixes: 6
P1R1#
```

Step 3   The stub designation bounds query traffic and helps the router avoid getting into a stuck-in-active state, where EIGRP is unable to resolve routes for long periods. To demonstrate this situation, use the **debug ip eigrp** command on the internal router.

Step 4   Shut down the serial interface between the edge routers (the S0/0/1 interface between P*x*R1 and P*x*R2).

Step 5   Compared to the time before the internal routers were configured as stubs, notice that no queries are now being sent to the internal router. You should *not* see the "processing incoming QUERY" debug message on the internal routers, because they are configured as stub routers.

Solution:

The following shows the required command on the P1R3 router, the configuration on the P1R1 router, and example output on the P1R3 router. Queries are no longer being sent to the internal routers. P1R1 only sends the Update packet to P1R3:

```
P1R3#debug ip eigrp
IP-EIGRP Route Events debugging is on

P1R1(config)#int s0/0/1
P1R1(config-if)#shutdown
```

```
P1R3#
*Mar  6 02:32:34.507: IP-EIGRP(Default-IP-Routing-Table:1): Processing incoming UPDATE
    packet
*Mar  6 02:32:34.507: IP-EIGRP(Default-IP-Routing-Table:1): Int 10.1.0.0/24 M
   4294967295 - 0 4294967295 SM 4294967295 - 0 4294967295
*Mar  6 02:32:34.507: IP-EIGRP(Default-IP-Routing-Table:1): Int 10.1.2.0/24 M
   4294967295 - 20000000 4294967295 SM 4294967295 - 20000000 4294967295
*Mar  6 02:32:34.523: IP-EIGRP(Default-IP-Routing-Table:1): Int 10.1.0.0/24 metric
   4294967295 - 0 4294967295
*Mar  6 02:32:34.523: IP-EIGRP(Default-IP-Routing-Table:1): Int 10.1.2.0/24 metric
   4294967295 - 20000000 4294967295
*Mar  6 02:32:34.543: IP-EIGRP(Default-IP-Routing-Table:1): Processing incoming REPLY
   packet
*Mar  6 02:32:34.543: IP-EIGRP(Default-IP-Routing-Table:1): Int 10.1.0.0/24 M
   4294967295 - 0 4294967295 SM 4294967295 - 0 4294967295
*Mar  6 02:32:34.543: IP-EIGRP(Default-IP-Routing-Table:1): Int 10.1.2.0/24 M
   4294967295 - 20000000 4294967295 SM 4294967295 - 20000000 4294967295
P1R3#
```

Step 6   Turn off debugging on the internal routers (P*x*R3 and P*x*R4).

Solution:

The following shows the required command on the P1R3 router:

```
P1R3#no debug all
All possible debugging has been turned off
P1R3#
```

Step 7   Reenable the serial interface between the edge routers (the S0/0/1 interface
between P*x*R1 and P*x*R2).

Solution:

The following shows the required configuration on the P1R1 router:

```
P1R1(config)#int s0/0/1
P1R1(config-if)#no shutdown
```

Task 4: Configuring an EIGRP Default Route

In this task, you advertise a default route from the edge routers to the internal routers via EIGRP.
This change adds stability and speed convergence to the network by minimizing update traffic and
routing table size. Follow these steps:

Step 1   Send a default route from the edge routers to the internal routers, and filter
all specific routes. You can do this by configuring a summary route of
0.0.0.0 0.0.0.0 on each edge router, on the interface to the internal router.

Solution:

The following shows the required configuration on the P1R1 router:

```
P1R1(config)#int fa0/0
P1R1(config-if)#ip summary-address eigrp 1 0.0.0.0 0.0.0.0
```

Step 2   Examine the routing table on the internal routers. You should see the default
routes and the connected routes, but the more specific routes from the edge
router should have been filtered.

Solution:

The following shows sample output on the P1R3 router. Notice that the gateway of last resort is
also now set on the internal routers:

```
P1R3#show ip route
<output omitted>
Gateway of last resort is 10.1.1.1 to network 0.0.0.0

     10.0.0.0/24 is subnetted, 1 subnets
C        10.1.1.0 is directly connected, FastEthernet0/0
D*   0.0.0.0/0 [90/30720] via 10.1.1.1, 00:01:58, FastEthernet0/0
```

Step 3   Ping the TFTP server (10.254.0.254) from the internal router to verify
connectivity.

Solution:

The following shows sample output on the P1R3 router. The ping is successful:

```
P1R3#ping 10.254.0.254

Type escape sequence to abort.
Sending 5, 100-byte ICMP Echos to 10.254.0.254, timeout is 2 seconds:
!!!!!
Success rate is 100 percent (5/5), round-trip min/avg/max = 28/30/32 ms
P1R3#
```

Step 4   Examine the EIGRP topology table, EIGRP traffic statistics, information
about interfaces configured for EIGRP, and EIGRP neighbors.

Solution:

The following shows sample output on the P1R1 router:

```
P1R1#show ip eigrp topology
IP-EIGRP Topology Table for AS(1)/ID(172.31.1.1)

Codes: P - Passive, A - Active, U - Update, Q - Query, R - Reply,
       r - reply Status, s - sia Status

P 0.0.0.0/0, 1 successors, FD is 28160
        via Summary (28160/0), Null0
P 10.1.2.0/24, 1 successors, FD is 20514560
        via 10.1.0.2 (20514560/28160), Serial0/0/1
P 10.1.1.0/24, 1 successors, FD is 28160
        via Connected, FastEthernet0/0
P 10.1.0.0/16, 1 successors, FD is 28160
        via Summary (28160/0), Null0
P 10.1.0.0/24, 1 successors, FD is 20512000
        via Connected, Serial0/0/1
P 172.31.2.0/24, 1 successors, FD is 21024000
        via 172.31.1.3 (21024000/20512000), Serial0/0/0
```

```
P 172.31.1.0/24, 1 successors, FD is 20512000
        via Connected, Serial0/0/0
P 10.254.0.0/24, 1 successors, FD is 20514560
        via 172.31.1.3 (20514560/28160), Serial0/0/0

P1R1#show ip eigrp traffic
IP-EIGRP Traffic Statistics for AS 1
  Hellos sent/received: 907/905
  Updates sent/received: 341/35
  Queries sent/received: 6/7
  Replies sent/received: 7/6
  Acks sent/received: 33/40
  Input queue high water mark 2, 0 drops
  SIA-Queries sent/received: 0/0
  SIA-Replies sent/received: 0/0
  Hello Process ID: 150
  PDM Process ID: 88

P1R1#show ip eigrp interfaces
IP-EIGRP interfaces for process 1

                    Xmit Queue   Mean   Pacing Time   Multicast    Pending
Interface   Peers   Un/Reliable  SRTT   Un/Reliable   Flow Timer   Routes
Fa0/0         1       0/0          4       0/10          50          0
Se0/0/1       1       0/0         35       5/190        346          0
Se0/0/0       2       0/0         75       5/190        748          0
P1R1#

P1R1#show ip eigrp neighbors
IP-EIGRP neighbors for process 1
H   Address              Interface    Hold Uptime   SRTT   RTO  Q   Seq
                                      (sec)         (ms)        Cnt Num
0   10.1.0.2             Se0/0/1       14 00:07:39   35   1140  0   65
1   10.1.1.3             Fa0/0         13 00:14:21    4    200  0   18
2   172.31.1.3           Se0/0/0      139 00:30:19  151   1140  0   4341
P1R1#
```

Step 5   Save your configurations to NVRAM.

Solution:

The following shows how to perform the required step on the P1R1 router:

```
P1R1#copy run start
Destination filename [startup-config]?
Building configuration...
[OK]
```

Exercise Verification

You have successfully completed this exercise when you achieve the following results:

- You have successfully implemented EIGRP and have observed EIGRP query traffic.

- You have summarized your pod addresses to the core.

- You have optimized performance on the internal routers.

Review Questions

Answer the following questions, and then refer to Appendix A, "Answers to Review Questions," for the answers.

1. What are some features of EIGRP?

2. Is EIGRP operational traffic multicast or broadcast?

3. What are the four key technologies employed by EIGRP?

4. How do IGRP and EIGRP differ in their metric calculation?

5. Which of the following best describes the EIGRP topology table?

    a. It is populated as a result of receiving hello packets.

    b. It contains all learned routes to a destination.

    c. It contains only the best routes to a destination.

6. Describe the five types of EIGRP packets.

7. True or false: EIGRP hello packets are sent every 5 seconds on LAN links.

8. What is the difference between the hold time and the hello interval?

9. Which of the following statements are true?

    a. A route is considered passive when the router is not performing recomputation on that route.

    b. A route is passive when it is undergoing recomputation.

    c. A route is active when it is undergoing recomputation.

    d. A route is considered active when the router is not performing recomputation on that route.

    e. Passive is the operational state for a route.

    f. Active is the operational state for a route.

10. Which command is used to see the RTO and hold time?

    a. **show ip eigrp traffic**

    b. **show ip eigrp timers**

    c. **show ip eigrp route**

    d. **show ip eigrp neighbors**

11. Why are EIGRP routing updates described as reliable?

12. What units are the bandwidth and delay parameters in the EIGRP metric calculation?

13. Which of the following statements are true regarding AD and FD?

    a. The AD is the EIGRP metric for a *neighbor router* to reach a particular network.

    b. The AD is the EIGRP metric for *this router* to reach a particular network.

    c. The FD is the EIGRP metric for *this router* to reach a particular network.

    d. The FD is the EIGRP metric for *the neighbor router* to reach a particular network.

14. What does it mean when a route is marked as an FS?

15. In the following table, place the letter of the description next to the term the description describes. The descriptions may be used more than once.

Descriptions:

    a. A network protocol that EIGRP supports.

    b. A table that contains FS information.

    c. The administrative distance determines routing information that is included in this table.

    d. A neighbor router that has the best path to a destination.

    e. A neighbor router that has a loop-free alternative path to a destination.

    f. An algorithm used by EIGRP that ensures fast convergence.

    g. A multicast packet used to discover neighbors.

    h. A packet sent by EIGRP routers when a new neighbor is discovered and when a change occurs.

Term	Description Letter
Successor	
Feasible successor	
Hello	
Topology table	
IP	
Update	
AppleTalk	
Routing table	
DUAL	
IPX	

16. Answer true or false to the following statements.

    a. EIGRP performs autosummarization.

    b. EIGRP autosummarization cannot be turned off.

    c. EIGRP supports VLSM.

    d. EIGRP can maintain three independent routing tables.

    e. The EIGRP hello interval is an unchangeable fixed value.

17. Which of the following are true?

    a. For Frame Relay point-to-point interfaces, set the **bandwidth** to the CIR.

    b. For Frame Relay point-to-point interfaces set the **bandwidth** to the sum of all CIRs.

    c. For Frame Relay multipoint connections, set the **bandwidth** to the sum of all CIRs.

    d. For generic serial interfaces such as PPP and HDLC, set the **bandwidth** to match the line speed.

    e. For Frame Relay multipoint connections, set the **bandwidth** to the CIR.

18. Router A has three interfaces with IP addresses 172.16.1.1/24, 172.16.2.3/24, and 172.16.5.1/24. What commands would be used to configure EIGRP to run in autonomous system 100 on only the interfaces with addresses 172.16.2.3/24 and 172.16.5.1/24?

19. Routers A and B are connected and are running EIGRP on all their interfaces. Router A has four interfaces, with IP addresses 172.16.1.1/24, 172.16.2.3/24, 172.16.5.1/24, and 10.1.1.1/24. Router B has two interfaces, with IP addresses 172.16.1.2/24 and 192.168.1.1/24. There are other routers in the network that are connected on each of the interfaces of these two routers that are also running EIGRP. Which summary routes does Router A generate automatically?

    a. 172.16.0.0/16

    b. 192.168.1.0/24

    c. 10.0.0.0/8

    d. 172.16.1.0/22

    e. 10.1.1.0/24

20. Router A has four EIGRP paths to a destination with the following EIGRP metrics. Assuming no potential routing loops exist and the command **variance 3** is configured on Router A, which paths are included for load balancing?

    a. Path 1: 1100

    b. Path 2: 1200

    c. Path 3: 2000

    d. Path 4: 4000

21. Router A has the following configuration:

```
interface s0
  ip bandwidth-percent eigrp 100 40
  bandwidth 256
router eigrp 100
  network 10.0.0.0
```

What is the maximum bandwidth that EIGRP uses on the S0 interface?

- a. 100
- b. 40
- c. 256
- d. 102
- e. 10
- f. 47

22. What is the default EIGRP authentication?

- a. Simple password
- b. MD5
- c. None
- d. IPsec

23. True or false: When configuring EIGRP authentication, each router must have a unique password configured.

24. What does the **accept-lifetime** command do for EIGRP authentication?

25. What command is used to troubleshoot EIGRP authentication?

- a. **debug eigrp authentication**
- b. **debug ip eigrp packets**
- c. **debug eigrp packets**
- d. **debug ip eigrp authentication**

26. What is the default EIGRP stuck-in-active timer?

27. With the EIGRP active process enhancement, when does the SIA-Query get sent?

28. How does EIGRP summarization limit the query range?

29. How does the EIGRP stub feature limit the query range?

30. What does the **eigrp stub receive-only** command do?

31. True or false: Goodbye messages are sent in hello packets.

32. The following is part of the output of the **show ip eigrp topology** command:

```
P 10.1.3.0/24, 1 successors, FD is 10514432
        via 10.1.2.2 (10514432/28160), Serial0/0/0
```

What are the two numbers in parentheses?

This chapter introduces the Open Shortest Path First (OSPF) protocol. It covers the following topics:

- OSPF Protocol Overview

- OSPF Packets

- Configuring Basic OSPF Routing

- OSPF Network Types

CHAPTER 4

Configuring the Open Shortest Path First Protocol

This chapter examines the Open Shortest Path First (OSPF) routing protocol, which is one of the most commonly used interior gateway protocols in IP networking. OSPF is an open-standard protocol based primarily on Requests For Comments (RFC) 2328. OSPF is a fairly complex protocol made up of several protocol handshakes, database advertisements, and packet types. This chapter also describes basic configuration of OSPF, in both single and multiple areas, and explores OSPF configuration over specific network types.

OSPF Protocol Overview

This section introduces the major characteristics of the OSPF routing protocol including a description of link-state routing protocols, area structures, link-state adjacencies, shortest path first (SPF) calculations, and link-state data structures.

Link-State Routing Protocols

The need to overcome the limitations of distance-vector routing protocols led to the development of link-state routing protocols. Link-state routing protocols have the following characteristics:

- They respond quickly to network changes.

- They send triggered updates when a network change occurs.

- They send periodic updates, known as link-state refresh, at long time intervals, such as every 30 minutes.

Link-state routing protocols generate routing updates only when a change occurs in the network topology. When a link changes state, the device that detected the change creates a link-state advertisement (LSA) concerning that link, as shown in Figure 4-1. The LSA propagates to all neighboring devices using a special multicast address. Each routing device takes a copy of the LSA, forwards the LSA to all neighboring devices (within an area; areas are described in the "OSPF Area Structure" section later in this chapter) and updates its link-state database (LSDB). This flooding of the LSA ensures that all routing devices can update their databases and then update their routing tables to reflect the new topology. As shown in Figure 4-1, the LSDB is used to calculate the best paths through the network. Link-state routers find the best paths to a destination by applying Dijkstra's algorithm, also known as SPF, against the LSDB to build the SPF tree. Each router selects the best paths from their SPF tree and places them in their routing table.

Figure 4-1 *Link-State Protocol Operation*

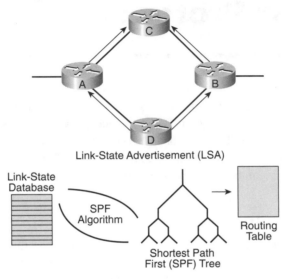

Link-State Routing Analogy

You can think of the LSDB as being like a map in a shopping mall—every map in the mall is the same, just as the LSDB is the same in all routers within an area.

The one difference between all the maps in a shopping mall is the "you are here" dot. By looking at this dot, you can determine the best way to get to every store from your current location; the best path to a specific store will be different from each location in the mall. Link-state routers function similarly; they each calculate the best way to every network within the area, from their own perspective, using the LSDB.

OSPF and Integrated Intermediate System-to-Intermediate System (IS-IS) are classified as link-state routing protocols because of the manner in which they distribute routing information and calculate routes.

Link-state routing protocols collect routing information from all other routers in the network or from within a defined area of the network. After link-state routing protocols have collected this information from all routers, each router independently calculates its best paths to all destinations in the network using Dijkstra's (SPF) algorithm. Incorrect information from any particular router is less likely to cause confusion, because each router maintains its own view of the network.

For all the routers in the network to make consistent routing decisions, each link-state router must keep a record of the following information:

- **Its immediate neighbor routers**—If the router loses contact with a neighbor router, within a few seconds it invalidates all paths through that router and recalculates its paths through the network. Adjacency information about neighbors is stored in the OSPF neighbor table, also known as an adjacency database.

- **All the other routers in the network, or in its area of the network, and their attached networks**—The router recognizes other routers and networks through LSAs, which are flooded through the network. LSAs are stored in a topology table or database (which is also called an LSDB).

- **The best paths to each destination**—Each router independently calculates the best paths to each destination in the network using Dijkstra's (SPF) algorithm. All paths are kept in the LSDB. The best paths are then offered to the routing table (or forwarding database). Packets arriving at the router are forwarded based on the information held in the routing table.

KEY POINT

OSPF Terminology

You might encounter different terminology for the various OSPF tables, as follows:

- OSPF neighbor table = adjacency database

- OSPF topology table = OSPF topology database = LSDB

- Routing table = forwarding database

The memory resources required to maintain these tables is one drawback to link-state protocols. However, because the topology table is identical for all OSPF routers in an area and contains full information about all the routers and links in an area, each router can independently select a loop-free and efficient path, based on cost (as described in the "OSPF Metric Calculation" section later in this chapter), to reach every network in the area. This benefit overcomes the "routing by rumor" limitations of distance vector routing.

KEY POINT

Distance Vector versus Link-State

With distance vector routing protocols, the routers rely on routing decisions from the neighbors. Routers do not have the full picture of the network topology.

With link-state routing protocols, each router has the full picture of the network topology, and it can independently make a decision based on an accurate picture of the network topology.

OSPF Area Structure

In small networks, the web of router links is not complex, and paths to individual destinations are easily deduced. However, in large networks, the resulting web is highly complex, and the number of potential paths to each destination is large. Therefore, the Dijkstra calculations comparing all of these possible routes can be very complex and can take significant time.

Link-state routing protocols usually reduce the size of the Dijkstra calculations by partitioning the network into areas. The number of routers in an area and the number of LSAs that flood only within the area are small, which means that the LSDB or topology database for an area is small. Consequently, the Dijkstra calculation is easier and takes less time.

OSPF uses a two-layer area hierarchy:

■ **Transit area**—An OSPF area whose primary function is the fast and efficient movement of IP packets. Transit areas interconnect with other OSPF area types. Generally, end users are not found within a transit area. OSPF area 0, also known as the *backbone area*, is by definition a transit area.

■ **Regular area**—An OSPF area whose primary function is to connect users and resources. Regular areas are usually set up along functional or geographic groupings. By default, a regular area does not allow traffic from another area to use its links to reach other areas; all traffic from other areas must cross a transit area such as area 0. An area that does not allow traffic to pass through it is known as a regular area, or nonbackbone area. It can have a number of subtypes, including standard area, stub area, a totally stubby area, and a not-so-stubby area (NSSA). Chapter 5, "Advanced Open Shortest Path First Protocol Configuration," discusses area types in further detail.

OSPF forces a rigid two-layer area hierarchy. The network's underlying physical connectivity must map to the two-layer area structure, with all nonbackbone areas attaching directly to area 0.

OSPF Areas

In link-state routing protocols, all routers must keep a copy of the LSDB; the more OSPF routers that exist, the larger the LSDB. It can be advantageous to have all information in all routers, but this approach does not scale to large network sizes. The area concept is a compromise. Routers inside an area maintain detailed information about the links and routers located within that area; OSPF can be configured so that only general or summary information about routers and links in other areas is maintained.

When OSPF is configured properly and a router or link fails, that information is flooded along adjacencies to only routers in the local area. Routers outside the area do not receive this information. By maintaining a hierarchical structure and limiting the number of routers in an area, an OSPF autonomous system can scale to very large sizes.

OSPF areas require a hierarchical structure, meaning that all areas must connect directly to area 0. In Figure 4-2, notice that links between area 1 routers and area 2 or 3 routers are not allowed. All interarea traffic must pass through the backbone area—area 0. The optimal number of routers per area varies based on factors such as network stability, but in the "Designing Large Scale IP Internetworks" document (you can search for this at http://www.cisco.com), Cisco recommends that there generally be no more than 50 routers per area.

Figure 4-2   *OSPF Areas*

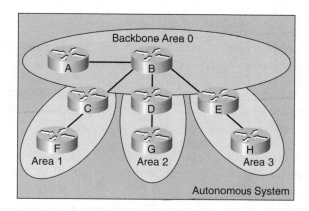

KEY POINT

OSPF Area Characteristics

OSPF requires a hierarchical network design. OSPF areas may do the following:

• Minimize routing table entries.

• Localize the impact of a topology change within an area.

• Stop detailed LSA flooding at the area boundary.

Area Terminology

Routers within area 0 are known as *backbone routers*. Hierarchical networking defines area 0 as the core and all other areas connect directly to the backbone area 0.

An area border router (ABR) connects area 0 to the nonbackbone areas. An OSPF ABR plays a very important role in network design and has the following characteristics:

■ It separates LSA flooding zones.

■ It becomes the primary point for area address summarization.

■ It functions regularly as the source of default routes.

■ It maintains the LSDB for each area with which it is connected.

The ideal design is to have each ABR connected to two areas only, the backbone and another area; three areas are the recommended upper limit.

OSPF Adjacencies

A router running a link-state routing protocol must first establish neighbor adjacencies with selected neighboring routers. A router achieves this neighbor adjacency by exchanging hello packets with the neighboring routers, as shown in Figure 4-3. In general, routers establish adjacencies as follows:

■ The router sends and receives hello packets to and from its neighboring routers. The format of the destination address is typically multicast.

■ The routers exchange hello packets subject to protocol-specific parameters, such as checking whether the neighbor is in the same area, using the same hello interval, and so on. Routers declare the neighbor up when the exchange is complete.

■ After two routers establish neighbor adjacency using hello packets, they synchronize their LSDBs by exchanging LSAs and confirming the receipt of LSAs from the adjacent router. The two neighbor routers now recognize that they have synchronized their LSDBs with each other. For OSPF, this means that the routers are now in full adjacency state with each other.

■ If necessary, the routers forward any new LSAs to other neighboring routers, ensuring complete synchronization of link-state information inside the area.

Figure 4-3 *Hello Exchange on a Broadcast Network*

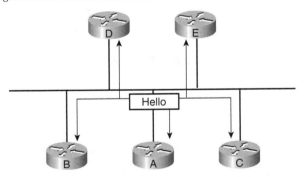

The two OSPF routers on a point-to-point serial link, usually encapsulated in High-Level Data Link Control (HDLC) or Point-to-Point Protocol (PPP), form a full adjacency with each other.

OSPF routers on LAN links elect one router as the Designated Router (DR) and another as the Backup Designated Router (BDR). All other routers on the LAN form full adjacencies with these two routers and pass LSAs only to them. The DR forwards updates received from one neighbor on the LAN to all other neighbors on that same LAN. One of the main functions of a DR is to ensure that all the routers on the same LAN have an identical LSDB.

The DR passes its LSDB to any new routers that join that LAN. Having all the routers on that LAN pass the same information to the new router is inefficient, so the one DR router represents the other routers to a new router on the LAN or to other routers in the area. Routers on the LAN also maintain a partial-neighbor relationship, called a *two-way adjacency state*, with the other routers on the LAN that are non-DR and non-BDR routers; these other routers are known as DROTHERs.

The exchange of link-state information occurs through LSAs, which are also called link-state protocol data units (PDUs).

KEY POINT	**Link State**
	LSAs report the state of routers and the links between routers—hence the term *link state*.

Link-state information must be synchronized between routers. To accomplish this, LSAs have the following characteristics:

- LSAs are reliable; there is a method for acknowledging their delivery.

- LSAs are flooded throughout the area (or throughout the domain if there is only one area).

- LSAs have a sequence number and a set lifetime, so each router recognizes that it has the most current version of the LSA.

- LSAs are periodically refreshed to confirm topology information before they age out of the LSDB.

Only by reliably flooding link-state information can every router in the area or domain ensure that it has the latest, most accurate view of the network. Only then can the router make reliable routing decisions that are consistent with the decisions of other routers in the network.

OSPF Metric Calculation

Edsger Dijkstra designed a mathematical algorithm for calculating the best paths through complex networks. Link-state routing protocols use Dijkstra's algorithm to calculate the best paths through a network. By assigning a cost to each link in the network, and by placing the specific node at the root of a tree and summing the costs toward each given destination, the branches of the tree can be calculated to determine the best path to each destination. The best paths are offered to the forwarding database (the routing table).

For OSPF, the default behavior is that the interface cost is calculated based on its configured bandwidth; the higher the bandwidth, the lower the cost. The default OSPF cost on Cisco routers is calculated using the formula 100 Mbps/(bandwidth in Mbps). You can also manually define an OSPF cost for each interface, which overrides the default cost value (as described in more detail in Chapter 5).

Figure 4-4 is an example of a Dijkstra calculation. The following steps occur:

■ Router H advertises its presence to Router E. Router E passes Router H's and its own advertisements to its neighbors (Routers C and G). Router G passes these and its own advertisements to D, and so on.

■ These LSAs follow the split-horizon rule, which dictates that a router should never advertise an LSA to the router from which it came. In this example, Router E does not advertise Router H's LSAs back to Router H.

■ Router *x* has four neighbor routers: A, B, C, and D. From these routers, it receives the LSAs from all other routers in the network. From these LSAs, it can also deduce the links between all routers and draw the web of routers shown in Figure 4-4.

■ Each FastEthernet link in Figure 4-4 is assigned an OSPF cost of 1. By summing the costs to each destination, the router can deduce the best path to each destination.

■ The right side of Figure 4-4 shows the resulting best paths (SPF tree). From these best paths, shown with solid lines, routes to destination networks attached to each router are offered to the routing table; for each route, the next-hop address is the appropriate neighboring router (A, B, C, or D).

Figure 4-4 *SPF Calculations*

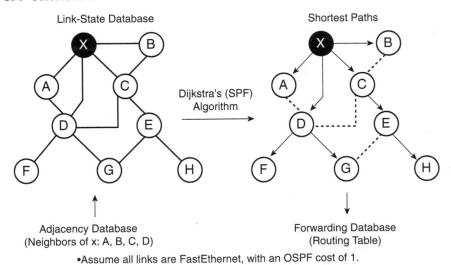

Link-State Database

Shortest Paths

Dijkstra's (SPF) Algorithm

Adjacency Database
(Neighbors of x: A, B, C, D)

Forwarding Database
(Routing Table)

•Assume all links are FastEthernet, with an OSPF cost of 1.

Link-State Data Structures

Each LSA entry has its own aging timer, which the link-state age field carries. The default timer value for OSPF is 30 minutes (expressed in seconds in the link-state age field). After an LSA entry ages, the router that originated the entry sends the LSA, with a higher sequence number, in a link-state update (LSU), to verify that the link is still active, as shown in Figure 4-5. The LSU can contain one or more LSAs. This LSA validation method saves on bandwidth compared to distance-vector routers, which send their entire routing table at short, periodic intervals.

When each router receives the LSU, it does the following:

■ If the LSA entry does not already exist, the router adds the entry to its LSDB, sends back a link-state acknowledgment (LSAck), floods the information to other routers, runs SPF, and updates its routing table.

■ If the entry already exists and the received LSA has the same sequence number, the router ignores the LSA entry.

■ If the entry already exists but the LSA includes newer information (it has a higher sequence number), the router adds the entry to its LSDB, sends back an LSAck, floods the information to other routers, runs SPF, and updates its routing table.

■ If the entry already exists but the LSA includes older information, it sends an LSU to the sender with its newer information.

Figure 4-5 *LSA Operations*

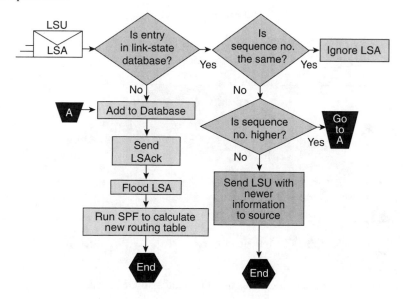

OSPF Packets

This section describes the five OSPF packet types and explains where and how these packets interact to build OSPF neighbor adjacencies and maintain the OSPF topology database.

Table 4-1 describes the five types of OSPF packets.

Table 4-1 *OSPF Packets*

Type	Packet Name	Description
1	Hello	Discovers neighbors and builds adjacencies between them
2	Database description (DBD)	Checks for database synchronization between routers
3	Link-state request (LSR)	Requests specific link-state records from another router
4	LSU	Sends specifically requested link-state records
5	LSAck	Acknowledges the other packet types

All five OSPF packets are encapsulated directly into an IP payload, as shown in Figure 4-6. The OSPF packet does not use Transmission Control Protocol (TCP) or User Datagram Protocol (UDP). OSPF requires a reliable packet transport scheme, and because TCP is not used, OSPF defines its own acknowledgment routine using an acknowledgment packet (OSPF packet type 5).

Figure 4-6 *OSPF Packet Header Format*

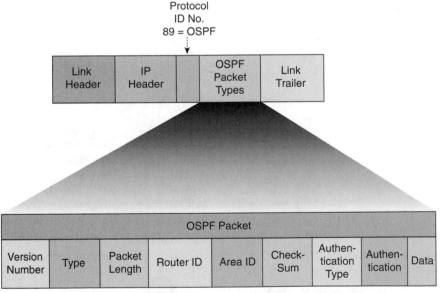

In the IP header, a protocol identifier of 89 indicates an OSPF packet. Each OSPF packet begins with the same header format. This header has the following fields:

- **Version Number**—For OSPF Version 2.

- **Type**—Differentiates the five OSPF packet types, as described in Table 4-1.

- **Packet Length**—The length of the OSPF packet in bytes.

- **Router ID**—Defines which router is the packet's source.

- **Area ID**—Defines the area where the packet originated.

- **Checksum**—Used for packet header error detection to ensure that the OSPF packet was not corrupted during transmission.

- **Authentication Type**—An option in OSPF that describes either no authentication, cleartext passwords, or encrypted Message Digest 5 (MD5) for router authentication.

- **Authentication**—Used with authentication type.

> **NOTE**   OSPF authentication is covered in Chapter 5.

- **Data**—Contains different information, depending on the OSPF packet type:

  — **For the hello packet**—Contains a list of known neighbors.

  — **For the DBD packet**—Contains a summary of the LSDB, which includes all known router IDs and their last sequence number, among a number of other fields.

  — **For the LSR packet**—Contains the type of LSU needed and the router ID of the router that has the needed LSU.

  — **For the LSU packet**—Contains the full LSA entries. Multiple LSA entries can fit in one OSPF update packet.

  — **For the LSAck packet**—This data field is empty.

Establishing OSPF Neighbor Adjacencies: Hello

Neighbor OSPF routers must recognize each other on the network before they can share information, because OSPF routing depends on the status of a link between two routers. This process is done using the Hello protocol. The Hello protocol establishes and maintains neighbor relationships by ensuring bidirectional (two-way) communication between neighbors. Bidirectional communication occurs when a router sees itself listed in the hello packet received from a neighbor.

Each interface participating in OSPF uses the IP multicast address 224.0.0.5 to send hello packets periodically. As shown in Figure 4-7, a hello packet contains the following information:

- **Router ID**—A 32-bit number that uniquely identifies the router. The highest IP address on an active interface is chosen by default unless a loopback interface exists or the router ID is manually configured (this process is described later, in the "OSPF Router ID" section). For example, IP address 172.16.12.1 would be chosen over 172.16.1.1. This identification is important in establishing neighbor relationships and coordinating LSU exchanges. The router ID is also used to break ties during the DR and BDR selection processes if the OSPF priority values are equal (as described in the "Electing a DR and BDR" section later in this chapter).

- **Hello and dead intervals**—The hello interval specifies how often, in seconds, a router sends hello packets (10 seconds is the default on multiaccess networks). The dead interval is the amount of time in seconds that a router waits to hear from a neighbor before declaring the neighbor router out of service (the dead interval is four times the hello interval by default). These timers must be the same on neighboring routers; otherwise an adjacency will not be established.

- **Neighbors**—The Neighbors field lists the adjacent routers with which this router has established bidirectional communication. Bidirectional communication is indicated when the router sees itself listed in the Neighbors field of the hello packet from the neighbor.

- **Area ID**—To communicate, two routers must share a common segment, and their interfaces must belong to the same OSPF area on that segment; they must also share the same subnet and mask. These routers will all have the same link-state information for that area.

- **Router priority**—An 8-bit number that indicates a router's priority. Priority is used when selecting a DR and BDR.

- **DR and BDR IP addresses**—If known, the IP addresses of the DR and BDR for the specific multiaccess network.

- **Authentication password**—If router authentication is enabled, two routers must exchange the same password. Authentication is not required, but if it is enabled, all peer routers must have the same password.

- **Stub area flag**—A stub area is a special area. The stub area technique reduces routing updates by replacing them with a default route. Two neighboring routers must agree on the stub area flag in the hello packets. Chapter 5 describes stub areas in greater detail.

Figure 4-7 *Establishing Neighbor Adjacencies*

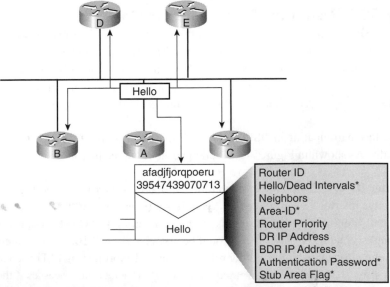

*Entry Must Match On Neighboring Routers

> **NOTE**   After a DR and BDR are selected, any router added to the network establishes adjacencies with the DR and BDR only.

Exchange Process and OSPF Neighbor Adjacency States

When routers running OSPF initialize, they first go through an exchange process, using the Hello protocol, as shown in Figure 4-8 and described as follows:

1. Router A is enabled on the LAN and is in a *down* state because it has not exchanged information with any other router. It begins by sending a hello packet through each of its interfaces participating in OSPF, even though it does not know the identity of the DR or of any other routers. The hello packet is sent out using the multicast address 224.0.0.5.

2. All directly connected routers running OSPF receive the hello packet from Router A and add Router A to their list of neighbors. This state is the *init* state.

3. All routers that received the hello packet send a unicast reply packet to Router A with their corresponding information. The Neighbor field in the hello packet includes all other neighboring routers, including Router A.

4. When Router A receives these hello packets, it adds all the routers that have its router ID in their hello packets to its own neighbor relationship database. These routers are now in the *two-way* state. At this point, all routers that have each other in their lists of neighbors have established bidirectional communication.

5. If the link type is a broadcast network, generally a LAN link such as Ethernet, then a DR and BDR must be selected. The DR forms bidirectional adjacencies with all other routers on the LAN link. This process must occur before the routers can begin exchanging link-state information.

> **NOTE**   If a router joins a broadcast network in which there is already a DR and BDR, it will get to the two-way state with all routers, including the DR and BDR, and those that are DROTHER. The joining router will form bidirectional adjacencies only with the DR and BDR.

6. Periodically (every 10 seconds by default on broadcast networks) the routers in a network exchange hello packets to ensure that communication is still working. The hello packets include the DR, the BDR, and the list of routers whose hello packets have been received by the router. Remember that "received" means that the receiving router recognizes itself as one of the neighbor list entries in the received hello packet.

Figure 4-8 *Establishing Bidirectional Communication*

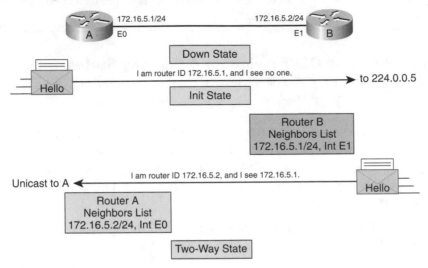

After the DR and BDR have been selected, the routers are considered to be in the *exstart* state and they are ready to discover the link-state information about the internetwork and create their LSDBs. The process used to discover the network routes is the exchange protocol, and it gets the routers to a *full* state of communication. The first step in this process is for the DR and BDR to establish adjacencies with each of the other routers. Once adjacent routers are in a full state, they do not repeat the exchange protocol unless the full state changes.

The exchange protocol, shown in Figure 4-9, operates as follows:

1. In the *exstart* state, a master and slave relationship is created between each router and its adjacent DR and BDR. The router with the higher router ID acts as the master during the exchange process.

> **NOTE**   Only the DR exchanges and synchronizes link-state information with the routers to which it has established adjacencies. Having the DR represent the network in this capacity reduces the amount of routing update traffic.

2. The master and slave routers exchange one or more DBD packets (also called DDPs). The routers are in the *exchange* state.

   A DBD includes information about the LSA entry header that appears in the router's LSDB. The entries can be about a link or about a network. Each LSA entry header includes information about the link-state type, the address of the advertising router, the link's cost, and the sequence number. The router uses the sequence number to determine the "newness" of the received link-state information.

3. When the router receives the DBD, it performs the following actions, as shown in Figure 4-10:

— It acknowledges the receipt of the DBD using the LSAck packet.

— It compares the information it received with the information it has in its own LSDB. If the DBD has a more current link-state entry, the router sends an LSR to the other router. The process of sending LSRs is called the *loading* state.

— The other router responds with the complete information about the requested entry in an LSU packet. Again, when the router receives an LSU, it sends an LSAck.

4. The router adds the new link-state entries into its LSDB.

Figure 4-9 *Discovering the Network Routes*

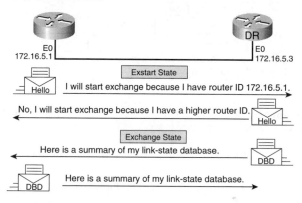

Figure 4-10 *Adding Link-State Entries*

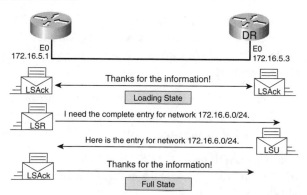

After all LSRs have been satisfied for a given router, the adjacent routers are considered synchronized and in a full state.

KEY POINT | **Routers Must Be in Full State to Route**

The routers must be in a full state before they can route traffic. At this point, all the routers in the area should have identical LSDBs.

Maintaining Routing Information

In a link-state routing environment, it is very important for the link-state databases of all routers to stay synchronized. When there is a change in a link state, as shown in Figure 4-11, the routers use a flooding process to notify the other routers in the network of the change. LSUs provide the mechanism for flooding LSAs.

Figure 4-11 *Maintaining Routing Information*

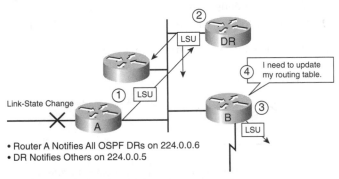

- Router A Notifies All OSPF DRs on 224.0.0.6
- DR Notifies Others on 224.0.0.5

> **NOTE**   Although it is not shown in Figure 4-11, all LSUs are acknowledged.

In general, the following are the flooding process steps in a multiaccess network:

1. A router notices a change in a link state and multicasts an LSU packet, which includes the updated LSA entry, to 224.0.0.6; this address goes to all OSPF DRs and BDRs. An LSU packet might contain several distinct LSAs.

2. The DR acknowledges the receipt of the change and floods the LSU to other routers on the network using the OSPF multicast address 224.0.0.5. After receiving the LSU, each router responds to the DR with an LSAck; to make the flooding procedure reliable, each LSA must be acknowledged separately.

3. If a router is connected to other networks, it floods the LSU to those other networks by forwarding the LSU to the DR of the multiaccess network (or to the adjacent router if in a point-to-point network). That DR, in turn, multicasts the LSU to the other routers in the network.

4. The router updates its LSDB using the LSU that includes the changed LSA. It then recomputes the SPF algorithm against the updated database after a short delay and updates the routing table as necessary.

> **NOTE**   The **timers throttle spf** router configuration command, introduced in Cisco IOS Software Release 12.2(14)S, enables the OSPF throttling feature so that the SPF calculations can be potentially delayed during network instability. The "OSPF Shortest Path First Throttling" section of the Cisco IOS IP Routing Protocols Configuration Guide provides details about this command; you can search for this document at http://www.cisco.com. This command replaces the **timers spf** command in earlier Cisco IOS Software releases.

OSPF Multicast Addresses

OSPF uses two multicast addresses:

- 224.0.0.5 goes to all OSPF routers.

- 224.0.0.6 goes to the DR and BDR.

OSPF simplifies the synchronization issue by requiring only adjacent routers to remain synchronized.

Summaries of individual link-state entries, not the complete link-state entries, are sent every 30 minutes to ensure LSDB synchronization. Each link-state entry has a timer to determine when the LSA refresh update must be sent.

Each link-state entry also has a maximum age (maxage) of 60 minutes. If a link-state entry is not refreshed within 60 minutes, it is removed from the LSDB.

NOTE   In a Cisco router, if a route already exists, the routing table is used at the same time the SPF algorithm is calculating. However, if the SPF is calculating a new route, the new route is used only after the SPF calculation is complete.

OSPF Link-State Sequence Numbers

A combination of the maxage and refresh timers, and link-state sequence numbers, helps OSPF maintain a database of only the most recent link-state records.

The link-state sequence number field in an LSA header is 32 bits long. Beginning with the leftmost bit set, the first legal sequence number is 0x80000001 and the last number is 0x7FFFFFFF. The sequence number is used to detect old or redundant LSA records. The larger the number, the more recent the LSA.

To ensure an accurate database, OSPF floods (refreshes) each LSA every 30 minutes; this interval is called the *LSRefreshTime*. Each time a record is flooded, the sequence number is incremented by 1. An LSA record resets its maximum age when it receives a new LSA update. An LSA never remains in the database for longer than the maximum age of 1 hour without a refresh.

It is possible for an LSA to exist in the database for long periods of time, being refreshed every 30 minutes. At some point the sequence number needs to wrap back to the starting sequence number. When this process occurs, the existing LSA is prematurely aged out (the maxage timer is immediately set to 1 hour) and flushed. The LSA then restarts its sequencing at 0x80000001.

The output of the **show ip ospf database** command in Example 4-1 demonstrates how the LS age and LS sequence numbers are kept in the database.

Every OSPF router announces a router LSA for those interfaces that it owns in that area. The link ID is the ID of the router that created the router LSA. The advertising router (shown as **ADV Router** in the output) is the router ID of the OSPF router that announced the router LSA. Generally, the link ID and advertising router for a router LSA are the same.

The first router LSA entry in the OSPF database shown in Example 4-1 indicates that the router LSA with link ID 192.168.1.67 has been updated eight times (because the sequence number is 0x80000008) and that the last update occurred 48 seconds ago.

Example 4-1 *LSA Database Sequence Numbers and Maxage*

```
RTC#show ip ospf database
OSPF Router with ID (192.168.1.67) (Process ID 10)
        Router Link States (Area 1)
Link ID          ADV Router       Age  Seq#         Checksum  Link count
192.168.1.67     192.168.1.67     48   0x80000008   0xB112    2
192.168.2.130    192.168.2.130    212  0x80000006   0x3F44    2
<output omitted>
```

The **debug ip ospf packet** command is used to troubleshoot and verify that OSPF packets are flowing properly between two routers. Example 4-2 demonstrates output from this **debug** command. Notice that the output shows the fields in the OSPF header, but they are not described in any detail. Table 4-2 describes the OSPF packet header fields represented in this output.

Example 4-2 *Debug of a Single Packet*

```
Router#debug ip ospf packet
OSPF packet debugging is on
R1#
*Apr 16 11:03:51.206: OSPF: rcv. v:2 t:1 l:48 rid:10.0.0.12
aid:0.0.0.1 chk:D882 aut:0 auk: from Serial0/0/0.2
```

Table 4-2 **debug ip ospf packet** *Command*

Field	Description
v:	Identifies the version of OSPF
t:	Specifies the OSPF packet type:
	1—Hello
	2—DBD
	3—LSR
	4—LSU
	5—LSAck

Table 4-2   **debug ip ospf packet** *Command (Continued)*

Field	Description
l:	Specifies the OSPF packet length in bytes
rid:	Displays the OSPF router ID
aid:	Shows the OSPF area ID
chk:	Displays the OSPF checksum
aut:	Provides the OSPF authentication type: 0—No authentication 1—Simple password 2—MD5
auk:	Specifies the OSPF authentication key, if used
keyid:	Displays the MD5 key ID; only used for MD5 authentication
seq:	Provides the sequence number; only used for MD5 authentication

Configuring Basic OSPF Routing

This section discusses the basic OSPF configuration commands for single-area and multiarea networks.

To configure the OSPF process, do the following:

Step 1   Enable the OSPF process on the router using the **router ospf** *process-id* [**vrf** *vpn-name*] global configuration command. Table 4-3 describes the parameters of the **router ospf** command.

Table 4-3   **router ospf** *Command*

Parameter	Description
process-id	An internally used number that identifies the OSPF routing process. The *process-id* does not need to match process IDs on other routers. Running multiple OSPF processes on the same router is not recommended, because it creates multiple database instances that add extra overhead.
vrf *vpn-name*	(Optional) Specifies the name of the virtual private network (VPN) routing and forwarding (VRF) instance to associate with OSPF VRF processes.

Step 2   Identify which interfaces on the router are part of the OSPF process
and the OSPF area to which the network belongs using the **network**
ip-address wildcard-mask **area** *area-id* router configuration command.
Table 4-4 describes the parameters of the **network** command in the
context of OSPF.

Table 4-4   **network** *Command Parameters with OSPF*

Parameter	Description
ip-address	Either the network address, subnet address, or the interface's address. This address instructs the router to determine which links to advertise to, which links to check for advertisements, and what networks to advertise.
wildcard-mask	Determines how to interpret the *ip-address*. The mask has wildcard bits, in which 0 is a match and 1 is "don't care." For example, 0.0.255.255 indicates a match in the first 2 bytes. To specify the interface address, use the mask 0.0.0.0 to match all 4 bytes of the address. An address and wildcard mask combination of 0.0.0.0 255.255.255.255 matches all interfaces on the router.
area-id	Specifies the OSPF area to be associated with the address. This parameter can be a decimal number or can be in dotted-decimal notation similar to an IP address, such as A.B.C.D.

Starting with Cisco IOS Software Release 12.3(11)T (and some specific versions of earlier
releases), OSPF can be enabled directly on the interface using the **ip ospf** *process-id* **area** *area-id*
[**secondaries none**] interface configuration command. This command simplifies the configuration
of unnumbered interfaces. Because the command is configured explicitly for the interface, it will
take precedence over the **network area** command. Table 4-5 describes the parameters of the
ip ospf area command.

Table 4-5   **ip ospf area** *Command*

Parameter	Description
process-id	An internally used number that identifies the OSPF routing process. The process ID is entered as a decimal number in the range from 1 to 65535.
area-id	Specifies the OSPF area to be associated with the interface. The area ID is entered either as a decimal value in the range from 0 to 4294967295 or can be in dotted-decimal notation similar to an IP address, such as A.B.C.D.
secondaries none	(Optional) Prevents secondary IP addresses on the interface from being advertised.

Single-Area OSPF Configuration Example

Figure 4-12 shows the OSPF configuration for FastEthernet broadcast networks and serial point-to-point links. All three routers in Figure 4-12 are assigned to area 0 and are configured for network 10.0.0.0.

Figure 4-12 *Configuring OSPF on Internal Routers of a Single Area*

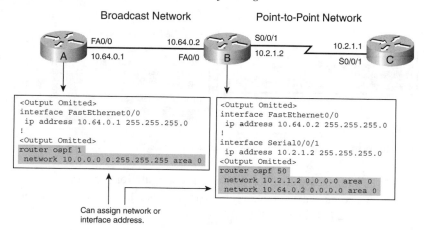

Router A uses a general **network 10.0.0.0 0.255.255.255** statement. This technique assigns all interfaces defined in the 10.0.0.0 network to OSPF process 1.

Router B uses a specific host address technique. The wildcard mask of 0.0.0.0 requires a match on all 4 bytes of the address. This technique allows the operator to define which specific interfaces will run OSPF.

Although the two examples shown in Figure 4-12 are a commonly used combination of a **network** statement and a wildcard mask, others could also work. For instance, a range of subnets could be specified.

KEY POINT

OSPF network Command

For OSPF, the **network** command and its wildcard mask are not used for route summarization purposes. The **network** statement is used strictly to enable OSPF for a single interface or for multiple interfaces.

Multiarea OSPF Configuration Example

Figure 4-13 shows an example of multiarea OSPF configuration. Router A is in area 0, router C is in area 1, and router B is the ABR between the two areas.

Figure 4-13 *Configuring OSPF for Mulitple Areas*

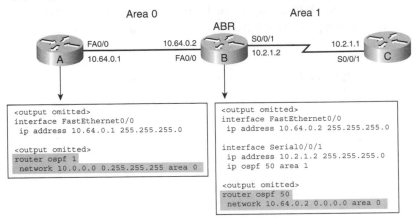

The configuration for router A is the same as it was in Figure 4-12.

Router B has a **network** statement for area 0. The configuration for area 1 in this example uses the **ip ospf 50 area 1** command; alternatively a separate **network** router configuration command, such as **network 10.2.1.2 0.0.0.0 area 1**, could have been used.

Verifying OSPF Operations

To verify that OSPF has been properly configured, use the following **show** commands:

■ The **show ip protocols** command displays IP routing protocol parameters including timers, filters, metrics, networks, and other information for the entire router.

■ The **show ip route ospf** command displays the OSPF routes known to the router. This command is one of the best ways to determine connectivity between the local router and the rest of the internetwork. This command also has optional parameters so that you can further specify the information to be displayed, including the OSPF *process-id*.

■ The **show ip ospf interface** [*type number*] [**brief**] command verifies that interfaces are configured in the intended areas. In addition, this command displays the timer intervals (including the hello interval) and shows the neighbor adjacencies.

■ The **show ip ospf** command displays the OSPF router ID (RID), OSPF timers, the number of times the SPF algorithm has been executed, and LSA information.

■ The **show ip ospf neighbor** [*type number*] [*neighbor-id*] [**detail**] command displays a list of neighbors, including their OSPF router ID, their OSPF priority, their neighbor adjacency state (such as init, exstart, or full), and the dead timer.

The **debug ip ospf events** command displays OSPF-related events, such as adjacencies, flooding information, DR selection, and SPF calculations. The **debug ip ospf adj** command tracks adjacencies as they go up and down.

The following sections illustrate example output from some of these commands, and the syntax of the command parameters.

> **NOTE**   Sample output from the **show ip ospf** command is provided in the "Verifying the OSPF Router ID" section later in this chapter.
>
> Sample output from the **debug ip ospf adj** command is provided in the "Displaying OSPF Adjacency Activity" section later in this chapter.

The show ip route ospf Command

As illustrated in Example 4-3, the **show ip route ospf** command is used to verify the OSPF routes in the IP routing table.

The O code indicates that the route was learned from OSPF; the IA code indicates that the learned route is in another area (interarea). In Example 4-3, the 10.2.1.0 subnet is recognized on FastEthernet 0/0 via neighbor 10.64.0.2. The [110/782] in the routing table represents the administrative distance assigned to OSPF (110) and the total cost of the route to subnet 10.2.1.0 (cost of 782).

Example 4-3   show ip route ospf *Command*

```
RouterA#show ip route ospf
     10.0.0.0/8 is variably subnetted, 3 subnets, 2 masks
O IA    10.2.1.0/24 [110/782] via 10.64.0.2, 00:03:05, FastEthernet0/0
RouterA#
```

The show ip ospf interface Command

Table 4-6 contains information about the parameters of the **show ip ospf interface** [*type number*] [**brief**] command.

Table 4-6   show ip ospf interface *Command*

Parameter	Description
type	(Optional) Specifies the interface type
number	(Optional) Specifies the interface number
brief	(Optional) Displays brief overview information for OSPF interfaces, states, addresses and masks, and areas on the router

The **show ip ospf interface** command output in Example 4-4 is from router A in the configuration example in Figure 4-13 and details the OSPF status of the FastEthernet 0/0 interface. This command verifies that OSPF is running on that particular interface and shows the OSPF area it is in. The command also displays other information, such as the OSPF process ID, the router ID, the OSPF network type, the DR and BDR, timers, and neighbor adjacency information.

Example 4-4 **show ip ospf interface** *Command on Router A in Figure 4-13*

```
RouterA#show ip ospf interface fastEthernet 0/0
FastEthernet0/0 is up, line protocol is up
  Internet Address 10.64.0.1/24, Area 0
  Process ID 1, Router ID 10.64.0.1, Network Type BROADCAST, Cost: 1
  Transmit Delay is 1 sec, State DROTHER, Priority 0
  Designated Router (ID) 10.64.0.2, Interface address 10.64.0.2
  No backup designated router on this network
  Timer intervals configured, Hello 10, Dead 40, Wait 40, Retransmit 5
    oob-resync timeout 40
    Hello due in 00:00:04
  Supports Link-local Signaling (LLS)
  Index 1/1, flood queue length 0
  Next 0x0(0)/0x0(0)
  Last flood scan length is 1, maximum is 4
  Last flood scan time is 0 msec, maximum is 4 msec
  Neighbor Count is 1, Adjacent neighbor count is 1
    Adjacent with neighbor 10.64.0.2  (Designated Router)
Suppress hello for 0 neighbor(s)
```

The show ip ospf neighbor Command

One of the most important OSPF troubleshooting commands is the **show ip ospf neighbor** [*type number*] [*neighbor-id*] [**detail**] command. OSPF does not send or receive updates without having full adjacencies between neighbors; this command displays OSPF neighbor information for each interface.

Table 4-7 contains information about the parameters of this command.

Table 4-7 **show ip ospf neighbor** *Command*

Parameter	Description
type	(Optional) Specifies the interface type
number	(Optional) Specifies the interface number
neighbor-id	(Optional) Specifies the neighbor ID
detail	(Optional) Displays details of all neighbors

Example 4-5 illustrates output from router B in Figure 4-13. Router B has two neighbors. The first entry in the table represents the adjacency formed on the FastEthernet interface. A FULL state means that the LSDB has been exchanged successfully. The **DROTHER** entry means that a router other than this neighboring router is the designated router. (Note that the OSPF priority on router A's FastEthernet 0/0 interface has been set to 0, indicating that it cannot be the DR or BDR on that interface.)

Example 4-5   show ip ospf neighbor *Command from Router B in Figure 4-13*

```
RouterB#show ip ospf neighbor

Neighbor ID   Pri   State          Dead Time   Address     Interface
10.64.0.1     0     FULL/DROTHER   00:00:30    10.64.0.1   FastEthernet0/0
10.2.1.1      0     FULL/  -       00:00:34    10.2.1.1    Serial0/0/1
```

The second line of output in Example 4-5 represents the neighbor of router B on the serial interface. DR and BDR are not used on point-to-point interfaces (as indicated by a dash [-]).

Example 4-6 shows further output from router B in Figure 4-13, providing details of router B's neighbors.

Example 4-6   show ip ospf neighbor detail *Command from Router B in Figure 4-13*

```
RouterB#show ip ospf neighbor detail
 Neighbor 10.64.0.1, interface address 10.64.0.1
    In the area 0 via interface FastEthernet0/0
    Neighbor priority is 0, State is FULL, 16 state changes
    DR is 10.64.0.2 BDR is 0.0.0.0
    Options is 0x52
    LLS Options is 0x1 (LR)
    Dead timer due in 00:00:35
    Neighbor is up for 00:07:14
    Index 2/2, retransmission queue length 0, number of retransmission 0
    First 0x0(0)/0x0(0) Next 0x0(0)/0x0(0)
    Last retransmission scan length is 0, maximum is 0
    Last retransmission scan time is 0 msec, maximum is 0 msec
 Neighbor 10.2.1.1, interface address 10.2.1.1
    In the area 1 via interface Serial0/0/1
    Neighbor priority is 0, State is FULL, 6 state changes
    DR is 0.0.0.0 BDR is 0.0.0.0
    Options is 0x52
    LLS Options is 0x1 (LR)
    Dead timer due in 00:00:39
    Neighbor is up for 00:01:50
    Index 1/1, retransmission queue length 0, number of retransmission 1
    First 0x0(0)/0x0(0) Next 0x0(0)/0x0(0)
    Last retransmission scan length is 1, maximum is 1
Last retransmission scan time is 0 msec, maximum is 0 msec
```

The debug ip ospf events Command

As illustrated in Example 4-7, the **debug ip ospf events** command is used to display OSPF-related events. This sample output shows that the router received a hello packet on its Serial 0/0/1 interface.

Example 4-7 **debug ip ospf events** *Command*

```
R1#debug ip ospf events
OSPF events debugging is on
*Apr 27 11:47:00.942: OSPF: Rcv hello from 10.0.0.12 area 1 from Serial0/0/1 10.1.0.2
*Apr 27 11:47:00.942: OSPF: End of hello processing
```

OSPF Router ID

An OSPF router ID uniquely identifies each OSPF router in the network. The OSPF routing process chooses a router ID for itself when it starts up. The router ID is a unique IP address that can be assigned in the following ways:

- By default, the highest IP address of any active physical interface when OSPF starts is chosen as the router ID. The interface does not have to be part of the OSPF process, but it has to be up. There must be at least one "up" IP interface on the router for OSPF to use as the router ID. If no up interface with an IP address is available when the OSPF process starts, the following error message occurs:

  ```
  p5r2(config)#router ospf 1
  2w1d: %OSPF-4-NORTRID: OSPF process 1 cannot start.
  ```

- Alternatively, if a loopback interface exists, its IP address will always be preferred as the router ID instead of the IP address of a physical interface, because a loopback interface never goes down. If there is more than one loopback interface, then the highest IP address on any active loopback interface becomes the router ID.

- Alternatively, if the **router-id** *ip-address* OSPF router configuration command is used, it will override the use of the address of a physical or loopback interface as the router ID. Using the **router-id** command is the preferred procedure for setting the router ID.

KEY POINT	**Router ID Should Be Unique**
	The OSPF database uses the router ID to uniquely describe each router in the network. Remember that every router keeps a complete topology database of all routers and links in an area and network; therefore, router IDs should be unique throughout the OSPF autonomous system, no matter how they are configured.

After the router ID has been set, it does not change, even if the interface that the router is using for the router ID goes down. The OSPF router ID changes only if the router reloads or if the OSPF routing process restarts.

Loopback Interfaces

To modify the router ID to a loopback address, first define a loopback interface as follows:

```
Router(config)#interface loopback number
```

Configuring an IP address on a loopback interface overrides the highest IP address on any active physical interface being used as the router ID. OSPF is more stable if a loopback interface is configured, because the interface is always active and cannot fail, whereas a real interface could go down. For this reason, you should use a loopback address on all key routers. If the loopback address is advertised with the **network** command, then this address can be pinged for testing purposes. A private IP address can be used to save registered public IP addresses.

OSPF Router ID Stability

As mentioned earlier, if a physical interface fails, the router ID does not change. But if the physical interface fails and the router (or OSPF process) is restarted, the router ID changes. This change in router ID makes it more difficult for network administrators to troubleshoot and manage. The stability provided by using a loopback interface for the router ID comes from the router ID staying the same, regardless of the state of the physical interfaces.

NOTE   A loopback address requires a different subnet for each router, unless the host address itself is advertised. By default, OSPF advertises loopbacks as /32 host routes.

OSPF router-id Command

The **router-id** *ip-address* OSPF router configuration command ensures that OSPF selects a specific planned router ID. The *ip-address* parameter can be any unique arbitrary 32-bit value in an IP address format (dotted decimal).

After the **router-id** command is configured, use the **clear ip ospf process** EXEC command to restart the OSPF routing process, so the router reselects the new IP address as its router ID.

CAUTION   The **clear ip ospf process** command temporarily disrupts an operational network.

For example, the commands shown in Example 4-8 ensure that OSPF selects the preconfigured router ID 172.16.1.1.

Example 4-8   router-id *Command*

```
Router(config)#router ospf  1
Router(config-router)#router-id  172.16.1.1

Router#clear ip ospf process
```

NOTE   Changing the OSPF router ID of a router whose router ID was set by configuring a loopback interface requires you to either reboot the router or to disable and then enable OSPF. Changing a router ID of a router whose router ID was set by configuring it under the OSPF process requires only that the OSPF process be cleared, a much less drastic move.

Verifying the OSPF Router ID

Use the **show ip ospf** command to verify the router ID. This command also displays OSPF timer settings and other statistics, including the number of times the shortest path first algorithm has been executed. Optional parameters allow you to specify other information to be displayed.

Example 4-9 shows example output from this command when executed on router B in Figure 4-13.

Example 4-9   show ip ospf *Command from Router B in Figure 4-13*

```
RouterB#show ip ospf
Routing Process "ospf 50" with ID 10.64.0.2
 Supports only single TOS(TOS0) routes
 Supports opaque LSA
 Supports Link-local Signaling (LLS)
 Supports area transit capability
 It is an area border router
 Initial SPF schedule delay 5000 msecs
 Minimum hold time between two consecutive SPFs 10000 msecs
 Maximum wait time between two consecutive SPFs 10000 msecs
 Incremental-SPF disabled
 Minimum LSA interval 5 secs
 Minimum LSA arrival 1000 msecs
 LSA group pacing timer 240 secs
 Interface flood pacing timer 33 msecs
 Retransmission pacing timer 66 msecs
 Number of external LSA 0. Checksum Sum 0x000000
 Number of opaque AS LSA 0. Checksum Sum 0x000000
 Number of DCbitless external and opaque AS LSA 0
 Number of DoNotAge external and opaque AS LSA 0
 Number of areas in this router is 2. 2 normal 0 stub 0 nssa
 Number of areas transit capable is 0
 External flood list length 0
    Area BACKBONE(0)
    Area BACKBONE(0)
        Area has no authentication
        SPF algorithm last executed 00:01:25.028 ago
        SPF algorithm executed 7 times
        Area ranges are
        Number of LSA 6. Checksum Sum 0x01FE3E
        Number of opaque link LSA 0. Checksum Sum 0x000000
        Number of DCbitless LSA 0
        Number of indication LSA 0
        Number of DoNotAge LSA 0
        Flood list length 0
    Area 1
        Number of interfaces in this area is 1
        Area has no authentication
```

Example 4-9 **show ip ospf** *Command from Router B in Figure 4-13 (Continued)*

```
        SPF algorithm last executed 00:00:54.636 ago
        SPF algorithm executed 3 times
        Area ranges are
        Number of LSA 4. Checksum Sum 0x01228A
        Number of opaque link LSA 0. Checksum Sum 0x000000
        Number of DCbitless LSA 0
        Number of indication LSA 0
        Number of DoNotAge LSA 0
        Flood list length 0

RouterB#
```

OSPF Network Types

Understanding that an OSPF area is made up of different types of network links is important because the adjacency behavior is different for each network type, and OSPF must be properly configured to function correctly over certain network types.

Types of OSPF Networks

OSPF defines distinct types of networks, based on their physical link type. OSPF operation on each type is different, including how adjacencies are established and the configuration required.

There are three types of networks that are defined by OSPF:

- **Point-to-point**—A network that joins a single pair of routers.

- **Broadcast**—A multiaccess broadcast network, such as Ethernet.

- **Nonbroadcast multiaccess (NBMA)**—A network that interconnects more than two routers but that has no broadcast capability. Frame Relay, ATM, and X.25 are examples of NBMA networks. There are five modes of OSPF operation available for NBMA networks, as described later in the "OSPF over Frame Relay Configuration Options" section of this chapter.

OSPF operation and configuration on each of these network types is the focus of the rest of this section.

Adjacency Behavior for a Point-to-Point Link

A point-to-point network joins a single pair of routers. A T1 serial line configured with a link-layer protocol such as PPP or HDLC is an example of a point-to-point network.

On point-to-point networks, the router dynamically detects its neighboring routers by multicasting its hello packets to all OSPF routers using the address 224.0.0.5. On point-to-point networks, neighboring routers become adjacent whenever they can communicate directly. No DR or BDR election is performed, because a point-to-point link can have only two routers, so there is no need for a DR or BDR.

Usually, the IP source address of an OSPF packet is set to the address of the outgoing interface on the router. It is possible to use IP unnumbered interfaces with OSPF. On unnumbered interfaces, the IP source address is set to the IP address of another interface on the router.

The default OSPF hello and dead intervals on point-to-point links are 10 seconds and 40 seconds, respectively.

Adjacency Behavior for a Broadcast Network

An OSPF router on a multiaccess broadcast network such as Ethernet forms an adjacency with its DR and BDR. Adjacent routers have synchronized LSDBs. A common media segment is the basis for adjacency, such as two routers connected on the same Ethernet segment. When routers first come up on the Ethernet, they perform the hello process and then elect the DR and BDR. The routers then attempt to form adjacencies with the DR and BDR.

The routers on a segment must elect a DR and BDR to represent the multiaccess broadcast network. The BDR does not perform any DR functions when the DR is operating. Instead, the BDR receives all the information, but the DR performs the LSA forwarding and LSDB synchronization tasks. The BDR performs the DR tasks only if the DR fails. If the DR fails, the BDR automatically becomes the DR, and a new BDR election occurs. The DR and BDR add value to the network in the following ways:

- **Reducing routing update traffic**—The DR and BDR act as a central point of contact for link-state information exchange on a given multiaccess broadcast network; therefore, each router must establish a full adjacency with the DR and the BDR only. Instead of each router exchanging link-state information with every other router on the segment, each router sends the link-state information to the DR and BDR only. The DR represents the multiaccess broadcast network in the sense that it sends link-state information from each router to all other routers in the network. This flooding process significantly reduces the router-related traffic on a segment.

- **Managing link-state synchronization**—The DR and BDR ensure that the other routers on the network have the same link-state information about the internetwork. In this way, the DR and BDR reduce the number of routing errors.

KEY POINT | **Adjacencies with DR and BDR**

After a DR and BDR have been selected, any router added to the network establishes adjacencies with the DR and BDR only.

Electing a DR and BDR

To elect a DR and BDR, the routers view the OSPF priority value of the other routers during the hello packet exchange process and then use the following conditions to determine which router to select:

- The router with the highest priority value is the DR, as shown in Figure 4-14.

Figure 4-14 *Electing the DR and BDR*

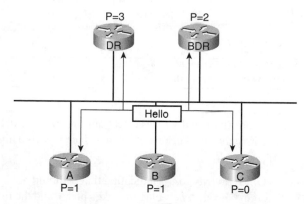

- The router with the second-highest priority value is the BDR.

- The default for the interface OSPF priority is 1. In case of a tie, the router ID is used. The router with the highest router ID becomes the DR. The router with the second-highest router ID becomes the BDR.

- A router with a priority of 0 cannot become the DR or BDR. A router that is not the DR or BDR is a DROTHER.

- If a router with a higher priority value gets added to the network, it does not preempt the DR and BDR. The only time a DR or BDR changes is if one of them is out of service. If the DR is out of service, the BDR becomes the DR, and a new BDR is selected. If the BDR is out of service, a new BDR is elected.

To determine whether the DR is out of service, the BDR uses the wait timer. This timer is a reliability feature. If the BDR does not confirm that the DR is forwarding LSAs before the wait timer expires, the BDR assumes that the DR is out of service.

KEY POINT

DR and BDR on Each Segment

The DR concept is at the link level; in a multiaccess broadcast environment each network segment has its own DR and BDR. A router connected to multiple multiaccess broadcast networks can be a DR on one segment and a regular (DROTHER) router on another segment.

Setting Priority for the DR Election

Use the **ip ospf priority** *number* interface configuration command to designate which router interfaces on a multiaccess link are the DR and the BDR. The default priority is 1, and the range is from 0 to 255. The highest priority interface becomes the DR, and the second-highest priority interface becomes the BDR. Any interfaces set to 0 priority cannot be involved in the DR or BDR election process.

Example 4-10 illustrates an example of configuring the FastEthernet interface on a router with an OSPF priority of 10.

Example 4-10 **ip ospf priority** *Command*

```
Router(config)#interface FastEthernet 0/0
Router(config-if)#ip ospf priority 10
```

> **NOTE**   An interface's priority usually takes effect only when the existing DR goes down. A DR does not relinquish its status just because a new interface reports a higher priority in its hello packet.
>
> Setting an interface's OSPF priority to 0—indicating that it should not be the DR or the BDR—takes effect immediately, however. A new election takes place, and the interface in question will not be elected for either the DR or BDR role.

Adjacency Behavior for a Nonbroadcast Multiaccess Network

When a single interface interconnects multiple sites over an NBMA network, the network's nonbroadcast nature can create reachability issues. NBMA networks can support more than two routers, but they have no inherent broadcast capability. To implement broadcasting or multicasting, the router replicates the packets to be broadcast or multicast and sends them individually on each permanent virtual circuit (PVC) to all destinations. This process is CPU- and bandwidth-intensive. If the NBMA topology is not fully meshed, a broadcast or multicast sent by one router does not reach all the other routers. Frame Relay, ATM, and X.25 are examples of NBMA networks.

The default OSPF hello and dead intervals on NBMA interfaces are 30 seconds and 120 seconds, respectively.

DR Election in an NBMA Topology

OSPF considers the NBMA environment to function similarly to other multiaccess media such as Ethernet. However, NBMA networks are usually hub-and-spoke topologies using PVCs or switched virtual circuits (SVCs). A hub-and-spoke topology means that the NBMA network is only a partial mesh. In these cases, the physical topology does not provide the multiaccess capability on which OSPF relies.

The election of the DR becomes an issue in NBMA topologies because the DR and BDR need to have full physical connectivity with all routers in the NBMA network. The DR and BDR also need to have a list of all the other routers so that they can establish adjacencies.

KEY POINT | **NBMA Adjacencies**

By default, OSPF cannot automatically build adjacencies with neighbor routers over NBMA interfaces.

OSPF over Frame Relay Configuration Options

Depending on the network topology, several OSPF configuration choices are available for a Frame Relay network.

With Frame Relay, remote sites interconnect in a variety of ways, as shown in Figure 4-15. By default, interfaces that support Frame Relay are multipoint connection types. The following examples are types of Frame Relay topologies:

■ **Star topology**—A star topology, also known as a hub-and-spoke configuration, is the most common Frame Relay network topology. In this topology, remote sites connect to a central site that generally provides a service or application. The star topology is the least expensive topology because it requires the fewest PVCs. The central router provides a multipoint connection because it typically uses a single interface to interconnect multiple PVCs.

■ **Full-mesh topology**—In a full-mesh topology, all routers have virtual circuits (VCs) to all other destinations. This method, although costly, provides direct connections from each site to all other sites and allows for redundancy. As the number of nodes in the full-mesh topology increases, the topology becomes increasingly expensive. To figure out how many VCs are needed to implement a full-mesh topology, use the formula $n(n-1)/2$, where n is the number of nodes in the network.

■ **Partial-mesh topology**—In a partial-mesh topology, not all sites have direct access to a central site. This method reduces the cost, compared to implementing a full-mesh topology.

Figure 4-15 *Frame Relay Topologies*

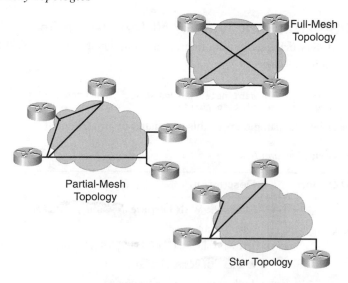

OSPF over NBMA Topology Modes of Operation

As described in RFC 2328, OSPF runs in one of the following two official modes in NBMA topologies:

- **Nonbroadcast**—The nonbroadcast (NBMA) mode simulates the operation of OSPF in broadcast networks. Neighbors must be configured manually, and DR and BDR election is required. This configuration is typically used with fully-meshed networks.

- **Point to multipoint**—Point-to-multipoint mode treats the nonbroadcast network as a collection of point-to-point links. In this environment, the routers automatically identify their neighboring routers but do not elect a DR and BDR. This configuration is typically used with partial-mesh networks.

The choice between nonbroadcast and point-to-multipoint modes determines how the Hello protocol and flooding work over the nonbroadcast network.

The main advantage of point-to-multipoint mode is that it requires less manual configuration. The main advantage of nonbroadcast mode is that there is less overhead traffic compared to point-to-multipoint mode.

In addition, Cisco offers the following modes for OSPF operation in an NBMA network:

- Point-to-multipoint nonbroadcast

- Broadcast

- Point-to-point

Selecting the OSPF Network Type for NBMA Networks

Use the **ip ospf network** interface configuration command to select the OSPF mode. The syntax of the command is as follows:

```
Router(config-if)#ip ospf network {broadcast | non-broadcast | point-to-multipoint
  [non-broadcast] | point-to-point}
```

Table 4-8 describes the parameters of this command in greater detail.

Table 4-8 ip ospf network *Command*

Command Options	Description
broadcast (Cisco mode)	Makes the WAN interface appear to be a LAN. One IP subnet. Uses a multicast OSPF hello packet to automatically discover the neighbors. DR and BDR are elected. Full- or partial-mesh topology.

Table 4-8 **ip ospf network** *Command (Continued)*

Command Options	Description
nonbroadcast (RFC-compliant mode)	One IP subnet. Neighbors must be manually configured. DR and BDR are elected. DR and BDR need to have full connectivity with all other routers. Full- or partial-mesh topology.
point-to-multipoint (RFC-compliant mode)	One IP subnet. Uses a multicast OSPF hello packet to automatically discover the neighbors. DR and BDR are not required. The router sends additional LSAs with more information about neighboring routers. Typically used in a partial-mesh or star topology.
point-to-multipoint nonbroadcast (Cisco mode)	If multicast and broadcast are not enabled on the VCs, the RFC-compliant point-to-multipoint mode cannot be used, because the router cannot dynamically discover its neighboring routers using the hello multicast packets; this Cisco mode should be used instead. Neighbors must be manually configured. DR and BDR election is not required.
point-to-point (Cisco mode)	Different IP subnet on each subinterface. No DR or BDR election. Used when only two routers need to form an adjacency on a pair of interfaces. Interfaces can be either LAN or WAN.

KEY POINT

Default OSPF Modes

The default OSPF mode on a point-to-point Frame Relay subinterface is the point-to-point mode.

The default OSPF mode on a Frame Relay multipoint subinterface is the nonbroadcast mode.

The default OSPF mode on a main Frame Relay interface is also the nonbroadcast mode.

OSPF Broadcast Mode Configuration

Broadcast mode is a workaround for statically listing all existing neighboring routers. The interface is set to broadcast and behaves as though the router connects to a LAN. DR and BDR election is still performed; therefore, take special care to ensure either a full-mesh topology or a static election of the DR based on the interface priority.

Example 4-11 shows a sample configuration of a Frame Relay router in a full-mesh topology, with the broadcast mode of operation defined.

Example 4-11 *Frame Relay Router in OSPF Broadcast Mode with Full-Mesh Topology*

```
Router(config)#interface serial 0/0/0
Router(config-if)#encapsulation frame-relay
Router(config-if)#ip ospf network broadcast
```

OSPF Nonbroadcast Mode Configuration   *NBMA*

In nonbroadcast mode, OSPF emulates operation over a broadcast network. A DR and BDR
are elected for the NBMA network, and the DR originates an LSA for the network. In this
environment, the routers are usually fully meshed to facilitate the establishment of adjacencies
among them. If the routers are not fully meshed, the DR and BDR should be selected manually
to ensure that the selected DR and BDR have full connectivity to all other neighbor routers.
Neighboring routers are statically defined to start the DR/BDR election process. When using
nonbroadcast mode, all routers are on one IP subnet.

For flooding over a nonbroadcast interface, the LSU packet must be replicated for each PVC. The
updates are sent to each of the interface's neighboring routers, as defined in the neighbor table.

When few neighbors exist in the network, nonbroadcast mode is the most efficient way to run
OSPF over NBMA networks because it has less overhead than point-to-multipoint mode.

Use the **neighbor** command to statically define adjacent relationships in NBMA networks using
the nonbroadcast mode. The syntax for this command is as follows:

```
Router(config-router)#neighbor ip-address [priority number] [poll-interval number]
   [cost number] [database-filter all]
```

Table 4-9 describes the **neighbor** command parameters in greater detail.

Table 4-9 **neighbor** *Command*

Parameter	Description
ip-address	Specifies the IP address of the neighboring router.
priority *number*	(Optional) Specifies priority of neighbor. The default is 0, which means that the neighboring router does not become the DR or BDR.
poll-interval *number*	(Optional) Specifies how long an NBMA interface waits before sending hellos to the neighbors even if the neighbor is inactive. The poll interval is defined in seconds.
cost *number*	(Optional) Assigns a cost to the neighbor in the form of an integer from 1 to 65535. Neighbors with no specific cost configured assume the cost of the interface based on the **ip ospf cost** command. For point-to-multipoint interfaces, the **cost** keyword and the *number* argument are the only options that are applicable. This keyword does not apply to nonbroadcast mode.
database-filter all	(Optional) Filters outgoing LSAs to an OSPF neighbor.

Figure 4-16 shows an example of statically defining adjacencies. All three routers are using the default nonbroadcast mode on their Frame Relay interfaces; therefore, neighboring routers must be manually configured on each. The **priority** parameter is set to 0 for routers B and C because a full-mesh topology does not exist. This configuration ensures that router A becomes the DR, because only router A has full connectivity to the other two routers. No BDR will be elected in this case.

Figure 4-16   *Using the* **neighbor** *Command in Nonbroadcast Mode*

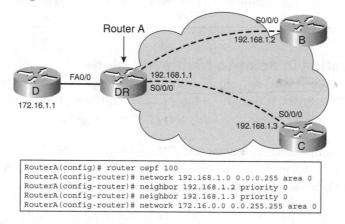

```
RouterA(config)# router ospf 100
RouterA(config-router)# network 192.168.1.0 0.0.0.255 area 0
RouterA(config-router)# neighbor 192.168.1.2 priority 0
RouterA(config-router)# neighbor 192.168.1.3 priority 0
RouterA(config-router)# network 172.16.0.0 0.0.255.255 area 0
```

> **NOTE**   The default priority on the **neighbor** command is supposed to be 0. However, during testing it was noted that configuring the priority in this way for nonbroadcast mode interfaces actually resulted in a priority of 1, not 0. Setting the OSPF priority to 0 at the interface level (with the **ip ospf priority** command) on routers B and C did result in a priority of 0 and the routers not being elected as DR or BDR.

In nonbroadcast mode, **neighbor** statements are required only on the DR and BDR. In a hub-and-spoke topology, **neighbor** statements must be placed on the hub, which must be configured to become the DR by being assigned a higher priority. **neighbor** statements are not mandatory on the spoke routers. In a full-mesh NBMA topology, you might need **neighbor** statements on all routers unless the DR and BDR are statically configured using the **ip ospf priority** command.

The **show ip ospf neighbor** command displays OSPF neighbor information on a per-interface basis, as described earlier in the "Verifying OSPF Operations" section.

Example 4-12 demonstrates sample output from the **show ip ospf neighbor** command for router A in Figure 4-16 (with the OSPF priorities of routers B and C set to 0 at the interface level, as noted). Router A has a serial Frame Relay interface and a FastEthernet interface. The serial 0/0/0 interface on this router has two neighbors; both have a state of **FULL/DROTHER**. **DROTHER** means that the neighboring router is not a DR or BDR (because Router A is the DR and there is no BDR in this network). The neighbor learned on FastEthernet 0/0 has a state of **FULL/BDR**, which means that it has successfully exchanged LSDB information with the router issuing the **show** command, and that it is the BDR.

Example 4-12 **show ip ospf neighbor** *Output for Router A in Figure 4-16*

```
RouterA#show ip ospf neighbor

Neighbor ID    Pri   State          Dead Time   Address        Interface
192.168.1.3     0   FULL/DROTHER    00:01:57    192.168.1.3    Serial0/0/0
192.168.1.2     0   FULL/DROTHER    00:01:33    192.168.1.2    Serial0/0/0
172.16.1.1      1   FULL/BDR        00:00:34    172.16.1.1     FastEthernet0/0
```

OSPF Configuration in Point-to-Multipoint Mode

Networks in RFC 2328-compliant point-to-multipoint mode are designed to work with partial-mesh or star topologies. In point-to-multipoint mode, OSPF treats all router-to-router connections over the nonbroadcast network as if they are point-to-point links.

In point-to-multipoint mode, DRs are not used, and a type 2 network LSA is not flooded to adjacent routers. (Chapter 5 covers the different types of LSAs in greater detail.) Instead, OSPF point-to-multipoint works by exchanging additional LSUs that are designed to automatically discover neighboring routers and add them to the neighbor table.

In large networks, using point-to-multipoint mode reduces the number of PVCs required for complete connectivity, because you are not required to have a full-mesh topology. In addition, not having a full-mesh topology reduces the number of neighbor entries in your neighborship table.

Point-to-multipoint mode has the following properties:

- **Does not require a full-mesh network**—This environment allows routing to occur between two routers that are not directly connected but that are connected through a router that has VCs to each of the two routers. All three routers connected to the Frame Relay network in Figure 4-17 could be configured for point-to-multipoint mode.

- **Does not require a static neighbor configuration**—In nonbroadcast mode, neighboring routers are statically defined to start the DR election process, and allow the exchange of routing updates. However, because point-to-multipoint mode treats the network as a collection of point-to-point links, multicast hello packets discover neighboring routers dynamically. Statically configuring neighboring routers is not necessary.

- **Uses one IP subnet**—As in nonbroadcast mode, when using point-to-multipoint mode, all routers are on one IP subnet.

- **Duplicates LSA packets**—Also as in nonbroadcast mode, when flooding out a nonbroadcast interface in point-to-multipoint mode, the router must replicate the LSU. The LSU packet is sent to each of the interface's neighboring routers, as defined in the neighbor table.

Figure 4-17 *Using OSPF Point-to-Multipoint Mode*

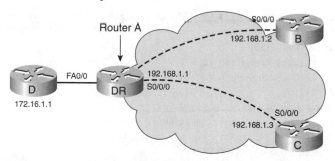

Example 4-13 shows partial configurations of routers A and C in Figure 4-17 in point-to-multipoint mode. This configuration does not require subinterfaces and uses only a single subnet. In point-to-multipoint mode, a DR or BDR is not required; therefore, DR and BDR election and priorities are not a concern.

Example 4-13 *Point-to-Multipoint Configuration for Routers A and C in Figure 4-17*

```
RouterA(config)#interface Serial0/0/0
RouterA(config-if)#ip address 192.168.1.1 255.255.255.0
RouterA(config-if)#encapsulation frame-relay
RouterA(config-if)#ip ospf network point-to-multipoint
<output omitted>
RouterA(config)#router ospf 100
RouterA(config-router)#log-adjacency-changes
RouterA(config-router)#network 172.16.0.0 0.0.255.255 area 0
RouterA(config-router)#network 192.168.1.0 0.0.0.255 area 0
RouterC(config)#interface Serial0/0/0
RouterC(config-if)#ip address 192.168.1.3 255.255.255.0
RouterC(config-if)#encapsulation frame-relay
RouterC(config-if)#ip ospf network point-to-multipoint
<output omitted>
RouterC(config)#router ospf 100
RouterC(config-router)#log-adjacency-changes
RouterC(config-router)#network 192.168.1.0 0.0.0.255 area 0
```

Example 4-14 demonstrates output from the **show ip ospf interface** command, which displays key OSPF details for each interface. This sample output is from router A in Figure 4-17.

Example 4-14 **show ip ospf interface** *Output from Router A in Figure 4-17*

```
RouterA#show ip ospf interface s0/0/0
Serial0/0/0 is up, line protocol is up
  Internet Address 192.168.1.1/24, Area 0
  Process ID 100, Router ID 192.168.1.1, Network Type POINT_TO_MULTIPOINT, Cost: 781
  Transmit Delay is 1 sec, State POINT_TO_MULTIPOINT
```

continues

Example 4-14 **show ip ospf interface** *Output from Router A in Figure 4-17 (Continued)*

```
   Timer intervals configured, Hello 30, Dead 120, Wait 120, Retransmit 5
     oob-resync timeout 120
     Hello due in 00:00:26
   Supports Link-local Signaling (LLS)
   Index 2/2, flood queue length 0
   Next 0x0(0)/0x0(0)
   Last flood scan length is 1, maximum is 1
   Last flood scan time is 0 msec, maximum is 4 msec
   Neighbor Count is 2, Adjacent neighbor count is 2
     Adjacent with neighbor 192.168.1.3
     Adjacent with neighbor 192.168.1.2
   Suppress hello for 0 neighbor(s)
RouterA#
```

The OSPF network type, area number, cost, and state of the interface are all displayed. The hello interval for a point-to-multipoint interface is 30 seconds and the dead interval is 120 seconds. Point-to-multipoint mode, point-to-multipoint nonbroadcast mode, and nonbroadcast mode use a 30-second hello timer, while point-to-point mode and broadcast mode use a 10-second hello timer. The hello and dead timers on the neighboring interfaces must match for the neighbors to form successful adjacencies.

The listed adjacent neighboring routers are all dynamically learned.

Cisco Point-to-Multipoint Nonbroadcast Mode

As mentioned, Cisco defines additional modes for OSPF neighbor relationships, including point-to-multipoint nonbroadcast. This mode is a Cisco extension of the RFC-compliant point-to-multipoint mode. You must statically define neighbors, and you can modify the cost of the link to the neighboring router to reflect the different bandwidths of each link. The RFC point-to-multipoint mode was developed to support underlying point-to-multipoint VCs that support multicast and broadcast. If multicast and broadcast are not enabled on the VCs, RFC-compliant point-to-multipoint mode cannot be used because the router cannot dynamically discover its neighboring routers using the hello multicast packets; the Cisco point-to-multipoint nonbroadcast mode should be used instead.

In point-to-multipoint nonbroadcast mode, you must statically define neighbors, like in nonbroadcast mode. As in point-to-multipoint mode, DRs and BDRs are not elected.

Using Subinterfaces in OSPF over Frame Relay Configuration

A physical interface can be split into multiple logical interfaces called subinterfaces. Each subinterface is defined as a point-to-point or multipoint interface. Subinterfaces were originally created to better handle issues caused by split horizon over NBMA for distance vector-based routing protocols. Each subinterface requires an IP subnet. A point-to-point subinterface has similar properties to a physical point-to-point interface.

Define subinterfaces using the **interface serial** *number.subinterface-number* {**multipoint** | **point-to-point**} global configuration command.

Table 4-10 lists the parameters of this command.

Table 4-10   **interface serial** *Command Parameters*

Parameter	Description
number.subinterface-number	Specifies the interface number and subinterface number. The subinterface number is in the range of 1 to 4294967293. The interface number that precedes the period (.) is the interface number to which this subinterface belongs.
multipoint	Specifies that the subinterface is multipoint; on multipoint subinterfaces routing IP, all routers are in the same subnet.
point-to-point	Specifies that the subinterface is point-to-point; on point-to-point subinterfaces routing IP, each pair of point-to-point routers is in its own subnet.

The choice of **point-to-point** or **multipoint** keywords affects the OSPF operation as described in the sections that follow.

Point-to-Point Subinterfaces

When point-to-point subinterfaces are configured, each virtual circuit (PVC and SVC) gets its own subinterface. A point-to-point subinterface has the properties of any physical point-to-point interface: there is no DR or BDR and neighbor discovery is automatic, so neighbors do not need to be configured.

Point-to-point mode is used when only two nodes exist on the NBMA network; this mode is typically used only with point-to-point subinterfaces. Each point-to-point connection is one IP subnet. An adjacency forms over the point-to-point network with no DR or BDR election.

In the example in Figure 4-18, Router A's serial 0/0/0 interface is configured with point-to-point subinterfaces. Although all three routers on the Frame Relay network have only one physical serial port, Router A appears to have two logical ports. Each logical port (subinterface) has its own IP address and operates as in OSPF point-to-point mode. Each subinterface is on its own IP subnet.

Figure 4-18 *OSPF Point-to-Point Subinterface Example*

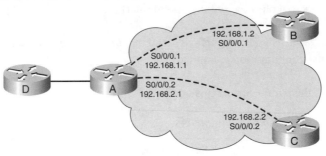

Point-to-Point Mode with NBMA

Point-to-point mode can also be used in the case of a single PVC on a serial interface where point-to-point behavior is desired. For example, this mode could be used to track the PVC when Hot Standby Router Protocol (HSRP) is used.

Multipoint Subinterfaces

When multipoint subinterfaces are configured, multiple virtual circuits (PVCs or SVCs) exist on a single subinterface. Multipoint Frame Relay subinterfaces default to OSPF nonbroadcast mode, which requires neighbors to be statically configured and a DR and BDR election.

In the example in Figure 4-19, router A has one point-to-point subinterface and one multipoint subinterface. The multipoint subinterface supports two other routers in a single subnet.

Figure 4-19 *Multipoint Subinterface Example*

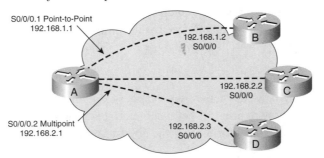

OSPF defaults to point-to-point mode on the point-to-point subinterface and to nonbroadcast mode on the multipoint subinterface.

OSPF Mode Summary

Table 4-11 briefly compares the different modes of operation for OSPF.

Table 4-11 *OSPF Mode Summary*

OSPF Mode	NBMA Preferred Topology	Subnet Address	Hello Timer	Adjacency	RFC or Cisco	Example
Broadcast	Full or partial mesh	Same	10 sec	Automatic DR/BDR elected	Cisco	LAN interface such as Ethernet
Nonbroadcast	Full or partial mesh	Same	30 sec	Manual configuration DR/BDR elected	RFC	Frame Relay configured on a serial interface
Point-to-multipoint	Partial mesh or star	Same	30 sec	Automatic No DR/BDR	RFC	OSPF over Frame Relay mode that eliminates the need for a DR; used when VCs support multicast and broadcast
Point-to-multipoint nonbroadcast	Partial mesh or star	Same	30 sec	Manual configuration No DR/BDR	Cisco	OSPF over Frame Relay mode that eliminates the need for a DR; used when VCs do not support multicast and broadcast
Point-to-point	Partial mesh or star, using subinterfaces	Different for each subinterface	10 sec	Automatic No DR/BDR	Cisco	Serial interface with point-to-point subinterfaces

Displaying OSPF Adjacency Activity

Use the **debug ip ospf adj** command to track OSPF adjacencies as they go up or down. Debugging allows you to see exactly which OSPF packets are being sent between routers. The ability to see packets as they are sent over a link is an invaluable tool to the troubleshooter.

> **NOTE** The last parameter in this command is **adj**, not **adjacency**.

The debug output in Example 4-15 illustrates the activity on a serial interface in point-to-point mode. No DR/BDR election occurs; however, the adjacency forms, allowing DBD packets to be sent during the exchange process. Notice that the neighbor relationship passes through the two-way phase and into the exchange phase. After database description packets are sent between routers, the neighbors move into the final state: full adjacency.

Example 4-15 **debug ip ospf adj** *Command Output for a Point-to-Point Serial Link*

```
RouterA# debug ip ospf adj
OSPF: Interface Serial0/0/0.1 going Up
OSPF: Build router LSA for area 0, router ID 192.168.1.1, seq 0x80000023
OSPF: Rcv DBD from 192.168.1.2 on Serial0/0/0.1 seq 0xCF0 opt 0x52 flag 0x7 len 32   mtu
    1500 state INIT
OSPF: 2 Way Communication to 192.168.1.2 on Serial0/0/0.1, state 2WAY
OSPF: Send DBD to 192.168.1.2 on Serial0/0/0.1 seq 0xF4D opt 0x52 flag 0x7 len 32
OSPF: NBR Negotiation Done. We are the SLAVE
OSPF: Send DBD to 192.168.1.2 on Serial0/0/0.1 seq 0xCF0 opt 0x52 flag 0x2 len 132
OSPF: Rcv DBD from 192.168.1.2 on Serial0/0/0.1 seq 0xCF1 opt 0x52 flag 0x3 len 132   mtu
    1500 state EXCHANGE
OSPF: Send DBD to 192.168.1.2 on Serial0/0/0.1 seq 0xCF1 opt 0x52 flag 0x0 len 32
OSPF: Database request to 192.168.1.2
OSPF: sent LS REQ packet to 192.168.1.2, length 12
OSPF: Rcv DBD from 192.168.1.2 on Serial0/0/0.1 seq 0xCF2 opt 0x52 flag 0x1 len 32   mtu
    1500 state EXCHANGE
OSPF: Exchange Done with 192.168.1.2 on Serial0/0/0.1
OSPF: Send DBD to 192.168.1.2 on Serial0/0/0.1 seq 0xCF2 opt 0x52 flag 0x0 len 32
OSPF: Synchronized with 192.168.1.2 on Serial0/0/0.1, state FULL
%OSPF-5-ADJCHG: Process 100, Nbr 192.168.1.2 on Serial0/0/0.1 from LOADING to FULL,
    Loading Done
OSPF: Build router LSA for area 0, router ID 192.168.1.1, seq 0x80000024
```

The debug output in Example 4-16 demonstrates the DR/BDR election process on a FastEthernet interface. The OSPF default behavior on a FastEthernet link is broadcast mode. First, the DR and BDR are selected, and then the exchange process occurs.

Example 4-16 **debug ip ospf adj** *Command Output for a FastEthernet Link*

```
RouterA#debug ip ospf adj
OSPF: Interface FastEthernet0/0 going Up
OSPF: Build router LSA for area 0, router ID 192.168.1.1,seq 0x80000008
%LINEPROTO-5-UPDOWN: Line protocol on Interface FastEthernet0/0, changed state to up
OSPF: 2 Way Communication to 172.16.1.1 on FastEthernet0/0, state 2WAY
OSPF: end of Wait on interface FastEthernet0/0
OSPF: DR/BDR election on FastEthernet0/0
OSPF: Elect BDR 192.168.1.1
OSPF: Elect DR 192.168.1.1
OSPF: Elect BDR 172.16.1.1
OSPF: Elect DR 192.168.1.1
DR: 192.168.1.1 (Id)   BDR: 172.16.1.1 (Id)
OSPF: Send DBD to 172.16.1.1 on FastEthernet0/0 seq 0xDCE opt 0x52 flag 0x7 len 32
OSPF: No full nbrs to build Net Lsa for interface FastEthernet0/0
```

Example 4-16   **debug ip ospf adj** *Command Output for a FastEthernet Link (Continued)*

```
OSPF: Neighbor change Event on interface FastEthernet0/0
OSPF; DR/BDR election on FastEthernet0/0
OSPF: Elect BDR 172.16.1.1
OSPF: Elect DR 192.168.1.1
DR: 192.168.1.1 (Id)   BDR: 172.16.1.1 (Id)
OSPF: Neighbor change Event on interface FastEthernet0/0
OSPF: DR/BDR election on FastEthernet0/0
OSPF: Elect BDR 172.16.1.1
OSPF: Elect DR 192.168.1.1
DR: 192.168.1.1 (Id)   BDR: 172.16.1.1 (Id)
OSPF: Rcv DBD from 172.16.1.1 on FastEthernet0/0 seq 0x14B 7 opt 0x52 flag 0x7 len 32  mtu
    1500 state EXSTART
OSPF: First DBD and we are not SLAVE-if)#
OSPF: Send DBD to 172.16.1.1 on FastEthernet0/0 seq 0xDCE opt 0x52 flag 0x7 len 32
OSPF: Retransmitting DBD to 172.16.1.1 on FastEthernet0/0[1]
OSPF: Rcv DBD from 172.16.1.1 on FastEthernet0/0 seq 0xDCE opt 0x52 flag 0x2 len 152  mtu
    1500 state EXSTART
OSPF: NBR Negotiation Done. We are the MASTER
OSPF: Send DBD to 172.16.1.1 on FastEthernet0/0 seq 0xDCF opt 0x52 flag 0x3 len 132
OSPF: Database request to 172.16.1.1
OSPF: sent LS REQ packet to 172.16.1.1, length 24
OSPF: Rcv DBD from 172.16.1.1 on FastEthernet0/0 seq 0xDCF opt 0x52 flag 0x0 len 32  mtu
    1500 state EXCHANGE
OSPF: Send DBD to 172.16.1.1 on FastEthernet0/0 seq 0xDD0
opt 0x52 flag 0x1 len 32
OSPF: No full nbrs to build Net Lsa for interface FastEthernet0/0
OSPF: Build network LSA for FastEthernet0/0, router ID 192.168.1.1
OSPF: Build network LSA for FastEthernet0/0, router ID 192.168.1.1
OSPF: Rcv DBD from 172.16.1.1 on FastEthernet0/0 seq 0xDD0 opt 0x52 flag 0x0 len 32  mtu
    1500 state EXCHANGE
OSPF: Exchange Done with 172.16.1.1 on FastEthernet0/0
OSPF: Synchronized with 172.16.1.1 on FastEthernet0/0, state FULL
%OSPF-5-ADJCHG: Process 100, Nbr 172.16.1.1 on FastEthernet0/0 from LOADING to FULL,
    Loading Done
OSPF: Build router LSA for area 0, router ID 192.168.1.1, seq 0x80000009
OSPF: Build network LSA for FastEthernet0/0, router ID 192.168.1.1
OSPF: Build network LSA for FastEthernet0/0, router ID 192.168.1.1
```

Summary

In this chapter you learned about the OSPF link-state routing protocol with a focus on the following topics:

- The OSPF tables—the neighbor table (also called the adjacency database), the topology table (also called the LSDB), and the routing table (also called the forwarding database).

- The two-tier hierarchical area structure, including how OSPF routers build adjacencies using the Hello protocol.

- The five types of OSPF packets—hello, DBD, LSR, LSU, and LSAck—and how they are used by OSPF.

- Basic OSPF configuration commands.

- The three types of networks defined by OSPF: point-to-point, broadcast, and NBMA.

- The five modes of OSPF operation available for NBMA networks: broadcast, nonbroadcast, point-to-multipoint, point-to-multipoint nonbroadcast, and point-to-point.

References

For additional information, refer to these resources:

- http://www.cisco.com document: "OSPF Design Guide"

- http://www.cisco.com document: "Designing Large-Scale IP Internetworks"

- Radia Perlman's book *Interconnections: Bridges, Routers, Switches, and Internetworking Protocols (2nd Edition)*, Addison-Wesley Professional (September 14, 1999), an excellent reference for understanding routing protocol sequence numbering and aging

Configuration Exercise: Configuring and Examining OSPF in a Single Area

In this exercise, you configure your pod as an OSPF single area.

Introduction to the Configuration Exercises

This book uses Configuration Exercises to help you practice configuring routers with the commands and topics presented. If you have access to real hardware, you can try these exercises on your routers. See Appendix B, "Configuration Exercise Equipment Requirements and Backbone Configurations," for a list of recommended equipment and configuration commands for the backbone routers. However, even if you don't have access to any routers, you can go through the exercises and keep a log of your own running configurations or just read through the solution. Commands used and solutions to the Configuration Exercises are provided within the exercises.

In the Configuration Exercises, the network is assumed to consist of two pods, each with four routers. The pods are interconnected to a backbone. You configure pod 1. No interaction between the two pods is required, but you might see some routes from the other pod in your routing tables in some exercises if you have it configured. In most of the exercises, the backbone has only one router; in some cases, another router is added to the backbone. Each Configuration Exercise assumes that you have completed the previous chapters' Configuration Exercises on your pod.

> **NOTE**   Throughout this exercise, the pod number is referred to as *x*, and the router number is referred to as *y*. Substitute the appropriate numbers as needed.

Exercise Objective

The objectives of this exercise are as follows:

■ Configure OSPF for a single area.

■ Configure a stable router ID.

■ Observe OSPF neighbor formation.

■ Observe OSPF DR and BDR elections.

Visual Objective

Figure 4-20 illustrates the topology used and what you will accomplish in this exercise.

Figure 4-20   *Configuring and Examining OSPF in a Single Area*

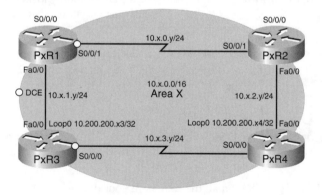

Command List

In this exercise, you use the commands in Table 4-12, listed in logical order. Refer to this list if you need configuration command assistance during the exercise.

> **CAUTION**   Although the command syntax is shown in this table, the addresses shown are typically for the P*x*R1 and P*x*R3 routers in Figure 4-20. Be careful when addressing your routers! Refer to the exercise instructions and the appropriate visual objective diagram for addressing details.

Table 4-12 *Configuration Exercise Command List*

Command	Description
(config)#**router ospf 1**	Turns on OSPF. The process number is not communicated to other routers.
(config-router)#**network 10.**x**.0.0 0.0.255.255 area x**	Specifies the interfaces on which OSPF will run in area x.
#**show ip ospf**	Shows OSPF process parameters.
(config)#**interface loopback 0**	Creates interface loopback 0.
(config-router)#**router-id 10.0.0.**xy	Configures the OSPF router ID.
#**clear ip ospf process**	Resets the OSPF process.
#**show ip ospf neighbor**	Shows all OSPF neighbors.
#**show ip ospf neighbor detail**	Displays details of all OSPF neighbors.
#**debug ip ospf events**	Displays OSPF process evolution.
(config-if)#**ip ospf priority 0**	Sets the OSPF priority to 0, which removes the router from being the DR or BDR on that interface.

NOTE   The exercise tasks include answers and solutions. Some answers cover multiple steps; the answers are given after the last step to which that answer applies.

Task 1: Cleaning Up

Before starting to investigate OSPF, you need to remove Enhanced Interior Gateway Routing Protocol (EIGRP) configuration.

Step 1   Disable EIGRP on all the routers in your pod.

Solution:

The following shows how to perform the required step on the P1R1 router:

```
P1R1(config)#no router eigrp 1
```

Step 2   Enable the serial interface S0/0/0 between the internal routers (PxR3 and PxR4).

Solution:

The following shows how to perform the required step on the P1R3 router:

```
P1R3(config)#int s0/0/0
P1R3(config-if)#no shutdown
```

Task 2: Configuring Single-Area OSPF Within Your Pod

In this task, you configure single-area OSPF within your pod. Complete the following steps:

Step 1   Shut down the serial 0/0/0 interfaces (the Frame Relay connections) on the edge routers P*x*R1 and P*x*R2, to isolate your pod.

Solution:

The following shows how to perform the required step on the P1R1 router:

```
P1R1(config)#int s0/0/0
P1R1(config-if)#shutdown
```

Step 2   Configure OSPF on all your pod routers in area *x*, where *x* is your pod number. To avoid problems in a later exercise, use the **network** command for your pod network 10.*x*.0.0, rather than the entire 10.0.0.0 network.

> **NOTE**   In this and subsequent OSPF exercises you may use the **ip ospf** *process-id* **area** *area-id* interface configuration command to enable OSPF explicitly on an interface, instead of using the **network** command. Note, however, that the examples shown use the **network** command.

Solution:

The following shows how to perform the required step on the P1R1 router:

```
P1R1(config)#router ospf 1
P1R1(config-router)#network 10.1.0.0 0.0.255.255 area 1
```

Step 3   Use the proper **show** command to verify the OSPF router ID on the pod routers.

What is the OSPF router ID of your pod routers? Is it what you expected it to be?

Solution:

The following shows the output on the P1R1 router:

```
P1R1#show ip ospf
 Routing Process "ospf 1" with ID 10.1.1.1
 Supports only single TOS(TOS0) routes
 Supports opaque LSA
 Supports Link-local Signaling (LLS)
 Supports area transit capability
 Initial SPF schedule delay 5000 msecs
 Minimum hold time between two consecutive SPFs 10000 msecs
 Maximum wait time between two consecutive SPFs 10000 msecs
 Incremental-SPF disabled
 Minimum LSA interval 5 secs
 Minimum LSA arrival 1000 msecs
 LSA group pacing timer 240 secs
```

```
Interface flood pacing timer 33 msecs
Retransmission pacing timer 66 msecs
Number of external LSA 0. Checksum Sum 0x000000
Number of opaque AS LSA 0. Checksum Sum 0x000000
Number of DCbitless external and opaque AS LSA 0
Number of DoNotAge external and opaque AS LSA 0
Number of areas in this router is 1. 1 normal 0 stub 0 nssa
Number of areas transit capable is 0
External flood list length 0
    Area 1
        Number of interfaces in this area is 2
        Area has no authentication
        SPF algorithm last executed 00:00:25.236 ago
        SPF algorithm executed 5 times
        Area ranges are
        Number of LSA 6. Checksum Sum 0x02B765
        Number of opaque link LSA 0. Checksum Sum 0x000000
        Number of DCbitless LSA 0
        Number of indication LSA 0
        Number of DoNotAge LSA 0
        Flood list length 0

P1R1#
```

The router IDs of the pod 1 routers are as follows:

■ **Router ID of P1R1**—10.1.1.1

■ **Router ID of P1R2**—10.1.2.2

■ **Router ID of P1R3**—10.1.3.3

■ **Router ID of P1R4**—10.1.3.4

The router IDs are what you would expect—by default, the router ID is the highest active IP address on the router. Notice that P1R1 and P1R2 have not chosen their Frame Relay IP addresses as their router IDs, because those interfaces were not active when OSPF started.

Task 3: Configuring a Stable OSPF Router ID

In this task, you create a stable OSPF router ID on all routers in your pod. Complete the following steps:

Step 1   Configure a loopback 0 interface on P*x*R3 and P*x*R4 with the IP address 10.200.200.*xy*/32, where *x* is the pod number and *y* is the router number.

Solution:

The following shows how to perform the required step on the P1R3 router:

```
P1R3(config)#int loopback 0
P1R3(config-if)#ip address 10.200.200.13 255.255.255.255
```

> **NOTE**   A mask of /32 is used so that the two loopback addresses do not appear to be on the same subnet.

Step 2   Use the proper **show** command to verify the OSPF router ID on the internal routers. The router ID is supposed to be the highest loopback IP address or, if there is no loopback address, the highest active IP address. What is the OSPF router ID of your pod's internal routers now? Is it what you expected it to be?

Solution:

The following shows the output on the P1R3 router:

```
P1R3#show ip ospf
 Routing Process "ospf 1" with ID 10.1.3.3
 Supports only single TOS(TOS0) routes
 Supports opaque LSA
 Supports Link-local Signaling (LLS)
 Supports area transit capability
 Initial SPF schedule delay 5000 msecs
 Minimum hold time between two consecutive SPFs 10000 msecs
 Maximum wait time between two consecutive SPFs 10000 msecs
 Incremental-SPF disabled
 Minimum LSA interval 5 secs
 Minimum LSA arrival 1000 msecs
 LSA group pacing timer 240 secs
 Interface flood pacing timer 33 msecs
 Retransmission pacing timer 66 msecs
 Number of external LSA 0. Checksum Sum 0x000000
 Number of opaque AS LSA 0. Checksum Sum 0x000000
 Number of DCbitless external and opaque AS LSA 0
 Number of DoNotAge external and opaque AS LSA 0
 Number of areas in this router is 1. 1 normal 0 stub 0 nssa
 Number of areas transit capable is 0
 External flood list length 0
    Area 1
        Number of interfaces in this area is 2
        Area has no authentication
        SPF algorithm last executed 00:07:54.996 ago
        SPF algorithm executed 4 times
        Area ranges are
        Number of LSA 6. Checksum Sum 0x02B765
        Number of opaque link LSA 0. Checksum Sum 0x000000
        Number of DCbitless LSA 0
        Number of indication LSA 0
        Number of DoNotAge LSA 0
        Flood list length 0

  P1R3#
```

The router ID of P1R3 is 10.1.3.3 (you might have expected it to be 10.200.200.13). The router ID of P1R4 is 10.1.3.4 (although you might have expected it to be 10.200.200.14).

Step 3   Notice that in the previous step, the router ID did not change; this is a stability feature of Cisco IOS. Because the loopback interface was configured after the OSPF process was configured, the router ID did not change. If the router ID did change, the LSAs would be invalid, and the network would have to reconverge. Save your configuration, and reload the internal routers so that their router IDs will change.

Solution:

The following shows how to perform the required step on the P1R3 router:

```
P1R3#copy run start
Destination filename [startup-config]?
Building configuration...
[OK]
P1R3#reload
Proceed with reload? [confirm]
```

Step 4   After the internal routers reload, use the proper **show** command to verify that their router IDs changed to the IP address of their loopback 0 interfaces.

Solution:

The following shows the output on the P1R3 router. The router ID did change as expected:

```
P1R3#show ip ospf
 Routing Process "ospf 1" with ID 10.200.200.13
 Supports only single TOS(TOS0) routes
 Supports opaque LSA
 Supports Link-local Signaling (LLS)
 Supports area transit capability
 Initial SPF schedule delay 5000 msecs
 Minimum hold time between two consecutive SPFs 10000 msecs
 Maximum wait time between two consecutive SPFs 10000 msecs
 Incremental-SPF disabled
 Minimum LSA interval 5 secs
 Minimum LSA arrival 1000 msecs
 LSA group pacing timer 240 secs
 Interface flood pacing timer 33 msecs
 Retransmission pacing timer 66 msecs
 Number of external LSA 0. Checksum Sum 0x000000
 Number of opaque AS LSA 0. Checksum Sum 0x000000
 Number of DCbitless external and opaque AS LSA 0
 Number of DoNotAge external and opaque AS LSA 0
 Number of areas in this router is 1. 1 normal 0 stub 0 nssa
 Number of areas transit capable is 0
 External flood list length 0
    Area 1
        Number of interfaces in this area is 2
        Area has no authentication
        SPF algorithm last executed 00:00:55.724 ago
        SPF algorithm executed 8 times
        Area ranges are
        Number of LSA 6. Checksum Sum 0x02E601
        Number of opaque link LSA 0. Checksum Sum 0x000000
        Number of DCbitless LSA 0
        Number of indication LSA 0
        Number of DoNotAge LSA 0
        Flood list length 0

    P1R3#
```

Step 5   On the PxR1 and PxR2 routers, set the OSPF router ID to 10.0.0.xy, where x is the pod number and y is the router number, using the **router-id** command in the OSPF router configuration mode. Note: Do not configure loopback interfaces on PxR1 and PxR2; loopback interfaces on these routers are configured in a later exercise, in Chapter 7, "Manipulating Routing Updates."

Step 6   Reset the OSPF process with the privileged mode command **clear ip ospf process** to make the **router-id** command take effect.

> **NOTE**   Changing the OSPF router ID of a router whose router ID was set by configuring a loopback interface requires you to either reboot the router or to disable and then enable OSPF. Changing a router ID of a router whose router ID was set by configuring it under the OSPF process requires only that the OSPF process be cleared, a much less drastic move.

Solution:

The following shows how to do the required steps on the P1R1 router:

```
P1R1(config)#router ospf 1
P1R1(config-router)#router-id 10.0.0.11
Reload or use "clear ip ospf process" command, for this to take effect
P1R1(config-router)#

P1R1#clear ip ospf process
Reset ALL OSPF processes? [no]: y
P1R1#
```

Step 7   Use the proper **show** command to verify that the router IDs of the edge routers have changed to 10.0.0.*xy* after the OSPF process was reset.

Solution:

The following shows the output on the P1R1 router. The router ID did change as expected:

```
P1R1#show ip ospf
 Routing Process "ospf 1" with ID 10.0.0.11
 Supports only single TOS(TOS0) routes
 Supports opaque LSA
 Supports Link-local Signaling (LLS)
 Supports area transit capability
 Initial SPF schedule delay 5000 msecs
 Minimum hold time between two consecutive SPFs 10000 msecs
 Maximum wait time between two consecutive SPFs 10000 msecs
 Incremental-SPF disabled
 Minimum LSA interval 5 secs
 Minimum LSA arrival 1000 msecs
 LSA group pacing timer 240 secs
 Interface flood pacing timer 33 msecs
 Retransmission pacing timer 66 msecs
 Number of external LSA 0. Checksum Sum 0x000000
 Number of opaque AS LSA 0. Checksum Sum 0x000000
 Number of DCbitless external and opaque AS LSA 0
 Number of DoNotAge external and opaque AS LSA 0
 Number of areas in this router is 1. 1 normal 0 stub 0 nssa
 Number of areas transit capable is 0
 External flood list length 0
    Area 1
        Number of interfaces in this area is 2
        Area has no authentication
        SPF algorithm last executed 00:00:01.412 ago
        SPF algorithm executed 4 times
        Area ranges are
```

```
            Number of LSA 6. Checksum Sum 0x04216C
            Number of opaque link LSA 0. Checksum Sum 0x000000
            Number of DCbitless LSA 0
            Number of indication LSA 0
            Number of DoNotAge LSA 0
            Flood list length 2

     P1R1#
```

Step 8   Before finishing, make sure that all neighbors are in communication (in the FULL state) on all your pod routers. This will help you avoid problems in future exercises.

Solution:

The following shows the output on the P1R1 router. P1R1 is in the FULL state with both of its neighbors:

```
P1R1#show ip ospf neighbor

Neighbor ID     Pri   State         Dead Time   Address     Interface
10.0.0.12        0    FULL/  -      00:00:33    10.1.0.2    Serial0/0/1
10.200.200.13    1    FULL/DR       00:00:33    10.1.1.3    FastEthernet0/0

P1R1#show ip ospf neighbor detail
 Neighbor 10.0.0.12, interface address 10.1.0.2
    In the area 1 via interface Serial0/0/1
    Neighbor priority is 0, State is FULL, 6 state changes
    DR is 0.0.0.0 BDR is 0.0.0.0
    Options is 0x52
    LLS Options is 0x1 (LR)
    Dead timer due in 00:00:39
    Neighbor is up for 00:03:28
    Index 1/1, retransmission queue length 0, number of retransmission 1
    First 0x0(0)/0x0(0) Next 0x0(0)/0x0(0)
    Last retransmission scan length is 1, maximum is 1
    Last retransmission scan time is 0 msec, maximum is 0 msec
 Neighbor 10.200.200.13, interface address 10.1.1.3
    In the area 1 via interface FastEthernet0/0
    Neighbor priority is 1, State is FULL, 6 state changes
    DR is 10.1.1.3 BDR is 10.1.1.1
    Options is 0x52
    LLS Options is 0x1 (LR)
    Dead timer due in 00:00:39
    Neighbor is up for 00:03:30
    Index 2/2, retransmission queue length 0, number of retransmission 1
    First 0x0(0)/0x0(0) Next 0x0(0)/0x0(0)
    Last retransmission scan length is 1, maximum is 1
    Last retransmission scan time is 0 msec, maximum is 0 msec
  P1R1#
```

Step 9   Display the IP routing table to be sure that you are getting OSPF routes.

Solution:

The following shows the output on the P1R1 router:

```
P1R1#show ip route
<output omitted>
Gateway of last resort is not set
```

```
         10.0.0.0/24 is subnetted, 4 subnets
O        10.1.3.0 [110/782] via 10.1.1.3, 00:04:47, FastEthernet0/0
O        10.1.2.0 [110/782] via 10.1.0.2, 00:04:47, Serial0/0/1
C        10.1.1.0 is directly connected, FastEthernet0/0
C        10.1.0.0 is directly connected, Serial0/0/1
P1R1#
```

All expected routes are present in the routing table.

Task 4: Observing the OSPF Process

In this task, you examine the **debug ip ospf events** command output to determine each step of the OSPF process, OSPF adjacency building, and election of the DR and BDR. Complete the following steps:

Step 1   Examine the OSPF process with the **debug ip ospf events** command on one of your pod routers.

Step 2   Reset the OSPF process with the **clear ip ospf process** command, and examine OSPF adjacency building and the election of a DR and BDR.

Solution:

The following shows the output on the P1R1 router. Comments have been added to explain some of the output; the comments begin with the exclamation point character (!):

```
P1R1#debug ip ospf events
OSPF events debugging is on
*Apr 25 19:40:00.942: OSPF: Rcv hello from 10.0.0.12 area 1 from Serial0/0/1 10.1.0.2
*Apr 25 19:40:00.942: OSPF: End of hello processing
*Apr 25 19:40:01.098: OSPF: Rcv hello from 10.200.200.13 area 1 from FastEthernet0/0
    10.1.1.3
*Apr 25 19:40:01.098: OSPF: End of hello processing
P1R1#
*Apr 25 19:40:02.970: OSPF: Send hello to 224.0.0.5 area 1 on Serial0/0/1 from 10.1.0.1
*Apr 25 19:40:02.974: OSPF: Send hello to 224.0.0.5 area 1 on FastEthernet0/0 from
    10.1.1.1
*Apr 25 19:40:00.942: OSPF: Rcv hello from 10.0.0.12 area 1 from Serial0/0/1 10.1.0.2
*Apr 25 19:40:00.942: OSPF: End of hello processing
*Apr 25 19:40:01.098: OSPF: Rcv hello from 10.200.200.13 area 1 from FastEthernet0/0
    10.1.1.3
*Apr 25 19:40:01.098: OSPF: End of hello processing
*Apr 25 19:40:02.970: OSPF: Send hello to 224.0.0.5 area 1 on Serial0/0/1 from 10.1.0.1
*Apr 25 19:40:02.974: OSPF: Send hello to 224.0.0.5 area 1 on FastEthernet0/0 from
    10.1.1.1
P1R1#clear ip ospf process
Reset ALL OSPF processes? [no]: y
P1R1#
*Apr 25 19:40:20.938: OSPF: Rcv hello from 10.0.0.12 area 1 from Serial0/0/1 10.1.0.2
*Apr 25 19:40:20.942: OSPF: End of hello processing
*Apr 25 19:40:21.098: OSPF: Rcv hello from 10.200.200.13 area 1 from FastEthernet0/0
    10.1.1.3
*Apr 25 19:40:21.098: OSPF: End of hello processing
*Apr 25 19:40:21.198: OSPF: Flushing External Links
*Apr 25 19:40:21.198: OSPF: Flushing Opaque AS Links
*Apr 25 19:40:21.234: OSPF: Flushing Link states in area 1
```

```
*Apr 25 19:40:21.270: OSPF: Interface Serial0/0/1 going Down
! Neighbor relationship goes to the DOWN state as the process is cleared.
*Apr 25 19:40:21.270: %OSPF-5-ADJCHG: Process 1, Nbr 10.0.0.12 on Serial0/0/1 from
   FULL to DOWN, Neighbor Down: Interface down or detached
*Apr 25 19:40:21.270: OSPF: Interface FastEthernet0/0 going Down
*Apr 25 19:40:21.270: OSPF: Neighbor change Event on interface FastEthernet0/0
*Apr 25 19:40:21.270: OSPF: DR/BDR election on FastEthernet0/0
*Apr 25 19:40:21.270: OSPF: Elect BDR 0.0.0.0
*Apr 25 19:40:21.270: OSPF: Elect DR 10.200.200.13
*Apr 25 19:40:21.270: OSPF: Elect BDR 0.0.0.0
*Apr 25 19:40:21.270: OSPF: Elect DR 10.200.200.13
*Apr 25 19:40:21.270:           DR: 10.200.200.13 (Id)    BDR: none
*Apr 25 19:40:21.270: %OSPF-5-ADJCHG: Process 1, Nbr 10.200.200.13 on FastEthernet0/0
   from FULL to DOWN, Neighbor Down: Interface down or detached
*Apr 25 19:40:21.270: OSPF: Neighbor change Event on interface FastEthernet0/0
*Apr 25 19:40:21.270: OSPF: DR/BDR election on FastEthernet0/0
*Apr 25 19:40:21.270: OSPF: Elect BDR 0.0.0.0
*Apr 25 19:40:21.270: OSPF: Elect DR 0.0.0.0
*Apr 25 19:40:21.270:           DR: none    BDR: none
*Apr 25 19:40:21.270: OSPF: Remember old DR 10.200.200.13 (id)
!OSPF process is starting up again; hellos are sent on each interface
*Apr 25 19:40:21.282: OSPF: Interface Serial0/0/1 going Up
*Apr 25 19:40:21.282: OSPF: Send hello to 224.0.0.5 area 1 on Serial0/0/1 from 10.1.0.1
*Apr 25 19:40:21.282: OSPF: Interface FastEthernet0/0 going Up
*Apr 25 19:40:21.282: OSPF: Send hello to 224.0.0.5 area 1 on FastEthernet0/0 from
   10.1.1.1
*Apr 25 19:40:30.938: OSPF: Rcv hello from 10.0.0.12 area 1 from Serial0/0/1 10.1.0.2
!After hellos sent and received, communication is in 2-Way state
*Apr 25 19:40:30.942: OSPF: 2 Way Communication to 10.0.0.12 on Serial0/0/1, state 2WAY
*Apr 25 19:40:30.942: OSPF: Send DBD to 10.0.0.12 on Serial0/0/1 seq 0xAED opt 0x52
   flag 0x7 len 32
*Apr 25 19:40:30.942: OSPF: End of hello processing
!Exchanging DBDs on Serial 0/0/1
*Apr 25 19:40:30.962: OSPF: Rcv DBD from 10.0.0.12 on Serial0/0/1 seq 0x1F9A opt 0x52
   flag 0x7 len 32 mtu 1500 state EXSTART
*Apr 25 19:40:30.962: OSPF: NBR Negotiation Done. We are the SLAVE
*Apr 25 19:40:30.962: OSPF: Send DBD to 10.0.0.12 on Serial0/0/1 seq 0x1F9A opt0x52
   flag 0x2 len 52
*Apr 25 19:40:30.994: OSPF: Rcv DBD from 10.0.0.12 on Serial0/0/1 seq 0x1F9B opt 0x52
   flag 0x3 len 112  mtu 1500 state EXCHANGE
*Apr 25 19:40:30.994: OSPF: Send DBD to 10.0.0.12 on Serial0/0/1 seq 0x1F9B opt0x52
   flag 0x0 len 32
*Apr 25 19:40:30.994: OSPF: Database request to 10.0.0.12
*Apr 25 19:40:30.994: OSPF: sent LS REQ packet to 10.1.0.2, length 48
*Apr 25 19:40:31.014: OSPF: Rcv DBD from 10.0.0.12 on Serial0/0/1 seq 0x1F9C opt 0x52
   flag 0x1 len 32  mtu 1500 state EXCHANGE
*Apr 25 19:40:31.014: OSPF: Exchange Done with 10.0.0.12 on Serial0/0/1
*Apr 25 19:40:31.014: OSPF: Send DBD to 10.0.0.12 on Serial0/0/1 seq 0x1F9C opt 0x52
   flag 0x0 len 32
*Apr 25 19:40:31.050: OSPF: Synchronized with 10.0.0.12 on Serial0/0/1, state FULL
!In FULL state on S0/0/1
*Apr 25 19:40:31.050: %OSPF-5-ADJCHG: Process 1, Nbr 10.0.0.12 on Serial0/0/1 from
   LOADING to FULL, Loading Done
*Apr 25 19:40:31.098: OSPF: Rcv hello from 10.200.200.13 area 1 from FastEthernet0/0
   10.1.1.3
*Apr 25 19:40:31.098: OSPF: 2 Way Communication to 10.200.200.13 on FastEthernet0/0,
   state 2WAY
*Apr 25 19:40:31.098: OSPF: Backup seen Event before WAIT timer on FastEthernet0/0
!Election on FastEthernet0/0
*Apr 25 19:40:31.098: OSPF: DR/BDR election on FastEthernet0/0
*Apr 25 19:40:31.098: OSPF: Elect BDR 10.0.0.11
*Apr 25 19:40:31.098: OSPF: Elect DR 10.200.200.13
*Apr 25 19:40:31.098: OSPF: Elect BDR 10.0.0.11
*Apr 25 19:40:31.098: OSPF: Elect DR 10.200.200.13
*Apr 25 19:40:31.098:           DR: 10.200.200.13 (Id)    BDR: 10.0.0.11 (Id)
*Apr 25 19:40:31.098: OSPF: Send DBD to 10.200.200.13 on FastEthernet0/0 seq 0x236D
   opt 0x52 flag 0x7 len 32
```

```
*Apr 25 19:40:31.098: OSPF: End of hello processing
*Apr 25 19:40:31.102: OSPF: Rcv DBD from 10.200.200.13 on FastEthernet0/0 seq 0x17A6
    opt 0x52 flag 0x7 len 32  mtu 1500 state EXSTART
*Apr 25 19:40:31.102: OSPF: NBR Negotiation Done. We are the SLAVE
*Apr 25 19:40:31.102: OSPF: Send DBD to 10.200.200.13 on FastEthernet0/0 seq 0x17A6
    opt 0x52 flag 0x2 len 132
*Apr 25 19:40:31.102: OSPF: Rcv DBD from 10.200.200.13 on FastEthernet0/0 seq 0x17A7
    opt 0x52 flag 0x3 len 112  mtu 1500 state EXCHANGE
*Apr 25 19:40:31.102: OSPF: Send DBD to 10.200.200.13 on FastEthernet0/0 seq 0x17A7
    opt 0x52 flag 0x0 len 32
*Apr 25 19:40:31.106: OSPF: Rcv DBD from 10.200.200.13 on FastEthernet0/0 seq 0x17A8
    opt 0x52 flag 0x1 len 32  mtu 1500 state EXCHANGE
*Apr 25 19:40:31.106: OSPF: Exchange Done with 10.200.200.13 on FastEthernet0/0
*Apr 25 19:40:31.106: OSPF: Synchronized with 10.200.200.13 on FastEthernet0/0,
    state FULL
!In FULL state on FastEthernet 0/0
*Apr 25 19:40:31.106: %OSPF-5-ADJCHG: Process 1, Nbr 10.200.200.13 on FastEthernet0/0
    from LOADING to FULL, Loading Done
*Apr 25 19:40:31.106: OSPF: Send DBD to 10.200.200.13 on FastEthernet0/0 seq 0x17A8
    opt 0x52 flag 0x0 len 32
!Exchanging hello packets with neighbors
*Apr 25 19:40:31.282: OSPF: Send hello to 224.0.0.5 area 1 on Serial0/0/1 from 10.1.0.1
*Apr 25 19:40:31.282: OSPF: Send hello to 224.0.0.5 area 1 on FastEthernet0/0 from
    10.1.1.1
*Apr 25 19:40:40.946: OSPF: Rcv hello from 10.0.0.12 area 1 from Serial0/0/1 10.1.0.2
*Apr 25 19:40:40.946: OSPF: End of hello processing
*Apr 25 19:40:41.098: OSPF: Rcv hello from 10.200.200.13 area 1 from FastEthernet0/0
    10.1.1.3
*Apr 25 19:40:41.098: OSPF: Neighbor change Event on interface FastEthernet0/0
*Apr 25 19:40:41.098: OSPF: DR/BDR election on FastEthernet0/0
*Apr 25 19:40:41.098: OSPF: Elect BDR 10.0.0.11
*Apr 25 19:40:41.098: OSPF: Elect DR 10.200.200.13
*Apr 25 19:40:41.098:         DR: 10.200.200.13 (Id)    BDR: 10.0.0.11 (Id)
*Apr 25 19:40:41.098: OSPF: End of hello processing
P1R1#
```

Task 5: Observing OSPF DR and BDR Elections

In this task, you further examine the DR/BDR election process. Complete the following steps:

Step 1   Determine the default OSPF priority and which router is the DR on the FastEthernet segment by using the **show ip ospf neighbor** command.

Solution:

The following shows the output on the P1R1 router:

```
P1R1#show ip ospf neighbor

Neighbor ID     Pri   State       Dead Time    Address      Interface
10.0.0.12        0    FULL/  -    00:00:38     10.1.0.2     Serial0/0/1
10.200.200.13    1    FULL/DR     00:00:38     10.1.1.3     FastEthernet0/0
P1R1#
```

P1R1's neighbor, P1R3, has a default priority of 1 and is the DR on the FastEthernet segment.

Step 2   Change the DR by adjusting the OSPF priority to 0 for the appropriate router's FastEthernet interface. Doing so removes this router from the election process. Observe the results when the edge router is elected as the DR (**debug ip ospf events** is still running).

Solution:

The following shows the required step on the P1R3 router:

```
P1R3(config)#int fa0/0
P1R3(config-if)#ip ospf priority 0
```

The following shows the output on the P1R1 router. Comments have been added to explain some of the output; the comments begin with the ! character:

```
P1R1#
*Apr 25 19:50:21.090: OSPF: Rcv hello from 10.200.200.13 area 1 from FastEthernet0/0
    10.1.1.3
*Apr 25 19:50:21.090: OSPF: Neighbor change Event on interface FastEthernet0/0
!An election is called on FastEthernet 0/0 because the priority has changed.
*Apr 25 19:50:21.090: OSPF: DR/BDR election on FastEthernet0/0
*Apr 25 19:50:21.090: OSPF: Elect BDR 10.0.0.11
*Apr 25 19:50:21.090: OSPF: Elect DR 10.0.0.11
*Apr 25 19:50:21.090: OSPF: Elect BDR 0.0.0.0
*Apr 25 19:50:21.090: OSPF: Elect DR 10.0.0.11
!P1R1 is elected as the DR. Because there are only 2 routers, and P1R3 cannot be DR
    or BDR, no BDR is elected.
*Apr 25 19:50:21.090:          DR: 10.0.0.11 (Id)    BDR: none
*Apr 25 19:50:21.090: OSPF: Remember old DR 10.200.200.13 (id)
*Apr 25 19:50:21.094: OSPF: End of hello processing
*Apr 25 19:50:21.282: OSPF: Send hello to 224.0.0.5 area 1 on Serial0/0/1 from
    10.1.0.1
*Apr 25 19:50:21.282: OSPF: Send hello to 224.0.0.5 area 1 on FastEthernet0/0 from
    10.1.1.1
*Apr 25 19:50:21.590: OSPF: Build network LSA for FastEthernet0/0, router ID
    10.0.0.11
*Apr 25 19:50:21.590: OSPF: Build network LSA for FastEthernet0/0, router ID
    10.0.0.11
*Apr 25 19:50:21.594: OSPF: Include link to old DR on FastEthernet0/0
P1R1#
*Apr 25 19:50:30.930: OSPF: Rcv hello from 10.0.0.12 area 1 from Serial0/0/1 10.1.0.2
*Apr 25 19:50:30.930: OSPF: End of hello processing
*Apr 25 19:50:31.090: OSPF: Rcv hello from 10.200.200.13 area 1 from FastEthernet0/0
    10.1.1.3
*Apr 25 19:50:31.090: OSPF: Neighbor change Event on interface FastEthernet0/0
*Apr 25 19:50:31.090: OSPF: DR/BDR election on FastEthernet0/0
*Apr 25 19:50:31.090: OSPF: Elect BDR 0.0.0.0
*Apr 25 19:50:31.090: OSPF: Elect DR 10.0.0.11
*Apr 25 19:50:31.090:          DR: 10.0.0.11 (Id)    BDR: none
*Apr 25 19:50:31.090: OSPF: End of hello processing
*Apr 25 19:50:31.282: OSPF: Send hello to 224.0.0.5 area 1 on Serial0/0/1 from
    10.1.0.1
*Apr 25 19:50:31.282: OSPF: Send hello to 224.0.0.5 area 1 on FastEthernet0/0 from
    10.1.1.1
*Apr 25 19:50:31.590: OSPF: Include link to old DR on FastEthernet0/0
*Apr 25 19:50:40.930: OSPF: Rcv hello from 10.0.0.12 area 1 from Serial0/0/1
    10.1.0.2
*Apr 25 19:50:40.930: OSPF: End of hello processing
*Apr 25 19:50:41.090: OSPF: Rcv hello from 10.200.200.13 area 1 from FastEthernet0/0
    10.1.1.3
*Apr 25 19:50:41.090: OSPF: End of hello processing
```

Step 3   After you have seen the DR and BDR election, turn off the debug. Why wasn't a BDR elected?

Solution:

The following shows the required step on the P1R1 router:

```
P1R1#no debug all
All possible debugging has been turned off
P1R1#
```

Because there are only two routers, and P1R3 cannot be DR or BDR because it has a priority of zero, no BDR is elected.

Step 4   Verify the results of the election by displaying the OSPF neighbor table.

Solution:

The following output is from the P1R1 router:

```
P1R1#show ip ospf neighbor

Neighbor ID     Pri   State          Dead Time   Address     Interface
10.0.0.12         0   FULL/   -      00:00:30    10.1.0.2    Serial0/0/1
10.200.200.13     0   FULL/DROTHER   00:00:31    10.1.1.3    FastEthernet0/0
P1R1#
```

P1R1's neighbor, P1R3, now shows DROTHER state, meaning that some other router is DR on this link. P1R1 is the only other router on the link, so therefore it is the DR.

Step 5   Save your configurations to NVRAM.

Solution:

The following shows how to perform the required step on the P1R1 router:

```
P1R1#copy run start
Destination filename [startup-config]?
Building configuration...
[OK]
```

Exercise Verification

You have completed this exercise when you achieve the following results:

■   EIGRP is removed from the routers.

■   OSPF is running in a single area and all pod routes are being passed.

■   You have configured stable OSPF router IDs.

■   You have observed OSPF neighbor formation.

■   You have observed the OSPF DR and BDR elections.

· **Review Questions**

Answer the following questions, and then refer to Appendix A, "Answers to Review Questions," for the answers.

1. Which of the following is not a characteristic of link-state routing protocols?

    a. They respond quickly to network changes.

    b. They broadcast every 30 minutes.

    c. They send triggered updates when a network change occurs.

    d. They may send periodic updates, known as link-state refresh, at long time intervals, such as every 30 minutes.

2. For all the routers in the network to make consistent routing decisions, each link-state router must keep a record of all the following items except which one?

    a. Its immediate neighbor routers

    b. All of the other routers in the network, or in its area of the network, and their attached networks

    c. The best paths to each destination

    d. The version of the routing protocol used

3. Link-state routing protocols use a two-layer area hierarchy composed of which two areas?

    a. Transit area

    b. Transmit area

    c. Regular area

    d. Linking area

4. Which of the following is not a characteristic of an OSPF area?

    a. It may minimize routing table entries.

    b. It requires a flat network design.

    c. It may localize the impact of a topology change within an area.

    d. It may stop detailed LSA flooding at the area boundary.

5. True or false: An ABR connects area 0 to the nonbackbone areas.

6. When a router receives an LSA (within an LSU), it does not do which of the following?

   a. If the LSA entry does not already exist, the router adds the entry to its LSDB, sends back an LSAck, floods the information to other routers, runs SPF, and updates its routing table.

   b. If the entry already exists and the received LSA has the same sequence number, the router overwrites the information in the LSDB with the new LSA entry.

   c. If the entry already exists but the LSA includes newer information (it has a higher sequence number), the router adds the entry to its LSDB, sends back an LSAck, floods the information to other routers, runs SPF, and updates its routing table.

   d. If the entry already exists but the LSA includes older information, it sends an LSU to the sender with its newer information.

7. What is an OSPF type 2 packet?

   a. Database description (DBD), which checks for database synchronization between routers

   b. Link-state request (LSR), which requests specific link-state records from router to router

   c. Link-state update (LSU), which sends specifically requested link-state records

   d. Link-state acknowledgment (LSAck), which acknowledges the other packet types

8. Which of the following is true of hellos and dead intervals?

   a. They don't need to be the same on neighboring routers, because the lowest common denominator is adopted.

   b. They don't need to be the same on neighboring routers, because the highest common denominator is adopted.

   c. They don't need to be the same on neighboring routers, because it is a negotiated interval between neighboring routers.

   d. They need to be the same on neighboring routers.

9. Which IP address is used to send an updated LSA entry to OSPF DRs and BDRs?

   a. Unicast 224.0.0.5

   b. Unicast 224.0.0.6

   c. Multicast 224.0.0.5

   d. Multicast 224.0.0.6

10. To ensure an accurate database, how often does OSPF flood (refresh) each LSA record?

    a. Every 60 minutes.

    b. Every 30 minutes.

    c. Every 60 seconds.

    d. Every 30 seconds.

    e. Flooding each LSA record would defeat the purpose of a link-state routing protocol, which strives to reduce the amount of routing traffic it generates.

11. What command is used to display the router ID, timers, and statistics?

    a. **show ip ospf**

    b. **show ip ospf neighbors**

    c. **show ip ospf stats**

    d. **show ip ospf neighborship**

12. Which of the following is not a way in which the OSPF router ID (a unique IP address) can be assigned?

    a. The highest IP address of any physical interface

    b. The lowest IP address of any physical interface

    c. The IP address of a loopback interface

    d. The **router-id** command

13. True or false: On point-to-point networks, the router dynamically detects its neighboring routers by multicasting its hello packets to all SPF routers using the address 224.0.0.6.

14. An adjacency is the relationship that exists where?

    a. Between routers located on the same physical network

    b. Between routers in different OSPF areas

    c. Between a router and its DR and BDR on different networks

    d. Between a backbone DR and a transit BDR

15. Which of the following is not true regarding the OSPF DR/BDR election?

   a. The router with the highest priority value is the DR.

   b. The router with the second-highest priority value is the BDR.

   c. If all routers have the default priority, the router with the lowest router ID becomes the DR.

   d. The router with a priority set to 0 cannot become the DR or BDR.

16. Which of the following is not true of OSPF point-to-multipoint mode?

   a. It does not require a full-mesh network.

   b. It does not require a static neighbor configuration.

   c. It uses multiple IP subnets.

   d. It duplicates LSA packets.

17. What is the default OSPF mode on a point-to-point Frame Relay subinterface?

   a. Point-to-point mode

   b. Multipoint mode

   c. Nonbroadcast mode

   d. Broadcast mode

18. What is the default OSPF mode on a Frame Relay multipoint subinterface?

   a. Point-to-point mode

   b. Multipoint mode

   c. Nonbroadcast mode

   d. Broadcast mode

19. What is the default OSPF mode on a main Frame Relay interface?

   a. Point-to-point mode

   b. Multipoint mode

   c. Nonbroadcast mode

   d. Broadcast mode

This chapter discusses advanced OSPF configuration. It covers the following topics:

■ Types of OSPF Routers and LSAs

■ Interpreting the OSPF LSDB and Routing Table

■ OSPF Route Summarization

■ Creating a Default Route in OSPF

■ OSPF Special Area Types

■ OSPF Virtual Links

■ Configuring OSPF Authentication

CHAPTER 5

Advanced Open Shortest Path First Protocol Configuration

This chapter introduces advanced operation, configuration, and verification of the Open Shortest Path First (OSPF) protocol. The different types of OSPF routers and link-state advertisements (LSAs) are introduced. Understanding the contents of the OSPF link-state database (LSDB) and IP routing table is key to understanding OSPF operation; both are investigated in this chapter. OSPF does not automatically summarize routes; route summarization configuration is covered, so that routing table size and the number of updates are reduced. Default routes are introduced next, followed by types of stub areas; both of these also reduce routing table size and the number of updates. Virtual links—links that allow discontiguous area 0s to be connected—are explored. The chapter concludes with a discussion of OSPF authentication configuration.

Types of OSPF Routers and LSAs

This section first describes the various OSPF router types, including backbone routers, area border routers (ABRs), autonomous system boundary routers (ASBRs), and internal routers. Each of the common LSA types and how they form the layout of the OSPF LSDB are then introduced.

Types of OSPF Routers

OSPF can operate within a single area; however issues may arise if the single area expands into hundreds of networks, as shown in Figure 5-1.

Figure 5-1 *Issues with Maintaining a Large OSPF Network*

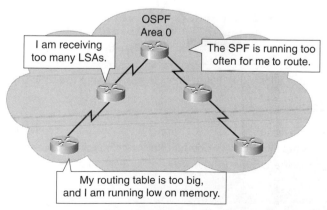

If an area becomes too big, the following issues need to be addressed:

- **Frequent shortest path first (SPF) algorithm calculations**—In a large network, changes are inevitable; therefore, the routers spend many CPU cycles recalculating the SPF algorithm and updating the routing table.

- **Large routing table**—OSPF does not perform route summarization by default. If the routes are not summarized, the routing table can become very large, depending on the size of the network.

- **Large LSDB**—Because the LSDB covers the topology of the entire network, each router must maintain an entry for every network in the area, even if not every route is selected for the routing table.

A solution to these issues is to divide the network into multiple OSPF areas. OSPF allows the separation of a large area into smaller, more manageable areas that still can exchange routing information.

Hierarchical area routing, shown in Figure 5-2, is OSPF's ability to separate a large internetwork into multiple areas. Using this technique, interarea routing still occurs, but many of the internal routing operations, such as SPF calculations, can remain within individual areas. For example, if area 1 is having problems with a link going up and down, routers in other areas do not need to continually run their SPF calculation, because they can be isolated from the problem in area 1.

Figure 5-2 *The Solution: OSPF Hierarchical Routing*

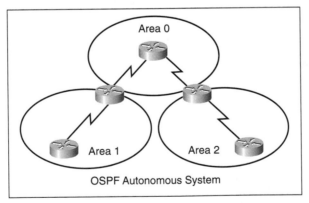

Assuming a proper IP addressing hierarchy is in place, using multiple OSPF areas has several important advantages:

- **Reduced frequency of SPF calculations**—Because detailed route information exists within each area, it is not necessary to flood all link-state changes to all other areas. Therefore, only routers that are affected by the change need to recalculate the SPF algorithm.

- **Smaller routing tables**—With multiple areas, detailed route entries for specific networks within an area can remain in the area. Instead of advertising these explicit routes outside the area, routers can be configured to summarize the routes into one or more summary addresses. Advertising these summaries reduces the number of LSAs propagated between areas but keeps all networks reachable.

- **Reduced link-state update (LSU) overhead**—LSUs contain a variety of LSA types, including link-state and summary information. Rather than send an LSU about each network within an area, a router can advertise a single summarized route or a small number of routes between areas, thereby reducing the overhead associated with LSUs when they cross areas.

Certain types of OSPF routers control the traffic types that go in and out of various areas. The following are the four router types, as shown in Figure 5-3:

- **Internal router**—Routers that have all of their interfaces in the same area; all routers within the same area have identical LSDBs.

- **Backbone router**—Routers that sit in the perimeter of the backbone area and that have at least one interface connected to area 0. Backbone routers maintain OSPF routing information using the same procedures and algorithms as internal routers.

- **ABR**—Routers that have interfaces attached to multiple areas, maintain separate LSDBs for each area to which they connect, and route traffic destined for or arriving from other areas. ABRs are exit points for the area, which means that routing information destined for another area can get there only via the ABR of the local area. ABRs can be configured to summarize the routing information from the LSDBs of their attached areas. ABRs distribute the routing information into the backbone. The backbone routers then forward the information to the other ABRs. An area can have one or more ABRs.

- **ASBR**—Routers that have at least one interface attached to an external internetwork (another autonomous system [AS]), such as a non-OSPF network. ASBRs can import non-OSPF network information to the OSPF network and vice versa; this process is called route redistribution (and is covered in Chapter 7, "Manipulating Routing Updates").

A router can be more than one router type. For example, if a router interconnects to area 0 and area 1, and to a non-OSPF network, it is both an ABR and an ASBR.

A router has a separate LSDB for each area to which it connects. Therefore, an ABR will have one LSDB for area 0 and another LSDB for the other area in which it participates. Two routers belonging to the same area maintain identical LSDBs for that area.

An LSDB is synchronized between pairs of adjacent routers. On broadcast networks such as Ethernet, an LSDB is synchronized between the DROTHER (a router that is not a Designated Router [DR] or a Backup Designated Router [BDR]) and its DR and BDR.

Figure 5-3   *Types of OSPF Routers*

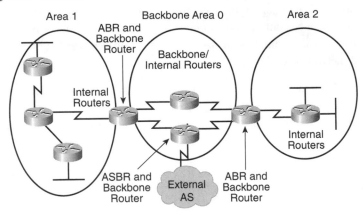

OSPF Design Guidelines

Studies and real-world implementations have led to the following OSPF design guidelines, as documented in the Cisco Press book *OSPF Network Design Solutions*.

Routers in a domain	Minimum 20	Mean 510	Maximum 1000
Routers per single area	Minimum 20	Mean 160	Maximum 350
Areas per domain	Minimum 1	Mean 23	Maximum 60

In "Designing Large-Scale IP Internetworks," Cisco recommends the following guidelines:

- An area should have no more than 50 routers.

- Each router should have no more than 60 OSPF neighbors.

- A router should not be in more than three areas.

These values are recommended to ensure that OSPF calculations do not overwhelm the routers. Of course, the network design and link stability can also affect the load on the routers.

OSPF LSA Types

LSAs are the building blocks of the OSPF LSDB. Table 5-1 summarizes the types of LSAs.

Table 5-1   *Summary of OSPF LSA Types*

LSA Type	Description
1	Router LSA
2	Network LSA
3 and 4	Summary LSAs

Table 5-1   *Summary of OSPF LSA Types (Continued)*

LSA Type	Description
5	AS external LSA
6	Multicast OSPF LSA
7	Defined for not-so-stubby areas (NSSAs)
8	External attributes LSA for Border Gateway Protocol (BGP)
9, 10, or 11	Opaque LSAs

Individually, LSAs act as database records; in combination, they describe the entire topology of an OSPF network or area. The following are descriptions of each type of LSA (with LSA types 1 to 5 explained in more detail in the following sections):

- **Type 1**—Every router generates router-link advertisements for each area to which it belongs. Router-link advertisements describe the states of the router's links to the area and are flooded only within a particular area. All types of LSAs have 20-byte LSA headers. One of the fields of the LSA header is the link-state ID. The link-state ID of the type 1 LSA is the originating router's ID.

- **Type 2**—DRs generate network link advertisements for multiaccess networks, which describe the set of routers attached to a particular multiaccess network. Network link advertisements are flooded in the area that contains the network. The link-state ID of the type 2 LSA is the DR's IP interface address.

- **Types 3 and 4**—ABRs generate summary link advertisements. Summary link advertisements describe the following interarea routes:

  — Type 3 describes routes to the area's networks (and may include aggregate routes).

  — Type 4 describes routes to ASBRs.

  The link-state ID is the destination network number for type 3 LSAs and the router ID of the described ASBR for type 4 LSAs.

  These LSAs are flooded throughout the backbone area to the other ABRs. Type 3 and type 4 LSAs are not flooded into totally stubby areas or totally stubby NSSAs. (Stub areas and NSSAs are discussed later in this chapter in the "OSPF Special Area Types" section.)

- **Type 5**—ASBRs generate autonomous system external link advertisements. External link advertisements describe routes to destinations external to the autonomous system and are flooded everywhere except to stub areas, totally stubby areas, and NSSAs. The link-state ID of the type 5 LSA is the external network number.

- **Type 6**—These LSAs are used in multicast OSPF applications.

- **Type 7**—These LSAs are used in NSSAs.

- **Type 8**—These LSAs are used to internetwork OSPF and BGP.

- **Types 9, 10, or 11**—These LSA types are designated for future upgrades to OSPF for application-specific purposes. For example, Cisco Systems uses opaque LSAs for Multiprotocol Label Switching (MPLS) with OSPF. Standard LSDB flooding mechanisms are used to distribute opaque LSAs. Each of the three types has a different flooding scope.

LSA Type 1: Router LSA

A router advertises a type 1 LSA that floods to all other routers in the area where it originated, as shown in Figure 5-4. A type 1 LSA describes the collective states of the router's directly connected links (interfaces).

Figure 5-4 *LSA Type 1: Router LSA*

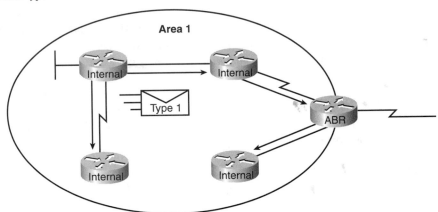

Each type 1 LSA is identified by the originating router's ID in the link-state ID field.

Each of the router's links (interfaces) is defined as one of four types: type 1, 2, 3, or 4. The LSA includes a link ID field to identify what is on the other end of the link; depending on the link type, the link ID field has different meanings. Type 1 LSA link types and their link ID meanings are described in Table 5-2.

Table 5-2 *LSA Type 1 (Router LSA) Link Types*

Link Type	Description	Link ID
1	Point-to-point connection to another router	Neighbor router ID
2	Connection to a transit network	DR's interface address
3	Connection to a stub network	IP network/subnet number
4	Virtual link	Neighbor router ID

> **NOTE**   A stub network is a dead-end link that has only one router attached. A virtual link is a special case in OSPF (and is described later in this chapter in the "OSPF Special Area Types" section).

A link data field is also specified for each link, providing 32 bits of extra information. For most link types this is the IP interface address of the associated router interface. For links to stub networks, this field provides the stub network's subnet mask.

In addition, the type 1 LSA indicates the OSPF cost for each link, and whether the router is an ABR or ASBR.

LSA Type 2: Network LSA

A type 2 LSA is generated for every transit broadcast or nonbroadcast multiaccess (NBMA) network within an area. A transit network has at least two directly attached OSPF routers, as shown in Figure 5-5. A multiaccess network such as Ethernet is an example of a transit network. A type 2 network LSA lists each of the attached routers that make up the transit network, including the DR itself, and the subnet mask of the link.

Figure 5-5   *LSA Type 2: Network LSA*

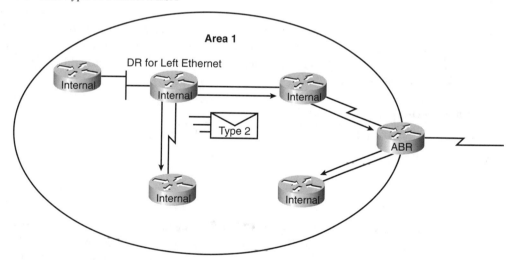

The transit link's DR is responsible for advertising the network LSA. The type 2 LSA then floods to all routers within the transit network area. Type 2 LSAs never cross an area boundary. The link-state ID for a network LSA is the IP interface address of the DR that advertises it.

LSA Type 3: Summary LSA

The ABR sends type 3 summary LSAs. A type 3 LSA advertises any networks owned by an area to the rest of the areas in the OSPF autonomous system, as shown in Figure 5-6.

Figure 5-6   *LSA Type 3: Summary LSA*

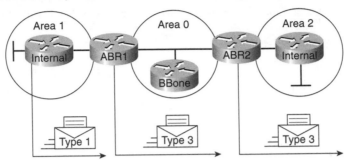

Type 3 LSAs Represent the Area's Type 1 LSAs

As Figure 5-6 illustrates, type 1 LSAs stay within an area. When an ABR receives type 1 LSAs from other routers within an area, it sends out type 3 summary LSAs to advertise the networks learned via these type 1 LSAs to other areas.

By default, OSPF does not automatically summarize groups of contiguous subnets, or even summarize a network to its classful boundary. The network operator, through configuration commands, must specify if and how the summarization will occur. Therefore, by default, a type 3 LSA is advertised into the backbone area for every subnet defined in the originating area, which can cause significant flooding problems. Consequently, manual route summarization at the ABR should always be considered. ABRs flood summary LSAs regardless of whether the routes listed in the LSAs are summarized. (OSPF route summarization is discussed later in this chapter, in the "OSPF Route Summarization" section.)

Summary LSAs

Summary LSAs do not, by default, contain summarized routes. Therefore, by default, all subnets in an area will be advertised.

LSA Type 4: Summary LSA

A type 4 summary LSA is used only when an ASBR exists within an area. A type 4 LSA identifies the ASBR and provides a route to it. The link-state ID is set to the ASBR's router ID. All traffic destined for an external autonomous system requires routing table knowledge of the ASBR that originated the external routes.

In Figure 5-7, the ASBR sends a type 1 router LSA with a bit (known as the external bit [e bit]) that is set to identify itself as an ASBR. When the ABR (identified with the border bit [b bit] in the router LSA) receives this type 1 LSA, it builds a type 4 LSA and floods it to the backbone, area 0. Subsequent ABRs regenerate a type 4 LSA to flood into their area.

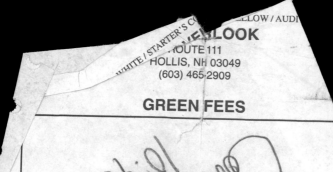

OVERLOOK
ROUTE 111
HOLLIS, NH 03049
(603) 465-2909

WHITE / STARTER'S CO... ...LLOW / AUDI...

GREEN FEES

CART

CART RENTAL AGREEMENT

For and in consideration of the use of the assigned golf cart, I represent and agree:

- I am familiar with the use and operation of the golf cart.
- I am at least 18 years old and I have a valid driver's license.
- I will not permit anyone under the age of 18 to operate the cart.
- I will keep the cart in my custody and control and I will operate it carefully.
- I will keep the cart on the property of the Overlook Golf course.
- I will return the golf cart immediately following the completion of my rental.
- I will return the golf cart in as good condition as I received it.
- I will not permit more than two (2) people to ride in the cart at any one (1) time.

I promise and agree to hold the Overlook Golf Course and its agents free and harmless from any claim of liability for damage or injury to myself or any other person or property which results from negligence in providing the cart to me or which results from the condition of the premises. I agree to be responsible for any damage to the cart, normal wear and tear, excepted. I accept full and all responsibility for any and all damage or injury.

I HAVE READ AND AGREE TO ALL TERMS AND CONDITIONS ABOVE.

NAME: _____ CART # _____

SIGNATURE: _____ DATE: _____

STARTERS NO.
17416

Thank You

RAIN CHECK

Good for ___2___ Player(s)

at $ ___17.50___ each.

towards greens Fees and

_____ towards power cart

$ _____

Date _6-12-3_ Signature _____

Overlook C.C.

| **Type 4 LSAs**

As Figure 5-7 again illustrates, type 1 LSAs stay within an area. When an ABR receives a type 1 LSA from an ASBR, it sends out a type 4 summary LSA to advertise the presence of the ASBR to other areas.

Figure 5-7 *LSA Type 4: Summary LSA*

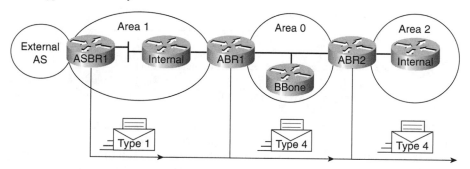

LSA Type 5: External LSA

Type 5 external LSAs describe routes to networks outside the OSPF autonomous system. Type 5 LSAs are originated by the ASBR and are flooded to the entire autonomous system, as shown in Figure 5-8. Because of the flooding scope and depending on the number of external networks, the default lack of route summarization can also be a major issue with external LSAs. The network operator should always attempt to summarize blocks of external network numbers at the ASBR to reduce flooding problems.

Figure 5-8 *LSA Type 5: External LSA*

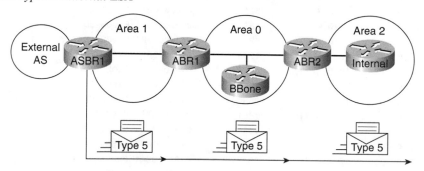

Interpreting the OSPF LSDB and Routing Table

This section explains the relationship between and how to interpret the OSPF LSDB and routing table. This section also describes the OSPF LSDB overload protection feature and how to change the OSPF cost metric.

OSPF LSDB

Example 5-1 illustrates output from the **show ip ospf database** command, used to get information about an OSPF LSDB, on an ABR. In this output, the router link states are type 1 LSAs, the net link states are type 2 LSAs, the summary net link states are type 3 LSAs, the summary ASB link states are type 4 LSAs, and the external link states are type 5 LSAs. (This output is from the P1R1 router in Configuration Exercise 5-3, later in this chapter.)

Example 5-1 **show ip ospf database** *Command*

```
P1R1#show ip ospf database

            OSPF Router with ID (10.0.0.11) (Process ID 1)

                Router Link States (Area 0)

Link ID          ADV Router       Age      Seq#       Checksum Link count
10.0.0.11        10.0.0.11        485      0x80000004 0x002EE5 2
10.0.0.12        10.0.0.12        540      0x80000002 0x0046CB 2
10.0.0.21        10.0.0.21        494      0x80000042 0x00F8E1 1
10.0.0.22        10.0.0.22        246      0x80000042 0x00F6E0 1
200.200.200.200 200.200.200.200 485      0x800001CB 0x00E504 6

                Summary Net Link States (Area 0)

Link ID          ADV Router       Age      Seq#       Checksum
10.1.0.0         10.0.0.11        486      0x8000001A 0x00C92A
10.1.0.0         10.0.0.12        541      0x8000001A 0x00C32F
10.1.1.0         10.0.0.11        486      0x8000001A 0x002BD6
10.1.1.0         10.0.0.12        521      0x8000001C 0x00BE30
10.1.2.0         10.0.0.11        486      0x8000001A 0x00BD33
10.1.2.0         10.0.0.12        521      0x8000001C 0x0016E7
10.1.3.0         10.0.0.11        487      0x8000001A 0x00B23D
10.1.3.0         10.0.0.12        527      0x80000001 0x00DE29
10.2.0.0         10.0.0.21        1759     0x8000003F 0x00378C
10.2.0.0         10.0.0.22        856      0x8000003F 0x003191
10.2.1.0         10.0.0.21        1861     0x80000041 0x00943B
10.2.1.0         10.0.0.22        856      0x8000003F 0x003090
10.2.2.0         10.0.0.21        1861     0x80000049 0x00179F
10.2.2.0         10.0.0.22        1359     0x80000044 0x007D4D
10.2.3.0         10.0.0.21        1861     0x8000003F 0x00209F
10.2.3.0         10.0.0.22        1359     0x80000041 0x0016A6
10.11.0.0        10.0.0.11        589      0x80000018 0x005596
10.11.0.0        10.0.0.12        619      0x80000001 0x007D84

                Router Link States (Area 1)

Link ID          ADV Router       Age      Seq#       Checksum Link count
10.0.0.11        10.0.0.11        613      0x80000006 0x000CF1 5
```

Example 5-1   show ip ospf database *Command (Continued)*

```
10.0.0.12        10.0.0.12        614        0x80000006 0x00F205 5
10.200.200.13    10.200.200.13    639        0x80000005 0x0006B4 3
10.200.200.14    10.200.200.14    635        0x80000005 0x00882C 3

                 Net Link States (Area 1)


Link ID          ADV Router       Age        Seq#       Checksum
10.1.1.1         10.0.0.11        640        0x80000001 0x00D485
10.1.2.2         10.0.0.12        635        0x80000001 0x00D183


                 Summary Net Link States (Area 1)


Link ID          ADV Router       Age        Seq#       Checksum
172.31.11.1      10.0.0.11        616        0x80000001 0x002F21
172.31.11.1      10.0.0.12        576        0x80000001 0x0064CA
172.31.11.2      10.0.0.11        576        0x80000001 0x0060CE
172.31.11.2      10.0.0.12        670        0x80000001 0x001F2F
172.31.11.4      10.0.0.11        576        0x80000001 0x00AE8E
172.31.11.4      10.0.0.12        630        0x80000001 0x00A893
172.31.22.4      10.0.0.11        576        0x80000001 0x0035FC
172.31.22.4      10.0.0.12        630        0x80000001 0x002F02


                 Summary ASB Link States (Area 1)


Link ID          ADV Router       Age        Seq#       Checksum
200.200.200.200 10.0.0.11         576        0x80000001 0x00688B
200.200.200.200 10.0.0.12         631        0x80000001 0x006290


                 Type-5 AS External Link States


Link ID          ADV Router       Age        Seq#       Checksum Tag
10.254.0.0       200.200.200.200 451         0x8000019D 0x00DADD 0
P1R1#
```

The database columns in Example 5-1 are as follows:

- **Link ID**—Identifies each LSA.

- **ADV Router**—Advertising router—the LSA's source router.

- **Age**—The maximum age counter in seconds. The maximum age is 1 hour, or 3600 seconds.

- **Seq#**—The LSA's sequence number. It begins at 0x80000001 and increases with each update of the LSA.

- **Checksum**—Checksum of the individual LSA to ensure reliable receipt of that LSA.

■ **Link count**—The total number of directly attached links; used only on router LSAs. The link count includes all point-to-point, transit, and stub links. Point-to-point serial links count as two; all other links, including Ethernet links, count as one.

OSPF Routing Table and Types of Routes

Table 5-3 describes each of the routing table designators for OSPF.

Table 5-3   *Types of OSPF Routes*

Route Designator	Description	
O	OSPF intra-area (router LSA) and network LSA	Networks from within the router's area. Advertised by way of router LSAs and network LSAs.
O IA	OSPF interarea (summary LSA)	Networks from outside the router's area but within the OSPF autonomous system. Advertised by way of summary LSAs.
O E1	Type 1 external routes	Networks from outside the router's autonomous system, advertised by way of external LSAs.
O E2	Type 2 external routes	Networks from outside the router's autonomous system, advertised by way of external LSAs. The difference between E1 and E2 external routes is described in the "Calculating the Costs of E1 and E2 Routes" section.

Router and network LSAs describe the details within an area. The routing table reflects this link-state information with a designation of O, meaning that the route is an intra-area.

When an ABR receives summary or external LSAs, it adds them to its LSDB and regenerates and floods them into the local area. The internal routers then assimilate the information into their databases. Summary LSAs appear in the routing table as IA (interarea) routes. External LSAs appear in the routing table marked as external type 1 (E1) or external type 2 (E2) routes.

The SPF algorithm is then run against the LSDB to build the SPF tree, which is used to determine the best paths. The following is the order in which the best paths are calculated:

1. All routers calculate the best paths to destinations within their area (intra-area) and add these entries to the routing table. These are the type 1 and type 2 LSAs, which are noted in the routing table with a routing designator of O (OSPF).

2. All routers calculate the best paths to the other areas in the internetwork. These best paths are the interarea route entries, or type 3 and type 4 LSAs. They are noted with a routing designator of O IA (interarea).

3. All routers (except those that are in the form of a stub area) calculate the best paths to the external autonomous system (type 5) destinations; these are noted with either an O E1 or O E2 route designator, depending on the configuration.

At this point, a router can communicate with any network within or outside the OSPF autonomous system.

Calculating the Costs of E1 and E2 Routes

The cost of an external route varies, depending on the external type configured on the ASBR, as shown in Figure 5-9.

Figure 5-9 *Calculating the Costs of E1 and E2 Routes*

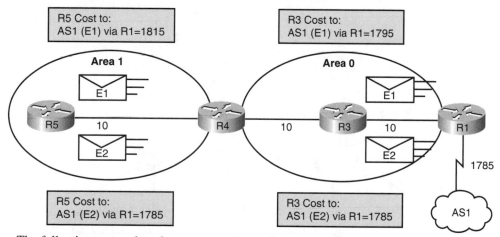

The following external packet types can be configured:

- **E1**—Type O E1 external routes calculate the cost by adding the external cost to the internal cost of each link the packet crosses. Use this type when multiple ASBRs are advertising an external route to the same autonomous system, to avoid suboptimal routing.

- **E2 (default)**—The external cost of O E2 packet routes is always the external cost only. Use this type if only one ASBR is advertising an external route to the autonomous system.

The **show ip route** command output shown in Example 5-2 depicts both external type routes (O E2) and interarea (O IA) routes. This output is taken from Router B in Figure 5-10.

Example 5-2 **show ip route** *Command Output with an External OSPF Route*

```
RouterB>show ip route
<output omitted>
Gateway of last resort is not set
```

continues

Example 5-2 **show ip route** *Command Output with an External OSPF Route (Continued)*

```
         172.31.0.0/24 is subnetted, 2 subnets
O IA    172.31.2.0 [110/1563] via 10.1.1.1, 00:12:35, FastEthernet0/0
O IA    172.31.1.0 [110/782] via 10.1.1.1, 00:12:35, FastEthernet0/0
         10.0.0.0/8 is variably subnetted, 6 subnets, 2 masks
C       10.200.200.13/32 is directly connected, Loopback0
C       10.1.3.0/24 is directly connected, Serial0/0/0
O       10.1.2.0/24 [110/782] via 10.1.3.4, 00:12:35, Serial0/0/0
C       10.1.1.0/24 is directly connected, FastEthernet0/0
O       10.1.0.0/24 [110/782] via 10.1.1.1, 00:12:37, FastEthernet0/0
O E2    10.254.0.0/24 [110/50] via 10.1.1.1, 00:12:37, FastEthernet0/0
```

Figure 5-10 *Network Used For Example 5-2*

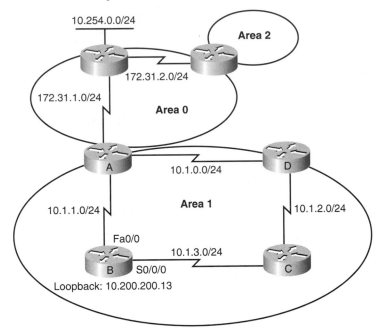

In Example 5-2, the last entry (O E2) is an external route from the ASBR, via the ABR. The two numbers in brackets [110/50] are the administrative distance and the total cost of the route to the specific destination network, respectively. In this case, the administrative distance is set to the default for all OSPF routes of 110, and the total cost of the route has been calculated as 50.

Configuring OSPF LSDB Overload Protection

If other routers are misconfigured, causing, for example, a redistribution of a large number of prefixes, large numbers of LSAs can be generated. These excessive LSAs can drain local CPU and memory resources. OSPF LSDB overload protection can be configured to protect against this issue with Cisco IOS Software Release 12.3(7)T and later (and some specific earlier releases) by using the **max-lsa** *maximum-number* [*threshold-percentage*] [**warning-only**] [**ignore-time** *minutes*] [**Ignore-count** *count-number*] [**reset-time** *minutes*] router configuration command.

Table 5-4 lists the parameters of the **max-lsa** command.

Table 5-4   **max-lsa** *Command Parameters*

Parameter	Description
maximum-number	Maximum number of non-self-generated LSAs that the OSPF process can keep in the OSPF LSDB.
threshold-percentage	(Optional) The percentage of the maximum LSA number, as specified by the *maximum-number* argument, at which a warning message is logged. The default is 75 percent.
warning-only	(Optional) Specifies that only a warning message is sent when the maximum limit for LSAs is exceeded; the OSPF process never enters ignore state. Disabled by default.
ignore-time *minutes*	(Optional) Specifies the time, in minutes, to ignore all neighbors after the maximum limit of LSAs has been exceeded. The default is 5 minutes.
ignore-count *count-number*	(Optional) Specifies the number of times that the OSPF process can consecutively be placed into the ignore state. The default is five times.
reset-time *minutes*	(Optional) Specifies the time, in minutes, after which the ignore count is reset to 0. The default is 10 minutes.

When this feature is enabled, the router keeps count of the number of received (non-self-generated) LSAs that it keeps in its LSDB. An error message is logged when this number reaches a configured threshold number, and a notification is sent when it exceeds the threshold number.

If the LSA count still exceeds the threshold after one minute, the OSPF process takes down all adjacencies and clears the OSPF database; this is called the *ignore* state. In this ignore state, no OSPF packets are sent or received by interfaces that belong to that OSPF process.

The OSPF process remains in the ignore state for the time that is defined by the **ignore-time** parameter. The **ignore-count** parameter defines the maximum number of times that the OSPF process can consecutively enter the ignore state before remaining permanently down and requiring manual intervention.

If the OSPF process remains normal for the time that is defined by the **reset-time** parameter, the ignore state counter is reset to 0.

Changing the Cost Metric

By default, OSPF calculates the OSPF metric for an interface according to the inverse of the interface's bandwidth. In general, the cost in Cisco routers is calculated using the formula 100 Mbps/(bandwidth in Mbps). For example, a 64-Kbps link gets a metric of 1562, and a T1 link gets a metric of 64. However, this formula is based on a maximum bandwidth of 100 Mbps, which results in a cost of 1. If you have faster interfaces, you may want to recalibrate the cost of 1 to a higher bandwidth.

When you are using the interface's bandwidth to determine OSPF cost, always remember to use the **bandwidth** *value* interface configuration command to accurately define the bandwidth per interface, in kilobits per second.

If interfaces that are faster than 100 Mbps are being used, you should use the **auto-cost reference-bandwidth** *ref-bw* router configuration command. Use this command on all routers in the network to ensure accurate route calculations.

The parameter for the **auto-cost reference-bandwidth** command is described in Table 5-5.

Table 5-5   **auto-cost reference-bandwidth** *Command Parameter*

Parameter	Description
ref-bw	The reference bandwidth in megabits per second. The range is from 1 to 4,294,967; the default is 100.

To override the default cost, manually define the cost using the **ip ospf cost** *interface-cost* configuration command on a per-interface basis. The *interface-cost* is an integer from 1 to 65,535. The lower the number, the better (and more preferred) the link.

KEY POINT

Manipulating the OSPF Cost Metric

The OSPF cost metric default is calculated according to the inverse of the bandwidth defined on an interface. The **ip ospf cost**, **bandwidth**, and **auto-cost reference-bandwidth** commands can be used to manipulate the cost metric.

OSPF Route Summarization

Route summarization involves consolidating multiple routes into a single advertisement. Proper route summarization directly affects the amount of bandwidth, CPU, and memory resources consumed by the OSPF routing process.

Without route summarization, every specific-link LSA is propagated into the OSPF backbone and beyond, causing unnecessary network traffic and router overhead. Whenever an LSA is sent, all affected OSPF routers have to recompute their LSDB and the SPF tree using the SPF algorithm.

With route summarization, only summarized routes propagate into the backbone (area 0), as shown in Figure 5-11. This summarization is important because it prevents every router from having to rerun the SPF algorithm, increases the network's stability, and reduces unnecessary LSA flooding. Also, if a network link fails, the topology change is not propagated into the backbone (and other areas by way of the backbone). Specific-link LSA flooding outside the area does not occur.

Figure 5-11 *Benefits of Route Summarization*

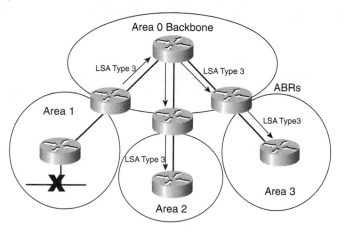

KEY
POINT
| **Summary LSAs Do Not Contain Summarized Routes**
Recall that summary LSAs (type 3 LSAs) and external LSAs (type 5 LSAs) by default do not contain summarized routes. By default, summary LSAs are not summarized.

The two types of summarization are as follows:

- **Interarea route summarization**—Interarea route summarization occurs on ABRs and applies to routes from within each area. It does not apply to external routes injected into OSPF via redistribution. To perform effective interarea route summarization, network numbers within areas should be assigned contiguously so that these addresses can be summarized into a minimal number of summary addresses. (Figure 5-12 later illustrates interarea summarization at the ABR for area 1.)

- **External route summarization**—External route summarization is specific to external routes that are injected into OSPF via route redistribution. Again, it is important to ensure the contiguity of the external address ranges that are being summarized. Summarizing overlapping ranges from two different routers can cause packets to be sent to the wrong destination. Generally, only ASBRs summarize external routes.

OSPF is a classless routing protocol, which means that it carries subnet mask information along with route information. Therefore, OSPF supports multiple subnet masks for the same major network, known as variable-length subnet masking (VLSM). OSPF also supports discontiguous subnets, because subnet masks are part of the LSDB. However, other protocols, such as Routing Information Protocol Version 1 (RIPv1), do not support VLSMs or discontiguous subnets. If the same major network crosses the boundaries of an OSPF and RIPv1 domain, VLSM information redistributed into RIPv1 is lost, and static routes have to be configured in the RIPv1 domain.

KEY
POINT

Contiguous Address Assignment

Network numbers in areas should be assigned contiguously to ensure that these addresses can be summarized into a minimal number of summary addresses.

For example, in Figure 5-12, the list of 12 networks in router B's routing table can be summarized into two summary address advertisements. The block of addresses from 172.16.8.0 to 172.16.15.0/24 can be summarized using 172.16.8.0/21, and the block from 172.16.16.0 to 172.16.19.0/24 can be summarized using 172.16.16.0/22.

Figure 5-12 *Using Route Summarization*

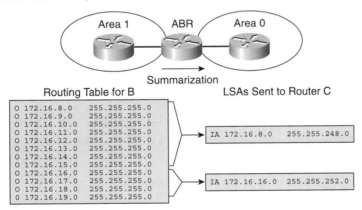

Configuring OSPF Route Summarization on an ABR

OSPF does not perform autosummarization on major network boundaries. To manually configure interarea route summarization on an ABR, use the following procedure:

Step 1   Configure OSPF.

Step 2   Use the **area** *area-id* **range** *address mask* [**advertise** | **not-advertise**] [**cost** *cost*] router configuration command, described in Table 5-6, to instruct the ABR to summarize routes for a specific area before injecting them into a different area via the backbone as type 3 summary LSAs.

Table 5-6 **area range** *Command Parameters*

Parameter	Description
area-id	Identifies the area subject to route summarization.
address	The summary address designated for a range of addresses.
mask	The IP subnet mask used for the summary route.
advertise	(Optional) Sets the address range status to advertise and generates a type 3 summary LSA.
not-advertise	(Optional) Sets the address range status to DoNotAdvertise. The type 3 summary LSA is suppressed, and the component networks remain hidden from other networks.
cost	(Optional) Metric or cost for this summary route, which is used during the OSPF SPF calculation to determine the shortest paths to the destination. The value can be 0 to 16777215.

The Cisco IOS Software creates a summary route to interface null 0 when manual summarization is configured, to prevent routing loops. For example, if the summarizing router receives a packet to an unknown subnet that is part of the summarized range, the packet matches the summary route based on the longest match. The packet is forwarded to the null 0 interface (in other words, it is dropped), which prevents the router from forwarding the packet to a default route and possibly creating a routing loop.

Configuring OSPF Route Summarization on an ASBR

To configure manual route summarization on an ASBR to summarize external routes, use the following procedure:

Step 1   Configure OSPF.

Step 2   Use the **summary-address** *ip-address mask* [**not-advertise**] [**tag** *tag*] router configuration command, described in Table 5-7, to instruct the ASBR to summarize external routes before injecting them into the OSPF domain as a type 5 external LSA.

Table 5-7 **summary-address** *Command Parameters*

Parameter	Description
ip-address	The summary address designated for a range of addresses
mask	The IP subnet mask used for the summary route
not-advertise	(Optional) Used to suppress routes that match the address/mask pair
tag *tag*	(Optional) A tag value that can be used as a "match" value to control redistribution via route maps

Route Summarization Configuration Example at an ABR

Figure 5-13 shows that route summarization can occur in both directions on an ABR—from a nonbackbone area to area 0 and from area 0 to a nonbackbone area. Example 5-3 illustrates the R1 and R2 configurations. For example, the R1 configuration specifies the following summarization:

- **area 0 range 172.16.96.0 255.255.224.0**—Identifies area 0 as the area containing the range of networks to be summarized into area 1. The ABR R1 summarizes the range of subnets from 172.16.96.0 to 172.16.127.0 into one range: 172.16.96.0 255.255.224.0.

- **area 1 range 172.16.32.0 255.255.224.0**—Identifies area 1 as the area containing the range of networks to be summarized into area 0. The ABR R1 summarizes the range of subnets from 172.16.32.0 to 172.16.63.0 into one range: 172.16.32.0 255.255.224.0.

Figure 5-13 *Route Summarization Example at the ABR*

Example 5-3 *Enabling OSPF Routing on R1 and R2 in Figure 5-13*

```
Router1(config)#router ospf 100
Router1(config-router)#network 172.16.32.1 0.0.0.0 area 1
Router1(config-router)#network 172.16.96.1 0.0.0.0 area 0
Router1(config-router)#area 0 range 172.16.96.0 255.255.224.0
Router1(config-router)#area 1 range 172.16.32.0 255.255.224.0

Router2(config)#router ospf 100
Router2(config-router)#network 172.16.64.1 0.0.0.0 area 2
Router2(config-router)#network 172.16.127.1 0.0.0.0 area 0
Router2(config-router)#area 0 range 172.16.96.0 255.255.224.0
Router2(config-router)#area 2 range 172.16.64.0 255.255.224.0
```

NOTE Depending on your network topology, you may not want to summarize area 0 networks into other areas. For example, if you have more than one ABR between an area and the backbone area, sending a type 3 (summary) LSA with the explicit network information into an area ensures that the shortest path to destinations outside the area is selected. If you summarize the addresses, suboptimal path selection may occur.

Route Summarization Configuration Example at an ASBR

Figure 5-14 depicts route summarization on an ASBR. On the left, an external autonomous system running RIPv2 has its routes redistributed into OSPF. Because of the contiguous subnet block in the external RIP network, it is possible to summarize the 32 different subnets into one summarized route.

Figure 5-14   *Route Summarization Example at the ASBR*

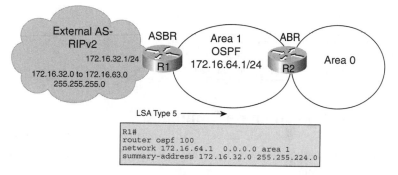

Instead of 32 external type 5 LSAs flooding into the OSPF network, there is only 1.

> **NOTE**   RIPv2 routes must also be redistributed into OSPF in this example; redistribution is covered in Chapter 7.

Creating a Default Route in OSPF

You may want to configure OSPF to advertise a default route into its autonomous system, as described in this section.

Figure 5-15 shows how OSPF injects a default route into a standard area (the different types of areas are covered in the "OSPF Special Area Types" section later in this chapter). Any OSPF router can originate default routes injected into a standard area. However, OSPF routers do not, by default, generate a default route into the OSPF domain. For OSPF to generate a default route, you must use the **default-information originate** command.

Figure 5-15   *Default Routes in OSPF*

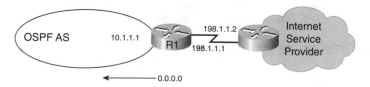

There are two ways to advertise a default route into a standard area. The first is to advertise 0.0.0.0 into the OSPF domain, provided that the advertising router already has a default route. The second is to advertise 0.0.0.0 regardless of whether the advertising router already has a default route. (The second method can be accomplished by adding the keyword **always** to the **default-information originate** command, as described in the next section.)

A default route shows up in the OSPF database as an external LSA type 5, as shown in Example 5-4.

Example 5-4 *Default Route in the OSPF Database*

```
Type-5 AS External Link States
Link ID    ADV Router   Age    Seq#        Checksum   Tag
0.0.0.0    198.1.1.1    601    0x80000001  0xD0D8     0
```

The default-information originate Command

To generate a default external route into an OSPF routing domain, use the **default-information originate** [**always**] [**metric** *metric-value*] [**metric-type** *type-value*] [**route-map** *map-name*] router configuration command.

To disable this feature, use the **no** form of the command. Table 5-8 explains the options of the **default-information originate** command.

Table 5-8 **default-information originate** *Command Parameters*

Parameter	Description
always	(Optional) Specifies that OSPF always advertises the default route regardless of whether the router has a default route in the routing table.
metric *metric-value*	(Optional) A metric used for generating the default route. If you omit a value and do not specify a value using the **default-metric** router configuration command, the default metric value is 1. Cisco IOS Software documentation indicates that the default metric value is 10; testing shows that it is actually 1. Refer to the "**default-information originate** Command Actual Behavior" sidebar for more details.
metric-type *type-value*	(Optional) External link type that is associated with the default route that is advertised into the OSPF routing domain. It can be one of the following values: **1**—Type 1 external route **2**—Type 2 external route. The default is type 2 external route (indicated by O*E2 in the routing table).
route-map *map-name*	(Optional) Specifies that the routing process generates the default route if the route map is satisfied.

default-information originate Command Actual Behavior

The Cisco IOS Software documentation for the **default-information originate** command
mentions that if you omit a value for the *metric* variable and do not specify a value using the
default-metric router configuration command, the default metric value for the **default-information originate** command is 10. Testing shows that it is actually 1.

To verify the default value of the *metric* when using the **default-information originate** command,
tests were performed on Ethernet, serial high-level data link control (HDLC), and serial Frame
Relay links. In all cases, the metric was 1. The following is the configuration used on two routers
in one of the tests:

```
Router R1:
interface Serial1
 no ip address
 encapsulation frame-relay
 !
interface Serial1.1 multipoint
 ip address 10.0.0.1 255.0.0.0
 ip ospf network broadcast
 frame-relay interface-dlci 120
 !
router ospf 10
 log-adjacency-changes
 network 10.0.0.0 0.0.0.255 area 0
 default-information originate always

Router R2:
interface Serial0
 ip address 10.0.0.2 255.0.0.0
 encapsulation frame-relay
 ip ospf network broadcast
 no fair-queue
 clockrate 2000000
 frame-relay interface-dlci 120
 frame-relay intf-type dce
 !
router ospf 10
 network 10.0.0.0 0.0.0.255 area 0
```

The following is the routing table on Router R2, when the command **default-information
originate** was issued on R1 without specifying a value for the *metric* variable. The metric
appearing in the routing table for the default route is 1, not 10 as mentioned in the documentation:

```
R2>show ip route
<output omitted>
Gateway of last resort is 10.0.0.1 to network 0.0.0.0

C    10.0.0.0/8 is directly connected, Serial0
O*E2 0.0.0.0/0 [110/1] via 10.0.0.1, 00:18:49, Serial0
```

Figure 5-16 shows an OSPF network multihomed to dual Internet service providers (ISPs). The
optional **metric** parameter has been used to prefer the default route to ISP A. The default route
being generated has a *metric-type* of E2 by default, so the metric does not increase as it goes
through the area. As a result, all routers, regardless of their proximity to the border router, prefer
ISP A over ISP B.

Figure 5-16 *Default Route Example*

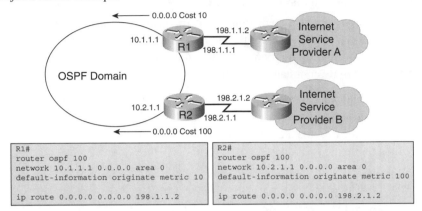

```
R1#                                      R2#
router ospf 100                          router ospf 100
network 10.1.1.1 0.0.0.0 area 0          network 10.2.1.1 0.0.0.0 area 0
default-information originate metric 10  default-information originate metric 100

ip route 0.0.0.0 0.0.0.0 198.1.1.2       ip route 0.0.0.0 0.0.0.0 198.2.1.2
```

> **NOTE**   The **default-information originate** command causes the router to send a default route to all its OSPF neighbors. In Figure 5-16, notice that the R1 and R2 routers are not running OSPF on their connections to the ISP routers, and are therefore not passing a default route to the ISP routers.

OSPF Special Area Types

The characteristics assigned to an area control the type of route information it receives. The purpose behind any type of stub area is to inject default routes into an area so that external and/or summary LSAs are not flooded into the area. This reduces the LSDB size and the routing table size in the routers within the area. The possible area types, some of which are shown in Figure 5-17, are as follows:

- **Standard area**—This default area accepts link updates, route summaries, and external routes.

- **Backbone area (transit area)**—The backbone area is the central entity to which all other areas connect. The backbone area is labeled area 0. All other areas connect to this area to exchange and route information. The OSPF backbone has all the properties of a standard OSPF area.

- **Stub area**—This area does not accept information about routes external to the autonomous system, such as routes from non-OSPF sources. If routers need to route to networks outside the autonomous system, they use a default route, indicated as 0.0.0.0. Stub areas cannot contain ASBRs (except that the ABRs may also be ASBRs).

- **Totally stubby area**—This area does not accept external autonomous system routes or summary routes from other areas internal to the autonomous system. If a router needs to send a packet to a network external to the area, it sends the packet using a default route. Totally stubby areas cannot contain ASBRs (except that the ABRs may also be ASBRs).

- **NSSA**—NSSA is an addendum to the OSPF Requests for Comments (RFC). This area defines a special LSA type 7. NSSA offers benefits that are similar to those of a stub or totally stubby area. However, NSSAs allow ASBRs, which is against the rules in a stub area. Cisco routers also allow an area to be configured as a totally stubby NSSA.

Figure 5-17   *Some Types of OSPF Areas*

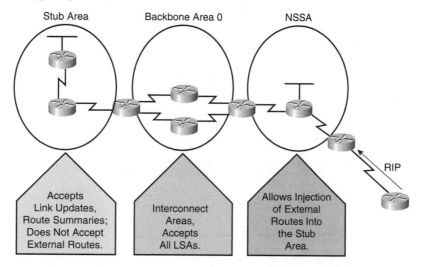

An area qualifies as stub or totally stubby area if it has the following characteristics:

- There is a single exit point from that area; or if there are multiple exits, one or more ABRs inject a default route into the stub area and suboptimal routing paths are acceptable. In other words, routing to other areas or autonomous systems can take a suboptimal path to reach the destination by exiting the area via a point that is farther from the destination than other exit points.

- All OSPF routers inside the stub area, including ABRs and internal routers, are configured as stub routers. All of these routers must be configured as stub routers before they can become neighbors and exchange routing information.

- The area is not needed as a transit area for virtual links (virtual links are described in the "OSPF Virtual Links" section later in this chapter).

- No ASBR is inside the stub area.

- The area is not the backbone area (area 0).

Configuring Stub Areas

Configuring a stub area reduces the size of the LSDB inside an area, resulting in reduced memory requirements for routers in that area. Routers within the stub area also do not have to run the SPF algorithm as often since they will receive less routing updates. External network LSAs (type 5), such as those redistributed from other routing protocols into OSPF, are not permitted to flood into a stub area, as shown in Figure 5-18. Routing from these areas to a route external to the OSPF autonomous system is based on a default route (0.0.0.0). If a packet is addressed to a network that is not in the routing table of an internal router, the router automatically forwards the packet to the ABR that originates a 0.0.0.0 LSA. Forwarding the packet to the ABR allows routers within the stub area to reduce the size of their routing tables, because a single default route replaces many external routes.

Figure 5-18 *Using Stub Areas*

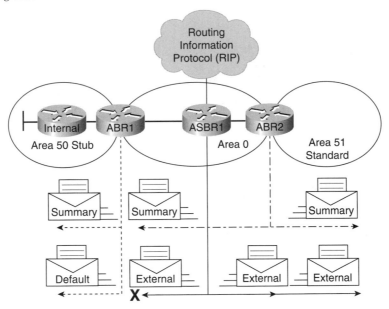

A stub area is typically created using a hub-and-spoke topology, with a spoke being a stub area, such as a branch office. In this case, the branch office does not need to know about every network at the headquarters site, because it can use a default route to reach the networks.

To configure an area as a stub, use the following procedure:

Step 1 Configure OSPF.

Step 2 Define an area as stub by adding the **area** *area-id* **stub** router configuration command to all routers within the area.

Table 5-9 describes the parameter of the **area stub** command.

Table 5-9 **area stub** *Command Parameter*

Parameter	Description
area-id	The identifier for the stub area. The identifier can be either a decimal value or a value in dotted-decimal format, like an IP address.

By default, the ABR of a stubby or totally stubby area advertises a default route with a cost of 1. An option is to change the cost of the default route by using the **area** *area-id* **default-cost** *cost* router configuration command. The parameters of this command are shown in Table 5-10.

Table 5-10 **area default-cost** *Command Parameters*

Parameter	Description
area-id	The identifier for the stub area, totally stubby area, or NSSA. The identifier can be either a decimal value or a value in dotted-decimal format, like an IP address.
cost	Cost for the default summary route. The acceptable values are 0 through 16777215.

Figure 5-19 illustrates an example. Area 2 is defined as the stub area. No routes from the external autonomous system are forwarded into the stub area.

Figure 5-19 *OSPF Stub Area Example*

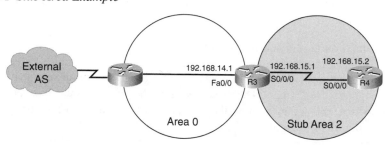

Example 5-5 shows the OSPF configuration on routers R3 and R4 including enabling an OSPF stub area.

Example 5-5 *OSPF Stub Area Configuration for Routers R3 and R4 in Figure 5-19*

```
Router R3:
R3(config)#interface FastEthernet0/0
R3(config-if)#ip address 192.168.14.1 255.255.255.0
R3(config)#interface Serial 0/0/0
R3(config-if)#ip address 192.168.15.1 255.255.255.252
```

continues

Example 5-5 *OSPF Stub Area Configuration for Routers R3 and R4 in Figure 5-19 (Continued)*

```
R3(config)#router ospf 100
R3(config-router)#network 192.168.14.0.0 0.0.0.255 area 0
R3(config-router)#network 192.168.15.0.0 0.0.0.255 area 2
R3(config-router)#area 2 stub

Router R4:
R4(config)#interface Serial 0/0/0
R4(config-if)#ip address 192.168.15.2 255.255.255.252

R4(config)#router ospf 100
R4(config-router)#network 192.168.15.0.0 0.0.0.255 area 2
R4(config-router)#area 2 stub
```

The last line in each configuration (**area 2 stub**) defines the stub area. The R3 router (the ABR) automatically advertises 0.0.0.0 (the default route) with a default cost metric of 1 into the stub area.

Each router in the stub area must be configured with the **area stub** command.

The routes that appear in the routing table of router R4 are as follows:

- Intra-area routes, which are designated with an O in the routing table

- The default route and interarea routes, which are both designated with an IA in the routing table

- The default route, which is also denoted with an asterisk (O*IA)

> **NOTE** The hello packet exchanged between OSPF routers contains a stub area flag that must match on neighboring routers. The **area** *area-id* **stub** command must be enabled on all routers in the stub area so that they all have the stub flag set; they can then become neighbors and exchange routing information.

Configuring Totally Stubby Areas

A totally stubby area is a Cisco-specific feature that further reduces the number of routes in the routing table. A totally stubby area blocks external type 5 LSAs and summary type 3 and type 4 LSAs (interarea routes) from entering the area, as shown in Figure 5-20. By blocking these routes, the totally stubby area recognizes only intra-area routes and the default route 0.0.0.0. ABRs inject the default summary link 0.0.0.0 into the totally stubby area. Each router picks the closest ABR as a gateway to everything outside the area.

Figure 5-20   *Using Totally Stubby Areas*

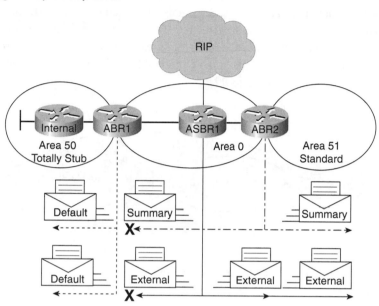

Totally stubby areas minimize routing information further than stub areas and increase stability and scalability of OSPF internetworks. Using totally stubby areas is typically a better solution than using stub areas, assuming the ABR is a Cisco router.

To configure an area as totally stubby, do the following:

Step 1   Configure OSPF.

Step 2   Define an area as totally stubby by adding the **area** *area-id* **stub** router configuration command to all routers in the area.

Step 3   At the ABR only, add the **no-summary** parameter to the **area** *area-id* **stub** command.

Table 5-11 explains the **area** *area-id* **stub no-summary** command.

Table 5-11   **area** *area-id* **stub no-summary** *Command Parameters*

Parameter	Description
area-id	The identifier for the stub or totally stubby area. It can be either a decimal value or a value in dotted-decimal format, like an IP address.
no-summary	Stops summary LSAs, in addition to external LSAs, from flooding into the totally stubby area.

Figure 5-21 shows an example of a totally stubby area topology. The configurations on routers R2, R3, and R4 are shown in Example 5-6. All routes advertised into area 1 (from area 0 and the external autonomous system) default to 0.0.0.0. The default route cost is set to 5 on R2 and to 10 on R4. Both default routes are advertised into area 1. However, the default route from R2 is advertised with a lower cost to make it more preferable if the internal cost from R3 to R4 is the same as the internal cost from R3 to R2.

Figure 5-21   *Totally Stubby Example*

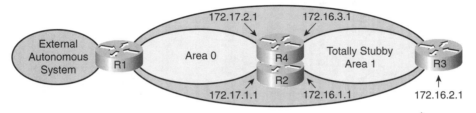

Example 5-6   *Totally Stubby Configuration for Routers in Figure 5-21*

```
Router R2:
R2(config)#router ospf 10
R2(config-router)#network 172.17.0.0 0.0.255.255 area 0
R2(config-router)#network 172.16.0.0 0.0.255.255 area 1
R2(config-router)#area 1 stub no-summary
R2(config-router)#area 1 default-cost 5

Router R3:
R3(config)#router ospf 10
R3(config-router)#network 172.16.0.0 0.0.255.255 area 1
R3(config-router)#area 1 stub

Router R4:
R4(config)#router ospf 10
R4(config-router)#network 172.17.0.0 0.0.255.255 area 0
R4(config-router)#network 172.16.0.0 0.0.255.255 area 1
R4(config-router)#area 1 stub no-summary
R4(config-router)#area 1 default-cost 10
```

Notice that R3 requires the **area 1 stub** command, yet the **no-summary** extension is not required. Only ABRs use **no-summary** to keep summary LSAs from being propagated into another area.

> **CAUTION**   Remember that all routers in a stub or totally stubby area must be configured as stubs. An OSPF adjacency will not form between stub and nonstub routers.

Interpreting Routing Tables in Different Types of OSPF Areas

This section illustrates routing tables when different area types are configured.

Example 5-7 shows how the routing table of an OSPF router in a standard area (without any kind of stub configuration) might look. Intra-area, interarea, and external routes are all maintained in a standard area.

Example 5-7 *Routing Table in a Standard Area*

```
P1R3#show ip route
<output omitted>

Gateway of last resort is not set
     172.31.0.0/32 is subnetted, 4 subnets
O IA    172.31.22.4 [110/782] via 10.1.1.1, 00:02:44, FastEthernet0/0
O IA    172.31.11.1 [110/1] via 10.1.1.1, 00:02:44, FastEthernet0/0
O IA    172.31.11.2 [110/782] via 10.1.3.4, 00:02:52, Serial0/0/0
                     [110/782] via 10.1.1.1, 00:02:52, FastEthernet0/0
O IA    172.31.11.4 [110/782] via 10.1.1.1, 00:02:44, FastEthernet0/0
     10.0.0.0/8 is variably subnetted, 7 subnets, 2 masks
O       10.11.0.0/24 [110/782] via 10.1.1.1, 00:03:22, FastEthernet0/0
C       10.200.200.13/32 is directly connected, Loopback0
C       10.1.3.0/24 is directly connected, Serial0/0/0
O       10.1.2.0/24 [110/782] via 10.1.3.4, 00:03:23, Serial0/0/0
C       10.1.1.0/24 is directly connected, FastEthernet0/0
O       10.1.0.0/24 [110/782] via 10.1.1.1, 00:03:23, FastEthernet0/0
O E2    10.254.0.0/24 [110/50] via 10.1.1.1, 00:02:39, FastEthernet0/0
P1R3#
```

Example 5-8 shows how the same routing table looks if the area is configured as a stub area. Intra-area and interarea routes are all maintained. However, external routes are not visible in the routing table; they are accessible via the intra-area default route.

Example 5-8 *Routing Table in a Stub Area*

```
P1R3#show ip route
<output omitted>

Gateway of last resort is 10.1.1.1 to network 0.0.0.0
     172.31.0.0/32 is subnetted, 4 subnets
O IA    172.31.22.4 [110/782] via 10.1.1.1, 00:01:49, FastEthernet0/0
O IA    172.31.11.1 [110/1] via 10.1.1.1, 00:01:49, FastEthernet0/0
O IA    172.31.11.2 [110/782] via 10.1.3.4, 00:01:49, Serial0/0/0
                     [110/782] via 10.1.1.1, 00:01:49, FastEthernet0/0
O IA    172.31.11.4 [110/782] via 10.1.1.1, 00:01:49, FastEthernet0/0
     10.0.0.0/8 is variably subnetted, 6 subnets, 2 masks
```

continues

Example 5-8 *Routing Table in a Stub Area (Continued)*

```
O       10.11.0.0/24 [110/782] via 10.1.1.1, 00:01:50, FastEthernet0/0
C       10.200.200.13/32 is directly connected, Loopback0
C       10.1.3.0/24 is directly connected, Serial0/0/0
O       10.1.2.0/24 [110/782] via 10.1.3.4, 00:01:50, Serial0/0/0
C       10.1.1.0/24 is directly connected, FastEthernet0/0
O       10.1.0.0/24 [110/782] via 10.1.1.1, 00:01:50, FastEthernet0/0
O*IA 0.0.0.0/0 [110/2] via 10.1.1.1, 00:01:51, FastEthernet0/0
P1R3#
```

Example 5-9 shows how the same routing table looks if summarization is performed on the ABR; the area is still configured as a stub area. Intra-area and summarized interarea routes are all maintained. External routes are not visible in the routing table but are accessible via the intra-area default route.

Example 5-9 *Routing Table in a Stub Area with Summarization*

```
P1R3#show ip route
<output omitted>

Gateway of last resort is 10.1.1.1 to network 0.0.0.0
     172.31.0.0/16 is variably subnetted, 2 subnets, 2 masks
O IA    172.31.22.4/32 [110/782] via 10.1.1.1, 00:13:08, FastEthernet0/0
O IA    172.31.11.0/24 [110/1] via 10.1.1.1, 00:02:39, FastEthernet0/0
     10.0.0.0/8 is variably subnetted, 6 subnets, 2 masks
O       10.11.0.0/24 [110/782] via 10.1.1.1, 00:13:08, FastEthernet0/0
C       10.200.200.13/32 is directly connected, Loopback0
C       10.1.3.0/24 is directly connected, Serial0/0/0
O       10.1.2.0/24 [110/782] via 10.1.3.4, 00:13:09, Serial0/0/0
C       10.1.1.0/24 is directly connected, FastEthernet0/0
O       10.1.0.0/24 [110/782] via 10.1.1.1, 00:13:09, FastEthernet0/0
O*IA 0.0.0.0/0 [110/2] via 10.1.1.1, 00:13:09, FastEthernet0/0
P1R3#
```

Example 5-10 shows how the same routing table looks if the area is configured as a totally stubby area. Notice that routers in the totally stubby area have the smallest routing tables. Intra-area routes are maintained. Interarea and external routes are not visible in the routing table but are accessible via the intra-area default route.

Example 5-10 *Routing Table in a Totally Stubby Area*

```
P1R3#show ip route
<output omitted>

Gateway of last resort is 10.1.1.1 to network 0.0.0.0
     10.0.0.0/8 is variably subnetted, 6 subnets, 2 masks
O       10.11.0.0/24 [110/782] via 10.1.1.1, 00:16:53, FastEthernet0/0
```

Example 5-10 *Routing Table in a Totally Stubby Area (Continued)*

```
C       10.200.200.13/32 is directly connected, Loopback0
C       10.1.3.0/24 is directly connected, Serial0/0/0
O       10.1.2.0/24 [110/782] via 10.1.3.4, 00:16:53, Serial0/0/0
C       10.1.1.0/24 is directly connected, FastEthernet0/0
O       10.1.0.0/24 [110/782] via 10.1.1.1, 00:16:53, FastEthernet0/0
O*IA 0.0.0.0/0 [110/2] via 10.1.1.1, 00:00:48, FastEthernet0/0
P1R3#
```

Configuring NSSAs

The OSPF NSSA feature is described by RFC 3101 and was introduced in Cisco IOS Software Release 11.2. It is a nonproprietary extension of the existing stub area feature that allows the injection of external routes in a limited fashion into the stub area.

Redistribution into an NSSA area creates a special type of LSA known as type 7, which can exist only in an NSSA area. An NSSA ASBR generates this LSA, and an NSSA ABR translates it into a type 5 LSA, which gets propagated into the OSPF domain.

The NSSA feature allows an area to retain the other stub area features—the ABR sends a default route into the NSSA instead of external routes from other ASBRs—while also allowing an ASBR to be inside of the area. Recall that one of the rules of stub areas is that there must not be an ASBR inside of a stub area; an NSSA—a *not-so-stubby* area—bends this rule. Figure 5-22 illustrates an NSSA.

Figure 5-22 *NSSA*

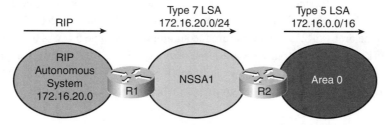

The type 7 LSA is described in the routing table as an O N2 or O N1 (N means NSSA). N1 means that the metric is calculated like external type 1; N2 means that the metric is calculated like external type 2. The default is O N2.

To configure an NSSA, the **area** *area-id* **nssa** [**no-redistribution**] [**default-information-originate**] [**metric** *metric*-value] [**metric-type** *type-value*] [**no-summary**] router configuration command is used in place of the **area** *area-id* **stub** command. Remember that all routers in the NSSA must have this command configured; two routers will not form an adjacency unless both are configured as NSSA.

Table 5-12 defines the parameters of the **area nssa** command.

Table 5-12 **area** *area-id* **nssa** *Command Parameters*

Parameter	Description
area-id	The identifier for the NSSA. It can be either a decimal value or a value in dotted-decimal format, like an IP address.
no-redistribution	(Optional) Used when the router is an NSSA ABR and you want the **redistribute** command to import routes only into the standard areas, but not into the NSSA area.
default-information-originate	(Optional) Used to generate a type 7 default LSA into the NSSA area. This keyword takes effect only on an NSSA ABR or an NSSA ASBR.
metric *metric-value*	(Optional) Metric that is used for generating the default route. Acceptable values are 0 through 16777214.
metric-type *type-value*	(Optional) OSPF metric type for default routes. It can be one of the following values: 1: type 1 external route 2: type 2 external route
no-summary	(Optional) Allows an area to be an NSSA but not have summary routes injected into it. Thus, the area is a totally stubby NSSA.

In Figure 5-23 and Example 5-11, R1 is the ASBR that redistributes RIP routes into area 1, the NSSA. R2 is the NSSA ABR; this router converts type 7 LSAs into type 5 LSAs for advertisement into backbone area 0. R2 is also configured to summarize the type 5 LSAs that originate from the RIP network; the 172.16.0.0 subnets are summarized to 172.16.0.0/16 and are advertised into area 0. To cause R2 (the NSSA ABR) to generate an O*N2 default route (O*N2 0.0.0.0/0) into the NSSA, the **default-information-originate** parameter is used on the **area** *area-id* **nssa** command on R2.

Figure 5-23 *NSSA Example*

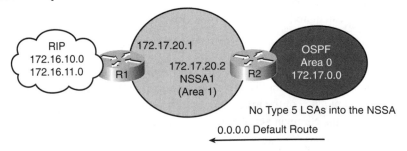

Example 5-11 *OSPF NSSA Configuration for Routers in Figure 5-23*

```
Router R1:
R1(config)#router ospf 10
R1(config-router)#redistribute rip subnets
R1(config-router)#default metric 150
R1(config-router)#network 172.17.0.0 0.0.255.255 area 1
R1(config-router)#area 1 nssa

Router R2:
R2(config)#router ospf 10
R2(config-router)#summary-address 172.16.0.0 255.255.0.0
R2(config-router)#network 172.17.20.0 0.0.0.255 area 1
R2(config-router)#network 172.17.0.0 0.0.255.255 area 0
R2(config-router)#area 1 nssa default-information-originate
```

In another example in Figure 5-24 and Example 5-12, notice that the ABR is using the **area 1 nssa no-summary** command. This command works exactly the same as the totally stubby technique. A single default route replaces both inbound external (type 5) LSAs and summary (type 3 and 4) LSAs into the area. The NSSA ABR, which is R2, automatically generates the O*N2 default route into the NSSA area when the **no-summary** option is configured at the ABR, so the **default-information-originate** parameter is not required.

Figure 5-24 *NSSA Totally Stubby*

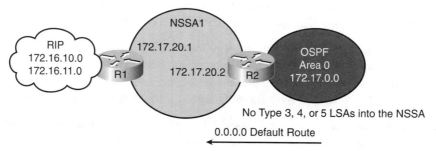

Example 5-12 *NSSA Totally Stubby Configuration for Routers in Figure 5-24*

```
Router R1:
R1(config)#router ospf 10
R1(config-router)#redistribute rip subnets
R1(config-router)#default metric 150
R1(config-router)#network 172.17.0.0 0.0.255.255 area 1
R1(config-router)#area 1 nssa

Router R2:
R2(config)#router ospf 10
R2(config-router)#summary-address 172.16.0.0 255.255.0.0
R2(config-router)#network 172.17.20.0 0.0.0.255 area 1
R2(config-router)#network 172.17.0.0 0.0.255.255 area 0
R2(config-router)#area 1 nssa no-summary
```

All other routers in the NSSA area require the **area 1 nssa** command only. The NSSA totally stubby configuration is a Cisco-specific feature, just as the totally stubby area feature is.

Verifying All Area Types

The **show** commands in Table 5-13 are used to display which area type has been configured and other information about the area.

Table 5-13   **show** *Commands for All Area Types*

Command	Description
show ip ospf	Displays OSPF information, including which areas are standard, stub, or NSSA
show ip ospf database	Displays details of LSAs
show ip ospf database nssa-external	Displays specific details of each LSA type 7 update in the database
show ip route	Displays all routes

How Does OSPF Generate Default Routes?

How OSPF generates default routes (0.0.0.0) varies depending on the type of area the default route is being injected into—a standard area, stub area, totally stubby area, or NSSA.

By default, in standard areas, routers don't generate default routes. To have an OSPF router generate a default route, use the **default-information originate** [**always**] [**metric** *metric-value*] [**metric-type** *type-value*] [**route-map** *map-name*] command. By default, this command generates an E2 route with link-state ID 0.0.0.0 and network mask 0.0.0.0, which makes the router an ASBR.

There are two ways to inject a default route into a standard area. If the ASBR already has the default route, you can advertise 0.0.0.0 into the area. If the ASBR doesn't have the route, you can add the keyword **always** to the **default-information originate** command, which then advertises 0.0.0.0.

For stub and totally stubby areas, the ABR generates a summary LSA with the link-state ID 0.0.0.0. This is true even if the ABR does not have a default route. In this scenario, you do not need to use the **default-information originate** command.

The ABR for an NSSA generates the default route, but not by default. To force the ABR to generate the default route, use the **area** *area-id* **nssa default-information-originate** command. The ABR generates a type 7 LSA with the link-state ID 0.0.0.0. If you want to import routes only into the standard areas, not into the NSSA area, you can use the **no-redistribution** option on the NSSA ABR. The ABR for a totally stubby NSSA automatically generates a default route.

OSPF Virtual Links

OSPF's two-tiered area hierarchy requires that all areas be directly connected to the backbone area, area 0, and that area 0 be contiguous.

A virtual link is a link that allows discontiguous area 0s to be connected, or a disconnected area to be connected to area 0, via a transit area. The OSPF virtual link feature should be used only in very specific cases, for temporary connections or backup after a failure. Virtual links should not be used as a primary backbone design feature.

Virtual links are part of the OSPF open standard and have been a part of Cisco IOS Software since software release 10.0. In Figure 5-25, area 0 is discontiguous because of a network failure. A logical link (virtual link) is built between the two ABRs, routers A and B. This virtual link is similar to a standard OSPF adjacency; however, in a virtual link, the routers do not have to be directly attached to neighboring routers.

Figure 5-25 *Virtual Links Are Used to Connect a Discontiguous Area 0*

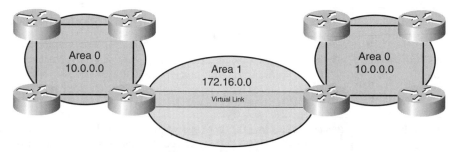

The Hello protocol works over virtual links as it does over standard links, in 10-second intervals. However, LSA updates work differently on virtual links. An LSA usually refreshes every 30 minutes; LSAs learned through a virtual link have the DoNotAge (DNA) option set, so that the LSA does not age out. This DNA technique is required to prevent excessive flooding over the virtual link.

Configuring OSPF Virtual Links

Use the **area** *area-id* **virtual-link** *router-id* [**authentication** [**message-digest** | **null**]] [**hello-interval** *seconds*] [**retransmit-interval** *seconds*] [**transmit-delay** *seconds*] [**dead-interval** *seconds*] [[**authentication-key** *key*] | [**message-digest-key** *key-id* **md5** *key*]] router configuration command to define an OSPF virtual link. To remove a virtual link, use the **no** form of this command.

Table 5-14 describes the options available with the **area** *area-id* **virtual-link** command. Make sure you understand the effect of these options before changing them. For instance, the smaller the hello interval, the faster the detection of topological changes; however, more routing traffic ensues.

You should be conservative with the setting of the retransmit interval, or the result is needless retransmissions; the value is larger for serial lines and virtual links. The transmit delay value should take into account the interface's transmission and propagation delays.

Table 5-14 **area** *area-id* **virtual-link** *Command Parameters*

Parameter	Description
area-id	Specifies the area ID of the transit area for the virtual link. This ID can be either a decimal value or in dotted-decimal format, like a valid IP address. There is no default. The transit area cannot be a stub area.
router-id	Specifies the router ID of the virtual link neighbor. The router ID appears in the **show ip ospf** display. This value is in an IP address format. There is no default.
authentication	(Optional) Specifies an authentication type.
message-digest	(Optional) Specifies the use of message digest 5 (MD5) authentication.
null	(Optional) Overrides simple password or MD5 authentication if configured for the area; no authentication is used.
hello-interval *seconds*	(Optional) Specifies the time (in seconds) between the hello packets that the Cisco IOS Software sends on an interface. The unsigned integer value is advertised in the hello packets. The value must be the same for all routers and access servers attached to a common network. The default is 10 seconds.
retransmit-interval *seconds*	(Optional) Specifies the time (in seconds) between LSA retransmissions for adjacencies belonging to the interface. The value must be greater than the expected round-trip delay between any two routers on the attached network. The default is 5 seconds.
transmit-delay *seconds*	(Optional) Specifies the estimated time (in seconds) to send an LSU packet on the interface. This integer value must be greater than 0. LSAs in the update packet have their age incremented by this amount before transmission. The default value is 1 second.
dead-interval *seconds*	(Optional) Specifies the time (in seconds) that must pass without hello packets being seen before a neighboring router declares the router down. This is an unsigned integer value. The default is four times the default hello interval, or 40 seconds. As with the hello interval, this value must be the same for all routers and access servers attached to a common network.
authentication-key *key*	(Optional) Specifies the password used by neighboring routers for simple password authentication. It is any continuous string of up to 8 characters. There is no default value.
message-digest-key *key-id* **md5** *key*	(Optional) Identifies the key ID and key (password) used between this router and neighboring routers for MD5 authentication. There is no default value.

NOTE   OSPF authentication, including details of the *key* and *key-id* parameters, is described further in the "Configuring OSPF Authentication" section later in this chapter.

The **area** *area-id* **virtual-link** command requires the router ID of the far-end router. To find the router ID of the far-end router, use the **show ip ospf** command, **show ip ospf interface** command, or **show ip protocol** command on that remote router.

Example 5-13 illustrates the output of the **show ip ospf** command, displaying the OSPF router ID.

Example 5-13   *Finding the OSPF Router ID for Use on a Virtual Link*

```
remoterouter#show ip ospf
 Routing Process "ospf 1000" with ID 10.2.2.2
 Supports only single TOS(TOS0) routes
 Supports opaque LSA
 Supports Link-local Signaling (LLS)
 Supports area transit capability
 It is an area border router
<output omitted>
```

In the example in Figure 5-26, area 0 is discontiguous (split into two pieces) because of network failure. A virtual link is used as a backup strategy to temporarily reconnect area 0; area 1 is used as the transit area. Router A builds a virtual link to router B, and router B builds a virtual link to the router A. Each router points at the other router's router ID.

Figure 5-26   *OSPF Virtual Link Configuration: Split Area 0*

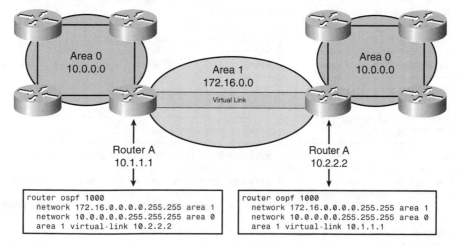

Verifying OSPF Virtual Link Operation

The **show ip ospf virtual-links** command is used to verify OSPF virtual link operation. Example 5-14 provides the output of the **show ip ospf virtual-links** command on router A in the example in Figure 5-26, verifying that the configured link works properly.

Example 5-14 **show ip ospf virtual-links** *Command Output from Router A in Figure 5-26*

```
RouterA#show ip ospf virtual-links
Virtual Link OSPF_VL0 to router 10.2.2.2 is up
  Run as demand circuit
  DoNotAge LSA allowed.
  Transit area 1, via interface Serial0/0/1, Cost of using 781
  Transmit Delay is 1 sec, State POINT_TO_POINT,
  Timer intervals configured, Hello 10, Dead 40, Wait 40, Retransmit 5
    Hello due in 00:00:07
    Adjacency State FULL (Hello suppressed)
    Index 1/2, retransmission queue length 0, number of retransmission 1
    First 0x0(0)/0x0(0) Next 0x0(0)/0x0(0)
    Last retransmission scan length is 1, maximum is 1
    Last retransmission scan time is 0 msec, maximum is 0 msec
RouterA#
```

Table 5-15 describes some of the fields of the output of the **show ip ospf virtual-links** command in detail.

Table 5-15 **show ip ospf virtual-links** *Command Fields*

Field	Description
Virtual Link OSPF_VL0 to router 10.2.2.2 is up	Specifies the OSPF neighbor and whether the link to that neighbor is up or down
Transit area 1	Specifies the transit area through which the virtual link is formed
Via interface Serial0/0/1	Specifies the interface through which the virtual link is formed
Cost of using 781	Specifies the cost of reaching the OSPF neighbor through the virtual link
Transmit Delay is 1 sec	Specifies the transmit delay on the virtual link
State POINT_TO_POINT	Specifies the state of the OSPF neighbor
Timer intervals configured	Specifies the various timer intervals configured for the link
Hello due in 0:00:07	Specifies when the next hello is expected from the neighbor
Adjacency State FULL	Specifies the adjacency state between the neighbors

Routers across a virtual link become adjacent and exchange LSAs via the virtual link, similar to the process over a physical link.

Other commands that are useful when troubleshooting virtual links are **show ip ospf neighbor**, **show ip ospf database**, and **debug ip ospf adj**.

Example output from the **show ip ospf neighbor** command is provided in Example 5-15.

Example 5-15   show ip ospf neighbor *Command Output from Router A in Figure 5-26*

```
RouterA#show ip ospf neighbor

Neighbor ID     Pri   State       Dead Time   Address      Interface
10.200.200.13    1    FULL/DR     00:00:33    10.1.1.3     FastEthernet0/0
10.2.2.2         0    FULL/  -        -        172.16.1.2   OSPF_VL0
10.2.2.2         0    FULL/  -     00:00:32    172.16.1.2   Serial0/0/1
RouterA#
```

Example output from the **show ip ospf database** command is shown in Example 5-16.

Example 5-16   show ip ospf database *Command Output from Router A in Figure 5-26*

```
RouterA#show ip ospf database router 10.2.2.2

            OSPF Router with ID (10.1.1.1) (Process ID 1000)

               Router Link States (Area 0)

  Routing Bit Set on this LSA
  LS age: 1 (DoNotAge)
  Options: (No TOS-capability, DC)
  LS Type: Router Links
  Link State ID: 10.2.2.2
  Advertising Router: 10.2.2.2
  LS Seq Number: 80000003
  Checksum: 0x8380
  Length: 48
  Area Border Router
  Number of Links: 2

    Link connected to: a Virtual Link
      (Link ID) Neighboring Router ID: 10.1.1.1
      (Link Data) Router Interface address: 172.16.1.2
       Number of TOS metrics: 0
        TOS 0 Metrics: 781
```

continues

Example 5-16 **show ip ospf database** *Command Output from Router A in Figure 5-26 (Continued)*

```
      Link connected to: a Transit Network
       (Link ID) Designated Router address: 10.1.2.2
       (Link Data) Router Interface address: 10.1.2.2
        Number of TOS metrics: 0
         TOS 0 Metrics: 1

                 Router Link States (Area 1)

 Routing Bit Set on this LSA
 LS age: 1688
 Options: (No TOS-capability, DC)
 LS Type: Router Links
 Link State ID: 10.2.2.2
 Advertising Router: 10.2.2.2
 LS Seq Number: 80000008
 Checksum: 0xCC81
 Length: 48
 Area Border Router
 Virtual Link Endpoint
 Number of Links: 2

   Link connected to: another Router (point-to-point)
    (Link ID) Neighboring Router ID: 10.1.1.1
    (Link Data) Router Interface address: 172.16.1.2
     Number of TOS metrics: 0
      TOS 0 Metrics: 781

   Link connected to: a Stub Network
    (Link ID) Network/subnet number: 172.16.1.0
    (Link Data) Network Mask: 255.255.255.0
     Number of TOS metrics: 0
      TOS 0 Metrics: 781



 RouterA#
```

Configuring OSPF Authentication

You can prevent your router from receiving fraudulent route updates by configuring neighbor router authentication. OSPF neighbor authentication (also called *neighbor router authentication* or *route authentication*) can be configured such that routers can participate in routing based on predefined passwords.

This section describes the types of OSPF authentication and how to configure and troubleshoot them.

Types of Authentication

Recall that when neighbor authentication has been configured on a router, the router authenticates the source of each routing update packet that it receives. This is accomplished by the exchange of an authenticating key (sometimes referred to as a *password*) that is known to both the sending and the receiving router.

By default, OSPF uses null authentication, which means that routing exchanges over a network are not authenticated. OSPF supports two other authentication methods: simple password authentication (also called plain text authentication), and MD5 authentication.

OSPF MD5 authentication includes a nondecreasing sequence number in each OSPF packet to protect against replay attacks.

Configuring Simple Password Authentication

To configure OSPF simple password authentication, complete the following steps:

Step 1   Assign a password to be used when using OSPF simple password authentication with neighboring routers, using the **ip ospf authentication-key** *password* interface configuration command. Table 5-16 describes the parameter of the **ip ospf authentication-key** command.

Table 5-16   **ip ospf authentication-key** *Command Parameter*

Parameter	Description
password	Any continuous string of characters that can be entered from the keyboard up to 8 bytes in length

NOTE   In Cisco IOS Release 12.4, the router will give a warning message if you try to configure a password longer than eight characters; only the first eight characters will be used. Some earlier Cisco IOS releases did not provide this warning.

The password created by this command is used as a "key" that is inserted directly into the OSPF header when the Cisco IOS Software originates routing protocol packets. A separate password can be assigned to each network on a per-interface basis. All neighboring routers on the same network must have the same password to be able to exchange OSPF information.

> **NOTE** If the **service password-encryption** command is not used when configuring OSPF authentication, the password will be stored as plain text in the router configuration. If you configure the **service password-encryption** command, the password will be stored and displayed in an encrypted form; when it is displayed, there will be an encryption type of 7 specified before the encrypted password.

Step 2 Specify the authentication type using the **ip ospf authentication** [**message-digest | null**] interface configuration command. Table 5-17 describes the parameters of the **ip ospf authentication** command.

Table 5-17 **ip ospf authentication** *Command Parameters*

Parameter	Description
message-digest	(Optional) Specifies that MD5 authentication will be used.
null	(Optional) No authentication is used. Useful for overriding simple password or MD5 authentication if configured for an area.

For simple password authentication, use the **ip ospf authentication** command with no parameters. Before using this command, configure a password for the interface using the **ip ospf authentication-key** command.

The **ip ospf authentication** command was introduced in Cisco IOS Software Release 12.0. For backward compatibility, authentication type for an area is still supported. If the authentication type is not specified for an interface, the authentication type for the area will be used (the area default is null authentication). To enable authentication for an OSPF area, use the **area** *area-id* **authentication** [**message-digest**] router configuration command. Table 5-18 describes the parameters of the **area authentication** command.

Table 5-18 **area authentication** *Command Parameters*

Parameter	Description
area-id	Identifier of the area for which authentication is to be enabled. The identifier can be specified as either a decimal value or an IP address.
message-digest	(Optional) Enables MD5 authentication for the area specified by the *area-id* argument.

For simple password authentication, use the **area authentication** command with no parameters.

Simple Password Authentication Example

Figure 5-27 shows the network used to illustrate the configuration, verification, and troubleshooting of simple password authentication. The configuration of the R1 and R2 routers are shown in Example 5-17.

Figure 5-27   *Simple Password Authentication Example*

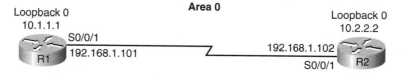

Example 5-17   *Configuration of Routers R1 and R2 in Figure 5-27*

```
Router R1:
<output omitted>
interface Loopback0
 ip address 10.1.1.1 255.255.255.0

<output omitted>
interface Serial0/0/1
 ip address 192.168.1.101 255.255.255.224
 ip ospf authentication
 ip ospf authentication-key plainpas

<output omitted>
router ospf 10
 log-adjacency-changes
 network 10.1.1.1 0.0.0.0 area 0
 network 192.168.1.0 0.0.0.255 area 0

Router R2:
<output omitted>
interface Loopback0
 ip address 10.2.2.2 255.255.255.0

<output omitted>
interface Serial0/0/1
 ip address 192.168.1.102 255.255.255.224
 ip ospf authentication
 ip ospf authentication-key plainpas

<output omitted>
router ospf 10
 log-adjacency-changes
 network 10.2.2.2 0.0.0.0 area 0
 network 192.168.1.0 0.0.0.255 area 0
```

Notice that the connecting interfaces on both R1 and R2 are configured for the same type of authentication with the same authentication key. Simple password authentication is configured on interface serial 0/0/1 on both routers, with the **ip ospf authentication** command. The interfaces are configured with an authentication key of *plainpas*.

Verifying Simple Password Authentication

Example 5-18 shows the output of the **show ip ospf neighbor** and **show ip route** commands on the R1 router in Figure 5-27. The results of a **ping** to the R2 loopback interface address are also displayed to illustrate that the link is working.

Example 5-18 *Verifying Simple Password Authentication on R1 in Figure 5-27*

```
R1#show ip ospf neighbor
Neighbor ID     Pri   State        Dead Time   Address         Interface
10.2.2.2          0   FULL/   -    00:00:32    192.168.1.102   Serial0/0/1

R1#show ip route
<output omitted>
Gateway of last resort is not set
     10.0.0.0/8 is variably subnetted, 2 subnets, 2 masks
O       10.2.2.2/32 [110/782] via 192.168.1.102, 00:01:17, Serial0/0/1
C       10.1.1.0/24 is directly connected, Loopback0
     192.168.1.0/27 is subnetted, 1 subnets
C       192.168.1.96 is directly connected, Serial0/0/1

R1#ping 10.2.2.2
Type escape sequence to abort.
Sending 5, 100-byte ICMP Echos to 10.2.2.2, timeout is 2 seconds:
!!!!!
Success rate is 100 percent (5/5), round-trip min/avg/max = 28/29/32 ms
```

Notice in the **show ip ospf neighbor** command output that the neighbor state is FULL, indicating that the two routers have successfully formed an OSPF adjacency. The routing table verifies that the 10.2.2.2 address has been learned via OSPF over the serial connection.

Troubleshooting Simple Password Authentication

The **debug ip ospf adj** command is used to display OSPF adjacency-related events and is useful when troubleshooting authentication.

Successful Simple Password Authentication Example

The output of the **debug ip ospf adj** command in Example 5-19 illustrates successful communication on the R1 router in Figure 5-27 after the serial 0/0/1 interface, on which simple password authentication has been configured, comes up.

NOTE   Although this **debug ip ospf adj** output does not indicate anything about the authentication, it does show that the two routers successfully form a FULL adjacency. As the output in the next section illustrates, this command output does display authentication failures if there are any. During testing we were unable to find any **debug** command output that displayed information about successful OSPF simple password authentication.

Example 5-19 *Successful: Simple Password Authentication on R1 in Figure 5-27*

```
*Apr 20 18:41:51.242: OSPF: Interface Serial0/0/1 going Up
*Apr 20 18:41:51.742: OSPF: Build router LSA for area 0, router ID 10.1.1.1, seq 0x80000013
*Apr 20 18:41:52.242: %LINEPROTO-5-UPDOWN: Line protocol on Interface Serial0/0/1, changed
   state to up
*Apr 20 18:42:01.250: OSPF: 2 Way Communication to 10.2.2.2 on Serial0/0/1, state 2WAY
*Apr 20 18:42:01.250: OSPF: Send DBD to 10.2.2.2 on Serial0/0/1 seq 0x9B6 opt 0x52 flag
   0x7 len 32
*Apr 20 18:42:01.262: OSPF: Rcv DBD from 10.2.2.2 on Serial0/0/1 seq 0x23ED opt0x52 flag
   0x7 len 32  mtu 1500 state EXSTART
*Apr 20 18:42:01.262: OSPF: NBR Negotiation Done. We are the SLAVE
*Apr 20 18:42:01.262: OSPF: Send DBD to 10.2.2.2 on Serial0/0/1 seq 0x23ED opt 0x52 flag
   0x2 len 72
*Apr 20 18:42:01.294: OSPF: Rcv DBD from 10.2.2.2 on Serial0/0/1 seq 0x23EE opt0x52 flag
   0x3 len 72  mtu 1500 state EXCHANGE
*Apr 20 18:42:01.294: OSPF: Send DBD to 10.2.2.2 on Serial0/0/1 seq 0x23EE opt 0x52 flag
   0x0 len 32
*Apr 20 18:42:01.294: OSPF: Database request to 10.2.2.2
*Apr 20 18:42:01.294: OSPF: sent LS REQ packet to 192.168.1.102, length 12
*Apr 20 18:42:01.314: OSPF: Rcv DBD from 10.2.2.2 on Serial0/0/1 seq 0x23EF opt0x52 flag
   0x1 len 32  mtu 1500 state EXCHANGE
*Apr 20 18:42:01.314: OSPF: Exchange Done with 10.2.2.2 on Serial0/0/1
*Apr 20 18:42:01.314: OSPF: Send DBD to 10.2.2.2 on Serial0/0/1 seq 0x23EF opt 0x52 flag
   0x0 len 32
*Apr 20 18:42:01.326: OSPF: Synchronized with 10.2.2.2 on Serial0/0/1, state FULL
*Apr 20 18:42:01.330: %OSPF-5-ADJCHG: Process 10, Nbr 10.2.2.2 on Serial0/0/1 from LOADING
   to FULL, Loading Done
*Apr 20 18:42:01.830: OSPF: Build router LSA for area 0, router ID 10.1.1.1, seq 0x80000014
```

The output of the **show ip ospf neighbor** command shown in Example 5-20 illustrates that R1 has successfully formed an adjacency with R2.

Example 5-20 *R1 and R2 in Figure 5-27 Have Formed an Adjacency*

```
R1#show ip ospf neighbor
Neighbor ID     Pri   State        Dead Time   Address        Interface
10.2.2.2          0   FULL/  -      00:00:34    192.168.1.102  Serial0/0/1
```

Example: Troubleshooting Simple Password Authentication Problems

Using the network in Figure 5-27, if simple password authentication is configured on the R1 serial 0/0/1 interface but no authentication is configured on the R2 serial 0/0/1 interface, the routers will not be able to form an adjacency over that link. The output of the **debug ip ospf adj** command shown in Example 5-21 illustrates that the routers report a mismatch in authentication type; no OSPF packets will be sent between the neighbors.

Example 5-21 *Simple Password Authentication on R1 and no Authentication on R2 in Figure 5-27*

```
R1#
*Apr 17 18:51:31.242: OSPF: Rcv pkt from 192.168.1.102, Serial0/0/1 : Mismatch
   Authentication type. Input packet specified type 0, we use type 1

R2#
*Apr 17 18:50:43.046: OSPF: Rcv pkt from 192.168.1.101, Serial0/0/1 : Mismatch
   Authentication type. Input packet specified type 1, we use type 0
```

> **NOTE** The different types of OSPF authentication have the following type codes:
>
> ■ **Null**—Type 0
>
> ■ **Simple password**—Type 1
>
> ■ **MD5**—Type 2

If simple password authentication is configured on the R1 serial 0/0/1 interface and on the R2 serial 0/0/1 interface, but with different passwords, the routers will not be able to form an adjacency over that link. The outputs of the **debug ip ospf adj** command shown in Example 5-22 illustrate that the routers report a mismatch in authentication key; no OSPF packets will be sent between the neighbors.

Example 5-22 *Simple Password Authentication on R1 and R2 in Figure 5-27, but with Different Passwords*

```
R1#
*Apr 17 18:54:01.238: OSPF: Rcv pkt from 192.168.1.102, Serial0/0/1 : Mismatch
   Authentication Key - Clear Text

R2#
*Apr 17 18:53:13.050: OSPF: Rcv pkt from 192.168.1.101, Serial0/0/1 : Mismatch
   Authentication Key - Clear Text
```

Configuring MD5 Authentication

With OSPF MD5 authentication, a key and key ID are configured on each router. To configure OSPF MD5 authentication, complete the following steps:

Step 1   Assign a key ID and key to be used with neighboring routers that are using the OSPF MD5 authentication, using the **ip ospf message-digest-key** *key-id* **md5** *key* interface configuration command. Table 5-19 describes the parameters in the **ip ospf message-digest-key** command.

Table 5-19 **ip ospf message-digest-key** *Command Parameters*

Parameter	Description
key-id	An identifier in the range from 1 to 255
key	Alphanumeric password of up to 16 bytes

The key and the key ID specified in this command are used to generate a message digest (also called a *hash*) of each OSPF packet; the message digest is appended to the packet. A separate password can be assigned to each network on a per-interface basis.

Usually, one key per interface is used to generate authentication information when sending packets and to authenticate incoming packets. All neighboring routers on the same network must have the same password to be able to exchange OSPF information; in other words, the same *key-id* on the neighbor router must have the same *key* value.

The key-id allows for uninterrupted transitions between keys, which is helpful for administrators who want to change the OSPF password without disrupting communication. If an interface is configured with a new key, the router will send multiple copies of the same packet, each authenticated by different keys. The router will stop sending duplicate packets when it detects that all of its neighbors have adopted the new key.

The process of changing keys is as follows. Suppose the current configuration is as follows:

```
interface FastEthernet 0/0
 ip ospf message-digest-key 100 md5 OLD
```

The following configuration is then added:

```
interface FastEthernet 0/0
 ip ospf message-digest-key 101 md5 NEW
```

The router assumes its neighbors do not have the new key yet, so it begins a rollover process. It sends multiple copies of the same packet, each authenticated by different keys. In this example, the router sends out two copies of the same packet: the first one authenticated by key 100 and the second one authenticated by key 101.

Rollover allows neighboring routers to continue communication while the network administrator is updating them with the new key. Rollover stops once the local system finds that all its neighbors know the new key. The system detects that a neighbor has the new key when it receives packets from the neighbor authenticated by the new key.

After all neighbors have been updated with the new key, the old key should be removed. In this example, you would enter the following:

```
interface FastEthernet 0/0
 no ip ospf message-digest-key 100
```

From then on, only key 101 is used for authentication on interface FastEthernet 0/0.

Cisco recommends that you not keep more than one key per interface. Every time you add a new key, you should remove the old key to prevent the local router from continuing to communicate with a hostile system that knows the old key.

> **NOTE** If the **service password-encryption** command is not used when implementing OSPF authentication, the key will be stored as plain text in the router configuration. If you configure the **service password-encryption** command, the key will be stored and displayed in an encrypted form; when it is displayed, there will be an *encryption-type* of 7 specified before the encrypted key.

Step 2　Specify the authentication type using the **ip ospf authentication [message-digest | null]** interface configuration command. The parameters for this command are as described in the earlier "Configuring Simple Password Authentication" section. For MD5 authentication, use the **ip ospf authentication** command with the **message-digest** parameter. Before using this command, configure the message digest key for the interface with the **ip ospf message-digest-key** command.

Recall that the **ip ospf authentication** command was introduced in Cisco IOS Software Release 12.0. As for simple password authentication, the MD5 authentication type for an area is still supported using the **area** *area-id* **authentication message-digest** router configuration command, for backward compatibility.

MD5 Authentication Example

Figure 5-28 shows the network used to illustrate the configuration, verification, and troubleshooting of MD5 authentication. The configuration of the R1 and R2 routers are shown in Example 5-23.

Figure 5-28 *MD5 Authentication Example*

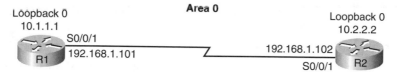

Example 5-23 *Configuration of Routers R1 and R2 in Figure 5-28*

```
Router R1:
<output omitted>
interface Loopback0
 ip address 10.1.1.1 255.255.255.0

<output omitted>
interface Serial0/0/1
 ip address 192.168.1.101 255.255.255.224
 ip ospf authentication message-digest
 ip ospf message-digest-key 1 md5 secretpass

<output omitted>
router ospf 10
 log-adjacency-changes
 network 10.1.1.1 0.0.0.0 area 0
 network 192.168.1.0 0.0.0.255 area 0

Router R2:
<output omitted>
interface Loopback0
 ip address 10.2.2.2 255.255.255.0

<output omitted>
interface Serial0/0/1
 ip address 192.168.1.102 255.255.255.224
 ip ospf authentication message-digest
 ip ospf message-digest-key 1 md5 secretpass

<output omitted>
router ospf 10
 log-adjacency-changes
 network 10.2.2.2 0.0.0.0 area 0
 network 192.168.1.0 0.0.0.255 area 0
```

Notice that the connecting interfaces on both R1 and R2 are configured for the same type of authentication with the same authentication key and key-id. MD5 authentication is configured on interface serial 0/0/1 on both routers with the **ip ospf authentication message-digest** command.

The interfaces on both routers are configured with an authentication key number 1 set to *secretpass*.

Verifying MD5 Authentication

Example 5-24 shows the output of the **show ip ospf neighbor** and **show ip route** commands on the R1 router in Figure 5-28. The results of a **ping** to the R2 loopback interface address is also displayed to illustrate that the link is working.

Example 5-24 *Verifying MD5 Authentication on R1 in Figure 5-28*

```
R1#show ip ospf neighbor
Neighbor ID     Pri   State         Dead Time   Address        Interface
10.2.2.2          0   FULL/  -      00:00:31    192.168.1.102  Serial0/0/1

R1#show ip route
<output omitted>
Gateway of last resort is not set
     10.0.0.0/8 is variably subnetted, 2 subnets, 2 masks
O       10.2.2.2/32 [110/782] via 192.168.1.102, 00:00:37, Serial0/0/1
C       10.1.1.0/24 is directly connected, Loopback0
     192.168.1.0/27 is subnetted, 1 subnets
C       192.168.1.96 is directly connected, Serial0/0/1

R1#ping 10.2.2.2
Type escape sequence to abort.
Sending 5, 100-byte ICMP Echos to 10.2.2.2, timeout is 2 seconds:
!!!!!
Success rate is 100 percent (5/5), round-trip min/avg/max = 28/28/32 ms
```

Notice in the **show ip ospf neighbor** command output that that the neighbor state is FULL, indicating that the two routers have successfully formed an OSPF adjacency. The routing table verifies that the 10.2.2.2 address has been learned via OSPF over the serial connection.

Troubleshooting MD5 Authentication

As for simple password authentication, the **debug ip ospf adj** command is used to display OSPF adjacency-related events and is very useful when troubleshooting MD5 authentication.

Successful MD5 Authentication Example

The output of the **debug ip ospf adj** command in Example 5-25 illustrates successful MD5 authentication on the R1 router in Figure 5-28 after the serial 0/0/1 interface, on which authentication has been configured, comes up.

Example 5-25 *Successful MD5 Authentication on R1 in Figure 5-28*

```
R1#debug ip ospf adj
OSPF adjacency events debugging is on
*Apr 20 17:13:56.530: %LINK-3-UPDOWN: Interface Serial0/0/1, changed state to up
*Apr 20 17:13:56.530: OSPF: Interface Serial0/0/1 going Up
*Apr 20 17:13:56.530: OSPF: Send with youngest Key 1
*Apr 20 17:13:57.030: OSPF: Build router LSA for area 0, router ID 10.1.1.1, seq 0x80000009
*Apr 20 17:13:57.530: %LINEPROTO-5-UPDOWN: Line protocol on Interface Serial0/0/1, changed
    state to up
*Apr 20 17:14:06.530: OSPF: Send with youngest Key 1
*Apr 20 17:14:06.546: OSPF: 2 Way Communication to 10.2.2.2 on Serial0/0/1, state 2WAY
*Apr 20 17:14:06.546: OSPF: Send DBD to 10.2.2.2 on Serial0/0/1 seq 0xB37 opt 0x52 flag
    0x7 len 32
*Apr 20 17:14:06.546: OSPF: Send with youngest Key 1
*Apr 20 17:14:06.562: OSPF: Rcv DBD from 10.2.2.2 on Serial0/0/1 seq 0x32F opt 0
x52 flag 0x7 len 32  mtu 1500 state EXSTART
*Apr 20 17:14:06.562: OSPF: NBR Negotiation Done. We are the SLAVE
*Apr 20 17:14:06.562: OSPF: Send DBD to 10.2.2.2 on Serial0/0/1 seq 0x32F opt 0x52 flag
    0x2 len 72
*Apr 20 17:14:06.562: OSPF: Send with youngest Key 1
*Apr 20 17:14:06.602: OSPF: Rcv DBD from 10.2.2.2 on Serial0/0/1 seq 0x330 opt 0x52 flag
0x3 len 72  mtu 1500 state EXCHANGE
*Apr 20 17:14:06.602: OSPF: Send DBD to 10.2.2.2 on Serial0/0/1 seq 0x330 opt 0x52 flag
    0x0 len 32
*Apr 20 17:14:06.602: OSPF: Send with youngest Key 1
*Apr 20 17:14:06.602: OSPF: Database request to 10.2.2.2
*Apr 20 17:14:06.602: OSPF: Send with youngest Key 1
*Apr 20 17:14:06.602: OSPF: sent LS REQ packet to 192.168.1.102, length 12
*Apr 20 17:14:06.614: OSPF: Send with youngest Key 1
*Apr 20 17:14:06.634: OSPF: Rcv DBD from 10.2.2.2 on Serial0/0/1 seq 0x331 opt 0x52 flag
    0x1 len 32  mtu 1500 state EXCHANGE
*Apr 20 17:14:06.634: OSPF: Exchange Done with 10.2.2.2 on Serial0/0/1
*Apr 20 17:14:06.634: OSPF: Send DBD to 10.2.2.2 on Serial0/0/1 seq 0x331 opt 0x52 flag
    0x0 len 32
*Apr 20 17:14:06.634: OSPF: Send with youngest Key 1
*Apr 20 17:14:06.650: OSPF: Synchronized with 10.2.2.2 on Serial0/0/1, state FULL
*Apr 20 17:14:06.650: %OSPF-5-ADJCHG: Process 10, Nbr 10.2.2.2 on Serial0/0/1 from LOADING
    to FULL, Loading Done
*Apr 20 17:14:07.150: OSPF: Send with youngest Key 1
*Apr 20 17:14:07.150: OSPF: Build router LSA for area 0, router ID 10.1.1.1, seq 0x8000000A
*Apr 20 17:14:09.150: OSPF: Send with youngest Key 1
```

The output of the **show ip ospf neighbor** command shown Example 5-26 illustrates that R1 has successfully formed an adjacency with R2.

Example 5-26 *R1 and R2 in Figure 5-28 Have Formed an Adjacency*

```
R1#show ip ospf neighbor
Neighbor ID     Pri   State           Dead Time   Address         Interface
10.2.2.2          0   FULL/   -       00:00:34    192.168.1.102   Serial0/0/1
```

Example: Troubleshooting MD5 Authentication Problems

Using the network in Figure 5-28, if MD5 authentication is configured on the R1 serial 0/0/1 interface and on the R2 serial 0/0/1 interface, but R1 has key 1 and R2 has key 2, the routers will not be able to form an adjacency over that link, even though both have the same passwords configured. The outputs of the **debug ip ospf adj** command shown in Example 5-27 illustrate that the routers report a mismatch in authentication key. No OSPF packets will be sent between the neighbors.

Example 5-27 *MD5 Authentication on R1 and R2 in Figure 5-28, but with Different Key-IDs*

```
R1#
*Apr 20 17:56:16.530: OSPF: Send with youngest Key 1
*Apr 20 17:56:26.502: OSPF: Rcv pkt from 192.168.1.102, Serial0/0/1 : Mismatch
   Authentication Key - No message digest key 2 on interface
*Apr 20 17:56:26.530: OSPF: Send with youngest Key 1

R2#
*Apr 20 17:55:28.226: OSPF: Send with youngest Key 2
*Apr 20 17:55:28.286: OSPF: Rcv pkt from 192.168.1.101, Serial0/0/1 : Mismatch
   Authentication Key - No message digest key 1 on interface
*Apr 20 17:55:38.226: OSPF: Send with youngest Key 2
```

Summary

In this chapter, you learned about advanced OSPF topics. The following topics were presented:

- The different types of OSPF routers: backbone routers, ABRs, ASBRs, and internal routers.

- The 11 different OSPF LSA types. The first five are the most commonly used: type 1 (router), type 2 (network), type 3 and 4 (summary), and type 5 (external).

- The three kinds of OSPF routes: intra-area, interarea, and external. External routes are either E1 or E2.

- Route summarization configuration to improve CPU utilization, reduce LSA flooding, and reduce LSDB and routing table sizes.

- How default routes can be used in OSPF to prevent the need for a specific route to all destination networks. The benefit is a much smaller routing table and LSDB, with complete reachability.

- The several area types defined in OSPF: standard areas, backbone (transit) areas, stub areas, totally stubby areas, NSSAs, and totally stubby NSSAs.

- The virtual link feature, used to *temporarily* mend backbone failures.

- The types of OSPF authentication: null, simple password authentication (also called plain-text authentication), and MD5 authentication.

References

For additional information, refer to these resources:

- http://www.cisco.com article, "OSPF Frequently Asked Questions"

- http://www.cisco.com article, "OSPF Not-So-Stubby Area (NSSA)"

- http://www.cisco.com article, "What Are OSPF Areas and Virtual Links?"

- http://www.cisco.com/univercd/cc/td/doc/cisintwk/idg4/nd2003.htm article, "Designing Large-Scale IP Internetworks"

Configuration Exercise 5-1: Configuring OSPF for Multiple Areas and Frame Relay Nonbroadcast

In this exercise, you configure OSPF ABRs to allow routes to pass between areas over a simple Frame Relay network.

Introduction to the Configuration Exercises

This book uses Configuration Exercises to help you practice configuring routers with the commands and topics presented. If you have access to real hardware, you can try these exercises on your routers. See Appendix B, "Configuration Exercise Equipment Requirements and Backbone Configurations," for a list of recommended equipment and configuration commands for the backbone routers. However, even if you don't have access to any routers, you can go through the exercises, and keep a log of your own running configurations, or just read through the solution. Commands used and solutions to the Configuration Exercises are provided within the exercises.

In the Configuration Exercises, the network is assumed to consist of two pods, each with four routers. The pods are interconnected to a backbone. You configure pod 1. No interaction between the two pods is required, but you might see some routes from the other pod in your routing tables in some exercises if you have it configured. In most of the exercises, the backbone has only one router; in some cases, another router is added to the backbone. Each Configuration Exercise assumes that you have completed the previous chapters' Configuration Exercises on your pod.

NOTE   Throughout this exercise, the pod number is referred to as *x*, and the router number is referred to as *y*. Substitute the appropriate numbers as needed.

Objectives

The objectives of this exercise are as follows:

■ Configure OSPF in a multiarea environment.

■ Configure OSPF in nonbroadcast mode over a Frame Relay network.

Visual Objective

Figure 5-29 illustrates the topology used in this exercise.

Figure 5-29 *Configuring OSPF for Multiple Areas and Frame Relay Nonbroadcast*

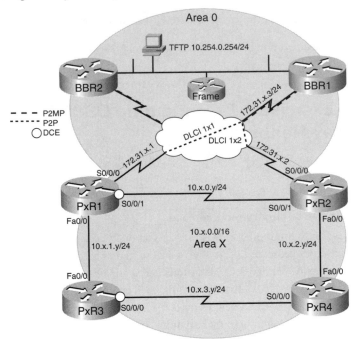

Command List

In this exercise, you use the commands in Table 5-20, listed in logical order. Refer to this list if you need configuration command assistance during the exercise.

> **CAUTION** Although the command syntax is shown in this table, the addresses shown are typically for the P*x*R1 and P*x*R3 routers. Be careful when addressing your routers! Refer to the exercise instructions and the appropriate visual objective diagram for addressing details.

Table 5-20 *Configuration Exercise 5-1 Commands*

Command	Description
(config-router)#**network 172.31.**x**.0 0.0.0.255 area 0**	Places a set of interfaces in OSPF area 0
(config-if)#**ip ospf priority 0**	Sets a port's OSPF priority to 0 to prevent it from participating in DR/BDR election
#**show ip ospf neighbor**	Displays a list of OSPF neighbors
#**show ip ospf interface**	Displays information about interfaces configured for OSPF

NOTE   The exercise tasks include answers and solutions. Some answers cover multiple steps; the answers are given after the last step to which that answer applies.

Task: Using the Nonbroadcast Network Type over Frame Relay

In this task, you configure ABRs, allowing OSPF to pass routes between areas. Follow these steps:

Step 1   Configure the edge routers (P*x*R1 and P*x*R2) as ABRs. You do this by placing the Frame Relay connection (the S0/0/0 interfaces on the edge routers) into OSPF area 0. Remember that the default OSPF network type (mode) for a Frame Relay interface is nonbroadcast.

Step 2   It is important that the core (BBR1) is the DR, because this is a hub-and-spoke network, and only the core (BBR1) has full connectivity to the spoke routers. Set the OSPF priority to 0 on the edge router's S0/0/0 interface to ensure this.

NOTE   In an NBMA network, **neighbor** statements are required only on the DR and BDR. In a hub-and-spoke topology, **neighbor** statements must be configured on the hub (which must become the DR) and are not mandatory on the spoke routers. However, in a full-mesh topology, you might need **neighbor** statements on all routers if you have not specified the DR and BDR with the **priority** command. The BBR1 router, with Router ID 100.100.100.100, has appropriate **neighbor** commands configured, as shown here:

```
BBR1#sh run | begin router ospf
router ospf 1
 router-id 100.100.100.100
 log-adjacency-changes
 redistribute connected metric 50 subnets
 network 172.31.0.0 0.0.255.255 area 0
 neighbor 172.31.2.2
 neighbor 172.31.2.1
 neighbor 172.31.1.2
 neighbor 172.31.1.1
```

Step 3   Enable the serial 0/0/0 interfaces on the edge routers.

Solution:

The following shows how to perform the required steps on the P1R1 router:

```
P1R1(config)#router ospf 1
P1R1(config-router)#network 172.31.1.0 0.0.0.255 area 0
P1R1(config-router)#exit
P1R1(config)#interface serial 0/0/0
P1R1(config-if)#ip ospf priority 0
P1R1(config-if)#no shutdown
```

Step 4   View the routing table on the internal routers to ensure that all appropriate OSPF routes are present. What is the difference between the O and O IA OSPF routes? Ping the TFTP server from the internal router to verify network connectivity.

Solution:

The following shows the output on the P1R3 router:

```
P1R3#show ip route
<output omitted>
Gateway of last resort is not set

     172.31.0.0/24 is subnetted, 2 subnets
O IA    172.31.2.0 [110/1563] via 10.1.1.1, 00:00:32, FastEthernet0/0
O IA    172.31.1.0 [110/782] via 10.1.1.1, 00:00:37, FastEthernet0/0
     10.0.0.0/8 is variably subnetted, 6 subnets, 2 masks
C       10.200.200.13/32 is directly connected, Loopback0
C       10.1.3.0/24 is directly connected, Serial0/0/0
O       10.1.2.0/24 [110/782] via 10.1.3.4, 00:02:52, Serial0/0/0
C       10.1.1.0/24 is directly connected, FastEthernet0/0
O       10.1.0.0/24 [110/782] via 10.1.1.1, 00:02:54, FastEthernet0/0
O E2    10.254.0.0/24 [110/50] via 10.1.1.1, 00:00:23, FastEthernet0/0
P1R3#
```

The O routes are intra-area routes, and the O IA routes are interarea routes.

```
P1R3#ping 10.254.0.254

Type escape sequence to abort.
Sending 5, 100-byte ICMP Echos to 10.254.0.254, timeout is 2 seconds:
!!!!!
Success rate is 100 percent (5/5), round-trip min/avg/max = 32/32/32 ms
P1R3#
```

The ping to the TFTP server is successful, verifying connectivity.

Step 5   At the edge routers, verify OSPF neighborship. Is BBR1 the DR for the 172.31.*x*.0/24 hub-and-spoke network?

Solution:

The following shows the output on the P1R1 router:

```
P1R1#show ip ospf neighbor

Neighbor ID       Pri   State          Dead Time   Address      Interface
100.100.100.100    1    FULL/DR        00:01:53    172.31.1.3   Serial0/0/0
10.0.0.12          0    FULL/ -        00:00:39    10.1.0.2     Serial0/0/1
10.200.200.13      0    FULL/DROTHER   00:00:39    10.1.1.3     FastEthernet0/0
```

Yes, BBR1 is the DR (it has a RID of 100.100.100.100 and it is the DR).

Step 6   Verify the OSPF network types on the interfaces on the pod edge routers, P*x*R1 and P*x*R2.

What is the OSPF network type on the Frame Relay interface?

What is the OSPF network type on the HDLC serial interface between P*x*R1 and P*x*R2?

What is the OSPF network type on the FastEthernet interface?

Solution:

The following shows the output on the P1R1 router:

```
P1R1#show ip ospf interface
Serial0/0/0 is up, line protocol is up
  Internet Address 172.31.1.1/24, Area 0
  Process ID 1, Router ID 10.0.0.11, Network Type NON_BROADCAST, Cost: 781
  Transmit Delay is 1 sec, State DROTHER, Priority 0
  Designated Router (ID) 100.100.100.100, Interface address 172.31.1.3
  No backup designated router on this network
  Timer intervals configured, Hello 30, Dead 120, Wait 120, Retransmit 5
    oob-resync timeout 120
    Hello due in 00:00:26
  Supports Link-local Signaling (LLS)
  Index 1/3, flood queue length 0
  Next 0x0(0)/0x0(0)
  Last flood scan length is 1, maximum is 1
  Last flood scan time is 0 msec, maximum is 0 msec
  Neighbor Count is 1, Adjacent neighbor count is 1
    Adjacent with neighbor 100.100.100.100  (Designated Router)
  Suppress hello for 0 neighbor(s)
Serial0/0/1 is up, line protocol is up
  Internet Address 10.1.0.1/24, Area 1
  Process ID 1, Router ID 10.0.0.11, Network Type POINT_TO_POINT, Cost: 781
  Transmit Delay is 1 sec, State POINT_TO_POINT
  Timer intervals configured, Hello 10, Dead 40, Wait 40, Retransmit 5
    oob-resync timeout 40
    Hello due in 00:00:07
  Supports Link-local Signaling (LLS)
  Index 2/2, flood queue length 0
  Next 0x0(0)/0x0(0)
  Last flood scan length is 1, maximum is 3
  Last flood scan time is 0 msec, maximum is 4 msec
```

```
    Neighbor Count is 1, Adjacent neighbor count is 1
      Adjacent with neighbor 10.0.0.12
    Suppress hello for 0 neighbor(s)
FastEthernet0/0 is up, line protocol is up
    Internet Address 10.1.1.1/24, Area 1
    Process ID 1, Router ID 10.0.0.11, Network Type BROADCAST, Cost: 1
    Transmit Delay is 1 sec, State DR, Priority 1
    Designated Router (ID) 10.0.0.11, Interface address 10.1.1.1
    No backup designated router on this network
    Timer intervals configured, Hello 10, Dead 40, Wait 40, Retransmit 5
      oob-resync timeout 40
      Hello due in 00:00:07
    Supports Link-local Signaling (LLS)
    Index 1/1, flood queue length 0
    Next 0x0(0)/0x0(0)
    Last flood scan length is 1, maximum is 2
    Last flood scan time is 0 msec, maximum is 0 msec
    Neighbor Count is 1, Adjacent neighbor count is 1
      Adjacent with neighbor 10.200.200.13
    Suppress hello for 0 neighbor(s)
P1R1#
```

The OSPF network type on the Frame Relay interface is nonbroadcast.

The OSPF network type on the HDLC serial interface between PxR1 and PxR2 is point to point.

The OSPF network type on the FastEthernet interface is broadcast.

Step 7   Save your configurations to NVRAM.

Solution:

The following shows how to perform the required step on the P1R1 router:

```
P1R1#copy run start
Destination filename [startup-config]?
Building configuration...
[OK]
```

Exercise Verification

You have completed this exercise when you have configured ABRs so that OSPF passes routes between areas over a simple Frame Relay network.

Configuration Exercise 5-2: Configuring OSPF for Multiple Areas and Frame Relay Point to Multipoint and Point to Point

In this exercise, you configure OSPF for use over a complex Frame Relay network.

> **NOTE**   Throughout this exercise, the pod number is referred to as *x*, and the router number is referred to as *y*. Substitute the appropriate numbers as needed.

Objectives

The objectives of this exercise are as follows:

- Configure OSPF over Frame Relay using the point-to-multipoint OSPF network type (mode).

- Configure OSPF over Frame Relay using the point-to-point OSPF network type (mode).

Visual Objective

Figure 5-30 illustrates the topology used in this exercise.

Figure 5-30 *Configuring OSPF for Multiple Areas and Frame Relay Point to Multipoint and Point to Point*

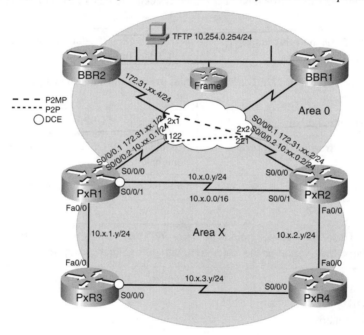

Command List

In this exercise, you use the commands in Table 5-21, listed in logical order. Refer to this list if you need configuration command assistance during the exercise.

> **CAUTION**   Although the command syntax is shown in this table, the addresses shown are typically for the PxR1 and PxR3 routers. Be careful when addressing your routers! Refer to the exercise instructions and the appropriate visual objective diagram for addressing details.

Table 5-21 *Configuration Exercise 5-2 Commands*

Command	Description
(config)#**default interface s0/0/0**	Erases the configuration on an interface
(config-if)#**encapsulation frame-relay**	Enables Frame Relay encapsulation
(config-if)#**no frame-relay inverse-arp**	Disables Frame Relay inverse Address Resolution Protocol (ARP) on the interface
(config)#**interface s0/0/0.1 multipoint | point-to-point**	Creates a subinterface (either multipoint or point to point)
(config-subif)#**ip ospf network point-to-multipoint**	Forces OSPF to treat this interface as point to multipoint
(config-subif)#**frame-relay map ip 172.31.xx.4 2xy broadcast**	Maps a next-hop IP address to a permanent virtual circuit (PVC) data-link connection identifier (DLCI)
(config-router)#**network 172.31.xx.0 0.0.0.255 area 0**	Sets interfaces that match this pattern to be in OSPF area 0
#**show ip ospf neighbor**	Displays a list of OSPF neighbors
(config-subif)#**frame-relay interface-dlci 122**	Specifies that DLCI 122 is associated with this point-to-point link
#**show ip ospf interface**	Displays information about interfaces configured for OSPF

NOTE   The exercise tasks include answers and solutions. Some answers cover multiple steps; the answers are given after the last step to which that answer applies.

Task 1: Cleaning Up
Follow these steps:

Step 1   Shut down the serial 0/0/0 interface (the Frame Relay interface) on the edge routers.

Step 2   To prepare the interface for use in this exercise, make the following interface configuration changes:

   • Remove all Frame Relay **map** statements.

   • Remove the IP address.

   • Remove the OSPF **priority** statement.

Alternatively, you may remove the entire configuration from the interface by issuing the **default interface s0/0/0** global configuration command.

Step 3   If you used the **default interface s0/0/0** command, enable Frame Relay encapsulation on the serial 0/0/0 interface. Turn off **frame-relay inverse-arp** on that interface.

Step 4   View the running configuration to verify that the edge routers' S0/0/0 interface is configured to use Frame Relay encapsulation and that **frame-relay inverse-arp** is disabled.

Solution:

The following shows how to perform the required steps on the P1R1 router:

```
P1R1(config)#interface s0/0/0
P1R1(config-if)#shutdown
*Apr 25 21:41:43.105: %OSPF-5-ADJCHG: Process 1, Nbr 100.100.100.100 on Serial0/
0/0 from FULL to DOWN, Neighbor Down: Interface down or detached
*Apr 25 21:41:45.105: %LINK-5-CHANGED: Interface Serial0/0/0, changed state to
    administratively down
*Apr 25 21:41:46.105: %LINEPROTO-5-UPDOWN: Line protocol on Interface Serial0/0/0,
    changed state to down
P1R1(config-if)#exit
P1R1(config)#default interface s0/0/0
Building configuration...

Interface Serial0/0/0 set to default configuration
P1R1(config)#int s0/0/0
P1R1(config-if)#encapsulation frame-relay
P1R1(config-if)#no frame-relay inverse-arp

P1R1#show run
Building configuration...
<output omitted>
interface Serial0/0/0
 no ip address
 encapsulation frame-relay
 shutdown
 no frame-relay inverse-arp
```

Step 5   In the OSPF configuration, remove the **network** command for the 172.31.x.0 network since the interface to BBR1 is not used in this exercise; the interface to BBR2 is used instead.

Solution:

The following shows how to perform the required step on the P1R1 router:

```
P1R1(config)#router ospf 1
P1R1(config-router)#no network 172.31.1.0 0.0.0.255 area 0
```

Task 2: Configuring OSPF over Frame Relay Using the Point-to-Multipoint OSPF Network Type

> **NOTE** For this exercise, you connect the edge routers to the BBR2 router over the 172.31.*xx*.0/24 network. The connection from the edge routers to the BBR1 router over the 172.31.*x*.0/24 network is not used.

Follow these steps:

Step 1 At the edge routers, create a multipoint subinterface numbered s0/0/0.1. You will use this interface to explore Frame Relay hub-and-spoke behavior using the OSPF point-to-multipoint network type.

Step 2 Change the s0/0/0.1 OSPF network type to point-to-multipoint. (The default OSPF network type for a Frame Relay multipoint subinterface is nonbroadcast.)

Step 3 Assign the IP address 172.31.*xx*.*y*/24 to S0/0/0.1, where *x* is the pod number and *y* is the router number. For example, for P2R2, the IP address is 172.31.22.2/24.

Step 4 Because you are not using **frame relay inverse arp**, you need to manually map the remote IP address to the local DLCI. Create a new Frame Relay **map** statement from each edge router to the BBR2 IP address of 172.31.*xx*.4 using a DLCI number of 2*xy,* where *x* is the pod number and *y* is the router number. Do not forget the **broadcast** option.

For example, for P1R2, the Frame Relay **map** statement is this:

```
frame-relay map ip 172.31.11.4 212 broadcast
```

For P1R1, the Frame Relay **map** statement is this:

```
frame-relay map ip 172.31.11.4 211 broadcast
```

Step 5 Enable the serial 0/0/0 interface on the edge routers.

Step 6 At the edge routers, add a new **network** statement to OSPF for the 172.31.*xx*.0 network that has been created on s0/0/0.1, placing it in area 0.

Solution:

The following shows how to perform the required steps on the P1R1 router:

```
P1R1(config)#int s0/0/0.1 multipoint
P1R1(config-subif)#ip ospf network point-to-multipoint
P1R1(config-subif)#ip address 172.31.11.1 255.255.255.0
```

```
P1R1(config-subif)#frame-relay map ip 172.31.11.4 211 broadcast
P1R1(config-subif)#exit

P1R1(config)#int s0/0/0
P1R1(config-if)#no shutdown
P1R1(config-if)#router ospf 1
P1R1(config-router)#network 172.31.11.0 0.0.0.255 area 0
```

Step 7   On the edge routers, use the proper **show** command to display the OSPF neighbor status. Is there a DR or BDR when using the point-to-multipoint OSPF network type?

Solution:

The following shows the output on the P1R1 router:

```
P1R1#show ip ospf neighbor

Neighbor ID      Pri   State          Dead Time   Address       Interface
200.200.200.200   0    FULL/  -       00:01:46    172.31.11.4   Serial0/0/0.1
10.0.0.12         0    FULL/  -       00:00:39    10.1.0.2      Serial0/0/1
10.200.200.13     0    FULL/DROTHER   00:00:39    10.1.1.3      FastEthernet0/0
P1R1#
```

No, there is no DR or BDR when using point-to-multipoint mode.

Step 8   View the routing table on the edge routers P*x*R1 and P*x*R2 to verify that they are receiving OSPF routes from the core.

Solution:

The following shows the output on the P1R1 router:

```
P1R1#show ip route
<output omitted>
Gateway of last resort is not set

     172.31.0.0/16 is variably subnetted, 4 subnets, 2 masks
O       172.31.22.4/32 [110/781] via 172.31.11.4, 00:01:23, Serial0/0/0.1
C       172.31.11.0/24 is directly connected, Serial0/0/0.1
O       172.31.11.2/32 [110/1562] via 172.31.11.4, 00:01:23, Serial0/0/0.1
O       172.31.11.4/32 [110/781] via 172.31.11.4, 00:01:23, Serial0/0/0.1
     10.0.0.0/24 is subnetted, 5 subnets
O       10.1.3.0 [110/782] via 10.1.1.3, 00:02:03, FastEthernet0/0
O       10.1.2.0 [110/782] via 10.1.0.2, 00:02:03, Serial0/0/1
C       10.1.1.0 is directly connected, FastEthernet0/0
C       10.1.0.0 is directly connected, Serial0/0/1
O E2    10.254.0.0 [110/50] via 172.31.11.4, 00:01:14, Serial0/0/0.1
P1R1#
```

The router is receiving OSPF routes from the core, over the Serial 0/0/0.1 interface.

Step 9   Ping BBR2's FastEthernet interface (10.254.0.2) from the edge routers to verify connectivity with the core.

Solution:

The following shows the successful ping output on the P1R1 router:

```
P1R1#ping 10.254.0.2

Type escape sequence to abort.
Sending 5, 100-byte ICMP Echos to 10.254.0.2, timeout is 2 seconds:
!!!!!
Success rate is 100 percent (5/5), round-trip min/avg/max = 28/29/32 ms
P1R1#
```

Task 3: Configuring OSPF over Frame Relay Using the Point-to-Point OSPF Network Type

Follow these steps:

Step 1   Create a new point-to-point subinterface to connect the two edge routers. Give the new subinterface the number S0/0/0.2. Address it as 10.*xx*.0.*y*/24, where *x* is the pod number and *y* is the router number. The DLCI from P*x*R1 to P*x*R2 is 122, and the DLCI from P*x*R2 to P*x*R1 is 221, in both pods.

Solution:

The following shows how to configure the required steps on the P1R1 router:

```
P1R1(config)#interface s0/0/0.2 point-to-point
P1R1(config-subif)#ip address 10.11.0.1 255.255.255.0
P1R1(config-subif)#frame-relay interface-dlci 122
```

Step 2   At each edge router, ping the s0/0/0.2 subinterface of the other edge router to verify connectivity.

Solution:

The following shows the output on the P1R1 router:

```
P1R1#ping 10.11.0.2

Type escape sequence to abort.
Sending 5, 100-byte ICMP Echos to 10.11.0.2, timeout is 2 seconds:
!!!!!
Success rate is 100 percent (5/5), round-trip min/avg/max = 28/31/32 ms
P1R1#
```

Step 3   At the edge routers, add the 10.*xx*.0.0 network to OSPF in area *x*.

Solution:

The following shows how to configure the required steps on the P1R1 router:

```
P1R1(config)#router ospf 1
P1R1(config-router)#network 10.11.0.0 0.0.0.255 area 1
```

Step 4   At the edge routers, verify the OSPF network type of the two subinterfaces. What is the default OSPF network type on the point-to-point subinterface?

Solution:

The following shows the output on the P1R1 router:

```
P1R1#show ip ospf interface
Serial0/0/0.1 is up, line protocol is up
  Internet Address 172.31.11.1/24, Area 0
  Process ID 1, Router ID 10.0.0.11, Network Type POINT_TO_MULTIPOINT, Cost: 781
  Transmit Delay is 1 sec, State POINT_TO_MULTIPOINT
  Timer intervals configured, Hello 30, Dead 120, Wait 120, Retransmit 5
    oob-resync timeout 120
    Hello due in 00:00:08
  Supports Link-local Signaling (LLS)
  Index 1/3, flood queue length 0
  Next 0x0(0)/0x0(0)
  Last flood scan length is 1, maximum is 3
  Last flood scan time is 0 msec, maximum is 0 msec
  Neighbor Count is 1, Adjacent neighbor count is 1
    Adjacent with neighbor 200.200.200.200
  Suppress hello for 0 neighbor(s)
Serial0/0/0.2 is up, line protocol is up
  Internet Address 10.11.0.1/24, Area 1
  Process ID 1, Router ID 10.0.0.11, Network Type POINT_TO_POINT, Cost: 781
  Transmit Delay is 1 sec, State POINT_TO_POINT
  Timer intervals configured, Hello 10, Dead 40, Wait 40, Retransmit 5
    oob-resync timeout 40
    Hello due in 00:00:05
  Supports Link-local Signaling (LLS)
  Index 3/4, flood queue length 0
  Next 0x0(0)/0x0(0)
  Last flood scan length is 1, maximum is 1
  Last flood scan time is 0 msec, maximum is 0 msec
  Neighbor Count is 1, Adjacent neighbor count is 1
    Adjacent with neighbor 10.0.0.12
  Suppress hello for 0 neighbor(s)
Serial0/0/1 is up, line protocol is up
  Internet Address 10.1.0.1/24, Area 1
  Process ID 1, Router ID 10.0.0.11, Network Type POINT_TO_POINT, Cost: 781
  Transmit Delay is 1 sec, State POINT_TO_POINT
  Timer intervals configured, Hello 10, Dead 40, Wait 40, Retransmit 5
    oob-resync timeout 40
    Hello due in 00:00:09
  Supports Link-local Signaling (LLS)
  Index 2/2, flood queue length 0
  Next 0x0(0)/0x0(0)
  Last flood scan length is 1, maximum is 3
  Last flood scan time is 0 msec, maximum is 4 msec
  Neighbor Count is 1, Adjacent neighbor count is 1
    Adjacent with neighbor 10.0.0.12
  Suppress hello for 0 neighbor(s)
FastEthernet0/0 is up, line protocol is up
  Internet Address 10.1.1.1/24, Area 1
  Process ID 1, Router ID 10.0.0.11, Network Type BROADCAST, Cost: 1
  Transmit Delay is 1 sec, State DR, Priority 1
  Designated Router (ID) 10.0.0.11, Interface address 10.1.1.1
  No backup designated router on this network
  Timer intervals configured, Hello 10, Dead 40, Wait 40, Retransmit 5
    oob-resync timeout 40
    Hello due in 00:00:04
  Supports Link-local Signaling (LLS)
```

```
        Index 1/1, flood queue length 0
        Next 0x0(0)/0x0(0)
        Last flood scan length is 1, maximum is 3
        Last flood scan time is 0 msec, maximum is 0 msec
        Neighbor Count is 1, Adjacent neighbor count is 1
          Adjacent with neighbor 10.200.200.13
        Suppress hello for 0 neighbor(s)
      P1R1#
```

The default OSPF network type on the point-to-point subinterface is point to point.

Step 5   At the edge routers, use the proper **show** command to verify the OSPF neighbor status. Is there a DR or BDR on s0/0/0.2 using the point-to-point OSPF network type?

Solution:

The following shows the output on the P1R1 router:

```
      P1R1#sh ip ospf neighbor

      Neighbor ID       Pri   State           Dead Time   Address       Interface
      200.200.200.200   0     FULL/   -       00:01:36    172.31.11.4   Serial0/0/0.1
      10.0.0.12         0     FULL/   -       00:00:33    10.11.0.2     Serial0/0/0.2
      10.0.0.12         0     FULL/   -       00:00:39    10.1.0.2      Serial0/0/1
      10.200.200.13     0     FULL/DROTHER    00:00:39    10.1.1.3      FastEthernet0/0
      P1R1#
```

No, there is no DR or BDR on the point-to-point S0/0/0.2 subinterface.

Step 6   At the edge routers, verify the OSPF routes in the IP routing table. (You might not see routes from the other pod, depending on if it is in use.)

Solution:

The following shows the output on the P1R1 router:

```
      P1R1#show ip route
      <output omitted>
      Gateway of last resort is not set

            172.31.0.0/16 is variably subnetted, 4 subnets, 2 masks
      O       172.31.22.4/32 [110/781] via 172.31.11.4, 00:03:37, Serial0/0/0.1
      C       172.31.11.0/24 is directly connected, Serial0/0/0.1
      O       172.31.11.2/32 [110/1562] via 172.31.11.4, 00:03:37, Serial0/0/0.1
      O       172.31.11.4/32 [110/781] via 172.31.11.4, 00:03:37, Serial0/0/0.1
            10.0.0.0/24 is subnetted, 6 subnets
      C       10.11.0.0 is directly connected, Serial0/0/0.2
      O       10.1.3.0 [110/782] via 10.1.1.3, 00:03:17, FastEthernet0/0
      O       10.1.2.0 [110/782] via 10.11.0.2, 00:03:18, Serial0/0/0.2
                       [110/782] via 10.1.0.2, 00:03:18, Serial0/0/1
      C       10.1.1.0 is directly connected, FastEthernet0/0
      C       10.1.0.0 is directly connected, Serial0/0/1
      O E2    10.254.0.0 [110/50] via 172.31.11.4, 00:03:18, Serial0/0/0.1
      P1R1#
```

Step 7   On the internal routers, verify the OSPF routes in the IP routing table. Why are some marked as "O IA" on the internal router, but not on the edge routers?

Solution:

The following shows the output on the P1R3 router:

```
P1R3#show ip route
<output omitted>
Gateway of last resort is not set

     172.31.0.0/32 is subnetted, 4 subnets
O IA   172.31.22.4 [110/782] via 10.1.1.1, 00:04:30, FastEthernet0/0
O IA   172.31.11.1 [110/1] via 10.1.1.1, 00:04:30, FastEthernet0/0
O IA   172.31.11.2 [110/782] via 10.1.3.4, 00:04:30, Serial0/0/0
                   [110/782] via 10.1.1.1, 00:04:30, FastEthernet0/0
O IA   172.31.11.4 [110/782] via 10.1.1.1, 00:04:30, FastEthernet0/0
     10.0.0.0/8 is variably subnetted, 7 subnets, 2 masks
O      10.11.0.0/24 [110/782] via 10.1.1.1, 00:04:30, FastEthernet0/0
C      10.200.200.13/32 is directly connected, Loopback0
C      10.1.3.0/24 is directly connected, Serial0/0/0
O      10.1.2.0/24 [110/782] via 10.1.3.4, 00:04:32, Serial0/0/0
C      10.1.1.0/24 is directly connected, FastEthernet0/0
O      10.1.0.0/24 [110/782] via 10.1.1.1, 00:04:32, FastEthernet0/0
O E2   10.254.0.0/24 [110/50] via 10.1.1.1, 00:04:33, FastEthernet0/0
P1R3#
```

The routes marked as "O IA" on the internal routers are from area 0. Because the internal routers are not connected to area 0, they see these routes as interarea—coming from another area. These routes are therefore marked as "O IA" on the internal routers.

The edge routers are in both area 0 and the pod's own area; the edge routers therefore see these routes are intra-area routes. These routes are therefore marked as "O" on the edge routers.

Step 8   Use the **show ip protocols** command to verify the OSPF routing process on the edge and internal routers. How many areas does the edge router belong to? How many areas does the internal router belong to?

Solution:

The following shows the output on the P1R1 and P1R3 routers:

```
P1R1#show ip protocols
Routing Protocol is "ospf 1"
  Outgoing update filter list for all interfaces is not set
  Incoming update filter list for all interfaces is not set
  Router ID 10.0.0.11
  It is an area border router
  Number of areas in this router is 2. 2 normal 0 stub 0 nssa
  Maximum path: 4
  Routing for Networks:
    10.1.0.0 0.0.255.255 area 1
    10.11.0.0 0.0.0.255 area 1
    172.31.11.0 0.0.0.255 area 0
```

```
        Routing Information Sources:
          Gateway          Distance      Last Update
          200.200.200.200     110        00:05:35
          100.100.100.100     110        00:29:26
          10.200.200.14       110        02:14:53
          10.0.0.12           110        00:05:35
          10.200.200.13       110        00:05:35
          10.1.3.3            110        02:53:40
          10.1.2.2            110        02:42:54
          10.1.3.4            110        02:45:05
        Distance: (default is 110)

    P1R3#show ip protocols
    Routing Protocol is "ospf 1"
      Outgoing update filter list for all interfaces is not set
      Incoming update filter list for all interfaces is not set
      Router ID 10.200.200.13
      Number of areas in this router is 1. 1 normal 0 stub 0 nssa
      Maximum path: 4
      Routing for Networks:
        10.1.0.0 0.0.255.255 area 1
      Routing Information Sources:
        Gateway          Distance      Last Update
        200.200.200.200     110        00:06:22
        100.100.100.100     110        00:30:14
        10.0.0.11           110        00:06:22
        10.200.200.14       110        02:15:40
        10.0.0.12           110        00:06:22
        10.1.2.2            110        02:42:54
        10.1.1.1            110        02:43:30
      Distance: (default is 110)
```

The edge routers belong to two areas, and the internal routers belong to one area.

> **NOTE** You may see some old addresses as routing information sources in the output of the **show ip protocols** command if you have not reloaded your router since you changed the other routers' OSPF router IDs, as is the case in the sample output.

Step 9   Save your configurations to NVRAM.

Solution:

The following shows how to perform the required step on the P1R1 router:

```
    P1R1#copy run start
    Destination filename [startup-config]?
    Building configuration...
    [OK]
```

Exercise Verification

You have successfully completed this exercise when you have configured OSPF over Frame Relay using the point-to-multipoint and point-to-point network types.

Configuration Exercise 5-3: Tuning OSPF

In this exercise, you use **show** commands to view the LSDB structure. You will also investigate the use of OSPF route summarization and stub areas.

> **NOTE**   Throughout this exercise, the pod number is referred to as *x*, and the router number is referred to as *y*. Substitute the appropriate numbers as needed.

Objectives

The objectives of this exercise are as follows:

- Examine the OSPF LSDB structure.

- Configure OSPF route summarization to limit the routing table size and update traffic.

- Configure an OSPF stub area and totally stubby area to limit the routing table size and update traffic.

Visual Objective

Figure 5-31 illustrates the topology used in this exercise.

Figure 5-31 *Tuning OSPF*

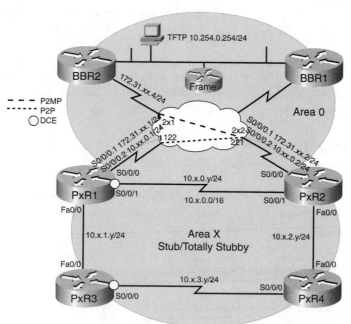

Command List

In this exercise, you use the commands in Table 5-22, listed in logical order. Refer to this list if you need configuration command assistance during the exercise.

> **CAUTION** Although the command syntax is shown in this table, the addresses shown are typically for the P*x*R1 and P*x*R3 routers. Be careful when addressing your routers! Refer to the exercise instructions and the appropriate visual objective diagram for addressing details.

Table 5-22 *Configuration Exercise 5-3 Commands*

Command	Description
#**show ip ospf database**	Shows the LSDB.
#**show ip ospf database external**	Shows external (type 5) LSAs.
(config-router)#**area** *x* **range 10.***x***.0.0 255.255.0.0**	On an ABR, configures route summarization of the address 10.x.0.0/16 for the area *x*.
(config-router)#**area** *x* **stub**	Configures the area to be a stub area. This blocks type 5 LSAs (external routes) from reaching this area and substitutes a default route to the ABR.
(config-router)#**area** *x* **stub no-summary**	Configures the area to be totally stubby. This blocks type 3, 4, and 5 LSAs (interarea and external routes) from reaching this area and substitutes a default route to the ABR.

> **NOTE** The exercise tasks include answers and solutions. Some answers cover multiple steps; the answers are given after the last step to which that answer applies.

Task 1: Examining the OSPF Database

In this task, you examine the OSPF LSDB. Follow these steps:

Step 1   On all your pod routers, use the **show ip ospf database** command to display the OSPF database. This database shows all LSAs stored in the router.

Do you see LSA types 1, 2, 3, 4, and 5 in the OSPF database?

On the edge routers, do you see LSA information about area 0 and area *x*?

On the internal routers, do you see LSA information about area *x* only?

Solution:

The following shows the output on the P1R1 and P1R3 routers:

```
P1R1#show ip ospf database

                OSPF Router with ID (10.0.0.11) (Process ID 1)

                    Router Link States (Area 0)

Link ID          ADV Router       Age       Seq#        Checksum Link count
10.0.0.11        10.0.0.11        485       0x80000004 0x002EE5 2
10.0.0.12        10.0.0.12        540       0x80000002 0x0046CB 2
10.0.0.21        10.0.0.21        494       0x80000042 0x00F8E1 1
10.0.0.22        10.0.0.22        246       0x80000042 0x00F6E0 1
200.200.200.200 200.200.200.200 485       0x800001CB 0x00E504 6

                    Summary Net Link States (Area 0)

Link ID          ADV Router       Age       Seq#        Checksum
10.1.0.0         10.0.0.11        486       0x8000001A 0x00C92A
10.1.0.0         10.0.0.12        541       0x8000001A 0x00C32F
10.1.1.0         10.0.0.11        486       0x8000001A 0x002BD6
10.1.1.0         10.0.0.12        521       0x8000001C 0x00BE30
10.1.2.0         10.0.0.11        486       0x8000001A 0x00BD33
10.1.2.0         10.0.0.12        521       0x8000001C 0x0016E7
10.1.3.0         10.0.0.11        487       0x8000001A 0x00B23D
10.1.3.0         10.0.0.12        527       0x80000001 0x00DE29
10.2.0.0         10.0.0.21        1759      0x8000003F 0x00378C
10.2.0.0         10.0.0.22        856       0x8000003F 0x003191
10.2.1.0         10.0.0.21        1861      0x80000041 0x00943B
10.2.1.0         10.0.0.22        856       0x8000003F 0x003090
10.2.2.0         10.0.0.21        1861      0x80000049 0x00179F
10.2.2.0         10.0.0.22        1359      0x80000044 0x007D4D
10.2.3.0         10.0.0.21        1861      0x8000003F 0x00209F
10.2.3.0         10.0.0.22        1359      0x80000041 0x0016A6
10.11.0.0        10.0.0.11        589       0x80000018 0x005596
10.11.0.0        10.0.0.12        619       0x80000001 0x007D84

                    Router Link States (Area 1)

Link ID          ADV Router       Age       Seq#        Checksum Link count
10.0.0.11        10.0.0.11        613       0x80000006 0x000CF1 5
10.0.0.12        10.0.0.12        614       0x80000006 0x00F205 5
10.200.200.13    10.200.200.13    639       0x80000005 0x0006B4 3
10.200.200.14    10.200.200.14    635       0x80000005 0x00882C 3

                    Net Link States (Area 1)

Link ID          ADV Router       Age       Seq#        Checksum
10.1.1.1         10.0.0.11        640       0x80000001 0x00D485
10.1.2.2         10.0.0.12        635       0x80000001 0x00D183

                    Summary Net Link States (Area 1)

Link ID          ADV Router       Age       Seq#        Checksum
172.31.11.1      10.0.0.11        616       0x80000001 0x002F21
172.31.11.1      10.0.0.12        576       0x80000001 0x0064CA
172.31.11.2      10.0.0.11        576       0x80000001 0x0060CE
172.31.11.2      10.0.0.12        670       0x80000001 0x001F2F
172.31.11.4      10.0.0.11        576       0x80000001 0x00AE8E
172.31.11.4      10.0.0.12        630       0x80000001 0x00A893
172.31.22.4      10.0.0.11        576       0x80000001 0x0035FC
172.31.22.4      10.0.0.12        630       0x80000001 0x002F02
```

```
                    Summary ASB Link States (Area 1)

     Link ID          ADV Router       Age        Seq#        Checksum
     200.200.200.200 10.0.0.11        576        0x80000001 0x00688B
     200.200.200.200 10.0.0.12        631        0x80000001 0x006290

                    Type-5 AS External Link States

     Link ID          ADV Router       Age        Seq#        Checksum Tag
     10.254.0.0       200.200.200.200 451        0x8000019D 0x00DADD 0
     P1R1#

P1R3#show ip ospf database

              OSPF Router with ID (10.200.200.13) (Process ID 1)

                 Router Link States (Area 1)

     Link ID          ADV Router       Age        Seq#        Checksum Link count
     10.0.0.11        10.0.0.11        669        0x80000006 0x000CF1 5
     10.0.0.12        10.0.0.12        670        0x80000006 0x00F205 5
     10.200.200.13    10.200.200.13    694        0x80000005 0x0006B4 3
     10.200.200.14    10.200.200.14    688        0x80000005 0x00882C 3

                 Net Link States (Area 1)

     Link ID          ADV Router       Age        Seq#        Checksum
     10.1.1.1         10.0.0.11        695        0x80000001 0x00D485
     10.1.2.2         10.0.0.12        689        0x80000001 0x00D183

                 Summary Net Link States (Area 1)

     Link ID          ADV Router       Age        Seq#        Checksum
     172.31.11.1      10.0.0.11        670        0x80000001 0x002F21
     172.31.11.1      10.0.0.12        630        0x80000001 0x0064CA
     172.31.11.2      10.0.0.11        630        0x80000001 0x0060CE
     172.31.11.2      10.0.0.12        724        0x80000001 0x001F2F
     172.31.11.4      10.0.0.11        631        0x80000001 0x00AE8E
     172.31.11.4      10.0.0.12        686        0x80000001 0x00A893
     172.31.22.4      10.0.0.11        631        0x80000001 0x0035FC
     172.31.22.4      10.0.0.12        686        0x80000001 0x002F02

                 Summary ASB Link States (Area 1)

     Link ID          ADV Router       Age        Seq#        Checksum
     200.200.200.200 10.0.0.11        631        0x80000001 0x00688B
     200.200.200.200 10.0.0.12        686        0x80000001 0x006290

                 Type-5 AS External Link States

     Link ID          ADV Router       Age        Seq#        Checksum Tag
     10.254.0.0       200.200.200.200 505        0x8000019D 0x00DADD 0
     P1R3#
```

LSA types 1 (Router), 2 (Net), 3 (Summary Net), 4 (Summary ASB), and 5 (AS External) are in the OSPF database.

The edge routers have LSA information about area 0 and area *x*; in this example P1R1 has information about area 0 and area 1.

The internal routers have LSA information about area *x* only; in this example P1R3 only has information about area 1.

Table 5-23 explains some of the fields in the output.

Table 5-23   **show ip ospf database** *Command Output*

Field	Information Provided
ADV Router	The advertising router's RID.
Age	The LSA's age.
Checksum	The checksum of the LSA's contents.
Link Count	The number of interfaces on the router. Each serial interface counts as two links, and each Ethernet interface counts as one link.
Link ID	A value that uniquely identifies a specific LSA.
Seq#	The sequence number, used to detect an older or duplicate LSA.
Tag	Administratively used to recognize routes that are introduced through a specific redistribution process.

Step 2   Use the **show ip ospf database external** command on your edge routers to display all the type 5 LSAs in the OSPF database. The core router, BBR2, is redistributing the 10.254.0.0/24 network into OSPF. Determine whether there is a type 5 LSA about the 10.254.0.0 network.

Solution:

The following shows the output on the P1R1 router:

```
P1R1#show ip ospf database external

                OSPF Router with ID (10.0.0.11) (Process ID 1)

                    Type-5 AS External Link States

    Routing Bit Set on this LSA
    LS age: 549
    Options: (No TOS-capability, DC)
    LS Type: AS External Link
    Link State ID: 10.254.0.0 (External Network Number )
    Advertising Router: 200.200.200.200
    LS Seq Number: 8000019D
    Checksum: 0xDADD
    Length: 36
    Network Mask: /24
          Metric Type: 2 (Larger than any link state path)
          TOS: 0
          Metric: 50
          Forward Address: 0.0.0.0
          External Route Tag: 0

    P1R1#
```

As can be seen in the output, there is a type 5 LSA about the 10.254.0.0 network.

Task 2: Configure OSPF Route Summarization

In this task, you limit routing table size and update traffic using OSPF route summarization. Follow these steps:

Step 1   Telnet to the BBR2 router (172.31.xx.4) and examine its routing table. Note the paths to the subnets of the pod 10.x.0.0/16 network.

Solution:

The following shows the output on the BBR2 router:

```
BBR2#show ip route ospf
      172.31.0.0/16 is variably subnetted, 6 subnets, 2 masks
O         172.31.11.1/32 [110/781] via 172.31.11.1, 00:23:21, Serial0/0/0.1
O         172.31.11.2/32 [110/781] via 172.31.11.2, 00:23:21, Serial0/0/0.1
      10.0.0.0/24 is subnetted, 7 subnets
O IA    10.11.0.0 [110/1562] via 172.31.11.2, 00:23:21, Serial0/0/0.1
                  [110/1562] via 172.31.11.1, 00:23:21, Serial0/0/0.1
O IA    10.1.3.0 [110/1563] via 172.31.11.2, 00:23:21, Serial0/0/0.1
                 [110/1563] via 172.31.11.1, 00:23:21, Serial0/0/0.1
O IA    10.1.2.0 [110/782] via 172.31.11.2, 00:23:21, Serial0/0/0.1
O IA    10.1.1.0 [110/782] via 172.31.11.1, 00:23:21, Serial0/0/0.1
O IA    10.1.0.0 [110/1562] via 172.31.11.2, 00:23:21, Serial0/0/0.1
                 [110/1562] via 172.31.11.1, 00:23:21, Serial0/0/0.1
BBR2#
```

Step 1   On the edge routers, summarize the pod networks to 10.x.0.0/16 from area x.

Solution:

The following shows how to do the required step on the P1R1 router:

```
P1R1(config)#router ospf 1
P1R1(config-router)#area 1 range 10.1.0.0 255.255.0.0
```

Step 2   From an edge router, Telnet to the BBR2 router (172.31.xx.4), and examine its routing table. Examine the paths to the subnets of the pod 10.x.0.0/16 network.

Solution:

The following shows the output on the BBR2 router:

```
BBR2#show ip route ospf
      172.31.0.0/16 is variably subnetted, 6 subnets, 2 masks
O         172.31.11.1/32 [110/781] via 172.31.11.1, 00:25:26, Serial0/0/0.1
O         172.31.11.2/32 [110/781] via 172.31.11.2, 00:25:26, Serial0/0/0.1
      10.0.0.0/8 is variably subnetted, 4 subnets, 2 masks
```

```
O IA    10.11.0.0/24 [110/1562] via 172.31.11.2, 00:25:26, Serial0/0/0.1
                     [110/1562] via 172.31.11.1, 00:25:26, Serial0/0/0.1
O IA    10.1.0.0/16 [110/782] via 172.31.11.2, 00:00:34, Serial0/0/0.1
                    [110/782] via 172.31.11.1, 00:00:34, Serial0/0/0.1
BBR2#
```

Notice that BBR2 recognizes two paths to the pod 10.*x*.0.0/16 network. It no longer recognizes each of the pod /24 links (10.*x*.0.0/24, 10.*x*.1.0/24, 10.*x*.2.0/24, and 10.*x*.3.0/24).

BBR2 still recognizes the 10.*xx*.0.0/24 link, because it is not part of the summarized range.

Step 3   Determine the changes summarization made to the routing table on the edge routers. Is the routing table reduced on the edge routers? Explain why there is a route to Null0.

Solution:

The following shows the output on the P1R1 router:

```
P1R1#show ip route
<output omitted>
Gateway of last resort is not set

     172.31.0.0/16 is variably subnetted, 4 subnets, 2 masks
O       172.31.22.4/32 [110/781] via 172.31.11.4, 00:01:41, Serial0/0/0.1
C       172.31.11.0/24 is directly connected, Serial0/0/0.1
O       172.31.11.2/32 [110/1562] via 172.31.11.4, 00:01:41, Serial0/0/0.1
O       172.31.11.4/32 [110/781] via 172.31.11.4, 00:01:41, Serial0/0/0.1
     10.0.0.0/8 is variably subnetted, 7 subnets, 2 masks
C       10.11.0.0/24 is directly connected, Serial0/0/0.2
O       10.1.3.0/24 [110/782] via 10.1.1.3, 00:01:42, FastEthernet0/0
O       10.1.2.0/24 [110/782] via 10.11.0.2, 00:01:42, Serial0/0/0.2
                    [110/782] via 10.1.0.2, 00:01:42, Serial0/0/1
C       10.1.1.0/24 is directly connected, FastEthernet0/0
C       10.1.0.0/24 is directly connected, Serial0/0/1
O       10.1.0.0/16 is a summary, 00:01:42, Null0
O E2    10.254.0.0/24 [110/50] via 172.31.11.4, 00:01:42, Serial0/0/0.1
P1R1#
```

The edge router P1R1 still has routes to the 10.1.*x*.0 subnets; those routes have a mask of /24. For network 10.1.0.0/16 P1R1 now has a route to interface Null0; in other words, it discards packets that belong to any of the subnets of 10.1.0.0/16 for which it doesn't have a more precise match of 24 bits. This route to Null0 route is the result of having "told the world" that it knows how to get to any of the subnets of 10.1.0.0/16 with the summarization command.

If pod 2 had also been configured similarly, P1R1 would see a summarized route to 10.2.0.0/16. If pod 2 had not summarized the routes, P1R1 would see detailed /24 subnet routes from pod 2.

Task 3: **Configure an OSPF Stub Area**

In this task, you limit routing table size and update traffic using OSPF stub area and totally stubby area features. Follow these steps:

Step 1 Configure the pod OSPF area as a stub area; remember to configure both the edge and internal routers because the stub flag is included in the hello packets and must match on all routers in the area. Notice the error messages and that no adjacency is established until both routers agree that they are stubs. What changes do you expect to occur with the implementation of a stub?

Solution:

The following shows how to do the required step on the P1R1 router:

```
P1R1(config)#router ospf 1
P1R1(config-router)#area 1 stub
```

All the routers in the pod must have this command configured.

With the implementation of a stub network, the routing tables of the internal routers should be smaller.

Step 2 Examine the edge (PxR1 or PxR2) and internal (PxR3 or PxR4) routing tables. Determine whether there are any interarea OSPF routes in the internal routers and the reason for their presence.

Solution:

The following shows the output on the P1R1 and P1R3 routers:

```
P1R1#show ip route
<output omitted>
Gateway of last resort is not set

     172.31.0.0/16 is variably subnetted, 4 subnets, 2 masks
O       172.31.22.4/32 [110/781] via 172.31.11.4, 00:02:12, Serial0/0/0.1
C       172.31.11.0/24 is directly connected, Serial0/0/0.1
O       172.31.11.2/32 [110/1562] via 172.31.11.4, 00:02:12, Serial0/0/0.1
O       172.31.11.4/32 [110/781] via 172.31.11.4, 00:02:12, Serial0/0/0.1
     10.0.0.0/8 is variably subnetted, 7 subnets, 2 masks
C       10.11.0.0/24 is directly connected, Serial0/0/0.2
O       10.1.3.0/24 [110/782] via 10.1.1.3, 00:01:18, FastEthernet0/0
O       10.1.2.0/24 [110/782] via 10.11.0.2, 00:01:18, Serial0/0/0.2
                    [110/782] via 10.1.0.2, 00:01:18, Serial0/0/1
C       10.1.1.0/24 is directly connected, FastEthernet0/0
C       10.1.0.0/24 is directly connected, Serial0/0/1
O       10.1.0.0/16 is a summary, 00:01:18, Null0
O E2    10.254.0.0/24 [110/50] via 172.31.11.4, 00:01:19, Serial0/0/0.1
P1R1#

P1R3#show ip route
```

```
<output omitted>
Gateway of last resort is 10.1.1.1 to network 0.0.0.0

     172.31.0.0/32 is subnetted, 4 subnets
O IA    172.31.22.4 [110/782] via 10.1.1.1, 00:02:01, FastEthernet0/0
O IA    172.31.11.1 [110/1] via 10.1.1.1, 00:02:01, FastEthernet0/0
O IA    172.31.11.2 [110/782] via 10.1.3.4, 00:02:01, Serial0/0/0
                    [110/782] via 10.1.1.1, 00:02:01, FastEthernet0/0
O IA    172.31.11.4 [110/782] via 10.1.1.1, 00:02:01, FastEthernet0/0
     10.0.0.0/8 is variably subnetted, 6 subnets, 2 masks
O       10.11.0.0/24 [110/782] via 10.1.1.1, 00:02:02, FastEthernet0/0
C       10.200.200.13/32 is directly connected, Loopback0
C       10.1.3.0/24 is directly connected, Serial0/0/0
O       10.1.2.0/24 [110/782] via 10.1.3.4, 00:02:02, Serial0/0/0
C       10.1.1.0/24 is directly connected, FastEthernet0/0
O       10.1.0.0/24 [110/782] via 10.1.1.1, 00:02:02, FastEthernet0/0
O*IA 0.0.0.0/0 [110/2] via 10.1.1.1, 00:02:03, FastEthernet0/0
P1R3#
```

There are interarea (IA) routes on the internal routers, showing routes outside of area 1.

The edge routers do have an external route (O E2). The internal routers do not have any external (O E2) routes; the ABR (edge router) generates a default route (O*IA) to the internal routers for reaching the external network.

Step 3   Configure the OSPF area of the pod as totally stubby. Remember that only the ABR requires the command to configure the area as totally stubby.

Solution:

The following shows how to do the required step on the P1R1 router:

```
P1R1(config)#router ospf 1
P1R1(config-router)#area 1 stub no-summary
```

Both of the edge routers in the pod must have this command configured.

Step 4   Examine the edge (P*x*R1 or P*x*R2) and internal (P*x*R3 or P*x*R4) routing tables. Determine whether any interarea OSPF routes are in the internal routers and the reason for their presence.

Solution:

The following shows the output on the P1R1 and P1R3 routers:

```
P1R1#show ip route
<output omitted>
Gateway of last resort is not set

     172.31.0.0/16 is variably subnetted, 4 subnets, 2 masks
O       172.31.22.4/32 [110/781] via 172.31.11.4, 00:00:58, Serial0/0/0.1
C       172.31.11.0/24 is directly connected, Serial0/0/0.1
O       172.31.11.2/32 [110/1562] via 172.31.11.4, 00:00:58, Serial0/0/0.1
```

```
O          172.31.11.4/32 [110/781] via 172.31.11.4, 00:00:58, Serial0/0/0.1
        10.0.0.0/8 is variably subnetted, 7 subnets, 2 masks
C          10.11.0.0/24 is directly connected, Serial0/0/0.2
O          10.1.3.0/24 [110/782] via 10.1.1.3, 00:01:00, FastEthernet0/0
O          10.1.2.0/24 [110/782] via 10.11.0.2, 00:01:00, Serial0/0/0.2
                       [110/782] via 10.1.0.2, 00:01:00, Serial0/0/1
C          10.1.1.0/24 is directly connected, FastEthernet0/0
C          10.1.0.0/24 is directly connected, Serial0/0/1
O          10.1.0.0/16 is a summary, 00:01:00, Null0
O E2    10.254.0.0/24 [110/50] via 172.31.11.4, 00:01:00, Serial0/0/0.1
P1R1#

P1R3#show ip route
<output omitted>
Gateway of last resort is 10.1.1.1 to network 0.0.0.0

        10.0.0.0/8 is variably subnetted, 6 subnets, 2 masks
O          10.11.0.0/24 [110/782] via 10.1.1.1, 00:05:22, FastEthernet0/0
C          10.200.200.13/32 is directly connected, Loopback0
C          10.1.3.0/24 is directly connected, Serial0/0/0
O          10.1.2.0/24 [110/782] via 10.1.3.4, 00:05:22, Serial0/0/0
C          10.1.1.0/24 is directly connected, FastEthernet0/0
O          10.1.0.0/24 [110/782] via 10.1.1.1, 00:05:22, FastEthernet0/0
O*IA 0.0.0.0/0 [110/2] via 10.1.1.1, 00:01:04, FastEthernet0/0
P1R3#
```

There are no interarea (IA) routes on the internal routers.

The edge routers do have an external route (O E2). The internal routers do not have any external (O E2) or interarea (IA) routes; the ABR (edge router) generates a default route (O*IA) to the internal routers for reaching all external and interarea networks.

Step 5   Ping the TFTP server from the internal routers to verify connectivity.

Solution:

The following shows the output on the P1R3 router:

```
P1R3#ping 10.254.0.254

Type escape sequence to abort.
Sending 5, 100-byte ICMP Echos to 10.254.0.254, timeout is 2 seconds:
!!!!!
Success rate is 100 percent (5/5), round-trip min/avg/max = 28/29/32 ms
P1R3#
```

Step 6   Save your configurations to NVRAM.

Solution:

The following shows how to perform the required step on the P1R1 router:

```
P1R1#copy run start
Destination filename [startup-config]?
Building configuration...
[OK]
```

Exercise Verification

You have successfully completed this exercise when you achieve these results:

- You have examined the OSPF LSDB, and you understand the tools necessary to investigate the LSDB.

- You have minimized routing table size by using route summarization without affecting reachability. You should still be able to ping all devices in your pod and in the core.

- You have configured your pod router area as an OSPF stub area and as a totally stubby area.

Review Questions

Answer the following questions, and then refer to Appendix A, "Answers to Review Questions," for the answers.

1. True or false: OSPF performs route summarization by default.

2. True or false: In a large network where topological changes are frequent, routers spend many CPU cycles recalculating the SPF algorithm and updating the routing table.

3. Match the type of router with its description:

Type of Router	Description
1—Internal router	**A**—A router that sits in the perimeter of the backbone area and that has at least one interface connected to area 0. It maintains OSPF routing information using the same procedures and algorithms as an internal router.
2—Backbone router	**B**—A router that has interfaces attached to multiple areas, maintains separate LSDBs for each area to which it connects, and routes traffic destined for or arriving from other areas. This router is an exit point for the area, which means that routing information destined for another area can get there only via the local area's router of this type. This kind of router can be configured to summarize the routing information from the LSDBs of its attached areas. This router distributes the routing information into the backbone.
3—ABR	**C**—A router that has all its interfaces in the same area.
4—ASBR	**D**—A router that has at least one interface attached to an external internetwork (another AS), such as a non-OSPF network. This router can import non-OSPF network information to the OSPF network and vice versa; this process is called route redistribution.

4. How many different types of LSAs are there?

   a. 5

   b. 9

   c. 10

   d. 11

5. What kind of router generates LSA type 5?

   a. DR

   b. ABR

   c. ASBR

   d. ADR

6. True or false: By default, OSPF does not automatically summarize groups of contiguous subnets.

7. Where does a type 1 LSA flood to?

   a. To immediate peers

   b. To all other routers in the area where it originated

   c. To routers located in other areas

   d. To all areas

8. How does a routing table reflect the link-state information of an intra-area route?

   a. The route is marked with O.

   b. The route is marked with I.

   c. The route is marked with IO.

   d. The route is marked with EA.

   e. The route is marked with O IA.

9. Which type of external route is the default?

   a. E1.

   b. E2.

   c. E5.

   d. There is no default external route. OSPF adapts and chooses the most accurate one.

10. E1 external routes calculate the cost by adding what?

    a. The internal cost of each link the packet crosses

    b. The external cost to the internal cost of each link the packet crosses

    c. The external cost only

    d. All area costs, even those that are not used

11. What does the OSPF **max-lsa** command do?

    a. Defines the maximum number of LSAs that the router can generate.

    b. Protects the router from an excessive number of received (non-self-generated) LSAs in its LSDB.

    c. Defines the maximum size of the LSAs that the router generates.

    d. Protects the router from excessively large received (non-self-generated) LSAs in its LSDB.

12. How is the OSPF metric calculated, by default?

    a. OSPF calculates the OSPF metric for a router according to the bandwidth of all its interfaces.

    b. OSPF calculates the OSPF metric by referencing the DR.

    c. OSPF calculates the OSPF metric for an interface according to the interface's inverse bandwidth.

    d. OSPF calculates the OSPF metric by using the lowest bandwidth value among all of its interfaces.

13. Why is configuring a stub area advantageous?

    a. It reduces the size of the LSDB inside an area.

    b. It increases the memory requirements for routers in that area.

    c. It further segments the hierarchy.

    d. It starts to behave like a distance vector routing protocol, thus speeding up convergence.

14. A stub area is typically created using what kind of topology?

    a. Point to point

    b. Broadcast

    c. Hub and spoke

    d. Full mesh

15. True or false: By default, in standard areas, routers generate default routes.

16. What command makes an OSPF router generate a default route?

    a. **ospf default-initiate**

    b. **default-information originate**

    c. **default information-initiate**

    d. **ospf information-originate**

17. If your router has an interface faster than 100 Mbps that is used with OSPF, consider using the _____ command under the _____ process.

    a. **auto-cost reference-bandwidth**, OSPF

    b. **auto-cost reference-bandwidth**, interface

    c. **autocost reference-speed**, OSPF

    d. **autocost reference-speed**, interface

18. True or false: OSPF design requires that all areas be directly connect to the backbone.

19. True or false: Virtual links are very useful, and you should include them in your network architecture when designing a completely new OSPF network.

20. Which of the following would result in the smallest routing tables on OSPF internal routers?

    a. Stub area

    b. Totally stubby area

    c. Standard area

    d. Transit area

21. What is the default OSPF authentication?

    a. Simple password

    b. MD5

    c. Null

    d. IPsec

22.   True or false: When configuring OSPF authentication, each router must have a unique password configured.

23.   What command is used to troubleshoot OSPF authentication?

   a. **debug ip ospf adj**

   b. **debug ip ospf auth**

   c. **debug ip ospf md5**

   d. **debug ip ospf packet**

24.   True or false: Only one MD5 OSPF authentication key can be configured at a time on a Cisco router.

This chapter introduces the Intermediate System-Intermediate System (IS-IS) protocol and covers the following topics:

- Introducing IS-IS and Integrated IS-IS Routing

- IS-IS Routing Operation

- Configuring Integrated IS-IS

- Verifying IS-IS Configuration and Structures

CHAPTER 6

Configuring the Integrated Intermediate System-to-Intermediate System Protocol

This chapter provides an overview of the Integrated Intermediate System-to-Intermediate System (IS-IS) protocol, including its operation and configuration. The IS-IS protocol is a part of the Open System Interconnection (OSI) suite of protocols. The OSI suite uses Connectionless Network Service (CLNS) to provide connectionless delivery of data, and the actual Layer 3 protocol is Connectionless Network Protocol (CLNP). CLNP is the solution for "unreliable" (connectionless) delivery of data, similar to IP. IS-IS uses CLNS addresses to identify the routers and build the link-state database (LSDB).

What's the Difference Between ISO and OSI?

The International Organization for Standardization (ISO) was constituted to develop standards for data networking.

OSI protocols represent an international standardization program that facilitates multivendor equipment interoperability.

IS-IS operates in strictly CLNS terms; however, Integrated IS-IS supports IP routing and CLNS. CLNS addresses are required to configure and troubleshoot Integrated IS-IS, even when it is used only for IP. IS-IS supports different data-link environments, such as Ethernet and Frame Relay.

IS-IS supports the most important characteristics of the Open Shortest Path First (OSPF) and Enhanced Interior Gateway Routing Protocol (EIGRP) routing protocols, because it supports variable-length subnet masking (VLSM) and converges quickly. Each protocol has advantages and disadvantages, but this commonality makes any of the three scalable and appropriate for supporting today's large-scale networks.

Introducing IS-IS and Integrated IS-IS Routing

Integrated IS-IS is a proven and extensible IP routing protocol that converges quickly and supports VLSM. IS-IS is a public standard, originally published as ISO 9542 and republished as Requests For Comments (RFC) 995, *End System to Intermediate System Routing Exchange*

Protocol. Integrated IS-IS (or dual IS-IS) is specified in RFC 1195, *Use of OSI IS-IS for routing in TCP/IP and dual environments*, and offers support for IP and OSI protocols. Although not as common, Integrated IS-IS is comparable to, and in some cases preferable to, OSPF. This section describes IS-IS and Integrated IS-IS routing and compares Integrated IS-IS with OSPF. It also explores some of the concepts necessary to develop an understanding of Integrated IS-IS.

IS-IS Routing

IS-IS is a popular IP routing protocol in the Internet service provider (ISP) industry. The simplicity and stability of IS-IS make it robust in large internetworks. IS-IS is found in large ISPs and in some networks that support OSI protocols.

IS-IS development began before OSPF development. Large ISPs chose IS-IS because of their unique requirement for scalability, convergence, and stability. The U.S. government also required support for OSI protocols in the early Internet. Although this requirement was later dropped, IS-IS met both constraints.

Later, businesses typically chose OSPF because it was a more widely supported native IP protocol. Today it is harder to find information and expertise on IS-IS than it is for OSPF. However, some of the largest networks in the world still persist with IS-IS, which is a tribute to its capabilities.

ISO specifications call routers "intermediate systems" (ISs). Thus, IS-IS is a protocol that allows routers to communicate with other routers.

KEY POINT | **OSI Suite Protocols**

The OSI suite uses CLNS to provide connectionless delivery of data.

The actual Layer 3 protocol is CLNP, which provides connectionless delivery of data, similar to what IP does for the TCP/IP suite.

The IS-IS routing protocol uses CLNS addresses to identify the routers and to build the LSDB. IS-IS serves as an Interior Gateway Protocol (IGP) for the CLNS.

IS-IS Routing Levels

IS-IS is the dynamic link-state routing protocol for the OSI protocol stack. It distributes routing information for routing CLNP data for the ISO CLNS environment.

IS-IS operates similarly to OSPF. IS-IS allows the routing domain to be partitioned into areas. IS-IS routers establish adjacencies using a Hello protocol and exchange link-state information, using link-state packets (LSPs), throughout an area to build the LSDB. Each router then runs Dijkstra's shortest path first (SPF) algorithm against its LSDB to pick the best paths. There is a minimal amount of information communicated between areas, which reduces the burden on routers supporting the protocol.

IS-IS routing takes place at two levels within an AS: Level 1 (L1) and Level 2 (L2).

L1 routing occurs within an IS-IS area and is responsible for routing to end systems (ESs) and ISs inside an area. All devices in an L1 routing area have the same area address. Routing within an area is accomplished by looking at the locally significant address portion, known as the system ID, and choosing the lowest-cost path.

L2 routing occurs between IS-IS areas. L2 routers learn the locations of L1 routing areas and build an interarea routing table. L2 routers use the destination area address to route traffic using the lowest-cost path.

KEY POINT	**Two IS-IS Routing Levels**
	IS-IS supports two routing levels:
	• L1 builds a common topology of system IDs in the local area and routes traffic within the area using the lowest-cost path.
	• L2 exchanges prefix information (area addresses) between areas and routes traffic to an area using the lowest-cost path.

IS-IS Routers

KEY POINT	**Three Types of IS-IS Routers**
	To support the two routing levels, IS-IS defines three types of routers, as follows:
	• L1 routers use LSPs to learn about paths within the areas they connect to (intra-area).
	• L2 routers use LSPs to learn about paths among areas (interarea).
	• Level 1/Level 2 (L1/L2) routers learn about paths both within and between areas. L1/L2 routers are equivalent to area border routers (ABRs) in OSPF.

The three types of IS-IS routers are shown in Figure 6-1.

Figure 6-1 *Three Types of IS-IS Routers*

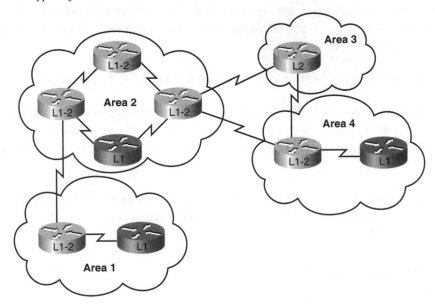

The path of connected L2 and L1/L2 routers is called the backbone. All areas and the backbone must be contiguous.

KEY POINT	**IS-IS Area Boundaries Are on Links**
	IS-IS area boundaries fall on the links, not within the routers. Each IS-IS router belongs to exactly one area. Neighboring routers learn that they are in the same or different areas and negotiate appropriate adjacencies—L1, L2, or both.

Integrated IS-IS Routing

Integrated IS-IS or dual IS-IS is an implementation of the IS-IS protocol for routing multiple network protocols, IP and CLNS, and is specified in RFC 1195 and ISO 10589.

> **NOTE** ISO 10589 is republished as RFC 1142, *OSI IS-IS Intradomain Routing Protocol.*

Integrated IS-IS tags CLNP routes with information about IP networks and subnets. Integrated IS-IS provides IP with an alternative to OSPF and combines ISO CLNS and IP routing in one protocol; it can be used for IP routing, CLNS routing, or for a combination of the two.

Integrated IS-IS uses its own protocol data units (PDUs) to transport information between routers, including IP reachability information. IS-IS information is not carried within a network layer protocol but is instead carried directly within data-link layer frames.

> **NOTE**   This protocol-independence makes IS-IS easily extensible; there is also a version of
> Integrated IS-IS that supports IP version 6 (IPv6), as described in Chapter 10, "Implementing
> IPv6."

Because IS-IS uses CLNS addresses to identify the routers and to build the LSDB, an
understanding of CLNS addresses is required to configure and troubleshoot IS-IS, even when it is
used only for routing IP.

Integrated IS-IS Design Principles

Effective networks are well-planned. The first and most important step in building a scalable
network is developing a good addressing plan that allows for route summarization. Route
summarization is possible only when using a hierarchical addressing structure.

Effective address planning presents opportunities to group devices into areas. Using areas confines
the scope of LSP propagation and saves bandwidth. L1/L2 routers, on the border between an L1
area and the L2 backbone, are logical places to implement route summarization, as shown in
Figure 6-2.

Figure 6-2   *L1/L2 Routers Should Implement Route Summarization*

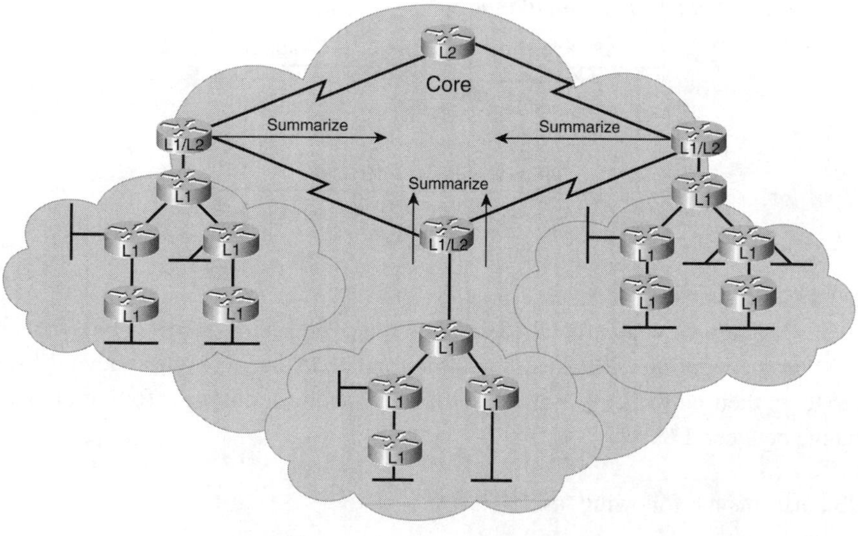

Route summarization has many benefits. It saves memory because each IS (router) is no longer
responsible for the LSPs of the entire routing domain. It also saves CPU usage, because a smaller
routing table is easier to maintain. Route summarization also results in a more stable network,
because topology changes can be isolated to a small portion of the network, and not propagate

8

throughout; routers in other portions of the network therefore do not have to run the routing algorithm and update their routing tables as often.

Issues with Integrated IS-IS

One issue with IS-IS is that older implementations default to using *narrow metrics*, which limit the maximum interface metric to 63 (6 bits) and the maximum total path metric to 1023 (10 bits). This provides little room to distinguish between paths.

Cisco IOS Software, beginning in Release 12.0, supports *wide metrics*, which allow a 24-bit interface and a 32-bit path metric. The default, however, is still narrow metrics.

> **NOTE** Complications can occur if you use wide metrics along with narrow metrics (for example, on older routers or in a multivendor environment).

Another issue is that IS-IS as implemented on Cisco routers does not automatically scale the interface metric. Instead, all IS-IS interfaces have a default metric of 10, as shown in Figure 6-3; this can be changed manually. If the default metric is not adjusted on each interface, the IS-IS metric becomes similar to the hop count metric used by the Routing Information Protocol (RIP).

Figure 6-3 *Default IS-IS Path Metric Calculation*

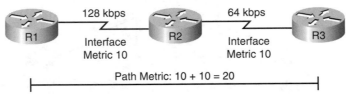

The ES-IS Protocol

Hosts in OSI terminology are called end systems. The End System-to-Intermediate System (ES-IS) protocol permits ESs (hosts) and ISs (routers) to discover one another. ES-IS also allows ESs to learn their network layer addresses. ES-IS handles topology information discovery and exchange between ESs and ISs.

ES-IS performs the following tasks:

- It identifies the area prefix to ESs.
- It creates adjacencies between ESs and ISs.
- It creates data link-to-network address mappings.

ESs send End System Hellos (ESHs) to well-known addresses that announce their presence to routers (ISs), as shown in Figure 6-4. Routers listen to ESHs to find the ESs on a segment. Routers include information on ESs in LSPs.

Figure 6-4 *End System-to-Intermediate System*

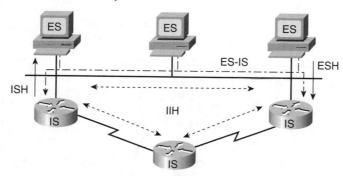

Routers transmit Intermediate System Hellos (ISHs) to well-known addresses, announcing their presence to ESs. ESs listen for these ISHs and randomly pick an IS to which they forward all their packets. When an ES needs to send a packet to another ES, it sends the packet to one of the ISs (routers) on its directly attached network.

Routers use IS-IS Hellos (IIHs) to establish and maintain adjacencies between ISs.

IP end host systems do not use ES-IS. IP has its own processes and applications to handle the same functions as ES-IS, such as Internet Control Message Protocol (ICMP), Address Resolution Protocol (ARP), and Dynamic Host Configuration Protocol (DHCP).

Although Integrated IS-IS can support IP exclusively, IS-IS still uses CLNS to transmit reachability information and still forms adjacencies using IIHs.

KEY POINT

ES-IS Protocol

The following summarizes the ES-IS protocol:

- ES-IS forms adjacencies between ESs (hosts) and ISs (routers).

  — IP end-systems do not use ES-IS.

- ESs transmit ESHs to announce their presence to ISs.

- ISs transmit ISHs to announce their presence to ESs.

- ISs transmit IIHs to other ISs.

OSI Routing Levels

The OSI specifications discuss four unique types of routing operations, numbered 0 to 3, as shown in Figure 6-5. As discussed earlier, IS-IS is responsible for L1 and L2 OSI routing.

Figure 6-5 *OSI Routing*

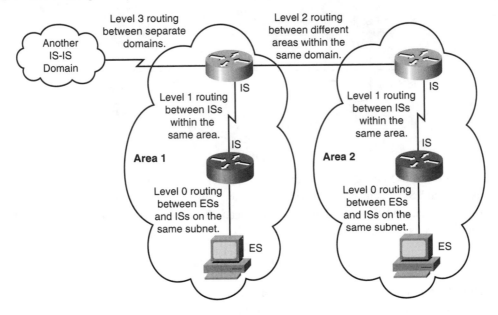

Level 0 (L0) Routing

OSI routing begins with ES-IS, when the ESs discover the nearest IS by listening to ISH packets.

When an ES needs to send a packet to another ES, it sends the packet to an IS on an attached network. This process is known as *L0 routing*.

IS-IS L1 Routing

Each ES and IS resides in a particular area. To pass traffic, the router looks up the destination address and forwards the packet along the best route. If the destination is on the same subnetwork, the IS knows the location (from listening to the ESH) and forwards the packet appropriately. The IS can also provide a redirect message back to the source that tells it that a more direct route is available. If the destination is on a different subnetwork but within the same area, the router identifies the best path, using the system ID, and forwards the traffic appropriately.

> **NOTE** L1 routing is also called intra-area routing.

IS-IS L2 Routing

If a destination address is in another area, the L1 IS sends the packet to the nearest L1/L2 IS. Packet forwarding continues through L2 and L1/L2 ISs, using the area address, until the packet reaches an L1/L2 IS in the destination area. This process is called L2 routing. Within the destination area, ISs forward the packet along the best path, based on system ID, until the packet reaches the destination.

> **NOTE**   L2 routing is also called interarea routing.

Level 3 (L3) Routing

Routing between separate domains is called L3 routing. L3 routing is comparable to Border Gateway Protocol (BGP) interdomain routing in IP. L3 routing passes traffic between different autonomous systems; these autonomous systems might have different routing logic, so metrics cannot be directly compared. L3 OSI routing is not implemented on Cisco routers but is specified as being accomplished through the Interdomain Routing Protocol (IDRP).

KEY POINT

Routing Levels

The following summarizes the OSI routing levels:

- L0 routing is conducted by ES-IS.

- L1 and L2 routing are functions of IS-IS.

- IDRP conducts L3 routing. IDRP is similar in purpose to BGP; Cisco routers do not support IDRP.

Comparing IS-IS to OSPF

Most of the development of the OSPF and IS-IS protocols was done concurrently. The cooperation and competition between the development groups produced two protocols that are very similar, and each is better because of the other. The practical differences between the two protocols deal with perceived issues of resource usage and customization.

IS-IS History

Most debates of the merits of these protocols are colored by their mutual history; different groups with different cultures developed them.

Digital Equipment Corporation (DEC) originally developed IS-IS for DECnet Phase V. In 1987, the American National Standards Institute (ANSI) chose it to be the OSI IGP. At that time it could route only CLNP.

A Condensed History of IS-IS

IS-IS was ad hoc in its evolution, whereas OSPF was more formal. The following is a brief history of IS-IS:

■ 1985: Originally called DECnet Phase V Routing.

■ 1988: Adopted by ISO and renamed IS-IS.

■ 1990: Publication of RFC 1142, *OSI IS-IS Intradomain Routing Protocol.*

■ 1990: Publication of RFC 1195, *Use of OSI IS-IS for routing in TCP/IP and dual environments.*

■ 1991: Cisco IOS Software starts supporting IS-IS.

■ 1995: ISPs start adopting IS-IS.

■ 2000: Publication of Internet Engineering Task Force (IETF) draft "IS-IS Extensions for Traffic Engineering."

■ 2001: Publication of IETF draft "IS-IS Extensions in Support of Generalized MPLS."

The ISO process is an international standards development process. According to an account given by Christian Huitema in his book *Routing in the Internet*, groups within ISO and outside the United States did not approve of TCP/IP because of its origin (it was also called the U.S. Department of Defense [DoD] protocol).

From the perspective of ISO, IP development was chaotic and imprecise, based on the famous maxim of "loose consensus and running code." From the perspective of the early Internet engineers, the ISO process was slow, irritating, and disenfranchising.

In 1988, the U.S. National Science Foundation Network (NSFnet) was created. The IGP used was based on an early draft of IS-IS. The extensions to IS-IS for handling IP were developed in 1988. OSPF development began during this time; it was loosely based on IS-IS.

In 1989, OSPF Version 1 (OSPFv1) was published, and conflict ensued between the proponents of IS-IS and OSPF. The IETF eventually supported both, although it continued to favor OSPF. With the unofficial endorsement of the IETF, OSPF eventually became more popular.

By the mid-1990s, large ISPs in need of an IGP selected IS-IS for two reasons. IS-IS supported IP and CLNS (and therefore solved two problems at once), and OSPF was seen as immature at the time.

Similarities Between IS-IS and OSPF

IS-IS and OSPF are more similar than dissimilar. Both routing protocols have the following characteristics:

■ They are open standard link-state routing protocols.

- They support VLSM.

- They use similar mechanisms (link-state advertisements [LSAs], link-state aging timers, and link-state database synchronization) to maintain the health of the LSDB.

- They use the SPF algorithm, with similar update, decision, and flooding processes.

- They are successful in the largest and most-demanding deployments (ISP networks).

- They converge quickly after network changes.

Differences Between Integrated IS-IS and OSPF

The differences between OSPF and Integrate IS-IS are small, but they do exist; these differences are explored in this section.

Area Design

With OSPF, network design is constrained because OSPF is based on a central backbone, area 0, with all other areas being physically attached to area 0, as shown in Figure 6-6.

The border between OSPF areas is inside the ABRs; each link is in only one area. When you use this type of hierarchical model, you need a consistent IP addressing structure to summarize addresses into the backbone. Summarization also reduces the amount of information carried in the backbone and advertised across the network.

Figure 6-6 *OSPF Area Design*

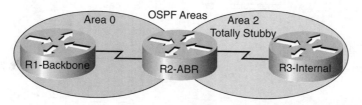

In comparison, IS-IS has a hierarchy of L1, L2/L1, and L2 routers, and the area borders lie on links, as shown in Figure 6-7. IS-IS permits a more flexible approach to extending the backbone. The backbone can be extended by simply adding more L2/L1 or L2 routers, a less-complex process than with OSPF.

Figure 6-7 *Integrated IS-IS Area Design*

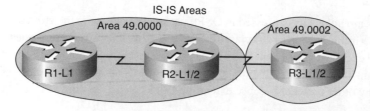

Advantages of Integrated IS-IS

OSPF produces many small LSAs, whereas a router groups IS-IS updates and sends them as one LSP. Thus, as network complexity increases, the number of IS-IS updates is not an issue. Each packet must be routed though, and routing takes network resources, so more packets represent a larger impact on the network. Because IS-IS uses significantly fewer LSPs, more routers, at least 1,000, can reside in a single area, making IS-IS more scalable than OSPF.

IS-IS is also more efficient than OSPF in the use of CPU resources and in how it processes routing updates, as shown in Figure 6-8. For one thing, there are fewer LSPs to process (LSAs in OSPF terminology). Also, the mechanism by which IS-IS installs and withdraws prefixes is less resource intensive because it uses network entity title (NET) addresses, which are already summarized. Recall that OSPF runs on top of IP, whereas IS-IS runs through CLNS.

Figure 6-8 *Comparing IS-IS and OSPF Routing Updates*

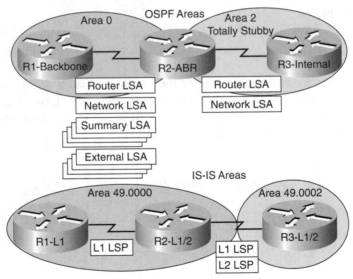

Both OSPF and IS-IS are link-state protocols and thus provide fast convergence. The convergence time depends on a number of factors, such as timers, number of nodes, and type of router. Based on the default timers, IS-IS detects a failure faster than OSPF; therefore, convergence occurs more rapidly. If there are many neighboring routers and adjacencies, the convergence time also might depend on the router's processing power; IS-IS is less CPU intensive than OSPF.

New ideas are not easily expressed in OSPF packets; they require the creation of a new LSA. The OSPF description schema is difficult to extend, because of compatibility issues, and because it was developed exclusively for IPv4. IS-IS is easy to extend through the Type, Length, and Value (TLV) mechanism. TLV strings, called tuples, encode all IS-IS updates. IS-IS can easily grow to cover IPv6 or any other protocol because extending IS-IS consists of simply creating new type codes.

Advantages of OSPF

An organization might choose OSPF over IS-IS because OSPF is more optimized and was designed exclusively as an IP routing protocol. For example, OSPF defines different area types (standard, stub, and not-so-stubby [NSSA]). On Cisco routers the default OSPF metric is related to the interface bandwidth, whereas IS-IS defaults to a metric of 10 on all interfaces.

If an organization does choose OSPF, it will require networking equipment that supports OSPF, and network engineers that are familiar with OSPF theory and operation. It is relatively easy to find both equipment and personnel to support an OSPF infrastructure. Furthermore, OSPF documentation is much more readily available than documentation for IS-IS.

Summary of Differences Between OSPF and Integrated IS-IS

Table 6-1 summarizes the differences between OSPF and Integrated IS-IS.

Table 6-1 *Summary of Differences Between OSPF and Integrated IS-IS*

OSPF	Integrated IS-IS
Area border inside routers (ABRs)	Area border on links
Each link in only 1 area	Each router in only 1 area
More complex to extend backbone	Simple extension of backbone
Many small LSAs sent	Fewer LSPs sent
Runs on top of IP	Runs on top of data-link layer
Requires IP addresses	Requires IP and CLNS addresses
Default metric is scaled by interface bandwidth	Default metric is 10 for all interfaces
Not easy to extend	Easy to support new protocols with new TLV tuples
Equipment, personnel, and information more readily available	Equipment, personnel, and information not as readily available

IS-IS Routing Operation

KEY POINT

CLNS Addresses Required Even if Routing Only for IP

Unlike IP addresses, CLNS addresses apply to entire nodes and not to interfaces. Because IS-IS was originally designed for CLNS, IS-IS requires CLNS node addresses even if the router is used for routing only IP.

CLNS addresses that are used by routers are called network service access points (NSAPs). One part of an NSAP address is the NSAP selector (NSEL) byte. When an NSAP is specified with an NSEL of 0, the NSAP is called the network entity title (NET).

This section starts by describing NSAP and NET addresses for use with Integrated IS-IS. The section then describes how CLNS addressing affects IS-IS operation and how the IS-IS protocol learns the network topology, makes routing decisions, and handles different types of data links.

NSAP Addresses

IS-IS LSPs use NSAP addresses to identify the router and build the topology table and the underlying IS-IS routing tree; therefore, IS-IS requires NSAP addresses to function properly, even if it is used only for routing IP.

NSAP addresses contain the following:

- The device's OSI address

- A link to the higher-layer process

The NSAP address is equivalent to the combination of the IP address and upper-layer protocol in an IP header.

NSAP addresses have a maximum size of 20 bytes. Various uses require definition of different address structures; the high-order bits identify the interarea structure, and the low-order bits identify unique systems within an area (intra-area).

Integrated IS-IS NSAP Address Structure

KEY POINT | **NSAP Address Structure**

The Cisco implementation of Integrated IS-IS divides the NSAP address into three fields: the area address, the system ID, and the NSEL.

The NSAP address structure is shown in Figure 6-9.

Figure 6-9 *Integrated IS-IS NSAP Address Structure*

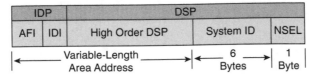

Cisco routers routing CLNS use addressing that conforms to the ISO 10589 standard. ISO NSAP addresses consist of the following:

- The authority and format identifier (AFI) and the initial domain identifier (IDI) make up the initial domain part (IDP) of the NSAP address. The IDP corresponds roughly to an IP classful major network.

    — The AFI byte specifies the format of the address and the authority that assigned that address. Some valid values are shown in Table 6-2.

Table 6-2   *Examples of AFI Values*

AFI	Address Domain
39	ISO Data Country Code (DCC)
45	E.164
47	ISO 6523 International Code Designation (ICD)
49	Locally administered (private)

    — Addresses starting with the AFI value of 49 are private addresses, analogous to RFC 1918 for IP addresses. IS-IS routes these addresses; however, this group of addresses should not be advertised to other CLNS networks because they are ad hoc addresses. Other companies that use a value of 49 may have created different numbering schemes that, when used together, could create confusion.

    — The IDI identifies a subdomain under the AFI. For instance, 47.0005 is assigned to civilian departments of the U.S. Government and 47.0006 to the U.S. Department of Defense.

- The domain-specific part (DSP) contributes to routing within an IS-IS routing domain. The DSP is comprised of the high-order domain-specific part (HODSP), the system ID, and the NSEL.

    — The HODSP subdivides the domain into areas. The HODSP is more or less the OSI equivalent of a subnet in IP.

    — The system ID identifies an individual OSI device. In OSI each *device* has an address, just as it does in DECnet, whereas in IP, each *interface* has an address.

    — The NSEL identifies a process on the device and corresponds roughly to a port or socket in IP. The NSEL is not used in routing decisions.

KEY POINT

NSAP Format

The simplest NSAP format, used by most companies running IS-IS as their IGP, comprises the following:

- The area address, which must be at least 1 byte, separated into two parts:

    — The AFI set to 49, which signifies that the AFI is locally administered and thus individual addresses can be assigned by the company.

    — The area identifier (ID), the octets of the area address after the AFI.

- A system ID. Cisco routers compliant with the U.S. Government OSI Profile (GOSIP) Version 2.0 standard require a 6-byte system ID.

- The NSEL, which must always be set to 0 for a router.

The NSAP is called the *NET* when it has an NSEL of 0. Routers use the NET to identify themselves in the IS-IS PDUs.

For example, you might assign 49.0001.0000.0c12.3456.00, which represents the following:

- AFI of 49

- Area ID of 0001

- System ID of 0000.0c12.3456, the Media Access Control (MAC) address of a LAN interface on the device

- NSEL of 0

> **NOTE**   The area address is also referred to as the *prefix*.
>
> Some IS-IS documentation uses the terms "area ID" and "area address" as synonyms.

IS-IS Area Addresses

The first part of an NSAP is the area address and is associated with the IS-IS routing process. Unlike OSPF, an IS-IS router can be a member of only one area, as shown in Figure 6-10.

All routers in an area must use the same area address, which actually defines the area. The area address is used in L2 routing.

ESs recognize only ISs and other ESs on the same subnetwork that share the same area address.

Figure 6-10 *IS-IS Routers Are Members of Only One Area*

49.0001.0000.0C11.1111.00

Area 1

49.0001.0000.0C22.2222.00

49.0004.0000.0C88.8888.00

Area 4

49.0004.0000.0C99.9999.00

IS-IS System ID

The 6-byte NSAP system ID must be unique within an area. It is customary to use a MAC address from the router as the system ID, as shown in Figure 6-11, or, for Integrated IS-IS, to encode an IP address into the system ID.

Figure 6-11 *System IDs Are Often the System MAC Address*

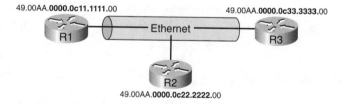

49.00AA.**0000.0c11.1111**.00

49.00AA.**0000.0c33.3333**.00

Ethernet

R1

R3

R2

49.00AA.**0000.0c22.2222**.00

All the system IDs in a domain must be of equal length. Cisco enforces this OSI directive by fixing the length of the system ID at 6 bytes in all cases.

Level 1 intra-area routing is based on system IDs; therefore, each ES and IS must have a unique system ID within the area.

All Level 2 ISs eventually recognize all other ISs in the Level 2 backbone; therefore, they must also have unique system IDs.

Thus, system IDs should remain unique across the domain. If the system IDs remain unique, there can never be a conflict at L1 or L2 if, for example, a device moves into a different area.

NET Addresses

As discussed earlier, NSAP address have a one octet NSEL field that identifies a process on the device, corresponding roughly to a port number in IP. NET addresses are NSAP addresses with an NSEL value of 0. A NET address is used to uniquely identify an OSI host within an IS-IS routing domain. Because IS-IS originates from the OSI world, NET addresses are required even if the only routed protocol is IP.

The NET refers to the device itself; that is, it is the equivalent of that device's Layer 3 OSI address.

Routers use the NET to identify themselves in the LSPs and, therefore, form the basis for the OSI routing calculation.

Three additional IS-IS terms related to NET addresses are introduced in Figure 6-12: subnetwork point of attachment (SNPA), circuit ID, and link.

Figure 6-12 *Subnetwork Point of Attachment, Local Circuit ID, and Link*

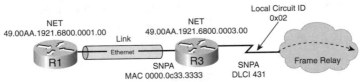

The SNPA is the point that provides subnetwork services. SNPA is the equivalent of the Layer 2 address corresponding to the NET or NSAP address. The SNPA is assigned by using one of the following:

■ The MAC address on a LAN interface

■ The virtual circuit ID from X.25 or ATM connections, or the data-link connection identifier (DLCI) from Frame Relay connections

■ For High-Level Data Link Control (HDLC) interfaces, the SNPA is simply set to "HDLC"

A *circuit* is the IS-IS term for an interface. Because the NSAP and NET refer to the entire device, a circuit ID is used to distinguish a particular interface. A router assigns a circuit ID (1 octet) to each of its interfaces as follows:

■ In the case of point-to-point interfaces, the SNPA is the sole identifier for the circuit. For example, on an HDLC point-to-point link, the circuit ID is 0x00.

- In the case of LAN interfaces, the circuit ID is tagged to the end of the system ID of the designated IS (DIS) to form a 7-byte LAN ID, for example, 1921.6800.0001.01. On Cisco routers, the router hostname is used instead of the system ID; therefore, the circuit ID of a LAN interface may look like R1.01. (The DIS is described in the "Implementing IS-IS in Broadcast Networks" section later in this chapter.)

A link is the path between two neighbor ISs and is defined as being up when communication is possible between the two neighbor SNPAs.

IS-IS Router Operation

Recall that IS-IS defines three types of routers as follows:

- **Level 1**—L1 routers learn about paths within the areas they connect to (intra-area). L1 routers are similar to OSPF internal nonbackbone routers.

- **Level 2**—L2 routers learn about paths between areas (interarea). L2 routers are similar to OSPF backbone routers.

- **Level 1-2**—L1/L2 routers learn about paths both within and between areas. L1/L2 routers are equivalent to ABRs in OSPF.

Intra-area (L1) routing enables ESs to communicate. An L1 area is a collection of L1 and L1/L2 routers.

The path of connected L2 and L1/L2 routers is called the backbone. All areas and the backbone must be contiguous.

Area boundaries fall on the links. Each IS-IS router belongs to exactly one area. Neighboring routers learn whether they are in the same area or different areas and negotiate appropriate adjacencies, L1, L2, or both.

L1 ISs maintain a copy of the L1 area LSDB. L2 ISs maintain a copy of the L2 area LSDB. Each router keeps a copy of the LSDBs for the levels it is responsible for.

An L1/L2 router automatically advertises to all L1 routers (within its area) that it is a potential exit point of the area. L1 routers will default to the nearest attached L1/L2 router.

Intra-Area and Interarea Addressing and Routing

IS-IS routing flows naturally from the OSI address plan in which areas are identified and unique system IDs are given to each device.

The area address portion of the NSAP address can range from 1 to 13 bytes in length, as specified by the ISO standard. Therefore, an NSAP for an IS-IS network can be as little as 8 bytes in length; the NSAP is usually longer to permit some granularity in the allocation of areas. The area address is common to all devices in an area and is unique for each area. ISs and ESs are in the same area if they share the same area address.

Routing within an area involves collecting system IDs and adjacencies for all ISs and ESs in an area and using Dijkstra's algorithm to compute best paths between devices. L1 routers are only aware of the local area topology. They pass the traffic destined outside the area to the closest L1/L2 router.

Routing between areas is based on area address. L2 (or L1/L2) routers in different areas exchange area address information and use Dijkstra's algorithm to compute best paths between areas. They pass traffic destined to another area to the best L2 or L1/L2 router to reach that specific area.

KEY POINT

Addressing and Routing

The area address is used to route between areas; the system ID is not considered.

The system ID is used to route within an area; the area address is not considered.

When an ES is required to send a packet to another ES, the packet goes to one of the ISs on a network directly attached to the ES. The router then searches for the destination address and forwards the packet along the best route. If the destination ES is in the same area, the local IS recognizes the location by listening to ESH packets and forwards the packet appropriately; routing is by system ID within the area. If the destination address is an ES in another area, the L1 IS sends the packet to the nearest L1/L2 IS.

The L1/L2 IS routes by area address to other L1/L2 or L2 ISs. Forwarding through L1/L2 or L2 ISs, by area address, continues until the packet reaches an L1/L2 or L2 IS in the destination area. Within the destination area, ISs forward the packet along the best path, routing by system ID, until the destination ES is reached.

Because each router makes its own best-path decisions at every hop along the way, there is a significant chance that paths will not be reciprocal. That is, return traffic can take a different path than the outgoing traffic. For this reason, it is important to know the traffic patterns within your network and tune IS-IS for optimal path selection if necessary.

IS-IS Routing Examples

Using Figure 6-13, the following list analyzes traffic from Router 7 (R7) to Router 9 (R9):

1. R7 recognizes that R9's prefix (49.00CC) is not the same as R7's prefix (49.00BB). R7 therefore passes the traffic to the closest L1/L2 router, Router 5 (R5). R7 uses its L1 topology database to find the best path to R5.

2. R5 uses its L2 topology database to pick the best next hop to reach the prefix 49.00CC: R3. R5 does not use the destination system ID in this decision.

3. R3 uses its L2 topology database to pick the best next hop to reach the prefix 49.00CC: R1. R3 does not use the destination system ID in this decision.

4. R1 uses its L2 topology database to pick the best next hop to reach the prefix 49.00CC: R8. R1 does not use the destination system ID in this decision.

5. R8 recognizes that R9's prefix (49.00CC) is the same as R8's prefix (49.00CC). R8 therefore passes the traffic to R9 using its L1 topology database to find the best path.

Figure 6-13 *Example of OSI Addressing*

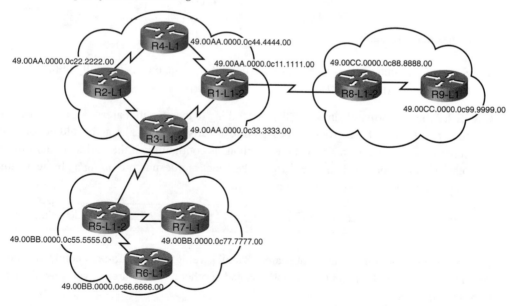

Figure 6-14 illustrates another example, this time with asymmetric routing. Area 1 contains the following two routers:

- One router borders area 2 and area 5; it is an L1/L2 IS.

- The other router is contained within the area and is an L1 IS only.

Figure 6-14 *OSI Area Routing*

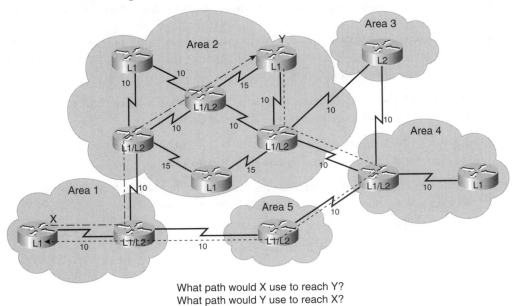

What path would X use to reach Y?
What path would Y use to reach X?

Area 2 has many routers:

■ Some of the routers are specified as L1. The routers route either internally to that area or to the exit points (the L1/L2 ISs).

■ L1/L2 routers form a chain across the area linking to the neighbor areas. Although the middle router of the three L1/L2 routers does not link directly to another area, the middle router must support L2 routing to ensure that the backbone is contiguous. If the middle router fails, the other L1-only routers cannot perform the L2 function (despite providing a physical path across the area), and the backbone is broken.

> **NOTE** The lower router in Area 2 in Figure 6-14 could be L1/L2, to provide redundancy.

Area 3 contains one router that borders areas 2 and 4, yet it has no intra-area neighbors and is currently performing L2 functions only. If you add another router to area 3, you should change it to be an L1/L2 IS.

Recall, as shown in Figure 6-14, the border between the areas in an IS-IS network is on the link between L2 routers. (This is in contrast to OSPF, where the border exists inside the ABR itself.)

KEY POINT | **L1 and L2 Are Separate**

In IS-IS, asymmetric routing (packets taking different paths in different directions) might occur because L1 and L2 computations are separate. The L2 details are hidden from the L1 routers.

In this example, symmetric routing does not occur because L2 details are hidden from L1 routers, which only recognize a default route to the nearest L1/L2 router. For example, traffic from Router X to Router Y flows from Router X to its closest L1/L2 router. The L1/L2 router then forwards the traffic along the shortest path to the destination area (area 2), where it is routed along the shortest intra-area path to Router Y.

Router Y routes return packets to Router X via its nearest L1/L2 router. The L1/L2 router recognizes the best route to area 1 via area 4 based on the lowest-cost L2 path. Because L1 and L2 computations are separate, the path taken from Router Y back to Router X is not necessarily the least-cost path from Router Y to Router X.

Asymmetric routing is not detrimental to the network. However, troubleshooting can be difficult, and this type of routing is sometimes a symptom of suboptimal design. Like EIGRP and OSPF, a good IS-IS design is generally hierarchical and symmetrical.

Route Leaking

Route leaking is a feature available since Cisco IOS Software Release 12.0 that helps avoid asymmetric routing and reduce suboptimal routing by providing a mechanism for leaking, or redistributing, L2 routes into L1 routers in a controlled manner. By having more detail about interarea routes, an L1 router is able to make a better choice with regard to which L1/L2 router to forward the packet.

Route leaking is defined in RFC 2966, *Domain-wide Prefix Distribution with Two-Level IS-IS*, for use with the narrow metric TLV types 128 and 130. The IETF has also defined route leaking for use with the wide metric (using TLV type 135).

To implement route leaking, an up/down bit in the TLV is used to indicate whether or not the route identified in the TLV has been leaked. If the up/down bit is set to 0 the route was originated within that L1 area. If the up/down bit is set to 1 the route has been redistributed into the area from L2. The up/down bit is used to prevent routing loops: An L1/L2 router does not re-advertise into L2 any L1 routes that have the up/down bit set.

Route leaking should be planned and deployed carefully to avoid the situation where any topology change in one area results in having to recompute many routes in all other areas.

OSI and IS-IS PDUs

This section describes the OSI PDUs and four types of IS-IS PDUs.

OSI PDUs

The OSI stack defines a unit of data as a PDU. OSI recognizes a frame as a data-link PDU and a packet (or datagram, in the IP environment) as a network PDU.

Figure 6-15 shows examples of three types of PDUs (all with IEEE 802.2 Logical Link Control [LLC] encapsulation). IS-IS and ES-IS PDUs are encapsulated directly in a data-link PDU (frame); there is no CLNP header and no IP header. (In other words, IS-IS and ES-IS do not put routing information in IP or CLNP packets; rather, they put routing information directly in a data-link layer frame.) True CLNP (data) packets contain a full CLNP header between the data-link header and any higher-layer CLNS information.

Figure 6-15 *OSI PDUs*

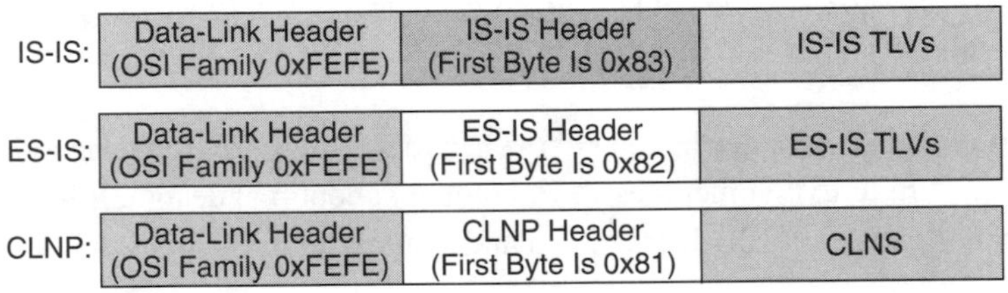

IS-IS:	Data-Link Header (OSI Family 0xFEFE)	IS-IS Header (First Byte Is 0x83)	IS-IS TLVs
ES-IS:	Data-Link Header (OSI Family 0xFEFE)	ES-IS Header (First Byte Is 0x82)	ES-IS TLVs
CLNP:	Data-Link Header (OSI Family 0xFEFE)	CLNP Header (First Byte Is 0x81)	CLNS

The IS-IS and ES-IS PDUs contain variable-length fields, depending on the function of the PDU. Each field contains a type code, a length, and the appropriate values; this information is known as the TLVs.

KEY POINT

OSI PDUs

OSI PDUs are between peers.

A network PDU is also called a *datagram* or *packet*.

A data-link PDU is also called a *frame*.

IS-IS PDUs

KEY POINT

IS-IS PDUs

As mentioned, IS-IS PDUs are encapsulated directly into an OSI data-link frame. There is no CLNP or IP header.

IS-IS defines the following four types of PDUs:

- **Hello PDU (ESH, ISH, IIH)**—Used to establish and maintain adjacencies

- **LSP**—Used to distribute link-state information

- **Partial sequence number PDU (PSNP)**—Used to acknowledge and request missing pieces of link-state information

- **Complete sequence number PDU (CSNP)**—Used to describe the complete list of LSPs in a router's LSDB

The Hello PDUs were described earlier in section "The ES-IS Protocol"; IIHs use is further explored later in this chapter in the "Implementing IS-IS in Different Network Types" section. LSPs are described in the next section. PSNPs and CSNPs use is described in the later "Link-State Database Synchronization" section.

IS-IS LSPs

In IS-IS, router characteristics are defined by an LSP. A router's LSP contains an LSP header followed by TLV fields, as shown in Figure 6-16.

Figure 6-16   *Link-State Packets Represent Routers*

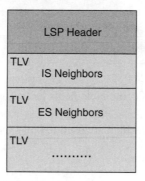

An LSP header describes the following:

- The PDU type and length

- The LSP ID

- The LSP sequence number, used to identify duplicate LSPs and to ensure that the latest LSP information is stored in the topology table

- The LSP's remaining lifetime, which is used to age out LSPs

LSP Sequence Number

The LSP sequence number allows receiving routers to do the following:

- Ensure that they use the latest LSPs in their route calculations

- Avoid entering duplicate LSPs in the topology tables

If a router reloads, the sequence number is set to 1. The router then receives its previous LSPs back from its neighbors. These LSPs have the last valid sequence number before the router reloaded. The router records this number and reissues its own LSPs with the next-highest sequence number.

LSP Remaining Lifetime

Each LSP has a remaining lifetime that is used by the LSP aging process to ensure the removal of outdated and invalid LSPs from the topology table after a suitable time period. This process uses a decreasing timer and is known as the count-to-zero operation; 1200 seconds is the default start value.

LSP TLVs

Each LSP includes specific information about networks and stations attached to a router. This information is found in multiple TLV fields that follow the LSP's common header. The TLV structure is a flexible way to add data to the LSP and an easy mechanism for adding new data fields that might be required in the future.

> **NOTE**   TLV is sometimes also called Code, Length, Value (CLV).

The TLV variable-length fields contain elements including the following:

- The router's neighbor ISs, which are used to build the map of the network

- The router's neighbor ESs

- Authentication information, which is used to secure routing updates

- Attached IP subnets (optional, for Integrated IS-IS)

Table 6-3 shows examples of TLVs.

Table 6-3   *LSP TLV Examples*

TLV	Type Code	Length Field	Value Variable Length
Area address	1	Area address length + 1	Area addresses
Intermediate system neighbors	2	Neighbor count + 1	IS neighbors
IP internal reachability	128	Number of connected IP prefixes	Connected IP prefixes: 4 octet metric, 4 octet prefix, 4 octet mask
IP external reachability	130	Number of redistributed IP prefixes	Redistributed IP prefixes: 4 octet metric, 4 octet prefix, 4 octet mask

You can find documentation on important TLVs in ISO 10589 and RFC 1195.

Implementing IS-IS in Different Network Types

Network topologies can be divided into the following two general types:

- **Point-to-point networks**—Point-to-point links that are either permanently established (leased line, permanent virtual circuit [PVC]) or dynamically established (ISDN, switched virtual circuit [SVC])

- **Broadcast networks**—Multipoint WAN links or LAN links such as Ethernet, Token Ring, or Fiber Distributed Data Interface (FDDI)

IS-IS supports only the following two media representations for its link states:

- **Broadcast**—For LANs and multipoint WAN links

- **Point to point**—For all other media

Implementing IS-IS in Nonbroadcast Multiaccess (NBMA) Networks

KEY POINT

IS-IS Does Not Know About NBMA

IS-IS has no concept of NBMA networks. It is recommended that you use point-to-point links, such as point-to-point subinterfaces, over NBMA networks, such as ATM, Frame Relay, or X.25.

Cisco IOS Software automatically uses broadcast mode for LAN links and multipoint WAN links. It uses point-to-point mode for point-to-point links, such as point-to-point subinterfaces and dialer interfaces.

IS-IS has no specific support for NBMA networks. When implemented in broadcast mode, Cisco IOS Software assumes that the NBMA environment features a full mesh of PVCs. When creating static maps to map the remote IP address to the local DLCI on a Frame Relay interface, you should use the **broadcast** keyword; this is because broadcast mode uses multicast updates, which will not be sent without this keyword set.

When you use multipoint WAN links such as multipoint Frame Relay interfaces, you must also allow CLNS broadcasts and multicasts. This can be done by using the **frame-relay map clns** *dlci-number* **broadcast** command (in addition to creating the IP maps).

Implementing IS-IS in Broadcast Networks

In IS-IS, broadcast networks are LAN interfaces or multipoint WAN interfaces.

KEY POINT

Use Broadcast Mode Only for LANs

Broadcast mode is recommended for use only on LAN interfaces, although it is also the default for multipoint WANs.

Separate IS-IS adjacencies are established for L1 and L2 processes. If two neighboring routers in the same area run both L1 and L2, they establish two adjacencies, one for each level. The router stores the L1 and L2 adjacencies in separate L1 and L2 adjacency tables. On LANs, routers establish the two adjacencies with specific Layer 1 and Layer 2 IIH PDUs.

KEY POINT

Adjacencies on a LAN

Routers on a LAN establish adjacencies with all other routers on the LAN (unlike OSPF, where routers establish full adjacencies only with the Designated Router [DR] and Backup Designated Router [BDR]).

IIH PDUs announce the area address; separate IIH packets announce the L1 and L2 neighbors. Adjacencies form based on the area address communicated in the incoming IIH and the type of router (L1 or L2). L1 routers accept L1 IIH PDUs from their own area and establish adjacencies with other routers in their own area. L2 routers (or the L2 process within any L1/L2 router) accept only L2 IIH PDUs and establish only Level 2 adjacencies.

Pseudonode and DIS

In IS-IS, a broadcast link itself is modeled as a pseudo-node that connects all attached routers to a star-shaped topology. The pseudo-node is represented by the DIS. Dijkstra's algorithm requires this virtual router (pseudo-node) to build a directed graph for broadcast media.

Criteria for DIS selection are, first, highest priority and second, highest SNPA (recall that on LANs the SNPA is the MAC address). Cisco router interfaces have a default L1 and L2 priority of 64. You can configure the priority from 0 to 127 using the **isis priority** *number-value* [**level-1** | **level-2**] interface configuration command. The L1 DIS and L2 DIS on a LAN may or may not be the same router, because an interface can have different L1 and L2 priorities.

In IS-IS, all routers on a LAN establish adjacencies with all other routers and with the DIS. Therefore, if the DIS fails, another router takes over immediately with little or no impact on the network's topology. There is no backup DIS. Contrast this behavior with OSPF, where the DR and BDR are selected and the other routers on the LAN establish full adjacencies only with the DR and BDR. In case of DR failure, the BDR is promoted to DR, and a new BDR is elected.

A selected router is not guaranteed to remain the DIS. Any adjacent IS with a higher priority automatically takes over the DIS role; this is called preemptive behavior. Because the IS-IS LSDB is synchronized frequently on a LAN, giving priority to another IS over the DIS is not a significant issue.

Rather than having each router connected to the LAN advertise an adjacency with every other router on the LAN, each router (including the DIS) just advertises a single adjacency to the pseudo-node. Otherwise, each IS on a broadcast network with *n* connected ISs would require $(n)(n-1)/2$ adjacency advertisements. Generating LSPs for each adjacency creates considerable overhead in terms of LSDB synchronization.

As shown in Figure 6-17, the DIS generates the pseudo-node LSPs. A pseudo-node LSP details only the adjacent ISs (for example, the ISs connected to that LAN). The pseudo-node LSP is used to build the map of the network and to calculate the SPF tree. The pseudo-node LSP is the equivalent of a network LSA in OSPF.

Figure 6-17   *LSP Representing Routers: LAN Representation*

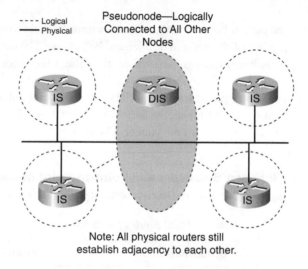

LSPs and IIHs

This section describes the LSPs and IIHs used by L1 and L2 routers.

L1 and L2 LSPs

The link-state information for the two levels is distributed separately, in L1 LSPs and L2 LSPs. Each IS originates its own LSPs (one for L1 and one for L2).

On a LAN, one router (the DIS, representing a pseudo-node) sends out LSP information on behalf of the LAN. The DIS sends out the separate L1 and L2 LSPs for the pseudo-node. Recall that the L1 DIS and the L2 DIS on a LAN may or may not be the same router, because an interface can have different L1 and L2 priorities.

LSPs on broadcast media (LANs) are sent as multicast, and LSPs on point-to-point links are sent as unicast.

L1 and L2 IIHs

IIHs are used to establish and maintain neighbor adjacency between ISs. The default hello interval is every 10 seconds; however, the hello interval timer is adjustable.

On a LAN, separate L1 and L2 IIHs are sent periodically as multicasts to a multicast MAC address. L1 announcements are sent to the AllL1IS multicast MAC address 0180.C200.0014, and L2 announcements are sent to the AllL2IS multicast MAC address 0180.C200.0015. The default hello interval for the DIS is 3 times faster (that is, it is 3 times smaller) than the interval for other routers, so that DIS failures can be detected quickly. Unlike DR/BDR in OSPF, there is no backup DIS in IS-IS.

A neighbor is declared dead if hellos are not received within the hold time. The hold time is calculated as the product of the hello multiplier and hello time. The default hello time is 10 seconds and the default multiplier is 3; therefore, the default hold time is 30 seconds.

Unlike LAN interfaces with separate L1 and L2 IIHs, point-to-point links have a common point-to-point IIH format that specifies whether the hello relates to L1 or L2 or both. Point-to-point hellos are sent to the unicast address of the connected router.

Summary of Differences Between Broadcast and Point-to-Point Modes

Table 6-4 summarizes the differences between broadcast and point-to-point links.

Table 6-4 *Comparing Broadcast and Point-to-Point Modes for IS-IS*

	Broadcast Mode	**Point-to-Point Mode**
Usage	LAN, full-mesh WAN	PPP, HDLC, partial-mesh WAN
Hello timer	3.3 seconds for DIS; otherwise 10 seconds	10 seconds
Adjacencies	$n(n-1)/2$	$n-1$
Uses DIS?	Yes	No
IIH type	L1 IIH and L2 IIH	Point-to-point IIH

Link-State Database Synchronization

This section describes how IS-IS LSDBs are synchronized between routers.

LSP Flooding

An IS-IS update process is responsible for flooding the LSPs throughout the IS-IS domain. An LSP is typically flooded to all adjacent neighbors except the neighbor from which it was received. L1 LSPs are flooded within their local areas. L2 LSPs are flooded throughout the backbone.

Each IS originates its own LSPs (one for L1 and one for L2). These LSPs are identified by the originator's system ID and an LSP fragment number starting at 0. If an LSP exceeds the maximum transmission unit (MTU), it is fragmented into several LSPs, numbered 1, 2, 3, and so on.

IS-IS maintains the L1 and L2 LSPs in separate LSDBs.

When an IS receives an LSP, it examines the checksum and discards any invalid LSPs, flooding them with an expired lifetime age. If the LSP is valid and newer than what is currently in the LSDB, it is retained, acknowledged, and given a lifetime of 1200 seconds. The age is decremented every second until it reaches 0, at which point the LSP is considered to have expired. If an LSP expires, it is kept for an additional 60 seconds before it is flooded as an expired LSP.

LSDB Synchronization

Sequence number PDUs (SNPs) are used to acknowledge the receipt of LSPs and to maintain LSDB synchronization. There are two types of SNPs: CSNP and PSNP. The use of SNPs differs between point-to-point and broadcast media.

KEY POINT

CSNPs and PSNPs

CSNPs and PSNPs share the same format; that is, each carries summarized LSP information.

The main difference is that CSNPs contain summaries of all LSPs in the LSDB, whereas PSNPs contain only a subset of LSP entries.

Separate CSNPs and PSNPs are used for L1 and L2 adjacencies.

Adjacent IS-IS routers exchange CSNPs to compare their LSDB. In broadcast networks, only the DIS transmits CSNPs. All adjacent neighbors compare the LSP summaries received in the CSNP with the contents of their local LSDBs to determine whether their LSDBs are synchronized (in other words, whether they have the same copies of LSPs as other routers for the appropriate levels and area of routing). CSNPs are periodically multicast (every 10 seconds) by the DIS on a LAN to ensure LSDB accuracy.

If there are too many LSPs to include in one CSNP, they are sent in ranges. The CSNP header indicates the starting and ending LSP ID in the range. If all LSPs fit the CSNP, the range is set to default values.

Adjacent IS-IS routers use PSNPs to acknowledge the receipt of LSPs and to request transmission of missing or newer LSPs.

On point-to-point networks, CSNPs are sent when the link comes up to synchronize the LSDBs.

LSDB Synchronization on a LAN Example

On a LAN the DIS periodically (every 10 seconds) sends CSNPs that list the LSPs it holds in its LSDB. This update is a multicast to all L1 or L2 IS-IS routers on the LAN.

Figure 6-18 illustrates an example. In this network, R1 compares the list of LSPs from the DIS with its topology table and realizes it is missing one LSP. Therefore, it sends a PSNP to the DIS (R2) to request the missing LSP.

Figure 6-18   *LSDB Synchronization on a LAN*

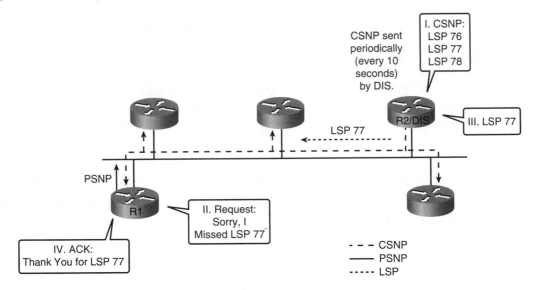

The DIS reissues only that missing LSP (LSP 77), and R1 acknowledges it with a PSNP.

LSDB Synchronization on Point-to-Point Links Example

Unlike on broadcast links, such as LAN links, CSNPs are not periodically sent on point-to-point links. A CSNP is sent only once, when the point-to-point link first comes up. After that, LSPs are sent to describe topology changes, and they are acknowledged with a PSNP.

Figure 6-19 shows an example of what happens on a point-to-point link when a link failure is detected.

Figure 6-19   *LSDB Synchronization: Point to Point*

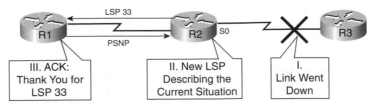

The steps shown in this example are as follows:

1. A link fails.

2. R2 notices this failure and issues a new LSP noting the change.

3. R1 receives the LSP, stores it in its topology table, and sends a PSNP back to R2 to acknowledge receipt of the LSP.

LAN Adjacencies

IIH PDUs announce the area address. On LANs, separate IIH packets announce the L1 and L2 neighbors.

For example, when a LAN has routers from two areas attached, as shown in Figure 6-20, the following process takes place:

■ The routers from one area accept L1 IIH PDUs only from their own area and therefore establish adjacencies only with their own area routers.

■ The routers from a second area similarly accept L1 IIH PDUs only from their own area.

■ The L2 routers (or the L2 process within any L1/L2 router) accept only L2 IIH PDUs and establish only L2 adjacencies.

Figure 6-20 *L1 and L2 Adjacencies on a LAN*

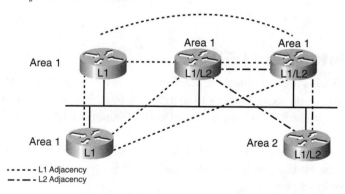

WAN Adjacencies

On point-to-point WAN links, the IIH PDUs are a common format to both levels. The level type and the area address are announced in the hellos, as follows:

■ L1 routers in the same area (which includes links between L1 and L1/L2 routers) exchange IIH PDUs that specify L1 and establish an L1 adjacency.

- L2 routers (in the same area or between areas, and including links between L2 only and L1/L2 routers) exchange IIH PDUs that specify L2 and establish an L2 adjacency.

- Two L1/L2 routers in the same area establish both L1 and L2 adjacencies and maintain these with a common IIH PDU format that specifies the L1 and L2 information.

Two L1 routers that are physically connected but are not in the same area can exchange IIHs, but they do not establish an adjacency, because the area addresses do not match.

Figure 6-21 shows the different permutations for WAN adjacencies.

Figure 6-21 *WAN Adjacencies*

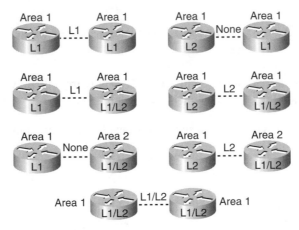

Configuring Integrated IS-IS

Even when IS-IS is used to support IP exclusively, network devices must also be configured to use the OSI CLNS protocol. Each IS-IS router requires a NET, and IS-IS packets are directly encapsulated onto the data link layer instead of traveling inside IP packets.

The commands to configure Integrated IS-IS are slightly different from those of the other IP routing protocols that you have studied earlier in this book, so it is important to understand how to enable IS-IS processes.

In addition, the default settings for IS-IS can result in the inefficient use of router and network resources and suboptimal routing; therefore, a network administrator also needs to know how to effectively tune IS-IS for optimum performance.

This section discusses the mechanics of Integrated IS-IS operation in an IP and CLNS environment and outlines specific commands necessary to implement Integrated IS-IS on a Cisco router.

Integrated IS-IS in a CLNS Environment

A NET address identifies a device (an IS or ES), not an interface. This is a critical difference between a NET address and an IP address.

Even if you use Integrated IS-IS only for IP routing, each IS-IS router must have a NET address configured, because Integrated IS-IS depends on the support of CLNS routing. The OSI protocols (hello PDUs) are used to form the neighbor relationship between routers, and the SPF calculations rely on a configured NET address to identify the routers.

A device identifies other devices within its own area based on matching area addresses in their NET. It then knows that it can communicate with these other devices without using a default route. A default route is injected into the area by the L1/L2 router. If the area addresses do not match, the device knows that it must forward that traffic to its nearest L1/L2 router.

When you are using IS-IS to route IP traffic, IP subnets are treated as leaf objects associated with IS-IS areas. When routing IP traffic, the router looks up the destination network in its routing table. If the network belongs to a different area, then that traffic must also be forwarded to the nearest L1/L2 router.

Scalability is achieved by minimizing the size of the LSDB and routing tables, the amount of processing, and the number of network updates—in other words, using route summarization wherever possible. Route summarization can be accomplished only where the address planning permits grouping addresses by a common prefix. This condition is true for OSI and IP. Therefore, it is very important to carefully plan the IS-IS areas, NET addresses, and IP addresses.

Building an OSI Routing Table

IS-IS uses an OSI forwarding database (routing table) to select the best path to a destination.

When the LSDBs are synchronized, routers use the LSDBs to calculate the SPF tree to OSI destinations (NETs). The total of the link metrics along each path determines the shortest path to any given destination. L1 and L2 routes have separate LSDBs; therefore, routers may run the SPF algorithm twice, once for each level, and create separate SPF trees for each level. Routers insert the best paths into the CLNS routing table (also called the OSI forwarding database).

Routers calculate ES reachability with a partial route calculation (PRC), based on the L1 and L2 SPF trees.

Building an IP Routing Table

KEY POINT | **IP Routes Only Require PRC**

While there are no OSI ESs in a pure IP Integrated IS-IS environment, Integrated IS-IS includes IP prefix reachability information in the LSPs, treating it as if it were ES information. In other words IP prefix information is treated as leaf connections to the SPF tree. Therefore, updating IP reachability requires only a PRC, similar to ES reachability in an OSI network.

The PRC generates best-path choices for IP routes and offers the routes to the IP routing table, where they are accepted based on normal IP routing table rules. For example, if more than one routing protocol is running, the router compares the administrative distances of routes to the same destination. When the IP IS-IS routes are entered into the routing table, they are shown as via L1 or L2, as appropriate.

The separation of IP reachability from the core IS-IS network architecture provides Integrated IS-IS better scalability than OSPF, as follows:

- OSPF sends LSAs for individual IP subnets. If an IP subnet fails, the LSA floods through the network and all routers must run a full SPF calculation, which is extremely CPU intensive.

- Integrated IS-IS builds the SPF tree from CLNS information. If an IP subnet fails, the LSP floods through the network, which is the same for OSPF. However, if this is a leaf (stub) IP subnet (that is, the loss of the subnet does not affect the underlying CLNS architecture), the SPF tree is unaffected; therefore, only a PRC occurs.

Integrated IS-IS Configuration

This section describes the configuration process for Integrated IS-IS in an IP environment.

The following four steps are required for the basic setup of Integrated IS-IS. Additional commands are available for fine-tuning the configuration.

Step 1 Before you can configure Integrated IS-IS, you must plan the areas, prepare the addressing plan (NETs) for the routers, and determine which interfaces to enable Integrated IS-IS on.

Step 2 Enable IS-IS on the router.

Step 3 Configure the router's NET.

Step 4 Enable Integrated IS-IS on the proper interfaces. Do not forget interfaces to stub IP networks, such as loopbacks (although there are no CLNS neighbors there).

Table 6-5 describes the three basic commands used to enable Integrated IS-IS.

Table 6-5 *Commands Necessary to Configure Integrated IS-IS*

Command	Description
(config)#**router isis** [*area-tag*]	Enables IS-IS as an IP routing protocol and assigns a tag to the process (optional).
(config-router)#**net** *network-entity-title*	Identifies the router for IS-IS by assigning a NET to the router.

Table 6-5 *Commands Necessary to Configure Integrated IS-IS (Continued)*

Command	Description
(config-if)#**ip router isis** [*area-tag*]	Enables an interface to use IS-IS to distribute its routing information. (This approach is slightly different from most other IP routing protocols, where the interfaces are defined by **network** commands; no **network** command exists under the IS-IS process.)

The following sections detail these four steps.

Step 1: Define the Area and Addressing

Recall that all interarea traffic in IS-IS must traverse the L2 backbone area. Thus, CLNS addresses must be planned to execute a two-level hierarchy. You must decide which routers will be backbone (L2) routers, which routers will be L1/L2, and which will be internal area (L1) routers. If some routers must do both L1 and L2 routing, the specific interfaces that will participate in each type of routing should be identified.

Remember that a router's CLNS address is called the NET, and it consists of three main parts:

- The area address (prefix), which identifies the area that the router is a part of

- The system ID, which uniquely identifies each device

- The NSEL, which must be 0

It is not enough to plan the IS-IS area addressing. You must also plan IP addressing to allow for summarization of addresses so that the network is scalable. Route summarization is the key that enables all the benefits of hierarchical addressing design. Route summarization minimizes routing update traffic and resource utilization.

Be particularly careful when you configure the IP addressing on the router, because it is more difficult to troubleshoot IP address misconfigurations with IS-IS. The IS-IS neighbor relationships are established over OSI CLNS, not over IP. Because of this approach, two ends of a CLNS adjacency can have IP addresses on different subnets, with no impact on the operation of IS-IS.

Step 2: Enable IS-IS on the Router

The **router isis** [*area-tag*] global configuration command enables Integrated IS-IS on the router. You can use the optional tag to identify multiple IS-IS processes. (Just as multiple OSPF processes can be present on the same router, multiple IS-IS processes are possible.) The process name is significant only to the local router. If it is omitted, the Cisco IOS Software assumes a tag of 0. If more than one IS-IS process is used, the network plan should indicate which interfaces will participate in which IS-IS process.

IP routing is enabled by default; CLNS routing is disabled by default. To enable CLNS routing, use the **clns routing** global configuration command. In addition, you must enable CLNS routing at each interface.

> **NOTE** By default, the Cisco IOS Software makes the router an L1/L2 router.

Step 3: Configure the NET

After the IS-IS process is enabled, the router's NET must be assigned, with the **net** *network-entity-title* router configuration command.

Even when you use IS-IS for IP routing only (with CLNS routing not enabled), you must still configure a NET. The NET is a combination of area number and a unique system identification number for each particular router, plus an NSEL of 00 at the end. The area number must be between 1 and 13 bytes in length. The system ID has a fixed length of 6 bytes in Cisco routers and must be unique throughout each area (L1) and throughout the backbone (L2).

Step 4: Enable Integrated IS-IS on Interfaces

The final step is to select which interfaces participate in IS-IS routing. Interfaces that use IS-IS to route IP (and thus must establish IS-IS adjacencies) must be configured using the **ip router isis** [*area-tag*] interface configuration command. Enable Integrated IS-IS on the appropriate interfaces—do not forget interfaces to stub IP networks, such as loopback interfaces (even though there are no CLNS neighbors on those interfaces).

If there is more than one IS-IS process, the IS-IS process to which the interface belongs must be specified using the appropriate process name in the optional *area-tag* field. If no *area-tag* is listed, the Cisco IOS Software assumes a tag value of 0. If only one IS-IS process is active on the router, no *area-tag* value is needed.

Use the **clns router isis** [*area-tag*] interface configuration command to enable the IS-IS routing process on an interface to support CLNS routing.

Simple Integrated IS-IS Example

Example 6-1 shows a simple Integrated IS-IS configuration for IP routing only; CLNS routing is not enabled. This configuration specifies only one IS-IS process, so the optional *area-tag* is not used. The **net** command configures the router to be in area 49.0001 and assigns a system ID of 0000.0000.0002. IS-IS is enabled on the Fast Ethernet 0/0 and serial 0/0/1 interfaces. This router acts as an L1/L2 router by default.

Example 6-1 *Simple Integrated IS-IS Example*

```
interface FastEthernet0/0
 ip address 10.1.1.2 255.255.255.0
 ip router isis
!
interface Serial 0/0/1
 ip address 10.2.2.2 255.255.255.0
 ip router isis
!

<output omitted>

router isis
net 49.0001.0000.0000.0002.00
```

Optimizing IS-IS

Optimizing IS-IS facilitates its proper functioning and maximizes its efficiency. Three commands that help optimize IS-IS operation are discussed in this section.

Changing the IS-IS Router Level

The default configuration of IS-IS leaves the router with an IS type of L1/L2. Although this configuration has the advantage of allowing all routers to learn of each other and pass routes without too much administrative oversight, it is not the most efficient way to build an IS-IS network. Routers with the default configuration send out both L1 and L2 hellos and maintain both L1 and L2 LSDBs.

Each router should be configured to support the minimum level of routing required, which does the following:

- **Saves memory**—If a router does not need the LSDB for one of the levels, it does not maintain one.

- **Saves bandwidth**—Hellos and LSPs are sent only for the necessary level.

If a router is to operate only as an internal area router or a backbone router, specify this configuration by entering the **is-type** {**level-1** | **level-1-2** | **level-2-only**} router configuration command. To specify that the router act only as an internal area (L1) router, use **is-type level-1**. To specify that the router act only as a backbone (L2) router, use **is-type level-2-only**. If the level type has been changed from the default, you can return to the default with the **is-type level-1-2** command.

Changing the IS-IS Interface Level

Although a router can be an L1/L2 router, it might not be required to establish both types of adjacencies over all interfaces.

If a particular interface only has L1 routers connected to it, there is no need for the router to send L2 hellos out that interface. Similarly, if an interface only has L2 routers connected to it, there is no need for the router to send L1 hellos out that interface. Extraneous hellos would waste bandwidth and router resources trying to establish adjacencies that do not exist.

To make IS-IS more efficient in these types of situations, configure the interface to send only the needed type of hellos by using the **isis circuit-type** {**level-1** | **level-1-2** | **level-2-only**} interface configuration command. The default is **level-1-2**; the router will attempt to establish both types of adjacencies over the interface.

Changing the IS-IS Metric

Unlike most other IP protocols, IS-IS on a Cisco router does not take into account line speed or bandwidth when it sets its link metrics; all interfaces are assigned a metric value of 10 by default. In a network with links of varying types and speeds, this assignment can result in suboptimal routing.

To change the metric value, use the **isis metric** *metric* [*delay-metric* [*expense-metric* [*error-metric*]]] {**level-1** | **level-2**} interface configuration command. The metric can have different values for L1 and L2 over the same interface. The *metric* value is from 1 to 63.

> **NOTE** The IS-IS specification defines four different types of metrics. Cost, being the default metric, is supported by all routers. Delay, expense, and error are optional metrics. The delay metric measures transit delay, the expense metric measures the monetary cost of link utilization, and the error metric measures the residual error probability associated with a link. The default Cisco implementation uses cost only. However, the Cisco IOS does now allow all four metrics to be set with the optional parameters in the **isis metric** command.

If the metric value for all interfaces needs to be changed from the default value of 10, then the change needs to be performed one by one on all IS-IS interfaces, which can be time-consuming and error-prone, especially for routers with many IS-IS interfaces. Alternately, the **metric** *default-value* {**level-1** | **level-2**} router configuration command can be used to change the metric value for all IS-IS interfaces. If the keyword **level-1** or **level-2** is not entered, the metric will be applied to both L1 and L2 IS-IS interfaces. This command is available only in Cisco IOS Software Release 12.3(4)T and later; it only supports the cost metric.

Tuning IS-IS Example

Figure 6-22 shows two different areas. The configurations of the routers are provided in Example 6-2.

Figure 6-22 *Tuning IS-IS Example*

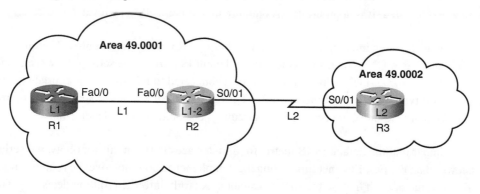

Example 6-2 *Configurations for Routers in Figure 6-22*

```
R1(config)#router isis
R1(config-router)#net 49.0001.0000.0000.0001.00
R1(config-router)#is-type level-1

R1(config)#interface FastEthernet0/0
R1(config-if)#ip router isis
R1(config-if)#isis circuit-type level-1
R2(config)#router isis
R2(config-router)#net 49.0001.0000.0000.0002.00

R2(config)#interface FastEthernet0/0
R2(config-if)#ip router isis
R2(config-if)#isis circuit-type level-1

R2(config)#interface serial 0/0/1
R2(config-if)#ip router isis
R2(config-if)#isis circuit-type level-2-only
R2(config-if)#isis metric 35 level-2
R3(config)#router isis
R3(config-router)#net 49.0002.0000.0000.0003.00
R3(config-router)#is-type level-2-only

R3(config)#interface Serial0/0/1
R3(config-if)#ip router isis
R3(config-if)#isis circuit-type level-2-only
R3(config-if)#isis metric 35 level-2
```

In this example, area 49.0002 contains only one router (R3) and needs to do only L2 routing.
Therefore, it is appropriate to change R3's IS type to level-2-only.

Area 49.0001 has two routers. R1 is strictly an internal area router; it does not connect to routers in any other area. It is appropriate to configure this router as IS type level-1.

R2 connects to the internal area router R1 and also to R3, in a different area. Therefore, R2 must do both L1 and L2 routing, so it is left at the default IS L1/L2 type setting. However, there is no need for R2 to send L2 hellos out the interface connected to R1, so it is appropriate to set the IS-IS circuit type of R2's FastEthernet 0/0 to L1. Similarly, because R2's Serial 0/0/1 interface connects only to an L2 router, the IS-IS circuit type should be set to level-2-only.

Remember that the default IS-IS metric for all interfaces is 10. In this topology, the serial link is slower than the Fast Ethernet link. Using the default metric does not give the routers a true picture of the value of each link, so the routers cannot make truly informed routing decisions. Therefore, the IS-IS metric on each serial interface should be changed to reflect the link preference; in Example 6-2, the metric is set to 35.

Configuring IP Route Summarization in IS-IS

Routing protocol scalability is a function of the appropriate use of route summarization.

An IS-IS router can be configured to aggregate a range of IP addresses into a summary address, using the **summary-address** *address mask* [**level-1** | **level-2** | **level-1-2**] [**tag** *tag-number*] [**metric** *metric-value*] router configuration command.

This command can be used on any router in an IS-IS network. The router summarizes IP routes into L1, L2, or both; the default is into L2 (**level-2**). The optional *tag-number* is used to tag the summary route. The optional *metric-value* is applied to the summary route.

As discussed earlier, the benefits of summarization include the following:

■ Reduced routing table size

■ Reduced LSP traffic and protection from flapping routes

■ Reduced memory requirements

■ Reduced CPU usage

■ A more stable network because topology changes can be isolated

The following is an example of the use of this command, summarizing 10.3.2.0/23 into L1/L2:

```
R1(config-router)#summary-address 10.3.2.0 255.255.254.0 level-1-2
```

Route summarization is removed with the **no** form of the command.

NOTE   The **summary-address** command works on all IS-IS routers (L1 and L2), but it will only summarize the *external* IS-IS L1 routes (routes that were redistributed into IS-IS L1). The description of the **level-1** parameter in the command documentation is consistent with this: "Only routes redistributed into Level 1 are summarized with the configured address and mask value." To test this functionality, three loopback interfaces were created, two of them running IS-IS and one redistributed into IS-IS. Only the redistributed route was summarized using the **summary-address** command on the L1 router.

The partial configuration of R3, an L1 router, is as follows:

```
!partial config of R3, an L1 router
!
 interface Loopback111
 ip address 3.3.3.3 255.255.255.255
 ip router isis
!
interface Loopback112
 ip address 3.3.3.4 255.255.255.255
 ip router isis
!
interface Loopback222
 ip address 122.122.122.122 255.255.255.255
!
router isis
 net 49.0011.3333.3333.3333.00
 summary-address 122.122.122.0 255.255.255.0 level-1
 summary-address 3.3.3.0 255.255.255.0 level-1
 redistribute connected level-1
 is-type level-1
!
```

The partial routing table on the R3 L1 router is as follows:

```
R3#show ip route
<output omitted>
     3.0.0.0/32 is subnetted, 2 subnets
C       3.3.3.3 is directly connected, Loopback111
C       3.3.3.4 is directly connected, Loopback112
<output omitted>
     122.0.0.0/8 is variably subnetted, 2 subnets, 2 masks
C       122.122.122.122/32 is directly connected, Loopback222
i su    122.122.122.0/24 [115/0] via 0.0.0.0, Null0
```

The partial routing table on R1, an L1/L2 upstream router, is as follows:

```
R1#show ip route
<output omitted>
     3.0.0.0/32 is subnetted, 2 subnets
i L1    3.3.3.3 [115/20] via 10.1.1.3, Ethernet0/0
i L1    3.3.3.4 [115/20] via 10.1.1.3, Ethernet0/0
<output omitted>
     122.0.0.0/24 is subnetted, 1 subnets
i L1     122.122.122.0 [115/10] via 10.1.1.3, Ethernet0/0
```

Only the redistributed route, 122.122.122.122/32, was summarized, to 122.122.122.0/24. The other two routes were not summarized.

Verifying IS-IS Configuration and Structures

This section describes some commands that can be used to verify IS-IS configuration and CLNS IS-IS structures.

Verifying IS-IS Configuration

To verify the IS-IS configuration and IP functionality of an Integrated IS-IS network, use the following commands; these commands can also be useful for troubleshooting problems with the IS-IS network:

- **show ip protocols**—Displays the active IP routing protocols, the interfaces on which they are active, and the networks for which they are routing.

- **show ip route** [*address* [*mask*]] | [*protocol* [*process-id*]]—Displays the IP routing table. You can specify the details for a particular route or a list of all routes in the routing table from a particular routing protocol process.

Example 6-3 is sample output from the **show ip protocols** command that displays information about IP routing being done by Integrated IS-IS. IS-IS is running, it is not redistributing any other protocols, and address summarization has not been configured. Example 6-3 also shows that interfaces FastEthernet 0/0, Loopback 0, and Serial 0/0/1 are taking part in Integrated IS-IS, that there are two sources of routing information (the neighboring routers), and that the administrative distance of Integrated IS-IS is 115.

Example 6-3 **show ip protocols** *Command to Examine IS-IS*

```
R2#show ip protocols
Routing Protocol is "isis"
  Invalid after 0 seconds, hold down 0, flushed after 0
  Outgoing update filter list for all interfaces is not set
  Incoming update filter list for all interfaces is not set
  Redistributing: isis
  Address Summarization:
    None
  Maximum path: 4
  Routing for Networks:
    FastEthernet0/0
    Loopback0
    Serial0/0/1
  Routing Information Sources:
    Gateway         Distance      Last Update
    10.10.10.10          115      00:00:02
    10.30.30.30          115      00:00:03
  Distance: (default is 115)
R2#
```

Sample output from the **show ip route isis** command in Example 6-4 displays only the IS-IS routes in the IP routing table. One route is from L1, as indicated by the **i L1** tag, and the other is from L2, as indicated by the **i L2** tag.

Example 6-4   show ip route isis *Command*

```
R2#show ip route isis
     10.0.0.0/24 is subnetted, 5 subnets
i L2   10.30.30.0 [115/45] via 10.2.2.3, Serial0/0/1
i L1   10.10.10.0 [115/20] via 10.1.1.1, FastEthernet0/0
R2#
```

Integrated IS-IS uses, by default, an administrative distance of 115. The metric shown for each route is the IS-IS cost to the destination. In Example 6-4, in the value [115/20], 115 is the Integrated IS-IS administrative distance, and 20 is the IS-IS metric.

Verifying CLNS IS-IS Structures

Many **show** commands are helpful when troubleshooting CLNS and IS-IS structures, as covered in this section.

Troubleshooting Commands: CLNS

You can use the following **show clns** commands to verify the router configuration and to troubleshoot the CLNS portion of an Integrated IS-IS network:

- **show clns**—This command displays general information about the CLNS network.

- **show clns** [*area-tag*] **protocol**—This command displays information for the specific IS-IS processes in the router.

- **show clns interface** [*type number*]—This command displays information about the interfaces that currently run CLNS.

- **show clns** [*area-tag*] **neighbors** [*type number*] [**detail**]—This command displays IS and ES neighbors, if there are any. The neighbor routers are the routers with which this router has IS-IS adjacencies. The optional keyword **detail** displays the area addresses advertised by the neighbor in the hello messages. You can reduce the list to those neighbors across a particular interface if you specify the interface in the command.

Troubleshooting Commands: CLNS and IS-IS

You can use the following **show** commands to verify the router configuration and to troubleshoot the CLNS and IS-IS portions of the Integrated IS-IS network:

- **show isis** [*area-tag*] **route**—This command displays the IS-IS L1 routing table, which includes all other system IDs in the area. This command is available only if CLNS routing is enabled both globally and at the interface level.

- **show clns route** [*nsap*]—This command displays the IS-IS L2 routing table, which includes the areas known to this router and the routes to them. Specify a specific address with the optional *nsap* parameter.

- **show isis** [*area-tag*] **database**—This command displays the contents of the IS-IS LSDB. To force IS-IS to refresh its LSDB and recalculate all routes, issue the **clear isis** command; an asterisk (*) can be used to clear all IS-IS processes.

- **show isis** [*area-tag*] **topology**—This command displays the L1 and L2 topology tables, which show the least-cost IS-IS paths to the ISs.

OSI Intra-Area and Interarea Routing Example

Figure 6-23 is a copy of Figure 6-22, repeated here for your convenience. The figure shows three routers in two areas; routers R1 and R2 belong to area 49.0001 and router R3 belongs to area 49.0002. R1 is an L1 router doing only L1 routing. R2 is an L1/L2 router doing both L1 and L2 routing. R3 is an L2 router doing only L2 routing. The configuration of the three routers is shown earlier, in Example 6-2.

Figure 6-23 *Routing in a Two-Level Area Structure*

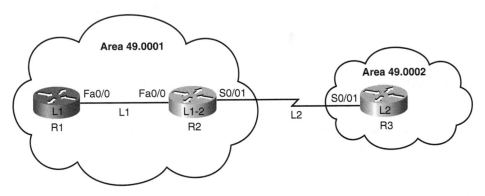

Figure 6-23 forms the basis of the following **show** command output examples.

Level 1 and Level 2 Topology Table

The **show isis topology** command, as shown in Example 6-5, displays the topology databases with the least-cost paths to destination ISs.

Example 6-5   show isis topology *Command Output*

```
R1#show isis topology
IS-IS paths to level-1 routers
System Id           Metric     Next-Hop   Interface   SNPA
R1                  --
R2                  10         R2         Fa0/0       0016.4650.c470
R2#show isis topology
IS-IS paths to level-1 routers
System Id           Metric     Next-Hop   Interface   SNPA
R1                  10         R1         Fa0/0       0016.4610.fdb0
R2                  --
IS-IS paths to level-2 routers
System Id           Metric     Next-Hop   Interface   SNPA
R1                  **
R2                  --
R3                  35         R3         Se0/0/1     *HDLC*
```

Notice in Example 6-5 that the output for Router R1 (an L1 router) shows the topology database for L1 only and the output for Router R2 (an L1/L2 router) shows that separate topology databases exist for L1 and L2.

The fields in the topology database are common for both levels of routing. They are as follows:

- The System ID column shows the NET of the destination IS. Cisco IOS Software uses dynamic hostname mapping (per RFC 2763, *Dynamic Hostname Exchange Mechanism for IS-IS*) to map the system ID to a hostname that is available to the router.

- The Metric column displays the sum of the metrics on the least-cost path to the destination.

- The Next-Hop column displays the next IS along the path to a destination.

- The Interface column shows the output interface that leads to the IS listed in Next-Hop.

- The SNPA column contains the OSI Layer 2 address of the next hop. HDLC is shown as the SNPA across an HDLC serial interface. The SNPA across the FastEthernet interface is the MAC address. For a Frame Relay interface, the SNPA would be the DLCI.

The topology database on R1 (an L1 router) in Example 6-5 shows only routers within the local area. R1 is doing only L1 routing, so it does not know of any routers outside its area. Traffic bound for other areas is forwarded to the nearest router doing L2 routing—in this case, R2.

R2 is doing both levels of routing. It thus maintains two topology databases. The L1 database looks very much like the R1 database; only routers within the local area are listed. The L2 database is where the external area router, R3, finally shows up.

The CLNS Protocol

In Example 6-6, the example output from the **show clns protocol** command displays the following information:

- The Integrated IS-IS process is running; its tag, if present, is also displayed.

- The system ID and area address for this router.

- The IS level types for the router.

- The interfaces using Integrated IS-IS for routing, including whether they are routing for IP, CLNS, or both.

- Any redistribution of other route sources.

- Information about the administrative distance for Level 2 CLNS routes and the acceptance and generation of metrics.

Example 6-6   **show clns protocol** *Command as a Troubleshooting Tool*

```
R2#show clns protocol
IS-IS Router: <Null Tag>
  System Id: 0000.0000.0002.00   IS-Type: level-1-2
  Manual area address(es):
        49.0001
  Routing for area address(es):
        49.0001
  Interfaces supported by IS-IS:
        Loopback0 - IP
        Serial0/0/1 - IP
        FastEthernet0/0 - IP
  Redistribute:
    static (on by default)
  Distance for L2 CLNS routes: 110
  RRR level: none
  Generate narrow metrics: level-1-2
  Accept narrow metrics:   level-1-2
  Generate wide metrics:   none
Accept wide metrics:       none
```

CLNS Neighbors

In the example output in Example 6-7, the **show clns neighbors** command displays the following information:

- The IS-IS neighbors with which this router has established adjacencies, and the interface on which each can be reached

- The SNPAs and state

- The holdtime, which is the timeout for receipt of no hellos, after which the neighbor is declared down

- The neighbor level type

Example 6-7 **show clns neighbors** *Command to Verify Adjacencies*

```
R2#show clns neighbors
System Id       Interface   SNPA            State  Holdtime  Type Protocol
R3              Se0/0/1     *HDLC*          Up     28        L2   IS-IS
R1              Fa0/0       0016.4610.fdb0  Up     23        L1   IS-IS
```

CLNS Interface

In Example 6-8, the output from the **show clns interface** command displays the following information:

- The interface runs IS-IS and attempts to establish L2 adjacencies.

- The interface numbers and circuit ID for IS-IS purposes.

- The ID of the neighbor.

- The metric or metrics for the interface.

- The priority for DIS negotiation. Priority is not relevant in this case because it is a serial HDLC interface.

- Information about hello timers and the number of established adjacencies.

- The state of the interface.

Example 6-8 **show clns interface** *Command Output*

```
R2#show clns interface s0/0/1
Serial0/0/1 is up, line protocol is up
  Checksums enabled, MTU 1500, Encapsulation HDLC
  ERPDUs enabled, min. interval 10 msec.
  CLNS fast switching enabled
  CLNS SSE switching disabled
  DEC compatibility mode OFF for this interface
  Next ESH/ISH in 45 seconds
  Routing Protocol: IS-IS
    Circuit Type: level-2
    Interface number 0x1, local circuit ID 0x100
    Neighbor System-ID: R3
    Level-2 Metric: 35, Priority: 64, Circuit ID: R2.00
    Level-2 IPv6 Metric: 10
    Number of active level-2 adjacencies: 1
    Next IS-IS Hello in 5 seconds
  if state UP
```

Summary

In this chapter, you learned about IS-IS, a proven IP routing protocol; the following topics were covered:

- History of IS-IS, as the routing protocol for the OSI protocol suite, and its use of CLNS addresses to identify routers and to build the LSDBs.

- The two IS-IS routing levels: L1 within areas and L2 between areas.

- The three types of IS-IS routers: L1, L2, and L1/L2.

- The IS-IS backbone, the path of connected L2 and L1/L2 routers.

- Integrated IS-IS, the implementation of the IS-IS protocol for routing multiple network protocols, including IP and CLNS.

- Various related protocols and hello messages, including ES-IS, ESHs, ISHs, and IIHs.

- The similarities and differences between IS-IS and OSPF.

- IS-IS routing operation, including NSAP and NET addresses, how CLNS addressing affects IS-IS operation, and how the IS-IS protocol learns the topology, makes routing decisions, and handles different types of data links.

- The OSI PDUs, including the IS-IS and ES-IS PDUs, and the four types of IS-IS PDUs: Hello PDUs, LSPs, PSNPs, and CSNPs.

- IS-IS configuration, including enabling the IS-IS protocol, configuring a NET, and enabling IS-IS on the appropriate interfaces.

- Optimizing IS-IS configuration, including changing the IS-IS router level and interface level, changing the IS-IS interface metric, and configuring IP route summarization.

- Verifying IS-IS configuration and CLNS IS-IS structures.

Configuration Exercise: Configuring Integrated IS-IS in Multiple Areas

In this exercise, you configure the routers in your pod for IS-IS routing in multiple areas.

Introduction to the Configuration Exercises

This book uses Configuration Exercises to help you practice configuring routers with the commands and topics presented. If you have access to real hardware, you can try these exercises on your routers. See Appendix B, "Configuration Exercise Equipment Requirements and

Backbone Configurations," for a list of recommended equipment and configuration commands for the backbone routers. However, even if you don't have access to any routers, you can go through the exercises and keep a log of your own running configurations or just read through the solution. Commands used and solutions to the Configuration Exercises are provided within the exercises.

In the Configuration Exercises, the network is assumed to consist of two pods, each with four routers. The pods are interconnected to a backbone. You configure pod 1. No interaction between the two pods is required, but you might see some routes from the other pod in your routing tables in some exercises if you have it configured. In most of the exercises, the backbone has only one router; in some cases, another router is added to the backbone. Each Configuration Exercise assumes that you have completed the previous chapters' Configuration Exercises on your pod.

NOTE   Throughout this exercise, the pod number is referred to as *x*, and the router number is referred to as *y*. Substitute the appropriate numbers as needed.

Objectives

The objective of this exercise is to connect the devices in your pod using IS-IS routes.

Visual Objective

Figure 6-24 illustrates the topology used and what you will accomplish in this exercise.

Figure 6-24   *IS-IS Configuration Exercise Topology*

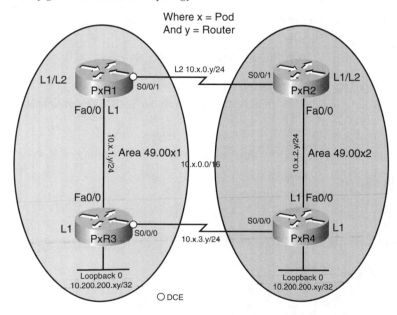

Command List

In this exercise, you use the commands in Table 6-6, listed in logical order. Refer to this list if you need configuration command assistance during the exercise.

> **CAUTION** Although the command syntax is shown in Table 6-6, the addresses shown are typically for the P*x*R1 and P*x*R3 routers. Be careful when addressing your routers! Refer to the exercise instructions and the appropriate visual objective diagram for addressing details.

Table 6-6 *Configuration Exercise Commands*

Command	Description
(config)#**router isis**	Enables IS-IS on the router.
(config-router)#**net 49.00**x**1.**yyyy.yyyy.yyyy**.00**	Identifies the NET to be used for this device. CLNS addresses identify a device, not an interface.
(config-if)#**ip router isis**	Enables IS-IS routing on an interface.
(config-router)#**is-type level-1**	Sets this router to participate in only L1 routing (used on internal routers only).
#**show isis topology**	Display the IS-IS topology table.
(config-if)#**isis circuit-type level-2-only**	Sets this interface to participate in only L2 routing.
(config-if)#**isis circuit-type level-1**	Sets this interface to participate in only L1 routing.
(config-router)#**summary-address 10.**x**.0.0 255.255.254.0**	Creates a summary route 10.x.0.0/23 (into L2 by default).

Task 1: Cleaning Up and Preparing

Before starting to investigate IS-IS, you need to remove the OSPF configuration and shut down interfaces to the core.

Step 1   Remove all OSPF configuration from the internal routers (P*x*R3 and P*x*R4).

Solution:

The following shows how to do the required step on the P1R3 router:

```
P1R3(config)#no router ospf 1
```

Step 2   Remove all OSPF configuration from the edge routers. Remember to remove the **ip ospf network point-to-multipoint** command on the S0/0/0.1 subinterface.

Step 3   Shut down the serial 0/0/0 interface on the edge routers (P*x*R1 and P*x*R2) to isolate your pod from the core for this exercise.

Solution:

The following shows how to do the required steps on the P1R1 router:

```
P1R1(config)#no router ospf 1
P1R1(config)#int s0/0/0
P1R1(config-if)#shutdown
P1R1(config-if)#int s0/0/0.1
P1R1(config-subif)#no ip ospf network point-to-multipoint
```

Task 2: Configuring Integrated IS-IS in Multiple Areas

In this task, you configure IS-IS in multiple areas.

Step 1   Configure IS-IS on the pod routers and assign a NET address to each router, as shown in Table 6-7. P*x*R1 and P*x*R3 should be in area 49.00*x*1. P*x*R2 and P*x*R4 should be in area 49.00*x*2.

Table 6-7   *Assigning NET Addresses*

Router	NET	Example (Pod 2)
P*x*R1	**49.00*x*1**.*yyyy.yyyy.yyyy*.**00**	49.0021.1111.1111.1111.00
P*x*R2	**49.00*x*2**.*yyyy.yyyy.yyyy*.**00**	49.0022.2222.2222.2222.00
P*x*R3	**49.00*x*1**.*yyyy.yyyy.yyyy*.**00**	49.0021.3333.3333.3333.00
P*x*R4	**49.00*x*2**.*yyyy.yyyy.yyyy*.**00**	49.0022.4444.4444.4444.00

Solution:

The following shows how to do the required steps on the P1R1 and P1R3 routers:

```
P1R1(config)#router isis
P1R1(config-router)#net 49.0011.1111.1111.1111.00

P1R3(config)#router isis
P1R3(config-router)#net 49.0011.3333.3333.3333.00
```

Step 2   Enable IS-IS on the active serial, loopback, and FastEthernet interfaces of all the routers within your pod. (Recall that only your P*x*R3 and P*x*R4 routers have loopback addresses at this point.)

Solution:

The following shows how to do the required steps on the P1R1 and P1R3 routers:

```
P1R1(config)#int fa0/0
P1R1(config-if)#ip router isis
P1R1(config-if)#int s0/0/1
P1R1(config-if)#ip router isis

P1R3(config)#int fa0/0
P1R3(config-if)#ip router isis
P1R3(config-if)#int s0/0/0
P1R3(config-if)#ip router isis
P1R3(config-if)#int loop 0
P1R3(config-if)#ip router isis
```

Step 3   Leave the edge routers as the default IS type of L1/L2; however, set up internal routers to participate only in L1 routing using the proper IS-IS router configuration command. When the setup is complete, all communication between the areas will go through the edge routers.

Solution:

The following shows how to do the required steps on the P1R3 router:

```
P1R3(config)#router isis
P1R3(config-router)#is-type level-1
```

Step 4   L1 communication takes place only if the areas match. Therefore, P*x*R3 and P*x*R4 will not form an L1 adjacency with each other, because they are in different areas. They form an adjacency only with their directly connected edge router. P*x*R1 and P*x*R2 form an L2 adjacency.

Look at the IS-IS topology on an internal router; the internal router should have an L1 adjacency with the edge router. Trace the path from one internal router to the loopback address of the opposite internal router. The trace should show that the path to reach the opposite internal router's loopback address goes through the edge router.

Solution:

The following shows the output on the P1R3 router. P1R3 has an L1 adjacency with the edge router P1R1. The trace shows that the path to reach the opposite internal router's (P1R4) loopback address goes through the edge router (P1R1, which has address 10.1.1.1).

```
P1R3#show isis topology

IS-IS paths to level-1 routers
System Id             Metric     Next-Hop          Interface   SNPA
P1R1                  10         P1R1              Fa0/0       0016.4650.c470

P1R3                  --

P1R3#trace 10.200.200.14

Type escape sequence to abort.
Tracing the route to 10.200.200.14

  1 10.1.1.1 0 msec 0 msec 4 msec
  2 10.1.0.2 12 msec 16 msec 12 msec
  3 10.1.2.4 16 msec *  12 msec
P1R3#
```

Step 5   Look at the routing table on the internal routers. Notice that IS-IS L1
routing tables resemble OSPF totally stubby areas. For instance, where is
the route to the loopback address you just traced to?

Solution:

The following shows the output on the P1R3 router:

```
P1R3#show ip route
<output omitted>
Gateway of last resort is 10.1.1.1 to network 0.0.0.0

       10.0.0.0/8 is variably subnetted, 4 subnets, 2 masks
C        10.200.200.13/32 is directly connected, Loopback0
C        10.1.3.0/24 is directly connected, Serial0/0/0
C        10.1.1.0/24 is directly connected, FastEthernet0/0
i L1     10.1.0.0/24 [115/20] via 10.1.1.1, FastEthernet0/0
i*L1 0.0.0.0/0 [115/10] via 10.1.1.1, FastEthernet0/0
P1R3#
```

The route to 10.200.200.14 is not shown in the routing table, so the router would use the default
route 0.0.0.0, through 10.1.1.1 (P1R1).

Step 6   Notice the 10.x.0.0/24 route in the routing table. Why is it there?

Solution:

The 10.x.0.0/24 route is the subnet between the edge routers. By default all interfaces on the edge
routers are participating in L1 and L2 routing. Therefore, the edge routers are advertising this
10.x.0.0/24 route to the internal routers, as an IS-IS L1 route (displayed as i L1 in the routing
table).

Step 7   Look at the IS-IS topology table on the edge routers. Although these routers
participate in L1 and L2 routing, they use only L1 on the FastEthernet
interface and only L2 on the serial interface.

Solution:

The following shows the output on the P1R1 router:

```
P1R1#show isis topology

IS-IS paths to level-1 routers
System Id         Metric      Next-Hop         Interface    SNPA
P1R1              - -
P1R3              10          P1R3             Fa0/0        0016.4610.fdb0

IS-IS paths to level-2 routers
System Id         Metric      Next-Hop         Interface    SNPA
P1R1              - -
P1R2              10          P1R2             Se0/0/1      *HDLC*
P1R3              **
P1R4              **
P1R1#
```

Step 8   Use the proper IS-IS interface configuration command to remove the
              redundant (and unused) hellos by forcing P*x*R1 and P*x*R2 to participate in
              a single routing level on each interface (L1 only on the FastEthernet
              interfaces and L2 only on the serial interfaces). Redundancy—forming
              both L1 and L2 adjacencies—wastes bandwidth and router resources to
              form both L1 and L2 adjacencies.

Solution:

The following shows how to do the required steps on the P1R1 router:

```
P1R1(config)#int s0/0/1
P1R1(config-if)#isis circuit level-2-only
P1R1(config-if)#int fa0/0
P1R1(config-if)#isis circuit level-1
```

Step 9   Look at the routing table on the internal routers; notice that the 10.x.0.0/24
              route is no longer there.

Solution:

The following shows the output on the P1R3 router; the 10.x.0.0/24 route is no longer there:

```
P1R3#show ip route
<output omitted>
Gateway of last resort is 10.1.1.1 to network 0.0.0.0

     10.0.0.0/8 is variably subnetted, 3 subnets, 2 masks
C       10.200.200.13/32 is directly connected, Loopback0
C       10.1.3.0/24 is directly connected, Serial0/0/0
C       10.1.1.0/24 is directly connected, FastEthernet0/0
i*L1 0.0.0.0/0 [115/10] via 10.1.1.1, FastEthernet0/0
P1R3#
```

Step 10   On P*x*R1, summarize the 10.*x*.0.0 and 10.*x*.1.0 networks to 10.*x*.0.0/23. On
              P*x*R2, summarize the 10.*x*.2.0/24 and 10.*x*.3.0/24 networks to 10.*x*.2.0/23.

Solution:

The following shows how to do the required steps on the P1R1 and P1R2 routers:

```
P1R1(config)#router isis
P1R1(config-router)#summary-address 10.1.0.0 255.255.254.0

P1R2(config)#router isis
P1R2(config-router)#summary-address 10.1.2.0 255.255.254.0
```

Step 11   Examine the routing tables on P*x*R1 and P*x*R2 to verify that the summary route appears.

Solution:

The following shows the output on the P1R1 router:

```
P1R1#show ip route
<output omitted>
Gateway of last resort is not set

     10.0.0.0/8 is variably subnetted, 7 subnets, 3 masks
i L2    10.200.200.14/32 [115/30] via 10.1.0.2, Serial0/0/1
i L1    10.200.200.13/32 [115/20] via 10.1.1.3, FastEthernet0/0
i L1    10.1.3.0/24 [115/20] via 10.1.1.3, FastEthernet0/0
i L2    10.1.2.0/23 [115/20] via 10.1.0.2, Serial0/0/1
C       10.1.1.0/24 is directly connected, FastEthernet0/0
C       10.1.0.0/24 is directly connected, Serial0/0/1
i su    10.1.0.0/23 [115/10] via 0.0.0.0, Null0
P1R1#
```

The summary route to 10.1.2.0/23, from P1R2, appears in P1R1's routing table. Note that the 10.1.3.0/24 route still appears in P1R1's routing table, but via its FastEthernet 0/0 interface. P1R1 is learning the /24 route from P1R3, and the /23 route from P1R2; it keeps both because they are different routes.

Step 12   Save your configurations to NVRAM.

Solution:

The following shows how to perform the required step on the P1R1 router:

```
P1R1#copy run start
Destination filename [startup-config]?
Building configuration...
[OK]
```

Exercise Verification

You have successfully completed this exercise when you achieve these results:

- IS-IS is configured properly and exchanging routes.

- IS-IS has been optimized to use only one type of hello over each link.

- IS-IS has been optimized to pass a summary route.

Review Questions

Answer the following questions, and then refer to Appendix A, "Answers to Review Questions," for the answers.

1. Which of the following does Integrated IS-IS support?

   a. BGP

   b. IP

   c. OSPF

   d. IPX

2. What is an IS? What is an ES?

3. Because IS-IS is protocol independent, it can support which of the following?

   a. IPv4

   b. IPv6

   c. OSI CLNS

   d. All of the above

4. IS-IS routers use what to establish and maintain neighbor relationships?

   a. OSHs

   b. IIHs

   c. ISKs

   d. CLHs

5. As soon as neighbor adjacency is established, IS-IS routers exchange link-state information using what?

   a. Link-state packets

   b. Logical state packets

   c. Adjacency state packets

   d. Reachability state packets

6. Describe the four OSI routing levels.

7. What are some of the similarities between OSPF and IS-IS?

8. What are CLNS addresses used by routers called?

   a. DSAPs

   b. NOTs

   c. MSAPs

   d. NETs

9. What are NSAP addresses equivalent to?

   a. A combination of the IP address and upper-layer protocol in an IP header

   b. Layer 2 addresses

   c. A combination of the transport layer address and data link address

   d. Layer 4 addresses

10. The Cisco implementation of Integrated IS-IS divides the NSAP address into what three fields?

    a. The data-link address, the logical address, and the upper-layer address

    b. The PDU address, the NSAP selector, and the cluster ID

    c. The area address, the system ID, and the NSAP selector

    d. The transport layer address, the CPU ID, and the NSAP selector

11. True or false: Cisco routers routing CLNS data do not use addressing that conforms to the ISO 10589 standard.

12. What is the first part of a NET?

    a. Zone address

    b. Area address

    c. Cluster address

    d. ISO address

13. How does an IS-IS L1/L2 router route a packet?

14. What kind of IS-IS router is aware of only the local area topology?

    a. External

    b. Level 2

    c. Internal

    d. Level 1

15. Routing between IS-IS areas is based on what?

    a. Area address

    b. IP address

    c. Level 2

    d. Level 1/Level 2

16. True or false: In IS-IS, area boundaries fall on the links.

17. True or false: Symmetrical routing is a feature of IS-IS.

18. What does the IS-IS route leaking feature do?

19. In IS-IS, PDUs are encapsulated directly into an OSI data-link frame, so there is no what?

    a. ISO or area address header

    b. CLNP or IP header

    c. ES or IP header

    d. CLNS or area address header

20. Cisco IOS Software automatically uses IS-IS broadcast mode for which two of the following?

    a. Dialer interfaces

    b. LAN interfaces

    c. Multipoint WAN interfaces

    d. Point-to-point subinterfaces

21. True or false: IS-IS offers support specifically for NBMA networks.

22. In IS-IS, rather than having each router connected to a LAN advertise an adjacency with every other router on the LAN, each router just advertises a single adjacency to what?

    a. Area

    b. Cluster

    c. LSDB

    d. Pseudo-node

23. True or false: IS-IS maintains the L1 and L2 LSPs in different LSDBs.

24. True or false: CSNPs are periodically sent on point-to-point links.

25. When configuring Integrated IS-IS for IP, which command is required to be configured on an interface?

   a. **ip router net**

   b. **router isis net**

   c. **ip router isis**

   d. **ip isis router**

26. What is the default IS-IS metric on an interface of a Cisco router? How can this be changed?

27. What does "i L2" indicate in the output of the **show ip route isis** command?

28. What is a subnetwork point of attachment (SNPA)?

This chapter discusses different means of controlling routing update information, and Cisco IOS support of DHCP. It covers the following topics:

- Using Multiple IP Routing Protocols

- Controlling Routing Update Traffic

- Configuring DHCP

CHAPTER 7

Manipulating Routing Updates

This chapter starts with a discussion of route redistribution between different routing protocols. Methods of controlling the routing information sent between these routing protocols include using distribute lists, using route maps, and changing the administrative distance; each of these methods are described. The chapter concludes with a discussion of the Dynamic Host Configuration Protocol (DHCP) and how to enable DHCP server functionality on a Cisco IOS device.

> **NOTE** This chapter on manipulating routing updates is placed before the chapter on Border Gateway Protocol (BGP) because knowledge of route redistribution and route maps is required for the BGP discussion.

Using Multiple IP Routing Protocols

Simple routing protocols work well for simple networks, but as networks grow and become more complex, it might be necessary to change routing protocols. Often the transition between routing protocols takes place gradually, so multiple routing protocols might run in a network for some time. This section examines several reasons for using more than one routing protocol, how routing information is exchanged between them, and how Cisco routers operate in a multiple routing protocol environment.

Considerations When Migrating to Another Routing Protocol

There are many reasons why a change in routing protocols might be required.

As a network grows and becomes more complex, the original routing protocol might not be the best choice anymore. For example, routers running Routing Information Protocol (RIP) periodically send their entire routing tables in their updates; as the network grows larger, the traffic from those updates can slow the network down, indicating that a change to a more scalable routing protocol might be necessary. Alternatively, the network might be using Cisco's Enhanced Interior Gateway Routing Protocol (EIGRP) and now a protocol that supports multiple vendors might be required, or a new policy that specifies a particular routing protocol might be introduced.

Whatever the reason for the change, network administrators must manage the migration from one routing protocol to another carefully and thoughtfully. An accurate topology map of the network and an inventory of all network devices are critical for success. The new routing protocol will most likely have different requirements and capabilities from the old one; it is important for network administrators to understand what must be changed and to create a detailed plan before making any changes. For example, link-state routing protocols, such as Open Shortest Path First (OSPF) and Intermediate System-to-Intermediate System (IS-IS), require a hierarchical network structure; network administrators need to decide which routers will reside in the backbone area and how to divide the other routers into areas. Although EIGRP does not require a hierarchical structure, it operates much more effectively within one.

During the transition, there will likely be a time when two (or more) routing protocols are running in the network; it might be necessary to redistribute routing information between the protocols. If so, the redistribution strategy must be carefully planned to avoid disrupting network traffic or causing suboptimal routing. The timing of the migration must also be determined. For example, will the entire network change all at once, or will it be done in stages? Where will the migration start? An administrator must understand the network to make these decisions.

Note that networks may run multiple routing protocols as part of their design, not only as part of a migration. Thus, redistribution of routing information might be required in other cases as well. The "Redistribution Overview" section discusses the need for redistribution.

Figure 7-1 shows a sample network migration. This network initially used RIP Version 1 (RIPv1) and is migrating to OSPF, necessitating the following changes:

■ Conversion of the old fixed-length subnet mask (FLSM) addressing scheme to a variable-length subnet mask (VLSM) configuration

■ Use of a hierarchical addressing scheme to facilitate route summarization and make the network more scalable

■ Division of the network from one large area into a transit backbone area and two other areas

Planning and Implementing a New IP Address Allocation

If the migration to a new routing protocol requires the IP address scheme to be changed, this must also be carefully planned. One of the first steps when migrating to a new address space is to determine the timeframe for the changeover: Will it be a gradual change, with migration of different remote sites each weekend? Or will the new addressing be put in all at once? Resources and schedules must be considered when migrating multiple remote sites to a new address space.

Figure 7-1   *Network Migration Might Require Readdressing and Other Changes*

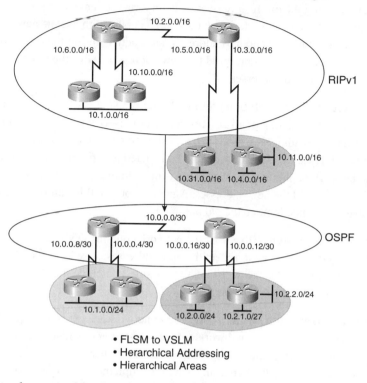

- FLSM to VSLM
- Herarchical Addressing
- Hierarchical Areas

The address plan created for the migration needs to be well-documented and accessible for review and reference by all internetworking personnel. If there are any questions or conflicts, this document helps settle the differences. For example, the new address space might have portions already in use, unbeknownst to the designer. Having remote personnel review and agree to the address assignments for the entire network helps prevent problems in the implementation stage.

After the IP addressing scheme has been determined, you must plan and execute its implementation. In most situations, the network must stay operational during the transition from one protocol to another and from one IP addressing plan to another. For successful implementation, carefully consider the following:

- **Host addressing**—If host IP addresses are statically assigned, this is an excellent time to migrate to using DHCP. If DHCP is already in use, changes in IP addressing are transparent to most end users. Configure the DHCP server to start assigning the new IP addresses to individual hosts. Configure new static IP addresses on devices such as servers. Remember to also change the assigned default gateways on devices (DHCP is described in the "Configuring DHCP" section later in this chapter). Update any applications that are referencing IP addresses instead of hostnames, and any documentation that specifically references IP addresses (such as router interface descriptions).

- **Access lists and other filters**—Firewalls and other types of traffic filters will have been configured using the old IP addresses. It is important to have complete documentation of all the filters within the network so that they can be updated to use the new IP address ranges. If you are keeping the old and new address ranges active during the transition, the access lists and filters need modification to add the new addresses. After the transition is complete, you must remove the old addresses.

- **Network Address Translation (NAT)**—If you're using NAT, it is also important to have complete documentation of all devices performing NAT within the network (such as servers, routers, and firewalls). NAT needs to be configured to recognize and use the new IP addresses. The new addresses also might need to be translated to different outside addresses, depending on the network configuration. If you are using both old and new address ranges during the transition, just add the new addresses. Again, if you use this approach, after the transition is complete, you must remove the old addresses.

- **Domain Name System (DNS)**—If the network contains DNS servers, decide which mappings must be redone to reflect the new addresses. Any DNS used for internal addresses needs mappings for the new IP addresses. Be sure to include the changes for any static hosts, such as web or application servers.

- **Timing and transition strategy**—In a large network, changes are typically done in stages. You might start at the core and work outward or start at the edges and work inward; base the decision on a thorough knowledge of the network. Other important decisions are the time of day and day of the week when changes will be implemented; be sure to allow enough time to test and verify the new configuration. Notify the Help Desk, and users, of the changes. If some portions of the network will be using both the old and new IP addresses for any length of time during the transition, configure the affected routers to recognize and use both address ranges. Secondary addresses may be used on the router interfaces.

> **NOTE** In this chapter, *core* and *edge* are generic terms used to simplify the discussion of redistribution.

> **NOTE** This list includes some of the items your transition plan needs to address. Depending on your network, there might be others.

For example, suppose that the migration shown in Figure 7-1 is being done because there are frequent changes in the network. These frequent changes cause frequent RIP updates to be sent, which uses up bandwidth. Network convergence is also slow with RIP. If OSPF were implemented in this network without changing the addressing so that route summarization could be implemented, triggered updates would still be sent frequently whenever any part of the network topology changed. The changes would cause the shortest path first (SPF) algorithm to be recomputed frequently, which in turn would disrupt routing. In this case, OSPF may be a worse choice than RIP. However, if a proper addressing plan were implemented, as is shown in the lower portion of Figure 7-1, this same network could run very efficiently. With route summarization in the right places, changes in the network topology would be hidden from most of the other routers, and the SPF algorithm would not need to run for every topology change.

Configuring a Secondary IP Address

If secondary addresses are required in the transition, they must be configured before any of the host addressing, NAT, or access lists can be changed. The old routing protocol also might need updating to include the new networks in its **network** commands if you want it to route for these networks.

Use the **ip address** *address mask* **secondary** interface configuration command to assign a secondary IP address to an interface.

Example 7-1 shows a sample configuration with a primary and a secondary address configured on FastEthernet 0/0.

Example 7-1 *Configuration with a Secondary Address Applied*

```
Router#show run
<output omitted>
interface FastEthernet0/0
ip address 172.17.1.3 255.255.255.240 secondary
ip address 10.1.2.3 255.255.255.0
```

Some routing protocols have issues with secondary addresses.

KEY POINT

EIGRP and OSPF Use Primary Interface Addresses

EIGRP and OSPF use an interface's primary IP address as the source of their updates. They expect the routers on both sides of a link to belong to the same subnet.

EIGRP and OSPF do not accept an update from, or form a neighbor relationship with, a router on the wrong subnet; EIGRP constantly generates error messages in this situation. Therefore, you must use the same subnet for the primary addresses on neighbor routers; do not use the same subnet for the secondary address on one router and the primary address on its neighbor.

KEY POINT

Make New Addresses Primary Addresses

As soon as all the routers in a portion of the network are using the new routing protocol and the new IP address ranges, the routers can be reconfigured to use the new IP addresses as primary. One way to introduce more fault tolerance into this process, and to make the final transition easier, is to configure the original addresses as secondary addresses and the new addresses as the primary addresses until the entire network has transitioned, everything has been tested, and the network is stable. The original IP addresses, now the secondary addresses, should be removed when they are no longer needed.

Migrating to a New Routing Protocol

Before making any changes to the routing protocol in a network, plan an escape route: Make sure you have backup copies of all device configurations. Network documentation should include information on packet-flow paths so that you can be sure that the changes will not create suboptimal paths or routing loops. Documentation should also include baseline statistics for data flows.

When planning the migration, consider the following steps:

Step 1   To avoid delays, you need a clear and comprehensive timeline for all steps in the migration, including for implementing and testing the new router configurations. Consider the impact of the changes on user traffic, and make changes when traffic is least likely to be affected (for example, during off-peak hours).

Be sure to allow time for testing and verifying changes and configuration. The migration to a new routing protocol typically is gradual—one section of the network is changed at a time. When the network's IP addressing was planned, the network was probably divided into either logical or physical hierarchical areas; plan when each of these areas will be migrated to the new routing protocol.

Step 2   Determine which routing protocol is the core and which is the edge. Usually, a choice must be made between starting the migration at the core of the network and working out to the edges, or starting at an edge router and working in toward the network core. Each approach has its pros and cons. For example, if you start at an edge, you can install and test the protocol without disrupting the main network traffic, and you can work out problems that might not have shown up in a testing lab in a more realistic, smaller-scale environment before progressing with the migration.

Migrations to protocols that require a backbone area (such as OSPF) should begin at the core of the network. Because all interarea traffic goes through the backbone, the backbone must be in place before the areas can communicate. Other reasons to begin with the network core include the fact that there are typically fewer devices at the core, and that redundancy is usually built into the core design, which helps minimize the effects of any problems. The most experienced network staff is also usually at the same location as the core network devices.

Step 3   Identify the boundary routers where the multiple routing protocols will run. Part of migrating to a new routing protocol includes redistribution between the old and new routing protocol. As part of the timeline, you must determine how many routers will be converted to the new routing protocol at one time. The routers that are the gateways between the old and the new routing protocols are the ones that may perform redistribution.

Step 4   Determine how you want to redistribute information between the core and edge routing protocols. Redistribution is covered in detail in the following sections.

Step 5   Verify that all devices support the new routing protocol. If not, you need to download, install, and test any required Cisco IOS Software upgrades before beginning the migration.

Step 6   Implement and test the routing solution in a lab environment. The migration strategy should be tested in as realistic an environment as possible to identify and correct any bugs ahead of time.

Each step of the migration must be documented, tested, and verified.

Redistribution Overview

The following are possible reasons why you might need multiple routing protocols running at the same time within your network:

■ You are migrating from an older Interior Gateway Protocol (IGP) to a new IGP. Multiple redistribution boundaries may exist until the new protocol has displaced the old protocol completely. Running multiple routing protocols during a migration is effectively the same as a network that has multiple routing protocols running as part of its design.

■ You want to use another protocol but need to keep the old routing protocol because of the host system's needs. For example, UNIX host-based routers might run only RIP.

■ Different departments might not want to upgrade their routers to support a new routing protocol.

■ If you have a mixed-router vendor environment, you can use a Cisco-specific routing protocol, such as EIGRP, in the Cisco portion of the network and then use a common standards-based routing protocol, such as OSPF, to communicate with non-Cisco devices.

When multiple routing protocols are running in different parts of the network, hosts in one part of the network might need to reach hosts in the other part. One way to accomplish this is to advertise a default route into each routing protocol, but default routes might not always be the best policy. For example, the network design might not allow default routes, and if there is more than one way to get to a destination network, routers might need information about routes in the other parts of the network to determine the best path to that destination. In addition, if multiple paths exist, a router must have sufficient information to determine a loop-free path to the remote networks.

When any of these situations arise, Cisco routers allow internetworks using different routing protocols (referred to as routing domains or autonomous systems) to exchange routing information through a feature called route redistribution.

<table>
<tr><td>**KEY POINT**</td><td>**Redistribution**

Redistribution is defined as the capability of boundary routers connecting different routing domains to exchange and advertise routing information between those routing domains (autonomous systems).</td></tr>
</table>

> **NOTE** The term autonomous system as used here denotes internetworks using different routing protocols. These routing protocols may be IGPs or Exterior Gateway Protocols (EGPs). This use of the term *autonomous system* is different than that used for BGP.

In some cases the same protocol may be used in multiple different domains or autonomous systems within a network. The multiple instances of the protocol are treated no differently than if they were distinct protocols; redistribution is required to exchange routes between them.

Within each autonomous system, the internal routers have complete knowledge of their network. The router that interconnects the autonomous systems is called a *boundary router*. The boundary router must be running all the routing protocols that will exchange routes. In most cases, route redistribution must be configured to redistribute routes from one routing protocol to another. The only time redistribution is automatic in IP routing protocols is between Interior Gateway Routing Protocol (IGRP) and EIGRP processes running on the same router and using the same autonomous system number.

> **NOTE** IGRP is no longer supported, as of Cisco IOS Release 12.3. It is included in this chapter for completeness.

When a router redistributes routes, it allows a routing protocol to advertise routes that were not learned through that routing protocol. These redistributed routes could have been learned via a different routing protocol, such as when redistributing between EIGRP and OSPF, or they could have been learned from static routes or by a direct connection to a network. (Routers can redistribute static and connected routes and routes from other routing protocols.)

Redistribution is always performed *outbound*; the router doing redistribution does not change its routing table. For example, when redistribution between OSPF and EIGRP is configured, the OSPF process on the boundary router takes the EIGRP routes in the routing table and advertises them as OSPF routes to its OSPF neighbors. Likewise, the EIGRP process on the boundary router takes the OSPF routes in the routing table and advertises them as EIGRP routes to its EIGRP neighbors. With this redistribution, both autonomous systems know about the routes of the other, and each autonomous system can then make informed routing decisions for these networks. The boundary router's neighbors see the redistributed routes as external routes. In this example, if a packet destined for one of the networks in the OSPF domain arrives from the EIGRP autonomous system, the boundary router must have the OSPF routes for the networks in the OSPF domain in its routing table to be able to forward the traffic.

KEY POINT | **Redistributed Routes**

Routes must be in the routing table for them to be redistributed.

This requirement might seem self-evident, but it can be a source of confusion. For instance, if a router learns about a network via EIGRP and OSPF, only the EIGRP route is put in the routing table because it has a lower administrative distance. Suppose RIP is also running on this router, and you want to redistribute OSPF routes into RIP. That network is not redistributed into RIP, because it is placed in the routing table as an EIGRP route, not as an OSPF route.

Figure 7-2 illustrates an autonomous system running OSPF that is connected to an autonomous system running EIGRP. The internal routers within each autonomous system have complete knowledge of their networks, but without redistribution, they do not know about the routes present in the other autonomous system. Router A is the boundary router, and it has active OSPF and EIGRP processes.

Figure 7-2 *Redistribution Between OSPF and EIGRP*

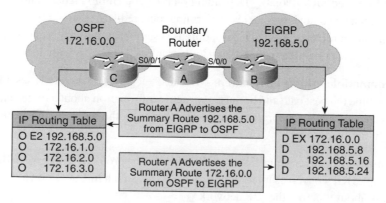

Without redistribution, Router A performs ships-in-the-night (SIN) routing: Router A passes OSPF route updates to its OSPF neighbors on the interfaces participating in OSPF, and it passes EIGRP route updates to its EIGRP neighbors on the interfaces participating in EIGRP. Router A does not exchange information between EIGRP and OSPF. If routers in the OSPF routing domain need to learn about the routes in the EIGRP domain, or vice versa, Router A must redistribute routes between EIGRP and OSPF.

Router A learns about network 192.168.5.0 from Router B via the EIGRP routing protocol running on its S0/0/0 interface. After redistribution is configured, Router A redistributes that information to Router C via OSPF on its S0/0/1 interface. Routing information is also passed in the other direction, from OSPF to EIGRP.

The routing table in Router B shows that it has learned about network 172.16.0.0 via EIGRP (as indicated by the D in the routing table) and that the route is external to this autonomous system (as indicated by the EX in the routing table). The routing table in Router C shows that it has learned about network 192.168.5.0 via OSPF (as indicated by the O in the routing table) and that the route is external (type 2) to this autonomous system (as indicated by the E2 in the routing table).

Note that in this example, Router A is redistributing routes that are summarized on the network class boundary. (Recall that EIGRP automatically summarizes on the class boundary, whereas OSPF must be configured to summarize.) This approach helps improve routing table stability and decreases the routing tables' size.

Redistribution Implementation Considerations

Redistribution of routing information, although powerful, adds to a network's complexity and increases the potential for routing confusion, so it should be used only when necessary. The key issues that arise when using redistribution are as follows:

- **Routing feedback (loops)**—Depending on how you employ redistribution—for example, if more than one boundary router is performing route redistribution—routers might send routing information received from one autonomous system back into that same autonomous system. The feedback is similar to the routing loop problem that occurs with distance vector protocols.

- **Incompatible routing information**—Because each routing protocol uses different metrics to determine the best path and because the metric information about a route cannot be translated exactly into a different protocol, path selection using the redistributed route information might not be optimal.

- **Inconsistent convergence times**—Different routing protocols converge at different rates. For example, RIP converges more slowly than EIGRP, so if a link goes down, the EIGRP network learns about it before the RIP network.

Good planning ensures that these issues do not cause problems in your network.

To understand why some of these problems might occur, you must first understand how Cisco routers select the best path when more than one routing protocol is running and how they convert the metrics used when importing routes from one autonomous system into another. These topics are discussed in the following sections.

Selecting the Best Route

Cisco routers use the following two parameters to select the best path when they learn two or more routes to the same destination from different routing protocols:

- **Administrative distance**—As discussed in Chapter 2, "Routing Principles," administrative distance is used to rate a routing protocol's believability. Each routing protocol is prioritized in order from most to least believable (or reliable or trustworthy) using a value called the administrative distance. This criterion is the first thing a router uses to determine which routing protocol to believe if more than one protocol provides route information for the same destination.

- **Routing metric**—The routing metric is a value representing the path between the local router and the destination network, according to the routing protocol being used. The metric is used to determine the routing protocol's "best" path to the destination.

Administrative Distance

Table 7-1 lists the default administrative distance (believability) of protocols supported by Cisco (this is a copy of Table 2-2).

Table 7-1   *Default Administrative Distances of Routing Protocols*

Routing Protocol	Default Administrative Distance Value
Connected interface	0
Static route out an interface	0
Static route to a next-hop address	1
EIGRP summary route	5
External BGP	20
Internal EIGRP	90
IGRP	100
OSPF	110

continues

Table 7-1 *Default Administrative Distances of Routing Protocols (Continued)*

Routing Protocol	Default Administrative Distance Value
IS-IS	115
RIPv1 and RIP Version 2 (RIPv2)	120
Exterior Gateway Protocol (EGP)	140
On-Demand Routing (ODR)	160
External EIGRP	170
Internal BGP	200
Unknown	255

KEY POINT

Administrative Distance

Lower administrative distances are considered more believable (better).

When using route redistribution, you might occasionally need to modify a protocol's administrative distance so that it is preferred. For example, if you want the router to select RIP-learned routes rather than OSPF-learned routes for some specific destination, you must increase the OSPF administrative distance or decrease the RIP administrative distance for the routes to that destination. Modifying the administrative distance is discussed in the later section "Using Administrative Distance to Influence the Route-Selection Process."

Seed Metrics

When a router is redistributing, it must assign a metric to the redistributed routes.

Redistributed routes are not physically connected to a router; rather, they are learned from other sources (such as other routing protocols). If a boundary router is to redistribute information between routing protocols, it must be capable of translating the metric of the received route from the source routing protocol into the other routing protocol. For example, if a boundary router receives a RIP route, the route has hop count as a metric. To redistribute the route into OSPF, the router must translate the hop count into a cost metric that the other OSPF routers will understand.

This metric, referred to as the seed or default metric, is defined during redistribution configuration. After the seed metric for a redistributed route is established, the metric increments normally within the autonomous system. (The exception to this rule is OSPF E2 routes, which hold their initial metric regardless of how far they are propagated across an autonomous system.)

> **KEY POINT**
>
> **Seed Metric for Directly Connected Networks**
>
> When a router advertises a link that is directly connected to one of its interfaces, the initial, or seed, metric used is derived from the characteristics of that interface, and the metric increments as the routing information is passed to other routers.
>
> For OSPF, the seed metric is based on the interface's bandwidth. For IS-IS, each interface has a default IS-IS metric of 10. For EIGRP and IGRP, the default seed metric is based on the interface bandwidth and delay. For RIP, the seed metric starts with a hop count of 0 and increases in increments from router to router.

The **default-metric** router configuration command establishes the seed metric for all redistributed routes. Cisco routers also allow the seed metric to be specified as part of the **redistribute** command, either with the **metric** option or by using a route map. These commands are discussed in detail in the later section "Configuring Redistribution."

> **KEY POINT**
>
> **Set The Seed Metric Larger Than the Largest Native Metric Within the Autonomous System**
>
> When redistributing routing information, set the seed metric to a value larger than the largest metric within the receiving autonomous system, to help prevent suboptimal routing and routing loops.

Default Seed Metrics

Table 7-2 lists the default seed metric value for routes that are redistributed into each IP routing protocol. A metric of infinity tells the router that the route is unreachable and, therefore, should not be advertised. Therefore, when redistributing routes into RIP, IGRP, and EIGRP, you must specify a seed metric, or the redistributed routes will not be advertised.

Table 7-2   *Default Seed Metrics*

Protocol That Route Is Redistributed Into	Default Seed Metric
RIP	ϕ, which is interpreted as infinity
IGRP/EIGRP	ϕ, which is interpreted as infinity
OSPF	20 for all except BGP routes, which have a default seed metric of 1
IS-IS	0
BGP	BGP metric is set to IGP metric value

For OSPF, the redistributed routes have a default type 2 (E2) metric of 20, except for redistributed BGP routes, which have a default type 2 metric of 1.

For IS-IS, the redistributed routes have a default metric of 0. But unlike RIP, IGRP, or EIGRP, a seed metric of 0 is not treated as unreachable by IS-IS. Configuring a seed metric for redistribution into IS-IS is recommended.

For BGP, the redistributed routes maintain the IGP routing metrics.

Figure 7-3 illustrates an example with an OSPF seed metric of 30 for redistributed RIP routes on Router C. The link cost of the Serial link to Router D is 100. The routes are redistributed as E2 routes, so the cost for networks 172.16.0.0, 172.17.0.0, and 172.18.0.0 in Router D is only the seed metric (30). Notice that the metrics of the three networks in the RIP cloud are irrelevant in the OSPF cloud, because the router in the OSPF network (Router D) forwards any traffic for these three networks to the border (redistributing) router, Router C. Router C then forwards the traffic within the RIP network appropriately.

Figure 7-3 *Redistribution Between OSPF and EIGRP*

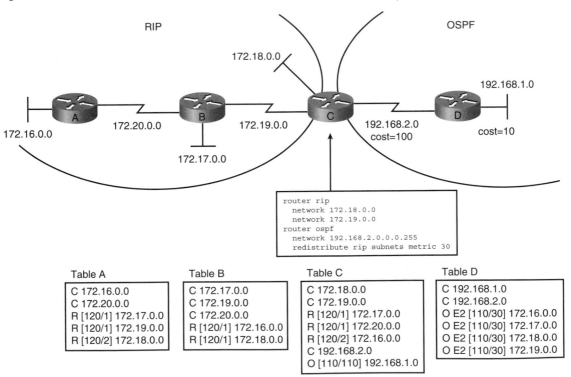

Redistribution Techniques

The following two methods of redistribution are available:

- **Two-way redistribution**—Redistributes all routes between the two routing processes

- **One-way redistribution**—Passes a default route into one routing protocol and redistributes only the networks learned from that routing protocol into the other routing protocol

| **One-Way Redistribution Is Safest**

The safest way to perform redistribution is to redistribute routes in only one direction, on only one boundary router within the network. (Note, however, that this results in a single point of failure in the network.)

If redistribution must be done in both directions or on multiple boundary routers, the redistribution should be tuned to avoid problems such as suboptimal routing and routing loops. Depending on your network design, you may use any of the following redistribution techniques, as illustrated in Figure 7-4:

- Redistribute a default route from the core autonomous system into the edge autonomous system, and redistribute routes from the edge routing protocols into the core routing protocol. This technique helps prevent route feedback, suboptimal routing, and routing loops.

- Redistribute multiple static routes about the core autonomous system networks into the edge autonomous system, and redistribute routes from the edge routing protocols into the core routing protocol. This method works if there is only one redistribution point; multiple redistribution points might cause route feedback.

- Redistribute routes from the core autonomous system into the edge autonomous system with filtering to block out inappropriate routes. For example, when there are multiple boundary routers, routes redistributed from the edge autonomous system at one boundary router should not be redistributed back into the edge autonomous system from the core at another redistribution point.

- Redistribute all routes from the core autonomous system into the edge autonomous system, and from the edge autonomous system into the core autonomous system, and then modify the administrative distance associated with redistributed routes so that they are not the selected routes when multiple routes exist for the same destination.

Figure 7-4 *Redistribution Techniques*

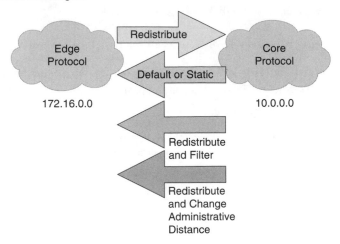

Configuring Redistribution

As shown in Example 7-2, redistribution supports all routing protocols. Static and connected routes can also be redistributed to allow the routing protocol to advertise these routes.

Example 7-2 *Redistribution Supports All Protocols*

```
RtrA(config)#router rip
RtrA(config-router)#redistribute ?
  bgp        Border Gateway Protocol (BGP)
  connected  Connected
  eigrp      Enhanced Interior Gateway Routing Protocol (EIGRP)
  isis       ISO IS-IS
  iso-igrp   IGRP for OSI networks
  metric     Metric for redistributed routes
  mobile     Mobile routes
  odr        On Demand stub Routes
  ospf       Open Shortest Path First (OSPF)
  rip        Routing Information Protocol (RIP)
  route-map  Route map reference
  static     Static routes
  <cr>
```

NOTE Note that IGRP is not in this list because it is no longer supported as of Cisco IOS Release 12.3.

KEY POINT	**Routes Are Redistributed into a Protocol**
	Routes are redistributed *into* a routing protocol, so the **redistribute** command is configured under the routing process that is to *receive* the redistributed routes.

Before implementing redistribution, consider the following points:

■ You can only redistribute routes from routing protocols that support the same protocol stack. For example, you can redistribute between IP RIP and OSPF because they both support the TCP/IP stack. You cannot redistribute between Internetwork Packet Exchange (IPX) RIP and OSPF because IPX RIP supports the IPX/Sequenced Packet Exchange (SPX) stack and OSPF does not. Although there are different protocol-dependent modules of EIGRP for IP, IPX, and AppleTalk, routes cannot be redistributed between them, because each protocol-dependent module supports a different protocol stack.

■ The method you use to configure redistribution varies among combinations of routing protocols. For example, redistribution occurs automatically between IGRP and EIGRP when they have the same autonomous system number, but redistribution must be configured between all other routing protocols. Some routing protocols require a metric to be configured during redistribution, but others do not.

The following steps for configuring redistribution are generic enough to apply to all routing protocol combinations. However, the commands used to implement the steps vary, as identified in the following sections. It is important that you review the Cisco IOS documentation for the configuration commands that apply to the specific routing protocols you want to redistribute.

> **NOTE**   Remember, in this chapter, the terms *core* and *edge* are generic terms used to simplify the discussion of redistribution.

Step 1   Locate the boundary router(s) on which redistribution is to be configured. Selecting a single boundary router for redistribution minimizes the likelihood of routing loops caused by feedback.

Step 2   Determine which routing protocol is the core or backbone protocol. Typically, this protocol is OSPF, IS-IS, or EIGRP.

Step 3   Determine which routing protocol is the edge or short-term (if you are migrating) protocol. Determine whether all routes from the edge protocol need to be propagated into the core. Consider methods that reduce the number of routes.

Step 4   Select a method for injecting the required edge protocol routes into the core. Simple redistribution using summarized routes at network boundaries minimizes the number of new entries in the routing table of the core routers.

Step 5   After you have planned the edge-to-core redistribution, consider how to inject the core routing information into the edge protocol. Your choice depends on your network.

The following sections examine the specific commands for redistributing routes into the various IP routing protocols. The **default-metric** and **passive-interface** commands are also described.

The redistribute Command for RIP

Use the **redistribute** *protocol* [*process-id*] [**match** *route-type*] [**metric** *metric-value*] [**route-map** *map-tag*] router configuration command to redistribute routes into RIP. This command is explained in Table 7-3.

Table 7-3   **redistribute** *Command for RIP*

Parameter	Description
protocol	The source protocol from which routes are redistributed. It can be one of the following keywords: **bgp**, **connected**, **eigrp**, **isis**, **iso-igrp**, **mobile**, **odr**, **ospf**, **rip**, or **static**.
process-id	For BGP or EIGRP, this value is an autonomous system number. For OSPF, this value is an OSPF process ID. This parameter is not required for IS-IS.
route-type	(Optional) A parameter used when redistributing OSPF routes into another routing protocol. It is the criterion by which OSPF routes are redistributed into other routing domains. It can be any of the following: **internal**—Redistributes routes that are internal to a specific autonomous system. **external 1**—Redistributes routes that are external to the autonomous system but are imported into OSPF as a type 1 external route. **external 2**—Redistributes routes that are external to the autonomous system but are imported into OSPF as a type 2 external route.
metric-value	(Optional) A parameter used to specify the RIP seed metric for the redistributed route. When redistributing into RIP (and all protocols other than OSPF and BGP), if this value is not specified and no value is specified using the **default-metric** router configuration command, the default metric is 0. For RIP (and all protocols other than IS-IS), the default metric of 0 is interpreted as infinity, and routes will not be redistributed. The metric for RIP is hop count.
map-tag	(Optional) Specifies the identifier of a configured route map to be interrogated to filter the importation of routes from the source routing protocol to the current RIP routing protocol.

Example 7-3 shows how to configure redistribution from OSPF process 1 into RIP. This example uses the **router rip** command to access the routing process *into* which routes need to be redistributed—the RIP routing process. The **redistribute** command is then used to specify the routing protocol to be redistributed into RIP. In this case, it is OSPF routing process number 1.

Example 7-3   *Configuring Redistribution into RIP*

```
RtrA(config)#router rip
RtrA(config-router)#redistribute ospf ?

 <1-65535>  Process ID
RtrA(config-router)#redistribute ospf 1 ?
  match      Redistribution of OSPF routes
  metric     Metric for redistributed routes
  route-map  Route map reference
...
  <cr>
```

NOTE   When redistributing into RIP, the default metric is infinity except when redistributing a static route (including a default static route defined using the **ip route 0.0.0.0 0.0.0.0** command) or connected route. In that case, the default metric is 1.

Figure 7-5 provides an example of redistributing routes into RIP. On Router A, routes from OSPF process 1 are redistributed into RIP and are given a seed metric of 3. Because no route type is specified, both internal and external OSPF routes are redistributed into RIP. Notice that Router B learns about the 172.16.0.0 network from Router A via RIP; Router B's routing table has 172.16.0.0 installed as a RIP route.

Figure 7-5   *Routes Redistributed into RIP*

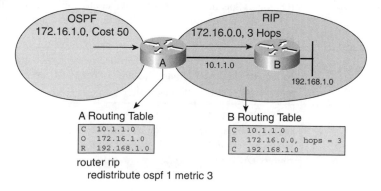

NOTE Notice that for RIP, the metric advertised to a router (3 in this case) is what that router uses as its metric. The sending router is assumed to have added 1 to the hop count; the receiving router does not add another hop. Notice also that the route is automatically summarized by Router A.

The redistribute Command for OSPF

Use the **redistribute** *protocol* [*process-id*] [**metric** *metric-value*] [**metric-type** *type-value*] [**route-map** *map-tag*] [**subnets**] [**tag** *tag-value*] router configuration command to redistribute routes into OSPF. This command is explained in Table 7-4.

Table 7-4 **redistribute** *Command for OSPF*

Parameter	Description
protocol	The source protocol from which routes are redistributed. It can be one of the following keywords: **bgp**, **connected**, **eigrp**, **isis**, **iso-igrp**, **mobile**, **odr**, **ospf**, **rip**, or **static**.
process-id	For BGP or EIGRP, this value is an autonomous system number. For OSPF, this value is an OSPF process ID. This parameter is not required for RIP or IS-IS.
metric-value	(Optional) A parameter that specifies the OSPF seed metric used for the redistributed route. When redistributing into OSPF, the default metric is 20 (except for BGP routes, which have a default metric of 1). The metric for OSPF is cost.
type-value	(Optional) An OSPF parameter that specifies the external link type associated with the external route advertised into the OSPF routing domain. This value can be **1** for type 1 external routes or **2** for type 2 external routes. The default is **2**.
map-tag	(Optional) Specifies the identifier of a configured route map to be interrogated to filter the importation of routes from the source routing protocol to the current OSPF routing protocol.
subnets	(Optional) An OSPF parameter that specifies that subnetted routes should also be redistributed. Only routes that are not subnetted are redistributed if the **subnets** keyword is not specified.
tag-value	(Optional) A 32-bit decimal value attached to each external route. The OSPF protocol itself does not use this parameter; it may be used to communicate information between OSPF autonomous system boundary routers (ASBRs).

Example 7-4 shows how to configure redistribution from EIGRP autonomous system 100 into OSPF. This example uses the **router ospf 1** command to access the OSPF routing process 1 into which routes need to be redistributed. The **redistribute** command is then used to specify the routing protocol to be redistributed into OSPF—in this case, the EIGRP routing process for autonomous system 100.

Example 7-4 *Configuring Redistribution into OSPF*

```
RtrA(config)#router ospf 1
RtrA(config-router)#redistribute eigrp ?

  <1-65535>  Autonomous system number
RtrA(config-router)#redistribute eigrp 100 ?

  metric        Metric for redistributed routes
  metric-type   OSPF/IS-IS exterior metric type for redistributed routes
  route-map     Route map reference
  subnets       Consider subnets for redistribution into OSPF
  tag           Set tag for routes redistributed into OSPF
  ...
  <cr>
```

KEY POINT

Redistributing into OSPF

When redistributing into OSPF, the default metric is 20, the default metric type is 2, and subnets are not redistributed by default.

Redistribution into OSPF can also be limited to a defined number of prefixes by the **redistribute maximum-prefix** *maximum* [*threshold*] [**warning-only**] router configuration command. The threshold parameter will default to logging a warning at 75 percent of the defined maximum value configured. After reaching the defined maximum number, no further routes are redistributed. If the **warning-only** parameter is configured, no limitation is placed on redistribution; the maximum value number simply becomes a second point where another warning messaged is logged. This command was introduced in Cisco IOS Version 12.0(25)S and was integrated into IOS versions 12.2(18)S and 12.3(4)T and later.

Figure 7-6 illustrates an example of redistributing EIGRP routes into OSPF. In this example, the default metric of 20 for OSPF is being used. The metric type is set to 1 (type 1 external [E1] routes), meaning that the metric increments whenever updates are passed through the network. Assuming the cost of the Ethernet link is 10, Router B's cost for the 172.16.1.0 route is 20 + 10 = 30. The command contains the **subnets** option, so subnets are redistributed.

Figure 7-6 *Routes Redistributed into OSPF*

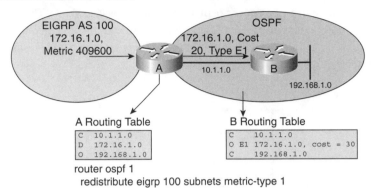

router ospf 1
  redistribute eigrp 100 subnets metric-type 1

| **Redistributing Subnets into OSPF**

In Figure 7-6, the **subnets** keyword is used. If this keyword were omitted, *no* subnets would be redistributed into the OSPF domain (including the 172.16.1.0 subnet). Omitting this keyword is a common configuration error.

The redistribute Command for EIGRP

Use the **redistribute** *protocol* [*process-id*] [**match** *route-type*] [**metric** *metric-value*] [**route-map** *map-tag*] router configuration command to redistribute routes into EIGRP. This command is explained in Table 7-5.

Table 7-5 **redistribute** *Command for EIGRP*

Parameter	Description
protocol	The source protocol from which routes are redistributed. It can be one of the following keywords: **bgp**, **connected**, **eigrp**, **isis**, **iso-igrp**, **mobile**, **odr**, **ospf**, **rip**, or **static**.
process-id	For BGP or EIGRP, this value is an autonomous system number. For OSPF, this value is an OSPF process ID. This parameter is not required for RIP or IS-IS.
route-type	(Optional) A parameter used when redistributing OSPF routes into another routing protocol. It is the criterion by which OSPF routes are redistributed into other routing domains. It can be one of the following: **internal**—Redistributes routes that are internal to a specific autonomous system. **external 1**—Redistributes routes that are external to the autonomous system but are imported into OSPF as a type 1 external route. **external 2**—Redistributes routes that are external to the autonomous system but are imported into OSPF as a type 2 external route.

Table 7-5 **redistribute** *Command for EIGRP (Continued)*

Parameter	Description
metric-value	(Optional) A parameter that specifies the EIGRP seed metric, in the order of bandwidth, delay, reliability, load, and maximum transmission unit (MTU), for the redistributed route. When redistributing into EIGRP (and all protocols other than OSPF and BGP), if this value is not specified and no value is specified using the **default-metric** router configuration command, the default metric is 0. For EIGRP (and all protocols other than IS-IS), the default metric of 0 is interpreted as infinity, and routes will not be redistributed. The metric for EIGRP is calculated based only on bandwidth and delay by default.
map-tag	(Optional) Specifies the identifier of a configured route map that is interrogated to filter the importation of routes from the source routing protocol to the current EIGRP routing protocol.

Example 7-5 shows how to configure redistribution from OSPF into EIGRP autonomous system 100. This example uses the **router eigrp 100** command to access the routing process into which routes need to be redistributed—in this case, the EIGRP routing process for autonomous system 100. The **redistribute** command is then used to specify the routing protocol to be redistributed into EIGRP autonomous system 100—in this case, OSPF routing process 1.

Example 7-5 *Configuring Redistribution into EIGRP*

```
RtrA(config)#router eigrp 100
RtrA(config-router)#redistribute ospf ?

  <1-65535>  Process ID
RtrA(config-router)#redistribute ospf 1 ?

  match       Redistribution of OSPF routes
  metric      Metric for redistributed routes
  route-map   Route map reference
...
  <cr>
```

NOTE   When redistributing routes from another routing protocol into EIGRP, the default metric is ɸ, which is interpreted infinity. When redistributing a static or connected route into EIGRP, the default metric is equal to the metric of the associated static or connected interface.

Table 7-6 shows the five parameters that comprise *metric-value* when redistributing into EIGRP.

Table 7-6 **metric-value** *Parameters for EIGRP*

metric-value Parameter	Description
bandwidth	The route's minimum bandwidth in kilobits per second (kbps).
delay	Route delay in tens of microseconds.
reliability	The likelihood of successful packet transmission, expressed as a number from 0 to 255, where 255 means that the route is 100 percent reliable.
loading	The route's effective loading, expressed as a number from 1 to 255, where 255 means that the route is 100 percent loaded.
mtu	Maximum transmission unit. The maximum packet size in bytes along the route; an integer greater than or equal to 1.

Figure 7-7 illustrates an example of redistributing OSPF routes into EIGRP autonomous system 100. In this case, a metric is specified to ensure that routes are redistributed. The redistributed routes appear in Router B's table as external EIGRP (D EX) routes. External EIGRP routes have a higher administrative distance than internal EIGRP (D) routes, so internal EIGRP routes are preferred over external EIGRP routes.

Figure 7-7 *Routes Redistributed into EIGRP*

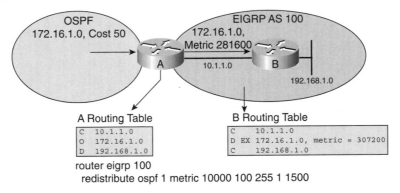

The metric used in this example is interpreted as follows:

- Bandwidth in kbps = 10,000

- Delay in tens of microseconds = 100

- Reliability = 255 (maximum)

- Load = 1 (minimum)

- MTU = 1500 bytes

The redistribute Command for IS-IS

Use the **redistribute** *protocol* [*process-id*] [**level** *level-value*] [**metric** *metric-value*] [**metric-type** *type-value*] [**route-map** *map-tag*] router configuration command to redistribute routes into IS-IS. This command is explained in Table 7-7.

Table 7-7 **redistribute** *Command for IS-IS*

Parameter	Description
protocol	The source protocol from which routes are redistributed. It can be one of the following keywords: **bgp**, **connected**, **eigrp**, **isis**, **iso-igrp**, **mobile**, **odr**, **ospf**, **rip**, or **static**.
process-id	For BGP or EIGRP, this value is an autonomous system number. For OSPF, this value is an OSPF process ID. This parameter is not required for RIP.
level-value	(Optional) A parameter that specifies how external routes are redistributed. They can be Level 1 (**level-1**), Level 1/Level 2 (**level-1-2**), or Level 2 (**level-2**) routes. The default is **level-2**.
metric-value	(Optional) A parameter that specifies the IS-IS seed metric used for the redistributed route. IS-IS uses a default metric of 0. Unlike RIP and EIGRP, a default metric of 0 is not treated as unreachable, so the route is redistributed. The metric is incremented as the route is propagated into the IS-IS domain. The IS-IS default metric value is cost.
type-value	(Optional) A parameter that specifies the IS-IS metric type as **external** or **internal**. The default is **internal**.
map-tag	(Optional) Specifies the identifier of a configured route map to be interrogated to filter the importation of routes from the source routing protocol to the current IS-IS routing protocol.

Example 7-6 shows how to configure redistribution from EIGRP autonomous system 100 into IS-IS. This example uses the **router isis** command to access the routing process into which routes need to be redistributed—the IS-IS routing process. The **redistribute** command is then used to specify the routing protocol to be redistributed into IS-IS—in this case, the EIGRP routing process for autonomous system 100.

Example 7-6 *Configuring Redistribution into IS-IS*

```
RtrA(config)#router isis
RtrA(config-router)#redistribute eigrp 100 ?

  level-1      IS-IS level-1 routes only
  level-1-2    IS-IS level-1 and level-2 routes
  level-2      IS-IS level-2 routes only
  metric       Metric for redistributed routes
  metric-type  OSPF/IS-IS exterior metric type for redistributed routes
  route-map    Route map reference
...
  <cr>
```

By default, routes are introduced into IS-IS as Level 2, with a metric of 0.

Redistribution into IS-IS can also be limited to a defined number of prefixes by the **redistribute maximum-prefix** *maximum* [*threshold*] [**warning-only** | **withdraw**] router configuration command. The threshold parameter will default to logging a warning at 75 percent of the defined maximum value configured. After reaching the defined maximum number, no further routes are redistributed. The optional **withdraw** parameter will also cause IS-IS to rebuild link-state protocol data units (PDUs) (link-state packets [LSPs]) without the external (redistributed) IP prefixes. If the **warning-only** parameter is configured, no limitation is placed on redistribution; the maximum value number simply becomes a second point where another warning messaged is logged. This command was introduced in Cisco IOS Version 12.0(25)S and was integrated into IOS versions 12.2(18)S and 12.3(4)T and later.

Figure 7-8 illustrates an example of redistributing from EIGRP autonomous system 100 into IS-IS, on Router A. No metric is configured, so these routes have a seed metric of 0. No level type is given, so the routes are redistributed as Level 2 routes (as shown by the L2 in Router B's routing table).

Figure 7-8 *Routes Redistributed into IS-IS*

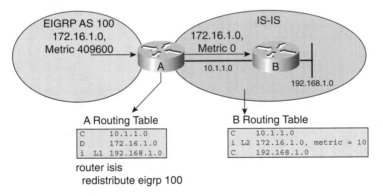

Redistributing IS-IS into Other Protocols

When redistributing IS-IS routes *into* other routing protocols, you have the option to include Level 1, Level 2, or both Level 1 and Level 2 routes. Example 7-7 shows the commands for choosing these routes. If no level is specified, all routes are redistributed.

Example 7-7 *Choosing the Level of Routes to Redistribute into IS-IS*

```
Router(config)#router ospf 1
Router(config-router)#redistribute isis ?
<output omitted>
  level-1            IS-IS level-1 routes only
  level-1-2          IS-IS level-1 and level-2 routes
  level-2            IS-IS level-2 routes only
<output omitted>
```

The default-metric Command

KEY
POINT

> **Changing Default Metrics**
>
> You can affect how routes are redistributed by changing the default metric associated with a protocol. You either specify the default metric with the **default-metric** router configuration command or use the *metric-value* parameter in the **redistribute** command.

If you use the **default-metric** command, the default metric you specify applies to all protocols being redistributed into this protocol.

If you use the **metric** parameter in the **redistribute** command, you can set a different default metric for each protocol being redistributed. A metric configured in a **redistribute** command overrides the value in the **default-metric** command for that one protocol.

When redistributing *into* EIGRP, use the **default-metric** *bandwidth delay reliability loading mtu* router configuration command to set the seed metric for all protocols. The parameters of this command are the same as those described earlier in Table 7-6.

When redistributing into OSPF, RIP, and BGP, use the **default-metric** *number* router configuration command for setting the seed metric. The *number* is the value of the metric, such as the number of hops for RIP.

The passive-interface Command

There are times when you must include a subnet in a routing protocols' **network** command, although you do not want the interface on which the subnet is connected to participate in the routing protocol.

KEY
POINT

> **passive-interface Command**
>
> The **passive-interface** *type number* [**default**] router configuration command prevents a routing protocol's routing updates from being sent through the specified router interface. This command is used to set either a particular interface or all router interfaces to passive; use the **default** option to set all router interfaces to passive.

Table 7-8 describes the parameters of this command.

Table 7-8   passive-interface *Command*

Parameter	Description
type number	Specifies the type of interface and interface number that will not send routing updates (or establish neighbor relationships for link-state routing protocols and EIGRP).
default	(Optional) A parameter that sets all interfaces on the router as passive by default.

When you use the **passive-interface** command with RIP and IGRP, routing updates are not sent out of the specified interface. However, the router still receives routing updates on that interface.

When you use the **passive-interface** command with EIGRP, hello messages are not sent out of the specified interface. Neighboring router relationships do not form with other routers that can be reached through that interface (because the hello protocol is used to verify bidirectional communication between routers). Because no neighbors are found on an interface, no other EIGRP traffic is sent.

Using the **passive-interface** command on a router running a link-state routing protocol also prevents the router from establishing neighboring router adjacencies with other routers connected to the interface specified in the command. The router does not send hello packets on the interface and therefore cannot establish neighbor adjacencies.

> **NOTE** During testing with **debug** commands, it was found that in some IOS versions OSPF sends hello and database description (DBD) packets on passive interfaces but does not send link state updates (LSUs).
>
> EIGRP does not send anything on passive interfaces.

In Internet service providers (ISPs) and large enterprise networks, many distribution routers have more than 200 interfaces. Before the introduction of the **passive-interface default** command in Cisco IOS Software Release 12.0, network administrators would configure the routing protocol on all interfaces and then manually set the **passive-interface** command on the interfaces where they did not require adjacency. However, this solution meant entering many **passive-interface** commands. A single **passive-interface default** command can now be used to set all interfaces to passive by default. To enable routing on individual interfaces where you require adjacencies, use the **no passive-interface** command.

For example, in Figure 7-9, Routers A and B run RIP and have a **network** command that encompasses all their interfaces. However, the network administrator wants to run RIP only on the link between Router A and Router B. Router A has several interfaces, so the **passive-interface default** command is configured, and then the **no passive-interface** command is used for the one interface from where RIP updates are advertised. Router B has only two interfaces, so the **passive-interface** command is used for the one interface that does not participate in RIP routing.

It is important to understand how this configuration affects the information exchanged between Routers A, B, and C. Unless you configure another routing protocol between Routers A and B and Router C, and redistribute between it and RIP, Router A does not tell Router C about the networks l from Router B via RIP (or about any of Router A's directly connected networks). Router B does not tell Router C that it has a way to reach the networks advertised by RIP (or about any of Router B's directly connected networks). Physical redundancy is built into this network; however, the three routers might not be able to use the redundancy effectively if they are not configured properly. For example, if the link between Routers C and A fails, Router C does not know that it has an alternative route through Router B to reach Router A.

Figure 7-9   **passive-interface** *Command Restricts Routing Traffic on an Interface*

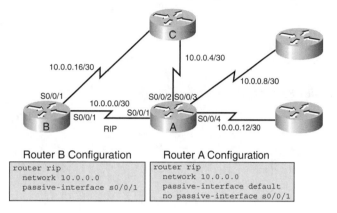

Route Redistribution Example

This section shows an example of route redistribution in a network using multiple routing protocols.

Figure 7-10 shows the network of a hypothetical company. The network begins with two routing domains (or autonomous systems)—one using OSPF and one using RIPv2. Router B is the boundary router; it connects directly to one router within each routing domain and runs both protocols. Router A is in the RIPv2 domain and advertises subnets 10.1.0.0, 10.2.0.0, and 10.3.0.0 to Router B. Router C is in the OSPF domain and advertises subnets 10.8.0.0, 10.9.0.0, 10.10.0.0, and 10.11.0.0 to Router B.

Figure 7-10   *Sample Network Before Redistribution*

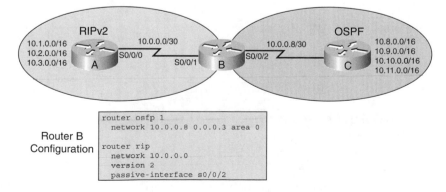

Figure 7-10 also shows the configuration of Router B. RIPv2 is required to run on the serial 0/0/1 interface only, so the **passive-interface** command is configured for interface serial 0/0/2 to prevent RIPv2 from sending route advertisements out that interface. OSPF is configured on interface serial 0/0/2.

Figure 7-11 shows the routing tables for Routers A, B, and C. Each routing domain is separate, and routers within them only recognize routes communicated from their own routing protocols. The only router with information on all the routes is Router B, the boundary router that runs both routing protocols and connects to both routing domains.

Figure 7-11 *Routing Tables Before Redistribution*

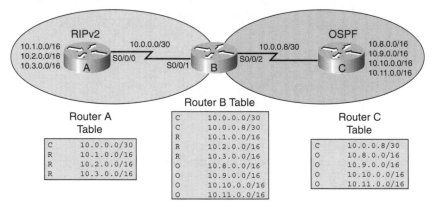

The goal of redistribution in this network is for all routers to recognize all routes within the company. To accomplish this goal, RIPv2 routes are redistributed into OSPF, and OSPF routes are redistributed into RIPv2. Router B is the boundary router, so the redistribution is configured on it, as shown in Figure 7-12.

Figure 7-12 *Redistribution Configured on Router B*

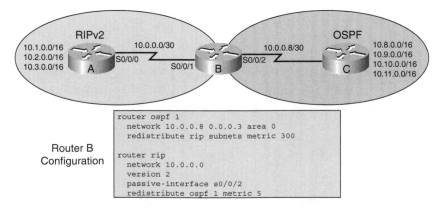

RIPv2 is redistributed into the OSPF process, and the metric is set using the **redistribute** command. A metric value of 300 is selected because it is a worse metric than any belonging to a native OSPF route.

Routes from OSPF process 1 are redistributed into the RIPv2 process with a metric of 5. A value of 5 is chosen because it is higher than any metric in the RIP network.

Figure 7-13 shows the routing tables of all three routers after redistribution is complete; Routers A and C now have routes to all the subnets that Router B learned from the other routing protocol. There is complete reachability; however, Routers A and C now have many more routes to keep track of than before. They also will be affected by any topology changes in the other routing domain.

Figure 7-13 *Routing Tables After Redistribution*

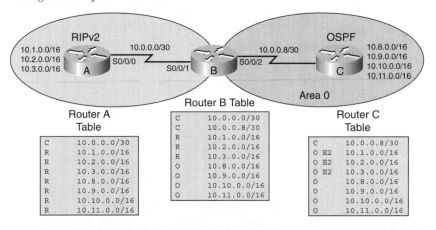

> **NOTE** Notice in Figure 7-13 that Router A does not see the 10.0.0.8/30 subnet, and Router C does not see the 10.0.0.0/30 subnet; these subnets are directly connected to Router B and therefore are not redistributed by the **redistribute rip** or **redistribute ospf** commands. You would need to add **redistribute connected** commands to Router B to redistribute these subnets.

Depending on the network requirements, you can increase efficiency by summarizing the routes before redistributing them. Remember that route summarization hides information, so if routers in the other autonomous systems are required to track topology changes within the entire network, route summarization should not be performed. A more typical case is that the routers need to recognize topology changes only within their own routing domains, so performing route summarization is appropriate.

> **NOTE** Remember from Chapter 2 that you must be careful when configuring route summarization. If a summarized route indicates that certain subnets can be reached via a router, when in fact those subnets are discontiguous or unreachable via that router, you may experience reachability problems.

If routes are summarized before redistribution, each router's routing tables are significantly smaller. Figure 7-14 shows the routing tables after summarization has been configured. Router B benefits the most; it now has only four routes to keep track of instead of nine. Router A has five routes instead of eight, and Router C has six routes to keep track of instead of eight. The configurations on Routers A and C are also shown in Figure 7-14.

For RIPv2 on Router A, the summarization command is configured on the interface connecting to Router B, interface S0/0/0. Interface S0/0/0 advertises the summary address instead of the individual subnets. (Note that when RIPv2 is configured, the subnet mask of the summary address must be greater than or equal to the default mask for the major classful network.) 10.0.0.0 255.252.0.0 summarizes the four subnets on Router A (including the 10.0.0.0/30 subnet).

Figure 7-14 *Routing Tables After Summarization*

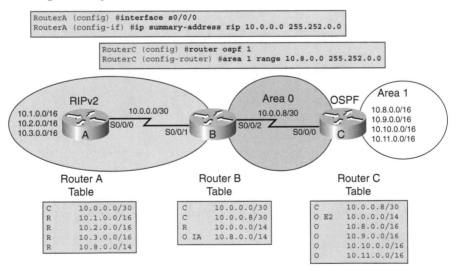

For OSPF, summarization must be configured on an area border router (ABR) or an ASBR. Therefore, OSPF area 1 is created to include the four subnets to be summarized. Router C becomes an ABR, and the summarization command is configured under the OSPF process on Router C. 10.8.0.0 255.252.0.0 summarizes the four subnets on Router C.

Controlling Routing Update Traffic

Routing updates compete with user data for bandwidth and router resources, yet routing updates are critical because they carry the information that routers need to make sound routing decisions. To ensure that the network operates efficiently, you must control and tune routing updates. Information about networks must be sent where it is needed and filtered from where it is not needed. No one type of route filter is appropriate for every situation; therefore, the more techniques you have at your disposal, the better your chance of having a smooth, well-run network.

This section discusses controlling the updates sent and received by dynamic routing protocols and controlling the routes redistributed into routing protocols. In many cases, you do not want to prevent all routing information from being advertised; you might want to block the advertisement of only certain routes. For example, you could use such a solution to prevent routing loops when implementing two-way route redistribution with dual redistribution points. The following are some ways to control or prevent dynamic routing updates from being generated:

- **Passive interface**—A passive interface prevents routing updates for the specified protocol from being sent through an interface.

- **Default routes**—A default route instructs the router that if it does not have a route for a given destination, it should send the packet to the default route. Therefore, no dynamic routing updates about the remote destinations are necessary.

- **Static routes**—A static route allows routes to remote destinations to be manually configured on the router. Therefore, no dynamic routing updates about the remote destinations are necessary.

- **Distribute lists**—A distribute list allows an access list to be applied to routing updates.

- **Route maps**—Route maps are complex access lists that allow conditions to be tested against a packet or route, and then actions taken to modify attributes of the packet or route.

- **Manipulating administrative distance**—The administrative distance of specific routes can be changed to indicate route selection preference.

Passive interfaces were discussed earlier in "The **passive-interface** Command" section. Static and default routes were discussed in Chapter 2; specifics related to controlling routing updates are explored in the next section, which is followed by a discussion of distribute lists, route maps, and manipulating administrative distances.

Static and Default Routes

Static routes are routes that you manually configure on a router. Static routes are used most often to do the following:

■ Define specific routes to use when two autonomous systems must exchange routing information, rather than having entire routing tables exchanged.

■ Define routes to destinations over a WAN link to eliminate the need for a dynamic routing protocol—that is, when you do not want routing updates to enable or cross the link.

When configuring static routes, keep in mind the following considerations:

■ When using static routes instead of dynamic routing updates, all participating routers must have static routes defined so that they can reach remote networks. Static route entries must be defined for all routes for which a router is responsible. To reduce the number of static route entries, you can define a default static route—for example, **ip route 0.0.0.0 0.0.0.0 S0/0/1**.

■ If you want a router to advertise a static route in a routing protocol, you might need to redistribute it.

You can configure default routes for routing protocols on Cisco routers. For example, when you create a default route on a router running RIP, the router advertises an address of 0.0.0.0. When a router receives this default route, it forwards any packets destined for a destination that does not appear in its routing table to the default route you configured.

You can also configure a default route by using the **ip default-network** *network-number* global configuration command. Figure 7-15 and Example 7-8 and Example 7-9 demonstrate the use of this command on a router running RIP. With the **ip default-network** command, you designate an actual network currently available in the routing table as the default path to use.

Figure 7-15 *Using the* **ip default-network** *Command*

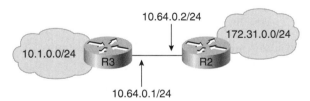

In Example 7-8, the R2 router has a directly connected interface onto the network specified in the **ip default-network** *network-number* command. RIP generates (sources) a default route, which appears as a 0.0.0.0 0.0.0.0 route to its RIP neighbor routers, as shown in Example 7-9 for R3.

Example 7-8 *Configuration on Router R2 in Figure 7-15*

```
R2#show run
<output omitted>
router rip
 network 10.0.0.0
 network 172.31.0.0
!
ip classless
ip default-network 10.0.0.0
```

Example 7-9 *Routing Table on R3 in Figure 7-15*

```
R3#show ip route
<output omitted>
Gateway of last resort is 10.64.0.2 to network 0.0.0.0
<Output Omitted>
R    172.31.0.0/16 [120/1] via 10.64.0.2, 00:00:16, FastEthernet0/0
R*   0.0.0.0/0 [120/1] via 10.64.0.2, 00:00:05, FastEthernet0/0
```

KEY POINT

Default Routes and Routing Protocols

The **ip default-network** command is used to distribute default route information to *other* routers. For RIP, this command provides no functionality for the router on which it is configured. Other protocols behave differently than RIP with the **ip default-network** and **ip route 0.0.0.0 0.0.0.0** commands.

For example, EIGRP does not redistribute the 0.0.0.0 0.0.0.0 default route by default. However, if the **network 0.0.0.0** command is added to the EIGRP configuration, it redistributes a default route as a result of the **ip route 0.0.0.0 0.0.0.0** *interface* command (but not as a result of the **ip route 0.0.0.0 0.0.0.0** *address* or **ip default-network** commands). Refer to the Cisco IOS documentation for further information.

ip default-network and Other IP Commands

The **ip default-network** command is used when routers do not know how to get to the outside world. This command is configured on the router that connects to the outside world and goes through a different major network to reach the outside world. If your environment is all one major network address, you probably would not want to use the **ip default-network** command, but rather a static route to 0.0.0.0 via a border router.

The **ip route 0.0.0.0 0.0.0.0** command is used on routers with IP routing enabled and that point to the outside world, for example for Internet connectivity. This route is advertised as the "gateway of last resort" if running RIP. The router that is directly connected to the border of the outside world is the preferred router, with the static route pointing to 0.0.0.0.

The **ip default-gateway** command is used on routers or communication servers that have IP routing turned off. The router or communication server acts just like a host on the network.

Using Distribute Lists to Control Routing Updates

Another way to control routing updates is to use a distribute list.

<table>
<tr><td>

**KEY
POINT**

</td><td>

Distribute List

A distribute list allows the application of an access list to routing updates.

</td></tr>
</table>

Access lists are usually associated with interfaces and are usually used to control *user* traffic. However, routers can have many interfaces, and route information can also be obtained through route redistribution, which does not involve a specific interface. In addition, access lists do not affect traffic originated by the router, so applying one on an interface has no effect on outgoing routing advertisements. However, when you configure an access list for a distribute list, routing updates can be controlled, no matter what their source is.

Access lists are configured in global configuration mode; the associated distribute list is configured under the routing protocol process. The access list should permit the networks that you want advertised or redistributed and deny the networks that you want to remain hidden. The router then applies the access list to routing updates for that protocol. Options in the **distribute-list** command allow updates to be filtered based on factors including the following:

■   Incoming interface

■   Outgoing interface

■   Redistribution from another routing protocol

Using a distribute list gives the administrator great flexibility in determining just which routes will be permitted and which will be denied.

Distribute List Processing

Figure 7-16 shows the general process that a router uses when filtering routing updates using a distribute list that is based on the incoming or outgoing interface. The process includes the following steps:

Step 1   The router receives a routing update or prepares to send an update about one or more networks.

Step 2   The router looks at the interface involved with the action: the interface on which an incoming update has arrived, or, for an update that must be advertised, the interface out of which it should be advertised.

Step 3   The router determines if a filter (distribute list) is associated with the interface.

Step 4   If a filter (distribute list) is not associated with the interface, the packet is processed normally.

Step 5   If a filter (distribute list) is associated with the interface, the router scans the access list referenced by the distribute list for a match for the given routing update.

Step 6   If there is a match in the access list, the route entry is processed as configured; it is either permitted or denied by the matching access list statement.

Step 7   If no match is found in the access list, the implicit **deny any** at the end of the access list causes the route entry to be dropped.

Figure 7-16   *Route Filters Using a Distribute List*

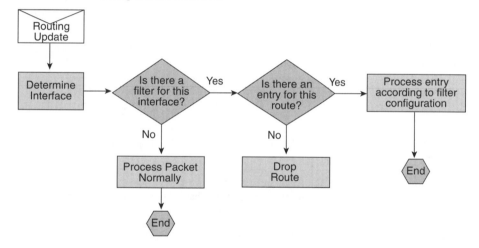

Configuring Distribute Lists

You can filter routing update traffic for any protocol by defining an access list and applying it to a specific routing protocol using the **distribute-list** command. A distribute list enables the filtering of routing updates coming into or out of a specific interface from neighboring routers using the same routing protocol. A distribute list also allows the filtering of routes redistributed from other routing protocols or sources. To configure a distribute list, follow this procedure:

Step 1   Identify the network addresses of the routes you want to filter, and create an access list.

Step 2   Determine whether you want to filter traffic on an incoming interface, traffic on an outgoing interface, or routes being redistributed from another routing source.

Step 3 Use the **distribute-list** {*access-list-number* | *name*} **out** [*interface-name* | *routing-process* [*routing-process parameter*]] router configuration command to assign the access list to filter outgoing routing updates. Table 7-9 explains this command. The **distribute-list out** command cannot be used with link-state routing protocols to block outbound link-state advertisements (LSAs) on an interface.

Step 4 Use the **distribute-list** {*access-list-number* | *name*} [**route-map** *map-tag*] **in** [*interface-type interface-number*] router configuration command to assign the access list to filter routing updates coming in through an interface. (This command also allows the use of a route map instead of an access list for OSPF.) Table 7-10 explains this command. This command prevents most routing protocols from placing the filtered routes in their database; when this command is used with OSPF, the routes are placed in the database, but not the routing table.

Table 7-9 **distribute-list out** *Command*

Parameter	Description
access-list-number	*name*	Specifies the standard access list number or name.
out	Applies the access list to outgoing routing updates.
interface-name	(Optional) Specifies the name of the interface out of which updates are filtered.
routing-process	(Optional) Specifies the name of the routing process, or the keyword **static** or **connected**, that is being redistributed and from which updates are filtered.
routing-process parameter	(Optional) Specifies a routing process parameter, such as the autonomous system number of the routing process.

NOTE OSPF outgoing updates cannot be filtered out of an interface.

Table 7-10 **distribute-list in** *Command*

Parameter	Description
access-list-number	*name*	Specifies the standard access list number or name.
map-tag	(Optional) Specifies the name of the route map that defines which networks are to be installed in the routing table and which are to be filtered from the routing table. This argument is supported by OSPF only.

Table 7-10   **distribute-list in** *Command (Continued)*

Parameter	Description
in	Applies the access list to incoming routing updates.
interface-type interface-number	(Optional) Specifies the interface type and number from which updates are filtered.

KEY POINT

Distribute List in Versus out

The **distribute-list out** command filters updates going *out of* the interface or routing protocol specified in the command, *into* the routing process under which it is configured.

The **distribute-list in** command filters updates going *into* the interface specified in the command, *into* the routing process under which it is configured.

IP Route Filtering with Distribution List Configuration Example

Figure 7-17 shows the topology of a WAN in which network 10.0.0.0 must be hidden from the devices in network 192.168.5.0.

Figure 7-17   *Network 10.0.0.0 Needs to Be Hidden from Network 192.168.5.0*

Example 7-10 is the configuration of Router B in Figure 7-17. In this example, the **distribute-list out** command applies access list 7 to packets going out interface Serial 0/0/0. The access list allows only routing information about network 172.16.0.0 to be distributed out Router B's Serial 0/0/0 interface. The implicit **deny any** at the end of the access list prevents updates about any other networks from being advertised. As a result, network 10.0.0.0 is hidden.

Example 7-10   *Filtering Out Network 10.0.0.0 on Router B in Figure 7-17*

```
router eigrp 1
  network 172.16.0.0
  network 192.168.5.0
  distribute-list 7 out Serial0/0/0
!
access-list 7 permit 172.16.0.0 0.0.255.255
```

NOTE   Another way to achieve the filtering of network 10.0.0.0 in this example would be to deny network 10.0.0.0 and permit any other networks. This method would be particularly efficient if the routing information contained multiple networks but only network 10.0.0.0 needed filtering.

Controlling Redistribution with Distribute Lists

With mutual redistribution, using a distribute list helps prevent route feedback and routing loops. Route feedback occurs when routes originally learned from one routing protocol are redistributed back into that protocol. Figure 7-18 illustrates an example in which redistribution is configured both ways between RIPv2 and OSPF (two-way redistribution). The configuration on Router B is shown in Example 7-11.

Figure 7-18   *Router B Controls Redistribution*

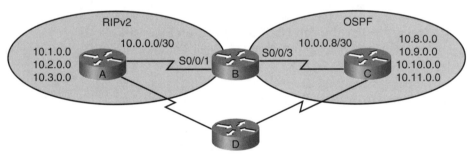

Example 7-11   *Configuration of Router B in Figure 7-18*

```
router ospf 1
  network 10.0.0.8 0.0.0.3 area 0
  redistribute rip subnets
  distribute-list 2 out rip

router rip
  network 10.0.0.0
  version 2
  passive-interface Serial0/0/3
  redistribute ospf 1 metric 5
  distribute-list 3 out ospf 1

access-list 2 deny 10.8.0.0 0.3.255.255
access-list 2 permit any

access-list 3 permit 10.9.0.0
```

Router B redistributes networks 10.1.0.0 to 10.3.0.0 from RIPv2 into OSPF. Route feedback could occur if Router D, another redistribution point, is configured, and OSPF on Router D then redistributes those same networks back into RIP. Router D's configuration would be similar to Router B's configuration.

Therefore, the configuration in Example 7-11 shows a distribute list configuration that prevents route feedback. Access list 2 denies the original OSPF routes and permits all others; the distribute list configured under OSPF refers to this access list. The result is that networks 10.8.0.0 to 10.11.0.0, originated by OSPF, are not redistributed back into OSPF from RIPv2. All other routes are redistributed into OSPF. Redistribution from OSPF into RIPv2 is filtered with access list 3; note that this is a more restrictive filter that permits only one route, 10.9.0.0, to be redistributed into RIPv2.

A distribute list hides network information, which could be considered a drawback in some circumstances. For example, in a network with redundant paths, a distribute list might permit routing updates for only specific paths, to avoid routing loops. In this case, other routers in the network might not know about the other ways to reach the filtered networks, so if the primary path goes down, the backup paths are not used because the rest of the network does not know they exist. When redundant paths exist, you should use other techniques, such as manipulating the administrative distance or metric, instead of distribute lists, to enable the use of an alternative path (with a worse administrative distance or metric) when the primary path goes down.

Using Route Maps to Control Routing Updates

Route maps provide another technique to manipulate and control routing protocol updates. Route maps may be used for a variety of purposes; after describing route map applications and operation, this section explores the use of route maps as a tool to filter and manipulate routing updates. All the IP routing protocols can use route maps for redistribution filtering.

Route Map Applications

Network administrators use route maps for a variety of purposes. Several of the more common applications for route maps are as follows:

- **Route filtering during redistribution**—Redistribution nearly always requires some amount of route filtering. Although distribute lists can be used for this purpose, route maps offer the added benefit of manipulating routing metrics through the use of **set** commands.

- **Policy-based routing (PBR)**—Route maps can be used to match source and destination addresses, protocol types, and end-user applications. When a match occurs, a **set** command can be used to define the interface or next-hop address to which the packet should be sent. PBR allows the operator to define routing policy other than basic destination-based routing using the routing table. PBR is discussed in Appendix D, "Manipulating Routing Updates Supplement."

- **NAT**—Route maps can better control which private addresses are translated to public addresses. Using a route map with NAT also provides more detailed **show** commands that describe the address-translation process.

- **BGP**—Route maps are the primary tools for implementing BGP policy. Network administrators assign route maps to specific BGP sessions (neighbors) to control which routes are allowed to flow in and out of the BGP process. In addition to filtering, route maps provide sophisticated manipulation of BGP path attributes. Route maps for BGP are discussed in Chapter 8, "Configuring the Border Gateway Protocol."

Understanding Route Maps

Route maps are complex access lists that allow some conditions to be tested against the packet or route in question using **match** commands. If the conditions match, some actions can be taken to modify attributes of the packet or route; these actions are specified by **set** commands.

A collection of route map statements that have the same route map name are considered one route map. Within a route map, each route map statement is numbered and therefore can be edited individually.

The statements in a route map correspond to the lines of an access list. Specifying the match conditions in a route map is similar in concept to specifying the source and destination addresses and masks in an access list.

KEY POINT

Route Maps Versus Access Lists

One big difference between route maps and access lists is that route maps can modify the packet or route by using **set** commands.

The **route-map** *map-tag* [**permit** | **deny**] [*sequence-number*] global configuration command can be used to define a route map. This command is explained in detail in Table 7-11.

Table 7-11 **route-map** *Command*

Parameter	Description
map-tag	Name of the route map.
permit	**deny**	(Optional) A parameter that specifies the action to be taken if the route map match conditions are met; the meaning of **permit** or **deny** is dependent on how the route map is used.
sequence-number	(Optional) A sequence number that indicates the position that a new route map statement will have in the list of route map statements already configured with the same name.

The default for the **route-map** command is **permit**, with a *sequence-number* of 10.

Route Map Sequence Numbering

If you leave out the sequence number when configuring all statements for the same route map name, the router will assume that you are editing and adding to the first statement, sequence number 10. Route map sequence numbers do not automatically increment!

A route map may be made up of multiple route map statements. The statements are processed top-down, similar to an access list. The first match found for a route is applied. The sequence number is also used for inserting or deleting specific route map statements in a specific place in the route map.

The **match** *condition* route map configuration commands are used to define the conditions to be checked. The **set** *condition* route map configuration commands are used to define the actions to be followed if there is a match and the action to be taken is permit. (The consequences of a deny action depend on how the route map is being used.)

A single **match** statement may contain multiple conditions. At least one condition in the **match** statement must be true for that **match** statement to be considered a match (this is a logical OR operation). A route map statement may contain multiple **match** statements. All **match** statements in the route map statement must be considered true for the route map statement to be considered matched. (This is a logical AND operation.)

Route Map Match Conditions

Only one condition listed on the same **match** statement must match for the entire statement to be considered a match.

However, all **match** statements within a route map statement must match for the route map to be considered matched.

For example, IP standard or extended access lists can be used to establish match criteria using the **match ip address** {*access-list-number* | *name*} [*...access-list-number* | *name*] route map configuration command. If multiple access lists are specified, matching any one results in a match. A standard IP access list can be used to specify match criteria for a packet's source address; extended access lists can be used to specify match criteria based on source and destination addresses, application, protocol type, type of service (ToS), and precedence.

The sequence number specifies the order in which conditions are checked. For example, if two statements in a route map are named MYMAP, one with sequence 10 and the other with sequence 20, sequence 10 is checked first. If the match conditions in sequence 10 are not met, sequence 20 is checked.

Like an access list, an implicit deny any appears at the end of a route map. The consequences of this deny depend on how the route map is being used.

Another way to explain how a route map works is to use a simple example and see how a router would interpret it. Example 7-12 shows a sample route map configuration. (Note that on a router, all the conditions and actions shown would be replaced with specific conditions and actions, depending on the exact **match** and **set** commands used.)

Example 7-12 *Demonstration of* **route-map** *Command*

```
route-map demo permit 10
  match x y z
  match a
  set b
  set c
route-map demo permit 20
  match q
  set r
route-map demo permit 30
```

The route map named **demo** in Example 7-12 is interpreted as follows:

> If {(x or y or z) and (a) match} then {set b and c}
> Else
> If q matches then set r
> Else
> Set nothing

Configuring Route Maps

The **redistribute** commands discussed in the "Configuring Redistribution" section all have a **route-map** option with a *map-tag* parameter. This parameter refers to a route map configured with the **route-map** *map-tag* [**permit** | **deny**] [*sequence-number*] global configuration command, as described earlier in Table 7-11.

KEY POINT

permit and deny For Redistribution

When used with a **redistribute** command, a route-map statement with **permit** indicates that the matched route is to be redistributed, while a **route-map** statement with **deny** indicates that the matched route is not to be redistributed.

The **match** *condition* route map configuration commands are used to define the conditions to be checked. Table 7-12 lists some of the variety of match criteria that can be defined; some of these commands are used for BGP policy, some for PBR, and some for redistribution filtering.

Table 7-12   match *Commands*

Command	Description
match ip address {*access-list-number* | *name*} [*...access-list-number* | *name*]	Matches any routes that have a network number that is permitted by a standard or extended access list. Multiple access lists can be specified; if multiple access lists are specified, matching any one results in a match.
match length *min max*	Matches based on a packet's Layer 3 length.
match interface *type number*	Matches any routes that have the next hop out of one of the interfaces specified.
match ip next-hop {*access-list-number* | *access-list-name*} [*...access-list-number* | *...access-list-name*]	Matches any routes that have a next-hop router address permitted by one of the access lists specified.
match ip route-source {*access-list-number* | *access-list-name*} [*...access-list-number* | *...access-list-name*]	Matches routes that have been advertised by routers and access servers that have an address permitted by one of the access lists specified.
match metric *metric-value*	Matches routes that have the metric specified.
match route-type [**external** | **internal** | **level-1** | **level-2** | **local**]	Matches routes of the specified type.
match community {*list-number* | *list-name*}	Matches a BGP community.
match tag *tag-value*	Matches based on the tag of a route.

The **set** *condition* route map configuration commands change or add characteristics, such as metrics, to any routes that have met a match criterion and the action to be taken is permit. (The consequences of a deny action depend on how the route map is being used.) Table 7-13 lists some of the variety of **set** commands that are available. Not all the **set** commands listed here are used for redistribution purposes; the table includes commands for BGP and PBR.

Table 7-13   set *Commands*

Command	Description
set metric *metric-value*	Sets the metric value for a routing protocol.
set metric-type [**type-1** | **type-2** | **internal** | **external**]	Sets the metric type for the destination routing protocol.
set default interface *type number* [*...type number*]	Indicates where to send output packets that pass a match clause of a route map for policy routing and for which the Cisco IOS Software has no explicit route to the destination.

continues

Table 7-13 set *Commands (Continued)*

Command	Description
set interface *type number* [...*type number*]	Indicates where to send output packets that pass a match clause of a route map for policy routing.
set ip default next-hop *ip-address* [...*ip-address*]	Indicates where to send output packets that pass a match clause of a route map for policy routing and for which the Cisco IOS Software has no explicit route to the destination.
set ip next-hop *ip-address* [...*ip-address*]	Indicates where to send output packets that pass a match clause of a route map for policy routing.
set level [**level-1** | **level-2** | **stub-area** | **backbone**]	Indicates at what level or type of area to import routes into (for IS-IS and OSPF routes).
set as-path {**tag** | **prepend** *as-path-string*}	Modifies an autonomous system path for BGP routes.
set automatic-tag	Automatically computes the BGP tag value.
set community {*community-number* [**additive**] [*well-known-community*] | **none**}	Sets the BGP communities attribute.
set local-preference *bgp-path-attributes*	Specifies a local preference value for the BGP autonomous system path.
set weight *bgp-weight*	Specifies the BGP weight value.
set origin *bgp-origin-code*	Specifies the BGP origin code.
set tag	Specifies the tag value for destination routing protocol.

Using Route Maps with Redistribution

Example 7-13 illustrates a route map being used to redistribute RIPv1 into OSPF 10. The route map, called redis-rip, is used in the **redistribute rip route-map redis-rip subnets** command under the OSPF process.

Example 7-13 *Redistributing RIPv1 into OSPF Using a Route Map*

```
router ospf 10
  redistribute rip route-map redis-rip subnets

route-map redis-rip permit 10
  match ip address 23 29
  set metric 500
  set metric-type type-1
```

Example 7-13 *Redistributing RIPv1 into OSPF Using a Route Map (Continued)*

```
route-map redis-rip deny 20
  match ip address 37

route-map redis-rip permit 30
  set metric 5000
  set metric-type type-2

access-list 23 permit 10.1.0.0 0.0.255.255
access-list 29 permit 172.16.1.0 0.0.0.255
access-list 37 permit 10.0.0.0 0.255.255.255
```

Sequence number 10 of the route map is looking for an IP address match in access list 23 or access list 29. Routes 10.1.0.0/16 and 172.16.1.0/24 match these lists. If a match is found, the router redistributes the route into OSPF with a cost metric of 500 and sets the new OSPF route to external type 1.

If there is no match to sequence number 10, sequence number 20 is checked. If there is a match in access list 37 (10.0.0.0/8), that route is not redistributed into OSPF, because sequence number 20 specifies **deny**.

If there is no match to sequence number 20, sequence number 30 is checked. Because sequence number 30 is a **permit** and there is no match criterion, all remaining routes are redistributed into OSPF with a cost metric of 5000 and an external metric of type 2.

Route Maps to Avoid Route Feedback

There is a possibility that routing feedback might cause suboptimal routing or a routing loop when routes are redistributed at more than one router. Figure 7-19 illustrates a network in which mutual redistribution (redistribution in both directions) is configured on Routers A and B. To prevent redistribution feedback loops, route maps are configured on both routers.

The potential for routing feedback becomes apparent if you follow the advertisements for a specific network before route maps are configured. For example, RIPv2 on Router C advertises network 192.168.1.0. Routers A and B redistribute the network into OSPF. OSPF then advertises the route to its neighbor OSPF routers as an OSPF external route. The route passes through the OSPF autonomous system and eventually makes its way back to the other edge router. Router B (or A) then redistributes 192.168.1.0 from OSPF back into the original RIPv2 network; this is a routing feedback loop.

Figure 7-19 *Route Maps Can Help Avoid Route Feedback Loops*

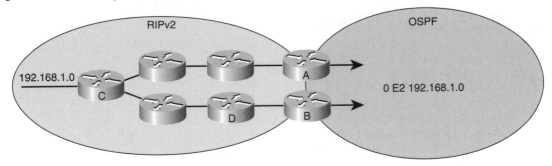

To prevent the routing feedback loop, a route map has been applied to Routers A and B, as shown in Example 7-14. The **route-map** statement with sequence number 10 refers to access list 1, which matches the original RIPv2 network. (The access list should include all networks in the RIPv2 domain.) This route map statement is a **deny**, so the 192.168.1.0 route is denied from being redistributed back into RIPv2. If the route does not match sequence number 10, the router then checks sequence number 20, which is an empty **permit** statement. This statement matches all routes, so all other routes are redistributed into RIP.

Example 7-14 *Partial Configuration on Routers A and B in Figure 7-19*

```
access-list 1 permit 192.168.1.0 0.0.0.255

route-map pacific deny 10
  match ip address 1

route-map pacific permit 20

router rip
  redistribute ospf 10 route-map pacific

router ospf 10
  redistribute rip subnets
```

Using Administrative Distance to Influence the Route-Selection Process

Multiple sources of routing information may be active at the same time, including static routes and routing protocols that use various methods of operation and metrics. In this situation, several sources of information may supply ambiguous next-hop addresses for a particular network, so routers must identify which routing information source is the most trustworthy and reliable. When routes are redistributed between two different methods of resolving the best path, important information may be lost—namely, the relative metrics of the routes—so route selection is sometimes confusing. One approach for correcting wayward choices is to control the administrative distance to indicate route selection preference and ensure that route selection is unambiguous. This approach does not always guarantee the *best* route is selected, only that route selection will be consistent.

You should change the default administrative distance carefully and by considering the network's specific requirements.

Selecting Routes with Administrative Distance

Recall that administrative distance is a way of ranking the trustworthiness of the sources of routing information. Administrative distance is expressed as an integer from 0 to 255, as shown earlier in Table 7-1; lower values indicate greater trustworthiness or believability.

For example, in Figure 7-20, R1 chooses different paths to get to the 10.0.0.0/8 network on R6, depending on the routing protocol configured. If RIP, IS-IS, OSPF, and EIGRP are all configured on all routers in this network, the protocols make the following path decisions:

- RIP, with an administrative distance of 120, chooses the R1 to R4 to R6 path based on hop count (two hops versus four hops the other way).

- IS-IS, with an administrative distance of 115 and using the default metric of 10 for each interface, also chooses the R1 to R4 to R6 path based on a metric of 20 versus 40 the other way. You can modify the IS-IS metrics to portray a more accurate view of the network. IS-IS is considered more trustworthy than RIP because it is a link-state routing protocol with fast convergence, so its routing information is more complete and up to date.

- OSPF, with an administrative distance of 110, typically calculates the default metric as 100 Mbps divided by the interface bandwidth, where the interface bandwidth is the speed of each link in Mbps. The path R1 to R4 to R6 default metric is (100 Mbps / 64 Kbps) + (100 Mbps / 1.544 Mbps) = (100 Mbps / .064 Mbps) + (100 Mbps / 1.544 Mbps) = (1562 + 64) = 1626. The R1 to R2 to R3 to R5 to R6 path default metric is 64 + 64 + 64 + 64 = 256. Therefore, OSPF chooses the R1 to R2 to R3 to R5 to R6 path. Although OSPF and IS-IS are both link-state routing protocols that converge quickly, OSPF is considered more trustworthy than IS-IS because OSPF bases its default metric on bandwidth and therefore is more likely to pick a faster path.

NOTE   By default, the Cisco routers calculate the OSPF cost using the formula 100 Mbps / bandwidth. However, this formula is based on a maximum bandwidth of 100 Mbps, resulting in a cost of 1. If you have faster interfaces, you might want to recalibrate the cost of 1 to a higher bandwidth. Chapter 5, "Advanced Open Shortest Path First Protocol Configuration," provides details about OSPF cost calculations.

- EIGRP, with an administrative distance of 90, calculates the default metric as BW + delay, where BW is [(10^7 / least bandwidth in the path in kbps) * 256], and delay is cumulative across the path, in tens of microseconds, multiplied by 256. Assuming a uniform link delay of 100 tens of microseconds, the R1 to R4 to R6 path default metric is ((10^7 / 64) * 256) + (200 * 256) = 40,051,200. The R1 to R2 to R3 to R5 to R6 path default metric is ((10^7 / 1544) * 256) + (400 * 256) = 1,760,431.

Therefore, EIGRP chooses the R1 to R2 to R3 to R5 to R6 path. Although EIGRP and OSPF routing protocols both converge quickly and consider bandwidth, EIGRP is considered more trustworthy than OSPF because EIGRP takes more information into account in its calculation.

Figure 7-20 *Path Selected Through a Network Depends on the Routing Protocols Configured*

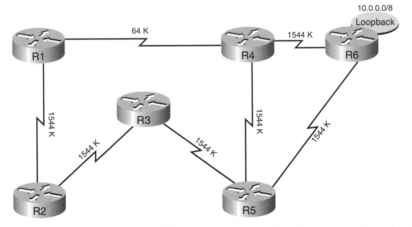

Because EIGRP has the lowest administrative distance of the four protocols, only the EIGRP path to 10.0.0.0/8 is put into the routing table.

NOTE The administrative distance affects only the choice of path for *identical* IP routes—in other words, for routes with the same prefix and mask. For example, because OSPF does not summarize by default, and all the other protocols do, the protocols might potentially provide different routing information. In this example, if OSPF advertised a route to 10.1.0.0/16 that was not advertised by any of the other protocols (because they automatically summarized to 10.0.0.0/8), the 10.1.0.0/16 route would be in the routing tables from OSPF, and the 10.0.0.0/8 route would be in the routing tables from EIGRP. As mentioned in Chapter 2, routers use the longest prefix match in the routing table if more than one entry in the routing table matches a particular destination. In this example, packets for 10.1.1.2 would be sent via the OSPF-learned route, while packets for 10.2.1.3 would be sent via the EIGRP-learned route.

Typically, multiple routing protocols are run only on the boundary routers in a network, not on *all* routers, so this situation should not be common.

Modifying Administrative Distance

In some cases, you will find that a router selects a suboptimal path because it believes a routing protocol that actually has a poorer route, because it has a better administrative distance. One way to make sure that routes from the desired routing protocol are selected is to assign a higher administrative distance to the route(s) from the undesired routing protocol.

> **NOTE**   Routes with a distance of 255 are not installed in the routing table.

For all protocols except EIGRP and BGP, use the **distance** *administrative-distance* [*address wildcard-mask* [*ip-standard- list*] [*ip-extended-list*]] router configuration command, as explained in Table 7-14, to change the default administrative distances.

Table 7-14   distance *Command (Except for EIGRP and BGP)*

Parameter	Description
administrative-distance	Sets the administrative distance, an integer from 10 to 255. (The values 0 to 9 are reserved for internal use and should not be used, even though values from 1 to 9 can be configured.)
address	(Optional) Specifies the IP address; this allows filtering of networks according to the IP address of the router supplying the routing information.
wildcard-mask	(Optional) Specifies the wildcard mask used to interpret the IP address. A bit set to 1 in the *wildcard-mask* argument instructs the software to ignore the corresponding bit in the *address* value. Use an address/mask of 0.0.0.0 255.255.255.255 to match any IP address (any source router supplying the routing information).
ip-standard-list *ip-extended-list*	(Optional) The number or name of a standard or extended access list to be applied to the incoming routing updates. Allows filtering of the networks being advertised.

> **NOTE**   The *ip-standard-list* and *ip-extended-list* parameters were added in Cisco IOS Release 12.0.

For EIGRP, use the **distance eigrp** *internal-distance external-distance* router configuration command, as explained in Table 7-15. By default, natively learned routes have an administrative distance of 90, but external routes have an administrative distance of 170.

Table 7-15 *distance eigrp* *Command*

Parameter	Description
internal-distance	Specifies the administrative distance for EIGRP internal routes. Internal routes are those that are learned from another entity within the same EIGRP autonomous system. The distance can be a value from 1 to 255; the default is 90.
external-distance	Specifies the administrative distance for EIGRP external routes. External routes are those for which the best path is learned from a neighbor external to the EIGRP autonomous system. The distance can be a value from 1 to 255; the default is 170.

For BGP, use the **distance bgp** *external-distance internal-distance local-distance* router configuration command to change the administrative distances, as explained in Table 7-16.

Table 7-16 *distance bgp* *Command*

Parameter	Description
external-distance	Specifies the administrative distance for BGP external routes. External routes are routes for which the best path is learned from a neighbor external to the autonomous system. Acceptable values are from 1 to 255. The default is 20.
internal-distance	Specifies the administrative distance for BGP internal routes. Internal routes are learned from another BGP entity within the same autonomous system. Acceptable values are from 1 to 255. The default is 200.
local-distance	Specifies the administrative distance for BGP local routes. Local routes are networks that are listed with a **network** router configuration command, often as back doors, for that router or for networks that are redistributed from another process. Acceptable values are from 1 to 255. The default is 200.

For OSPF, you can also use the **distance ospf** {[**intra-area** *dist1*] [**inter-area** *dist2*] [**external** *dist3*]} router configuration command to define the OSPF administrative distances based on route type, as explained in Table 7-17.

Table 7-17 *distance ospf* *Command*

Parameter	Description
dist1	(Optional) Specifies the administrative distance for all OSPF routes within an area. Acceptable values are from 1 to 255. The default is 110.
dist2	(Optional) Specifies the administrative distance for all OSPF routes from one area to another area. Acceptable values are from 1 to 255. The default is 110.
dist3	(Optional) Specifies the administrative distance for all routes from other routing domains, learned by redistribution. Acceptable values are from 1 to 255. The default is 110.

An Example of Redistribution Using Administrative Distance

Figure 7-21 illustrates a network using multiple routing protocols, RIPv2 and OSPF. There are a number of ways to correct path-selection problems in a redistribution environment. The purpose of this example is to show how a problem can occur, where it appears, and one possible way to resolve it.

Recall that OSPF is by default considered more believable than RIPv2 because it has an administrative distance of 110 and RIPv2 has an administrative distance of 120. For example, if a boundary router (P3R1 or P3R2) learns about network 10.3.3.0 via RIPv2 and also via OSPF, the OSPF route is inserted into the routing table. This route is used because OSPF has a lower administrative distance than RIPv2, even though the path via OSPF might be the longer (worse) path.

Example 7-15 and Example 7-16 illustrate the configurations for the P3R1 and P3R2 routers. These configurations redistribute RIPv2 into OSPF and OSPF into RIPv2 on both routers.

Figure 7-21 *Sample Redistribution Network Topology*

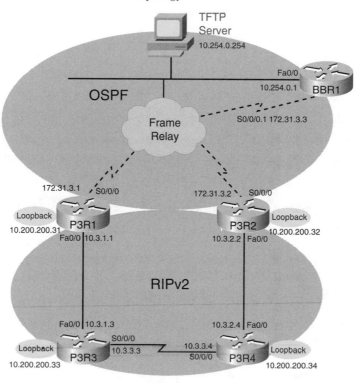

Example 7-15 *Configuration of Redistribution on Router P3R1 in Figure 7-21*

```
hostname P3R1
!
router ospf 1
 redistribute rip metric 10000 metric-type 1 subnets
 network 172.31.0.0 0.0.255.255 area 0
!
router rip
 version 2
 redistribute ospf 1 metric 5
 network 10.0.0.0
 no auto-summary
```

Example 7-16 *Configuration of Redistribution on Router P3R2 in Figure 7-21*

```
hostname P3R2
!
router ospf 1
 redistribute rip metric 10000 metric-type 1 subnets
 network 172.31.0.0 0.0.255.255 area 0
!
router rip
 version 2
 redistribute ospf 1 metric 5
 network 10.0.0.0
 no auto-summary
```

The RIPv2 routes redistributed into OSPF have an OSPF seed metric of 10,000 to make these routes less preferred than native OSPF routes and to protect against route feedback. The **redistribute** command also sets the metric type to 1 (external type 1) so that the route metrics continue to accrue. The routers also redistribute subnet information.

The OSPF routes redistributed into RIPv2 have a RIP seed metric of five hops to also protect against route feedback.

Example 7-17 displays the routing table on the P3R2 router after redistribution has occurred. Even though the P3R2 router learns RIPv2 and OSPF routes, it lists only OSPF routes in the routing table, because they have a lower administrative distance.

Example 7-17 *Routing Table on Router P3R2 in Figure 7-21 with Redistribution Configured*

```
P3R2#show ip route
<output omitted>
Gateway of last resort is not set

     172.31.0.0/24 is subnetted, 1 subnet
```

Example 7-17 *Routing Table on Router P3R2 in Figure 7-21 with Redistribution Configured (Continued)*

```
C        172.31.3.0/24 is directly connected, Serial0/0/0
         10.0.0.0/8 is variably subnetted, 8 subnets, 2 masks
O E1     10.3.1.0/24 [110/10781] via 172.31.3.1, 00:09:47, Serial0/0/0
O E1     10.3.3.0/24 [110/10781] via 172.31.3.1, 00:04:51, Serial0/0/0
C        10.3.2.0/24 is directly connected, FastEthernet0/0
O E1     10.200.200.31/32 [110/10781] via 172.31.3.1, 00:09:48, Serial0/0/0
O E1     10.200.200.34/32 [110/10781] via 172.31.3.1, 00:04:52, Serial0/0/0
C        10.200.200.32/32 is directly connected, Loopback0
O E1     10.200.200.33/32 [110/10781] via 172.31.3.1, 00:04:52, Serial0/0/0
O E2     10.254.0.0/24 [110/50] via 172.31.3.3, 00:09:48, Serial0/0/0
P3R2#
```

The first edge router on which redistribution is configured, P3R1 in this case, has a routing table that contains both OSPF and RIPv2 routes, as you would expect. The routers in the OSPF domain learn about the routes from the RIPv2 domain via redistribution; they then advertise these RIPv2 routes via OSPF routes to their neighboring routers. Thus, the second edge router, P3R2, receives information about the RIPv2 domain routes (also called the native RIPv2 routes) from both OSPF and RIPv2. P3R2 prefers the OSPF routes because OSPF has a lower administrative distance; therefore, none of the RIPv2 routes appears in the P3R2 routing table.

Refer to Figure 7-21 to trace some of the routes. The redistribution has resulted in suboptimal paths to many of the networks. For instance, 10.200.200.34 is a loopback interface on router P3R4. P3R4 is directly attached to P3R2; however, from P3R2 the OSPF path to that loopback interface goes through P3R1, and then P3R3, and then P3R4 before it reaches its destination. The OSPF path taken is actually a longer (worse) path than the more direct RIPv2 path.

You can change the administrative distance of the redistributed RIPv2 routes to ensure that the boundary routers select the native RIPv2 routes. Example 7-18 and Example 7-19 show the configurations on the P3R1 and P3R2 routers. The **distance** command changes the administrative distance of the OSPF routes to the networks that match access list 64 to 125 (from 110). Table 7-18 describes some of the command parameters used in the example configurations.

Example 7-18 *Configuration to Change the Administrative Distance on Router P3R1 in Figure 7-21*

```
hostname P3R1
!
router ospf 1
 redistribute rip metric 10000 metric-type 1 subnets
 network 172.31.0.0 0.0.255.255 area 0
 distance 125 0.0.0.0 255.255.255.255 64
!
router rip
 version 2
```

Example 7-18 *Configuration to Change the Administrative Distance on Router P3R1 in Figure 7-21 (Continued)*

```
 redistribute ospf 1 metric 5
 network 10.0.0.0
 no auto-summary
!
access-list 64 permit 10.3.1.0
access-list 64 permit 10.3.3.0
access-list 64 permit 10.3.2.0
access-list 64 permit 10.200.200.31
access-list 64 permit 10.200.200.32
access-list 64 permit 10.200.200.33
access-list 64 permit 10.200.200.34
```

Example 7-19 *Configuration to Change the Administrative Distance on Router P3R2 in Figure 7-21*

```
hostname P3R2
!
router ospf 1
 redistribute rip metric 10000 metric-type 1 subnets
 network 172.31.0.0 0.0.255.255 area 0
 distance 125 0.0.0.0 255.255.255.255 64
!
router rip
 version 2
 redistribute ospf 1 metric 5
 network 10.0.0.0
 no auto-summary
!
access-list 64 permit 10.3.1.0
access-list 64 permit 10.3.3.0
access-list 64 permit 10.3.2.0
access-list 64 permit 10.200.200.31
access-list 64 permit 10.200.200.32
access-list 64 permit 10.200.200.33
access-list 64 permit 10.200.200.34
```

Table 7-18 **distance** *Command Parameters Used in Example 7-18 and Example 7-19*

Parameter	Description
125	Defines the administrative distance that specified routes are assigned.
0.0.0.0 255.255.255.255	Defines the source address of the router supplying the routing information—in this case, any router.
64	Defines the access list to be used to filter incoming routing updates to determine which will have their administrative distance changed.

Access list 64 is used to match all the native RIPv2 routes. The **access-list 64 permit 10.3.1.0** command configures a standard access list to permit the 10.3.1.0 network; similar access list statements permit the other internal native RIPv2 networks. Table 7-19 describes some of the command parameters used in the examples.

Table 7-19   **access-list** *Command Parameters Used in Example 7-18 and Example 7-19*

Parameter	Description
64	The access list number.
permit	Allows all networks that match the address to be permitted—in this case, to have their administrative distance changed.
10.3.1.0	A network to be permitted—in this case, to have its administrative distance changed.

Both P3R1 and P3R2 are configured to assign an administrative distance of 125 to routes listed in access list 64, which it learns from OSPF. Access list 64 has permit statements for the internal native RIPv2 networks 10.3.1.0, 10.3.2.0, and 10.3.3.0 and the loopback networks 10.200.200.31, 10.200.200.32, 10.200.200.33, and 10.200.200.34. Therefore, when either of these routers learns about these networks from both RIPv2 and OSPF, it selects the routes learned from RIPv2—with a lower administrative distance of 120—over the same routes learned from OSPF (via redistribution from the other boundary router)—with an administrative distance of 125—and puts only the RIPv2 routes in the routing table.

KEY POINT

The distance Command

Notice in this example that the **distance** command is part of the OSPF routing process configuration because the administrative distance should be changed for these routes when they are learned by OSPF, not by RIPv2.

You need to configure the **distance** command on both redistributing routers because either one can have suboptimal routes, depending on which redistributing router sends the OSPF updates about the RIPv2 networks to the other redistributing router first.

Example 7-20 shows that Router P3R2 now retains the more direct paths to the internal networks by learning them from RIPv2.

Example 7-20 *Routing Table on Router P3R2 in Figure 7-21 with the Administrative Distance Changed*

```
P3R2#show ip route
<output omitted>
Gateway of last resort is not set

     172.31.0.0/24 is subnetted, 1 subnet
C       172.31.3.0/24 is directly connected, Serial0/0/0
     10.0.0.0/8 is variably subnetted, 8 subnets, 2 masks
R       10.3.1.0/24 [120/2] via 10.3.2.4, 00:00:03, FastEthernet0/0
R       10.3.3.0/24 [120/1] via 10.3.2.4, 00:00:03, FastEthernet0/0
C       10.3.2.0/24 is directly connected, FastEthernet0/0
R       10.200.200.31/32 [120/3] via 10.3.2.4, 00:00:04, FastEthernet0/0
R       10.200.200.34/32 [120/1] via 10.3.2.4, 00:00:04, FastEthernet0/0
C       10.200.200.32/32 is directly connected, Loopback0
R       10.200.200.33/32 [120/2] via 10.3.2.4, 00:00:04, FastEthernet0/0
O E2    10.254.0.0/24 [110/50] via 172.31.3.3, 00:00:04, Serial0/0/0

P3R2#
```

However, some routing information is lost with this configuration. For example, depending on the actual bandwidths, the OSPF path might have been better for the 10.3.1.0 network; it might have made sense not to include 10.3.1.0 in the access list for P3R2.

This example illustrates the importance of knowing your network before implementing redistribution and closely examining which routes the routers select after redistribution is enabled. You should pay particular attention to routers that can select from a number of possible redundant paths to a network, because they may select suboptimal paths.

KEY POINT | **No Path Information Is Lost When You Modify the Administrative Distance**

The most important feature of using administrative distance to control route preference is that no path information is lost; in this example, the OSPF information is still in the OSPF database. If the primary path (via the RIPv2 routes) is lost, the OSPF path reasserts itself, and the router maintains connectivity with those networks.

Verifying Redistribution Operation

The best way to verify redistribution operation is as follows:

■ Know your network topology, particularly where redundant routes exist.

- Study the routing tables on a variety of routers in the internetwork using the **show ip route** [*ip-address*] EXEC command. For example, check the routing table on the boundary router and on some of the internal routers in each autonomous system.

- Perform a trace using the **traceroute** [*ip-address*] EXEC command on some of the routes that go across the autonomous systems to verify that the shortest path is being used for routing. Be sure to run traces to networks for which redundant routes exist.

- If you encounter routing problems, use the **traceroute** and **debug** commands to observe the routing update traffic on the boundary routers and on the internal routers.

NOTE   Running **debug** requires extra processing by the router, so if the router is already overloaded, initiating **debug** is not recommended.

Configuring DHCP

DHCP is used to provide dynamic IP address allocation to TCP/IP hosts. DHCP uses a client/ server model; the DHCP server can be a Windows server, a UNIX-based server, or a Cisco IOS device. Cisco IOS devices can also be DHCP relay agents and DHCP clients.

Using this DHCP functionality allows a network administrator to implement more options and levels of DHCP service for a more robust and efficient network solution. This Cisco IOS functionality also allows existing equipment to be leveraged more effectively, in lieu of purchasing and installing separate devices.

DHCP Overview

DHCP is structured on the Bootstrap Protocol (BOOTP) Server (also known as BOOTPS) and BOOTP well-known User Datagram Protocol (UDP) protocols. Before these protocols existed, IP addresses were manually administered to IP hosts, which was a tedious, error-prone, and labor-intensive process.

DHCP allows IP addresses to be automatically assigned to DHCP clients. The DHCP service can be implemented with a server or with a Cisco IOS device.

Figure 7-22 illustrates where DHCP can be implemented within the Enterprise Composite Network Model.

Figure 7-22 *DHCP in an Enterprise Network*

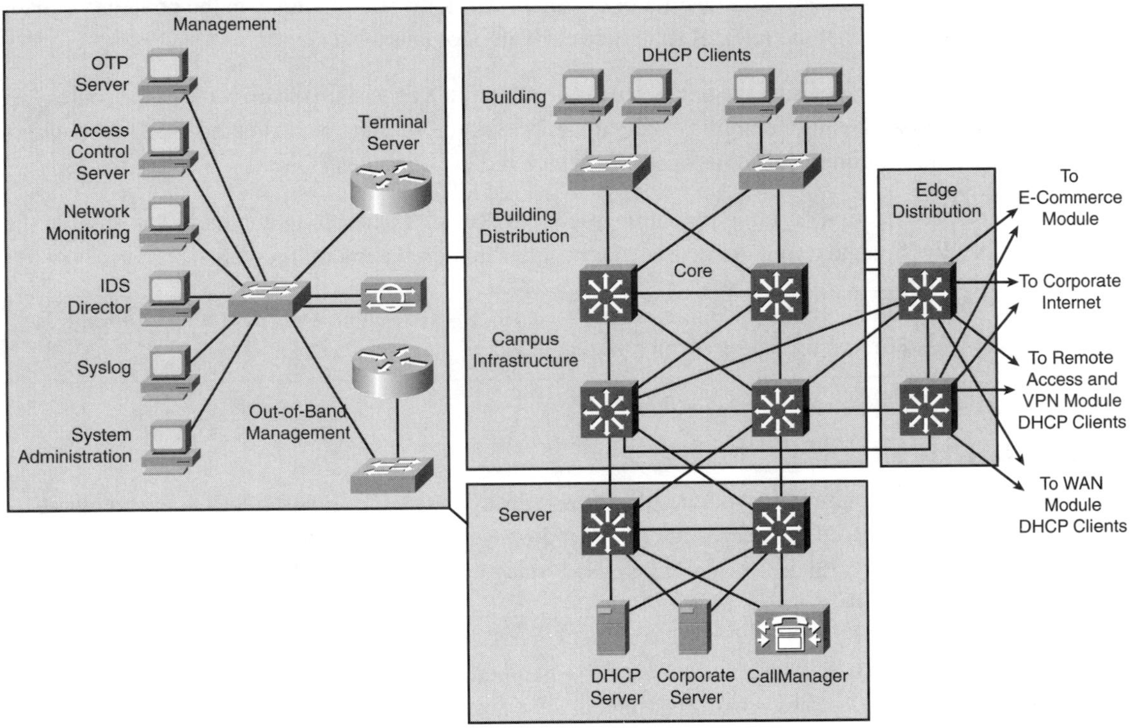

DHCP Operation

Figure 7-23 shows the steps that occur when a DHCP client requests an IP address from a DHCP server.

Step 1   The host sends a DHCPDISCOVER broadcast message to locate a DHCP server.

Step 2   A DHCP server offers configuration parameters such as an IP address, a media access control (MAC) address, a domain name, a default gateway, and a lease for the IP address to the client in a DHCPOFFER unicast message. This message may also include IP telephony DHCP options such as option 150, which is used for Trivial File Transfer Protocol (TFTP) configuration of IP telephones.

Step 3   The client returns a formal request for the offered IP address to the DHCP server in a DHCPREQUEST broadcast message.

Step 4   The DHCP server confirms that the IP address has been allocated to the client by returning a DHCPACK unicast message to the client.

Figure 7-23 *DHCP Operation*

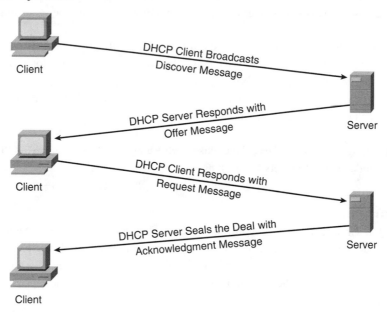

A DHCP client may receive offers from multiple DHCP servers and can accept any one of the offers; the client usually accepts the first offer it receives. An offer from the DHCP server is not a guarantee that the IP address will be allocated to the client; however, the server usually reserves the address until the client has had a chance to formally accept the address.

DHCP supports three possible address allocation mechanisms:

- **Manual**—The network administrator assigns an IP address to a specific MAC address. DHCP is used to dispatch the assigned address to the host.

- **Automatic**—The IP address is permanently assigned to a host.

- **Dynamic**—The IP address is assigned to a host for a limited time or until the host explicitly releases the address. This mechanism supports automatic address reuse when the host to which the address has been assigned no longer needs the address.

DHCP Bindings

An *address binding* is the mapping between the client's IP and hardware (MAC) addresses. The client's IP address can be configured by the administrator (manual address allocation) or assigned from a pool by the DHCP server.

On Cisco IOS devices, DHCP *address pools* are stored in nonvolatile RAM (NVRAM). There is no limit on the number of address pools.

Manual bindings are also stored in NVRAM. Manual bindings are just special address pools configured by a network administrator. There is no limit on the number of manual bindings.

Automatic bindings are IP addresses that have been automatically mapped to the MAC addresses of hosts that are found in the DHCP database. Automatic bindings are stored on a remote host called the *database agent*, which is any host—for example, a File Transfer Protocol (FTP), TFTP, or Remote Copy Protocol (RCP) server—that stores the DHCP bindings database. The bindings are saved as text records for easy maintenance.

You can configure multiple DHCP database agents and you can configure the interval between database updates and transfers for each agent.

Attribute Inheritance

The DHCP server database is organized as a tree. The root of the tree is the address pool for networks, branches are subnetwork address pools, and leaves are bindings to clients. Subnetworks inherit network parameters and clients inherit subnetwork parameters. Therefore, common parameters, for example the domain name, should be configured at the highest (network or subnetwork) level of the tree.

Inherited parameters can be overridden. For example, if a parameter is defined for both the network and a subnetwork, the definition of the subnetwork is used.

Address leases are not inherited. If a lease is not specified for an IP address, by default, the DHCP server assigns a one-day lease for the address.

DHCP Options and Suboptions

Configuration parameters and other control information are carried in tagged data items that are stored in the options field of the DHCP message. Options provide a method of appending additional information.

The Cisco IOS DHCP implementation also allows most DHCP server options to be customized. For example, the Cisco IOS image can be customized with option 150 to support intelligent IP phones.

Configuring a DHCP Server

The Cisco IOS DHCP server accepts address assignment requests and renewals and assigns the addresses from predefined groups of addresses contained within DHCP address pools. These address pools can also be configured to supply additional information to the requesting client such as the IP address of the DNS server, the default router, and other configuration parameters.

The Cisco IOS DHCP server can accept broadcasts from locally attached LAN segments or from DHCP requests that have been forwarded by other DHCP relay agents within the network.

The Cisco IOS DHCP server can allocate dynamic IP addresses based on the relay information option (option 82) information sent by the relay agent. Automatic DHCP address allocation is typically based on an IP address, whether it be the gateway address (in the *giaddr* field of the DHCP packet) or the incoming interface IP address. In some networks, it is necessary to use additional information to further determine which IP addresses to allocate. By using option 82, the Cisco IOS relay agent has long been able to include additional information about itself when forwarding client-originated DHCP packets to a DHCP server. The Cisco IOS DHCP server can also use option 82 as a means to provide additional information to properly allocate IP addresses to DHCP clients.

Preparing for DHCP Configuration

Before configuring a Cisco IOS DHCP server, the following items should be identified:

Step 1   An external FTP, TFTP, or RCP server that will be used to store the DHCP bindings database.

Step 2   The IP address range to be assigned by the DHCP server and the IP addresses to be excluded (for example, the addresses of default routers and other statically assigned addresses within the dynamically assigned range).

Step 3   DHCP options for devices where necessary, including the following:

- Default boot image name

- Default routers

- DNS servers

- Network Basic Input/Output System (NetBIOS) name server and NetBIOS node type

- IP telephony options, such as option 150

Step 4   The DNS domain name.

DHCP Server Configuration Tasks

The Cisco IOS DHCP server and relay agent are enabled by default. You can verify if they have been disabled by checking your configuration file. If they have been disabled, the **no service dhcp** command will appear in the configuration file; use the **service dhcp** global configuration command to reenable the functionality if necessary.

The following are some of the possible tasks when configuring a Cisco IOS DHCP server. (The commands are described in Table 7-20 later in this section.)

■ **Configuring a DHCP database agent or disabling DHCP conflict logging (required)—** A DHCP database agent stores the DHCP automatic bindings database. An address conflict occurs when two hosts use the same IP address. During address assignment, DHCP checks for conflicts using ping and gratuitous address resolution protocol (ARP). If a conflict is detected, the address is removed from the pool and the address will not be assigned until the administrator resolves the conflict. Cisco strongly recommends using database agents. However, if you choose not to configure a DHCP database agent, disable the recording of DHCP address conflicts on the DHCP server. If there is conflict logging but no database agent configured, bindings are lost across router reboots and possible false conflicts can occur causing the address to be removed from the address pool until the network administrator intervenes.

■ **Excluding IP addresses from the pool—**The IP address configured on the router interface is automatically excluded from the DHCP address pool; the DHCP server assumes that all other IP addresses in a DHCP address pool subnet are available for assigning to DHCP clients. You need to exclude addresses from the pool if the DHCP server should not allocate those IP addresses.

■ **Configuring a DHCP address pool (required)—**You can configure a DHCP address pool with a symbolic name (such as "building2") or an integer (such as 3). Configuring a DHCP address pool also places you in DHCP pool configuration mode—identified by the Router(dhcp-config)# prompt—from which you can configure pool parameters, including the following:

— The subnet network number and mask of the DHCP address pool

— The domain name for the client

— The IP address of a DNS server (or servers) that is available to a DHCP client

— (Optional) The name of the default boot image for a DHCP client

— (Optional) The next server in the boot process of a DHCP client

— (Optional) The NetBIOS WINS server that is available to a Microsoft DHCP client

— (Optional) The NetBIOS node type for a Microsoft DHCP client

— (Optional) The IP address of the default router for a DHCP client

— (Optional) DHCP server options

— (Optional) The duration of the lease

NOTE Notice that the DHCP pool configuration mode is identified by the Router(dhcp-config)# prompt; the prompt is *not* Router(config-dhcp)#, as you might expect.

■ **Configuring manual bindings**—Manual bindings are IP addresses that have been manually mapped to the MAC addresses of hosts and are stored in NVRAM on the DHCP server. You cannot configure manual bindings within the same pool that is configured for automatic bindings.

■ **Configuring DHCP static mapping**—Static mapping enables static IP addresses to be assigned without creating numerous host pools with manual bindings; the mappings are created by creating a text file that the DHCP server reads.

■ **Customizing DHCP server operation**—Customizing includes the following:

— **Configuring the number of ping packets and timeout**—By default, the DHCP server pings a pool address twice before assigning a particular address to a requesting client. If the ping is unanswered, the DHCP server assumes (with a high probability) that the address is not in use and assigns the address to the requesting client. By default, the DHCP server waits 2 seconds before timing out a ping packet. Both of these parameters can be changed.

— **Ignore all BOOTP requests**—You can configure the DHCP server to ignore and not reply to received BOOTP requests, when there is a mix of BOOTP and DHCP clients in a network segment and there is both a BOOTP server and a Cisco IOS DHCP server servicing the network segment. Because a DHCP server can also respond to a BOOTP request, an address offer may be made by the DHCP server causing the BOOTP clients to boot with the address from the DHCP server, instead of the address from the BOOTP server. The Cisco IOS Software can forward these ignored BOOTP request packets to another DHCP server if the **ip helper-address** interface configuration command is configured on the incoming interface (as described in the later "IP Helper Addresses" section).

■ **Configuring a remote router to import DHCP server options from a central DHCP server**—Network administrators can configure one or more centralized DHCP servers to update specific DHCP options within the DHCP pools. The remote servers can request or "import" these option parameters from the centralized servers.

■ **Configuring DHCP address allocation using Option 82**—Option 82 is organized as a single DHCP option that contains information known by a relay agent. The Cisco IOS DHCP server uses option 82 information to help determine which IP addresses to allocate to clients. The information sent via option 82 is used to identify which port the DHCP request came in on. This feature does not parse out the individual suboptions contained within option 82. Rather, the address allocation is done by matching a configured pattern byte by byte.

■ **Configuring a static route with the next-hop dynamically obtained through DHCP**—Static routes can be assigned using a DHCP default gateway as the next-hop router. The static routes are installed in the routing table when the default gateway is assigned by the DHCP server.

DHCP Server Configuration Commands

Table 7-20 describes some of the commands used to configure a Cisco IOS DHCP server, in logical order.

> **NOTE** Not all commands are listed here; for additional information see the DHCP documentation at http://www.cisco.com/univercd/cc/td/doc/product/software/ios124/124cg/hiad_c/ch10/index.htm.

Table 7-20 *DHCP Server Configuration Commands*

Command and Parameters	Description
Router(config)#**service dhcp**	Enables DHCP features on router; it is on by default.
Router(config)#**ip dhcp database** *url* [**timeout** *seconds* | **write-delay** *seconds*]	Specifies the database agent and the interval between database updates and database transfers.
Router(config)#**no ip dhcp conflict logging**	Disables DHCP conflict logging. (Used if a DHCP database agent is not configured.)
Router(config)#**ip dhcp excluded-address** *low-address* [*high address*]	Specifies the IP addresses that the DHCP server should not assign to DHCP clients.
Router(config)#**ip dhcp pool** *name*	Creates a name for the DCHP server address pool and places you in DHCP pool configuration mode (indicated by the Router(dhcp-config)# prompt).
Router(dhcp-config)#**network** *network-number* [*mask* | */prefix-length*]	Specifies the subnet/network number and mask of the DHCP address pool.
Router(dhcp-config)#**domain-name** *domain*	Specifies the domain name for the client.
Router(dhcp-config)#**dns-server** *address* [*address2....address8*]	Specifies the IP address of a DNS server that is available to a DHCP client. One is required, but up to eight can be specified, listed in order of preference.
Router(dhcp-config)#**bootfile** *filename*	Specifies the name of the default boot image for a DHCP client; the boot image is generally the operating system the client uses to load.
Router(dhcp-config)#**next-server** *address* [*address2 ... address8*]	Specifies the next server in the boot process of a DHCP client. If multiple servers are specified, DHCP assigns them to clients in round-robin order.
Router(dhcp-config)#**netbios-name-server** *address* [*address2....address8*]	Specifies the NetBIOS WINS server that is available to a Microsoft DHCP client. One address is required; however, you can specify up to eight addresses, listed in order of preference.

Table 7-20 *DHCP Server Configuration Commands (Continued)*

Command and Parameters	Description
Router(dhcp-config)#**netbios-node-type** *type*	Specifies the NetBIOS node type for a Microsoft DHCP client.
Router(dhcp-config)#**default-router** *address* [*address2... ...address8*]	Specifies the IP address of the default router for a DHCP client. One IP address is required; however, you can specify up to eight addresses, listed in order of preference.
Router(dhcp-config)#**option** *code* [**instance** *number*] {**ascii** *string* | **hex** *string* | *ip-address*}	Specifies DHCP server options.
Router(dhcp-config)#**lease** {*days* [*hours*] [*minutes*] | **infinite**}	Specifies the duration of the lease. The default is a one day. The **infinite** keyword specifies that the duration of the lease is unlimited.
Router(dhcp-config)#**host** *address* [*mask* | */prefix-length*]	Specifies the IP address and subnet mask of the client for which a manual binding is to be created.
Router(dhcp-config)#**hardware-address** *hardware-address type* or Router(dhcp-config)**client-identifier** *unique-identifier*	Specifies a hardware address for a client, or specifies the unique identifier for a Microsoft DHCP client, for which a manual binding is to be created.
Router(dhcp-config)#**client-name** *name*	Specifies the name of the client for which a manual binding is to be created.
Router(dhcp-config)#**ip dhcp ping packets** *number*	Specifies the number of ping packets the DHCP server sends to a pool address before assigning the address to a requesting client; the default is 2.
Router(dhcp-config)#**ip dhcp ping timeout** *milliseconds*	Specifies the amount of time the DHCP server waits for a ping reply from an address pool. The default is 2 seconds (2000 milliseconds).
Router(dhcp-config)#**ip dhcp bootp ignore**	Allows the DHCP server to selectively ignore and not reply to received BOOTP requests.
Router(dhcp-config)#**import all**	Imports DHCP option parameters into the DHCP server database. Used for remote DHCP pools.

DHCP Server Example

In Example 7-21, three DHCP address pools are created: one in network 172.16.0.0, one in subnetwork 172.16.1.0, and one in subnetwork 172.16.2.0. Attributes from network 172.16.0.0—such as the domain name, DNS server, NetBIOS name server, and NetBIOS node type—are inherited in subnetworks 172.16.1.0 and 172.16.2.0. In pools 1 and 2, clients are granted 30-day leases. All addresses in each subnetwork, except the excluded addresses, are available to the DHCP server for assigning to clients. Table 7-21 lists the IP addresses for the devices in three DHCP address pools.

Table 7-21 *DHCP Address Pool Configuration Example*

Pool 0 (Network 172.16.0.0/16)		Pool 1 (Subnetwork 172.16.1.0/24)		Pool 2 (Subnetwork 172.16.2.0/24)	
Device	**IP Address**	**Device**	**IP Address**	**Device**	**IP Address**
Default routers	—	Default routers	172.16.1.100 172.16.1.101	Default routers	172.16.2.100 172.16.2.101
DNS server	172.16.1.102 172.16.2.102				
NetBIOS name server	172.16.1.103 172.16.2.103				
NetBIOS node type	h-node				

Example 7-21 *DHCP Address Pool Configuration Example*

```
ip dhcp database ftp://user:password@172.16.4.253/router-dhcp write-delay 120
ip dhcp excluded-address 172.16.1.100 172.16.1.103
ip dhcp excluded-address 172.16.2.100 172.16.2.103
!
ip dhcp pool 0
 network 172.16.0.0 /16
 domain-name cisco.com
 dns-server 172.16.1.102 172.16.2.102
 netbios-name-server 172.16.1.103 172.16.2.103
 netbios-node-type h-node
!
ip dhcp pool 1
 network 172.16.1.0 /24
 default-router 172.16.1.100 172.16.1.101
 lease 30
!
ip dhcp pool 2
 network 172.16.2.0 /24
 default-router 172.16.2.100 172.16.2.101
 lease 30
```

DHCP Server Options Import Example

In the past, each Cisco IOS DHCP server had to be configured separately with all parameters and options. The Cisco IOS has been revised to allow remote Cisco IOS DHCP servers to import option parameters from a centralized server.

Figure 7-24 and Example 7-22 and Example 7-23 illustrate a central and remote server configured to support the importing of DHCP options. The central server is configured with DHCP options, such as DNS and WINS addresses. In response to a DHCP request from a local client, the remote server can request or "import" these option parameters from the centralized server.

Figure 7-24   *DHCP Options Import*

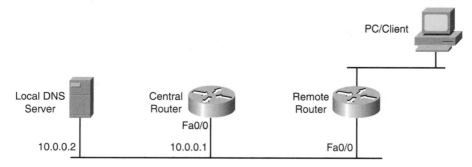

Example 7-22   *DHCP Import Option Example: Configuration of Central Router in Figure 7-24*

```
! Do not assign this range to DHCP clients
ip dhcp-excluded address 10.0.0.1 10.0.0.5
!
ip dhcp pool central
! Specifies the network number and mask for DHCP clients
 network 10.0.0.0 255.255.255.0
! Specifies the domain name for the client
 domain-name central
! Specifies the DNS server that will respond to DHCP clients when they
! need to correlate host name to IP address
 dns-server 10.0.0.2
! Specifies the NETBIOS WINS server
 netbios-name-server 10.0.0.2
!
interface FastEthernet0/0
 ip address 10.0.0.1 255.255.255.0
 duplex auto
 speed auto
```

Example 7-23 *DHCP Import Option Example: Configuration of Remote Router in Figure 7-24*

```
ip dhcp pool client
! Specifies the network number and mask for DHCP clients
 network 172.16.1.0 255.255.255.0
! Import DHCP option parameters into DHCP server database
 import all
!
interface FastEthernet0/0
! Specifies that the interface acquires an IP address through DHCP
 ip address dhcp
 duplex auto
 speed auto
```

Configuring a DHCP Relay Agent

A DHCP relay agent is any host that forwards DHCP packets between clients and servers. Relay agents are used to forward requests and replies between clients and servers when they are not on the same physical subnet. Relay agents receive DHCP messages and then generate a new DHCP message to send out on another interface.

IP Helper Addresses

The Cisco IOS DHCP server and relay agent are enabled by default. However, the Cisco IOS DHCP relay agent is enabled on an interface only when a helper address is configured to enable DHCP broadcasts received on the interface to be forwarded to the configured DHCP server.

DHCP clients use UDP broadcasts to send their initial DHCPDISCOVER message, because they do not have information about the network to which they are attached. If the client is on a network that does not include a server, UDP broadcasts are normally not forwarded by the attached router, as illustrated in Figure 7-25.

Figure 7-25 *Routers Do Not Forward Broadcasts, by Default*

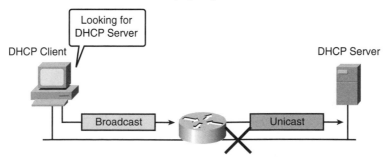

The **ip helper-address** *address* interface configuration command causes UDP broadcasts received on the interface to be changed to a unicast and forwarded out another interface to the unicast IP address specified by the command. The relay agent sets the gateway address (the *giaddr* field of the DHCP packet) and, if configured, adds the relay agent information option (option 82) in the packet and forwards it to the DHCP server. The reply from the server is forwarded back to the client after removing option 82. Figure 7-26 illustrates the use of the **ip helper-address** command to implement a DHCP relay agent. Example 7-24 provides the helper address configuration for the router in this figure.

Figure 7-26 *IP Helper Address Example*

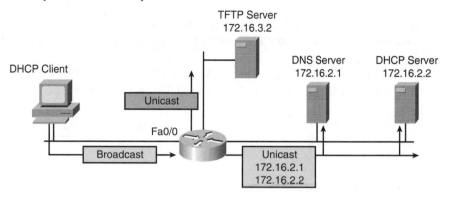

Example 7-24 *Configuration of the Router in Figure 7-26*

```
interface FastEthernet0/0
 ip address 172.16.1.100 255.255.255.0
 ip helper-address 172.16.2.1
 ip helper-address 172.16.2.2
 ip helper-address 172.16.3.2
```

KEY POINT

IP Helper Addresses

The **ip helper-address** command is configured on the interface on which the broadcasts are expected to be received.

By default, the **ip helper-address** command enables forwarding of packets sent to all the well-known UDP ports that may be included in a UDP broadcast message, which are the following:

- Time: 37

- TACACS: 49

- DNS: 53

- BOOTP/DHCP server: 67

- BOOTP/DHCP client: 68

- TFTP: 69

- NetBIOS name service: 137

- NetBIOS datagram service: 138

The **ip forward-protocol udp** [*port*] global configuration command can be used to customize this feature to network requirements. Ports can be eliminated from the forwarding service with the **no ip forward-protocol** *port* global configuration command, and ports can be added to the forwarding service with the **ip forward-protocol** *port* global configuration command.

Example 7-25 illustrates an example. This configuration would cause packets sent to the Time and NetBIOS ports to not be forwarded; packets sent to UDP port 8000 would be forwarded.

Example 7-25 *Modifying Forwarded UDP Ports*

```
interface FastEthernet0/0
 ip address 10.3.3.3 255.255.255.0
 ip helper-address 10.1.1.1
 no ip forward-protocol udp 137
 no ip forward-protocol udp 138
 no ip forward-protocol udp 37
 ip forward-protocol udp 8000
```

DHCP Relay Agent Configuration Tasks

The following are some of the possible tasks when configuring a Cisco IOS DHCP relay agent (the commands are described in Table 7-22 later in this section):

- **Specifying the Packet Forwarding Address (required)**—Use the **ip helper-address** command, as described in the previous section, to define the address of the DHCP server.

- **Configuring Relay Agent Information Option Support (option 82) (optional)**—By using the relay agent information option (option 82), the Cisco IOS relay agent can include additional information (the circuit identifier suboption and the remote ID suboption) about itself when forwarding client-originated DHCP packets to a DHCP server. The DHCP server can use this information to assign IP addresses, perform access control, and set QoS and security policies (or other parameter-assignment policies) for each subscriber of a service provider network. Figure 7-27 shows how the relay agent information option is inserted into the DHCP packet as follows:

  1. The DHCP client generates a DHCP request and broadcasts it on the network.

  2. The DHCP relay agent intercepts the broadcast DHCP request packet and inserts the relay agent information option (82) in the packet. The relay agent option contains the related suboptions.

Figure 7-27 *DHCP Relay Agent Option*

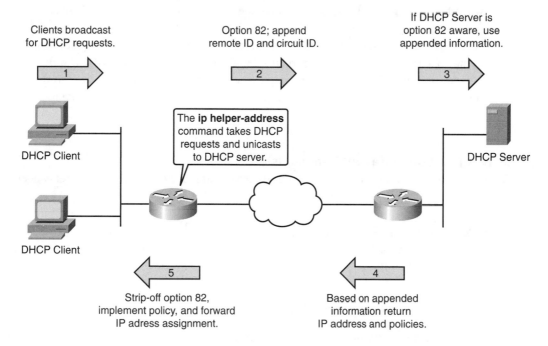

3. The DHCP relay agent unicasts the DHCP packet to the DHCP server.

4. The DHCP server receives the packet and uses the suboptions to assign IP addresses and other configuration parameters and forwards them back to the client.

5. The suboption fields are stripped off of the packet by the relay agent while forwarding to the client.

■ **Configuring the Subscriber Identifier Suboption of the Relay Agent Information Option (optional)**—An ISP can add a unique identifier to the subscriber-identifier suboption of the relay agent information option, so that the ISP can identify a subscriber, assign specific actions to that subscriber (for example, assignment of host IP address, subnet mask, and DNS), and trigger accounting.

■ **Configuring DHCP Relay Agent Support for Multiprotocol Label Switching (MPLS) Virtual Private Networks (VPNs) (optional)**—DHCP relay support for MPLS VPNs enables a network administrator to conserve address space by allowing overlapping addresses. The relay agent can support multiple clients on different VPNs, and many of these clients from different VPNs can share the same IP address.

■ **Setting the Gateway Address of the DHCP Broadcast to a secondary address using Smart Relay Agent Forwarding (optional)**—You only need to configure helper addresses on the interface where the UDP broadcasts that you want to forward to the DHCP server are being received, and you only need the **ip dhcp smart-relay** command configured if you have secondary addresses on that interface and you want the router to step through each IP network when forwarding DHCP requests. Without the smart relay agent configured, all requests are forwarded using the primary IP address on the interface. If the **ip dhcp smart-relay** command is configured, the relay agent counts the number of times the client retries sending a request to the DHCP server when there is no DHCPOFFER message from the DHCP server. After three retries, the relay agent sets the gateway address to the secondary address. If the DHCP server still does not respond after three more retries, then the next secondary address is used as the gateway address.

DHCP Relay Agent Configuration Commands

Table 7-22 describes some of the commands used to configure a Cisco IOS DHCP relay agent, in logical order.

> **NOTE**   Not all commands are listed here; for additional information, refer to the DHCP documentation at http://www.cisco.com/univercd/cc/td/doc/product/software/ios124/124cg/hiad_c/ch10/index.htm.

Table 7-22   *DHCP Relay Agent Configuration Commands*

Command and Parameters	Description
Router(config)#**ip dhcp information option**	Enables the system to insert the DHCP relay agent information option (82) in forwarded BOOTREQUEST messages to a DHCP server. Disabled by default.
Router(config)#**ip dhcp information check**	Configures DHCP to check that the relay agent information option in forwarded BOOTREPLY messages is valid. Enabled by default.
Router(config)#**ip dhcp information policy {drop | keep | replace}**	A DHCP relay agent may receive a message from another DHCP relay agent that already contains relay information. By default, the relay information from the previous relay agent is replaced. This command configures the reforwarding policy for the relay agent (what the relay agent should do if a message already contains relay information).
Router(config)#**ip dhcp relay information trust-all**	Configures all interfaces on a router as trusted sources of the DHCP relay information option. By default, if the gateway address is set to all zeros in the DHCP packet and the relay agent information option is already present in the packet, the DHCP relay agent will discard the packet; use this command to override this behavior and accept the packet. This is useful when Ethernet switches that may insert option 82 are involved in delivery of the packet from the client to the server. For an individual interface, the **ip dhcp relay information trusted** command can be used.

Configuring a DHCP Client

A DHCP client is a host using DHCP to obtain configuration parameters such as an IP address.

A Cisco IOS device can be configured to be a DHCP client and obtain an interface address dynamically from a DHCP server with the **ip address dhcp** interface configuration command. A router can act as both the DHCP client and DHCP server.

There are optional **ip dhcp client** interface configuration commands available; if used, these must be configured before entering the **ip address dhcp** command on the interface to ensure that the DHCPDISCOVER messages that are generated contain the correct option values. If any of the **ip dhcp client** commands are entered after an IP address has been acquired from DHCP, it will not take effect until the next time the router acquires an IP address from DHCP.

You can release the DHCP lease for the interface and deconfigure the IP address for the interface with the privileged EXEC command **release dhcp** *interface-type interface-number*. The lease can be renewed with the privileged EXEC command **renew dhcp** *interface-type interface-number*.

Verifying DHCP

Table 7-23 describes some of the commands used to verify DHCP on an IOS device.

Table 7-23 *DHCP Verification Commands*

Command and Parameters	Description
show ip dhcp database	Displays recent activity in the DHCP database.
show ip dhcp server statistics	Displays server statistics and counts of the number of messages sent and received.
show ip route dhcp {*ip-address*}	Displays the routes added to the routing table by the Cisco IOS DHCP server and relay agent.
show ip dhcp binding {*address*}	Displays a list of all bindings created on a specific DHCP server.
show ip dhcp conflict	Displays a list of all address conflicts recorded by a specific DHCP server.
show ip dhcp import	Displays the option parameters that were imported into the DHCP server database.

continues

Table 7-23 *DHCP Verification Commands (Continued)*

Command and Parameters	Description
show ip dhcp-relay information trusted-sources	Displays all interfaces configured to be a trusted source for the DHCP relay information option.
clear ip dhcp binding {*address* | ***}	Deletes an automatic address binding from the DHCP database.
clear ip dhcp conflict {*address* | ***}	Clears an address conflict from the DHCP database.
clear ip dhcp server statistics	Resets all DHCP server counters to 0.
clear ip route dhcp {*ip-address*}	Removes routes from the routing table added by the Cisco IOS DHCP server and relay agent.
debug dhcp detail	Displays the DHCP packets that were sent and received.
debug ip dhcp server {**events** | **packets** | **linkage**}	Displays the server side of the DHCP interaction.

Summary

In this chapter, you learned about why multiple routing protocols may run in a network and how to control routing update information between them, and about Cisco IOS support of DHCP; the following topics were presented:

- Reasons for using more than one routing protocol, how routing information can be exchanged between them (referred to as redistribution), and how Cisco routers operate in a multiple routing protocol environment

- Planning and implementing a new IP address scheme

- The roles that the administrative distance and the routing metric play in route selection

- The two methods of route redistribution: two-way and one-way

- Configuration of redistribution between various IP routing protocols

- Configuration of the default metric associated with a protocol

- How to control routing update traffic, including using passive interfaces, default routes, static routes, distribute lists, and route maps, and manipulating the administrative distance

- Configuring your router to be a DHCP server, relay agent, or client

Configuration Exercise 7-1: Configuring Basic Redistribution

In this Configuration Exercise, you configure your routers to redistribute routes from RIPv2 into OSPF and to supply a default route to the RIPv2 routing domain.

Introduction to the Configuration Exercises

This book uses Configuration Exercises to help you practice configuring routers with the commands and topics presented. If you have access to real hardware, you can try these exercises on your routers; see Appendix B, "Configuration Exercise Equipment Requirements and Backbone Configurations," for a list of recommended equipment and initial configuration commands for the backbone routers. However, even if you don't have access to any routers, you can go through the exercises and keep a log of your own running configurations or just read through the solution. Commands used and solutions to the Configuration Exercises are provided within the exercises.

In the Configuration Exercises, the network is assumed to consist of two pods, each with four routers. The pods are interconnected to a backbone. You configure pod 1. No interaction between the two pods is required, but you might see some routes from the other pod in your routing tables in some exercises if you have it configured. In most of the exercises, the backbone has only one router; in some cases, another router is added to the backbone. Each Configuration Exercise assumes that you have completed the previous chapters' Configuration Exercises on your pod.

NOTE   Throughout this exercise, the pod number is referred to as *x*, and the router number is referred to as *y*. Substitute the appropriate numbers as needed.

Exercise Objectives

The objectives of this exercise are to redistribute routes from RIPv2 into OSPF and to supply a default route to the RIPv2 routing domain.

Visual Objective

Figure 7-28 illustrates the topology used and what you will accomplish in this exercise.

Figure 7-28 *Basic Redistribution Configuration Exercise Topology*

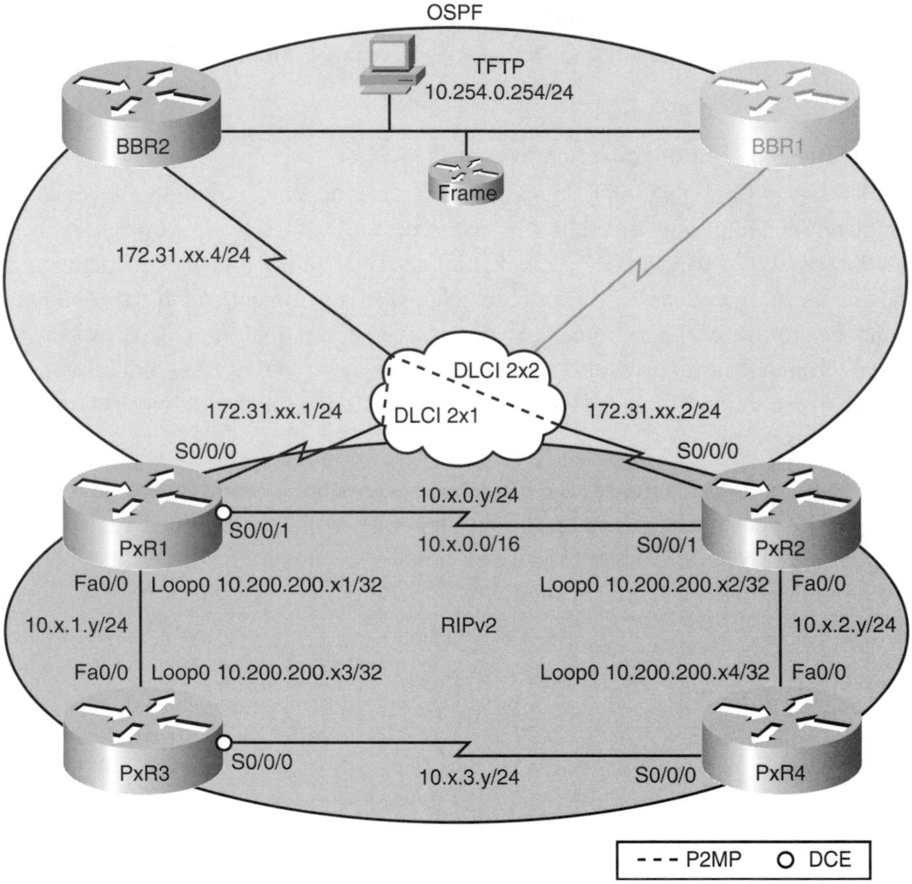

Command List

In this exercise, you use the commands in Table 7-24, listed in logical order. Refer to this list if you need configuration command assistance during the exercise.

> **CAUTION** Although the command syntax is shown in this table, the addresses shown are typically for the P*x*R1 and P*x*R3 routers. Be careful when addressing your routers! Refer to the exercise instructions and the appropriate visual objective diagram for addressing details.

Table 7-24 *Basic Redistribution Configuration Exercise Commands*

Command	Description
(config)#**router ospf 1**	Enters configuration mode for OSPF.
(config-router)#**network 172.31.***xx***.0 0.0.0.255 area 0**	Configures OSPF to run for interfaces 172.31.*xx*.0/24 in area 0.

Table 7-24 *Basic Redistribution Configuration Exercise Commands (Continued)*

Command	Description
(config-if)#**ip ospf network point-to-multipoint**	Configures the point-to-multipoint network type for OSPF on an interface.
(config)#**router rip**	Enters configuration mode for RIP.
(config-router)#**version 2**	Configures RIPv2.
(config-router)#**network 10.0.0.0**	Configures RIP to run on interfaces that belong to network 10.0.0.0.
(config-router)#**no auto-summary**	Turns off automatic summarization of routes at classful boundaries.
(config-router)#**default-information originate**	Advertises the default route through RIP.
(config)#**ip route 0.0.0.0 0.0.0.0 172.31.**xx**.4**	Creates a static default route.
(config-router)#**redistribute rip subnets**	Redistributes RIP routes into OSPF. The **subnets** keyword enables the passing of subnetted routes into OSPF.
>**show ip ospf database**	Displays the OSPF database.
(config)#**access-list 64 permit 10.1.0.0 0.0.255.255**	Configures access list 64 to permit any IP address that matches the first 16 bits of 10.1.0.0.
(config-router)#**distance 125 0.0.0.0 255.255.255.255 64**	Changes the administrative distance to 125 for routes from any source that match access list 64.

Task 1: Cleaning Up

In this task, you remove IS-IS and change the configuration of the Serial 0/0/0 interfaces on the edge routers, before configuring redistribution. Follow these steps:

Step 1   Remove the IS-IS configuration from all the pod routers using the **no router isis** global configuration command.

Step 2   Create a loopback interface on your edge routers with the IP address of 10.200.200.*xy* /32, where *x* is the pod number and *y* is the router number. (Your internal routers already have loopback interfaces with these addresses configured, from a previous exercise.)

Solution:

The following shows the required steps on the P1R1 router:

```
P1R1(config)#no router isis
P1R1(config)#int loopback 0
P1R1(config-if)#ip address 10.200.200.11 255.255.255.255
```

Step 3   The s0/0/0 interfaces on the edge routers have subinterfaces configured.
                Delete this configuration with the **default interface s0/0/0** command.
                Reconfigure the interface with an IP address of 172.31.xx.y /24, Frame
                Relay encapsulation, a Frame Relay static map to BBR2 using DLCI 2xy
                (do not forget the **broadcast** option), and Frame Relay Inverse ARP turned
                off. Enable the interface.

Solution:

The following shows the required steps on the P1R1 router:

```
P1R1(config)#default interface s0/0/0
Building configuration...

Interface Serial0/0/0 set to default configuration
P1R1(config)#interface s0/0/0
P1R1(config-if)#encapsulation frame
P1R1(config-if)#ip address 172.31.11.1 255.255.255.0
P1R1(config-if)#frame-relay map ip 172.31.11.4 211 broadcast
P1R1(config-if)#no frame inverse-arp
P1R1(config-if)#no shutdown
```

Task 2: Setting Up the Routing Protocols

In this task, you configure OSPF and RIPv2 on your pod routers. Follow these steps:

Step 1   BBR2 is in OSPF area 0. Each pod's edge routers will run both OSPF
                and RIPv2.

                On the edge routers, put the S0/0/0 interface in OSPF area 0. Because
                BBR2 is configured with a point-to-multipoint interface, configure the edge
                router's S0/0/0 interface with the OSPF point-to-multipoint network type.

                Configure the edge routers to also run RIPv2 internally to the pod. Turn off
                autosummarization for RIPv2.

Solution:

The following shows the required steps on the P1R1 router:

```
P1R1(config)#router ospf 1
P1R1(config-router)#network 172.31.11.0 0.0.0.255 area 0
P1R1(config-router)#interface s0/0/0
```

```
P1R1(config-if)#ip ospf network point-to-multipoint
P1R1(config-if)#router rip
P1R1(config-router)#version 2
P1R1(config-router)#network 10.0.0.0
P1R1(config-router)#no auto-summary
```

Step 2   Configure the internal routers to run only RIPv2 with autosummarization
turned off.

Solution:

The following shows the required steps on the P1R3 router:

```
P1R3(config)#router rip
P1R3(config-router)#version 2
P1R3(config-router)#network 10.0.0.0
P1R3(config-router)#no auto-summary
```

Step 3   Show the IP routing table on both edge routers. Verify that both edge
routers are learning both OSPF and RIPv2 routes. What is the highest hop
count on the RIPv2 routes to the networks within your pod?

Solution:

The following shows sample output on the P1R1 and P1R2 routers; the highest RIP hop count is
two hops:

```
P1R1#show ip route
<output omitted>
Gateway of last resort is not set

     172.31.0.0/16 is variably subnetted, 3 subnets, 2 masks
C       172.31.11.0/24 is directly connected, Serial0/0/0
O       172.31.11.2/32 [110/1562] via 172.31.11.4, 00:01:15, Serial0/0/0
O       172.31.11.4/32 [110/781] via 172.31.11.4, 00:01:15, Serial0/0/0
     10.0.0.0/8 is variably subnetted, 9 subnets, 2 masks
C       10.200.200.11/32 is directly connected, Loopback0
R       10.200.200.14/32 [120/2] via 10.1.1.3, 00:00:19, FastEthernet0/0
                         [120/2] via 10.1.0.2, 00:00:10, Serial0/0/1
R       10.200.200.12/32 [120/1] via 10.1.0.2, 00:00:10, Serial0/0/1
R       10.200.200.13/32 [120/1] via 10.1.1.3, 00:00:19, FastEthernet0/0
R       10.1.3.0/24 [120/1] via 10.1.1.3, 00:00:19, FastEthernet0/0
R       10.1.2.0/24 [120/1] via 10.1.0.2, 00:00:10, Serial0/0/1
C       10.1.1.0/24 is directly connected, FastEthernet0/0
C       10.1.0.0/24 is directly connected, Serial0/0/1
O E2    10.254.0.0/24 [110/50] via 172.31.11.4, 00:01:18, Serial0/0/0
P1R1#

P1R2#show ip route
<output omitted>
Gateway of last resort is not set

     172.31.0.0/16 is variably subnetted, 3 subnets, 2 masks
C       172.31.11.0/24 is directly connected, Serial0/0/0
O       172.31.11.1/32 [110/1562] via 172.31.11.4, 00:01:33, Serial0/0/0
O       172.31.11.4/32 [110/781] via 172.31.11.4, 00:01:33, Serial0/0/0
     10.0.0.0/8 is variably subnetted, 9 subnets, 2 masks
R       10.200.200.11/32 [120/1] via 10.1.0.1, 00:00:17, Serial0/0/1
R       10.200.200.14/32 [120/1] via 10.1.2.4, 00:00:14, FastEthernet0/0
C       10.200.200.12/32 is directly connected, Loopback0
```

```
R        10.200.200.13/32 [120/2] via 10.1.2.4, 00:00:14, FastEthernet0/0
                          [120/2] via 10.1.0.1, 00:00:18, Serial0/0/1
R        10.1.3.0/24 [120/1] via 10.1.2.4, 00:00:14, FastEthernet0/0
C        10.1.2.0/24 is directly connected, FastEthernet0/0
R        10.1.1.0/24 [120/1] via 10.1.0.1, 00:00:19, Serial0/0/1
C        10.1.0.0/24 is directly connected, Serial0/0/1
O E2     10.254.0.0/24 [110/50] via 172.31.11.4, 00:01:34, Serial0/0/0
P1R2#
```

Task 3: Configuring Basic Redistribution

In this task, you configure basic redistribution between OSPF and RIPv2. Follow these steps:

Step 1   Configure both edge routers to pass a default route into RIPv2, using the
               default-information originate command. Remember that a RIPv2 router
               needs a static default route configured with the appropriate next-hop (in this
               case, the next-hop is BBR2) to advertise it to other RIPv2 routers; configure
               the static default route on both edge routers.

Solution:

The following shows the required steps on the P1R1 router:

```
P1R1(config)#router rip
P1R1(config-router)#default-information originate
P1R1(config-router)#exit
P1R1(config)#ip route 0.0.0.0 0.0.0.0 172.31.11.4
```

Step 2   Examine the routing table on the internal routers. Is the default route
               present? What are its path and metric?

Solution:

The following shows sample output on the P1R3 router; the default route is present, with a next-hop of P1R1 and a metric of one hop:

```
P1R3#show ip route
<output omitted>
Gateway of last resort is 10.1.1.1 to network 0.0.0.0

     10.0.0.0/8 is variably subnetted, 8 subnets, 2 masks
R        10.200.200.11/32 [120/1] via 10.1.1.1, 00:00:23, FastEthernet0/0
R        10.200.200.14/32 [120/1] via 10.1.3.4, 00:00:19, Serial0/0/0
R        10.200.200.12/32 [120/2] via 10.1.3.4, 00:00:19, Serial0/0/0
                          [120/2] via 10.1.1.1, 00:00:23, FastEthernet0/0
C        10.200.200.13/32 is directly connected, Loopback0
C        10.1.3.0/24 is directly connected, Serial0/0/0
R        10.1.2.0/24 [120/1] via 10.1.3.4, 00:00:20, Serial0/0/0
C        10.1.1.0/24 is directly connected, FastEthernet0/0
R        10.1.0.0/24 [120/1] via 10.1.1.1, 00:00:24, FastEthernet0/0
R*   0.0.0.0/0 [120/1] via 10.1.1.1, 00:00:24, FastEthernet0/0
P1R3#
```

Step 3   Configure both edge routers to redistribute RIPv2 routes into OSPF without specifying a metric value. What default metric will OSPF use when the RIPv2 routes are redistributed? (Remember to include the **subnets** keyword in the **redistribute** command.)

Solution:

The following shows the required steps on the P1R1 router:

```
P1R1(config)#router ospf 1
P1R1(config-router)#redistribute rip subnets
```

The default metric used by OSPF is 20.

Step 4   Telnet to the BBR2 core router and examine the OSPF database. Which routes in the routing table were redistributed from your pod? What type of routes do the networks from your pod appear as?

Solution:

The following shows sample output on the BBR2 router; the networks from pod 1 appear as type 5 LSAs:

```
BBR2>show ip ospf database

        OSPF Router with ID (200.200.200.200) (Process ID 1)

            Router Link States (Area 0)

Link ID          ADV Router       Age     Seq#       Checksum Link count
10.200.200.11    10.200.200.11    247     0x80000004 0x00638C 2
10.200.200.12    10.200.200.12    43      0x80000004 0x007774 2
200.200.200.200  200.200.200.200  553     0x800001E4 0x001697 6

            Type-5 AS External Link States

Link ID          ADV Router       Age     Seq#       Checksum Tag
10.1.0.0         10.200.200.11    68      0x80000001 0x00F8F5 0
10.1.0.0         10.200.200.12    46      0x80000001 0x00F2FA 0
10.1.1.0         10.200.200.11    71      0x80000001 0x00EDFF 0
10.1.2.0         10.200.200.12    46      0x80000001 0x00DC0F 0
10.1.3.0         10.200.200.11    71      0x80000001 0x00D714 0
10.200.200.11    10.200.200.11    71      0x80000001 0x008CC6 0
10.200.200.12    10.200.200.12    46      0x80000001 0x007CD4 0
10.200.200.13    10.200.200.11    71      0x80000001 0x0078D8 0
10.200.200.14    10.200.200.11    71      0x80000001 0x006EE1 0
10.254.0.0       200.200.200.200  1463    0x800001B2 0x00B0F2 0
BBR2>
```

Step 5   Examine the routing tables of both edge routers. Are all the routes optimal (in other words, are they going where you would expect them to)? If not, why?

Solution:

The following shows sample output on the P1R1 and P1R2 routers. On P1R1, the routes to P1R2's loopback and the 10.1.2.0/24 subnet are all going through BBR2 via OSPF rather than directly to P1R2 via RIP. On P1R2, the routes to all subnets within the pod are going through BBR2 via OSPF rather than staying internal to the pod via RIP.

> **NOTE** In this task, one of your edge routers will learn the route to 10.x.3.0 via RIPv2 while the other will learn it via OSPF; it depends which is configured first as to which will learn via which protocol.

```
P1R1#show ip route
<output omitted>
Gateway of last resort is 172.31.11.4 to network 0.0.0.0

     172.31.0.0/16 is variably subnetted, 3 subnets, 2 masks
C       172.31.11.0/24 is directly connected, Serial0/0/0
O       172.31.11.2/32 [110/1562] via 172.31.11.4, 00:03:24, Serial0/0/0
O       172.31.11.4/32 [110/781] via 172.31.11.4, 00:03:24, Serial0/0/0
     10.0.0.0/8 is variably subnetted, 9 subnets, 2 masks
C       10.200.200.11/32 is directly connected, Loopback0
R       10.200.200.14/32 [120/2] via 10.1.1.3, 00:00:11, FastEthernet0/0
O E2    10.200.200.12/32 [110/20] via 172.31.11.4, 00:03:25, Serial0/0/0
R       10.200.200.13/32 [120/1] via 10.1.1.3, 00:00:11, FastEthernet0/0
R       10.1.3.0/24 [120/1] via 10.1.1.3, 00:00:11, FastEthernet0/0
O E2    10.1.2.0/24 [110/20] via 172.31.11.4, 00:03:25, Serial0/0/0
C       10.1.1.0/24 is directly connected, FastEthernet0/0
C       10.1.0.0/24 is directly connected, Serial0/0/1
O E2    10.254.0.0/24 [110/50] via 172.31.11.4, 00:03:26, Serial0/0/0
S*   0.0.0.0/0 [1/0] via 172.31.11.4
P1R1#

P1R2#show ip route
<output omitted>
Gateway of last resort is 172.31.11.4 to network 0.0.0.0

     172.31.0.0/16 is variably subnetted, 3 subnets, 2 masks
C       172.31.11.0/24 is directly connected, Serial0/0/0
O       172.31.11.1/32 [110/1562] via 172.31.11.4, 00:04:06, Serial0/0/0
O       172.31.11.4/32 [110/781] via 172.31.11.4, 00:04:06, Serial0/0/0
     10.0.0.0/8 is variably subnetted, 9 subnets, 2 masks
O E2    10.200.200.11/32 [110/20] via 172.31.11.4, 00:04:06, Serial0/0/0
O E2    10.200.200.14/32 [110/20] via 172.31.11.4, 00:04:07, Serial0/0/0
C       10.200.200.12/32 is directly connected, Loopback0
O E2    10.200.200.13/32 [110/20] via 172.31.11.4, 00:04:07, Serial0/0/0
O E2    10.1.3.0/24 [110/20] via 172.31.11.4, 00:04:07, Serial0/0/0
C       10.1.2.0/24 is directly connected, FastEthernet0/0
O E2    10.1.1.0/24 [110/20] via 172.31.11.4, 00:04:07, Serial0/0/0
C       10.1.0.0/24 is directly connected, Serial0/0/1
O E2    10.254.0.0/24 [110/50] via 172.31.11.4, 00:04:08, Serial0/0/0
S*   0.0.0.0/0 [1/0] via 172.31.11.4
P1R2#
```

Step 6   Examine the IP routing table on both internal routers.

Solution:

The following shows sample output on the P1R3 and P1R4 routers:

```
P1R3#show ip route
<output omitted>
Gateway of last resort is 10.1.1.1 to network 0.0.0.0

      10.0.0.0/8 is variably subnetted, 8 subnets, 2 masks
R        10.200.200.11/32 [120/1] via 10.1.1.1, 00:00:27, FastEthernet0/0
R        10.200.200.14/32 [120/1] via 10.1.3.4, 00:00:24, Serial0/0/0
R        10.200.200.12/32 [120/2] via 10.1.3.4, 00:00:24, Serial0/0/0
C        10.200.200.13/32 is directly connected, Loopback0
C        10.1.3.0/24 is directly connected, Serial0/0/0
R        10.1.2.0/24 [120/1] via 10.1.3.4, 00:00:24, Serial0/0/0
C        10.1.1.0/24 is directly connected, FastEthernet0/0
R        10.1.0.0/24 [120/1] via 10.1.1.1, 00:00:28, FastEthernet0/0
R*  0.0.0.0/0 [120/1] via 10.1.1.1, 00:00:28, FastEthernet0/0
P1R3#

P1R4#show ip route
<output omitted>
Gateway of last resort is 10.1.2.2 to network 0.0.0.0

      10.0.0.0/8 is variably subnetted, 8 subnets, 2 masks
R        10.200.200.11/32 [120/2] via 10.1.3.3, 00:00:07, Serial0/0/0
C        10.200.200.14/32 is directly connected, Loopback0
R        10.200.200.12/32 [120/1] via 10.1.2.2, 00:00:25, FastEthernet0/0
R        10.200.200.13/32 [120/1] via 10.1.3.3, 00:00:07, Serial0/0/0
C        10.1.3.0/24 is directly connected, Serial0/0/0
C        10.1.2.0/24 is directly connected, FastEthernet0/0
R        10.1.1.0/24 [120/1] via 10.1.3.3, 00:00:08, Serial0/0/0
R        10.1.0.0/24 [120/1] via 10.1.2.2, 00:00:01, FastEthernet0/0
R*  0.0.0.0/0 [120/1] via 10.1.2.2, 00:00:01, FastEthernet0/0
P1R4#
```

Task 4: Filtering Routing Updates

Because the core router BBR2 is exchanging OSPF routes with your pod edge routers, the OSPF administrative distance of 110 causes packets from your edge routers to directly connected interfaces on other pod routers to go through the backbone router. In this task, you configure your edge routers to change the administrative distance of routes to internal pod networks that have been redistributed to the core by the edge routers to 125, to make them less attractive than the RIPv2 routes to the same networks. Follow these steps:

Step 1   On your edge routers, create an access list that matches all the network addresses in your pod. Hint: This can be done with two **permit** statements.

Step 2   Use the **distance** command and the access list you configured to make the routes to the networks in your pod learned via RIPv2 more attractive to the edge routers than the routes to the same networks that have been redistributed into OSPF; give the redistributed routes an administrative distance of 125.

Solution:

The following shows the required steps on the P1R1 router:

```
P1R1(config)#access-list 64 permit 10.1.0.0 0.0.255.255
P1R1(config)#access-list 64 permit 10.200.200.0 0.0.0.255
P1R1(config)#router ospf 1
P1R1(config-router)#distance 125 0.0.0.0 255.255.255.255 64
```

Step 3   Examine the routing table in the edge routers. Are the paths to the networks
in the pod correct? They should now be in the routing table as RIP routes,
in other words to routers within the pod, not as OSPF routes via BBR2.
Ping and trace to the networks in the pod to ensure that they are going the
way you expect them to.

Solution:

The following shows sample output on the P1R1 and P1R2 routers. The paths to the networks are
correct:

```
P1R1#show ip route
Gateway of last resort is 172.31.11.4 to network 0.0.0.0
     172.31.0.0/16 is variably subnetted, 3 subnets, 2 masks
C        172.31.11.0/24 is directly connected, Serial0/0/0
O        172.31.11.2/32 [110/1562] via 172.31.11.4, 00:03:02, Serial0/0/0
O        172.31.11.4/32 [110/781] via 172.31.11.4, 00:03:02, Serial0/0/0
     10.0.0.0/8 is variably subnetted, 9 subnets, 2 masks
C        10.200.200.11/32 is directly connected, Loopback0
R        10.200.200.14/32 [120/2] via 10.1.1.3, 00:00:19, FastEthernet0/0
                          [120/2] via 10.1.0.2, 00:00:07, Serial0/0/1
R        10.200.200.12/32 [120/1] via 10.1.0.2, 00:00:07, Serial0/0/1
R        10.200.200.13/32 [120/1] via 10.1.1.3, 00:00:19, FastEthernet0/0
R        10.1.3.0/24 [120/1] via 10.1.1.3, 00:00:19, FastEthernet0/0
R        10.1.2.0/24 [120/1] via 10.1.0.2, 00:00:07, Serial0/0/1
C        10.1.1.0/24 is directly connected, FastEthernet0/0
C        10.1.0.0/24 is directly connected, Serial0/0/1
O E2     10.254.0.0/24 [110/50] via 172.31.11.4, 00:03:03, Serial0/0/0
S*    0.0.0.0/0 [1/0] via 172.31.11.4
P1R1#

P1R2#show ip route
Gateway of last resort is 172.31.11.4 to network 0.0.0.0

     172.31.0.0/16 is variably subnetted, 3 subnets, 2 masks
C        172.31.11.0/24 is directly connected, Serial0/0/0
O        172.31.11.1/32 [110/1562] via 172.31.11.4, 00:00:28, Serial0/0/0
O        172.31.11.4/32 [110/781] via 172.31.11.4, 00:00:28, Serial0/0/0
     10.0.0.0/8 is variably subnetted, 9 subnets, 2 masks
R        10.200.200.11/32 [120/1] via 10.1.0.1, 00:00:24, Serial0/0/1
R        10.200.200.14/32 [120/1] via 10.1.2.4, 00:00:18, FastEthernet0/0
C        10.200.200.12/32 is directly connected, Loopback0
R        10.200.200.13/32 [120/2] via 10.1.2.4, 00:00:18, FastEthernet0/0
                          [120/2] via 10.1.0.1, 00:00:24, Serial0/0/1
R        10.1.3.0/24 [120/1] via 10.1.2.4, 00:00:18, FastEthernet0/0
C        10.1.2.0/24 is directly connected, FastEthernet0/0
R        10.1.1.0/24 [120/1] via 10.1.0.1, 00:00:25, Serial0/0/1
C        10.1.0.0/24 is directly connected, Serial0/0/1
O E2     10.254.0.0/24 [110/50] via 172.31.11.4, 00:00:29, Serial0/0/0
S*    0.0.0.0/0 [1/0] via 172.31.11.4
P1R2#
```

The following show sample traces to various addresses within pod 1 from P1R1 and P1R2, illustrating that the path stays within the pod;

```
P1R1#trace 10.1.3.4

Type escape sequence to abort.
Tracing the route to 10.1.3.4

  1 10.1.1.3 0 msec 0 msec 4 msec
  2 10.1.3.4 12 msec *  12 msec
P1R1#trace 10.1.2.4

Type escape sequence to abort.
Tracing the route to 10.1.2.4

  1 10.1.0.2 12 msec 12 msec 16 msec
  2 10.1.2.4 12 msec *  12 msec
P1R1#

P1R2#trace 10.1.1.3

Type escape sequence to abort.
Tracing the route to 10.1.1.3

  1 10.1.0.1 16 msec 12 msec 16 msec
  2 10.1.1.3 12 msec *  12 msec
P1R2#trace 10.1.3.3

Type escape sequence to abort.
Tracing the route to 10.1.3.3

  1 10.1.2.4 4 msec 0 msec 0 msec
  2 10.1.3.3 16 msec *  12 msec
P1R2#
```

Step 4   Save your configurations to NVRAM.

Solution:

The following shows the required step on the P1R1 router:

```
P1R1#copy run start
Destination filename [startup-config]?
Building configuration...
[OK]
```

Exercise Verification

You have successfully completed this exercise when you achieve the following results:

■ You have established OSPF adjacencies between the edge routers and the core BBR2 router and exchanged the routing updates.

■ You have established that the RIPv2 updates are exchanged between the internal routers and edge routers.

■ You have established that redistribution is configured from RIPv2 to OSPF.

■ You have configured your edge routers to eliminate suboptimal routes.

Configuration Exercise 7-2: Tuning Basic Redistribution

In this exercise, you configure a route map to change the metric of redistributed routes. You also configure a distribute list to filter routes into the core.

> **NOTE** Throughout this exercise, the pod number is referred to as *x*, and the router number is referred to as *y*. Substitute the appropriate numbers as needed.

Objectives

Your task in this Configuration Exercise is to configure a route map and a distribute list to control redistribution.

Visual Objective

Figure 7-29 illustrates the topology used in this exercise.

Figure 7-29 *Tuning Basic Redistribution Configuration Exercise Topology*

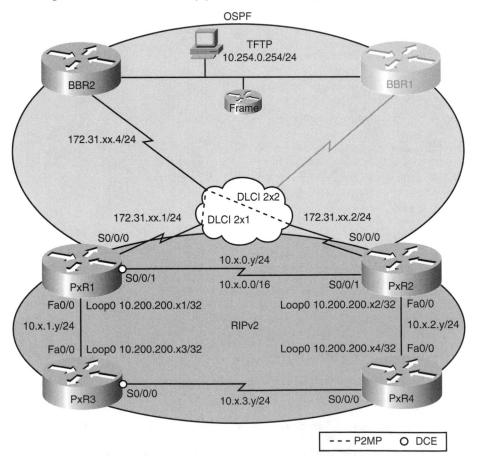

Command List

In this exercise, you use the commands in Table 7-25, listed in logical order. Refer to this list if you need configuration command assistance during the exercise.

> **CAUTION** Although the command syntax is shown in this table, the addresses shown are typically for the P*x*R1 and P*x*R3 routers. Be careful when addressing your routers! Refer to the exercise instructions and the appropriate visual objective diagram for addressing details.

Table 7-25 *Tuning Basic Redistribution Exercise Commands*

Command	Description
(config)#**route-map CONVERT permit 10**	Creates a route map statement.
(config-route-map)#**match metric 1**	Matches the source protocol metric.
(config-route-map)#**set metric 1000**	Sets the destination protocol metric.
(config-router)#**redistribute rip subnets route-map CONVERT**	Redistributes RIP routes using the route map.
(config)#**access-list 61 deny 10.200.200.0 0.0.0.255**	Configures access list 61 to deny any IP address that matches the first 24 bits of 10.200.200.0.
(config-router)#**distribute-list 61 out rip**	Configures a distribute list to use access list 61 to determine which routes will be distributed from RIP (into OSPF).

Task 1: Tuning Basic Redistribution with Route Maps

In this task, you use route maps to tune the redistribution. Follow these steps:

Step 1   Telnet to BBR2 and display the IP routing table. Notice that all your pod routes (10.*x*.0.0 and 10.200.200.*xy*) have the same OSPF metric of 20.

Solution:

The following shows sample output on the BBR2 router:

```
BBR2>show ip route
<output omitted>
Gateway of last resort is not set

     172.31.0.0/16 is variably subnetted, 4 subnets, 2 masks
B       172.31.1.0/24 [20/0] via 10.254.0.1, 06:14:15
C       172.31.11.0/24 is directly connected, Serial0/0.1
O       172.31.11.1/32 [110/781] via 172.31.11.1, 06:13:24, Serial0/0.1
O       172.31.11.2/32 [110/781] via 172.31.11.2, 06:13:24, Serial0/0.1
     10.0.0.0/8 is variably subnetted, 9 subnets, 2 masks
O E2    10.200.200.11/32 [110/20] via 172.31.11.2, 06:13:24, Serial0/0.1
                         [110/20] via 172.31.11.1, 06:13:24, Serial0/0.1
O E2    10.200.200.14/32 [110/20] via 172.31.11.2, 06:13:24, Serial0/0.1
                         [110/20] via 172.31.11.1, 06:13:24, Serial0/0.1
O E2    10.200.200.12/32 [110/20] via 172.31.11.2, 06:13:24, Serial0/0.1
                         [110/20] via 172.31.11.1, 06:13:24, Serial0/0.1
```

```
O E2    10.200.200.13/32 [110/20] via 172.31.11.2, 06:13:24, Serial0/0/0.1
                          [110/20] via 172.31.11.1, 06:13:24, Serial0/0/0.1
O E2    10.1.3.0/24 [110/20] via 172.31.11.2, 06:13:24, Serial0/0/0.1
                    [110/20] via 172.31.11.1, 06:13:24, Serial0/0/0.1
O E2    10.1.2.0/24 [110/20] via 172.31.11.2, 06:13:24, Serial0/0/0.1
                    [110/20] via 172.31.11.1, 06:13:24, Serial0/0/0.1
O E2    10.1.1.0/24 [110/20] via 172.31.11.2, 06:13:24, Serial0/0/0.1
                    [110/20] via 172.31.11.1, 06:13:24, Serial0/0/0.1
O E2    10.1.0.0/24 [110/20] via 172.31.11.2, 06:13:24, Serial0/0/0.1
                    [110/20] via 172.31.11.1, 06:13:24, Serial0/0/0.1
C       10.254.0.0/24 is directly connected, FastEthernet0/0
BBR2>
```

Step 2   Having the same metric for all the redistributed RIP routes prevents the core from making accurate routing decisions for those routes. The central OSPF domain needs to have different OSPF metrics based on how far the network is from the redistribution point.

At the edge routers, create a route map for altering the metric of the redistributed routes. Match the RIP metric and set an appropriate OSPF metric as follows:

- For a RIP hop count of 1, set the OSPF metric to 1000.

- For a RIP hop count of 2, set the OSPF metric to 2000.

- Permit all other routes to be redistributed, with the default metric.

Step 3   On the edge routers, change the redistribution from RIPv2 into OSPF to use this route map.

Solution:

The following shows the required steps on the P1R1 router:

```
P1R1(config)#route-map CONVERT permit 10
P1R1(config-route-map)#match metric 1
P1R1(config-route-map)#set metric 1000
P1R1(config-route-map)#route-map CONVERT permit 20
P1R1(config-route-map)#match metric 2
P1R1(config-route-map)#set metric 2000
P1R1(config-route-map)#route-map CONVERT permit 30
P1R1(config-route-map)#router ospf 1
P1R1(config-router)#no redistribute rip subnets
P1R1(config-router)#redistribute rip subnets route-map CONVERT
```

Step 4   View the routing table on BBR2. Did this route map convert the metrics appropriately?

Why are there no routes with a metric of 2000 in the routing table even though your route map specified it?

Look at the routing table on both edge routes for RIP metric 120/2. Remember that both routers are applying the route map and BBR2 will place the lowest metric in the routing table.

Why are there routes with a metric of 20 in BBR2's routing table?

Solution:

The following shows sample output on the BBR2 and P1R1 routers; the metrics were converted appropriately. Some routes would have been converted to an OSPF metric of 2000, but there are no routes with a metric of 2000 in the routing table because BBR2 learns routes from both pod edge routers via OSPF, and chooses the one with the lowest metric to be put in to the routing table. For example, BBR2 learns the 10.200.200.14/32 route via 172.31.11.2 at a cost of 1000; it also learns the same route via 172.31.11.1 at a cost of 2000 (2 RIP hops), but it chooses the lower cost of 1000.

The BBR2 routes with a metric of 20 are the routes that had a RIP hop count of 0 before they were redistributed. These routes did not match either of the two **match** commands in the route-map, and therefore their metric was not changed.

```
BBR2>show ip route
<output omitted>
Gateway of last resort is not set

     172.31.0.0/16 is variably subnetted, 4 subnets, 2 masks
B       172.31.1.0/24 [20/0] via 10.254.0.1, 00:26:56
C       172.31.11.0/24 is directly connected, Serial0/0/0.1
O       172.31.11.1/32 [110/781] via 172.31.11.1, 00:25:13, Serial0/0/0.1
O       172.31.11.2/32 [110/781] via 172.31.11.2, 00:25:13, Serial0/0/0.1
     10.0.0.0/8 is variably subnetted, 9 subnets, 2 masks
O E2    10.200.200.11/32 [110/20] via 172.31.11.1, 00:05:16, Serial0/0/0.1
O E2    10.200.200.14/32 [110/1000] via 172.31.11.2, 00:05:16, Serial0/0/0.1
O E2    10.200.200.12/32 [110/20] via 172.31.11.2, 00:02:22, Serial0/0/0.1
O E2    10.200.200.13/32 [110/1000] via 172.31.11.1, 00:05:16, Serial0/0/0.1
O E2    10.1.3.0/24 [110/1000] via 172.31.11.2, 00:05:16, Serial0/0/0.1
                    [110/1000] via 172.31.11.1, 00:05:16, Serial0/0/0.1
O E2    10.1.2.0/24 [110/20] via 172.31.11.2, 00:02:22, Serial0/0/0.1
O E2    10.1.1.0/24 [110/20] via 172.31.11.1, 00:05:17, Serial0/0/0.1
O E2    10.1.0.0/24 [110/20] via 172.31.11.2, 00:02:22, Serial0/0/0.1
                    [110/20] via 172.31.11.1, 00:02:22, Serial0/0/0.1
C       10.254.0.0/24 is directly connected, FastEthernet0/0
BBR2>

P1R1#show ip route
<output omitted>
Gateway of last resort is 172.31.11.4 to network 0.0.0.0

     172.31.0.0/16 is variably subnetted, 3 subnets, 2 masks
C       172.31.11.0/24 is directly connected, Serial0/0/0
O       172.31.11.2/32 [110/1562] via 172.31.11.4, 00:27:24, Serial0/0/0
O       172.31.11.4/32 [110/781] via 172.31.11.4, 00:27:24, Serial0/0/0
     10.0.0.0/8 is variably subnetted, 9 subnets, 2 masks
C       10.200.200.11/32 is directly connected, Loopback0
R       10.200.200.14/32 [120/2] via 10.1.1.3, 00:00:27, FastEthernet0/0
                         [120/2] via 10.1.0.2, 00:00:07, Serial0/0/1
R       10.200.200.12/32 [120/1] via 10.1.0.2, 00:00:07, Serial0/0/1
R       10.200.200.13/32 [120/1] via 10.1.1.3, 00:00:27, FastEthernet0/0
R       10.1.3.0/24 [120/1] via 10.1.1.3, 00:00:00, FastEthernet0/0
R       10.1.2.0/24 [120/1] via 10.1.0.2, 00:00:08, Serial0/0/1
C       10.1.1.0/24 is directly connected, FastEthernet0/0
C       10.1.0.0/24 is directly connected, Serial0/0/1
O E2    10.254.0.0/24 [110/50] via 172.31.11.4, 00:27:26, Serial0/0/0
S*   0.0.0.0/0 [1/0] via 172.31.11.4
P1R1#
```

Task 2: Filtering Routing Updates

In this task, you configure your edge routers to filter information about the loopback addresses to the core. Because the core is exchanging OSPF routes with your pod, use a distribute list to block these routes from being redistributed into OSPF.

Follow these steps:

Step 1   Create an access list that will match the four loopback addresses.

Step 2   Use a distribute list to block the RIPv2 routes specified by this access list from being redistributed into OSPF.

Solution:

The following shows the required steps on the P1R1 router:

```
P1R1(config)#access-list 61 deny 10.200.200.0 0.0.0.255
P1R1(config)#access-list 61 permit any
P1R1(config)#router ospf 1
P1R1(config-router)#distribute-list 61 out rip
```

Step 3   Examine the routing table on BBR2. Verify that the loopback addresses are not listed.

Solution:

The following shows sample output on the BBR2 router; the loopback addresses are not listed:

```
BBR2>show ip route
<output omitted>
Gateway of last resort is not set

     172.31.0.0/16 is variably subnetted, 4 subnets, 2 masks
B       172.31.1.0/24 [20/0] via 10.254.0.1, 13:27:53
C       172.31.11.0/24 is directly connected, Serial0/0/0.1
O       172.31.11.1/32 [110/781] via 172.31.11.1, 00:00:05, Serial0/0/0.1
O       172.31.11.2/32 [110/781] via 172.31.11.2, 00:00:05, Serial0/0/0.1
     10.0.0.0/24 is subnetted, 5 subnets
O E2    10.1.3.0 [110/1000] via 172.31.11.2, 00:00:06, Serial0/0/0.1
                 [110/1000] via 172.31.11.1, 00:00:06, Serial0/0/0.1
O E2    10.1.2.0 [110/20] via 172.31.11.2, 00:00:06, Serial0/0/0.1
O E2    10.1.1.0 [110/20] via 172.31.11.1, 00:00:06, Serial0/0/0.1
O E2    10.1.0.0 [110/20] via 172.31.11.2, 00:00:06, Serial0/0/0.1
                 [110/20] via 172.31.11.1, 00:00:06, Serial0/0/0.1
C       10.254.0.0 is directly connected, FastEthernet0/0
BBR2>
```

Step 4   Can the core ping your loopback addresses?

Solution:

No, the core cannot ping the loopback addresses because it does not have a route to them.

Step 5   Save your configurations to NVRAM.

Solution:

The following shows the required step on the P1R1 router:

```
P1R1#copy run start
Destination filename [startup-config]?
Building configuration...
[OK]
```

Exercise Verification

You have completed this exercise when have tuned the basic redistribution configuration using route maps and have configured your edge routers to filter information about the loopback addresses to the core.

Review Questions

Answer the following questions, and then refer to Appendix A, "Answers to Review Questions," for the answers.

1. What are some of the things you need to consider when migrating to another routing protocol?

2. List some things you may need to consider when transitioning to a new IP addressing plan.

3. A router is configured with a primary and secondary address on its FastEthernet 0/0 interface. It is also configured to run EIGRP on this interface. How will the secondary address interact with EIGRP?

4. What steps are involved when migrating to a new routing protocol?

5. List some reasons why you might use multiple routing protocols in a network.

6. What is redistribution?

7. Does redistributing between two routing protocols change the routing table on the router that is doing the redistribution?

8. What are some issues that arise with redistribution?

9. What may be the cause of a routing loop in a network that has redundant paths between two routing processes?

10. What two parameters do routers use to select the best path when they learn two or more routes to the same destination from different routing protocols?

11. Fill in the default administrative distances for the following routing protocols.

Routing Protocols	Default Administrative Distance Value
Connected interface	
Static route out an interface	
Static route to a next-hop address	
EIGRP summary route	
External BGP	
Internal EIGRP	

continues

(Continued)

Routing Protocols	Default Administrative Distance Value
IGRP	
OSPF	
IS-IS	
RIPv1 and RIPv2	
EGP	
ODR	
External EIGRP	
Internal BGP	
Unknown	

12. When configuring a default metric for redistributed routes, should the metric be set to a value *larger* or *smaller* than the largest metric within the receiving autonomous system?

13. Fill in the default seed metrics for the following protocols.

Protocol That the Route Is Redistributed Into	Default Seed Metric
RIP	
IGRP/EIGRP	
OSPF	
IS-IS	
BGP	

14. What is the safest way to perform redistribution between two routing protocols?

15. Can redistribution be configured between IPX RIP and IP RIP? Between IPX EIGRP and IP EIGRP? Between IP EIGRP and OSPF?

16. When configuring redistribution into RIP, what is the *metric-value* parameter?

17. Router A is running RIPv2 and OSPF. In the RIPv2 domain, it learns about the 10.1.0.0/16 and 10.3.0.0/16 routes. In the OSPF domain, it learns about the 10.5.0.0/16 and 172.16.1.0/24 routes. What is the result of the following configuration on Router A?

```
router ospf 1
  redistribute rip metric 20
```

18. What are the five components of the EIGRP routing metric?

19. When redistributing routes into IS-IS, what is the default *level-value* parameter?

20. What happens if you use the **metric** parameter in a **redistribute** command and you use the **default-metric** command?

21. What does the **passive-interface default** command do?

22. Suppose you have a dialup WAN connection between site A and site B. What can you do to prevent excess routing update traffic from crossing the link but still have the boundary routers know the networks that are at the remote sites?

23. A distribute list allows routing updates to be filtered based on what?

24. What is the difference between the **distribute-list out** and **distribute-list in** commands?

25. What command is used to configure filtering of the routing update traffic from an interface? At what prompt is this command entered?

26. True or false: In a route map statement with multiple **match** commands, all **match** statements in the route map statement must be considered true for the route map statement to be considered matched.

27. True or false: In a **match** statement with multiple conditions, all conditions in the **match** statement must be true for that **match** statement to be considered a match.

28. What are some applications of route maps?

29. What is the *map-tag* parameter in a **route-map** command?

30. What commands would be used to configure the use of a route map called TESTING when redistributing OSPF 10 traffic into RIP?

31. What does the following command do?

    ```
    distance 150 0.0.0.0 255.255.255.255 3
    ```

32. What command can be used to discover the path that a packet takes through a network?

33. What are the three DHCP roles that a Cisco IOS device can perform?

34. In what ways can DHCP addresses be allocated?

35. What does the **service dhcp** command do?

36. What must be enabled on an interface for the IOS DHCP relay agent to be enabled?

37. Packets sent to which ports are forwarded by default when the **ip helper-address** command is configured on an interface?

This chapter introduces Border Gateway Protocol (BGP), including the fundamentals of BGP operation. This chapter covers the following topics:

- BGP Terminology, Concepts, and Operation

- Configuring BGP

- Verifying and Troubleshooting BGP

- Basic BGP Path Manipulation Using Route Maps

CHAPTER **8**

Configuring the Border Gateway Protocol

The Internet is becoming a vital resource in many organizations, resulting in redundant connections to multiple Internet service providers (ISPs). With multiple connections, Border Gateway Protocol (BGP) is an alternative to using default routes to control path selections.

Configuring and troubleshooting BGP can be complex. A BGP administrator must understand the various options involved in properly configuring BGP for scalable internetworking. This chapter introduces BGP terminology and concepts, and BGP configuration and troubleshooting techniques. The chapter also introduces route maps for manipulating BGP path attributes.

BGP Terminology, Concepts, and Operation

This section provides an introduction to BGP, and an explanation of various BGP terminology and concepts.

Autonomous Systems

To understand BGP, you first need to understand how it is different than the other protocols discussed so far in this book, including an understanding of autonomous systems.

One way to categorize routing protocols is by whether they are interior or exterior:

- **Interior Gateway Protocol (IGP)**—A routing protocol that exchanges routing information *within* an autonomous system (AS). Routing Information Protocol (RIP), Open Shortest Path First (OSPF), Intermediate System-to-Intermediate System (IS-IS), and Enhanced Interior Gateway Routing Protocol (EIGRP) are examples of IGPs for IP.

- **Exterior Gateway Protocol (EGP)**—A routing protocol that exchanges routing information *between* different autonomous systems. BGP is an example of an EGP.

Figure 8-1 illustrates the concept of IGPs and EGPs.

Figure 8-1 *IGPs Operate Within an Autonomous System, and EGPs Operate Between Autonomous Systems*

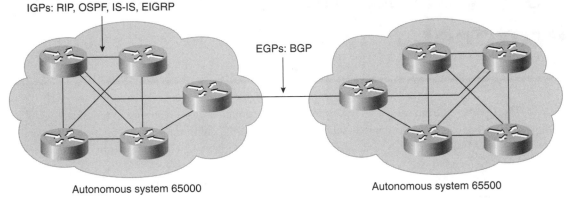

BGP is an Interdomain Routing Protocol (IDRP), which is also known as an EGP. All of the routing protocols you have seen so far in this book are IGPs.

> **NOTE** The term IDRP as used in this sense is a generic term, not the IDRP defined in ISO/IEC International Standard 10747, *Protocol for the Exchange of Inter-Domain Routing Information Among Intermediate Systems to Support Forwarding of ISO 8473 PDUs.*

BGP version 4 (BGP-4) is the latest version of BGP. It is defined in Requests for Comments (RFC) 4271, *A Border Gateway Protocol (BGP-4)*. As noted in this RFC, the classic definition of an AS is "a set of routers under a single technical administration, using an Interior Gateway Protocol (IGP) and common metrics to determine how to route packets within the AS, and using an inter-AS routing protocol to determine how to route packets to other [autonomous systems]."

> **NOTE** Extensions to BGP-4, known as BGP4+, have been defined to support multiple protocols, including IP version 6 (IPv6). These multiprotocol extensions to BGP are defined in RFC 2858, *Multiprotocol Extensions for BGP-4.*

Autonomous systems might use more than one IGP, with potentially several sets of metrics. The important characteristic of an AS from the BGP point of view is that the AS appears to other autonomous systems to have a single coherent interior routing plan, and it presents a consistent picture of which destinations can be reached through it. All parts of the AS must be connected to each other.

The Internet Assigned Numbers Authority (IANA) is the umbrella organization responsible for allocating AS numbers. Regional Internet Registries (RIRs) are nonprofit corporations established for the purpose of administration and registration of IP address space and autonomous system numbers. There are five RIRs, as follows:

- African Network Information Centre (AfriNIC) is responsible for the continent of Africa.

- Asia Pacific Network Information Centre (APNIC) administers the numbers for the Asia Pacific region.

- American Registry for Internet Numbers (ARIN) has jurisdiction over assigning numbers for Canada, the United States, and several islands in the Caribbean Sea and North Atlantic Ocean.

- Latin American and Caribbean IP Address Regional Registry (LACNIC) is responsible for allocation in Latin America and portions of the Caribbean.

- Réseaux IP Européens Network Coordination Centre (RIPE NCC) administers the numbers for Europe, the Middle East, and Central Asia.

This AS designator is a 16-bit number, with a range of 1 to 65535. RFC 1930, *Guidelines for Creation, Selection, and Registration of an Autonomous System (AS)*, provides guidelines for the use of AS numbers. A range of AS numbers, 64512 to 65535, is reserved for private use, much like the private IP addresses. All of the examples and exercises in this book use private AS numbers, to avoid publishing AS numbers belonging to an organization.

You need to use the IANA-assigned AS number, rather than a private AS number, only if your organization plans to use an EGP, such as BGP, to connect to a public network such as the Internet.

BGP Use Between Autonomous Systems

BGP is used between autonomous systems, as illustrated in Figure 8-2.

KEY POINT | **BGP Provides Interdomain Routing**

The main goal of BGP is to provide an interdomain routing system that guarantees the loop-free exchange of routing information between autonomous systems. BGP routers exchange information about paths to destination networks.

BGP is a successor to Exterior Gateway Protocol (EGP). (Note the dual use of the EGP acronym.) The EGP protocol was developed to isolate networks from each other at the early stages of the Internet.

There is a distinction between an ordinary autonomous system and one that has been configured with BGP to implement a transit policy. The latter is called an ISP or a service provider.

Figure 8-2 *BGP-4 Is Used Between Autonomous Systems on the Internet*

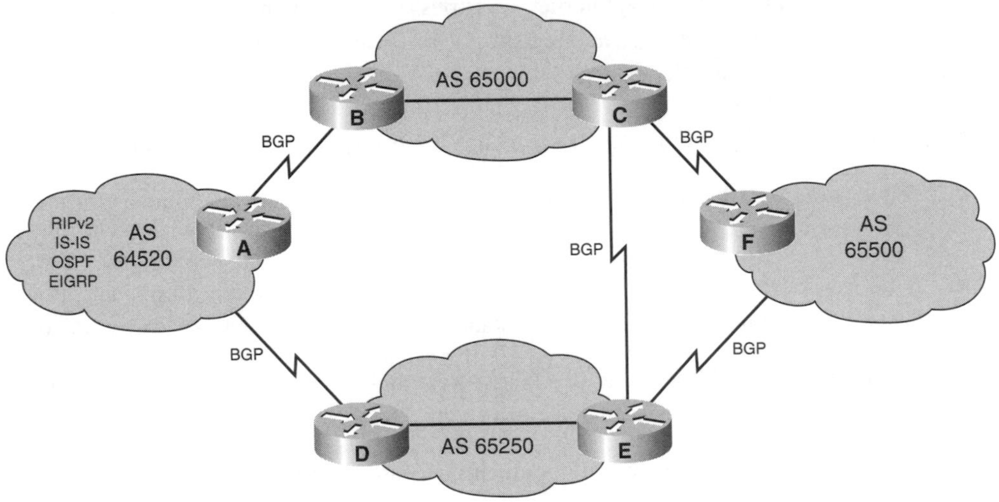

Many RFCs relate to BGP-4, including those listed in Table 8-1.

Table 8-1 *RFCs Relating to BGP-4*

RFC Number	RFC Title
RFC 1771	*A Border Gateway Protocol 4 (BGP-4)* (made obsolete by RFC 4271)
RFC 1772	*An Application of BGP on the Internet*
RFC 1773	*Experience with the BGP-4 Protocol*
RFC 1774	*BGP-4 Protocol Analysis*
RFC 1863	*A BGP/IDRP Route Server Alternative to a Full-Mesh Routing* (made obsolete by RFC 4223)
RFC 1930	*Guidelines for Creation, Selection, and Registration of an Autonomous System (AS)*
RFC 1965	*AS Confederations for BGP* (made obsolete by RFC 3065)
RFC 1966	*BGP Route Reflection—An Alternative to Full-Mesh IBGP* (updated by RFC 2796)
RFC 1997	*BGP Communities Attribute*
RFC 1998	*Application of the BGP Community Attribute in Multihome Routing*
RFC 2042	*Registering New BGP Attribute Types*

Table 8-1   *RFCs Relating to BGP-4 (Continued)*

RFC Number	RFC Title
RFC 2283	*Multiprotocol Extensions for BGP-4* (made obsolete by RFC 2858)
RFC 2385	*Protection of BGP Sessions via TCP MD5 Signature Option*
RFC 2439	*BGP Route Flap Damping*
RFC 2545	*Use of BGP-4 Multiprotocol Extensions for IPv6 Interdomain Routing*
RFC 2547	*BGP/MPLS VPNs*
RFC 2796	*BGP Route Reflection—An Alternative to Full-Mesh IBGP* (updates RFC 1966)
RFC 2842	*Capabilities Advertisement with BGP-4* (made obsolete by RFC 3392)
RFC 2858	*Multiprotocol Extensions for BGP-4* (makes RFC 2283 obsolete)
RFC 2918	*Route Refresh Capability for BGP-4*
RFC 3065	*Autonomous System Confederations for BGP* (makes RFC 1965 obsolete)
RFC 3107	*Carrying Label Information in BGP-4*
RFC 3392	*Capabilities Advertisement with BGP-4* (makes RFC 2842 obsolete)
RFC 4223	*Reclassification of RFC 1863 to Historic* (makes RFC 1863 obsolete)
RFC 4271	*A Border Gateway Protocol 4 (BGP-4)* (makes RFC 1771 obsolete)

NOTE   You can search for RFCs by number at http://www.rfc-editor.org/rfcsearch.html.

BGP-4 has many enhancements over earlier protocols. It is used extensively on the Internet today to connect ISPs and to interconnect enterprises to ISPs.

BGP-4 and its extensions are the only acceptable version of BGP available for use on the public Internet. BGP-4 carries a network mask for each advertised network and supports both variable-length subnet mask (VLSM) and classless interdomain routing (CIDR). BGP-4 predecessors did not support these capabilities, which are currently mandatory on the Internet. When CIDR is used on a core router for a major ISP, the IP routing table, which is composed mostly of BGP routes, has more than 190,000 CIDR blocks; not using CIDR at the Internet level would cause the IP routing table to have more than 2,000,000 entries. Using CIDR, and, therefore, BGP-4, prevents the Internet routing table from becoming too large for interconnecting millions of users.

Comparison with Other Scalable Routing Protocols

Table 8-2 compares some of BGP's key characteristics to the other scalable routing protocols discussed in this book.

Table 8-2 *Comparison of Scalable Routing Protocols*

Protocol	Interior or Exterior	Type	Hierarchy Required?	Metric
OSPF	Interior	Link state	Yes	Cost
IS-IS	Interior	Link state	Yes	Metric
EIGRP	Interior	Advanced distance vector	No	Composite
BGP	Exterior	Path vector	No	Path vectors (attributes)

As shown in Table 8-2, OSPF, IS-IS, and EIGRP are interior protocols, whereas BGP is an exterior protocol.

Chapter 2, "Routing Principles," discusses the characteristics of distance vector and link-state routing protocols. OSPF and IS-IS are link-state protocols, whereas EIGRP is an advanced distance vector protocol. BGP is also a distance vector protocol, with many enhancements; it is also called a path vector protocol.

Most link-state routing protocols, including OSPF and IS-IS, require a hierarchical design, especially to support proper address summarization. OSPF and IS-IS let you separate a large internetwork into smaller internetworks called areas. EIGRP and BGP do not require a hierarchical topology.

BGP works differently than IGPs. Internal routing protocols look at the path cost to get somewhere, usually the quickest path from one point in a corporate network to another based upon certain metrics. RIP uses hop count and looks to cross the fewest Layer 3 devices to reach the destination network. OSPF uses cost, which on Cisco routers is based on bandwidth, as its metric. The IS-IS metric is typically based on bandwidth (but it defaults to 10 on all interfaces on Cisco routers). EIGRP uses a composite metric, with bandwidth and accumulated delay considered by default.

In contrast, BGP does not look at speed for the best path. Rather, BGP is a policy-based routing protocol that allows an AS to control traffic flow using multiple BGP attributes. Routers running BGP exchange network reachability information, called path vectors or attributes, including a list of the full path of BGP AS numbers that a router should take to reach a destination network. BGP allows a provider to fully use all of its bandwidth by manipulating these path attributes.

Using BGP in an Enterprise Network

The Internet is a collection of autonomous systems that are interconnected to allow communication among them. BGP provides the routing between these autonomous systems.

Enterprises that want to connect to the Internet do so through one or more ISPs. If your organization has only one connection to one ISP, then you probably do not need to use BGP; instead you would use a default route. If you have multiple connections to one or to multiple ISPs, however, then BGP might be appropriate because it allows manipulation of path attributes, facilitating selection of the optimal path.

When BGP is running between routers in different autonomous systems, it is called *External BGP (EBGP)*. When BGP is running between routers in the same autonomous system, it is called *Internal BGP (IBGP)*.

Understanding how BGP works is important to avoid creating problems for your AS as a result of running BGP. For example, enterprise AS 65500 in Figure 8-3 is learning routes from both ISP-A and ISP-B via EBGP and is also running IBGP on all of its routers. Autonomous system 65500 learns about routes and chooses the best way to each one based on the configuration of the routers in the AS and the BGP routes passed from the ISPs. If one of the connections to the ISPs goes down, traffic will be sent through the other ISP.

Figure 8-3   *Using BGP to Connect to the Internet*

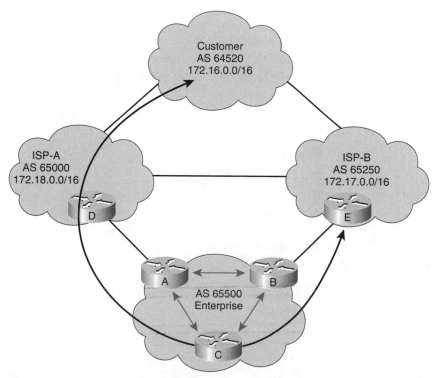

One of the routes that AS 65500 learns from ISP-A is the route to 172.18.0.0/16. If that route is passed through AS 65500 using IBGP and is mistakenly announced to ISP-B, then ISP-B might decide that the best way to get to 172.18.0.0/16 is through AS 65500, instead of through the Internet. AS 65500 would then be considered a transit AS (an ISP); this would be a very undesirable situation. AS 65500 wants to have a redundant Internet connection, but does not want to act as a transit AS between ISP-A and ISP-B. Careful BGP configuration is required to avoid this situation.

BGP Multihoming Options

Multihoming is when an AS has more than one connection to the Internet. Two typical reasons for multihoming are as follows:

- **To increase the reliability of the connection to the Internet**—If one connection fails, the other connection remains available.

- **To increase the performance of the connection**—Better paths can be used to certain destinations.

The benefits of BGP are apparent when an AS has multiple EBGP connections to either a single ISP or multiple ISPs. Having multiple connections enables an organization to have redundant connections to the Internet so that if a single path becomes unavailable, connectivity can still be maintained.

An organization can be multihomed to either a single ISP or to multiple ISPs. A drawback to having all of your connections to a single ISP is that connectivity issues in that single ISP can cause your AS to lose connectivity to the Internet. By having connections to multiple ISPs, an organization gains the following benefits:

- Has redundancy with the multiple connections

- Is not tied into the routing policy of a single ISP

- Has more paths to the same networks for better policy manipulation

A multihomed AS will run EBGP with its external neighbors and might also run IBGP internally.

If an organization has determined that it will perform multihoming with BGP, three common ways to do this are as follows:

- **Each ISP passes only a default route to the AS**—The default route is passed to the internal routers.

- **Each ISP passes only a default route and provider-owned specific routes to the AS—** These routes can be passed to internal routers, or all internal routers in the transit path can run BGP and pass these routes between them.

- **Each ISP passes all routes to the AS—**All internal routers in the transit path run BGP and pass these routes between them.

The sections that follow describe these options in greater detail.

Multihoming with Default Routes from All Providers

The first multihoming option is to receive only a default route from each ISP. This configuration requires the least resources within the AS because a default route is used to reach any external destinations. The AS sends all of its routes to the ISPs, which process and pass the routes on to other autonomous systems.

If a router in the AS learns about multiple default routes, the local IGP installs the best default route into the routing table. From the perspective of this router, it takes the default route with the least-cost IGP metric. This IGP default route will route packets that are destined to the external networks to an edge router of this AS, which is running EBGP with the ISPs. The edge router will use the BGP default route to reach all external networks.

The route that inbound packets take to reach the AS is decided outside of the AS (within the ISPs and other autonomous systems).

Regional ISPs that have multiple connections to national or international ISPs commonly implement this option. The regional ISPs do not use BGP for path manipulation; however, they require the capability of adding new customers and the networks of the customers. If the regional ISP does not use BGP, then each time that the regional ISP adds a new set of networks, the customers must wait until the national ISPs add these networks to their BGP process and place static routes pointing at the regional ISP. By running EBGP with the national or international ISPs, the regional ISP needs to add only the new networks of the customers to its BGP process. These new networks automatically propagate across the Internet with minimal delay.

A customer that chooses to receive default routes from all providers must understand the following limitations of this option:

- Path manipulation cannot be performed because only a single route is being received from each ISP.

- Bandwidth manipulation is extremely difficult and can be accomplished only by manipulating the IGP metric of the default route.

- Diverting some of the traffic from one exit point to another is challenging because all destinations are using the same default route for path selection.

Figure 8-4 illustrates an example. AS 65000 and AS 65250 send default routes into AS 65500. The ISP that a specific router within AS 65500 uses to reach any external address is decided by the IGP metric that is used to reach the default route within the autonomous system. For example, if AS 65500 uses RIP, Router C selects the route with the lowest hop count to the default route when sending packets to network 172.16.0.0.

Figure 8-4 *Default Routes from All ISPs*

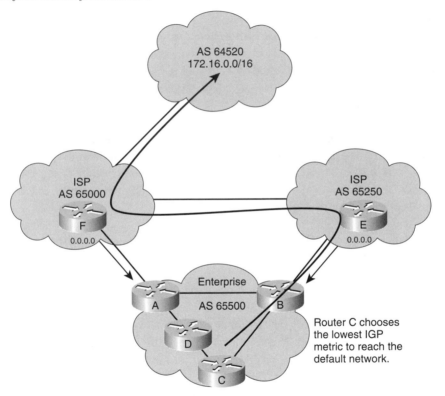

Multihoming with Default Routes and Partial Table from All Providers

In the second design option for multihoming, all ISPs pass default routes plus select specific routes to the AS.

An enterprise that is running EBGP with an ISP and that wants a partial routing table generally receives the networks that the ISP and its other customers own. The enterprise can also receive the routes from any other AS.

Major ISPs are assigned between 2000 and 10,000 CIDR blocks of IP addresses from the IANA, which they reassign to their customers. If the ISP passes this information to a customer that wants only a partial BGP routing table, the customer can redistribute these routes into its IGP. The internal routers of the customer (these routers are not running BGP) can then receive these routes via redistribution. They can take the nearest exit point based on the best metric of specific networks instead of taking the nearest exit point based on the default route.

Acquiring a partial BGP table from each provider is beneficial because path selection will be more predictable than when using a default route.

Figure 8-5 illustrates an example. ISPs in AS 65000 and AS 64900 send default routes and the routes that each ISP owns to AS 64500. The enterprise (AS 64500) asked both providers to also send routes to networks in AS 64520 because of the amount of traffic between AS 64520 and AS 64500.

Figure 8-5 *Default Routes and Partial Table from All ISPs*

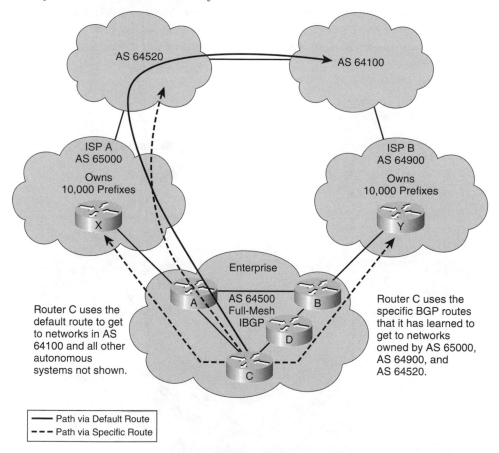

By running IBGP between the internal routers within AS 64500, AS 64500 can choose the optimal path to reach the customer networks (AS 64520 in this case). The routes to AS 64100 and to other autonomous systems (not shown in the figure) that are not specifically advertised to AS 64500 by ISP A and ISP B are decided by the IGP metric that is used to reach the default route within the AS.

Multihoming with Full Routes from All Providers

In the third multihoming option, all ISPs pass all routes to the AS, and IBGP is run on at least all the routers in the transit path in this AS. This option allows the internal routers of the AS to take the path through the best ISP for each route.

This configuration requires a lot of resources within the AS because it must process all the external routes.

The AS sends all its routes to the ISPs, which process the routes and pass them to other autonomous systems.

Figure 8-6 illustrates an example. AS 65000 and AS 64900 send all routes into AS 64500. The ISP that a specific router within AS 64500 uses to reach the external networks is determined by the BGP protocol. The routers in AS 64500 can be configured to influence the path to certain networks. For example, Router A and Router B can influence the outbound traffic from AS 64500.

Figure 8-6 *Full Routes from All ISPs*

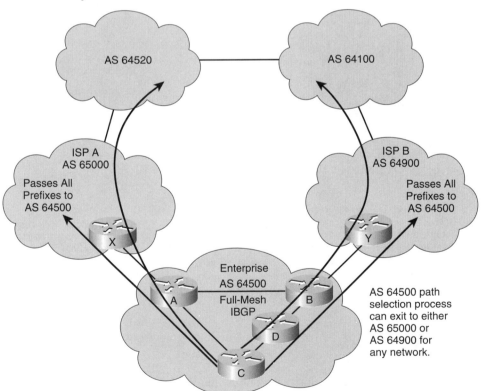

BGP Path Vector Characteristics

Internal routing protocols announce a list of networks and the metrics to get to each network. In contrast, BGP routers exchange network reachability information, called path vectors, made up of path attributes, as illustrated in Figure 8-7. The path vector information includes a list of the full path of BGP AS numbers (hop-by-hop) necessary to reach a destination network. Other attributes include the IP address to get to the next AS (the *next-hop* attribute) and how the networks at the end of the path were introduced into BGP (the *origin code* attribute); the later "BGP Attributes" section describes all the BGP attributes in detail.

Figure 8-7   *BGP Uses Path Vector Routing*

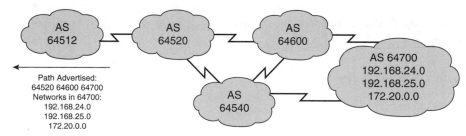

This AS path information is used to construct a graph of loop-free autonomous systems and is used to identify routing policies so that restrictions on routing behavior can be enforced based on the AS path.

KEY POINT

The BGP AS Path Is Guaranteed to Be Loop Free

The BGP AS path is guaranteed to always be loop free. A router running BGP does not accept a routing update that already includes its AS number in the path list, because the update has already passed through its AS, and accepting it again will result in a routing loop.

BGP is designed to scale to huge internetworks, such as the Internet.

BGP allows routing-policy decisions to be applied to the path of BGP AS numbers so that routing behavior can be enforced at the AS level and to determine how data will flow through the AS. These policies can be implemented for all networks owned by an AS, for a certain CIDR block of network numbers (prefixes), or for individual networks or subnetworks. The policies are based on the attributes carried in the routing information and configured on the routers.

KEY POINT

BGP Can Advertise Only the Routes It Uses

BGP specifies that a BGP router can advertise to its peers in neighboring autonomous systems only those routes that it uses. This rule reflects the hop-by-hop routing paradigm generally used throughout the current Internet.

Some policies cannot be supported by the hop-by-hop routing paradigm and, thus, require techniques such as source routing to enforce. For example, BGP does not allow one AS to send traffic to a neighboring AS, intending that the traffic take a different route from that taken by traffic originating in that neighboring AS. In other words, you cannot influence how a neighboring AS will route your traffic, but you can influence how your traffic gets to a neighboring AS. However, BGP can support any policy conforming to the hop-by-hop routing paradigm.

Because the current Internet uses only the hop-by-hop routing paradigm, and because BGP can support any policy that conforms to that paradigm, BGP is highly applicable as an inter-AS routing protocol for the current Internet.

For example, in Figure 8-8, the following paths are possible for AS 64512 to reach networks in AS 64700, through AS 64520:

■ 64520 64600 64700

■ 64520 64600 64540 64550 64700

■ 64520 64540 64600 64700

■ 64520 64540 64550 64700

Figure 8-8 *BGP Supports Routing Policies*

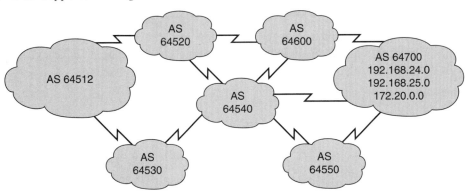

Autonomous system 64512 does not see all these possibilities. Autonomous system 64520 advertises to AS 64512 only its best path, 64520 64600 64700, the same way that IGPs announce only their best least-cost routes. This path is the only path through AS 64520 that AS 64512 sees. All packets that are destined for 64700 via 64520 take this path, because it is the AS-by-AS (hop-by-hop) path that AS 64520 uses to reach the networks in AS 64700. Autonomous system 64520 does not announce the other paths, such as 64520 64540 64600 64700, because it does not choose any of those paths as the best path, based on the BGP routing policy in AS 64520.

AS 64512 does not learn of the second-best path, or any other paths from 64520, unless the best path through AS 64520 becomes unavailable.

Even if AS 64512 were aware of another path through AS 64520 and wanted to use it, AS 64520 would not route packets along that other path, because AS 64520 selected 64520 64600 64700 as its best path, and all AS 64520 routers will use that path as a matter of BGP policy. BGP does not let one AS send traffic to a neighboring AS, intending that the traffic take a different route from that taken by traffic originating in the neighboring AS.

To reach the networks in AS 64700, AS 64512 can choose to use the path through AS 64520 or it can choose to go through the path that AS 64530 is advertising. Autonomous system 64512 selects the best path to take based on its own BGP routing policies.

When to Use BGP

BGP use in an AS is most appropriate when the effects of BGP are well-understood and at least one of the following conditions exists:

- The AS allows packets to transit through it to reach other autonomous systems (for example, it is a service provider).

- The AS has multiple connections to other autonomous systems.

- Routing policy and route selection for traffic entering and leaving the AS must be manipulated.

If an enterprise has a policy that requires it to differentiate between its traffic and traffic from its ISP, the enterprise must connect to its ISP using BGP. If, instead, an enterprise is connected to its ISP with a static route, traffic from that enterprise is indistinguishable from traffic from the ISP for policy decision-making purposes.

BGP was designed to allow ISPs to communicate and exchange packets. These ISPs have multiple connections to one another and have agreements to exchange updates. BGP is the protocol that is used to implement these agreements between two or more autonomous systems. If BGP is not properly controlled and filtered, it has the potential to allow an outside AS to affect the traffic flow to your AS. For example, if you are a customer connected to ISP-A and ISP-B (for redundancy), you want to implement a routing policy to ensure that ISP-A does not send traffic to ISP-B via your AS. You want to be able to receive traffic destined for your AS through each ISP, but you do not want to waste valuable resources and bandwidth within your AS to route traffic for your ISPs. This chapter focuses on how BGP operates and how to configure it properly so that you can prevent this from happening.

When Not to Use BGP

BGP is not always the appropriate solution to interconnect autonomous systems. For example, if there is only one exit path from the AS, a default or static route is appropriate; using BGP will not accomplish anything except to use router CPU resources and memory. If the routing policy that will be implemented in an AS is consistent with the policy implemented in the ISP AS, it is not necessary or even desirable to configure BGP in that AS. The only time BGP will be required is when the local policy differs from the ISP policy.

Do not use BGP if one or more of the following conditions exist:

- A single connection to the Internet or another AS

- Lack of memory or processor power on routers to handle constant BGP updates

- You have a limited understanding of route filtering and the BGP path-selection process

In these cases, use static or default routes instead, as discussed in Chapter 2.

BGP Characteristics

What type of protocol is BGP? Chapter 2 covers the characteristics of distance vector and link-state routing protocols. BGP is sometimes categorized as an advanced distance vector protocol, but it is actually a path vector protocol. BGP has many differences from standard distance vector protocols, such as RIP.

BGP uses the Transmission Control Protocol (TCP) as its transport protocol, which provides connection-oriented reliable delivery. In this way, BGP assumes that its communication is reliable and, therefore, BGP does not have to implement any retransmission or error-recovery mechanisms, like EIGRP does. BGP information is carried inside TCP segments using protocol 179; these segments are carried inside IP packets. Figure 8-9 illustrates this concept.

Figure 8-9 *BGP Is Carried Inside TCP Segments, Which Are Inside IP Packets*

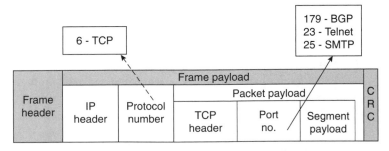

NOTE BGP is the only IP routing protocol to use TCP as its transport layer. OSPF and EIGRP reside directly above the IP layer. IS-IS is at the network layer. RIP uses the User Datagram Protocol (UDP) for its transport layer.

KEY POINT	**BGP Uses TCP to Communicate Between Neighbors**

Two routers speaking BGP establish a TCP connection with one another and exchange messages to open and confirm the connection parameters. These two routers are called BGP peer routers or BGP neighbors.

After the TCP connection is made, full BGP routing tables (described in the later "BGP Tables" section) are exchanged. However, because the connection is reliable, BGP routers need to send only changes (incremental updates) after that. Periodic routing updates are not required on a reliable link, so triggered updates are used. BGP sends keepalive messages, similar to the hello messages sent by OSPF, IS-IS, and EIGRP.

OSPF and EIGRP have their own internal functions to ensure that update packets are explicitly acknowledged. These protocols use a one-for-one window so that if either OSPF or EIGRP has multiple packets to send, the next packet cannot be sent until an acknowledgment from the first update packet is received. This process can be very inefficient and cause latency issues if thousands of update packets must be exchanged over relatively slow serial links; however, OSPF and EIGRP rarely have thousands of update packets to send. For example, EIGRP can hold more than 100 networks in one EIGRP update packet, so 100 EIGRP update packets can hold up to 10,000 networks. Most organizations do not have 10,000 subnets.

BGP, on the other hand, has more than 190,000 networks (and growing) on the Internet to advertise, and it uses TCP to handle the acknowledgment function. TCP uses a dynamic window, which allows for up to 65,576 bytes to be outstanding before it stops and waits for an acknowledgment. For example, if 1000-byte packets are being sent and the maximum window size is being used, BGP would have to stop and wait for an acknowledgment only when 65 packets had not been acknowledged.

NOTE   The CIDR report, at http://www.cidr-report.org/, is a good reference site to see the current size of the Internet routing tables and other related information.

TCP is designed to use a sliding window, where the receiver acknowledges at the halfway point of the sending window. This method allows any TCP application, such as BGP, to continue streaming packets without having to stop and wait, as OSPF or EIGRP would require.

BGP Neighbor Relationships

No single router can handle communications with the tens of thousands of the routers that run BGP and are connected to the Internet, representing more than 22,000 autonomous systems. A BGP router forms a direct neighbor relationship with a limited number of other BGP routers. Through these BGP neighbors, a BGP router learns of the paths through the Internet to reach any advertised network.

Any router that runs BGP is called a BGP speaker.

BGP Peer = BGP Neighbor

A BGP peer, also known as a BGP neighbor, is a BGP speaker that is configured to form a neighbor relationship with another BGP speaker for the purpose of directly exchanging BGP routing information with one another.

A BGP speaker has a limited number of BGP neighbors with which it peers and forms a TCP-based relationship, as illustrated in Figure 8-10. BGP peers can be either internal or external to the AS.

Figure 8-10 *Routers That Have Formed a BGP Connection Are BGP Neighbors or Peers*

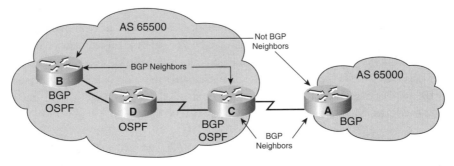

NOTE A BGP peer must be configured under the BGP process with a **neighbor** command. This command instructs the BGP process to establish a relationship with the neighbor at the address listed in the command and to exchange BGP routing updates with that neighbor.

BGP configuration is described later, in the "Configuring BGP" section.

External BGP Neighbors

Recall that when BGP is running between routers in different autonomous systems, it is called EBGP. Routers running EBGP are usually directly connected to each other, as shown in Figure 8-11.

An EBGP neighbor is a router outside this AS; an IGP is not run between the EBGP neighbors. For two routers to exchange BGP routing updates, the TCP reliable transport layer on each side must successfully pass the TCP three-way handshake before the BGP session can be established. Therefore, the IP address used in the **neighbor** command must be reachable without using an IGP. This can be accomplished by pointing at an address that can be reached through a directly connected network or by using static routes to that IP address. Generally, the neighbor address used is the address of the directly connected network.

Figure 8-11 *EBGP Neighbors Belong to Different Autonomous Systems*

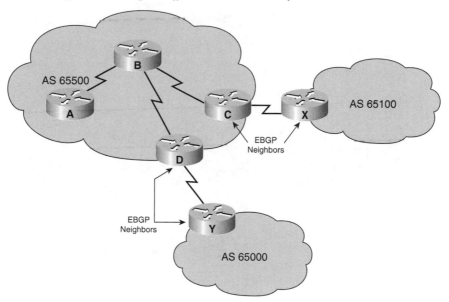

Internal BGP Neighbors

Recall that when BGP is running between routers within the same AS, it is called IBGP. IBGP is run within an AS to exchange BGP information so that all internal BGP speakers have the same BGP routing information about outside autonomous systems and so this information can be passed to other autonomous systems.

Routers running IBGP do not have to be directly connected to each other, as long as they can reach each other so that TCP handshaking can be performed to set up the BGP neighbor relationships. The IBGP neighbor can be reached by a directly connected network, static routes, or an internal routing protocol. Because multiple paths generally exist within an AS to reach other routers, a loopback address is usually used in the BGP **neighbor** command to establish the IBGP sessions.

For example, in Figure 8-12, Routers A, D, and C learn the paths to the external autonomous systems from their respective EBGP neighbors (Routers Z, Y, and X). If the link between Routers D and Y goes down, Router D must learn new routes to the external autonomous systems. Other BGP routers within AS 65500 that were using Router D to get to external networks must also be informed that the path through Router D is unavailable. Those BGP routers within AS 65500 need to have the alternative paths through Routers A and C in their BGP topology database. You must set up IBGP sessions between all routers in the transit path in AS 65500 so that each router in the transit path within the AS learns about paths to the external networks via IBGP.

Figure 8-12 *IBGP Neighbors Are in the Same AS*

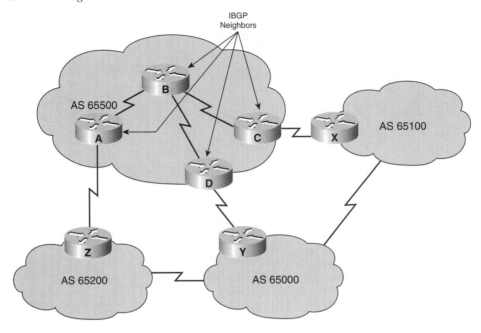

IBGP on All Routers in a Transit Path

This section explains why IBGP route propagation requires all routers in the transit path in an AS to run IBGP.

IBGP in a Transit AS

BGP was originally intended to run along the borders of an AS, with the routers in the middle of the AS ignorant of the details of BGP—hence the name "*Border Gateway* Protocol." A transit AS, such as the one shown in Figure 8-13, is an AS that routes traffic from one external AS to another external AS. As mentioned earlier, transit autonomous systems are typically ISPs. All routers in a transit AS must have complete knowledge of external routes. Theoretically, one way to achieve this goal is to redistribute BGP routes into an IGP at the edge routers; however, this approach has problems.

Because the current Internet routing table is very large, redistributing all the BGP routes into an IGP is not a scalable way for the interior routers within an AS to learn about the external networks. Another method that you can use is to run IBGP on all routers within the AS.

Figure 8-13 *BGP in a Transit AS*

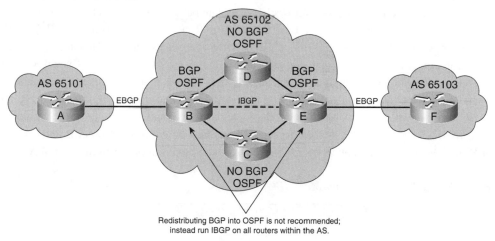

Redistributing BGP into OSPF is not recommended;
instead run IBGP on all routers within the AS.

IBGP in a Nontransit AS

A nontransit AS, such as an organization that is multihoming with two ISPs, does not pass routes between the ISPs. To make proper routing decisions, however, the BGP routers within the AS still require knowledge of all BGP routes passed to the AS.

BGP does not work in the same manner as IGPs. Because the designers of BGP could not guarantee that an AS would run BGP on all routers, a method had to be developed to ensure that IBGP speakers could pass updates to one another while ensuring that no routing loops would exist.

To avoid routing loops within an AS, BGP specifies that routes learned through IBGP are never propagated to other IBGP peers. Recall that the **neighbor** command enables BGP updates between BGP speakers. By default, each BGP speaker is assumed to have a **neighbor** statement for all other IBGP speakers in the AS—this is known as *full mesh IBGP*.

If the sending IBGP neighbor is not fully meshed with each IBGP router, the routers that are not peering with this router will have different IP routing tables than the routers that are peering with it. The inconsistent routing tables can cause routing loops or routing black holes, because the default assumption by all routers running BGP within an AS is that each BGP router exchanges IBGP information directly with all other BGP routers in the AS.

By fully meshing all IBGP neighbors, when a change is received from an external AS, the BGP router for the local AS is responsible for informing all other IBGP neighbors of the change. IBGP neighbors that receive this update do not send it to any other IBGP neighbor, because they assume that the sending IBGP neighbor is fully meshed with all other IBGP speakers and has sent each IBGP neighbor the update.

BGP Partial-Mesh and Full-Mesh Examples

The top network in Figure 8-14 shows IBGP update behavior in a partially meshed neighbor environment. Router B receives a BGP update from Router A. Router B has two IBGP neighbors, Routers C and D, but does not have an IBGP neighbor relationship with Router E. Routers C and D learn about any networks that were added or withdrawn behind Router B. Even if Routers C and D have IBGP neighbor sessions with Router E, they assume that the AS is fully meshed for IBGP and do not replicate the update and send it to Router E. Sending the IBGP update to Router E is Router B's responsibility, because it is the router with firsthand knowledge of the networks in and beyond AS 65101. Router E does not learn of any networks through Router B and does not use Router B to reach any networks in AS 65101 or other autonomous systems behind AS 65101.

Figure 8-14 *Partial-Mesh Versus Full-Mesh IBGP*

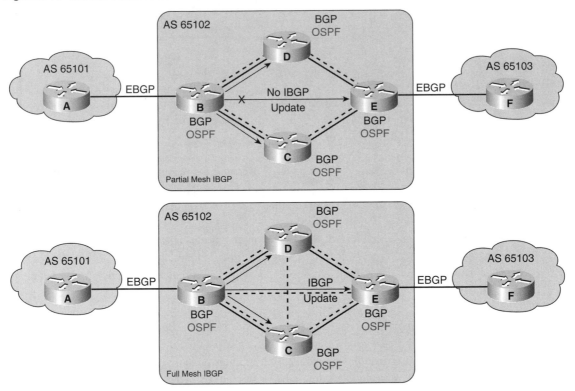

In the lower portion of Figure 8-14, IBGP is fully meshed. When Router B receives an update from Router A, it updates all three of its IBGP peers, Router C, Router D, and Router E. OSPF, the IGP, is used to route the TCP segment containing the BGP update from Router A to Router E, because these two routers are not directly connected. The update is sent once to each neighbor and not duplicated by any other IBGP neighbor, which reduces unnecessary traffic. In fully meshed IBGP, each router assumes that every other internal router has a **neighbor** statement that points to each IBGP neighbor.

TCP and Full Mesh

TCP was selected as the transport layer for BGP because TCP can move a large volume of data reliably. With the very large full Internet routing table changing constantly, using TCP for windowing and reliability was determined to be the best solution, as opposed to developing a BGP one-for-one windowing capability like OSPF or EIGRP.

TCP sessions cannot be multicast or broadcast because TCP has to ensure the delivery of packets to each recipient. Because TCP cannot use broadcasting, BGP cannot use it either.

Because each IBGP router needs to send routes to all the other IBGP neighbors in the same AS (so that they all have a complete picture of the routes sent to the AS) and they cannot use broadcast, they must use fully meshed BGP (TCP) sessions.

When all routers running BGP in an AS are fully meshed and have the same database as a result of a consistent routing policy, they can apply the same path-selection formula. The path-selection results will therefore be uniform across the AS. Uniform path selection across the AS means no routing loops and a consistent policy for exiting and entering the AS.

Routing Issues if BGP Not on in All Routers in a Transit Path

Figure 8-15 illustrates how routing might not work if all routers in a transit path are not running BGP.

Figure 8-15 *Routing Might Not Work if BGP Not Run on All Routers in a Transit Path*

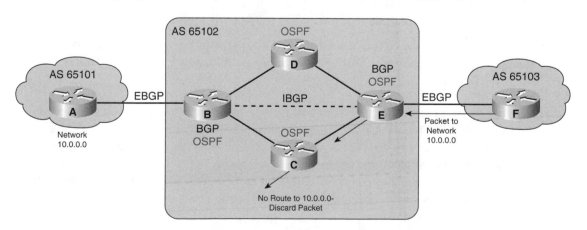

In this example, Routers A, B, E, and F are the only ones running BGP. Router B has an EBGP **neighbor** statement for Router A and an IBGP **neighbor** statement for Router E. Router E has an EBGP **neighbor** statement for Router F and an IBGP **neighbor** statement for Router B. Routers C and D are not running BGP. Routers B, C, D and E are running OSPF as their IGP.

Network 10.0.0.0 is owned by AS 65101 and is advertised by Router A to Router B via an EBGP session. Router B advertises it to Router E via an IBGP session. Routers C and D never learn about this network because it is not redistributed into the local routing protocol (OSPF in this example), and Routers C and D are not running BGP. If Router E advertises this network to Router F in AS 65103, and Router F starts forwarding packets to network 10.0.0.0 through AS 65102, where would Router E send the packets?

Router E would send the packets to its BGP peer, Router B. To get to Router B, however, the packets must go through Router C or D, but those routers do not have an entry in their routing tables for network 10.0.0.0. Thus, when Router E forwards packets with a destination address in network 10.0.0.0 to either Routers C or D, those routers discard the packets.

Even if Routers C and D have a default route going to the exit points of the AS (Routers B and E), there is a good chance that when Router E sends a packet for network 10.0.0.0 to Routers C or D, those routers may send it back to Router E, which will forward it again to Routers C or D, causing a routing loop. To solve this problem, BGP must be implemented on Routers C and D.

KEY POINT | **Routers in Transit Path Must Run BGP**

All routers in the path between IBGP neighbors within an AS, known as the transit path, must also be running BGP. These IBGP sessions must be fully meshed.

BGP Synchronization

KEY POINT | **BGP Synchronization Rule**

The BGP synchronization rule states that a BGP router should not use, or advertise to an external neighbor, a route learned by IBGP, unless that route is local or is learned from the IGP.

In the past, best practice dictated redistributing BGP into the IGP running in an autonomous system, so that IBGP was not needed in every router in the transit path. In this case, synchronization was needed to make sure that packets did not get lost, so synchronization was on by default. As the Internet grew, the number of routes in the BGP table became too much for the IGPs to handle, so the best practice was changed to not redistributing BGP into the IGP, but instead using IBGP on all routers in the transit path. In this case, synchronization is not needed; thus, it is now off by default.

KEY POINT

Synchronization Is Disabled by Default

BGP synchronization is disabled by default in Cisco IOS Software Release 12.2(8)T and later; it was on by default in earlier Cisco IOS Software releases.

With the default of synchronization disabled, BGP can use and advertise to external BGP neighbor routes learned from an IBGP neighbor that are not present in the local routing table.

BGP synchronization is unnecessary in some situations. It is safe to have BGP synchronization off (disabled) only if all routers in the transit path in the autonomous system are running full-mesh IBGP, for the reasons discussed in the previous section.

If synchronization is enabled and your autonomous system is passing traffic from one autonomous system to another, BGP should not advertise a route before all routers in your autonomous system have learned about the route via IGP. In other words, BGP and the IGP must be synchronized before networks learned from an IBGP neighbor can be used.

If synchronization is enabled, a router learning a route via IBGP waits until the IGP has propagated the route within the autonomous system and then advertises it to external peers. This is done so that all routers in the autonomous system are synchronized and can route traffic that the autonomous system advertises to other autonomous systems it can route. The BGP synchronization rule also ensures consistency of information throughout the autonomous system and avoids *black holes* (for example, advertising a destination to an external neighbor when not all the routers within the autonomous system can reach the destination) within the autonomous system.

Having synchronization disabled allows the routers to carry fewer routes in IGP and allows BGP to converge more quickly because it can advertise the routes as soon as it learns them.

Enable synchronization if there are routers in the BGP transit path in the autonomous system that are not running BGP (and therefore the routers do not have full-mesh IBGP within the autonomous system).

Figure 8-16 illustrates an example. Routers A, B, C, and D are all running IBGP and an IGP with each other (full-mesh IBGP). There are no matching IGP routes for the BGP routes (Routers A and B are not redistributing the BGP routes into the IGP). Routers A, B, C, and D have IGP routes to the internal networks of autonomous system 65500 but do not have IGP routes to external networks, such as 172.16.0.0.

Figure 8-16 *BGP Synchronization Example*

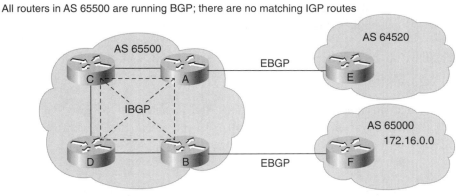

All routers in AS 65500 are running BGP; there are no matching IGP routes

Router B advertises the route to 172.16.0.0 to the other routers in AS 65500 using IBGP.

If synchronization is on in AS 65500 in Figure 8-16, the following happens:

- Router B uses the route to 172.16.0.0 and installs it in its routing table.

- Routers A, C, and D do not use or advertise the route to 172.16.0.0.

- Router E does not hear about 172.16.0.0. If Router E receives traffic destined for network 172.16.0.0, it does not have a route for that network and cannot forward the traffic.

If synchronization is off (the default) in AS 65500 in Figure 8-16, the following happens:

- Routers A, C, and D use and advertise the route to 172.16.0.0 that they receive via IBGP and install it in their routing tables (assuming, of course, that Routers A, C, and D can reach the next-hop address for 172.16.0.0).

- Router E hears about 172.16.0.0 from Router A. Router E has a route to 172.16.0.0 and can send traffic destined for that network.

- If Router E sends traffic for 172.16.0.0, Routers A, C, and D route the packets correctly to Router B. Router E sends the packets to Router A, and Router A forwards them to Router C. Router C has learned a route to 172.16.0.0 via IBGP and, therefore, forwards the packets to Router D. Router D forwards the packets to Router B. Router B forwards the packets to Router F, which routes them to network 172.16.0.0.

In modern autonomous systems, because the size of the Internet routing table is large, redistributing from BGP into an IGP is not scalable; therefore, most modern autonomous systems run full-mesh IBGP and do not require synchronization. Some advanced BGP configuration methods, such as route reflectors and confederations, reduce the IBGP full-mesh requirements (route reflectors are discussed in Appendix E, "BGP Supplement").

BGP Tables

As shown in Figure 8-17, a router running BGP keeps its own table for storing BGP information received from and sent to other routers.

Figure 8-17   *Router Running BGP Keeps a BGP Table, Separate from the IP Routing Table*

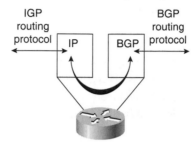

KEY POINT

BGP Table

This table of BGP information is known by many names in various documents, including

- BGP table

- BGP topology table

- BGP topology database

- BGP routing table

- BGP forwarding database

This table is separate from the IP routing table in the router.

The router can be configured to share information between the BGP table and the IP routing table.

BGP also keeps a neighbor table containing a list of neighbors with which it has a BGP connection.

For BGP to establish an adjacency, you must configure it explicitly for each neighbor. BGP forms a TCP relationship with each of the configured neighbors and keeps track of the state of these relationships by periodically sending a BGP/TCP keepalive message.

NOTE   BGP sends BGP/TCP keepalives by default every 60 seconds.

After establishing an adjacency, the neighbors exchange the BGP routes that are in their IP routing table. Each router collects these routes from each neighbor with which it successfully established an adjacency and places them in its BGP forwarding database. All routes that have been learned from each neighbor are placed in the BGP forwarding database. The best routes for each network are selected from the BGP forwarding database using the BGP route selection process (discussed in the section "The Route Selection Decision Process," later in this chapter) and then are offered to the IP routing table.

Each router compares the offered BGP routes to any other possible paths to those networks in its IP routing table, and the best route, based on administrative distance, is installed in the IP routing table. EBGP routes (BGP routes learned from an external AS) have an administrative distance of 20. IBGP routes (BGP routes learned from within the AS) have an administrative distance of 200.

BGP Message Types

BGP defines the following message types:

- Open

- Keepalive

- Update

- Notification

After a TCP connection is established, the first message sent by each side is an open message. If the open message is acceptable, a keepalive message confirming the open message is sent back by the side that received the open message.

When the open is confirmed, the BGP connection is established, and update, keepalive, and notification messages can be exchanged.

BGP peers initially exchange their full BGP routing tables. From then on, incremental updates are sent as the routing table changes. Keepalive packets are sent to ensure that the connection is alive between the BGP peers, and notification packets are sent in response to errors or special conditions.

An open message includes the following information:

- **Version**—This 8-bit field indicates the message's BGP version number. The highest common version that both routers support is used. Most BGP implementations today use the current version, BGP-4.

- **My autonomous system**—This 16-bit field indicates the sender's AS number. The peer router verifies this information; if it is not the AS number expected, the BGP session is torn down.

- **Hold time**—This 16-bit field indicates the maximum number of seconds that can elapse between the successive keepalive or update messages from the sender. Upon receipt of an open message, the router calculates the value of the hold timer to use by using the smaller of its configured hold time and the hold time received in the open message.

- **BGP router identifier (router ID)**—This 32-bit field indicates the sender's BGP identifier. The BGP router ID is an IP address assigned to that router and is determined at startup. The BGP router ID is chosen the same way the OSPF router ID is chosen; it is the highest active IP address on the router, unless a loopback interface with an IP address exists, in which case it is the highest such loopback IP address. Alternatively, the router ID can be statically configured, overriding the automatic selection.

- **Optional parameters**—A length field indicates the total length of the optional parameters field in octets. These parameters are Type, Length, and Value (TLV)-encoded. An example of an optional parameter is session authentication.

BGP does not use any transport protocol-based keepalive mechanism to determine whether peers can be reached. Instead, keepalive messages are exchanged between peers often enough to keep the hold timer from expiring. If the negotiated hold time interval is 0, periodic keepalive messages are not sent. A keepalive message consists of only a message header.

An update message has information on one path only; multiple paths require multiple messages. All the attributes in the message refer to that path, and the networks are those that can be reached through that path. An update message might include the following fields:

- **Withdrawn routes**—A list of IP address prefixes for routes that are being withdrawn from service, if any.

- **Path attributes**—The AS-path, origin, local preference, and so forth, as discussed in the next section. Each path attribute includes the attribute type, attribute length, and attribute value (TLV). The attribute type consists of the attribute flags, followed by the attribute type code.

- **Network layer reachability information**—A list of IP address prefixes that can be reached by this path.

A BGP router sends a notification message when it detects an error condition. The BGP router closes the BGP connection immediately after sending the notification message. Notification messages include an error code, an error subcode, and data related to the error.

BGP Neighbor States

BGP is a state machine that takes a router through the following states with its neighbors:

- Idle

- Connect

- Active

- Open sent

- Open confirm

- Established

Only when the connection is in the established state are update, keepalive, and notification messages exchanged.

Neighbor states are discussed in more detail in the "Understanding and Troubleshooting BGP Neighbor States" section later in this chapter.

NOTE Keepalive messages consist of only a message header and have a length of 19 bytes; they are sent every 60 seconds by default. Other messages might be between 19 and 4096 bytes long. The default hold time is 180 seconds.

BGP Attributes

BGP routers send BGP update messages about destination networks to other BGP routers. As described in the previous section, update messages can contain network layer reachability information, which is a list of one or more networks (IP address prefixes), and path attributes, which are a set of BGP metrics describing the path to these networks (routes). The following are some terms defining how these attributes are implemented:

- An attribute is either well-known or optional, mandatory or discretionary, and transitive or nontransitive. An attribute might also be partial.

- Not all combinations of these characteristics are valid; path attributes fall into four separate categories:

   — Well-known mandatory

   — Well-known discretionary

— Optional transitive

— Optional nontransitive

■ Only optional transitive attributes might be marked as partial.

These characteristics are described in the following sections.

BGP Update Message Contents

A BGP update message includes a variable-length sequence of path attributes describing the route. A path attribute is of variable length and consists of three fields:

■ Attribute type, which consists of a 1-byte attribute flags field and a 1-byte attribute-type code field

■ Attribute length

■ Attribute value

The first bit of the attribute flags field indicates whether the attribute is optional or well-known. The second bit indicates whether an optional attribute is transitive or nontransitive. The third bit indicates whether a transitive attribute is partial or complete. The fourth bit indicates whether the attribute length field is 1 or 2 bytes. The rest of the flag bits are unused and are set to 0.

Well-Known Attributes

A well-known attribute is one that all BGP implementations must recognize and propagate to BGP neighbors.

A well-known mandatory attribute *must* appear in all BGP updates. A well-known discretionary attribute does not have to be present in all BGP updates.

Optional Attributes

Attributes that are not well-known are called optional. Optional attributes are either transitive or nontransitive.

BGP routers that implement an optional attribute might propagate it to other BGP neighbors, based on its meaning.

BGP routers that do not implement an optional transitive attribute should pass it to other BGP routers untouched and mark the attribute as partial.

BGP routers that do not implement an optional nontransitive attribute must delete the attribute and must not pass it to other BGP routers.

Defined BGP Attributes

The attributes defined by BGP include the following:

- Well-known mandatory attributes:

    — AS-path

    — Next hop

    — Origin

- Well-known discretionary attributes:

    — Local preference

    — Atomic aggregate

- Optional transitive attributes:

    — Aggregator

    — Community

- Optional nontransitive attribute:

    — Multiexit-discriminator (MED)

In addition, Cisco has defined a weight attribute for BGP. The weight is configured locally on a router and is not propagated to any other BGP routers.

The AS-path, next-hop, origin, local preference, community, MED, and weight attributes are expanded upon in the following sections. The atomic aggregate and aggregator attributes are discussed in Appendix E, as is BGP community configuration.

BGP Attribute Type Codes

Cisco uses the following attribute type codes:

- Origin—type code 1

- AS-path—type code 2

- Next-hop—type code 3

- MED—type code 4

- Local-preference—type code 5

- Atomic-aggregate—type code 6

- Aggregator—type code 7

- Community—type code 8 (Cisco-defined)

- Originator-ID—type code 9 (Cisco-defined)

- Cluster list—type code 10 (Cisco-defined)

The originator ID and cluster list attributes are discussed in Appendix E.

The AS-Path Attribute

The AS-path attribute is a well-known mandatory attribute. Whenever a route update passes through an AS, the AS number is *prepended* to that update (in other words, it is put at the beginning of the list) when it is advertised to the next EBGP neighbor.

KEY POINT | **AS-Path Attribute**

The AS-path attribute is the list of AS numbers that a route has traversed to reach a destination, with the number of the AS that originated the route at the end of the list.

In Figure 8-18, Router A advertises network 192.168.1.0 in AS 64520. When that route traverses AS 65500, Router C prepends its own AS number to it. When the route to 192.168.1.0 reaches Router B, it has two AS numbers attached to it. From Router B's perspective, the path to reach 192.168.1.0 is (65500, 64520).

Figure 8-18 *Router C Prepends Its Own Autonomous System Number as It Passes Routes from Router A to Router B*

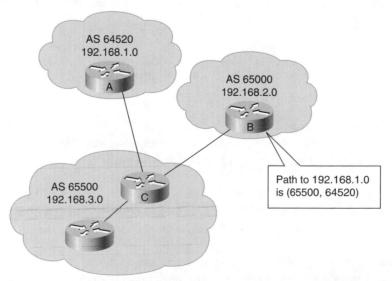

The same applies for 192.168.2.0 and 192.168.3.0. Router A's path to 192.168.2.0 is (65500 65000)—it traverses AS 65500 and then AS 65000. Router C has to traverse path (65000) to reach 192.168.2.0 and path (64520) to reach 192.168.1.0.

BGP routers use the AS-path attribute to ensure a loop-free environment. If a BGP router receives a route in which its own AS is part of the AS-path attribute, it does not accept the route.

Autonomous system numbers are prepended only by routers advertising routes to EBGP neighbors. Routers advertising routes to IBGP neighbors do not change the AS-path attribute.

The Next-Hop Attribute

The BGP next-hop attribute is a well-known mandatory attribute that indicates the next-hop IP address that is to be used to reach a destination. BGP, like IGPs, is a hop-by-hop routing protocol. However, unlike IGPs, BGP routes AS-by-AS, not router-by-router, and the default next-hop is the next AS. The next-hop address for a network from another AS is an IP address of the entry point of the next AS along the path to that destination network.

KEY POINT

EBGP Next Hop

For EBGP, the next hop is the IP address of the neighbor that sent the update.

In Figure 8-19, Router A advertises 172.16.0.0 to Router B, with a next hop of 10.10.10.3, and Router B advertises 172.20.0.0 to Router A, with a next hop of 10.10.10.1. Therefore, Router A uses 10.10.10.1 as the next-hop attribute to get to 172.20.0.0, and Router B uses 10.10.10.3 as the next-hop attribute to get to 172.16.0.0.

KEY POINT

IBGP Next Hop

For IBGP, the protocol states that the next hop advertised by EBGP should be carried into IBGP.

Because of this rule, Router B in Figure 8-19 advertises 172.16.0.0 to its IBGP peer Router C, with a next hop of 10.10.10.3 (Router A's address). Therefore, Router C knows that the next hop to reach 172.16.0.0 is 10.10.10.3, not 172.20.10.1, as you might expect.

It is very important, therefore, that Router C knows how to reach the 10.10.10.0 subnet, either via an IGP or a static route; otherwise, it will drop packets destined for 172.16.0.0, because it will not be able to get to the next-hop address for that network.

The IBGP neighboring router performs a recursive lookup to find out how to reach the BGP next-hop address by using its IGP entries in the routing table. For example, Router C in Figure 8-19 learns in a BGP update about network 172.16.0.0/16 from the route source 172.20.10.1, Router B, with a next hop of 10.10.10.3, Router A. Router C installs the route to 172.16.0.0/16 in the routing table with a next hop of 10.10.10.3. Assuming that Router B announces network 10.10.10.0/24 using its IGP to Router C, Router C installs that route in its routing table with a next hop of 172.20.10.1. An IGP uses the source IP address of a routing update (route source) as the next-hop address, whereas BGP uses a separate field for each network to record the next-hop address. If Router C has a packet to send to 172.16.100.1, it looks up the network in the routing table and finds a BGP route with a next hop of 10.10.10.3. Because it is a BGP entry, Router C completes a recursive lookup in the routing table for a path to network 10.10.10.3; there is an IGP route to network 10.10.10.0 in the routing table with a next hop of 172.20.10.1. Router C then forwards the packet destined for 172.16.100.1 to 172.20.10.1.

Figure 8-19 *BGP Next-Hop Attribute*

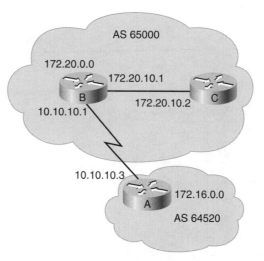

When running BGP over a multiaccess network such as Ethernet, a BGP router uses the appropriate address as the next-hop address (by changing the next-hop attribute) to avoid inserting additional hops into the path. This feature is sometimes called a *third-party next hop*.

For example, in Figure 8-20, assume that Routers B and C in AS 65000 are running an IGP, so that Router B can reach network 172.30.0.0 via 10.10.10.2. Router B is also running EBGP with Router A. When Router B sends a BGP update to Router A about 172.30.0.0, it uses 10.10.10.2 as the next hop, not its own IP address (10.10.10.1). This is because the network among the three routers is a multiaccess network, and it makes more sense for Router A to use Router C as a next hop to reach 172.30.0.0, rather than making an extra hop via Router B.

The third-party next-hop address issue also makes sense when you review it from an ISP perspective. A large ISP at a public peering point has multiple routers peering with different neighboring routers; it is not possible for one router to peer with every neighboring router at the major public peering points. For example, in Figure 8-20, Router B might peer with AS 64520, and Router C might peer with AS 64600; however, each router must inform the other IBGP neighbor of reachable networks from other autonomous systems. From the perspective of Router A, it must transit AS 65000 to get to networks in and behind AS 64600. Router A has a neighbor relationship with only Router B in AS 65000; however, Router B does not handle traffic going to AS 64600. Router B gets to AS 64600 through Router C, 10.10.10.2, and Router B must advertise the networks for AS 64600 to Router A, 10.10.10.3. Router B notices that Routers A and C are on the same subnet, so Router B tells Router A to install the AS 64600 networks with a next hop of 10.10.10.2, not 10.10.10.1.

Figure 8-20 *Multiaccess Network: Router A Has 10.10.10.2 as the Next-Hop Attribute to Reach 172.30.0.0*

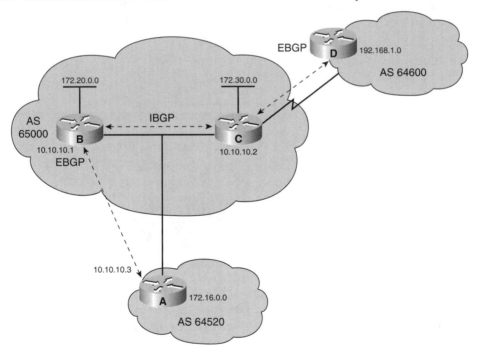

However, if the common medium between routers is a nonbroadcast multiaccess (NBMA) medium, complications might occur.

For example, in Figure 8-21, Routers A, B, and C are connected by Frame Relay. Router B can reach network 172.30.0.0 via 10.10.10.2. When Router B sends a BGP update to Router A about 172.30.0.0, it uses 10.10.10.2 as the next hop, not its own IP address (10.10.10.1). A problem arises if Routers A and C do not know how to communicate directly—in other words, if Routers A and C do not have a Frame Relay map entry to reach each other, Router A does not know how to reach the next-hop address on Router C.

This behavior can be overridden in Router B by configuring it to advertise itself as the next-hop address for routes sent to Router A; this configuration is described in the later section "Changing the Next-Hop Attribute."

Figure 8-21 *NBMA Network: Router A Has 10.10.10.2 as the Next-Hop Attribute to Reach 172.30.0.0, but It Might Be Unreachable*

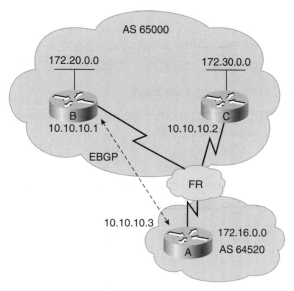

The Origin Attribute

The origin is a well-known mandatory attribute that defines the origin of the path information. The origin attribute can be one of three values:

- **IGP**—The route is interior to the originating AS. This normally happens when a **network** command is used to advertise the route via BGP. An origin of IGP is indicated with an i in the BGP table.

- **EGP**—The route is learned via EGP. This is indicated with an e in the BGP table. EGP is considered a historic routing protocol and is not supported on the Internet because it performs only classful routing and does not support CIDR.

- **Incomplete**—The route's origin is unknown or is learned via some other means. This usually occurs when a route is redistributed into BGP. (Redistribution is discussed in Chapter 7, "Manipulating Routing Updates," and Appendix E.) An incomplete origin is indicated with a ? in the BGP table.

The Local Preference Attribute

Local preference is a well-known discretionary attribute that indicates to routers in the AS which path is preferred to exit the AS.

KEY POINT | **Higher Local Preference Is Preferred**

A path with a *higher* local preference is preferred.

Local preference is an attribute that is configured on a router and exchanged only among routers within the same AS. The default value for local preference on a Cisco router is 100.

KEY POINT | **Local Preference Is Only for Internal Neighbors**

The term *local* refers to *inside* the AS. The local preference attribute is sent only to internal BGP neighbors; it is not passed to EBGP peers.

For example, in Figure 8-22, AS 64520 receives updates about network 172.16.0.0 from two directions. Router A and Router B are IBGP neighbors. Assume that the local preference on Router A for network 172.16.0.0 is set to 200 and that the local preference on Router B for network 172.16.0.0 is set to 150. Because the local preference information is exchanged within AS 64520, all traffic in AS 64520 addressed to network 172.16.0.0 is sent to Router A as an exit point from AS 64520.

Figure 8-22 *Local Preference Attribute: Router A Is the Preferred Router to Get to 172.16.0.0*

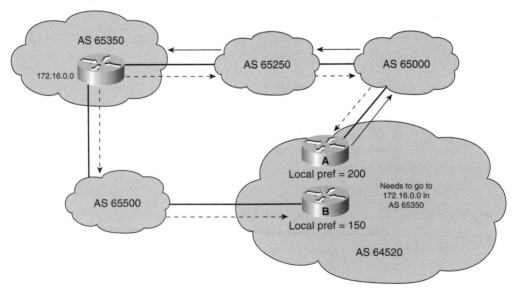

The Community Attribute

BGP communities are one way to filter incoming or outgoing routes. BGP communities allow routers to *tag* routes with an indicator (the *community*) and allow other routers to make decisions based on that tag. Any BGP router can tag routes in incoming and outgoing routing updates, or when doing redistribution. Any BGP router can filter routes in incoming or outgoing updates or can select preferred routes based on communities (the tag).

BGP communities are used for destinations (routes) that share some common properties and, therefore, share common policies; thus, routers act on the community rather than on individual routes. Communities are not restricted to one network or one AS, and they have no physical boundaries.

Communities are optional transitive attributes. If a router does not understand the concept of communities, it defers to the next router. However, if the router does understand the concept, it must be configured to propagate the community; otherwise, communities are dropped by default.

> **NOTE** BGP community configuration is detailed in Appendix E.

The MED Attribute

The MED attribute, also called the *metric*, is an optional nontransitive attribute. The MED was known as the inter-AS attribute in BGP-3.

> **NOTE** The MED attribute is called the metric in the Cisco IOS; in the output of the **show ip bgp** command for example, the MED is displayed in the *metric* column.

KEY POINT

> **MED**
>
> The MED indicates to *external* neighbors the preferred path into an AS. This is a dynamic way for an AS to try to influence another AS as to which way it should choose to reach a certain route if there are multiple entry points into the AS.
>
> A *lower* metric value is preferred.

Unlike local preference, the MED is exchanged between autonomous systems. The MED is sent to EBGP peers; those routers propagate the MED within their AS, and the routers within the AS use the MED, but do not pass it on to the next AS. When the same update is passed on to another AS, the metric will be set back to the default of 0.

KEY POINT

> **MED and Local Preference**
>
> MED influences inbound traffic to an AS, whereas local preference influences outbound traffic from an AS.

By default, a router compares the MED attribute only for paths from neighbors in the same AS.

By using the MED attribute, BGP is the only protocol that can affect how routes are sent into an AS.

For example, in Figure 8-23, Router B has set the MED attribute to 150, and Router C has set the MED attribute to 200. When Router A receives updates from Routers B and C, it picks Router B as the best next hop to get to AS 65500, because 150 is less than 200.

Figure 8-23   *MED Attribute: Router B Is the Best Next Hop to Get to AS 65500*

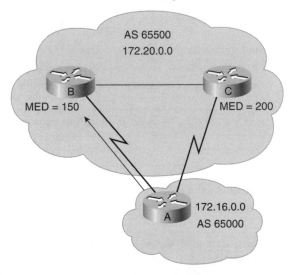

> **NOTE**   By default, the MED comparison is done only if the neighboring autonomous system is the same for all routes considered. For the router to compare metrics from neighbors coming from different autonomous systems, the **bgp always-compare-med** router configuration command must be configured on the router.

The Weight Attribute (Cisco Only)

The weight attribute is a Cisco-defined attribute used for the path-selection process. The weight is configured locally to a router and is not propagated to any other routers.

KEY POINT

Weight Attribute

The weight attribute provides local routing policy only and is *not* propagated to *any* BGP neighbors.

Routes with a *higher* weight are preferred when multiple routes to the same destination exist.

The weight can have a value from 0 to 65535. Paths that the router originates have a weight of 32768 by default, and other paths have a weight of 0 by default.

The weight attribute applies when using one router with multiple exit points out of an AS, as compared to the local preference attribute, which is used when two or more routers provide multiple exit points.

In Figure 8-24, Routers B and C learn about network 172.20.0.0 from AS 65250 and propagate the update to Router A. Router A has two ways to reach 172.20.0.0 and must decide which way to go. In the example, Router A is configured to set the weight of updates coming from Router B to 200 and the weight of those coming from Router C to 150. Because the weight for Router B is higher than the weight for Router C, Router A uses Router B as a next hop to reach 172.20.0.0.

Figure 8-24 *Weight Attribute: Router A Uses Router B as the Next Hop to Reach 172.20.0.0*

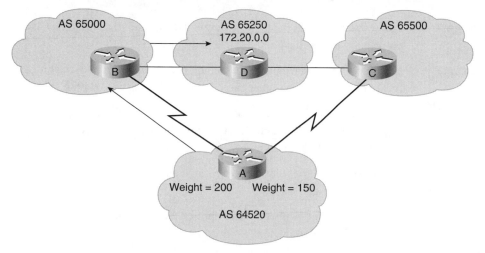

The Route Selection Decision Process

After BGP receives updates about different destinations from different autonomous systems, it decides which path to choose to reach each specific destination. Multiple paths might exist to reach a given network; these are kept in the BGP table. As paths for the network are evaluated, those determined not to be the best path are eliminated from the selection criteria but kept in the BGP table in case the best path becomes inaccessible.

KEY POINT

BGP Chooses Only a Single Best Path

BGP chooses only a single best path to reach a specific destination.

BGP is not designed to perform load balancing; paths are chosen because of policy, not based on bandwidth. The BGP selection process eliminates any multiple paths until a single best path is left.

The best path is submitted to the routing table manager process and is evaluated against any other routing protocols that can also reach that network. The route from the routing protocol with the lowest administrative distance is installed in the routing table.

The decision process is based on the attributes discussed earlier in the "BGP Attributes" section. When faced with multiple routes to the same destination, BGP chooses the best route for routing traffic toward the destination. A path is not considered if it is internal, synchronization is on, and the route is not synchronized (in other words, the route is not in the IGP routing table), or if the path's next-hop address cannot be reached. Thus, to choose the best route, BGP considers only synchronized routes with no AS loops and a valid next-hop address. The following process summarizes how BGP chooses the best route on a Cisco router:

Step 1   Prefer the route with the highest weight. (Recall that the weight is Cisco-proprietary and is local to the router only.)

Step 2   If multiple routes have the same weight, prefer the route with the highest local preference. (Recall that the local preference is used within an AS.)

Step 3   If multiple routes have the same local preference, prefer the route that was originated by the local router. (A locally originated route has a next hop of 0.0.0.0 in the BGP table.)

Step 4   If none of the routes were originated by the local router, prefer the route with the shortest AS-path.

Step 5   If the AS-path length is the same, prefer the lowest-origin code (IGP < EGP < incomplete).

Step 6   If all origin codes are the same, prefer the path with the lowest MED. (Recall that the MED is exchanged between autonomous systems.)

Ê Ê Ê Ê Ê Ê Ê ÊThe MED comparison is done only if the neighboring AS is the same for all routes considered, unless the **bgp always-compare-med** router configuration command is enabled.

NOTE   The most recent Internet Engineering Task Force (IETF) decision about BGP MED assigns a value of infinity to a missing MED, making a route lacking the MED variable the least preferred. The default behavior of BGP routers running Cisco IOS Software is to treat routes without the MED attribute as having a MED of 0, making a route lacking the MED variable the most preferred. To configure the router to conform to the IETF standard, use the **bgp bestpath med missing-as-worst** router configuration command.

Step 7   If the routes have the same MED, prefer external paths (EBGP) over internal paths (IBGP).

Step 8   If synchronization is disabled and only internal paths remain, prefer the path through the closest IGP neighbor. This means that the router prefers the shortest internal path within the AS to reach the destination (the shortest path to the BGP next-hop).

Step 9   For EBGP paths, select the oldest route, to minimize the effect of routes going up and down (flapping).

Step 10   Prefer the route with the lowest neighbor BGP router ID value.

Step 11   If the BGP router IDs are the same, prefer the route with the lowest neighbor IP address.

Only the best path is entered in the routing table and propagated to the router's BGP neighbors.

NOTE   The route selection decision process summarized here does not cover all cases, but it is sufficient for a basic understanding of how BGP selects routes.

For example, suppose that there are seven paths to reach network 10.0.0.0. All paths have no AS loops and valid next-hop addresses, so all seven paths proceed to Step 1, which examines the weight of the paths. All seven paths have a weight of 0, so they all proceed to Step 2, which examines the paths' local preference. Four of the paths have a local preference of 200, and the other three have a local preference of 100, 100, and 150. The four with a local preference of 200 continue the evaluation process to the next step. The other three remain in the BGP forwarding table but are currently disqualified as the best path.

BGP continues the evaluation process until only a single best path remains. The single best path that remains is offered to the IP routing table as the best BGP path.

Multiple Path Selection

BGP chooses only a single best path for each destination.

The **maximum-paths** *paths* router configuration command for BGP works if your router has multiple parallel paths to different routers in the same remote AS; this command affects only the number of routes kept in the IP routing table, not the number of paths selected as best by BGP. For BGP, the *paths* parameter defaults to one. For example, consider three routers: R1 is in AS 65201, and both R2 and R3 are in AS 65301, as shown in Figure 8-25. R1 is running EBGP to R2 and R3. R2 and R3 are advertising network 10.0.0.0. Without the **maximum-paths** command under the **router bgp 65201** command on R1, there is only one path to 10.0.0.0 in R1's routing table. After the **maximum-paths 2** command is added to the R1 BGP configuration, both paths appear in the IP routing table, as shown in Example 8-1. However, as also shown in Example 8-1, only one path is still selected as the best in the BGP table (as indicated by the > symbol); this is the path the router advertises to its BGP neighbors.

Figure 8-25 *BGP Maximum Paths Example*

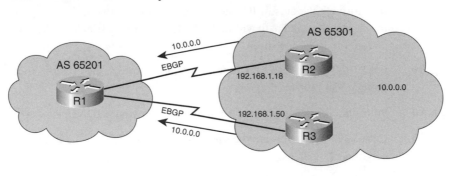

Example 8-1 *Output from Testing of the* **maximum-paths** *Command for BGP*

```
R1#show ip route bgp
B    10.0.0.0/8 [20/0] via 192.168.1.18, 00:00:41
                [20/0] via 192.168.1.50, 00:00:41

R1#show ip bgp
BGP table version is 3, local router ID is 192.168.1.49
Status codes: s suppressed, d damped, h history, * valid, > best, i ->internal
Origin codes: i - IGP, e - EGP, ? - incomplete

   Network          Next Hop          Metric LocPrf Weight Path
*> 10.0.0.0         192.168.1.18           0             0 65301 i
*                   192.168.1.50           0             0 65301 i
```

Configuring BGP

This section covers the commands used to configure some of the BGP features discussed in this chapter. The concept of peer groups is described first, because peer groups appear in many of the configuration commands.

> **NOTE** The syntax of some BGP configuration commands is similar to the syntax of commands used to configure internal routing protocols. However, there are significant differences in how BGP functions.

Peer Groups

In BGP, many neighbors are often configured with the same update policies (for example, they have the same filtering applied). On a Cisco Systems router, neighbors with the same update policies can be grouped into peer groups to simplify configuration and, more importantly, to make updating more efficient and improve performance. When you have many peers, this approach is highly recommended.

**KEY
POINT**
| **BGP Peer Group**

A BGP peer group is a group of BGP neighbors of the router being configured that all have the same update policies.

Instead of separately defining the same policies for each neighbor, a peer group can be defined with these policies assigned to the peer group. Individual neighbors are then made members of the peer group. The policies of the peer group are similar to a template; the template is then applied to the individual members of the peer group.

Members of the peer group inherit all the peer group's configuration options. The router can also be configured to override these options for some members of the peer group if these options do not affect outbound updates. In other words, only options that affect the inbound updates can be overridden.

> **NOTE**   Some earlier IOS releases had a restriction that all EBGP neighbors in a peer group had to be reachable over the same interface. This is because the next-hop attribute would be different for EBGP neighbors accessible on different interfaces. You can get around this restriction by configuring a loopback source address for EBGP peers. This restriction was removed starting in Cisco IOS Software Releases 11.1(18)CC, 11.3(4), and 12.0.

Peer groups are more efficient than defining the same policies for each neighbor, because updates are generated only once per peer group rather than repetitiously for each neighboring router; the generated update is replicated for each neighbor that is part of the peer group.

Thus, peer groups save processing time in generating the updates for all IBGP neighbors and make the router configuration easier to read and manage.

The **neighbor** *peer-group-name* **peer-group** router configuration command is used to create a BGP peer group. The *peer-group-name* is the name of the BGP peer group to be created. The *peer-group-name* is local to the router on which it is configured; it is not passed to any other router. You can use another syntax form of the **neighbor peer-group** command, the **neighbor** *ip-address* **peer-group** *peer-group-name* router configuration command, to assign neighbors as part of the group after the group has been created. Table 8-3 provides details of this command. Using this command allows you to type the peer group name instead of typing the IP addresses of individual neighbors in other commands, for example, to link a policy to the group of neighboring routers. (Note that you must enter the **neighbor** *peer-group-name* **peer-group** command before the router will accept this second command.)

Table 8-3 **neighbor peer-group** *Command Description*

Parameter	Description
ip-address	The IP address of the neighbor that is to be assigned as a member of the peer group.
peer-group-name	The name of the BGP peer group.

A neighboring router can be part of only one peer group.

> **NOTE** Release 12.0(24)S of Cisco IOS Software introduced the BGP Dynamic Update Peer-Groups feature using peer templates to dynamically optimize update-groups of neighbors for shared outbound policies. More information on this feature can be found at http://www.cisco.com.

The **clear ip bgp peer-group** *peer-group-name* EXEC command is used to reset the BGP connections for all members of a BGP peer group. The *peer-group-name* is the name of the BGP peer group for which connections are to be cleared.

> **CAUTION** Resetting BGP sessions will disrupt routing. See the "Resetting BGP Sessions" section later in this chapter for more information about how the **clear ip bgp** commands operate.

Entering BGP Configuration Mode

Use the **router bgp** *autonomous-system* global configuration command to enter BGP configuration mode, and identify the local AS in which this router belongs. In the command, *autonomous-system* identifies the local AS. The BGP process needs to be informed of its AS so that when BGP neighbors are configured it can determine whether they are IBGP or EBGP neighbors.

The **router bgp** command alone does not activate BGP on a router. You must enter at least one subcommand under the **router bgp** command to activate the BGP process on the router.

Only one instance of BGP can be configured on a router at a time. For example, if you configure your router in AS 65000 and then try to configure the **router bgp 65100** command, the router informs you that you are currently configured for AS 65000.

Defining BGP Neighbors and Activating BGP Sessions

Use the **neighbor** {*ip-address* | *peer-group-name*} **remote-as** *autonomous-system* router configuration command to activate a BGP session for external and internal neighbors and to identify a peer router with which the local router will establish a session, as described in Table 8-4.

Table 8-4   **neighbor remote-as** *Command Description*

Parameter	Description
ip-address	Identifies the peer router.
peer-group-name	Identifies the name of a BGP peer group.
autonomous-system	Identifies the peer router's AS.

The IP address used in the **neighbor remote-as** command is the destination address for all BGP packets going to this neighboring router. For a BGP relationship to be established, this address must be reachable, because BGP attempts to establish a TCP session and exchange BGP updates with the device at this IP address.

The value placed in the *autonomous-system* field of the **neighbor remote-as** command determines whether the communication with the neighbor is an EBGP or IBGP session. If the *autonomous-system* field configured in the **router bgp** command is identical to the field in the **neighbor remote-as** command, BGP initiates an internal session, and the IP address specified does not have to be directly connected. If the field values are different, BGP initiates an external session, and the IP address specified must be directly connected, by default.

The network shown in Figure 8-26 uses the BGP **neighbor** commands; the configurations of Routers A, B, and C are shown in Examples 8-2, 8-3, and 8-4. Router A in AS 65101 has two **neighbor** statements. In the first statement, neighbor 10.2.2.2 (Router B) is in the same AS as Router A (65101); this **neighbor** statement defines Router B as an IBGP neighbor. Autonomous system 65101 runs EIGRP between all internal routers. Router A has an EIGRP path to reach IP address 10.2.2.2; as an IBGP neighbor, Router B can be multiple routers away from Router A.

Figure 8-26   *BGP Network with IBGP and EBGP Neighbor Relationships*

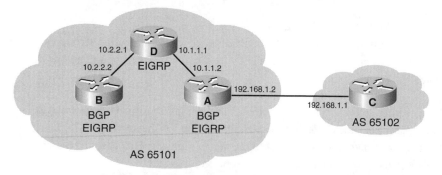

Example 8-2   *Configuration of Router A in Figure 8-26*

```
router bgp 65101
  neighbor 10.2.2.2 remote-as 65101
  neighbor 192.168.1.1 remote-as 65102
```

Example 8-3 *Configuration of Router B in Figure 8-26*

```
router bgp 65101
  neighbor 10.1.1.2 remote-as 65101
```

Example 8-4 *Configuration of Router C in Figure 8-26*

```
router bgp 65102
  neighbor 192.168.1.2 remote-as 65101
```

Router A in Figure 8-26 knows that Router C is an external neighbor because the **neighbor** statement for Router C uses AS 65102, which is different from the AS number of Router A, AS 65101. Router A can reach AS 65102 via 192.168.1.1, which is directly connected to Router A.

> **NOTE**   The network in Figure 8-26 is only used to illustrate the difference between configuring IBGP and EBGP sessions. As mentioned earlier, if Router B connects to another autonomous system then all routers in the transit path (Routers A, D, and B in this figure) should be running fully meshed BGP.

Shutting Down a BGP Neighbor

To disable (administratively shut down) an existing BGP neighbor or peer group, use the **neighbor** {*ip-address* | *peer-group-name*} **shutdown** router configuration command. To enable a previously existing neighbor or peer group that had been disabled using the **neighbor shutdown** command, use the **no neighbor** {*ip-address* | *peer-group-name*} **shutdown** router configuration command. If you want to implement major policy changes to a neighboring router and you change multiple parameters, you must administratively shut down the neighboring router, implement the changes, and then bring the neighboring router back up.

Defining the Source IP Address

The BGP **neighbor** statement tells the BGP process the destination IP address of each update packet. The router must decide which IP address to use as the source IP address in the BGP routing update.

When a router creates a packet, whether it is a routing update, a ping, or any other type of IP packet, the router does a lookup in the routing table for the destination address; the routing table lists the appropriate interface to get to the destination address. The address of this outbound interface is used as that packet's source address by default.

For BGP packets, this source IP address must match the address in the corresponding **neighbor** statement on the other router. (In other words, the other router must have a BGP relationship with the packet's source IP address.) Otherwise, the routers will not be able to establish the BGP session, and the packet will be ignored. BGP does not accept unsolicited updates; it must be aware of every neighboring router and have a neighbor statement for it.

For example, in Figure 8-27, assume that Router D uses the **neighbor 10.3.3.1 remote-as 65102** command to establish a relationship with Router A. If Router A is sending the BGP packets to Router D via Router B, the source IP address of the packets will be 10.1.1.1. When Router D receives a BGP packet via Router B, it does not recognize the sender of the BGP packet, because 10.1.1.1 is not configured as a neighbor of Router D. Therefore, the IBGP session between Router A and Router D cannot be established.

Figure 8-27 *BGP Source Address Must Match the Address in the neighbor Command*

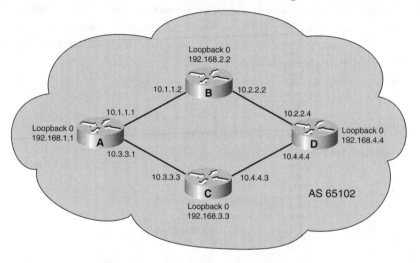

A solution to this problem is to establish the IBGP session using a loopback interface when there are multiple paths between the IBGP neighbors.

If the IP address of a loopback interface is used in the **neighbor** command, some extra configuration must be done on the neighbor router. You must tell BGP to use a loopback interface address rather than a physical interface address as the source address for all BGP packets, including those that initiate the BGP neighbor TCP connection. Use the **neighbor** {*ip-address* | *peer-group-name*} **update-source loopback** *interface-number* router configuration command to cause the router to use the address of the specified loopback interface as the source address for BGP connections to this neighbor.

The **update-source** option in the **neighbor** command overrides the default source IP address for BGP packets. This peering arrangement also adds resiliency to the IBGP sessions, because the routers are not tied into a physical interface, which might go down for any number of reasons. For example, if a BGP router is using a neighbor address that is assigned to a specific physical interface on another router, and that interface goes down, the router pointing at that address loses its BGP session with that other BGP neighbor. If, instead, the router peers with the loopback interface of the other router, the BGP session is not lost, because the loopback interface is always available as long as the router itself does not fail.

To peer with the loopback interface of an IBGP neighbor, configure each router with a **neighbor** command using the loopback address of the other neighbor. Both routers must have a route to the loopback address of the other neighbor in their routing table; check to ensure that both routers are announcing their loopback addresses into their local routing protocol. The **neighbor update-source** command is necessary for both routers.

For example, in Figure 8-28, Router B has Router A as an EBGP neighbor and Router C as an IBGP neighbor. The configurations for Routers B and C are shown in Examples 8-5 and 8-6. The only reachable address that Router B can use to establish a BGP neighbor relationship with Router A is the directly connected address 172.16.1.1. However, Router B has multiple paths to reach Router C, an IBGP neighbor. All networks, including the IP network for Router C's loopback interface, can be reached from Router B because these two routers exchange EIGRP updates. (Router B and Router A do not exchange EIGRP updates.) The neighbor relationship between Routers B and C is not tied to a physical interface, because each router peers with the loopback interface on the other router and uses its loopback address as the BGP source IP address. If Router B instead peered with 10.1.1.2 on Router C and that interface went down, the BGP neighbor relationship would be lost.

Figure 8-28 *BGP Sample Network Using Loopback Addresses*

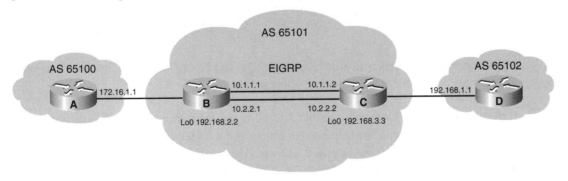

Example 8-5 *Configuration of Router B in Figure 8-28*

```
router bgp 65101
  neighbor 172.16.1.1 remote-as 65100
  neighbor 192.168.3.3 remote-as 65101
  neighbor 192.168.3.3 update-source loopback0
!
router eigrp 1
  network 10.0.0.0
  network 192.168.2.0
```

Example 8-6   *Configuration of Router C in Figure 8-28*

```
router bgp 65101
  neighbor 192.168.1.1 remote-as 65102
  neighbor 192.168.2.2 remote-as 65101
  neighbor 192.168.2.2 update-source loopback0
!
router eigrp 1
  network 10.0.0.0
  network 192.168.3.0
```

If Router B points at loopback address 192.168.3.3 on Router C and Router C points at loopback address 192.168.2.2 on Router B, but neither uses the **neighbor update-source** command, a BGP session is not established between these routers. Without this command, Router B will send a BGP open packet to Router C with a source IP address of either 10.1.1.1 or 10.2.2.1. Router C will examine the source IP address and attempt to match it against its list of known neighbors; because Router C will not find a match, it will not respond to the open message from Router B.

EBGP Multihop

When peering with an external neighbor, the only address that an EBGP router can reach without further configuration is the interface that is directly connected to that EBGP router. Because IGP routing information is not exchanged with external peers, the router must point to a directly connected address for external neighbors. A loopback interface is never directly connected. Therefore, if you want to peer with a loopback interface instead, you have to add a static route to the loopback pointing to the physical address of the directly connected network (the next-hop address). You must also enable multihop EBGP, with the **neighbor** {*ip-address* | *peer-group-name*} **ebgp-multihop** [*ttl*] router configuration command.

This command allows the router to accept and attempt BGP connections to external peers residing on networks that are not directly connected. This command increases the default of one hop for EBGP peers by changing the default Time to Live (TTL) value of 1 and therefore allowing routes to the EBGP loopback address. By default, the TTL is set to 255 with this command. This command is of value when redundant paths exist between EBGP neighbors.

For example, in Figure 8-29, Router A in AS 65102 has two paths to Router B in AS 65101. If Router A uses a single **neighbor** statement that points to 192.168.1.18 on Router B and that link goes down, the BGP session between these autonomous systems is lost, and no packets pass from one AS to the next, even though another link exists. This problem can be solved if Router A uses two **neighbor** statements pointing to 192.168.1.18 and 192.168.1.34 on Router B. However, every BGP update that Router A receives will be sent to Router B twice because of the two **neighbor** statements.

Figure 8-29 *EBGP Multihop Is Required if Loopback Is Used Between External Neighbors*

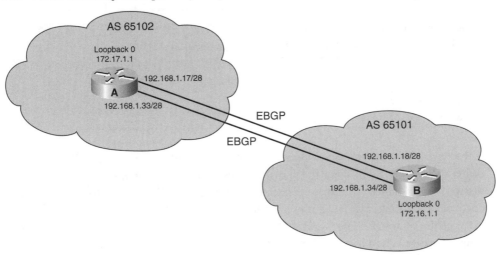

The configurations of Routers A and B are shown in Examples 8-7 and 8-8. As these configurations show, each router instead points to the loopback address of the other router and uses its loopback address as the source IP address for its BGP updates. Because an IGP is not used between autonomous systems, neither router can reach the loopback of the other router without assistance. Each router needs to use two static routes to define the paths available to reach the loopback address of the other router. The **neighbor ebgp-multihop** command must also be configured to change the default setting of BGP and inform the BGP process that this neighbor IP address is more than one hop away. In these examples, the commands used on Routers A and B inform BGP that the neighbor address is two hops away.

Example 8-7 *Configuration of Router A in Figure 8-29*

```
router bgp 65102
  neighbor 172.16.1.1 remote-as 65101
  neighbor 172.16.1.1 update-source loopback0
  neighbor 172.16.1.1 ebgp-multihop 2
ip route 172.16.1.1 255.255.255.255 192.168.1.18
ip route 172.16.1.1 255.255.255.255 192.168.1.34
```

Example 8-8 *Configuration of Router B in Figure 8-29*

```
router bgp 65101
  neighbor 172.17.1.1 remote-as 65102
  neighbor 172.17.1.1 update-source loopback0
  neighbor 172.17.1.1 ebgp-multihop 2
ip route 172.17.1.1 255.255.255.255 192.168.1.17
ip route 172.17.1.1 255.255.255.255 192.168.1.33
```

> **NOTE**   Recall that BGP is not designed to perform load balancing; paths are chosen because of policy, not based on bandwidth. BGP will choose only a single best path. Using the loopback addresses and the **neighbor ebgp-multihop** command as shown in this example allows load balancing, and redundancy, across the two paths between the autonomous systems.

Changing the Next-Hop Attribute

As discussed in the section "The Next-Hop Attribute" earlier in this chapter, it is sometimes necessary (for example, in an NBMA environment) to override a router's default behavior and force it to advertise itself as the next-hop address for routes sent to a neighbor.

An internal protocol, such as RIP, EIGRP, or OSPF, always uses the source IP address of a routing update as the next-hop address for each network from that update that is placed in the routing table. The **neighbor** {*ip-address* | *peer-group-name*} **next-hop-self** router configuration command is used to force BGP to use the source IP address of the update as the next hop for each network it advertises to the neighbor, rather than letting the protocol choose the next-hop address to use. This command is described in Table 8-5.

Table 8-5   **neighbor next-hop-self** *Command Description*

Parameter	Description
ip-address	Identifies the peer router to which advertisements will be sent, with this router identified as the next hop.
peer-group-name	Gives the name of a BGP peer group to which advertisements will be sent, with this router identified as the next hop.

For example, in Figure 8-30, Router B views all routes learned from AS 65100 as having a next hop of 172.16.1.1, which is the entrance to AS 65100 for Router B. When Router B announces those networks to its IBGP neighbors in AS 65101, the BGP default setting is to announce that the next hop to reach each of those networks is the entrance to AS 65100 (172.16.1.1), because BGP is an AS-by-AS routing protocol. With the default settings, a BGP router needs to reach the 172.16.1.1 next hop to reach networks in or behind AS 65100. Therefore, the network that represents 172.16.1.1 will have to be advertised in the internal routing protocol.

In this example, however, the configuration for Router B is as shown in Example 8-9. Router B uses the **neighbor next-hop-self** command to change the default BGP next-hop settings. After this command is given, Router B advertises a next hop of 192.168.2.2 (the IP address of its loopback interface) to its IBGP neighbor, because that is the source IP address of the routing update to its IBGP neighbor (set with the **neighbor update-source** command).

Figure 8-30   **neighbor next-hop-self** *Command Allows Router B to Advertise Itself as the Next Hop*

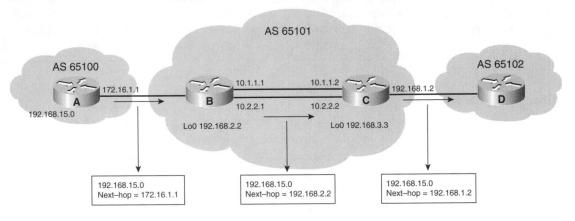

Example 8-9   *Configuration of Router B in Figure 8-30*

```
router bgp 65101
  neighbor 172.16.1.1 remote-as 65100
  neighbor 192.168.3.3 remote-as 65101
  neighbor 192.168.3.3 update-source loopback0
  neighbor 192.168.3.3 next-hop-self
!
router eigrp 1
  network 10.0.0.0
  network 192.168.2.0
```

When Router C announces networks that are in or behind AS 65101 to its EBGP neighbors, such as Router D in AS 65102, Router C, by default, uses its outbound interface address 192.168.1.2 as the next-hop address. This address is the default next-hop address for Router D to use to reach any networks in or behind AS 65101.

Defining the Networks That BGP Advertises

Use the **network** *network-number* [**mask** *network-mask*] [**route-map** *map-tag*] router configuration command to permit BGP to advertise a network if it is present in the IP routing table, as described in Table 8-6.

Table 8-6   *network Command Description*

Parameter	Description
network-number	Identifies an IP network to be advertised by BGP.
network-mask	(Optional) Identifies the subnet mask to be advertised by BGP. If the network mask is not specified, the default mask is the classful mask.
map-tag	(Optional) Identifies a configured route map. The route map is examined to filter the networks to be advertised. If not specified, all networks are advertised. If the **route-map** keyword is specified, but no route map tag is listed, no networks will be advertised.

The BGP network Command

The BGP **network** command determines which networks this router advertises. This is a different concept from what you are used to when configuring IGPs. Unlike for IGPs, the **network** command does not start BGP on specific interfaces; rather, it indicates to BGP which networks it should originate from this router. The **mask** parameter indicates that BGP-4 can handle subnetting and supernetting. The list of **network** commands must include all networks in your AS that you want to advertise, not just those locally connected to your router.

The **network** command allows classless prefixes; the router can advertise individual subnets, networks, or supernets. Note that the prefix must exactly match (address and mask) an entry in the IP routing table. A static route to null 0 might be used to create a supernet entry in the IP routing table.

Before Cisco IOS Software Release 12.0, there was a limit of 200 **network** commands per BGP router; this limit has now been removed. The router's resources, such as the configured NVRAM or RAM, determine the maximum number of **network** commands that you can now use.

The network Command Versus the neighbor Command

The **neighbor** command tells BGP *where* to advertise. The **network** command tells BGP *what* to advertise.

The sole purpose of the **network** command is to notify BGP which networks to advertise. If the mask is not specified, this command announces only the classful network number; at least one subnet of the specified major network must be present in the IP routing table to allow BGP to start announcing the classful network as a BGP route. However, if you specify the *network-mask*, an exact match to the network (both address and mask) must exist in the routing table for the network to be advertised.

Before BGP announces a route, it checks to see whether it can reach it. For example, if you configure **network 192.168.1.1 mask 255.255.255.0** by mistake, BGP looks for 192.168.1.1/24 in the routing table. It might find 192.168.1.0/24 or 192.168.1.1/32, but it will never find 192.168.1.1/24. Because the routing table does not contain a specific match to the network, BGP does not announce the 192.168.1.1/24 network to any neighbors.

In another example, if you configure **network 192.168.0.0 mask 255.255.0.0** to advertise a CIDR block, BGP looks for 192.168.0.0/16 in the routing table. It might find 192.168.1.0/24 or 192.168.1.1/32; however, if it never finds 192.168.0.0/16, BGP does not announce the 192.168.0.0/16 network to any neighbors. In this case, you can configure the static route **ip route 192.168.0.0 255.255.0.0 null0** toward the null interface so that BGP can find an exact match in the routing table. After finding an exact match in the routing table, BGP announces the 192.168.0.0/16 network to any neighbors.

> **NOTE** The BGP **auto-summary** router configuration command determines how BGP handles redistributed routes. With BGP summarization enabled (with **auto-summary**), all redistributed subnets are summarized to their classful boundaries in the BGP table. When disabled (with **no auto-summary**), all redistributed subnets are present in their original form in the BGP table, so only those subnets would be advertised.
>
> In Cisco IOS Software Release 12.2(8)T, the default behavior of the **auto-summary** command was changed to disabled (**no auto-summary**); prior to that the default was enabled (**auto-summary**).
>
> BGP route summarization is covered in Appendix E.

BGP Neighbor Authentication

You can configure BGP neighbor authentication on a router so that the router authenticates the source of each routing update packet that it receives. This is accomplished by the exchange of an authenticating key (sometimes referred to as a password) that is known to both the sending and the receiving router. BGP supports Message Digest 5 (MD5) neighbor authentication. MD5 sends a "message digest" (also called a "hash") which is created using the key and a message. The message digest is then sent instead of the key. The key itself is not sent, preventing it from being read by someone eavesdropping on the line while it is being transmitted.

To enable MD5 authentication on a TCP connection between two BGP peers, use the **neighbor** {*ip-address* | *peer-group-name*} **password** *string* router configuration command. Table 8-7 describes the **neighbor password** command parameters.

Table 8-7 **neighbor password** *Command Description*

Parameter	Description
ip-address	IP address of the BGP-speaking neighbor.
peer-group-name	Name of a BGP peer group.
string	Case-sensitive password of up to 25 characters. The first character cannot be a number. The string can contain any alphanumeric characters, including spaces. You cannot specify a password in the format *number-space-anything*. The space after the number can cause authentication to fail.

> **NOTE** If the **service password-encryption** command is not used when configuring BGP authentication, the password will be stored as plain text in the router configuration. If you configure the **service password-encryption** command, the password will be stored and displayed in an encrypted form; when it is displayed, there will be an encryption type of 7 specified before the encrypted password.

When MD5 authentication is configured between two BGP peers, each segment sent on the TCP connection between the peers is verified. MD5 authentication must be configured with the same password on both BGP peers; otherwise, the connection between them will not be made. Configuring MD5 authentication causes the Cisco IOS Software to generate and check the MD5 digest of every segment sent on the TCP connection.

> **CAUTION**   If the authentication string is configured incorrectly, the BGP peering session will not be established. You should enter the authentication string carefully and verify that the peering session is established after authentication is configured.

If a router has a password configured for a neighbor, but the neighbor router does not have a password configured, a message such as the following will appear on the console when the routers attempt to send BGP messages between themselves:

```
%TCP-6-BADAUTH: No MD5 digest from 10.1.0.2(179) to 10.1.0.1(20236)
```

Similarly, if the two routers have different passwords configured, a message such as the following will appear on the screen:

```
%TCP-6-BADAUTH: Invalid MD5 digest from 10.1.0.1(12293) to 10.1.0.2(179)
```

If you configure or change the password or key used for MD5 authentication between two BGP peers, the local router will not tear down the existing session after you configure the password. The local router will attempt to maintain the peering session using the new password until the BGP holddown timer expires. The default time period is 180 seconds. If the password is not entered or changed on the remote router before the holddown timer expires, the session will time out.

> **NOTE**   Configuring a new timer value for the holddown timer will take effect only after the session has been reset. So, it is not possible to change the configuration of the holddown timer to avoid resetting the BGP session.

Examples 8-10 and 8-11 show the configurations for the routers in Figure 8-31. MD5 authentication is configured for the BGP peering session between Routers A and B. The same password must be configured on the remote peer before the holddown timer expires.

Figure 8-31 *BGP Neighbor Authentication*

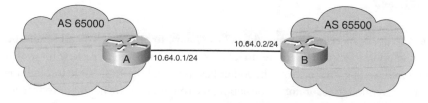

Example 8-10 *Configuration of Router A in Figure 8-31*

```
router bgp 65000
  neighbor 10.64.0.2 remote-as 65500
  neighbor 10.64.0.2 password v61ne0qke1336
```

Example 8-11 *Configuration of Router B in Figure 8-31*

```
router bgp 65500
  neighbor 10.64.0.1 remote-as 65000
  neighbor 10.64.0.1 password v61ne0qke1336
```

Configuring BGP Synchronization

Recall that the BGP synchronization rule states that that a BGP router should not use, or advertise to an external neighbor, a route learned by IBGP, unless that route is local or is learned from the IGP.

BGP synchronization is disabled by default in Cisco IOS Software Release 12.2(8)T and later; it was on by default in earlier Cisco IOS Software releases. With the default of synchronization disabled, BGP can use and advertise to an external BGP neighbor routes learned from an IBGP neighbor that are not present in the local routing table.

Use the **synchronization** router configuration command to enable BGP synchronization so that a router will not advertise routes in BGP until it learns them in an IGP. The **no synchronization** router configuration command disables synchronization if it was enabled.

Resetting BGP Sessions

BGP can potentially handle huge volumes of routing information. When a BGP policy configuration change occurs (such as when access lists, timers, or attributes are changed), the router cannot go through the huge table of BGP information and recalculate which entry is no longer valid in the local table. Nor can the router determine which route or routes, already advertised, should be withdrawn from a neighbor. There is an obvious risk that the first configuration change will immediately be followed by a second, which would cause the whole process to start all over again. To avoid such a problem, the Cisco IOS Software applies changes on only those updates received or transmitted after the BGP policy configuration change has been performed. The new policy, enforced by the new filters, is applied only on routes received or sent after the change.

If the network administrator wants the policy change to be applied on all routes, he or she must trigger an update to force the router to let all routes pass through the new filter. If the filter is applied to outgoing information, the router has to resend the BGP table through the new filter. If the filter is applied to incoming information, the router needs its neighbor to resend its BGP table so that it passes through the new filter.

There are three ways to trigger an update:

- Hard reset

- Soft reset

- Route refresh

The sections that follow discuss all three methods of triggering an update in greater detail.

Hard Reset of BGP Sessions

Resetting a session is a method of informing the neighbor or neighbors of a policy change. If BGP sessions are reset, all information received on those sessions is invalidated and removed from the BGP table. The remote neighbor detects a BGP session down state and, likewise, invalidates the received routes. After a period of 30 to 60 seconds, the BGP sessions are reestablished automatically, and the BGP table is exchanged again, but through the new filters. However, resetting the BGP session disrupts packet forwarding.

Use the **clear ip bgp *** or **clear ip bgp** {*neighbor-address*} privileged EXEC command to cause a hard reset of the BGP neighbors that are involved, where * indicates all sessions and the *neighbor-address* identifies the address of a specific neighbor for which the BGP sessions will be reset. A "hard reset" means that the router issuing either of these commands will close the appropriate TCP connections, reestablish those TCP sessions as appropriate, and resend all information to each of the neighbors affected by the particular command that is used.

> **CAUTION**   Clearing the BGP table and resetting BGP sessions will disrupt routing, so do not use these commands unless you have to.

The **clear ip bgp *** command causes the BGP forwarding table on the router on which this command is issued to be completely deleted; all networks must be relearned from every neighbor. If a router has multiple neighbors, this action is a very dramatic event. This command forces all neighbors to resend their entire tables simultaneously.

For example, assume that Router A has eight neighbors and that each neighbor sends Router A the full Internet table (assume that is about 32 MB in size). If the **clear ip bgp *** command is issued on Router A, all eight routers resend their 32-MB table at the same time. To hold all of these updates, Router A will need 256 MB of RAM. Router A will also need to be able to process all of this information. Processing 256 MB of updates will take a considerable number of CPU cycles for Router A, further delaying the routing of user data.

If, instead, the **clear ip bgp** *neighbor-address* command is used, one neighbor is reset at a time. The impact is less severe on the router issuing this command; however, it takes longer to change policy to all the neighbors, because each must be done individually rather than all at once as it is with the **clear ip bgp *** command. The **clear ip bgp** *neighbor-address* command still performs a hard reset and must reestablish the TCP session with the specified address used in the command, but this command affects only a single neighbor at a time, not all neighbors at once.

Soft Reset of BGP Sessions Outbound

Use the **clear ip bgp** { * | *neighbor-address* } [**soft out**] privileged EXEC command to cause BGP to do a soft reset for outbound updates. The router issuing the **clear ip bgp soft out** command does not reset the BGP session; instead, the router creates a new update and sends the whole table to the specified neighbors. This update includes withdrawal commands for networks that the other neighbor will not see anymore based on the new outbound policy.

> **NOTE** The **soft** keyword of this command is optional; **clear ip bgp out** does a soft reset for outbound updates.

Outbound BGP soft configuration does not have any memory overhead. This command is highly recommended when you are changing an outbound policy, but does not help if you are changing an inbound policy.

Soft Reset of BGP Sessions Inbound

There are two ways to perform an inbound soft reconfiguration: using stored routing update information and dynamically.

Inbound Soft Reset Using Stored Information

To use stored information, first enter the **neighbor** [*ip-address*] **soft-reconfiguration inbound** router configuration command to inform BGP to save all updates that were learned from the neighbor specified. The BGP router retains an unfiltered table of what that neighbor has sent. When the inbound policy is changed, use the **clear ip bgp** { * | *neighbor-address* } **soft in** privileged EXEC command to cause the router to use the stored unfiltered table to generate new inbound updates; the new results are placed in the BGP forwarding database. Thus, if you make changes, you do not have to force the other side to resend everything.

Route Refresh: Dynamic Inbound Soft Reset

Cisco IOS Software releases 12.0(2)S and 12.0(6)T introduced a BGP soft reset enhancement feature, also known as route refresh, that provides automatic support for dynamic soft reset of inbound BGP routing table updates that is not dependent on stored routing table update information. This new method requires no preconfiguration (using the **neighbor soft-reconfiguration** command) and requires significantly less memory than the previous soft reset method for inbound routing table updates. The **clear ip bgp** {* | *neighbor-address*} [**soft in** | **in**] privileged EXEC command is the only command required for this dynamic soft reconfiguration.

The **soft in** option generates new inbound updates without resetting the BGP session, but it can be memory intensive. BGP does not allow a router to force another BGP speaker to resend its entire table. If you change the inbound BGP policy and you do not want to complete a hard reset, use this command to cause the router to perform a soft reconfiguration.

> **NOTE**   To determine whether a BGP router supports this route refresh capability, use the **show ip bgp neighbors** command. The following message is displayed in the output when the router supports the route refresh capability:
>
> ```
> Received route refresh capability from peer.
> ```

If all BGP routers support the route refresh capability, use the **clear ip bgp** {* | *address* | *peer-group-name*} **in** command. You need not use the **soft** keyword, because soft reset is automatically assumed when the route refresh capability is supported.

> **NOTE**   The **clear ip bgp soft** command performs a soft reconfiguration of both inbound and outbound updates.

BGP Configuration Examples

This section provides some configuration examples using the commands discussed.

Basic BGP Example

Figure 8-32 shows a sample BGP network. Example 8-12 provides the configuration of Router A in Figure 8-32, and Example 8-13 provides the configuration of Router B.

Figure 8-32   *Sample BGP Network*

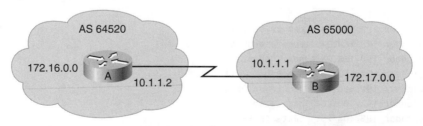

Example 8-12   *Configuration of Router A in Figure 8-32*

```
router bgp 64520
  neighbor 10.1.1.1 remote-as 65000
  network 172.16.0.0
```

Example 8-13 *Configuration of Router B in Figure 8-32*

```
router bgp 65000
  neighbor 10.1.1.2 remote-as 64520
  network 172.17.0.0
```

In this example, Routers A and B define each other as BGP neighbors, and start an EBGP session. Router A advertises the network 172.16.0.0/16, and Router B advertises the network 172.17.0.0/16.

Peer Group Example

In Figure 8-33, AS 65100 has four routers running IBGP. All of these IBGP neighbors are peering with each others' loopback 0 interface (shown in the figure) and are using the IP address of their loopback 0 interface as the source IP address for all BGP packets. Each router is using one of its own IP addresses as the next-hop address for each network advertised through BGP. These are outbound policies.

Figure 8-33 *Peer Groups Simplify Configuration*

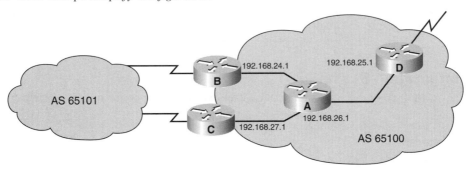

Example 8-14 shows the configuration of Router C when it is not using a peer group.

Example 8-14 *Configuration of Router C in Figure 8-33 Without Using a Peer Group*

```
router bgp 65100
  neighbor 192.168.24.1 remote-as 65100
  neighbor 192.168.24.1 update-source loopback 0
  neighbor 192.168.24.1 next-hop-self
  neighbor 192.168.24.1 distribute-list 20 out
  neighbor 192.168.25.1 remote-as 65100
  neighbor 192.168.25.1 update-source loopback 0
  neighbor 192.168.25.1 next-hop-self
  neighbor 192.168.25.1 distribute-list 20 out
  neighbor 192.168.26.1 remote-as 65100
  neighbor 192.168.26.1 update-source loopback 0
  neighbor 192.168.26.1 next-hop-self
  neighbor 192.168.26.1 distribute-list 20 out
```

Router C has an outbound distribution list associated with each IBGP neighbor. This outbound filter performs the same function as the **distribute-list** command you use for internal routing protocols; however, when used for BGP, it is linked to a specific neighbor. For example, the ISP behind Router C might be announcing private address space to Router C, and Router C does not want to pass these networks to other routers running BGP in AS 65100.

To accomplish this, **access-list 20** might look like the following:

- **access-list 20 deny 10.0.0.0 0.255.255.255**

- **access-list 20 deny 172.16.0.0 0.31.255.255**

- **access-list 20 deny 192.168.0.0 0.0.255.255**

- **access-list 20 permit any**

As shown in Example 8-14, all IBGP neighbors have the outbound distribution list linked to them individually. If Router C receives a change from AS 65101, it must generate an individual update for each IBGP neighbor and run each update against distribute-list 20. If Router C has a large number of IBGP neighbors, the processing power needed to inform the IBGP neighbors of the changes in AS 65101 could be extensive.

Example 8-15 shows the configuration of Router C when it is using a peer group called *internal*. The **neighbor remote-as**, **neighbor update-source**, **neighbor next-hop-self**, and **neighbor distribute-list 20 out** commands are all linked to peer group *internal*, which in turn is linked to each of the IBGP neighbors. If Router C receives a change from AS 65101, it creates a single update and processes it through distribute-list 20 once. The update is replicated for each neighbor that is part of the internal peer group. This action saves processing time in generating the updates for all IBGP neighbors. Thus, the use of peer groups can improve efficiency when processing updates for BGP neighbors that have a common outbound BGP policy.

Example 8-15 *Configuration of Router C in Figure 8-33 Using a Peer Group*

```
router bgp 65100
  neighbor internal peer-group
  neighbor internal remote-as 65100
  neighbor internal update-source loopback 0
  neighbor internal next-hop-self
  neighbor internal distribute-list 20 out
  neighbor 192.168.24.1 peer-group internal
  neighbor 192.168.25.1 peer-group internal
  neighbor 192.168.26.1 peer-group internal
```

Adding a new neighbor with the same policies as the other IBGP neighbors to Router C when it is using a peer group requires adding only a single **neighbor** statement to link the new neighbor to the peer group. Adding that same neighbor to Router C if it does not use a peer group requires four **neighbor** statements.

Using a peer group also makes the configuration easier to read and change. If you need to add a new policy, such as a route map, to all IBGP neighbors on Router C, and you are using a peer group, you need only to link the route map to the peer group. If Router C does not use a peer group, you need to add the new policy to each neighbor.

IBGP and EBGP Example

Figure 8-34 shows another BGP example.

Example 8-16 shows the configuration for Router B in Figure 8-34 (note that line numbers have been added to this example to simplify the discussion). The first two commands under the **router bgp 65000** command establish that Router B has the following two BGP neighbors:

■ Router A in AS 64520

■ Router C in AS 65000

Figure 8-34 *IBGP and EBGP Example*

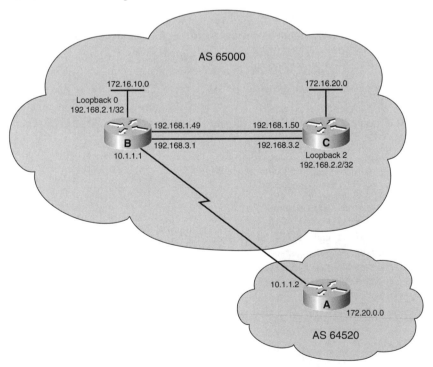

Example 8-16 *Configuration of Router B in Figure 8-34*

```
1.    router bgp 65000
2.    neighbor 10.1.1.2 remote-as 64520
3.    neighbor 192.168.2.2 remote-as 65000
4.    neighbor 192.168.2.2 update-source loopback 0
5.    neighbor 192.168.2.2 next-hop-self
6.    network 172.16.10.0 mask 255.255.255.0
7.    network 192.168.1.0
8.    network 192.168.3.0
9.    no synchronization
```

From the perspective of Router B, Router A is an EBGP neighbor, and Router C is an IBGP neighbor.

The **neighbor** statement on Router B for Router A is pointing to the directly connected IP address to reach Router A. However, the **neighbor** statement on Router B for Router C points to Router C's loopback interface. Router B has multiple paths to reach Router C. If Router B pointed to the 192.168.3.2 IP address of Router C and that interface went down, Router B would be unable to reestablish the BGP session until the link came back up. By pointing to the loopback interface of Router C, the link stays established as long as any path to Router C is available. (Router C should also point to Router B's loopback address in its configuration.)

Line 4 in the configuration forces Router B to use its loopback 0 address, 192.168.2.1, as the source IP address when sending an update to Router C, 192.168.2.2.

In line 5, Router B changes the next-hop address for networks that can be reached through it. The default next-hop for networks from AS 64520 is 10.1.1.2. With the **neighbor next-hop-self** command, Router B sets the next-hop address to the source IP address of the routing update, which is Router B's loopback 0 address, as set by the **neighbor update-source** command.

Lines 6, 7, and 8 tell BGP which networks to advertise. Line 6 contains a subnet of a Class B address using the **mask** option. Lines 7 and 8 contain two **network** statements for the two Class C networks that connect Routers B and C. The default mask for these networks is 255.255.255.0, so it is not needed in the commands.

In line 9, synchronization is disabled (this command is not needed if the router is running Cisco IOS Software Release 12.2(8)T or later, because then synchronization is off by default). If Router A is advertising 172.20.0.0 in BGP, Router B receives that route and advertises it to Router C. Because synchronization is off, Router C can use this route. If Router C had EBGP neighbors of its own and Router B wanted to use Router C as the path to those networks, synchronization on Router B would also need to be off. In this network, synchronization can be off because all the routers within the transit path in AS are running IBGP.

Verifying and Troubleshooting BGP

You can verify BGP operation using **show** EXEC commands, including the following:

■ **show ip bgp**—Displays entries in the BGP topology database (BGP table). Specify a network number to get more specific information about a particular network.

■ **show ip bgp rib-failure**—Displays BGP routes that were not installed in the routing information base (RIB), and the reason that they were not installed.

■ **show ip bgp neighbors**—Displays detailed information about the TCP and BGP connections to neighbors.

■ **show ip bgp summary**—Displays the status of all BGP connections.

Use the **show ip bgp ?** command on a router to see other BGP **show** commands.

debug commands display events as they happen on the router. For BGP, the **debug ip bgp** privileged EXEC command has many options, including the following:

■ **dampening**—BGP dampening

■ **events**—BGP events

■ **keepalives**—BGP keepalives

■ **updates**—BGP updates

The following sections provide sample output for some of these commands.

show ip bgp Command Output Example

Use the **show ip bgp** command to display the BGP topology database (the BGP table).

Example 8-17 is a sample output for the **show ip bgp** command. The status codes are shown at the beginning of each line of output, and the origin codes are shown at the end of each line. In this output, most of the rows have an asterisk (*) in the first column. This means that the next-hop address (in the fifth column) is valid. The next-hop address is not always the router that is directly connected to this router. Other options for the first column are as follows:

■ An s indicates that the specified routes are suppressed (usually because routes have been summarized and only the summarized route is being sent).

■ A d, for dampening, indicates that the route is being dampened (penalized) for going up and down too often. Although the route might be up right now, it is not advertised until the penalty has expired.

- An h, for history, indicates that the route is unavailable and is probably down; historic information about the route exists, but a best route does not exist.

- An r, for RIB failure, indicates that the route was not installed in the RIB. The reason that the route is not installed can be displayed using the **show ip bgp rib-failure** command, as described in the next section.

- An S, for stale, indicates that the route is stale (this is used in a nonstop forwarding-aware router).

Example 8-17 **show ip bgp** *Command Output*

```
RouterA#show ip bgp
BGP table version is 14, local router ID is 172.31.11.1
Status codes: s suppressed, d damped, h history, * valid, > best, i - internal, r RIB-
  failure, S Stale
Origin codes: i - IGP, e - EGP, ? - incomplete
   Network          Next Hop          Metric LocPrf Weight Path
*> 10.1.0.0/24      0.0.0.0                0            32768 i
* i                 10.1.0.2               0    100        0 i
*> 10.1.1.0/24      0.0.0.0                0            32768 i
*>i10.1.2.0/24      10.1.0.2               0    100        0 i
*> 10.97.97.0/24    172.31.1.3                             0 64998 64997 i
*                   172.31.11.4                            0 64999 64997 i
* i                 172.31.11.4            0    100        0 64999 64997 i
*> 10.254.0.0/24    172.31.1.3             0               0 64998 i
*                   172.31.11.4                            0 64999 64998 i
* i                 172.31.1.3             0    100        0 64998 i
r> 172.31.1.0/24    172.31.1.3             0               0 64998 i
r                   172.31.11.4                            0 64999 64998 i
r i                 172.31.1.3             0    100        0 64998 i
*> 172.31.2.0/24    172.31.1.3             0               0 64998 i
<output omitted>
```

A greater-than sign (>) in the second column indicates the best path for a route selected by BGP; this route is offered to the IP routing table.

The third column is either blank or has an i in it. If it is blank, BGP learned that route from an external peer. If it has an i, an IBGP neighbor advertised this route to this router.

The fourth column lists the networks that the router learned.

The fifth column lists all the next-hop addresses for each route. This next-hop address column might contain 0.0.0.0, which signifies that this router originated the route.

The next three columns list three BGP path attributes associated with the path: metric (MED), local preference, and weight.

The column with the "Path" header may contain a sequence of autonomous systems in the path. From left to right, the first AS listed is the adjacent AS from which this network was learned. The last number (the rightmost AS number) is this network's originating AS. The AS numbers between these two represent the exact path that a packet takes back to the originating AS. If the path column is blank, the route is from the current AS.

The last column signifies how this route was entered into BGP on the original router (the origin attribute). If the last column has an i in it, the original router probably used a **network** command to introduce this network into BGP. The character e signifies that the original router learned this network from EGP, which is the historic predecessor to BGP. A question mark (?) signifies that the original BGP process cannot absolutely verify this network's availability, because it is redistributed from an IGP into the BGP process.

show ip bgp rib-failure Command Output Example

Use the **show ip bgp rib-failure** command to display BGP routes that were not installed in the RIB, and the reason that they were not installed. In Example 8-18 the displayed routes were not installed because a route or routes with a better administrative distance already existed in the RIB.

Example 8-18 **show ip bgp rib-failure** *Command Output*

```
RouterA#show ip bgp rib-failure
Network           Next Hop                    RIB-failure      RIB-NH Matches
172.31.1.0/24     172.31.1.3        Higher admin distance              n/a
172.31.11.0/24    172.31.11.4       Higher admin distance              n/a
```

show ip bgp summary Command Output Example

The **show ip bgp summary** command is one way to verify the BGP neighbor relationship. Example 8-19 presents sample output from this command. Here are some of the highlights:

- **BGP router identifier**—IP address that all other BGP speakers recognize as representing this router.

- **BGP table version**—Increases in increments when the BGP table changes.

- **Main Routing table version**—Last version of BGP database that was injected into the main routing table.

- **Neighbor**—The IP address, used in the **neighbor** statement, with which this router is setting up a relationship.

- **Version (V)**—The version of BGP this router is running with the listed neighbor.

- **AS**—The listed neighbor's AS number.

- **Messages received (MsgRcvd)**—The number of BGP messages received from this neighbor.

■ **Messages sent (MsgSent)**—The number of BGP messages sent to this neighbor.

■ **TblVer**—The last version of the BGP table that was sent to this neighbor.

■ **In queue (InQ)**—The number of messages from this neighbor that are waiting to be processed.

■ **Out queue (OutQ)**—The number of messages queued and waiting to be sent to this neighbor. TCP flow control prevents this router from overwhelming a neighbor with a large update.

■ **Up/Down**—The length of time this neighbor has been in the current BGP state (established, active, or idle).

■ **State**—The current state of the BGP session—active, idle, open sent, open confirm, or idle (admin). The admin state is new to Cisco IOS Software Release 12.0; it indicates that the neighbor is administratively shut down. This state is created by using the **neighbor** *ip-address* **shutdown** router configuration command. (Neighbor states are discussed in more detail in the "Understanding and Troubleshooting BGP Neighbor States" section later in this chapter.) Note that if the session is in the established state, a state is not displayed; instead, a number representing the PfxRcd is displayed, as described next.

> **NOTE**   If the state field of the **show ip bgp summary** command indicates active, the router is attempting to create a TCP connection to this neighbor.

■ **Prefix received (PfxRcd)**—When the session is in the established state, this value represents the number of BGP network entries received from this neighbor.

Example 8-19   **show ip bgp summary** *Command Output*

```
RouterA#show ip bgp summary
BGP router identifier 10.1.1.1, local AS number 65001
BGP table version is 124, main routing table version 124
9 network entries using 1053 bytes of memory
22 path entries using 1144 bytes of memory
12/5 BGP path/bestpath attribute entries using 1488 bytes of memory
6 BGP AS-PATH entries using 144 bytes of memory
0 BGP route-map cache entries using 0 bytes of memory
0 BGP filter-list cache entries using 0 bytes of memory
BGP using 3829 total bytes of memory
BGP activity 58/49 prefixes, 72/50 paths, scan interval 60 secs

Neighbor        V    AS MsgRcvd MsgSent    TblVer  InQ OutQ Up/Down   State/PfxRcd

10.1.0.2        4 65001      11      11       124    0    0 00:02:28         8
172.31.1.3      4 64998      21      18       124    0    0 00:01:13         6
172.31.11.4     4 64999      11      10       124    0    0 00:01:11         6
```

> **NOTE** Example output of the **show ip bgp neighbors** command is provided in the "Understanding and Troubleshooting BGP Neighbor States" section later in this chapter.

debug ip bgp updates Command Output Example

Example 8-20 shows partial output from the **debug ip bgp updates** command on Router A after the **clear ip bgp** command is issued to clear BGP sessions with its IBGP neighbor 10.1.0.2.

Example 8-20 **debug ip bgp updates** *Command Output*

```
RouterA#debug ip bgp updates
Mobile router debugging is on for address family: IPv4 Unicast
RouterA#clear ip bgp 10.1.0.2
<output omitted>
*May 24 11:06:41.309: %BGP-5-ADJCHANGE: neighbor 10.1.0.2 Up
*May 24 11:06:41.309: BGP(0): 10.1.0.2 send UPDATE (format) 10.1.1.0/24, next 10.1.0.1,
  metric 0, path Local
*May 24 11:06:41.309: BGP(0): 10.1.0.2 send UPDATE (prepend, chgflags: 0x0) 10.1.0.0/24,
  next 10.1.0.1, metric 0, path Local
*May 24 11:06:41.309: BGP(0): 10.1.0.2 NEXT_HOP part 1 net 10.97.97.0/24, next 172.31.11.4
*May 24 11:06:41.309: BGP(0): 10.1.0.2 send UPDATE (format) 10.97.97.0/24, next
  172.31.11.4, metric 0, path 64999 64997
*May 24 11:06:41.309: BGP(0): 10.1.0.2 NEXT_HOP part 1 net 172.31.22.0/24, next 172.31.11.4
*May 24 11:06:41.309: BGP(0): 10.1.0.2 send UPDATE (format) 172.31.22.0/24, next
  172.31.11.4, metric 0, path 64999
<output omitted>
*May 24 11:06:41.349: BGP(0): 10.1.0.2 rcvd UPDATE w/ attr: nexthop 10.1.0.2, origin i,
  localpref 100, metric 0
*May 24 11:06:41.349: BGP(0): 10.1.0.2 rcvd 10.1.2.0/24
*May 24 11:06:41.349: BGP(0): 10.1.0.2 rcvd 10.1.0.0/24
```

After the neighbor adjacency is reestablished, Router A creates and sends updates to 10.1.0.2. The first update highlighted in the example, **10.1.1.0/24, next 10.1.0.1**, is an update about network 10.1.1.0/24, with a next hop of 10.1.0.1, which is Router A's address. The second update highlighted in the example, **10.97.97.0/24, next 172.31.11.4**, is an update about network 10.97.97.0/24, with a next hop of 172.31.11.4, which is the address of one of Router A's EBGP neighbors. The EBGP next-hop address is being carried into IBGP.

Router A later receives updates from 10.1.0.2. The update highlighted in the example contains a path to two networks, 10.1.2.0/24 and 10.1.0.0/24.

> **NOTE** Debugging uses up router resources and should be turned on only when necessary.

Understanding and Troubleshooting BGP Neighbor States

After the TCP handshake is complete, the BGP application tries to set up a session with the neighbor. BGP is a state machine that takes a router through the following states with its neighbors:

- **Idle**—The router is searching the routing table to see whether a route exists to reach the neighbor.

- **Connect**—The router found a route to the neighbor and has completed the three-way TCP handshake.

- **Open sent**—An open message was sent, with the parameters for the BGP session.

- **Open confirm**—The router received agreement on the parameters for establishing a session.

    Alternatively, the router goes into **Active** state if there is no response to the open message.

- **Established**—Peering is established and routing begins.

After you enter the **neighbor** command, BGP starts in the *idle* state, and the BGP process checks that it has a route to the IP address listed. BGP should be in the idle state for only a few seconds. If BGP does not find a route to the neighboring IP address, it stays in the idle state. If it finds a route, it goes to the *connect* state when the TCP handshaking synchronize acknowledge (SYN ACK) packet returns (when the TCP three-way handshake is complete). After the TCP connection is set up, the BGP process creates a BGP open message and sends it to the neighbor. After BGP dispatches this open message, the BGP peering session changes to the *open sent* state. If there is no response for 5 seconds, the state changes to the *active* state. If a response does come back in a timely manner, BGP goes to the *open confirm* state and starts scanning (evaluating) the routing table for the paths to send to the neighbor. When these paths have been found, BGP then goes to the *established* state and begins routing between the neighbors.

The BGP state is shown in the last column of the **show ip bgp summary** command output.

NOTE   You can observe the states that two BGP routers are going through to establish a session using **debug** commands. In Cisco IOS Software Release 12.4, you can use the **debug ip bgp ipv4 unicast** command to see this process. In earlier IOS releases, the **debug ip bgp events** command gave similar output.

Debugging consumes router resources and should be turned on only when necessary.

Idle State Troubleshooting

The idle state indicates that the router does not know how to reach the IP address listed in the **neighbor** statement. The router is idle for one of the following reasons:

■ It is waiting for a static route to that IP address or network to be configured.

■ It is waiting for the local routing protocol (IGP) to learn about this network through an advertisement from another router.

The most common reason for the idle state is that the neighbor is not announcing the IP address or network that the **neighbor** statement of the router is pointing to. Check the following two conditions to troubleshoot this problem:

■ Ensure that the neighbor announces the route in its local routing protocol (IGP).

■ Verify that you have not entered an incorrect IP address in the **neighbor** statement.

Active State Troubleshooting

If the router is in the active state, this means that it has found the IP address in the **neighbor** statement and has created and sent out a BGP open packet but has not received a response (open confirm packet) back from the neighbor.

One common cause of this is when the neighbor does not have a return route to the source IP address. Ensure that the source IP address or network of the packets is advertised into the local routing protocol (IGP) on the neighboring router.

Another common problem associated with the active state is when a BGP router attempts to peer with another BGP router that does not have a **neighbor** statement peering back at the first router, or the other router is peering with the wrong IP address on the first router. Check to ensure that the other router has a **neighbor** statement peering at the correct address of the router that is in the active state.

If the state toggles between idle and active, the AS numbers might be misconfigured. You see the following console message at the router with the wrong **remote-as** number configured in the **neighbor** statement:

```
%BGP-3-NOTIFICATION: sent to neighbor 172.31.1.3 2/2 (peer in wrong AS) 2 bytes FDE6
FFFF FFFF FFFF FFFF FFFF FFFF FFFF FFFF 002D 0104 FDE6 00B4 AC1F 0203 1002 0601 0400
  0100 0102 0280 0002 0202 00
```

At the remote router, you see the following message:

```
%BGP-3-NOTIFICATION: received from neighbor 172.31.1.1 2/2 (peer in wrong AS) 2 bytes
  FDE6
```

Established State

The established state is the desired state for a neighbor relationship. This state means that both routers agree to exchange BGP updates with one another and routing has begun. If the state column in the **show ip bgp summary** command output is blank or has a number in it, BGP is in the established state. The number shown is the number of routes that have been learned from this neighbor.

Use the **show ip bgp neighbors** command to display information about the BGP connections to neighbors. In Example 8-21, the BGP state is established, which means that the neighbors have established a TCP connection and the two peers have agreed to use BGP to communicate.

Example 8-21 **show ip bgp neighbors** *Command Output*

```
RouterA#show ip bgp neighbors
BGP neighbor is 172.31.1.3,  remote AS 64998, external link
  BGP version 4, remote router ID 172.31.2.3
  BGP state = Established, up for 00:19:10
 Last read 00:00:10, last write 00:00:10, hold time is 180, keepalive interval is 60 seconds
  Neighbor capabilities:
    Route refresh: advertised and received(old & new)
    Address family IPv4 Unicast: advertised and received
  Message statistics:
    InQ depth is 0
    OutQ depth is 0
                      Sent        Rcvd
    Opens:             7           7
    Notifications:     0           0
    Updates:          13          38
<output omitted>
```

Basic BGP Path Manipulation Using Route Maps

Manipulating path-selection criteria can affect the inbound and outbound traffic policies of an AS. This section discusses path manipulation and how to configure an AS using route maps to manipulate the BGP local preference and MED attributes to influence BGP path selection. This section also describes changing the value of the weight attribute.

BGP Path Manipulation

Unlike local routing protocols, BGP was never designed to choose the quickest path. Rather, it was designed to manipulate traffic flow to maximize or minimize bandwidth use. Figure 8-35 demonstrates a common situation that can result when using BGP without any policy manipulation.

Figure 8-35 *BGP Network Without Policy Manipulation*

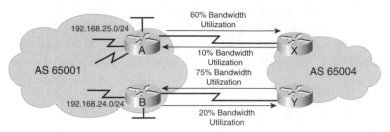

Using default settings for path selection in BGP might cause uneven use of bandwidth. In Figure 8-35, Router A in AS 65001 is using 60 percent of its outbound bandwidth to Router X in 65004, but Router B is using only 20 percent of its outbound bandwidth. If this utilization is acceptable to the administrator, no manipulation is needed. But if the load averages 60 percent and has temporary bursts above 100 percent of the bandwidth, this situation will cause lost packets, higher latency, and higher CPU usage because of the number of packets being routed. When another link to the same location is available and is not heavily used, it makes sense to divert some of the traffic to the other path. To change outbound path selection from AS 65001, the local preference attribute must be manipulated.

Recall that a higher local preference is preferred. To determine which path to manipulate, the administrator performs a traffic analysis on Internet-bound traffic by examining the most heavily visited addresses, web pages, or domain names. This information can usually be found by examining network management records or firewall accounting information.

Assume that in Figure 8-35, 35 percent of all traffic from AS 65001 has been going to www.cisco.com. The administrator can obtain the Cisco address or AS number by performing a reverse Domain Name System (DNS) lookup or by going to ARIN (at www.arin.net) and looking up the AS number of Cisco Systems or the address space assigned to the company. After this information has been determined, the administrator can use route maps to change the local preference to manipulate path selection for the Cisco network.

Using a route map, Router B can announce, to all routers within AS 65001, all networks associated with the Cisco Systems AS with a higher local preference than Router A announces for those networks. Because routers running BGP prefer routes with the highest local preference, other BGP routers in AS 65001 send all traffic destined for the Cisco Systems AS to exit AS 65001 via Router B. The outbound load for Router B increases from its previous load of 20 percent to account for the extra traffic from AS 65001 destined for the Cisco networks. The outbound load for Router A, which was originally 60 percent, should decrease. This change will make the outbound load on both links more balanced. The administrator should monitor the outbound loads and adjust the configuration accordingly as traffic patterns change over time.

Just as there was a loading issue outbound from AS 65001, there can be a similar problem inbound. For example, if the inbound load to Router B has a much higher utilization than the inbound load to Router A, the BGP MED attribute can be used to manipulate how traffic enters AS 65001. Router A in AS 65001 can announce a lower MED for network 192.168.25.0/24 to AS 65004 than Router B announces. This MED recommends to the next AS how to enter AS 65001. However, MED is not considered until later in the BGP path-selection process than local preference. Therefore, if AS 65004 prefers to leave its AS via Router Y (to Router B in AS 65001), Router Y should be configured to announce a higher local preference to the BGP routers in AS 65004 for network 192.168.25.0/24 than Router X announces. The local preference that Routers X and Y advertise to other BGP routers in AS 65004 is evaluated before the MED coming from Routers A and B. MED is considered a *recommendation*, because the receiving AS can override it by manipulating another variable that is considered before the MED is evaluated.

As another example using Figure 8-35, assume that 55 percent of all traffic is going to the 192.168.25.0/24 subnet (on Router A). The inbound utilization to Router A is averaging only 10 percent, but the inbound utilization to Router B is averaging 75 percent. The problem is that if the inbound load for Router B spikes to more than 100 percent and causes the link to flap, all the sessions crossing that link could be lost. For example, if these sessions were purchases being made on AS 65001 web servers, revenue would be lost, which is something administrators want to avoid. If AS 65001 were set to prefer to have all traffic that is going to 192.168.25.0/24 enter through Router A, the load inbound on Router A should increase, and the load inbound on Router B should decrease.

If load averages less than 50 percent for an outbound or inbound case, path manipulation might not be needed. However, as soon as a link starts to reach its capacity for an extended period of time, either more bandwidth is needed or path manipulation should be considered. The administrator should monitor the inbound loads and adjust the configuration accordingly as traffic patterns change over time.

The Path-Selection Decision Process with a Multihomed Connection

An AS rarely implements BGP with only one EBGP connection, so generally multiple paths exist for each network in the BGP forwarding database.

> **NOTE**   If you are running BGP in a network with only one EBGP connection, it is loop free. If synchronization is disabled or BGP is synchronized with the IGP for IBGP connections, and the next hop can be reached, the path is submitted to the IP routing table. Because there is only path, there is no benefit to manipulating its attributes.

Recall, from the "The Route Selection Decision Process" section earlier in this chapter, that when faced with multiple routes to the same destination, BGP chooses the best route for routing traffic toward the destination. Using the 11-step route selection process, only the best path is put in the routing table and propagated to the router's BGP neighbors. Without route manipulation, the most common reason for path selection is Step 4, the preference for the shortest AS-path.

Step 1 looks at weight, which by default is set to 0 for routes that were not originated by this router.

Step 2 compares local preference, which by default is set to 100 for all networks. Both of these steps have an effect only if the network administrator configures the weight or local preference to a nondefault value.

Step 3 looks at networks that are owned by this AS. If one of the routes is injected into the BGP table by the local router, the local router prefers it to any routes received from other BGP routers.

Step 4 selects the path that has the fewest autonomous systems to cross. This is the most common reason a path is selected in BGP. If a network administrator does not like the path with the fewest autonomous systems, he or she needs to manipulate weight or local preference to change which outbound path BGP chooses.

Step 5 looks at how a network was introduced into BGP. This introduction is usually either with **network** statements (i for an origin code) or through redistribution (? for an origin code).

Step 6 looks at MED to judge where the neighbor AS wants this AS to send packets for a given network. The Cisco IOS Software sets the MED to 0 by default; therefore, MED does not participate in path selection unless the network administrator of the neighbor AS manipulates the paths using MED.

If multiple paths have the same number of autonomous systems to traverse, the second most common decision point is Step 7, which states that an externally learned path from an EBGP neighbor is preferred over a path learned from an IBGP neighbor. A router in an AS prefers to use the ISP's bandwidth to reach a network rather than using internal bandwidth to reach an IBGP neighbor on the other side of its own AS.

If the AS path length is equal and the router in an AS has no EBGP neighbors for that network (only IBGP neighbors), it makes sense to take the quickest path to the nearest exit point. Step 8 looks for the closest IBGP neighbor; the IGP metric determines what closest means (for example, RIP uses hop count, and OSPF uses the least cost, based on bandwidth).

If the AS path length is equal and the costs via all IBGP neighbors are equal, or if all neighbors for this network are EBGP, the oldest path (step 9) is the next common reason for selecting one path over another. EBGP neighbors rarely establish sessions at the exact same time. One session is likely older than another, so the paths through that older neighbor are considered more stable, because they have been up longer.

If all these criteria are equal, the next most common decision is to take the neighbor with the lowest BGP router ID, which is Step 10.

If the BGP router IDs are the same (for example, if the paths are to the same BGP router), Step 11 states that the route with the lowest neighbor IP address is used.

Setting Local Preference

Local preference is used only within an AS between IBGP speakers to determine the best path to leave the AS to reach an outside network. The local preference is set to 100 by default; higher values are preferred.

> **NOTE**   If for some reason an EBGP neighbor did receive a local preference value (such as because of faulty software), the EBGP neighbor ignores it.

Changing Local Preference for All Routes

The **bgp default local-preference** *value* router configuration command changes the default local preference to the value specified; all BGP routes that are advertised include this local preference value. The value can be set to a number between 0 and 4294967295.

Manipulating the default local preference can have an immediate and dramatic effect on traffic flow leaving an AS. Before making any changes to manipulate paths, the network administrator should perform a thorough traffic analysis to understand the effects of the change. For example, the configurations for Routers A and B in Figure 8-36 are shown in Examples 8-22 and 8-23, respectively. In this network, the administrator changed the default local preference for all routes on Router B to 500 and on Router A to 200. All BGP routers in AS 65001 send all traffic destined for the Internet to Router B, causing its outbound utilization to be much higher and the utilization out Router A to be reduced to a minimal amount. This change is probably not what the network administrator intended. Instead, the network administrator should use route maps to set only certain networks to have a higher local preference through Router B to decrease some of the original outbound load that was being sent out Router A.

Figure 8-36   *Setting a Default Local Preference for All Routes*

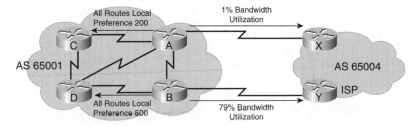

Example 8-22   *Configuration for Router A in Figure 8-36*

```
router bgp 65001
  bgp default local-preference 200
```

Example 8-23 *Configuration for Router B in Figure 8-36*

```
router bgp 65001
  bgp default local-preference 500
```

Local Preference Example

Figure 8-37 illustrates a sample network running BGP that will be used to demonstrate how local preference can be manipulated. This network initially has no commands configured to change the local preference.

Figure 8-37 *Network for Local Preference Example*

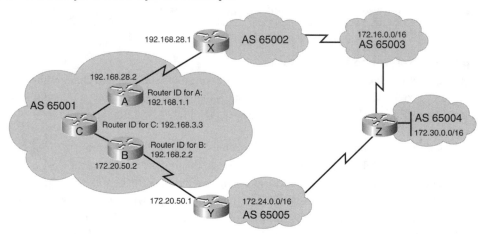

Example 8-24 illustrates the BGP forwarding table on Router C in Figure 8-37, showing only the networks of interest to this example:

- 172.16.0.0 in AS 65003

- 172.24.0.0 in AS 65005

- 172.30.0.0 in AS 65004

Example 8-24 *BGP Table for Router C in Figure 8-37 Without Path Manipulation*

```
RouterC#show ip bgp
BGP table version is 7, local router ID is 192.168.3.3
Status codes: s suppressed, d damped, h history, * valid, > best, i - internal,  r RIB-
   failure, S Stale
Origin codes: i - IGP, e - EGP, ? - incomplete
Network            Next Hop        Metric LocPrf  Weight Path
* i172.16.0.0      172.20.50.1               100      0 65005 65004 65003 i
*>i                192.168.28.1              100      0 65002 65003 i
*>i172.24.0.0      172.20.50.1               100      0 65005 i
* i                192.168.28.1              100      0 65002 65003 65004 65005 i
*>i172.30.0.0      172.20.50.1               100      0 65005 65004 i
* i                192.168.28.1              100      0 65002 65003 65004i
```

The best path is indicated with a > in the second column of the output.

Each network has two paths that are loop-free and synchronization-disabled and that have a valid next-hop address (that can be reached from Router C). All routes have a weight of 0 and a default local preference of 100, so Steps 1 and 2 in the BGP path-selection process do not select the best route.

This router does not originate any of the routes (Step 3), so the process moves to Step 4, and BGP uses the shortest AS-path to select the best routes as follows:

- For network 172.16.0.0, the shortest AS-path of two autonomous systems (65002 65003) is through the next hop of 192.168.28.1.

- For network 172.24.0.0, the shortest AS-path of one AS (65005) is through the next hop of 172.20.50.1.

- For network 172.30.0.0, the shortest AS-path of two autonomous systems (65005 65004) is through the next hop of 172.20.50.1.

Neither Routers A nor B are using the **neighbor next-hop-self** command in this example.

A traffic analysis reveals the following:

- The link going through Router B to 172.20.50.1 is heavily used, and the link through Router A to 192.168.28.1 is hardly used at all.

- The three largest-volume destination networks on the Internet from AS 65001 are 172.30.0.0, 172.24.0.0, and 172.16.0.0.

- Thirty percent of all Internet traffic is going to network 172.24.0.0 (via Router B), 20 percent is going to network 172.30.0.0 (via Router B), and 10 percent is going to network 172.16.0.0 (via Router A); the other 40 percent is going to other destinations. Thus, considering only these three largest-volume destinations, only 10 percent of the traffic is using the link out Router A to 192.168.28.1, and 50 percent of the traffic is using the link out Router B to 172.20.50.1.

The network administrator has decided to divert traffic to network 172.30.0.0 and send it out Router A to the next hop of 192.168.28.1, so that the loading between Routers A and B is more balanced.

Changing Local Preference Using Route Maps

A route map is added to Router A in Figure 8-37, as shown in the BGP configuration in Example 8-25. The route map alters the network 172.30.0.0 BGP update from Router X (192.168.28.1) to have a high local preference value of 400 so that it will be more preferred.

Example 8-25 *BGP Configuration for Router A in Figure 8-37 with a Route Map*

```
router bgp 65001
  neighbor 192.168.2.2 remote-as 65001
  neighbor 192.168.3.3 remote-as 65001
  neighbor 192.168.2.2 remote-as 65001 update-source loopback0
  neighbor 192.168.3.3 remote-as 65001 update-source loopback0
  neighbor 192.168.28.1 remote-as 65002
  neighbor 192.168.28.1 route-map local_pref in
!
route-map local_pref permit 10
  match ip address 65
  set local-preference 400
!
route-map local_pref permit 20
!
access-list 65 permit 172.30.0.0 0.0.255.255
```

The first line of the route map called local_pref is a **permit** statement with a sequence number of 10; this defines the first **route-map** statement. The **match** condition for this statement checks all networks to see which are permitted by access list 65. Access list 65 permits all networks that start with the first two octets of 172.30.0.0; the route map sets these networks to a local preference of 400.

The second statement in the route map called local_pref is a **permit** statement with a sequence number of 20, but it does not have any **match** or **set** statements. This statement is similar to a **permit any** statement in an access list. Because there are no **match** conditions for the remaining networks, they are all permitted with their current settings. In this case, the local preference for networks 172.16.0.0 and 172.24.0.0 stays set at the default of 100. The sequence number 20 (rather than 11) is chosen for the second statement in case other policies have to be implemented later before this **permit any** statement.

This route map is linked to neighbor 192.168.28.1 as an inbound route map. Therefore, as Router A receives updates from 192.168.28.1, it processes them through the local_pref route map and sets the local preference accordingly as the networks are placed in Router A's BGP forwarding table.

Example 8-26 illustrates the BGP table on Router C in Figure 8-37, after the route map has been applied on Router A and the BGP sessions have been reset. Router C learns about the new local preference value (400) coming from Router A for network 172.30.0.0. The only difference in this table compared to the original in Example 8-24 is that the best route to network 172.30.0.0 is now through 192.168.28.1 because its local preference of 400 is higher than the local preference of 100 for the next hop of 172.20.50.1. The AS-path through 172.20.50.1 is still shorter than the path through 192.168.28.1, but AS-path length is not evaluated until Step 4, whereas local preference is examined in Step 2. Therefore, the higher local preference path was chosen as the best path.

Example 8-26 *BGP Table for Router C in Figure 8-37 with a Route Map for Local Preference*

```
RouterC#show ip bgp
BGP table version is 7, local router ID is 192.168.3.3
Status codes: s suppressed, d damped, h history, * valid, > best, i - internal,  r RIB-
  failure, S Stale
Origin codes: i - IGP, e - EGP, ? - incomplete
   Network          Next Hop        Metric LocPrf Weight Path
* i172.16.0.0       172.20.50.1           100       0 65005 65004 65003 i
*>i                 192.168.28.1          100       0 65002 65003 i
*>i172.24.0.0       172.20.50.1           100       0 65005 i
* i                 192.168.28.1          100       0 65002 65003 65004 65005 i
* i172.30.0.0       172.20.50.1           100       0 65005 65004 i
*>i                 192.168.28.1          400       0 65002 65003 65004i
```

Setting the MED with Route Maps

Recall that MED is used to decide how to enter an AS when multiple paths exist between two autonomous systems and one AS is trying to influence the incoming path from the other AS. Because MED is evaluated late in the BGP path-selection process (Step 6), it usually has no influence on the process. For example, an AS receiving a MED for a route can change its local preference on how to leave the AS to override what the other AS is advertising with its MED value.

When comparing MED values for the same destination network in the BGP path-selection process, the lowest MED value is preferred.

Changing the MED for All Routes

The default MED value for each network an AS owns and advertises to an EBGP neighbor is set to 0. To change this value, use the **default-metric** *number* router configuration command. The *number* parameter is the MED value.

Manipulating the default MED value can have an immediate and dramatic effect on traffic flow entering your AS. Before making any changes to manipulate the path, you should perform a thorough traffic analysis to ensure that you understand the effects of the change.

For example, the configurations of Routers A and B in Figure 8-38 are shown in Examples 8-27 and 8-28, respectively. The network administrator in AS 65001 tries to manipulate how AS 65004 chooses its path to reach routes in AS 65001. By changing the default metric under the BGP process on Router A to 1001, Router A advertises a MED of 1001 for all routes to Router X. Router X then informs all the other routers in AS 65004 of the MED through Router X to reach networks originating in AS 65001. A similar event happens on Router B, but Router B advertises a MED of 99 for all routes to Router Y. All routers in AS 65004 see a MED of 1001 through the next hop of Router A and a MED of 99 through the next hop of Router B to reach networks in AS 65001. (The **neighbor next-hop self** command is not used on either Router X or Router Y.) If AS 65004 has no overriding policy, all routers in AS 65004 choose to exit their AS through Router Y to reach the networks in AS 65001; this traffic goes through Router B. This selection causes Router A's inbound bandwidth utilization to decrease to almost nothing except for BGP routing updates, and it causes the inbound utilization on Router B to increase and account for all returning packets from AS 65004 to AS 65001.

Figure 8-38   *Changing the Default MED for All Routes*

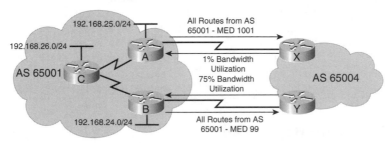

Example 8-27   *BGP Configuration for Router A in Figure 8-38*

```
router bgp 65001
  default-metric 1001
```

Example 8-28   *BGP Configuration for Router B in Figure 8-38*

```
router bgp 65001
  default-metric 99
```

This situation is probably not what the network administrator intended. Instead, to load-share the inbound traffic to AS 65001, the AS 65001 network administrator should configure some networks to have a lower MED through Router B and other networks to have a lower MED through Router A. Route maps should be used to set the appropriate MED values for various networks.

Changing the MED Using Route Maps

The network shown in Figure 8-39 is used as an example to demonstrate how to manipulate inbound traffic using route maps to change the BGP MED attribute. The intention of these route maps is to designate Router A as the preferred entry point to reach networks 192.168.25.0/24 and 192.168.26.0/24 and Router B as the preferred entry point to reach network 192.168.24.0/24. The other networks should still be reachable through each router in case of a link or router failure.

The MED is set outbound when advertising to an EBGP neighbor. In the configuration for Router A shown in Example 8-29, a route map named med_65004 is linked to neighbor 192.168.28.1 (Router X) as an outbound route map. When Router A sends an update to neighbor 192.168.28.1, it processes the outbound update through route map med_65004 and changes any values specified in a **set** command as long as the corresponding **match** command conditions in that section of the route map are met.

Figure 8-39 *Network for MED Examples*

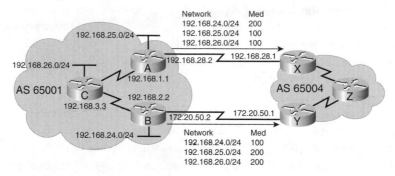

Example 8-29 *BGP Configuration for Router A in Figure 8-39 with a Route Map*

```
router bgp 65001
  neighbor 192.168.2.2 remote-as 65001
  neighbor 192.168.3.3 remote-as 65001
  neighbor 192.168.2.2 update-source loopback0
  neighbor 192.168.3.3 update-source loopback0
  neighbor 192.168.28.1 remote-as 65004
  neighbor 192.168.28.1 route-map med_65004 out
!
route-map med_65004 permit 10
  match ip address 66
  set metric 100
route-map med_65004 permit 100
  set metric 200
!
access-list 66 permit 192.168.25.0.0 0.0.0.255
access-list 66 permit 192.168.26.0.0 0.0.0.255
```

The first line of the route map called med_65004 is a **permit** statement with a sequence number of 10; this defines the first **route-map** statement. The **match** condition for this statement checks all networks to see which are permitted by access list 66. The first line of access list 66 permits any networks that start with the first three octets of 192.168.25.0, and the second line of access list 66 permits networks that start with the first three octets of 192.168.26.0.

Any networks that are permitted by either of these lines will have the MED set to 100 by the route map. No other networks are permitted by this access list (there is an implicit deny all at the end of all access lists), so their MED is not changed. These other networks must proceed to the next **route-map** statement in the med_65004 route map.

The route map's second statement is a **permit** statement with a sequence number of 100. The route map does not have any **match** statements, just a **set metric 200** statement. This statement is a

permit any statement for route maps. Because the network administrator does not specify a **match** condition for this portion of the route map, all networks being processed through this section of the route map (sequence number 100) are permitted, and they are set to a MED of 200. If the network administrator did not set the MED to 200, by default it would have been set to a MED of 0. Because 0 is less than 100, the routes with a MED of 0 would have been the preferred paths to the networks in AS 65001.

Similarly, the configuration for Router B is shown in Example 8-30. A route map named med_65004 is linked to neighbor 172.20.50.1 as an outbound route map. Before Router B sends an update to neighbor 172.20.50.1, it processes the outbound update through route map med_65004, and changes any values specified in a **set** command as long as the preceding **match** command conditions in that section of the route map are met.

Example 8-30 *BGP Configuration for Router B in Figure 8-39 with a Route Map*

```
router bgp 65001
  neighbor 192.168.1.1 remote-as 65001
  neighbor 192.168.3.3 remote-as 65001
  neighbor 192.168.1.1 update-source loopback0
  neighbor 192.168.3.3 update-source loopback0
  neighbor 172.20.50.1 remote-as 65004
  neighbor 172.20.50.1 route-map med_65004 out
!
route-map med_65004 permit 10
  match ip address 66
  set metric 100
route-map med_65004 permit 100
  set metric 200
!
access-list 66 permit 192.168.24.0.0 0.0.0.255
```

The first line of the route map called med_65004 is a **permit** statement with a sequence number of 10; this defines the first **route-map** statement. The **match** condition for this statement checks all networks to see which are permitted by access list 66. Access list 66 on Router B permits any networks that start with the first three octets of 192.168.24.0. Any networks that are permitted by this line have the MED set to 100 by the route map. No other networks are permitted by this access list, so their MED is unchanged. These other networks must proceed to the next **route-map** statement in the med_65004 route map.

The second statement of the route map is a **permit** statement with a sequence number of 100, but it does not have any **match** statements, just a **set metric 200** statement. This statement is a **permit any** statement for route maps. Because the network administrator does not specify a **match** condition for this portion of the route map, all networks being processed through this section of the route map are permitted, but they are set to a MED of 200. If the network administrator did not set the MED to 200, by default it would have been set to a MED of 0. Because 0 is less than 100, the routes with a MED of 0 would have been the preferred paths to the networks in AS 65001.

Example 8-31 shows the BGP forwarding table on Router Z in AS 65004 indicating the networks learned from AS 65001. (Other networks that do not affect this example have been omitted.) Note that in this command output, the MED is shown in the column labeled Metric.

Example 8-31 *BGP Table for Router Z in Figure 8-39 with a Route Map*

```
RouterZ#show ip bgp
BGP table version is 7, local router ID is 192.168.1.1
Status codes: s suppressed, d damped, h history, * valid, > best, i - internal,  r RIB-
   failure, S Stale
Origin codes: i - IGP, e - EGP, ? - incomplete
   Network          Next Hop         Metric LocPrf Weight Path
*>i192.168.24.0     172.20.50.2        100    100       0 65001 i
* i                 192.168.28.2       200    100       0 65001 i
* i192.168.25.0     172.20.50.2        200    100       0 65001 i
*>i                 192.168.28.2       100    100       0 65001 i
* i192.168.26.0     172.20.50.2        200    100       0 65001 i
*>i                 192.168.28.2       100    100       0 65001 i
```

Router Z has multiple paths to reach each network. These paths all have valid next-hop addresses and synchronization disabled and are loop free. All networks have a weight of 0 and a local preference of 100, so Steps 1 and 2 in the route-selection decision process do not determine the best path. None of the routes were originated by this router or any router in AS 65004; all networks came from AS 65001, so Step 3 does not apply. All networks have an AS-path of one AS (65001) and were introduced into BGP with **network** statements (i is the origin code), so Steps 4 and 5 are equal. The route selection decision process therefore gets to Step 6, which states that BGP chooses the lowest MED if all preceding steps are equal or do not apply.

For network 192.168.24.0, the next hop of 172.20.50.2 has a lower MED than the next hop of 192.168.28.2. Therefore, for network 192.168.24.0, the path through 172.20.50.2 is the preferred path. For networks 192.168.25.0 and 192.168.26.0, the next hop of 192.168.28.2 has a lower MED (100) than the next hop of 172.20.50.2 (with a MED of 200). Therefore, 192.168.28.2 is the preferred path for those two networks.

Configuring Weight

Recall that the weight attribute influences only the local router. Routes with a higher weight are preferred.

The **neighbor** {*ip-address* | *peer-group-name*} **weight** *weight* router configuration command is used to assign a weight to updates from a neighbor connection, as described in Table 8-8.

Table 8-8 **neighbor weight** *Command Description*

Parameter	Description
ip-address	The BGP neighbor's IP address.
peer-group-name	The name of a BGP peer group.
weight	The weight to assign. Acceptable values are 0 to 65535. The default is 32768 for local routes (routes that the router originates). Other routes have a weight of 0 by default.

Implementing BGP in an Enterprise Network

Figure 8-40 depicts a typical enterprise BGP implementation. The enterprise is multihomed to two ISPs, to increase the reliability and performance of its connection to the Internet. The ISPs might pass only default routes or might also pass other specific routes, or even all routes, to the enterprise. The enterprise routers connected to the ISPs run EBGP with the ISP routers and IBGP between themselves; thus all routers in the transit path within the enterprise AS run IBGP. These routers pass default routes to the other routers in the enterprise, rather than redistributing BGP into the interior routing protocol.

Figure 8-40 *BGP in an Enterprise*

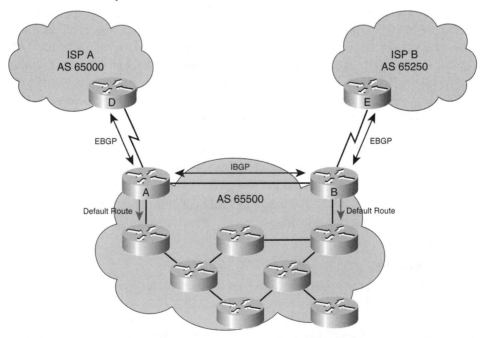

BGP attributes can be manipulated, using the methods discussed in this section, by any of the routers running BGP, to affect the path of the traffic to and from the autonomous systems.

Summary

This chapter covered the basics of BGP, the EGP used on the Internet, through discussion of the following topics:

- BGP terminology and concepts, including BGP's use between autonomous systems, BGP neighbor relationships and the difference between IBGP and EBGP, multihoming options, when to use BGP and when not to use BGP, BGP's use of TCP, and the use of IBGP on all routers in the transit path within the AS.

- The three tables used by BGP: the BGP table, IP routing table, and BGP neighbor table.

- The four BGP message types: open, keepalive, update, and notification.

- The BGP attributes that can be either well-known or optional, mandatory or discretionary, and transitive or nontransitive; an attribute might also be partial. The BGP attributes are AS-path, next-hop, origin, local preference, atomic aggregate, aggregator, community, MED, and the Cisco-defined weight.

- The 11-step route selection decision process.

- BGP configuration, verification and troubleshooting commands and examples, including BGP neighbor authentication.

- Understanding and troubleshooting the BGP states: idle, connect, active, open sent, open confirm, and established.

- BGP path manipulation using route maps, including changing the local preference and MED attributes.

References

For additional information, refer to Cisco's command reference and configuration guides available from the Documentation DVD home page at http://www.cisco.com/univercd/cc/td/doc/.

Configuration Exercise 8-1: Configuring Multihome BGP

In this Configuration Exercise, you configure EBGP between your P*x*R1 and P*x*R2 routers and the two backbone routers, BBR1 and BBR2.

Introduction to the Configuration Exercises

This book uses Configuration Exercises to help you practice configuring routers with the commands and topics presented. If you have access to real hardware, you can try these exercises on your routers. See Appendix B, "Configuration Exercise Equipment Requirements and Backbone Configurations," for a list of recommended equipment and initial configuration commands for the backbone routers. However, even if you do not have access to any routers, you can go through the exercises, and keep a log of your own running configurations, or just read through the solution. Commands used and solutions to the Configuration Exercises are provided within the exercises.

In the Configuration Exercises, the network is assumed to consist of two pods, each with four routers. The pods are interconnected to a backbone. You configure pod 1. No interaction between the two pods is required, but you might see some routes from the other pod in your routing tables in some exercises if you have it configured. In most of the exercises, the backbone has only one router; in some cases, another router is added to the backbone. Each Configuration Exercise assumes that you have completed the previous chapters' Configuration Exercises on your pod.

NOTE Throughout this exercise, the pod number is referred to as *x*, and the router number is referred to as *y*. Substitute the appropriate numbers as needed.

Objectives

The objectives of this exercise are to configure EBGP on your edge routers which are multihomed to the backbone, to simulate multihomed ISP connections.

Visual Objective

Figure 8-41 illustrates the topology used and what you will accomplish in this exercise.

NOTE The Frame Relay router is in AS 64997. However, it is provided only for communication with the backbone routers; it is not used in this exercise.

Command List

In this exercise, you use the commands in Table 8-9, listed in logical order. Refer to this list if you need configuration command assistance during the exercise.

CAUTION Although the command syntax is shown in this table, the addresses shown are typically for the P*x*R1 and P*x*R3 routers. Be careful when addressing your routers! Refer to the exercise instructions and the appropriate visual objective diagram for addressing details.

Figure 8-41   *Multihomed BGP Configuration Exercise Topology*

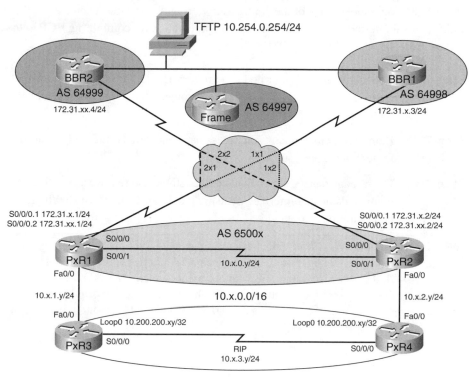

Table 8-9   *Multihomed BGP Configuration Exercise Commands*

Command	Description
(config)#**router bgp 6500***x*	Enters BGP router configuration mode. This router is in AS 6500*x*.
(config-router)#**neighbor 10.200.200.***xy* **remote-as 6500***x*	Identifies a BGP neighbor.
(config-router)#**neighbor 10.200.200.***xy* **update-source loopback 0**	Sets the source address of BGP updates with the neighbor to be the address of the loopback 0 interface.
(config-router)#**network 10.***x.***0.0 mask 255.255.255.0**	Advertises a network in BGP.
#**show ip bgp summary**	Displays a summary of BGP neighbor status and activities.
#**show ip bgp**	Displays the BGP table.
#**show ip route**	Displays the IP routing table.
(config-router)#**passive-interface s0/0/1**	Configures a routing protocol not to send updates or hellos out the specified interface.
#**show ip protocols**	Displays a summary of the IP routing protocols running on the router.

Task 1: Cleaning Up

In this task, you remove some of the configuration from the previous exercises, and create two multipoint subinterfaces on your edge routers in preparation for configuring BGP in the next task. Follow these steps:

Step 1 Connect to each of your pod edge routers (P*x*R1 and P*x*R2). Remove all OSPF configurations from these edge routers, but leave RIPv2 enabled on them.

Step 2 Remove any route maps and access lists that were configured on the edge routers in the previous exercises.

Step 3 On the edge routers, shut down interface s0/0/0 and remove all configuration commands on that interface by using the **default interface s0/0/0** global configuration command.

> **NOTE** If your edge routers have not been reloaded in the Configuration Exercises in Chapter 7, you have to save your configuration and then reload your edge routers after using the **default interface s0/0/0** command. Even though this command deletes the s0/0/0 subinterfaces, it does not remove the subinterface configuration from the router's memory, and you will not be able to change the link type of the s0/0/0.2 subinterface (from point-to-point to multipoint) until the router has been reloaded.

Solution:

The following shows the required steps on the P1R1 router:

```
P1R1(config)#no router ospf 1
P1R1(config)#no route-map CONVERT
P1R1(config)#no access-list 61
P1R1(config)#no access-list 64
P1R1(config)#default interface s0/0/0
Building configuration...

Interface Serial0/0/0 set to default configuration
P1R1(config)#

P1R1#copy run start
Destination filename [startup-config]?
Building configuration...
[OK]
P1R1#reload
Proceed with reload? [confirm]
```

Step 4 On the edge routers' s0/0/0 interface, enable Frame Relay encapsulation, and then disable Frame Relay Inverse Address Resolution Protocol (ARP).

Step 5   Create two multipoint subinterfaces on each edge router's serial 0/0/0
interface. These subinterfaces will be used to connect to both core routers
(BBR1 and BBR2) in this exercise.

Step 6   Configure subinterface s0/0/0.1 with an IP address of 172.31.*x.y*/24 and a
Frame Relay map statement pointing to the BBR1 address of 172.31.*x*.3;
do not forget the **broadcast** option. P*x*R1 uses DLCI 1x1 and P*x*R2 uses
DLCI 1x2 to reach 172.31.*x*.3/24.

Step 7   Configure the second subinterface, s0/0/0.2, with an IP address of
172.31.*xx.y*/24 and a Frame Relay map statement pointing to the BBR2
address of 172.31.*xx*.4; do not forget the **broadcast** option. P*x*R1 uses
DLCI 2x1 and P*x*R2 uses DLCI 2x2 to reach 172.31.*xx*.4/24.

Step 8   Enable interface s0/0/0 on the edge routers.

Solution:

The following shows the required steps on the P1R1 router:

```
P1R1(config)#int s0/0/0
P1R1(config-if)#encapsulation frame-relay
P1R1(config-if)#no frame-relay inverse-arp
P1R1(config-if)#int s0/0/0.1 multipoint
P1R1(config-subif)#ip address 172.31.1.1 255.255.255.0
P1R1(config-subif)#frame-relay map ip 172.31.1.3 111 broadcast
P1R1(config-subif)#int s0/0/0.2 multipoint
P1R1(config-subif)#ip address 172.31.11.1 255.255.255.0
P1R1(config-subif)#frame-relay map ip 172.31.11.4 211 broadcast
P1R1(config-subif)#int s0/0/0
P1R1(config-if)#no shutdown
```

Step 9   Test each subinterface by pinging the BBR1 and BBR2 routers from both
edge routers.

Solution:

The following shows sample output on the P1R1 router:

```
P1R1#ping 172.31.1.3

Type escape sequence to abort.
Sending 5, 100-byte ICMP Echos to 172.31.1.3, timeout is 2 seconds:
!!!!!
Success rate is 100 percent (5/5), round-trip min/avg/max = 28/30/32 ms
P1R1#ping 172.31.11.4

Type escape sequence to abort.
Sending 5, 100-byte ICMP Echos to 172.31.11.4, timeout is 2 seconds:
!!!!!
Success rate is 100 percent (5/5), round-trip min/avg/max = 28/29/32 ms
P1R1#
```

Task 2: Configuring BGP

In this task, you configure basic BGP on the edge routers. Follow these steps:

Step 1   Configure BGP on the edge routers in the pod (P*x*R1 and P*x*R2) using AS 6500*x*, where *x* is the pod number.

> **NOTE**   Only the edge routers run BGP in this exercise. The internal routers continue to use RIPv2.

Step 2   Configure P*x*R1 and P*x*R2 with two EBGP neighbors, BBR1 (in AS 64998) and BBR2 (in AS 64999), and as IBGP neighbors to each other. BBR1 has IP address 172.31.*x*.3, and BBR2 has IP address 172.31.*xx*.4. Use the loopback addresses (10.200.200.*xy*) to establish the IBGP session between the two edge routers, and remember to configure the loopbacks as the source address of the IBGP updates.

Step 3   Configure the edge routers to advertise your pod networks 10.*x*.0.0/24, 10.*x*.1.0/24, 10.*x*.2.0/24, and 10.*x*.3.0/24 to the core routers. There are two points to remember:

   - The 10.0.0.0 network is subnetted, so you need to use the **mask** option of the **network** command to announce the subnets.

   - The networks listed in the **network** command must match the networks in the routing table exactly.

Solution:

The following shows the required steps on the P1R1 router:

```
P1R1(config)#router bgp 65001
P1R1(config-router)#neighbor 172.31.1.3 remote-as 64998
P1R1(config-router)#neighbor 172.31.11.4 remote-as 64999
P1R1(config-router)#neighbor 10.200.200.12 remote-as 65001
P1R1(config-router)#neighbor 10.200.200.12 update-source loop 0
P1R1(config-router)#network 10.1.0.0 mask 255.255.255.0
P1R1(config-router)#network 10.1.1.0 mask 255.255.255.0
P1R1(config-router)#network 10.1.2.0 mask 255.255.255.0
P1R1(config-router)#network 10.1.3.0 mask 255.255.255.0
```

Step 4   At the edge routers, verify that all three BGP neighbor relationships are established using the **show ip bgp summary** command.

Do you see one IBGP neighbor and two EBGP neighbors on each edge router?

How many prefixes have been learned from each BGP neighbor?

Solution:

The following shows sample output on the P1R1 router. Each router has one IBGP neighbor and two EBGP neighbors. The number in the State/PfxRcd column indicates the number of prefixes received from the neighbor; the presence of a number in that column indicates that the BGP session with that neighbor is in the established state.

```
P1R1#show ip bgp summary
BGP router identifier 10.200.200.11, local AS number 65001
BGP table version is 13, main routing table version 13
10 network entries using 1170 bytes of memory
25 path entries using 1300 bytes of memory
14/5 BGP path/bestpath attribute entries using 1736 bytes of memory
6 BGP AS-PATH entries using 144 bytes of memory
0 BGP route-map cache entries using 0 bytes of memory
0 BGP filter-list cache entries using 0 bytes of memory
BGP using 4350 total bytes of memory
BGP activity 10/0 prefixes, 25/0 paths, scan interval 60 secs

Neighbor        V    AS MsgRcvd MsgSent   TblVer  InQ OutQ Up/Down  State/PfxRcd
10.200.200.12   4 65001     12      11       13    0    0 00:01:59           9
172.31.1.3      4 64998     17      14       13    0    0 00:04:58           6
172.31.11.4     4 64999     19      14       13    0    0 00:04:51           6
P1R1#
```

Step 5   At the edge routers, display the BGP table. Verify that you have received routes from the core and from the other edge router. Look at the IP routing table on the edge routers. Are the BGP routes present?

Solution:

The following shows sample output on the P1R1 router. P1R1 has received routes from all three of its neighbors.

```
P1R1#show ip bgp
BGP table version is 13, local router ID is 10.200.200.11
Status codes: s suppressed, d damped, h history, * valid, > best, i - internal,
              r RIB-failure, S Stale
Origin codes: i - IGP, e - EGP, ? - incomplete

   Network          Next Hop         Metric LocPrf Weight Path
* i10.1.0.0/24      10.200.200.12         0    100      0 i
*>                  0.0.0.0               0         32768 i
*> 10.1.1.0/24      0.0.0.0               0         32768 i
* i10.1.2.0/24      10.200.200.12         0    100      0 i
*>                  10.1.0.2              1         32768 i
* i10.1.3.0/24      10.1.2.4              1    100      0 i
*>                  10.1.1.3              1         32768 i
* i10.97.97.0/24    172.31.1.3            0    100      0 64998 64997 i
*                   172.31.11.4                        0 64999 64997 i
*>                  172.31.1.3                         0 64998 64997 i
* i10.254.0.0/24    172.31.1.3            0    100      0 64998 i
*                   172.31.11.4                        0 64999 64998 i
*>                  172.31.1.3            0              0 64998 i
r i172.31.1.0/24    172.31.1.3            0    100      0 64998 i
r                   172.31.11.4                        0 64999 64998 i
r>                  172.31.1.3            0              0 64998 i
```

```
* i172.31.2.0/24     172.31.1.3                    0    100      0 64998 i
*                    172.31.11.4                                 0 64999 64998 i
*>                   172.31.1.3                    0             0 64998 i
r i172.31.11.0/24    172.31.11.4                   0    100      0 64999 i
r>                   172.31.11.4                   0             0 64999 i
r                    172.31.1.3                                  0 64998 64999 i
* i172.31.22.0/24    172.31.11.4                   0    100      0 64999 i
*>                   172.31.11.4                   0             0 64999 i
*                    172.31.1.3                                  0 64998 64999 i
P1R1#
```

The following shows sample output on the P1R1 router. There are BGP routes in the IP routing table.

```
P1R1#show ip route
<output omitted>
Gateway of last resort is 172.31.11.4 to network 0.0.0.0

     172.31.0.0/24 is subnetted, 4 subnets
B       172.31.22.0 [20/0] via 172.31.11.4, 00:13:46
B       172.31.2.0 [20/0] via 172.31.1.3, 00:13:46
C       172.31.1.0 is directly connected, Serial0/0/0.1
C       172.31.11.0 is directly connected, Serial0/0/0.2
     10.0.0.0/8 is variably subnetted, 10 subnets, 2 masks
C       10.200.200.11/32 is directly connected, Loopback0
R       10.200.200.14/32 [120/2] via 10.1.1.3, 00:00:07, FastEthernet0/0
                         [120/2] via 10.1.0.2, 00:00:18, Serial0/0/1
R       10.200.200.12/32 [120/1] via 10.1.0.2, 00:00:19, Serial0/0/1
R       10.200.200.13/32 [120/1] via 10.1.1.3, 00:00:08, FastEthernet0/0
R       10.1.3.0/24 [120/1] via 10.1.1.3, 00:00:08, FastEthernet0/0
R       10.1.2.0/24 [120/1] via 10.1.0.2, 00:00:19, Serial0/0/1
B       10.97.97.0/24 [20/0] via 172.31.1.3, 00:13:48
C       10.1.1.0/24 is directly connected, FastEthernet0/0
C       10.1.0.0/24 is directly connected, Serial0/0/1
B       10.254.0.0/24 [20/0] via 172.31.1.3, 00:13:48
S*   0.0.0.0/0 [1/0] via 172.31.11.4
P1R1#
```

Step 6   Telnet to the core routers, BBR1 (172.31.x.3) and BBR2 (172.31.xx.4).
Look at the IP routing table. Are the BGP routes present for your pod? Exit
the Telnet sessions.

Solution:

The following shows sample output on the BBR1 and BBR2 routers. The routes from pod 1 are highlighted.

```
BBR1#show ip route
<output omitted>
Gateway of last resort is not set

     172.31.0.0/24 is subnetted, 4 subnets
B       172.31.22.0 [20/0] via 10.254.0.2, 2w5d
C       172.31.2.0 is directly connected, Serial0/0/0.2
C       172.31.1.0 is directly connected, Serial0/0/0.1
B       172.31.11.0 [20/0] via 10.254.0.2, 00:33:01
S    192.168.11.0/24 [1/0] via 172.31.1.2
     10.0.0.0/24 is subnetted, 6 subnets
B       10.1.3.0 [20/1] via 172.31.1.2, 00:18:00
B       10.1.2.0 [20/0] via 172.31.1.2, 00:18:00
```

```
B        10.97.97.0 [20/0] via 10.254.0.3, 2w5d
B        10.1.1.0 [20/0] via 172.31.1.1, 00:19:49
B        10.1.0.0 [20/0] via 172.31.1.1, 00:20:20
C        10.254.0.0 is directly connected, FastEthernet0/0
S     192.168.22.0/24 [1/0] via 172.31.2.2
S     192.168.1.0/24 [1/0] via 172.31.1.1
S     192.168.2.0/24 [1/0] via 172.31.2.1
BBR1#


BBR2#show ip route
<output omitted>
Gateway of last resort is not set

      172.31.0.0/24 is subnetted, 4 subnets
C        172.31.22.0 is directly connected, Serial0/0/0.2
B        172.31.2.0 [20/0] via 10.254.0.1, 2w5d
B        172.31.1.0 [20/0] via 10.254.0.1, 00:30:54
C        172.31.11.0 is directly connected, Serial0/0/0.1
      10.0.0.0/24 is subnetted, 6 subnets
B        10.1.3.0 [20/1] via 172.31.11.2, 00:20:12
B        10.1.2.0 [20/0] via 172.31.11.2, 00:20:12
B        10.97.97.0 [20/0] via 10.254.0.3, 2w5d
B        10.1.1.0 [20/0] via 172.31.11.1, 00:22:00
B        10.1.0.0 [20/0] via 172.31.11.1, 00:22:31
C        10.254.0.0 is directly connected, FastEthernet0/0
BBR2#
```

Step 7   RIPv2 is running between P*x*R1 and P*x*R2, because the network statement
for RIPv2 includes the entire 10.0.0.0 network.

For this exercise, you only want to run IBGP between P*x*R1 and P*x*R2.
Configure interface serial 0/0/1 as a passive interface for RIPv2 on both
edge routers.

Solution:

The following shows the required step on the P1R1 router:

```
P1R1(config)#router rip
P1R1(config-router)#passive-interface s0/0/1
```

Step 8   At the edge routers, use the **show ip protocols** command to verify the
RIPv2 passive interface and the BGP configuration.

Solution:

The following shows sample output on the P1R1 router. The passive interface for RIPv2 is
indicated, as is BGP.

```
P1R1#show ip protocols
Routing Protocol is "rip"
  Outgoing update filter list for all interfaces is not set
  Incoming update filter list for all interfaces is not set
  Sending updates every 30 seconds, next due in 21 seconds
  Invalid after 180 seconds, hold down 180, flushed after 240
  Redistributing: rip
```

```
    Default version control: send version 2, receive version 2
      Interface          Send  Recv  Triggered RIP  Key-chain
      FastEthernet0/0      2     2
      Loopback0            2     2
    Automatic network summarization is not in effect
    Maximum path: 4
    Routing for Networks:
      10.0.0.0
    Passive Interface(s):
      Serial0/0/1
    Routing Information Sources:
      Gateway         Distance      Last Update
      10.1.1.3            120       00:00:06
      10.1.0.2            120       00:02:28
    Distance: (default is 120)

  Routing Protocol is "bgp 65001"
    Outgoing update filter list for all interfaces is not set
    Incoming update filter list for all interfaces is not set
    IGP synchronization is disabled
    Automatic route summarization is disabled
    Neighbor(s):
      Address           FiltIn FiltOut DistIn DistOut Weight RouteMap
      10.200.200.12
      172.31.1.3
      172.31.11.4
    Maximum path: 1
    Routing Information Sources:
      Gateway         Distance      Last Update
      172.31.1.3          20        00:30:23
      172.31.11.4         20        00:30:23
    Distance: external 20 internal 200 local 200

    P1R1#
```

Step 9   You are not redistributing BGP into RIPv2, so the internal routers P*x*R3
and P*x*R4 do not know any routes outside your pod. In a previous exercise,
you configured RIPv2 to pass a default route to the internal pod routers
using the **default-information originate** command under the RIP router
configuration. View the running configuration to verify that this command
and the default route are still present.

Step 10   Verify connectivity by pinging the TFTP server (10.254.0.254) from the
edge routers. If this works, ping the TFTP server from internal routers.

Solution:

The following shows sample output on the P1R1 and P1R3 routers. Both pings work.

```
P1R1#ping 10.254.0.254

Type escape sequence to abort.
Sending 5, 100-byte ICMP Echos to 10.254.0.254, timeout is 2 seconds:
!!!!!
Success rate is 100 percent (5/5), round-trip min/avg/max = 28/31/32 ms
P1R1#

P1R3#ping 10.254.0.254
```

```
Type escape sequence to abort.
Sending 5, 100-byte ICMP Echos to 10.254.0.254, timeout is 2 seconds:
!!!!!
Success rate is 100 percent (5/5), round-trip min/avg/max = 28/30/32 ms
P1R3#
```

Step 11   Save your configurations to NVRAM.

Solution:

The following shows the required step on the P1R1 router.

```
P1R1#copy run start
Destination filename [startup-config]?
Building configuration...
[OK]
```

Exercise Verification

You have successfully completed this exercise when you achieve the following results:

- You have successfully configured IBGP between P*x*R1 and P*x*R2 and EBGP between P*x*R1, P*x*R2, BBR1, and BBR2.

- You can ping the TFTP server from all pod routers.

Configuration Exercise 8-2: Configuring Full-Mesh IBGP

In this exercise, you configure and verify full-mesh IBGP in your pod.

> **NOTE**   Throughout this exercise, the pod number is referred to as *x*, and the router number is referred to as *y*. Substitute the appropriate numbers as needed.

Objectives

The objective of this exercise is to configure a full-mesh IBGP network.

Visual Objective

Figure 8-42 illustrates the topology used in this exercise.

> **NOTE**   The Frame Relay router is in AS 64997. However, it is provided only for communication with the backbone routers; it is not used in this exercise.

Figure 8-42 *Full-Mesh IBGP Configuration Exercise Topology*

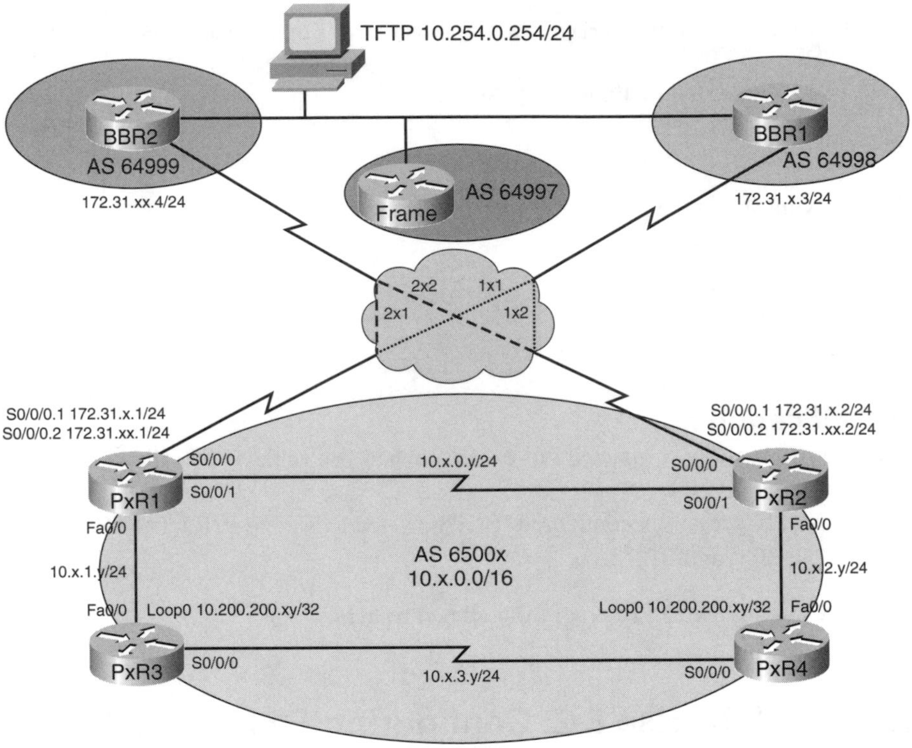

Command List

In this exercise, you use the commands in Table 8-10, listed in logical order. Refer to this list if you need configuration command assistance during the exercise.

> **CAUTION** Although the command syntax is shown in this table, the addresses shown are typically for the P*x*R1 and P*x*R3 routers. Be careful when addressing your routers! Refer to the exercise instructions and the appropriate visual objective diagram for addressing details.

Table 8-10 *Full-Mesh IBGP Configuration Exercise Commands*

Command	Description
(config)#**router bgp 6500***x*	Enters BGP router configuration mode. This router is in AS 6500*x*.
(config-router)#**neighbor 10.200.200.***xy* **remote-as 6500***x*	Identifies a BGP neighbor.

Table 8-10 *Full-Mesh IBGP Configuration Exercise Commands (Continued)*

Command	Description
(config-router)#**neighbor 10.200.200.***xy* **update-source loopback0**	Sets the source address of BGP updates with the neighbor to be the address of the loopback 0 interface.
(config-router)#**network 10.200.200.***xy* **mask 255.255.255.255**	Advertises a network in BGP.
#**show ip bgp summary**	Displays a summary of BGP neighbor status and activities.
#**show lp bgp**	Displays the BGP table.
#**show ip bgp 10.254.0.0**	Displays the BGP table entry for the 10.254.0.0 network.
(config-router)#**neighbor 10.200.200.***xy* **next-hop-self**	Advertises the router's own address as the next hop to this neighbor.

Task: Configuring Full-Mesh IBGP

In this task, you configure and verify full-mesh IBGP in your pod. Follow these steps:

Step 1   Remove the default static route and the RIPv2 default route advertisement on the edge routers.

Solution:

The following shows the required step on the P1R1 router:

```
P1R1(config)#no ip route 0.0.0.0 0.0.0.0 172.31.11.4
P1R1(config)#router rip
P1R1(config-router)#no default-information originate
```

Step 2   Configure full-mesh IBGP between the P*x*R1, P*x*R2, P*x*R3, and P*x*R4 routers. Use the loopback address 10.200.200.*xy* to establish the IBGP session between the edge routers and the internal routers, and the IBGP session between the internal routers. Remember to configure the address of the loopback interface as the source address of the IBGP updates. Recall that RIPv2 is advertising this network, so the routers can use their loopback IP address to establish the IBGP sessions.

For example, Figure 8-43 illustrates the BGP peering sessions for pod 1. The dotted lines indicate EBGP peers, and the solid lines indicate IBGP peers. There are six IBGP sessions; the one between the two edge routers was configured in the preceding exercise along with the EBGP sessions.

Figure 8-43 *BGP Peering Sessions for Pod 1*

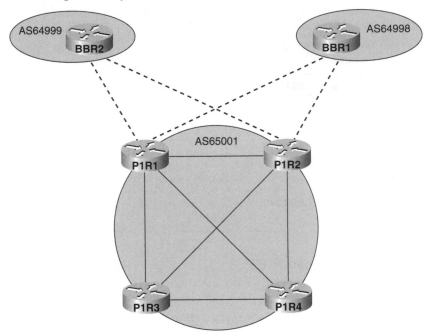

Step 3   Configure each internal router to advertise its loopback interface
(10.200.200.*xy*/32) in BGP.

Solution:

The following shows the required steps on the P1R1 and P1R3 routers:

```
P1R1(config)#router bgp 65001
P1R1(config-router)#neighbor 10.200.200.13 remote-as 65001
P1R1(config-router)#neighbor 10.200.200.14 remote-as 65001
P1R1(config-router)#neighbor 10.200.200.13 update-source loopback 0
P1R1(config-router)#neighbor 10.200.200.14 update-source loopback 0

P1R3(config)#router bgp 65001
P1R3(config-router)#neighbor 10.200.200.11 remote-as 65001
P1R3(config-router)#neighbor 10.200.200.12 remote-as 65001
P1R3(config-router)#neighbor 10.200.200.14 remote-as 65001
P1R3(config-router)#neighbor 10.200.200.11 update-source loopback 0
P1R3(config-router)#neighbor 10.200.200.12 update-source loopback 0
P1R3(config-router)#neighbor 10.200.200.14 update-source loopback 0
P1R3(config-router)#network 10.200.200.13 mask 255.255.255.255
```

Step 4   Verify that the appropriate BGP neighbor relationships have been
established. Each edge router should see two EBGP neighbors and three
IBGP neighbors. Each internal router should see three IBGP neighbors.

Solution:

The following shows sample output on the P1R1 router, indicating that this router has two EBGP neighbors and three IBGP neighbors:

```
P1R1#show ip bgp summary
BGP router identifier 10.200.200.11, local AS number 65001
BGP table version is 17, main routing table version 17
12 network entries using 1404 bytes of memory
28 path entries using 1456 bytes of memory
16/7 BGP path/bestpath attribute entries using 1984 bytes of memory
6 BGP AS-PATH entries using 144 bytes of memory
0 BGP route-map cache entries using 0 bytes of memory
0 BGP filter-list cache entries using 0 bytes of memory
BGP using 4988 total bytes of memory
BGP activity 12/0 prefixes, 28/0 paths, scan interval 60 secs

Neighbor        V    AS MsgRcvd MsgSent   TblVer  InQ OutQ Up/Down  State/PfxRcd
10.200.200.12   4 65001      11      11       17    0    0 00:01:36           10
10.200.200.13   4 65001       5      10       17    0    0 00:00:13            1
10.200.200.14   4 65001       5      10       17    0    0 00:00:13            1
172.31.1.3      4 64998      13      12       15    0    0 00:01:40            6
172.31.11.4     4 64999      13      12       15    0    0 00:01:46            6
P1R1#
```

Step 5   Display the BGP table on the internal routers to determine the next hop for the route to the 10.254.0.0/24 network in the core.

Step 6   Which path on the internal routers is selected as the best path to the 10.254.0.0/24 network?

Solution:

The following shows sample output on the P1R3 router, indicating that the next hop is 172.31.1.3. However, there is no > beside either of the routes to 10.254.0.0/24 network, thus no path is selected as the best path to this network.

```
P1R3#show ip bgp
BGP table version is 408, local router ID is 10.200.200.13
Status codes: s suppressed, d damped, h history, * valid, > best, i - internal,
              r RIB-failure, S Stale
Origin codes: i - IGP, e - EGP, ? - incomplete

   Network          Next Hop         Metric LocPrf Weight Path
r>i10.1.0.0/24      10.200.200.11         0    100      0 i
r i                 10.200.200.12         0    100      0 i
r>i10.1.1.0/24      10.200.200.11         0    100      0 i
r i                 10.1.2.4              2    100      0 i
r>i10.1.2.0/24      10.200.200.12         0    100      0 i
r>i10.1.3.0/24      10.1.2.4              1    100      0 i
*  i10.97.97.0/24   172.31.1.3            0    100      0 64998 64997 i
*  i                172.31.1.3            0    100      0 64998 64997 i
*> 10.200.200.13/32 0.0.0.0               0           32768 i
r>i10.200.200.14/32 10.200.200.14         0    100      0 i
*  i10.254.0.0/24   172.31.1.3            0    100      0 64998 i
*  i                172.31.1.3            0    100      0 64998 i
```

```
* i172.31.1.0/24    172.31.1.3             0    100      0 64998 i
* i                 172.31.1.3             0    100      0 64998 i
* i172.31.2.0/24    172.31.1.3             0    100      0 64998 i
* i                 172.31.1.3             0    100      0 64998 i
* i172.31.11.0/24   172.31.11.4            0    100      0 64999 i
  Network           Next Hop          Metric LocPrf Weight Path
* i                 172.31.11.4            0    100      0 64999 i
* i172.31.22.0/24   172.31.11.4            0    100      0 64999 i
* i                 172.31.11.4            0    100      0 64999 i
P1R3#
```

Step 7   Display the IP routing table of the edge routers. Is there a route to the 10.254.0.0/24 network?

Solution:

The following shows sample output on the P1R1 router, indicating that there is a route to 10.254.0.0/24 network.

```
P1R1#show ip route
<output omitted>
Gateway of last resort is not set

     172.31.0.0/24 is subnetted, 4 subnets
B       172.31.22.0 [20/0] via 172.31.11.4, 00:08:19
B       172.31.2.0 [20/0] via 172.31.1.3, 00:08:19
C       172.31.1.0 is directly connected, Serial0/0/0.1
C       172.31.11.0 is directly connected, Serial0/0/0.2
     10.0.0.0/8 is variably subnetted, 10 subnets, 2 masks
C       10.200.200.11/32 is directly connected, Loopback0
R       10.200.200.14/32 [120/2] via 10.1.1.3, 00:00:10, FastEthernet0/0
R       10.200.200.12/32 [120/3] via 10.1.1.3, 00:00:11, FastEthernet0/0
R       10.200.200.13/32 [120/1] via 10.1.1.3, 00:00:11, FastEthernet0/0
R       10.1.3.0/24 [120/1] via 10.1.1.3, 00:00:11, FastEthernet0/0
R       10.1.2.0/24 [120/2] via 10.1.1.3, 00:00:11, FastEthernet0/0
B       10.97.97.0/24 [20/0] via 172.31.1.3, 00:08:21
C       10.1.1.0/24 is directly connected, FastEthernet0/0
C       10.1.0.0/24 is directly connected, Serial0/0/1
B       10.254.0.0/24 [20/0] via 172.31.1.3, 00:08:21
P1R1#
```

Step 8   Display the IP routing table of the internal routers. Is there a route to the 10.254.0.0/24 network? Why or why not? Try the **show ip bgp 10.254.0.0** command on the internal routers to display the BGP table entry for 10.254.0.0.

Solution:

The following shows sample output on the P1R3 router. There is no route to the 10.254.0.0/24 network. The output of the **show ip bgp 10.254.0.0** command indicates that the next-hop address, 172.31.1.3, is inaccessible.

```
P1R3#show ip route
<output omitted>
Gateway of last resort is not set
```

```
        10.0.0.0/8 is variably subnetted, 8 subnets, 2 masks
R        10.200.200.11/32 [120/1] via 10.1.1.1, 00:00:00, FastEthernet0/0
R        10.200.200.14/32 [120/1] via 10.1.3.4, 00:00:18, Serial0/0/0
R        10.200.200.12/32 [120/2] via 10.1.3.4, 00:00:18, Serial0/0/0
C        10.200.200.13/32 is directly connected, Loopback0
C        10.1.3.0/24 is directly connected, Serial0/0/0
R        10.1.2.0/24 [120/1] via 10.1.3.4, 00:00:18, Serial0/0/0
C        10.1.1.0/24 is directly connected, FastEthernet0/0
R        10.1.0.0/24 [120/1] via 10.1.1.1, 00:00:02, FastEthernet0/0
P1R3#


P1R3#show ip bgp 10.254.0.0
BGP routing table entry for 10.254.0.0/24, version 382
Paths: (2 available, no best path)
  Not advertised to any peer
  64998
    172.31.1.3 (inaccessible) from 10.200.200.11 (10.200.200.11)
      Origin IGP, metric 0, localpref 100, valid, internal
  64998
    172.31.1.3 (inaccessible) from 10.200.200.12 (10.200.200.12)
      Origin IGP, metric 0, localpref 100, valid, internal
P1R3#
```

Step 9   The internal routers do not know how to reach the next-hop address; they do not install the routes in their routing table if the next-hop is not reachable. To correct this problem, you can either advertise the next-hop network via an IGP or configure the edge routers to advertise themselves as the next hop. Choose the second alternative.

On each edge router (P*x*R1 and P*x*R2), change the next-hop address that is advertised into the pod to be its own address.

Solution:

The following shows the required steps on the P1R1 router:

```
P1R1(config)#router bgp 65001
P1R1(config-router)#neighbor 10.200.200.13 next-hop-self
P1R1(config-router)#neighbor 10.200.200.14 next-hop-self
```

Step 10   On the internal routers, display the BGP table once more and display the BGP table entry for 10.254.0.0 again. What are the next-hop IP addresses for the routes to the 10.254.0.0/24 network now?

Have the internal routers installed these BGP routes in their routing table? Why or why not?

Solution:

The following shows sample output on the P1R3 router. The next-hop addresses for the routes to the 10.254.0.0/24 network are 10.200.200.11 and 10.200.200.12. The output of the **show ip bgp**

10.254.0.0 command indicates that the next-hop addresses are accessible. There is now a > beside one of the routes to 10.254.0.0/24 network in the BGP table; this is the path selected as the best path to this network and is offered to the IP routing table.

```
P1R3#show ip bgp
BGP table version is 415, local router ID is 10.200.200.13
Status codes: s suppressed, d damped, h history, * valid, > best, i - internal,
              r RIB-failure, S Stale
Origin codes: i - IGP, e - EGP, ? - incomplete

   Network          Next Hop         Metric LocPrf Weight Path
r>i10.1.0.0/24      10.200.200.11        0    100      0 i
r i                 10.200.200.12        0    100      0 i
r>i10.1.1.0/24      10.200.200.11        0    100      0 i
r i                 10.200.200.12        2    100      0 i
r i10.1.2.0/24      10.200.200.11        2    100      0 i
r>i                 10.200.200.12        0    100      0 i
r>i10.1.3.0/24      10.200.200.11        1    100      0 i
r i                 10.200.200.12        1    100      0 i
*>i10.97.97.0/24    10.200.200.11        0    100      0 64998 64997 i
* i                 10.200.200.12        0    100      0 64998 64997 i
*> 10.200.200.13/32 0.0.0.0              0          32768 i
r>i10.200.200.14/32 10.200.200.14        0    100      0 i
*>i10.254.0.0/24    10.200.200.11        0    100      0 64998 i
* i                 10.200.200.12        0    100      0 64998 i
*>i172.31.1.0/24    10.200.200.11        0    100      0 64998 i
* i                 10.200.200.12        0    100      0 64998 i
*>i172.31.2.0/24    10.200.200.11        0    100      0 64998 i
   Network          Next Hop         Metric LocPrf Weight Path
* i                 10.200.200.12        0    100      0 64998 i
*>i172.31.11.0/24   10.200.200.11        0    100      0 64999 i
* i                 10.200.200.12        0    100      0 64999 i
*>i172.31.22.0/24   10.200.200.11        0    100      0 64999 i
* i                 10.200.200.12        0    100      0 64999 i
P1R3#

P1R3#show ip bgp 10.254.0.0
BGP routing table entry for 10.254.0.0/24, version 415
Paths: (2 available, best #1, table Default-IP-Routing-Table)
  Not advertised to any peer
  64998
    10.200.200.11 (metric 1) from 10.200.200.11 (10.200.200.11)
      Origin IGP, metric 0, localpref 100, valid, internal, best
  64998
    10.200.200.12 (metric 2) from 10.200.200.12 (10.200.200.12)
      Origin IGP, metric 0, localpref 100, valid, internal
```

Step 11   Recall that BGP synchronization is off by default. Because you are running full-mesh IBGP in your AS, it is safe to have BGP synchronization disabled on all the pod routers.

What is the BGP synchronization rule?

Solution:

The BGP synchronization rule states that a BGP router should not use, or advertise to an external neighbor, a route learned by IBGP, unless that route is local or is learned from the IGP. BGP synchronization is disabled by default in Cisco IOS Software Release 12.2(8)T and later; it was on by default in earlier Cisco IOS Software releases.

Step 12   From the internal routers, ping the TFTP server (10.254.0.254) to test connectivity.

Step 13   What is the path each internal router is using to reach the TFTP server?

Solution:

The following sample output is from the P1R3 router; it illustrates that there is connectivity to the TFTP server. The path to the TFTP server from P1R3 is via P1R1, then BBR1.

```
P1R3#ping 10.254.0.254

Type escape sequence to abort.
Sending 5, 100-byte ICMP Echos to 10.254.0.254, timeout is 2 seconds:
!!!!!
Success rate is 100 percent (5/5), round-trip min/avg/max = 28/30/32 ms
P1R3#

P1R3#trace 10.254.0.254

Type escape sequence to abort.
Tracing the route to 10.254.0.254

  1 10.1.1.1 0 msec 4 msec 0 msec
  2 172.31.1.3 [AS 64998] 16 msec 16 msec 16 msec
  3 10.254.0.254 [AS 64998] 16 msec 12 msec 12 msec
P1R3#
```

Step 14   Save your configurations to NVRAM.

Solution:

The following shows the required step on the P1R1 router.

```
P1R1#copy run start
Destination filename [startup-config]?
Building configuration...
[OK]
```

Exercise Verification

You have successfully completed this exercise if you have configured full-mesh IBGP within your pod and your routing tables contain BGP routes to the networks advertised by the core.

Configuration Exercise 8-3: BGP Path Manipulation Using MED and Local Preference with Route Maps

In this exercise, you use route maps to change BGP MED and local preference values and verify how this changes the path selection.

> **NOTE** Throughout this exercise, the pod number is referred to as *x*, and the router number is referred to as *y*. Substitute the appropriate numbers as needed.

Objectives

The objective of this exercise is to use route maps to change BGP MED and local preference values, affecting path selection.

Visual Objective

Figure 8-44 illustrates the topology used in this exercise.

Figure 8-44 *BGP Path Manipulation Configuration Exercise Topology*

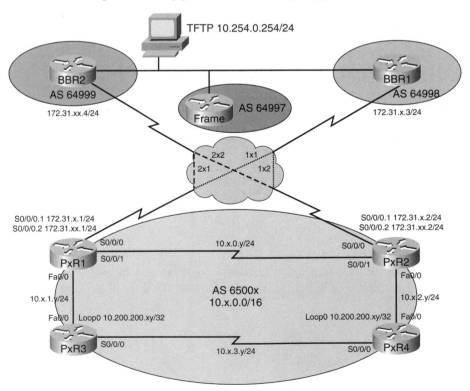

> **NOTE**   The Frame Relay router is in AS 64997. However, it is provided only for communication with the backbone routers; it is not used in this exercise.

Command List

In this exercise, you use the commands in Table 8-11, listed in logical order. Refer to this list if you need configuration command assistance during the exercise.

> **CAUTION**   Although the command syntax is shown in this table, the addresses shown are typically for the P*x*R1 and P*x*R3 routers. Be careful when addressing your routers! Refer to the exercise instructions and the appropriate visual objective diagram for addressing details.

Table 8-11   *BGP Path Manipulation Configuration Exercise Commands*

Command	Description
#**show ip bgp**	Displays the BGP table.
(config)#**route-map SET_PREF permit 10**	Creates a route map named SET_PREF.
(config-route-map)#**match ip address 3**	Used in a route map to match an IP address to routes that are permitted by access list 3.
(config-route-map)#**set local-preference 300**	Used in a route map to set the BGP local preference.
(config)#**access-list 3 permit 172.31.0.0 0.0.255.255**	Creates access list 3.
(config-router)#**neighbor 172.31.***xx***.4 route-map SET_PREF in**	Applies a route map to the incoming updates from a BGP neighbor.
#**clear ip bgp 172.31.***xx***.4 in**	Performs a BGP route refresh that provides a dynamic soft reset of inbound BGP routing table updates.
(config-route-map)#**set metric 200**	Used in a route map to set the BGP MED.
#**clear ip bgp 172.31.11.4 out**	Performs a BGP soft reset for outbound updates.

Task: Using MED and Local Preference with Route Maps for BGP Path Manipulation

In this task, you change the MED and local preference to manipulate the BGP path-selection process, as shown in Figure 8-45.

Figure 8-45 *BGP Paths That Will Be Manipulated*

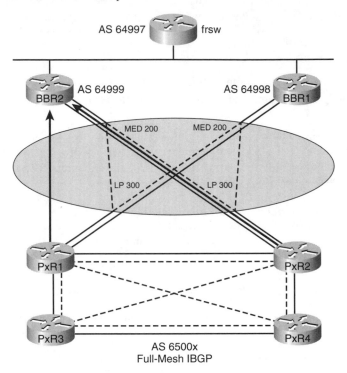

Step 1 On the edge routers, look at the BGP table, and notice the next hop for routes to the 172.31.*x*.0 and 172.31.*xx*.0 networks in the *other* pod (in other words, the networks that connect the BBR1 and BBR2 routers to the other pod); these networks are referred to as the *remote* networks in this exercise. For example, if you are using pod 1, look for pod 2 routes.

Solution:

The following shows sample output on the P1R1 router. The highlighted lines show the networks 172.31.2.0 and 172.31.22.0, which are the networks that connect pod 2 to the BBR1 and BBR2 routers.

```
P1R1#show ip bgp
BGP table version is 17, local router ID is 10.200.200.11
Status codes: s suppressed, d damped, h history, * valid, > best, i - internal,
              r RIB-failure, S Stale
Origin codes: i - IGP, e - EGP, ? - incomplete

   Network          Next Hop          Metric LocPrf Weight Path
*  i10.1.0.0/24     10.200.200.12          0    100      0 i
*>                  0.0.0.0                0           32768 i
*  i10.1.1.0/24     10.1.2.4               2    100      0 i
*>                  0.0.0.0                0           32768 i
*  i10.1.2.0/24     10.200.200.12          0    100      0 i
*>                  10.1.1.3               2           32768 i
```

```
   * i10.1.3.0/24       10.1.2.4                  1     100      0 i
   *>                   10.1.1.3                  1           32768 i
   *> 10.97.97.0/24     172.31.1.3                             0 64998 64997 i
   * i                  172.31.1.3                0     100      0 64998 64997 i
   *                    172.31.11.4                            0 64999 64997 i
   r>i10.200.200.13/32 10.200.200.13              0     100      0 i
   r>i10.200.200.14/32 10.200.200.14              0     100      0 i
   *> 10.254.0.0/24     172.31.1.3                0              0 64998 i
   * i                  172.31.1.3                0     100      0 64998 i
   *                    172.31.11.4                            0 64999 64998 i
   r> 172.31.1.0/24     172.31.1.3                0              0 64998 i
   r i                  172.31.1.3                0     100      0 64998 i
   r                    172.31.11.4                            0 64999 64998 i
   *> 172.31.2.0/24     172.31.1.3                0              0 64998 i
   * i                  172.31.1.3                0     100      0 64998 i
   *                    172.31.11.4                            0 64999 64998 i
   r  172.31.11.0/24    172.31.1.3                             0 64998 64999 i
   r i                  172.31.11.4               0     100      0 64999 i
   r>                   172.31.11.4               0              0 64999 i
   *  172.31.22.0/24    172.31.1.3                             0 64998 64999 i
   * i                  172.31.11.4               0     100      0 64999 i
   *>                   172.31.11.4               0              0 64999 i
P1R1#
```

Step 2   Which path does the edge router use to reach the remote 172.31.*x*.0 networks? Why does BGP choose that path?

Which path does the edge router use to reach the remote 172.31.*xx*.0 networks? Why does BGP choose that path?

Solution:

P1R1 and P1R2 use 172.31.1.3 (BBR1) to reach 172.31.2.0/24 and use 172.31.11.4 (BBR2) to reach 172.31.22.0/24. These are the shortest AS-path external routes to these networks; there is one AS in the selected path.

Step 3   This company has established a policy that all traffic exiting the AS bound for any of the remote 172.31.*x*.0 and 172.31.*xx*.0 networks should take the path through BBR2.

To comply with this policy, configure the edge routers, P*x*R1 and P*x*R2, with a route map setting local preference to 300 for any routes to the remote 172.31.*x*.0 and 172.31.*xx*.0 networks that are advertised by BBR2.

Solution:

The following shows the required steps on the P1R1 router:

```
P1R1(config)#route-map SET_PREF permit 10
P1R1(config-route-map)#match ip address 3
P1R1(config-route-map)#set local-preference 300
P1R1(config-route-map)#route-map SET_PREF permit 20
P1R1(config-route-map)#exit
P1R1(config)#access-list 3 permit 172.31.0.0 0.0.255.255
P1R1(config)#router bgp 65001
P1R1(config-router)#neighbor 172.31.11.4 route-map SET_PREF in
```

Step 4 Look at the BGP table on the edge routers. Has the local preference for the routes learned from BBR2 changed?

Solution:

The following shows the BGP table on the P1R1 router. The local preference has not changed.

```
P1R1#show ip bgp
BGP table version is 17, local router ID is 10.200.200.11
Status codes: s suppressed, d damped, h history, * valid, > best, i - internal,
              r RIB-failure, S Stale
Origin codes: i - IGP, e - EGP, ? - incomplete

   Network          Next Hop         Metric LocPrf Weight Path
*  i10.1.0.0/24     10.200.200.12         0    100      0 i
*>                  0.0.0.0               0         32768 i
*  i10.1.1.0/24     10.1.2.4              2    100      0 i
*>                  0.0.0.0               0         32768 i
*  i10.1.2.0/24     10.200.200.12         0    100      0 i
*>                  10.1.1.3              2         32768 i
*  i10.1.3.0/24     10.1.2.4              1    100      0 i
*>                  10.1.1.3              1         32768 i
*> 10.97.97.0/24    172.31.1.3            0             0 64998 64997 i
*  i                172.31.1.3            0    100      0 64998 64997 i
*                   172.31.11.4                         0 64999 64997 i
r>i10.200.200.13/32 10.200.200.13         0    100      0 i
r>i10.200.200.14/32 10.200.200.14         0    100      0 i
*> 10.254.0.0/24    172.31.1.3            0             0 64998 i
*  i                172.31.1.3            0    100      0 64998 i
*                   172.31.11.4                         0 64999 64998 i
r> 172.31.1.0/24    172.31.1.3            0             0 64998 i
r  i                172.31.1.3            0    100      0 64998 i
r                   172.31.11.4                         0 64999 64998 i
*> 172.31.2.0/24    172.31.1.3            0             0 64998 i
*  i                172.31.1.3            0    100      0 64998 i
*                   172.31.11.4                         0 64999 64998 i
r  172.31.11.0/24   172.31.1.3                          0 64998 64999 i
r  i                172.31.11.4           0    100      0 64999 i
r>                  172.31.11.4           0             0 64999 i
*  172.31.22.0/24   172.31.1.3                          0 64998 64999 i
*  i                172.31.11.4           0    100      0 64999 i
*>                  172.31.11.4           0             0 64999 i
P1R1#
```

Step 5 When you configure a policy, it is not automatically applied to routes already in the BGP table. You can perform a hard or soft reset of the BGP relationship with BBR2, or use the route refresh feature that provides a dynamic soft reset of inbound BGP routing table updates. To use the route refresh feature to apply the policy to the routes that have come in from BBR2, use the **clear ip bgp 172.31.xx.4 soft in** command. (Recall that you do not actually need to use the **soft** keyword, because soft reset is assumed when the route refresh capability is supported.)

Step 6 Look at the BGP table again. Have the local preference values changed?

Solution:

The following shows the route refresh on P1R1, and the BGP table on the same P1R1 router. The local preference has now changed.

```
P1R1#clear ip bgp 172.31.11.4 in
P1R1#show ip bgp
BGP table version is 21, local router ID is 10.200.200.11
Status codes: s suppressed, d damped, h history, * valid, > best, i - internal,
              r RIB-failure, S Stale
Origin codes: i - IGP, e - EGP, ? - incomplete

   Network          Next Hop         Metric LocPrf Weight Path
* i10.1.0.0/24      10.200.200.12         0    100      0 i
*>                  0.0.0.0               0          32768 i
* i10.1.1.0/24      10.1.2.4              2    100      0 i
*>                  0.0.0.0               0          32768 i
* i10.1.2.0/24      10.200.200.12         0    100      0 i
*>                  10.1.1.3              2          32768 i
* i10.1.3.0/24      10.1.2.4              1    100      0 i
*>                  10.1.1.3              1          32768 i
*> 10.97.97.0/24    172.31.1.3                         0 64998 64997 i
* i                 172.31.1.3            0    100      0 64998 64997 i
*                   172.31.11.4                         0 64999 64997 i
r>i10.200.200.13/32 10.200.200.13        0    100      0 i
r>i10.200.200.14/32 10.200.200.14        0    100      0 i
*> 10.254.0.0/24    172.31.1.3            0               0 64998 i
* i                 172.31.1.3            0    100      0 64998 i
*                   172.31.11.4                         0 64999 64998 i
r i172.31.1.0/24    172.31.11.4          0    300      0 64999 64998 i
r                   172.31.1.3           0               0 64998 i
r>                  172.31.11.4               300      0 64999 64998 i
* i172.31.2.0/24    172.31.11.4          0    300      0 64999 64998 i
*                   172.31.1.3           0               0 64998 i
*>                  172.31.11.4               300      0 64999 64998 i
r i172.31.11.0/24   172.31.11.4          0    300      0 64999 i
r                   172.31.1.3                          0 64998 64999 i
r>                  172.31.11.4          0    300      0 64999 i
* i172.31.22.0/24   172.31.11.4          0    300      0 64999 i
*                   172.31.1.3                          0 64998 64999 i
*>                  172.31.11.4          0    300      0 64999 i
P1R1#
```

Step 7   Which path does the edge router use to reach the remote 172.31.*x*.0 networks now? Why does BGP choose that path even though the AS-path is longer?

Which path does the edge router use to reach the remote 172.31.*xx*.0 networks now? Why does BGP choose that path?

Solution:

P1R1 is using 172.31.11.4 (BBR2) to reach the 172.31.2.0 and 172.31.22.0 networks. The path to 172.31.2.0 through BBR2 was chosen because the local preference is higher; local preference is looked at before AS-path length. Of the two routes with the same local preference, the EBGP route is chosen, because EBGP routes are preferred over IBGP routes.

Step 8   Both of the core routers (BBR1 and BBR2) have multiple ways into each
              pod. For example, BBR1 could take the direct path through your pod's
              P*x*R1 or P*x*R2 router, or it could take a path through BBR2 and then to one
              of the pod's edge routers.

              Telnet to BBR1 and examine the BGP table. Which path does the BBR1
              router use to reach your pod's 10.*x*.0.0/24 network? Why does BGP choose
              that path?

Solution:

The following output is from the BBR1 router. BBR1 uses the 172.31.1.2 path (through P1R2) to
get to 10.1.0.0/24. Because all the other parameters are equal, the AS-path is considered when
choosing the best route. Of the two routes with an AS-path length of 1, this route was chosen. It
must therefore be an older route than the route through P1R1. We know this because if the routes
were the same age, the lower neighbor router ID would be considered. The BGP router IDs are the
routers' loopback addresses: P1R1 has a router ID of 10.200.200.11, and P1R2 (172.31.1.2) has a
router ID of 10.200.200.12; P1R1's router ID is lower than P1R2's router ID, and P1R1 would
therefore have been chosen if router IDs were considered.

```
BBR1#show ip bgp
BGP table version is 216, local router ID is 172.31.2.3
Status codes: s suppressed, d damped, h history, * valid, > best, i - internal,
              r RIB-failure, S Stale
Origin codes: i - IGP, e - EGP, ? - incomplete

     Network          Next Hop          Metric LocPrf Weight Path
*    10.1.0.0/24      172.31.1.1             0             0 65001 i
*                     10.254.0.2                           0 64999 65001 i
*>                    172.31.1.2             0             0 65001 i
*>   10.1.1.0/24      172.31.1.1             0             0 65001 i
*                     172.31.1.2             2             0 65001 i
*                     10.254.0.2                           0 64999 65001 i
*    10.1.2.0/24      172.31.1.1             2             0 65001 i
*>                    172.31.1.2             0             0 65001 i
*                     10.254.0.2                           0 64999 65001 i
*    10.1.3.0/24      172.31.1.1             1             0 65001 i
*>                    172.31.1.2             1             0 65001 i
*                     10.254.0.2                           0 64999 65001 i
*    10.97.97.0/24    10.254.0.3                           0 64999 64997 i
*>                    10.254.0.3             0             0 64997 i
*    10.200.200.13/32 172.31.1.1                           0 65001 i
*>                    172.31.1.2                           0 65001 i
*                     10.254.0.2                           0 64999 65001 i
*    10.200.200.14/32 172.31.1.1                           0 65001 i
*                     10.254.0.2                           0 64999 65001 i
*>                    172.31.1.2                           0 65001 i
*>   10.254.0.0/24    0.0.0.0                0         32768 i
*>   172.31.1.0/24    0.0.0.0                0         32768 i
*>   172.31.2.0/24    0.0.0.0                0         32768 i
*    172.31.11.0/24   172.31.1.1                           0 65001 64999 i
*                     172.31.1.2                           0 65001 64999 i
*                     10.254.0.2                           0 64997 64999 i
*>                    10.254.0.2             0             0 64999 i
```

```
    *  172.31.22.0/24    172.31.1.1                              0 65001 64999 i
    *                    172.31.1.2                              0 65001 64999 i
    *                    10.254.0.2                              0 64997 64999 i
    *>                   10.254.0.2                 0            0 64999 i
    BBR1#
```

Step 9   Telnet to BBR2 and examine the BGP table. Which path does the BBR2 router use to reach your pod's 10.*x*.0.0/24 network? Why does BGP choose that path?

Solution:

The following output is from the BBR2 router. BBR2 uses the 172.31.11.2 path (through P1R2) to get to 10.1.0.0/24. Because all the other parameters are equal, the AS-path is considered when choosing the best route. Of the two routes with an AS-path length of 1, this route was chosen. It must therefore be an older route than the route through P1R1, for the same reasons as described in the solution for the previous step.

```
BBR2#show ip bgp
BGP table version is 220, local router ID is 172.31.22.4
Status codes: s suppressed, d damped, h history, * valid, > best, i - internal,
              r RIB-failure, S Stale
Origin codes: i - IGP, e - EGP, ? - incomplete

      Network            Next Hop         Metric LocPrf Weight Path
*   10.1.0.0/24          172.31.11.1           0             0 65001 i
*>                       172.31.11.2           0             0 65001 i
*                        10.254.0.1                          0 64997 64998 65001 i
*                        10.254.0.1                          0 64998 65001 i
*>  10.1.1.0/24          172.31.11.1           0             0 65001 i
*                        172.31.11.2           2             0 65001 i
*                        10.254.0.1                          0 64997 64998 65001 i
*                        10.254.0.1                          0 64998 65001 i
*   10.1.2.0/24          172.31.11.1           2             0 65001 i
*>                       172.31.11.2           0             0 65001 i
*                        10.254.0.1                          0 64997 64998 65001 i
*                        10.254.0.1                          0 64998 65001 i
*   10.1.3.0/24          172.31.11.1           1             0 65001 i
*>                       172.31.11.2           1             0 65001 i
*                        10.254.0.1                          0 64997 64998 65001 i
*                        10.254.0.1                          0 64998 65001 i
*   10.97.97.0/24        172.31.11.1                         0 65001 64998 64997 i
*                        172.31.11.2                         0 65001 64998 64997 i
*                        10.254.0.3                          0 64998 64997 i
*>                       10.254.0.3            0             0 64997 i
*   10.200.200.13/32 172.31.11.1                             0 65001 i
*>                       172.31.11.2                         0 65001 i
*                        10.254.0.1                          0 64997 64998 65001 i
*                        10.254.0.1                          0 64998 65001 i
*   10.200.200.14/32 172.31.11.1                             0 65001 i
*>                       172.31.11.2                         0 65001 i
*                        10.254.0.1                          0 64997 64998 65001 i
*                        10.254.0.1                          0 64998 65001 i
r   10.254.0.0/24        172.31.11.1                         0 65001 64998 i
r                        172.31.11.2                         0 65001 64998 i
r                        10.254.0.1                          0 64997 64998 i
r>                       10.254.0.1            0             0 64998 i
```

```
*   172.31.1.0/24    10.254.0.1                              0 64997 64998 i
*>                   10.254.0.1              0               0 64998 i
*   172.31.2.0/24    10.254.0.1                              0 64997 64998 i
*>                   10.254.0.1              0               0 64998 i
*> 172.31.11.0/24    0.0.0.0                 0           32768 i
*> 172.31.22.0/24    0.0.0.0                 0           32768 i
BBR2#
```

Step 10   Suppose this company has also established a policy for traffic inbound from the core. This policy states the following:

- Traffic from BBR1 to your pod 10.*x*.0.0/24 network should enter your pod through P*x*R1.

- Traffic from BBR2 to your pod 10.*x*.0.0/24 network should enter your pod through P*x*R2.

To accomplish this policy, you do the following:

- Make the paths through P*x*R1 look unattractive to BBR2.

- Make the paths through P*x*R2 look unattractive to BBR1.

Currently, the MED for both paths is 0 in the BGP table of both BBR1 and BBR2, so BBR1 and BBR2 pick the oldest EBGP path.

On P*x*R1, configure a route map that sets the MED to 200 for routes to your pod's internal network (10.*x*.0.0/24); apply the route map to updates sent to BBR2. (Remember that a lower MED is more attractive to BGP.)

On P*x*R2, configure a route map that sets the MED to 200 for routes to your pod's internal network (10.*x*.0.0/24); apply the route map to updates sent to BBR1.

Solution:

The following shows the required configuration on P1R1 and P1R2:

```
P1R1(config)#route-map SET_MED_HI permit 10
P1R1(config-route-map)#match ip address 4
P1R1(config-route-map)#set metric 200
P1R1(config-route-map)#route-map SET_MED_HI permit 20
P1R1(config-route-map)#exit
P1R1(config)#access-list 4 permit 10.1.0.0 0.0.255.255
P1R1(config)#router bgp 65001
P1R1(config-router)#neighbor 172.31.11.4 route-map SET_MED_HI out

P1R2(config)#route-map SET_MED_HI permit 10
P1R2(config-route-map)#match ip address 4
P1R2(config-route-map)#set metric 200
P1R2(config-route-map)#route-map SET_MED_HI permit 20
P1R2(config-route-map)#exit
P1R2(config)#access-list 4 permit 10.1.0.0 0.0.255.255
P1R2(config)#router bgp 65001
P1R2(config-router)#neighbor 172.31.1.3 route-map SET_MED_HI out
```

Step 11   Perform a soft reconfiguration after you apply the policy to the BGP neighbor (BBR1 or BBR2) by using the **clear ip bgp** *ip-address* **soft out** command. (Recall that you do not actually need to use the **soft** keyword, because soft reset is assumed.)

Solution:

The following shows the required command applied to the P1R1 and P1R2 routers:

```
P1R1#clear ip bgp 172.31.11.4 out
P1R2#clear ip bgp 172.31.1.3 out
```

Step 12   Telnet to the core routers, and examine the BGP table. Verify that the MED changes have taken effect.

Solution:

The following output from the BBR1 and BBR2 routers shows that the MED changes have taken effect:

```
BBR1#show ip bgp
BGP table version is 217, local router ID is 172.31.2.3
Status codes: s suppressed, d damped, h history, * valid, > best, i - internal,
              r RIB-failure, S Stale
Origin codes: i - IGP, e - EGP, ? - incomplete

     Network          Next Hop            Metric LocPrf Weight Path
*>  10.1.0.0/24       172.31.1.1               0             0 65001 i
*                     10.254.0.2                             0 64999 65001 i
*                     172.31.1.2             200             0 65001 i
*>  10.1.1.0/24       172.31.1.1               0             0 65001 i
*                     172.31.1.2               2             0 65001 i
*                     10.254.0.2                             0 64999 65001 i
*   10.1.2.0/24       172.31.1.1               2             0 65001 i
*>                    172.31.1.2               0             0 65001 i
*                     10.254.0.2                             0 64999 65001 i
*   10.1.3.0/24       172.31.1.1               1             0 65001 i
*>                    172.31.1.2               1             0 65001 i
*                     10.254.0.2                             0 64999 65001 i
*   10.97.97.0/24     10.254.0.3                             0 64999 64997 i
*>                    10.254.0.3               0             0 64997 i
*   10.200.200.13/32  172.31.1.1                             0 65001 i
*>                    172.31.1.2                             0 65001 i
*                     10.254.0.2                             0 64999 65001 i
*   10.200.200.14/32  172.31.1.1                             0 65001 i
*                     10.254.0.2                             0 64999 65001 i
*>                    172.31.1.2                             0 65001 i
*>  10.254.0.0/24     0.0.0.0                  0         32768 i
*>  172.31.1.0/24     0.0.0.0                  0         32768 i
*>  172.31.2.0/24     0.0.0.0                  0         32768 i
*   172.31.11.0/24    172.31.1.1                             0 65001 64999 i
*                     172.31.1.2                             0 65001 64999 i
*                     10.254.0.2                             0 64997 64999 i
*>                    10.254.0.2               0             0 64999 i
```

```
*   172.31.22.0/24   172.31.1.1                                    0 65001 64999 i
*                    172.31.1.2                                    0 65001 64999 i
*                    10.254.0.2                                    0 64997 64999 i
*>                   10.254.0.2                 0                  0 64999 i
BBR1#

BBR2#show ip bgp
BGP table version is 220, local router ID is 172.31.22.4
Status codes: s suppressed, d damped, h history, * valid, > best, i - internal,
              r RIB-failure, S Stale
Origin codes: i - IGP, e - EGP, ? - incomplete

     Network          Next Hop          Metric LocPrf Weight Path
*    10.1.0.0/24      172.31.11.1          200           0 65001 i
*>                    172.31.11.2            0           0 65001 i
*                     10.254.0.1                         0 64997 64998 65001 i
*                     10.254.0.1                         0 64998 65001 i
*>   10.1.1.0/24      172.31.11.1            0           0 65001 i
*                     172.31.11.2            2           0 65001 i
*                     10.254.0.1                         0 64997 64998 65001 i
*                     10.254.0.1                         0 64998 65001 i
*    10.1.2.0/24      172.31.11.1            2           0 65001 i
*>                    172.31.11.2            0           0 65001 i
*                     10.254.0.1                         0 64997 64998 65001 i
*                     10.254.0.1                         0 64998 65001 i
*    10.1.3.0/24      172.31.11.1            1           0 65001 i
*>                    172.31.11.2            1           0 65001 i
*                     10.254.0.1                         0 64997 64998 65001 i
*                     10.254.0.1                         0 64998 65001 i
*    10.97.97.0/24    172.31.11.1                        0 65001 64998 64997 i
*                     172.31.11.2                        0 65001 64998 64997 i
*                     10.254.0.3                         0 64998 64997 i
*>                    10.254.0.3             0           0 64997 i
*    10.200.200.13/32 172.31.11.1                        0 65001 i
*>                    172.31.11.2                        0 65001 i
*                     10.254.0.1                         0 64997 64998 65001 i
*                     10.254.0.1                         0 64998 65001 i
*    10.200.200.14/32 172.31.11.1                        0 65001 i
*>                    172.31.11.2                        0 65001 i
*                     10.254.0.1                         0 64997 64998 65001 i
*                     10.254.0.1                         0 64998 65001 i
r    10.254.0.0/24    172.31.11.1                        0 65001 64998 i
r                     172.31.11.2                        0 65001 64998 i
r                     10.254.0.1                         0 64997 64998 i
r>                    10.254.0.1             0           0 64998 i
*    172.31.1.0/24    10.254.0.1                         0 64997 64998 i
*>                    10.254.0.1             0           0 64998 i
*    172.31.2.0/24    10.254.0.1                         0 64997 64998 i
*>                    10.254.0.1             0           0 64998 i
*>   172.31.11.0/24   0.0.0.0               0        32768 i
*>   172.31.22.0/24   0.0.0.0               0        32768 i
BBR2#
```

Step 13   Notice that the path with a MED of 200 is not chosen as the best path. What is the best path from BBR1 to your pod 10.x.0.0 network now?

What is the best path from BBR2 to your pod 10.x.0.0 network now?

Solution:

The best path from BBR1 to 10.1.0.0 is via 172.31.1.1 (P1R1). When selecting the best path in this case, BGP considers the AS-path length. There are two routes with an AS-path length of 1, but with different MED values. The one with the lower MED, via 172.31.1.1, is selected as the best path.

Similarly, the best path from BBR2 to 10.1.0.0 is via 172.31.11.2 (P1R2). The AS-path is considered before the MED, so the two routes with an AS-path length of 1, through 172.31.11.2 and 172.31.11.1, are considered. The latter has a MED of 200, and the former has a default MED of 0. Because a lower MED is preferred, the route through 172.31.11.2 is selected as the best path.

Step 14   Save your configurations to NVRAM.

Solution:

The following shows the required step on the P1R1 router.

```
P1R1#copy run start
Destination filename [startup-config]?
Building configuration...
[OK]
```

Exercise Verification

You have successfully completed this exercise when you achieve the following results:

- You have changed the local preference of the specified routes.

- You have changed the MED of the specified routes.

Review Questions

Answer the following questions, and then refer to Appendix A, "Answers to Review Questions," for the answers.

1. What is the difference between an IGP and an EGP?

2. What type of routing protocol is BGP?

3. What is BGP multihoming?

4. What are three common design options for BGP multihoming?

5. What are some advantages of getting default routes and selected specific routes from your ISPs?

6. What is a disadvantage of having all ISPs pass all BGP routes into your AS?

7. A BGP router knows of three paths to a network and has chosen the best path. Can this BGP router advertise to its peer routers a route to that network other than the best path?

8. When is it appropriate to use BGP to connect to other autonomous systems?

9. When is it appropriate to use static routes rather than BGP to interconnect autonomous systems?

10. What protocol does BGP use as its transport protocol? What port number does BGP use?

11. How does BGP guarantee a loop-free AS path?

12. Any two routers that have formed a BGP connection can be referred to by what two terms?

13. Write a brief definition for each of the following:

— IBGP

— EBGP

— Well-known attribute

— Transitive attribute

— BGP synchronization

14. What tables are used by BGP?

15. What are the four BGP message types?

16. How is the BGP router ID selected?

17. What are the BGP states a router can be in with its neighbors?

18. What type of BGP attributes are the following?

— AS-path

— Next-hop

— Origin

— Local preference

— Atomic aggregate

— Aggregator

— Community

— Multiexit-discriminator

19. When IBGP advertises an external update, where does the value for the next-hop attribute of an update come from?

20. Describe the complication that an NBMA network can cause for an update's next-hop attribute.

21. Complete the following table to answer these questions about three BGP attributes:

— In which order are the attributes preferred (1, 2, or 3)?

— For the attribute, is the highest or lowest value preferred?

— Which other routers, if any, is the attribute sent to?

Attribute	Order Preferred In	Highest or Lowest Value Preferred?	Sent to Which Other Routers?
Local preference		Highest	
MED		Lowest	
Weight		Highest	

22. When is it safe to have BGP synchronization disabled?

23. What does the **neighbor 10.1.1.1 ebgp-multihop** command do?

24. Which commands are used to configure Routers A and B if Router A is to run BGP in AS 65000 and establish a neighbor relationship with Router B in AS 65001? The two routers are directly connected but should use their loopback 0 addresses to establish the BGP connection; Router A has loopback 0 address 10.1.1.1/24, and Router B has loopback 0 address 10.2.2.2/24.

25. What command disables BGP synchronization if it is enabled?

26. Which command would Router A in AS 65000 use to activate an IBGP session with Router B, 10.1.1.1, also in AS 65000?

27. What is the difference between the BGP **neighbor** command and the BGP **network** command?

28. What does the BGP **network 192.168.1.1 mask 255.255.255.0** command do?

29. What does the **clear ip bgp 10.1.1.1 soft out** command do?

30. Which command is used to display detailed information about BGP connections to neighbors?

31. What does a > in the output of the **show ip bgp** command mean?

32. What column in the **show ip bgp** command output displays the MED?

33. How is the *established* neighbor state represented in the output of the **show ip bgp summary** command?

34. What type of authentication does BGP support?

35. How can BGP path manipulation affect the relative bandwidth used between two connections to the Internet?

36. Describe what the following configuration on Router A does:

```
route-map local_pref permit 10
 match ip address 65
 set local-preference 300
route-map local_pref permit 20
router bgp 65001
 neighbor 192.168.5.3 remote-as 65002
 neighbor 192.168.5.3 route-map local_pref in
```

37. Place the BGP route selection criteria in order from the first step to the last step evaluated by placing a number in the blank provided.

_____ Prefer the path with the lowest neighbor BGP router ID.

_____ Prefer the lowest MED.

_____ Prefer the shortest AS-path.

_____ Prefer the oldest route for EBGP paths.

_____ Prefer the lowest origin code.

_____ Prefer the highest weight.

_____ Prefer the path through the closest IGP neighbor.

_____ Prefer the highest local preference.

_____ Prefer the route originated by the local router.

_____ Prefer the route with the lowest neighbor IP address.

_____ Prefer the EBGP path over the IBGP path.

38. What command is used to assign a weight to updates from a BGP neighbor connection?

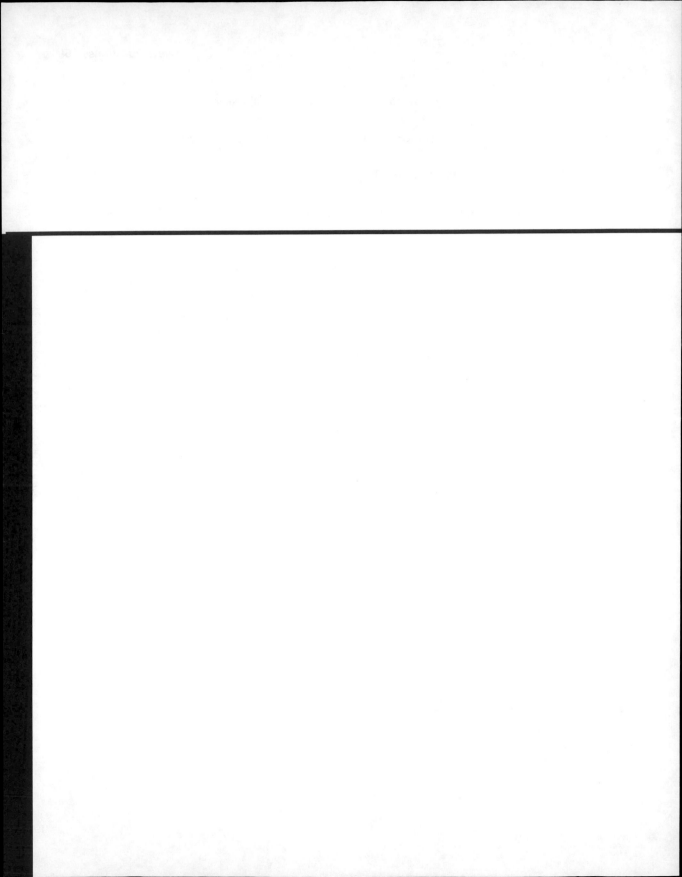

Part III: IP Multicast

This chapter introduces IP multicast and covers the following topics:

- Introduction to Multicast

- IGMP and CGMP

- PIM Routing Protocol

- IP Multicast Configuration and Verification

CHAPTER 9

Implementing IP Multicast

Many types of data can be transferred between devices over an IP network, including, for example, document files, voice, and video. However, a traditional IP network is not efficient when sending the same data to many locations; the data is sent in unicast packets and is therefore replicated on the network for each destination. For example, if a CEO's annual video address is sent out on a company's network for all employees to watch, the same data stream must be replicated for each employee. Obviously, this would consume many resources, including precious wide-area network (WAN) bandwidth.

IP multicast technology enables data to be sent over networks to a group of destinations in the most efficient way. The data is sent from the source as one stream; this single data stream travels as far as it can in the network. Devices only replicate the data if they need to send it out on multiple interfaces to reach all members of the destination group.

Multicast groups are identified by Class D IP addresses, which are in the range from 224.0.0.0 to 239.255.255.255. IP multicast involves some new protocols for network devices, including two for informing network devices which hosts require which multicast data stream—Internet Group Management Protocol (IGMP) and Cisco Group Management Protocol (CGMP)— and one for determining the best way to route multicast traffic—Protocol Independent Multicast (PIM).

This chapter provides an introduction to IP multicast, multicast addressing, the IGMP, CGMP, and PIM protocols, and the implementation of IP multicast on Cisco devices.

Introduction to Multicast

This section compares multicast with unicast and introduces the concept of a multicast group. The types of applications that benefit from the use of multicasting are discussed, as are basic IP and Layer 2 multicast addressing. The section concludes with a discussion of how an application or user learns about available multicast sessions.

Multicast Versus Unicast

When IP multicast is used to send data packets to multiple receivers, the packets are not duplicated for every receiver, but instead are sent in a single stream. Downstream routers replicate the packets only on links where receiving hosts exist.

The sender, or source, of multicast traffic does not have to know the unicast addresses of the receivers.

In contrast, unicast transmission sends multiple copies of data packets, one copy for each receiver.

The unicast example in Figure 9-1 shows a host transmitting three copies of a data packet, and a network forwarding each packet to three separate receivers. The host sends to only one receiver at a time, because it has to create a packet with a different destination address for each receiver.

Figure 9-1 *Unicast Versus Multicast*

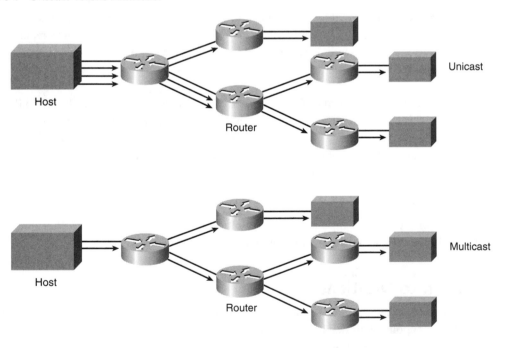

The multicast example in Figure 9-1 shows a host transmitting one copy of a data packet and a network replicating the packet at the last possible router for each receiver.

KEY POINT | **Multicast Sends Only a Single Copy of a Packet**

There is only a single copy of each multicast packet on any given network. A host sends to multiple receivers simultaneously because it is sending only one packet, with one multicast destination address. Downstream multicast routers replicate and forward the data packet to segments where there may be receivers.

> **NOTE**   Some web technologies (for example, webcasting) use a "push" method to deliver the same data to multiple users. Instead of users clicking on a link to get the data, the data is delivered automatically. Users first have to subscribe to a channel to receive the data, and then the data is periodically "pushed" to the user. The problem with the webcast is that the transport is still done using unicast.

Multicast Applications

IP multicast is used when simultaneous delivery for a group of receivers is required; hence, it is also called a *simulcast*.

There are various types of multicast applications. Two of the most common models are one-to-many and many-to-many.

In one-to-many applications, one sender sends data to many (two or more) receivers. This type of application may be used for audio or video distribution, push-media, announcements, monitoring, and so on. If a one-to-many application needs feedback from receivers, it may become a many-to-many application.

In many-to-many applications, any number of hosts send to the same multicast group. Two or more receivers also act as senders and a host can be a sender and a receiver simultaneously. Receiving data from several sources increases the complexity of applications and creates different management challenges. Using a many-to-many multicast concept as a foundation, a whole new range of applications may be built (for example, collaboration, concurrent processing, and distributed interactive simulations).

Other models (for example, many to one or few to many) are also used, especially in financial applications. The many-to-one multicast model is when many receivers are sending data back to one sender (via unicast or multicast) and may be used for resource discovery, data collection, auctions, polling, and similar applications.

Many new multicast applications are emerging as demand for them grows. Real-time applications include live TV, radio, and corporate broadcasts, financial data delivery, whiteboard collaboration, e-learning or distance learning, and videoconferencing.

Non-real-time applications include file transfer, data and file replication, and video on demand (VoD). Ghosting multiple PC images simultaneously is a common file transfer application. Some forms of e-learning are also non-real time.

Advantages of Multicast

Multicast transmission provides many advantages over unicast transmission in a one-to-many or many-to-many environment, including the following:

- **Enhanced efficiency**—As illustrated in Figure 9-2, available network bandwidth is used more efficiently because multiple streams of data are replaced with a single transmission. Server and CPU loads are also reduced. Multicast packets do not impose as high a rate of bandwidth utilization as unicast packets, so there is a greater possibility that they will arrive almost simultaneously at the receivers.

- **Optimized performance**—Multicast eliminates traffic redundancy because fewer copies of the data require forwarding and processing. The sender also needs much less processing power and bandwidth for the equivalent amount of multicast traffic.

- **Support for distributed applications**—As demand and usage grows, distributed multipoint applications will not be possible with unicast transmission, because it does not scale well (traffic levels and the number of clients increase at a 1:1 rate with unicast transmission). Multicast enables a whole range of new applications that were not possible with unicast, including for example, VoD.

Figure 9-2 *Multicast Reduces Traffic Load*

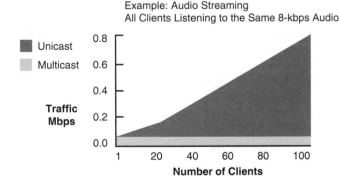

Disadvantages of Multicast

Most multicast applications are User Datagram Protocol (UDP) based. This foundation results in some undesirable consequences when compared to similar unicast, Transmission Control Protocol (TCP) based applications. UDP has no reliability mechanisms, so reliability issues have to be addressed in multicast applications if reliable data transfer is necessary. Some of the disadvantages of multicast that need to be considered include the following:

- UDP's best-effort delivery results in occasional packet drops. Thus, multicast applications must not expect reliable delivery of data and should be designed accordingly; in other words the multicast application itself must be reliable (at the application layer).

Many multicast applications that operate in real time (for example, video and audio) may be affected by these losses; requesting retransmission of the lost data at the application layer in these real-time applications is not feasible. For example, high packet-drop rates in voice applications may result in jerky, missed speech patterns that can make the content unintelligible. Moderate to heavy drops in video are sometimes tolerated by the human eye and appear as unusual "artifacts" in the picture. However, some compression algorithms may be severely affected by even low drop rates, which might cause the picture to become jerky or to freeze for several seconds while the decompression algorithm recovers.

- UDP's lack of congestion control (due to not having a windowing or slow-start mechanism like TCP has) may result in network congestion and overall network degradation as the popularity of UDP-based multicast applications grow. If possible, multicast applications should attempt to detect and avoid congestion conditions.

- Duplicate packets may occasionally be generated when multicast network topologies change. Multicast applications should be designed to expect occasional duplicate packets to arrive and must handle them accordingly.

- Out-of-sequence delivery of packets to the application may also result during network topology changes or other network events that affect the flow of multicast traffic. Multicast applications must be designed to handle these packets appropriately.

Some security issues with multicast, such as how to restrict multicast traffic to only a selected group of receivers to avoid eavesdropping, are not sufficiently resolved yet.

Some commercial applications (for example, financial data delivery) will become possible only when these reliability and security issues are fully resolved.

Multicast IP Addresses

KEY POINT | **Multicast IP Address Range**

Multicast IP addresses use the Class D address space, which is indicated by the high-order 4 bits set to binary 1110. Thus, the Class D multicast address range is 224.0.0.0 through 239.255.255.255.

The Internet Assigned Numbers Authority (IANA) assigns ranges and specific multicast addresses; a current list is available at http://www.iana.org/assignments/multicast-addresses.

Local scope addresses are addresses in the range 224.0.0.0 through 224.0.0.255 and are reserved by the IANA for network protocol use. This range of addresses is also known as the *local network control block*. Packets with multicast addresses in this range are never forwarded off the local network regardless of the Time to Live (TTL) field in the IP packet header; the TTL is usually set to 1. Examples of local scope IP multicast addresses include the following:

- **224.0.0.1**—All hosts

- **224.0.0.2**—All multicast routers

- **224.0.0.4**—All Distance Vector Multicast Routing Protocol (DVMRP) routers

- **224.0.0.5**—All Open Shortest Path First (OSPF) routers

- **224.0.0.6**—All OSPF Designated Routers (DRs)

- **224.0.0.9**—All Routing Information Protocol Version 2 (RIPv2) routers

- **224.0.0.10**—All Enhanced Interior Gateway Protocol (EIGRP) routers

For multicast applications, transient addresses are dynamically assigned and then returned for others to use when no longer needed. These addresses are assigned from the remainder of the IP multicast address space, which is divided into the following two types:

- Globally scoped addresses, in the range 224.0.1.0 through 238.255.255.255, to be allocated dynamically throughout the Internet. For example, the 224.2.0.0/16 range may be used in Multicast Backbone (Mbone) applications. Mbone is a collection of Internet routers that support IP multicasting and is used as a virtual network (multicast channel) on which various public and private audio and video programs are sent. Mbone was originally created by the Internet Engineering Task Force (IETF) in an effort to multicast audio and video meetings.

- Limited, or administratively, scoped addresses in the range 239.0.0.0 through 239.255.255.255. As defined by Requests for Comments (RFC) 2365, *Administratively Scoped IP Multicast*, these addresses are reserved for use inside private domains.

The administratively scoped multicast address space includes the following scopes, per the IANA:

- Site-local scope (239.255.0.0/16; 239.252.0.0/16, 239.253.0.0/16, and 239.254.0.0/16 are also reserved for this purpose)

- Organization local scope (239.192.0.0 to 239.251.255.255)

The IANA has further refined these ranges, as detailed in the IANA multicast address assignment list referenced earlier.

Layer 2 Multicast Addresses

Normally, devices on a local area network (LAN) segment will receive only packets destined for their own MAC address or the broadcast MAC address. For multicast to work, some means had to be devised so that multiple hosts could receive the same packet and still be capable of differentiating among multicast groups. The IEEE LAN specifications have provisions for the transmission of broadcast and/or multicast packets. In the 802.3 standard, bit 0 of the first octet is used to indicate a broadcast and/or multicast frame, as illustrated in Figure 9-3.

Figure 9-3 *IEEE 802.3 MAC Address Format*

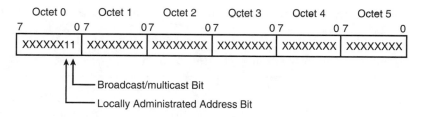

This bit indicates that the frame is destined for an arbitrary group of hosts (multicast) or all hosts on the network (broadcast); in the case of broadcast, the broadcast address is 0xFFFF.FFFF.FFFF. IP multicast makes use of this bit to transmit IP packets to a group of hosts on a LAN segment.

The IANA owns a block of Ethernet MAC addresses that start with hexadecimal 01:00:5E. The lower half of this block is allocated for multicast addresses, resulting in the range of available MAC addresses of 0100.5e00.0000 through 0100.5e7f.ffff.

The translation between IP multicast and Layer 2 multicast MAC address is achieved by the mapping of the low-order 23 bits of the IP (Layer 3) multicast address into the low-order 23 bits of the MAC (Layer 2) address, as shown in Figure 9-4.

Figure 9-4 *IP Multicast to Ethernet MAC Address Mapping*

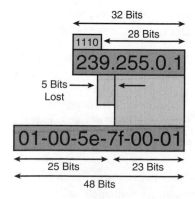

KEY POINT | **32 IP Multicast Addresses Map to One MAC Multicast Address**

Because there are 28 bits of unique address space for an IP multicast address (32 minus the first 4 bits containing the 1110 Class D prefix) and there are only 23 bits mapped into the IEEE MAC address, there are five (28 − 23 = 5) bits of overlap. These 5 bits represent 2^5 = 32 addresses. Therefore, there is a 32:1 overlap of IP addresses to MAC addresses, so 32 IP multicast addresses map to the same MAC multicast address.

For example, all the IP multicast addresses in Table 9-1 map to the same Layer 2 multicast MAC address 01-00-5e-0a-00-01.

Table 9-1   *Many IP Multicast Addresses Match One MAC Address*

224.10.0.1	225.10.0.1	226.10.0.1	227.10.0.1	228.10.0.1
229.10.0.1	230.10.0.1	231.10.0.1	232.10.0.1	233.10.0.1
234.10.0.1	235.10.0.1	236.10.0.1	237.10.0.1	238.10.0.1
239.10.0.1	224.138.0.1	225.138.0.1	226.138.0.1	227.138.0.1
228.138.0.1	229.138.0.1	230.138.0.1	231.138.0.1	232.138.0.1
233.138.0.1	234.138.0.1	235.138.0.1	236.138.0.1	237.138.0.1
238.138.0.1	239.138.0.1			

Learning About Multicast Sessions

Whenever a multicast application is started on a receiver, the application has to learn about the available sessions or streams, which typically map to one or more IP multicast groups. The application may then request to join the appropriate multicast groups.

These are several possibilities for applications to learn about the sessions, including the following:

■ The application may join a well-known, predefined group to which another multicast application sends announcements about available sessions.

■ Some type of directory services may be available, and the application may contact the appropriate directory server.

■ The application may be launched from a web page on which the sessions are listed as URLs.

■ An e-mail may be sent announcing the session; the user clicks on the link in the e-mail to join the session.

Another option is the use of the application called Session Directory (sd) that acts like a TV guide for displaying multicast content. A client application runs on a PC and lets the user know what content is available. This directory application uses either the Session Description Protocol (SDP) or the Session Announcement Protocol (SAP) to learn about the content. (Note that both the Session Directory application and the Session Description Protocol are sometimes called SDR or sdr, and that in Cisco documentation SDP/SAP is referred to as sdr.)

The original session directory application served as a means to announce available sessions and to assist in creating new sessions. The initial sd tool was revised resulting in the Session Description Protocol tool (referred to in this book as SDR), which is an applications tool that allows the following:

- Session description and its announcement

- Transport of session announcement via well-known multicast groups (224.2.127.254)

- Creation of new sessions

When SDR is used at the receiver side, it allows receivers to learn about available groups/sessions. If a user clicks on an icon describing a multicast stream listed via SDR, a join to that multicast group is initiated.

When SDR is used at the sender side, it allows new sessions to be created and address conflicts to be avoided. At the time of session creation, senders consult their respective SDR caches (senders are also receivers) and choose one of the unused multicast addresses. When the session is created, the senders start announcing it with all the information that is needed by receivers to successfully join the session.

RFC 3266, *Support for IPv6 in Session Description Protocol (SDP)*, which defines SDP, defines the standard set of variables that describe the sessions. Most of those variables were inherited from the SDR tool. The transport itself is not defined in this RFC. The packets describing the session may be transported across the multicast-enabled network via one of the following mechanisms:

- SAP, which is defined in RFC 2974, *Session Announcement Protocol*, carries the session information.

- Session Initiation Protocol (SIP), which is defined in RFC 3261, *SIP: Session Initiation Protocol*, is a signaling protocol for Internet conferencing, telephony, presence, events notification, and instant messaging.

- Real Time Streaming Protocol (RTSP), which is defined in RFC 2326, *Real Time Streaming Protocol (RTSP)*, serves mainly as a control protocol in a multimedia environment; RTSP allows videocassette recorder (VCR)-like controls (select, forward, rewind, pause, stop, and so on) and also carries information on a session.

- E-mail (in Multipurpose Internet Mail Extensions [MIME] format) may carry SDR packets describing the session.

- Web pages may provide session descriptions in standardized SDR format.

Cisco IP/TV is an example of an IP multicast application. Cisco IP/TV generally has three components: the server (the source), the content manager (the directory server), and the viewer (the receiver). Viewers may contact the content manager directly (by unicast) and request the list of available programs (sessions, streams) from it, as illustrated in Figure 9-5. Alternatively, viewers may listen to periodic SAP announcements. Cisco IP/TV uses SAP to transport the SDR sessions to the viewer. The standard SDR format for session description is used.

Figure 9-5 *Cisco IP/TV*

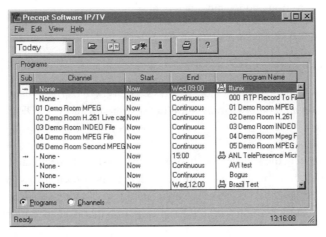

> **NOTE** Cisco has announced the end-of-sale and end-of life dates for the Cisco IP/TV 3400 Series products. See http://www.cisco.com/en/US/products/hw/contnetw/ps1863/ prod_eol_notice0900aecd804445b5.html for more details.

IGMP and CGMP

KEY POINT | **IGMP**
| IGMP is used between hosts and their local router.

Hosts use IGMP to register with the router to join (and leave) specific multicast groups; the router is then aware that it needs to forward the data stream destined to a specific multicast group to the registered hosts.

This section first introduces IGMP, which has evolved through three versions (1, 2, and 3). Understanding this protocol is fundamental in comprehending the multicast group membership join and leave process, which is a required function of multicasting.

Multicasting in Layer 2 switches is also discussed in this section; without control, Ethernet switches flood multicast packets in the same way that unknown unicast frames are flooded. IGMP snooping and CGMP are used to solve this problem.

IGMP Version 1 (IGMPv1)

With IGMPv1, specified in RFC 1112, *Host Extensions for IP Multicasting,* multicast routers periodically send membership queries (usually every 60 to 120 seconds) to the all-hosts multicast address 224.0.0.1. Hosts wanting to receive specific multicast group traffic send membership reports to the multicast address of the group they want to join. Hosts either send reports when they want to first join a group or in response to membership queries. On each subnet, only one member per group responds to a query, to save bandwidth on the subnet and minimize processing by hosts; this process is called *report suppression*.

There must be at least one active member of a multicast group on a local segment if multicast traffic is to be forwarded to that segment.

IGMPv1 does not have a mechanism defined for hosts to leave a multicast group. IGMPv1 hosts therefore leave a group silently, at any time, without any notification to the router. This is not a problem if there are multiple members on a segment, because the multicast traffic must still be delivered to the segment. However, when the last member on a segment leaves the multicast group, there will be a period when the router continues to forward the multicast traffic onto the segment needlessly. The IGMP router will time out the group after several query intervals without a response. This process is inefficient, especially if there are many groups or there is a lot of traffic in the groups.

IGMP Version 2 (IGMPv2)

Because of some of the limitations discovered in IGMPv1, work was begun on IGMPv2 in an attempt to remove these restrictions. IGMPv2 is specified in RFC 2236, *Internet Group Management Protocol, Version 2*. Most of the changes between IGMPv1 and IGMPv2 deal with the issues of leave and join latencies and ambiguities in the original protocol specification. IGMPv2 is backward compatible with IGMPv1.

The following are some important changes in IGMPv2:

- Group-specific queries

- Leave Group message

- Querier election mechanism

- Query-interval response time

A group-specific query allows a router to query membership only in a single group instead of in all groups, providing an optimized way to quickly find out whether any members are left in a group without asking all groups for a report. The difference between the group-specific query and the membership query is that a membership query is multicast to the all-hosts (224.0.0.1) address, whereas a group-specific query for group "G" is multicast to the group "G" multicast address.

A Leave Group message allows hosts to tell the router that they are leaving the group. This information reduces the leave latency for the group on the segment when the member who is leaving is the last member of the group. The specification includes the timing of when Leave Group messages must be sent.

When there are two IGMP routers on the same segment (broadcast domain), the router with the highest IP address is the designated querier.

The query-interval response time is used to control the "burstiness" of reports, and is specified in a query. It indicates to the members how much time they have to respond to a query by issuing a report.

IGMPv2: Joining a Group

Members joining a multicast group do not have to wait for a query to join; rather, they send an unsolicited report indicating their interest. This procedure reduces join latency for an end system joining if no other members are present.

In the example in Figure 9-6, after host H2 sends the join group message for group 224.1.1.1, group 224.1.1.1 is active on the router's FastEthernet 0/0 interface. The output of the **show ip igmp group** command provided in Example 9-1 reveals the following:

- Group 224.1.1.1 has been active on this interface for 1 hour and 3 minutes.

- Group 224.1.1.1 expires (and will be deleted) in 2 minutes and 31 seconds if an IGMP host membership report for this group is not heard in that time.

- The last host to report membership was 10.1.1.11 (H2).

Figure 9-6 *IGMPv2: Joining a Group*

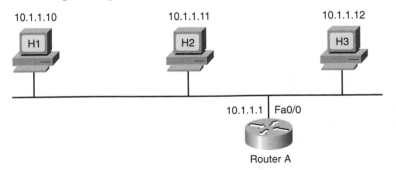

Example 9-1 **show ip igmp group** *Command Output for Router A in Figure 9-6*

```
RouterA#show ip igmp group
IGMP Connected Group Membership
Group Address    Interface       Uptime      Expires      Last Reporter
224.1.1.1        FastEthernet0/0  0d1h3m      00:02:31     10.1.1.11
```

IGMPv2: Leaving a Group

In IGMPv1, hosts leave passively—they just stop reporting their membership by responding to membership queries. IGMPv2 has explicit Leave Group messages.

When an IGMPv2 router receives a Leave Group message, it responds by sending a group-specific query for the associated group to see whether there are still other hosts interested in receiving traffic for the group. This process helps to reduce overall leave latency.

In the example in Figure 9-7, both hosts H2 and H3 are members of multicast group 224.1.1.1. Host H2 leaves the group and announces its departure by sending a Leave Group message to multicast address 224.0.0.2 (all multicast routers). The router hears the Leave Group message and sends a group-specific query to see whether any other group members are present. Host H3 has not left the multicast group 224.1.1.1 yet, so it responds with a Report message. This response tells the router to keep sending multicast for 224.1.1.1, because there is still at least one member present. The output from Router A in Example 9-2 illustrates the IGMP state after H2 leaves.

Figure 9-7 *IGMPv2: Leaving a Group*

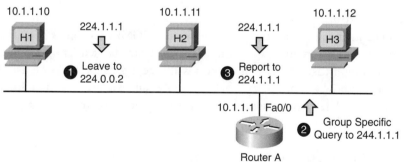

1. H2 sends a leave message.
2. Router A sends a group-specific query.
3. A remaining member host (H3) sends a report, so group remains active.

Example 9-2 **show ip igmp group** *Command Output for Router A in Figure 9-7*

```
RouterA#show ip igmp group
IGMP Connected Group Membership
Group Address    Interface       Uptime      Expires      Last Reporter
224.1.1.1        FastEthernet0/0  0d1h3m      00:01:47     10.1.1.12
```

Host H3 is the last host to send an IGMP group membership report.

If H3 leaves the group, it sends a Leave Group message. After receiving a Leave Group message from H3, the router sends a group-specific query to see whether any other group members are present. Because H3 was the last remaining member of the multicast group 224.1.1.1, no IGMP membership report for group 224.1.1.1 is received, and the group times out. This activity typically takes from 1 to 3 seconds from the time that the Leave Group message is sent until the group-specific query times out and multicast traffic stops flowing for that group.

The output in Example 9-3 indicates the IGMP state after all hosts have left the 224.1.1.1 group on FastEthernet 0/0.

Example 9-3 **show ip igmp group** *Command Output for Router A in Figure 9-7 When No Hosts Remain in Group*

```
RouterA#show ip igmp group
IGMP Connected Group Membership
Group Address    Interface      Uptime     Expires    Last Reporter
```

IGMP Version 3 (IGMPv3)

IGMPv3 is a proposed standard, documented in RFC 3376, *Internet Group Management Protocol, Version 3*, that adds the ability to filter multicasts based on multicast source so that hosts can indicate that they want to receive traffic only from particular sources within a multicast group. This enhancement makes the utilization of routing resources more efficient.

IGMPv3: Joining a Group

As illustrated in Figure 9-8, a joining member sends an IGMPv3 report to 224.0.0.22 immediately upon joining. This report might specify a source list, which is used for source filtering. A source list is a list of multicast sources that the host will accept packets from or a list of multicast sources that the host will not accept packets from. Using a source list, a multicast router can, for example, avoid delivering multicast packets from specific sources to networks where there are no interested receivers.

Figure 9-8 *IGMPv3: Joining a Group*

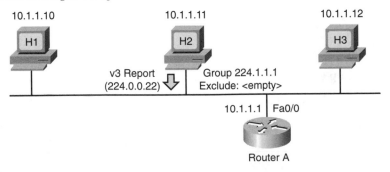

> **NOTE**   In IGMPv3, reports are sent to 224.0.0.22 rather than 224.0.0.2. Note that in the IANA
> multicast addresses document referenced earlier, 224.0.0.22 is called the "IGMP" address.

IGMPv3: Operation

Figure 9-9 illustrates IGMPv3 operation. The router sends periodic queries and all IGMPv3
members respond with reports that contain multiple group state records.

Figure 9-9   *IGMPv3 Operation*

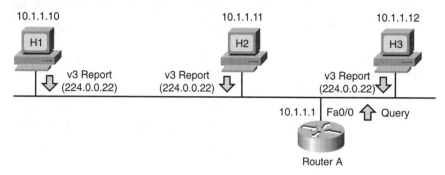

Determining Which IGMP Version Is Running

Use the **show ip igmp interface** command to determine which version of IGMP is currently active
on an interface, as illustrated by the example output in Example 9-4. The router in this example is
running IGMPv2.

Example 9-4   show ip igmp interface *Command Output*

```
RouterA#show ip igmp interface Fa0/0
FastEthernet0/0 is up, line protocol is up
  Internet address is 10.1.1.1, subnet mask is 255.255.255.0
  IGMP is enabled on interface
  Current IGMP version is 2
  CGMP is disabled on interface
  IGMP query interval is 60 seconds
  IGMP querier timeout is 120 seconds
  IGMP max query response time is 10 seconds
  Inbound IGMP access group is not set
  Multicast routing is enabled on interface
  Multicast TTL threshold is 0
  Multicast designated router (DR) is 10.1.1.1 (this system)
  IGMP querying router is 10.1.1.1 (this system)
  Multicast groups joined: 224.0.1.40 224.2.127.254
```

Multicast with Layer 2 Switches

In a typical network, hosts are not directly connected to routers but are connected to a Layer 2 switch, which is in turn connected to a router.

KEY POINT | **IGMP Is a Layer 3 Protocol**

IGMP is a network layer—Layer 3—protocol. Therefore, Layer 2 switches do not participate in IGMP and are not aware of which hosts attached to them might be part of a particular multicast group. By default, Layer 2 switches flood multicast frames to all ports within a virtual LAN (VLAN) (except the port from which the frame originated), which means that all multicast traffic received by a switch would be sent out on all ports within a VLAN, even if only one device on one port required the data stream.

One method Cisco Catalyst switches use to circumvent this is by allowing the administrator to configure the switch to manually associate a multicast MAC address with various ports: For example, the administrator may configure ports 5, 6, and 7 so that only those ports receive the multicast traffic destined for a specific multicast group. This method works but is not scalable because IP multicast hosts dynamically join and leave groups, using IGMP to signal to the multicast router.

To improve the behavior of the switches when they receive multicast frames, there have been many multicast switching solutions developed, including CGMP and IGMP snooping.

> **NOTE** The "Multicast Catalyst Switches Support Matrix" document, available at http://www.cisco.com/warp/public/473/167.html, includes a list of which switches support CGMP and which switches support IGMP snooping.

CGMP

KEY POINT | **CGMP Is Used Between a Router and a Switch**

CGMP is a Cisco Systems proprietary protocol that runs between a multicast router and a switch. The routers inform each of their directly connected switches of IGMP registrations that were received from hosts through the switch (in other words, from hosts accessible through the switch). The switch then forwards the multicast traffic only to ports that those requesting hosts are on rather than flooding the data to all ports.

CGMP is the most common multicast switching solution designed by Cisco and is based on a client/server model, where the router may be considered a CGMP server, and the switch a client.

When the router sees an IGMP control message, it creates a CGMP packet that contains the request type (join or leave), the Layer 2 multicast MAC address, and the actual MAC address of the client.

This packet is sent to the well-known CGMP multicast MAC address 0x0100.0cdd.dddd to which all CGMP switches listen. The switch interprets the CGMP control message and creates the proper entries in its MAC address table (also called its forwarding table or *content-addressable memory* [CAM] table) to constrain the forwarding of multicast traffic for this group to only the appropriate ports.

Figure 9-10 illustrates the interaction of the IGMP and CGMP protocols. Hosts A and D register, using IGMP, to join the multicast group to receive data from the server. The router informs both switches of these registrations, using CGMP. When the router forwards the multicast data to the hosts via the switches, the switches ensure that the data only goes out of the ports on which hosts A and D are connected. The ports on which hosts B and C are connected do not receive the multicast data.

Figure 9-10 *IGMP and CGMP Inform Network Devices About Which Hosts Want Which Multicast Data*

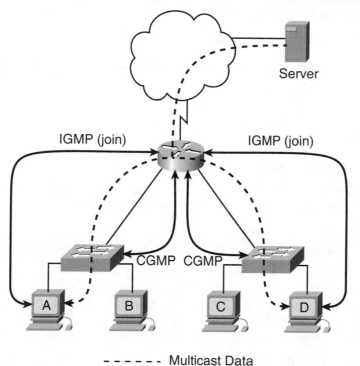

IGMP Snooping

KEY POINT

IGMP Snooping

With IGMP snooping, the switch eavesdrops on the IGMP messages sent between routers and hosts, and updates its MAC address table accordingly.

As its name implies, a switch must be IGMP aware to listen in on the IGMP conversations between hosts and routers. This activity requires the switch's processor to identify and intercept all IGMP packets flowing between routers and hosts and vice versa, including IGMP membership reports and IGMP Leave Group messages.

A switch may have to intercept all Layer 2 multicast packets to identify IGMP packets, which can have a significant impact on switch performance. Therefore, switches must effectively become Layer 3 aware to avoid serious performance problems because of IGMP snooping. Proper designs require special hardware (Layer 3 application specific integrated circuits [ASICs]) to avoid this problem, which may directly affect the overall cost of the switch.

PIM Routing Protocol

PIM is used by routers that are forwarding multicast packets. The "protocol-independent" part of the name indicates that PIM is independent of the unicast routing protocol (for example, EIGRP or OSPF) running in the network.

KEY POINT | **PIM Uses the Normal Routing Table**

PIM uses the normal routing table, populated by the unicast routing protocol, in its multicast routing calculations.

Unlike other routing protocols, no routing updates are sent between PIM routers.

KEY POINT | **Unicast Routing Protocols**

EIGRP, OSPF, and so forth are called *unicast routing protocols* because they are used for creating and maintaining unicast routing information in the routing table.

Recall, however, that unicast routing protocols use multicast packets (or broadcast packets in some protocols) to send their routing update traffic.

> **NOTE** A variant of OSPF, called multicast OSPF, supports multicast routing. Cisco routers do not support multicast OSPF.

This section explores the operation of PIM.

PIM Terminology

This section introduces some PIM terminology.

When a router is forwarding a unicast packet, it looks up the destination address in its routing table and forwards the packet out of the appropriate interface. However, when forwarding a multicast packet, the router might have to forward the packet out of multiple interfaces, toward all the receiving hosts. Multicast-enabled routers use PIM to dynamically create distribution trees that control the path that IP multicast traffic takes through the network to deliver traffic to all receivers.

Distribution Trees

There are two types of distribution trees: source trees and shared trees.

KEY POINT | **Source Tree**

A source tree is created for each source sending to each multicast group. The source tree has its root at the source and has branches through the network to the receivers.

Source trees are also called source-routed or shortest path trees (SPTs) because the tree takes a direct, or the shortest, path from source to its receivers.

KEY POINT | **Shared Tree**

A shared tree is a single tree that is shared between all sources for each multicast group. The shared tree has a single common root, called a *rendezvous point* (RP). Sources initially send their multicast packets to the RP, which in turn forwards data through a shared tree to the members of the group.

Distribution trees are further explored in the later "Multicast Distribution Trees" section.

Reverse Path Forwarding

Multicast routers consider the source address and the destination address of the multicast packet, and use the distribution tree to forward the packet away from the source toward the destination.

KEY POINT | **Reverse Path Forwarding**

Forwarding multicast traffic away from the source, rather than to the receiver, is called *Reverse Path Forwarding* (RPF); this is just the opposite of unicast routing. For multicast, the source IP address denotes the known source, and the destination IP address denotes a group of unknown receivers.

To avoid routing loops, RPF uses the unicast routing table to determine the upstream (toward the source) and downstream (away from the source) neighbors and ensures that only one interface on the router is considered to be an incoming interface for data from a specific source. For example, data received on one router interface and forwarded out another interface might loop around the network and come back into the same router on a different interface; RPF ensures that this data is not forwarded again.

PIM Modes

PIM operates in one of the following two main modes: PIM sparse mode (PIM-SM) or PIM dense mode (PIM-DM). PIM sparse-dense mode, a hybrid of the two, is another option.

KEY **POINT**	**Sparse Mode** Sparse mode uses a "pull" model to send multicast traffic. It uses a shared tree and therefore requires an RP to be defined.

In sparse mode, sources register with the RP. Routers along the path from active receivers that have explicitly requested to join a specific multicast group register to join that group. These routers calculate, using the unicast routing table, whether they have a better metric to the RP or to the source itself; they forward the join message to the device with which they have the better metric.

KEY **POINT**	**Dense Mode** Dense mode uses a "push" model that floods multicast traffic to the entire network. Dense mode uses source trees.

In dense mode, routers that have no need for the data (because they are not connected to receivers that want the data or to other routers that want it) request that the tree is pruned so that they no longer receive the data.

PIM sparse-dense mode allows the router to operate in sparse mode for sparse mode groups (those with known RPs) and in dense mode for other groups. PIM sparse-dense mode also supports automatic RP discovery.

PIM modes are further explored in the "PIM-DM," "PIM-SM," and "PIM Sparse-Dense Mode" sections later in this chapter.

Multicast Distribution Trees

This section further describes multicast source and shared trees.

Source Distribution Trees

Figure 9-11 illustrates a source tree between Source 1 and Receiver 1 and Receiver 2. The path between the source and receivers over Routers A, C, and E is the path with the lowest cost.

Packets are forwarded according to the source and group address pair along the tree. For this reason, the forwarding state associated with the source tree is referred to by the notation (S, G) (pronounced "S comma G"), where S is the IP address of the source, and G is the multicast group address.

Figure 9-12 shows the same network as in Figure 9-11, but with Source 2 active and sending multicast packets to Receiver 1 and Receiver 2. A separate source tree is built for this purpose, this time with Source 2 at the root of the tree.

Figure 9-11 *Source Distribution Tree*

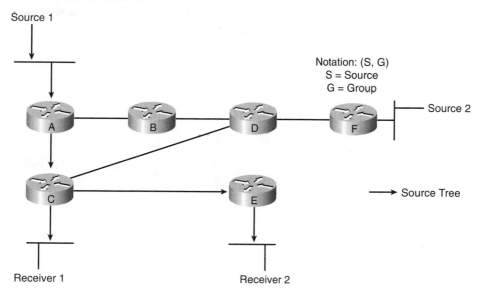

Figure 9-12 *A Separate Source Tree Is Built for Each Source Sending to Each Group*

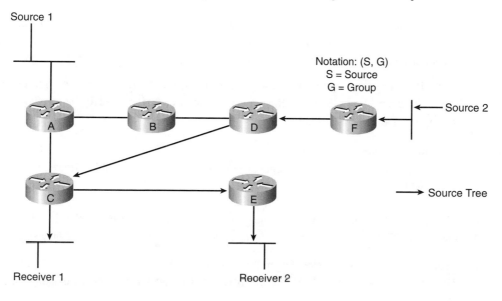

Source Tree

With source trees, a separate tree is built for every source S sending to group G.

Shared Distribution Trees

Figure 9-13 shows a shared distribution tree. Router D is the root of this shared tree, the RP. The tree is built from Router D to Routers C and E toward Receiver 1 and Receiver 2.

Figure 9-13 *The RP Is the Root of the Shared Distribution Tree*

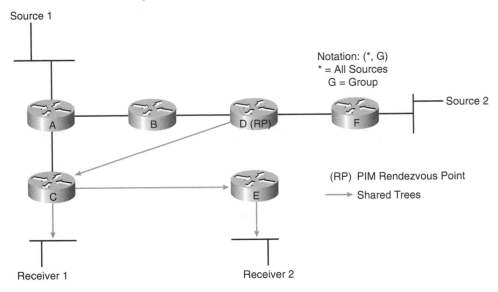

Packets are forwarded down the shared distribution tree to the receivers. The default forwarding state for the shared tree is identified by the notation (*, G) (pronounced "star comma G"), where * is a wildcard entry, meaning any source, and G is the multicast group address.

Figure 9-14 illustrates the operation of the network in Figure 9-13. Source 1 and Source 2 are sending multicast packets toward the RP via source path trees; from the RP, the multicast packets are flowing via a shared distribution tree toward Receiver 1 and Receiver 2.

Multicast Distribution Tree Notation

The multicast forwarding entries that appear in multicast forwarding tables are read in the following way:

- **(S, G)**—For the source S sending to the group G; traffic is forwarded via the shortest path from the source. These entries typically reflect a source tree, but may also appear on a shared tree.

- **(*, G)**—For any source (*) sending to the group G; traffic is forwarded via an RP for this group. These entries reflect a shared tree, but are also created in Cisco routers for any existing (S, G) entry.

SPT state entries (S, G) use more router memory because there is an entry for each source and group pair. The traffic is sent over the optimal path to each receiver, thus minimizing the delay in packet delivery.

Shared distribution tree state entries (*, G) consume less router CPU and memory, but may result in suboptimal paths from a source to receivers, thus introducing extra delay in packet delivery.

Figure 9-14 *Sources Send Toward the RP and the RP Sends to the Receivers*

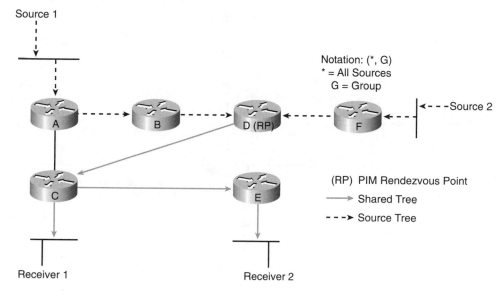

PIM-DM

PIM-DM initially floods multicast traffic to all parts of the network. The traffic is sent out of all non-RPF interfaces where there is another PIM-DM neighbor or a directly connected member of the group.

For example, in Figure 9-15, multicast traffic being sent by the source is flooded throughout the entire network. As each router receives the multicast traffic via its RPF interface (the interface in the direction of the source), it forwards the multicast traffic to all of its PIM-DM neighbors.

Note that this flooding may result in some traffic arriving via a non-RPF interface as is the case for Routers A, B, C, and D in Figure 9-15. Packets arriving via the non-RPF interfaces are discarded.

In Figure 9-16, PIM-DM prune messages are sent to stop unwanted traffic. Prune messages are sent on an RPF interface only when the router has no downstream receivers for multicast traffic from the specific source. In this example, there is only one receiver, so all other paths are pruned.

Figure 9-15 *PIM-DM Initial Flooding*

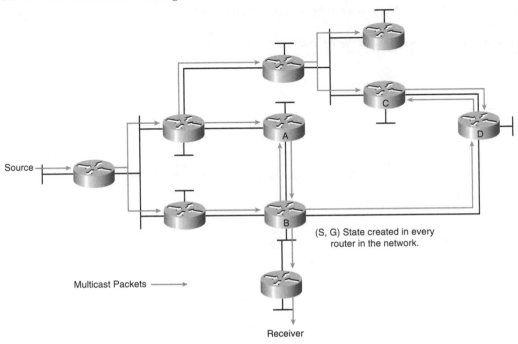

Figure 9-16 *PIM-DM Pruning Unwanted Traffic*

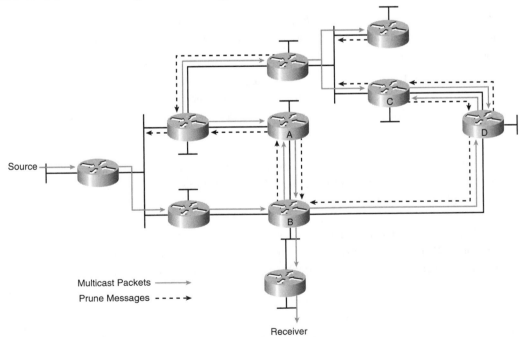

Prune messages are also sent on non-RPF interfaces to shut off the flow of multicast traffic because it is arriving via an interface that is not on the shortest path to the source.

Figure 9-17 shows the source tree resulting from pruning the unwanted multicast traffic in the network.

Figure 9-17   *PIM-DM Results After Pruning*

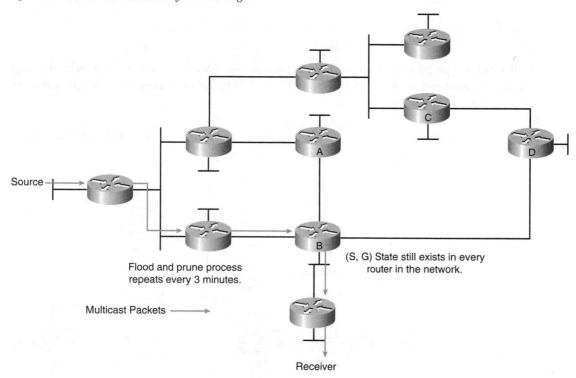

Although the flow of multicast traffic is no longer reaching most of the routers in the network, the (S, G) state still remains in all of them and will remain there until the source stops sending.

In PIM-DM, all prune messages expire in 3 minutes. After that, the multicast traffic is flooded again to all the routers. This periodic flood and prune behavior is normal and must be taken into account when a network is designed to use PIM-DM.

PIM-SM

PIM-SM is described in RFC 2362, *Protocol Independent Multicast-Sparse Mode (PIM-SM): Protocol Specification.* Similar to PIM-DM, it is also independent of underlying unicast protocols. PIM-SM uses shared distribution trees, but it may also switch to use source distribution trees.

PIM-SM is based on a pull model so that traffic is forwarded only to those parts of the network that need it. PIM-SM uses an RP to coordinate forwarding of multicast traffic from a source to receivers. Senders register with the RP and send a single copy of multicast data through the RP to the registered receivers. Group members are joined to the shared tree by their local designated router (DR). A shared tree that is built this way is always rooted at the RP.

> **NOTE** DR election is described in the "PIM Interfaces and Neighbors" section later in this chapter.

PIM-SM is appropriate for wide-scale deployment for both densely and sparsely populated groups in the enterprise network. It is preferred over PIM-DM for all production networks regardless of size and membership density.

Figure 9-18 illustrates an example. In this network, an active receiver (attached to the leaf Router E at the bottom of the figure) wants to join multicast group G.

Figure 9-18 *PIM-SM Shared Tree Join*

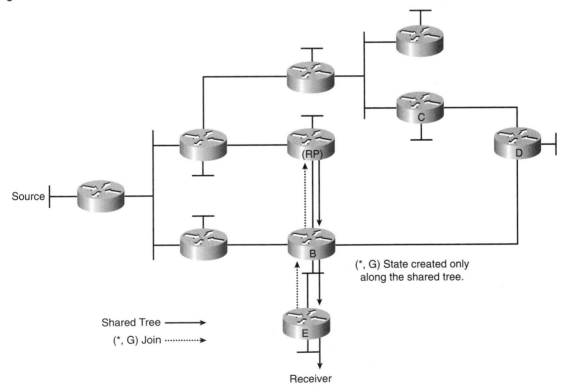

The last-hop router (Router E in this figure) knows the IP address of the RP router for group G, and it sends a (*, G) join for this group toward the RP. This (*, G) join travels hop-by-hop toward the RP building a branch of the shared tree that extends from the RP to the last-hop router directly connected to the receiver. At this point, group G traffic may flow down the shared tree to the receiver.

There are many optimizations and enhancements to PIM, including the following:

■ Bidirectional PIM mode, which is designed for many-to-many applications (that is, many hosts all multicasting to each other)

■ Source Specific Multicast (SSM), which is a variant of PIM-SM that builds only source specific shortest path trees and does not need an active RP for source-specific groups (in the address range 232.0.0.0/8)

PIM Sparse-Dense Mode

PIM sparse-dense mode allows the router to operate in sparse mode for sparse mode groups (those with known RPs) and in dense mode for other groups.

For maximum efficiency, multiple RPs can be implemented with each RP in an optimum location. Configuring, managing, and troubleshooting multiple RPs can be difficult if done manually. However, PIM sparse-dense mode supports automatic selection of RPs for each multicast source. For example, in Figure 9-19 Router A could be the RP for Source 1 and Router D could be the RP for Source 2.

Figure 9-19 *Multiple RPs Are Supported with PIM Sparse Dense Mode*

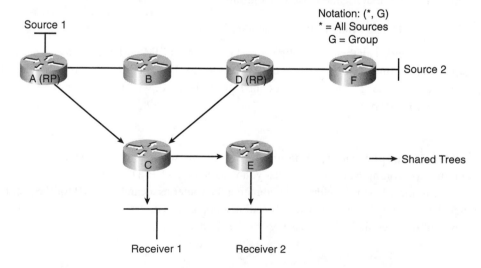

KEY POINT

PIM Sparse-Dense Mode Recommended

Cisco recommends PIM sparse-dense mode for IP multicast, because PIM-DM does not scale well and requires a lot of router resources, and PIM-SM has limited RP configuration options.

If no RP is discovered for the multicast group or none is manually configured, PIM sparse-dense mode will operate in dense mode. Therefore, automatic RP discovery should be implemented with PIM sparse-dense mode.

IP Multicast Configuration and Verification

This section describes how to configure PIM-SM and PIM sparse-dense mode and how to configure a router to become a member of a multicast group. Verification of IP multicast and IGMP groups on a router, and verification of IGMP snooping on a switch, are also explored.

Configuring PIM-SM and PIM Sparse-Dense Mode

This section examines the commands needed for simple PIM-SM and sparse-dense mode configuration.

First, use the **ip multicast-routing** global configuration command to enable IP multicast on a router.

Use the **ip pim sparse-mode** interface configuration command to enable PIM-SM operation on the selected interface. Use the **ip pim sparse-dense-mode** interface configuration command to enable the interface on the router to operate in sparse mode for sparse mode groups (those with known RPs) and in dense mode for other groups.

KEY POINT

PIM Sparse-Dense Mode Is Recommended Method

The recommended method for configuring an interface for PIM-SM operation is to use the **ip pim sparse-dense-mode** interface configuration command. This method permits either auto-RP, bootstrap router (BSR), or statically defined RPs to be used, with the least amount of configuration effort.

Configure the **ip pim send-rp-announce** *interface type* **scope** *ttl* **group-list** *access-list* global configuration command on a router that you want to be an RP. This router sends an auto-RP message to the 224.0.1.39 address, announcing the router as a candidate RP for the groups in the range described by the access list, only within a hop radius dictated by the scope *ttl* value. The address of the specified interface is used as the RP address.

The **ip pim send-rp-discovery** *interface type* **scope** *ttl* global configuration command configures a router as an RP mapping agent; it listens to the 224.0.1.39 address and sends a RP-to-group mapping message to the 224.0.1.40 address, only within a hop radius dictated by the scope *ttl* value. Other PIM routers listen to the 224.0.1.40 address to automatically discover the RP. The address of the specified interface is used as the RP mapping agent address.

The **ip pim spt-threshold** {*rate* | **infinity**} [**group-list** *access-list*] global configuration command controls when a PIM leaf router will switchover from the shared tree to the source tree in sparse mode. The keyword **infinity** means the switchover will never occur. If a source sends at a rate greater than or equal to the *rate*, in kbps, a PIM join message is triggered toward the source to construct a source tree. If the traffic rate from the source drops below the threshold traffic rate, the leaf router will switch back to the shared tree and send a prune message toward the source. Specifying an *access-list* defines the multicast groups to which the threshold applies.

Configuring a Router to Be a Member of a Group or a Statically Connected Member

Sometimes you want multicast traffic to go to a network segment but there is either no group member on the segment or a host cannot report its group membership using IGMP. This is often the situation in lab environments where no multicast servers and receivers are configured. The following are two ways to cause multicast traffic to flow to a network segment:

■ Use the **ip igmp join-group** *group-address* interface configuration command. With this command, the router joins the specified group; the router accepts multicast packets in addition to forwarding them. (Note that accepting the multicast packets prevents the router from fast switching.)

This command is often used in lab environments, where no multicast servers and receivers are configured, for determining multicast reachability. For example, if a device is configured to be a multicast group member and it supports the protocol that is being transmitted to the group, it can respond to requests addressed to the group. Examples of requests include Internet Control Message Protocol (ICMP) echo request packets sent by the **ping** command, and the multicast traceroute tools provided in the Cisco IOS Software.

■ Use the **ip igmp static-group** *group-address* interface configuration command. With this command, the router itself is a statically connected member of the group. The router does not accept the group's packets itself, but only forwards them. Hence, this method allows fast switching. The outgoing interface appears in the IGMP cache, but the router itself is not a member, as evidenced by lack of an L (local) flag in the multicast route entry (as displayed by the **show ip mroute** command, described in the next section).

Verifying IP Multicast

This section describes commands used to verify IP multicast operation.

Inspecting the IP Multicast Routing Table

The **show ip mroute** [*group-address*] [**summary**] [**count**] [**active** *kbps*] command displays the IP multicast routing table and is the most useful command for determining the state of multicast sources and groups, from the selected router perspective. The output of the command represents a part of the multicast distribution tree with an incoming interface and a list of outgoing interfaces. Table 9-2 explains the parameters of this command.

Table 9-2 **show ip mroute** *Command Parameters*

Parameter	Description
group-address	(Optional) IP address of multicast group.
summary	(Optional) Displays a one-line, abbreviated summary of each entry in the IP multicast routing table.
count	(Optional) Displays statistics about the group and source, including number of packets, packets per second, average packet size, and bytes per second.
active *kbps*	(Optional) Displays the rate at which active sources are sending to multicast groups. Active sources are those sending at a rate specified in the *kbps* value or higher. The *kbps* argument defaults to 4 kbps.

The output of the **show ip mroute** command in Example 9-5 illustrates a multicast routing table in a PIM-SM environment. The following two entries are displayed:

■ **(*, G) entry**—Timers, the RP address for the group, and the flags for the group ("S" indicates Sparse) are listed.

The incoming interface is the interface toward the RP. If this is Null, the router itself is the RP. The RPF neighbor (shown as RPF nbr in the output) is the next-hop address toward the RP; if it is 0.0.0.0, this router is the RP for the group.

The outgoing interface list is a list of outgoing interfaces along with the modes and timers associated with each.

■ **(S, G) entry**—Timers and flags for the entry are listed ("T" indicates that it is on the SPT; "A" indicates that it is to be advertised by the Multicast Source Discovery Protocol [MSDP]).

The incoming interface is the interface toward the source S. The RPF neighbor (shown as RPF nbr in the output) is the next-hop address toward the source; if it is 0.0.0.0, the source is directly attached.

The outgoing interface list is a list of outgoing interfaces, along with the modes and timers associated with each.

Example 9-5 *show ip mroute Command Output*

```
RouterA#show ip mroute
IP Multicast Routing Table
Flags: D - Dense, S - Sparse, B - Bidir Group, s - SSM Group, C - Connected
       L - Local, P - Pruned, R - RP-bit set, F - Register flag,
       T - SPT-bit set, J - Join SPT, M - MSDP created entry,
       X - Proxy Join Timer Running, A - Advertised via MSDP, U - URD,
       I - Received Source Specific Host Report
Outgoing interface flags: H - Hardware switched
Timers: Uptime/Expires
Interface state: Interface, Next-Hop or VCD, State/Mode

(*, 224.1.1.1), 00:07:54/00:02:59, RP 10.127.0.7, flags: S
  Incoming interface: Null, RPF nbr 0.0.0.0
  Outgoing interface list:
    Serial1/3, Forward/Sparse, 00:07:54/00:02:32

(172.16.8.1, 224.1.1.1), 00:01:29/00:02:08, flags: TA
  Incoming interface: Serial1/4, RPF nbr 10.139.16.130
  Outgoing interface list:
    Serial1/3, Forward/Sparse, 00:00:57/00:02:02
```

PIM Interfaces and Neighbors

The first step in checking the proper operation of PIM-SM is to check PIM-enabled interfaces and to determine whether the PIM neighbors are correct, using the following commands:

- **show ip pim interface** [*type number*] [**count**]—Displays information about interfaces configured for PIM

- **show ip pim neighbor** [*type number*]—Displays the discovered PIM neighbors

- **mrinfo** [*hostname | address*]—Displays information about multicast routers that are peering with the local router (if no address is specified) or with the specified router

The **show ip pim interface** command output in Example 9-6 displays the following information:

- **Address**—IP address of the interface.

- **Interface**—Type and number of the interface configured for PIM.

- **Ver/Mode**—PIM version (1 or 2) that is running on the interface and the mode (D = dense mode, S = sparse mode, SD = sparse-dense mode).

- **Nbr Count**—Number of neighbors on this link.

- **Query Intvl**—Frequency at which PIM hello messages (PIM queries) are sent; the default is 30 seconds.

- **DR Prior**—Priority used in DR election; if all the routers on a multiaccess link have the same priority (default = 1), the highest IP address is the tiebreaker.

- **DR**—IP address of the DR. Point-to-point links do not have DRs, so the output shows 0.0.0.0.

Example 9-6   **show ip pim interface** *Command Output*

```
RouterA#show ip pim interface
Address          Interface      Ver/   Nbr    Query  DR     DR
                                Mode   Count  Intvl  Prior
10.139.16.133    Serial0/0      v2/S   1      30     1      0.0.0.0
10.127.0.170     Serial1/2      v2/S   1      30     1      0.0.0.0
10.127.0.242     Serial1/3      v2/S   1      30     1      0.0.0.0
```

The **show ip pim neighbor** command output in Example 9-7 displays the following information:

- **Neighbor Address**—IP address of the PIM neighbor.

- **Interface**—Interface where the PIM hello message (or PIM Query in PIM Version 1 [PIMv1]) of this neighbor was received.

- **Uptime**—Period of time (in hours:minutes:seconds) that this PIM neighbor has been active.

- **Expires**—Period of time (holdtime) (in hours:minutes:seconds) after which this PIM neighbor will no longer be considered as active; receipt of another PIM Hello or PIM Query resets the timer.

- **Ver**—PIM version the neighbor is using (v1 or v2).

- **DR Prio/Mode**—Priority and mode of the DR. Possible modes are S (sparse mode), B (bidirectional mode), N (none—the neighbor does not include the DR-Priority Option in its Hello messages), and P (RPF vector proxy is received).

Example 9-7   **show ip pim neighbor** *Command Output*

```
RouterB#show ip pim neighbor
PIM Neighbor Table
Neighbor         Interface              Uptime/Expires     Ver    DR
Address                                                           Prio/Mode
10.31.1.3        Serial0/0/0.1          00:00:10/00:01:34 v2      1 / DR S
10.31.11.4       Serial0/0/0.2          00:00:04/00:01:40 v2      1 / DR S
```

Example 9-8 provides sample **mrinfo** command output. The flags indicate the following:

- P: prune capable

- M: mtrace capable

- S: SNMP capable

- A: auto-RP capable

Example 9-8 **mrinfo** *Command Output*

```
RouterC#mrinfo
10.1.1.1 [version  12.4] [flags: PMA]:
  10.200.200.11 -> 0.0.0.0 [1/0/pim/querier/leaf]
  10.1.1.1 -> 10.1.1.3 [1/0/pim]
  172.31.1.1 -> 172.31.1.3 [1/0/pim]
  10.1.0.1 -> 10.1.0.2 [1/0/pim]
```

Checking RP Information

The RP for a multicast group operating in PIM sparse mode has to be reachable and known to the router. Troubleshooting RP information includes (in addition to the standard tools such as unicast **ping** to check the RP reachability) the use of the following commands:

- **show ip pim rp** [*group-name* | *group-address* | **mapping**]—Without arguments, this command displays RP information about active groups. If the group address or name is provided, only the RP information for the selected group is shown (assuming that it is an active group). With the **mapping** argument, this command displays the contents of the Group-to-RP mapping cache indicating which RP is active for which group range. This cache is populated via the auto-RP or BSR mechanisms, or via static RP assignments.

- **show ip rpf** {*address* | *name*}—Displays RPF information for the RP or source specified.

The output of **show ip pim rp** command simply lists all active groups and their associated RPs, as illustrated in Example 9-9. This form of the command is becoming increasingly obsolete, because it offers limited information.

Example 9-9 **show ip pim rp** *Command Output*

```
RouterA#show ip pim rp
 Group: 224.1.2.3, RP: 10.127.0.7, uptime 00:00:20, expires never
```

Instead, the **show ip pim rp mapping** command, illustrated in Example 9-10, should be used in most cases because it supplies details on the actual contents of the Group-to-RP mapping cache, such as the following:

- The IP address of the router that distributed the information, or *local* when the source of the information is a local router that either has manual RP configuration or is a source of automatically distributed information

■ The mechanism by which this information was determined—by auto-RP, BSR, or static

■ Whether this router is operating as a candidate-RP, mapping agent, or BSR

Example 9-10 **show ip pim rp mapping** *Command Output*

```
RouterA#show ip pim rp mapping
PIM Group-to-RP Mappings

Group(s) 224.0.1.39/32
  RP 10.127.0.7 (NA-1), v1
    Info source: local, via Auto-RP
        Uptime: 00:00:21, expires: never
Group(s) 224.0.1.40/32
  RP 10.127.0.7 (NA-1), v1
    Info source: local, via Auto-RP
        Uptime: 00:00:21, expires: never
Group(s): 224.0.0.0/4, Static
    RP: 10.127.0.7 (NA-1)
```

The output of the **show ip rpf** command displays RPF information associated with the specified source address. The specified address does not necessarily have to be a currently active source. In fact, it may be any IP address, including the address of the RP. Specifying the address of the RP is useful in determining the RPF information for the shared tree.

Examples 9-11 and 9-12 illustrate output of this command toward an RP and toward a source, respectively. In the command output, "RPF interface" is the interface in the direction of the source (or RP), while "RPF neighbor" is the address of the next-hop router in the direction of the source (or RP).

Example 9-11 **show ip rpf** *Command Output Toward an RP*

```
RouterA#show ip rpf 10.127.0.7
RPF information for NA-1 (10.127.0.7)
  RPF interface: Serial1/3
  RPF neighbor: ? (10.127.0.241)
  RPF route/mask: 10.127.0.7/32
  RPF type: unicast (ospf 1)
  RPF recursion count: 0
  Doing distance-preferred lookups across tables
```

Example 9-12 **show ip rpf** *Command Output Toward a Source*

```
RouterA#show ip rpf 10.139.17.126
RPF information for ? (10.139.17.126)
  RPF interface: Serial0/0
  RPF neighbor: ? (10.139.16.134)
```

Example 9-12 **show ip rpf** *Command Output Toward a Source (Continued)*

```
RPF route/mask: 10.139.17.0/25
RPF type: unicast (ospf 1)
RPF recursion count: 0
Doing distance-preferred lookups across tables
```

The "RPF type" indicates the source of RPF information. In these examples, unicast indicates that the information was derived from the unicast routing table (in this case, from the OSPF). Other RPF types include DVMRP, Multiprotocol Border Gateway Protocol (MBGP) Extensions for IP Multicast, or static. RPF information is essential in multicast routing, and special care has to be taken when inspecting the PIM-SM information because of the possible coexistence of shared and source trees.

Verifying IGMP Groups

This section explains how to verify IGMP groups on a router.

Enabling PIM on an interface also enables IGMP operation on that interface (by default the router uses IGMPv2). An interface can be configured to be in PIM dense mode, sparse mode, or sparse-dense mode. The mode determines how the router populates its multicast routing table and how the router forwards multicast packets it receives from its directly connected LANs. You must enable PIM in one of these modes for an interface to perform IP multicast routing.

If multicast traffic is not flowing to receivers, the IGMP group membership should be checked on the leaf routers. The **show ip igmp interface** [*type number*] command shows multicast-related information about the selected interface, and **show ip igmp groups** [*group-address* | *type number*] command lists the multicast groups known to the router—both local groups (directly connected) and those that were learned via IGMP.

As illustrated in Example 9-13, the **show ip igmp interface** command output includes the following information:

- That the interface is configured for IGMP

- The version of IGMP running

- The address of the multicast DR

- The address of the IGMPv2 querier on the multiaccess network

- The multicast groups joined by the current router

Example 9-13 **show ip igmp interface** *Command Output*

```
RouterA#show ip igmp interface fa0/0
FastEthernet0/0 is up, line protocol is up
  Internet address is 10.1.1.1, subnet mask is 255.255.255.0
  IGMP is enabled on interface
  Current IGMP version is 2
  CGMP is disabled on interface
  IGMP query interval is 60 seconds
  IGMP querier timeout is 120 seconds
  IGMP max query response time is 10 seconds
  Inbound IGMP access group is not set
  Multicast routing is enabled on interface
  Multicast TTL threshold is 0
  Multicast designated router (DR) is 10.1.1.1 (this system)
  IGMP querying router is 10.1.1.1 (this system)
  Multicast groups joined: 224.0.1.40 224.2.127.254
```

In Example 9-13, the router has joined two groups:

- **224.0.1.40**—This is the auto-RP group, which the router joined automatically.

- **224.2.127.254**—This is the Session Description Protocol (SDR) group, which was joined because the **ip sdr listen** command was configured on the interface.

The **show ip igmp groups** command output illustrated in Example 9-14 indicates that the router recognizes two multicast groups:

- Group 224.1.1.1 is active on FastEthernet 0/0 and has been active on this interface for 6 days and 17 hours. This group expires (and will be deleted) in 1 minute and 47 seconds if an IGMP host membership report for this group is not heard in that time. The last host to report membership was 10.1.1.12.

- Group 224.0.1.40 (auto-RP) is automatically joined by all Cisco routers. Therefore, its expiration shows "never."

Example 9-14 **show ip igmp groups** *Command Output*

```
RouterA#show ip igmp groups
IGMP Connected Group Membership
Group Address    Interface         Uptime    Expires    Last Reporter
224.1.1.1        FastEthernet0/0   6d17h     00:01:47   10.1.1.12
224.0.1.40       FastEthernet0/0   6d17h     never      10.1.1.17
```

Verifying IGMP Snooping

This section explains how to verify IGMP snooping on a switch.

> **NOTE**   The commands and sample outputs in this section are from a Cisco Catalyst switch running non-Cisco IOS Software, for example purposes. Other switches might use different commands to display similar information.

When verifying IGMP snooping on a switch, use the **show multicast group** [**igmp**] [*mac-addr*] [*vlan-id*] command to display the multicast group configuration. If the **igmp** keyword is used, only IGMP-learned information is displayed.

Use the **show multicast router** [**igmp**] [*mod-num/port-num*] [*vlan-id*] command to display the information about ports that have IGMP multicast routers, both dynamically learned and manually configured, connected to them. Use the **igmp** keyword to specify that only the configuration information learned through IGMP is to be displayed.

Use the **show igmp statistics** *vlan-id* command to view IGMP statistics, for all VLANs or for a particular VLAN.

Figure 9-20 shows an IGMP-enabled multicast router with IP address 10.0.0.1 and a multicast receiver with IP address 10.0.0.2 connected to the router via a switch that has IGMP snooping enabled over ports 4/1 and 4/2. Both ports are in a VLAN 10.

Figure 9-20   *Network Used to Illustrate IGMP Snooping Verification*

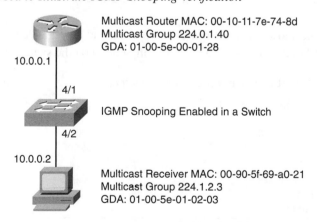

Multicast Router MAC: 00-10-11-7e-74-8d
Multicast Group 224.0.1.40
GDA: 01-00-5e-00-01-28

10.0.0.1

4/1

IGMP Snooping Enabled in a Switch

4/2

10.0.0.2

Multicast Receiver MAC: 00-90-5f-69-a0-21
Multicast Group 224.1.2.3
GDA: 01-00-5e-01-02-03

The IGMP router with the MAC address 00-10-11-7e-74-8d is a member of multicast group 224.0.1.40. The multicast receiver with the MAC address 00-90-5f-69-a0-21 is receiving multicast traffic from multicast group 224.1.2.3. The Layer 2 multicast group destination addresses (GDAs) are also shown in the figure.

The output of the **show igmp statistics** command shown in Example 9-15 displays statistics for VLAN 10 on the switch in Figure 9-20. The number of the group-specific queries and general queries is shown in addition to the number of host membership reports and Leave Group messages. The statistics are split into Receive and Transmit information.

Example 9-15 **show igmp statistics** *Command Output*

```
Switch>show igmp statistics 10
IGMP enabled

IGMP statistics for vlan 10:
    Transmit:
                        General Queries: 0
                Group Specific Queries: 0
                                Reports: 0
                                 Leaves: 0

    Receive:
                        General Queries: 1
                Group Specific Queries: 0
                                Reports: 2
                                 Leaves: 0
                       Total Valid pkts: 4
                     Total Invalid pkts: 0
                             Other pkts: 1
             MAC-Based General Queries: 0
         Failures to add GDA to EARL: 0
                 Topology Notifications: 0
```

The output of the **show multicast router igmp** command in Example 9-16 displays information about the IGMP router port and the VLAN configuration on the switch in Figure 9-20.

Example 9-16 **show multicast router igmp** *Command Output*

```
Switch>show multicast router igmp
Port        Vlan
---------  ----------------
 4/1        10

Total Number of Entries = 1
'*' - Configured
'+' - RGMP-capable
```

The output of the **show multicast group igmp** command in Example 9-17 lists information about the VLAN, multicast group, and ports that are joined to that multicast group on the switch in Figure 9-20.

Example 9-17   **show multicast group igmp** *Command Output*

```
Switch>show multicast group igmp

VLAN  Dest MAC/Route Des  [CoS]  Destination Ports or VCs / [Protocol Type]
----  -------------------------------------------------------------------
10    01-00-5e-00-01-28          4/1
10    01-00-5e-01-02-03          4/1-2


Total Number of Entries = 2
```

Summary

In this chapter, you learned the basics of IP multicast; the following topics were presented:

- The difference between multicast and unicast

- The advantages and disadvantages of using multicast

- The organization of the multicast IP addressing space

- How IP multicast addresses are mapped to Layer 2 multicast addresses

- Multicast applications and how users might learn about available sessions

- IGMP, IGMP snooping, and CGMP—protocols used by routers and switches within a multicast environment

- The PIM routing protocol, used by routers to forward multicast traffic, including the related terminology:

    — Source trees

    — Shared trees

    — RPF

    — PIM-SM

    — PIM-DM

    — PIM sparse-dense mode

    — RPs

- Basic IP multicast configuration and verification

References

For additional information, refer to the following:

■ The IANA's IP multicast addressing assignments reference, available at http://www.iana.org/ assignments/multicast-addresses

■ The Internet Protocol Multicast chapter of the Internetworking Technology Handbook, available at http://www.cisco.com/univercd/cc/td/doc/cisintwk/ito_doc/ipmulti.htm

■ Multicast in a Campus Network: CGMP and IGMP Snooping, available at http:// www.cisco.com/warp/public/473/22.html

Configuration Exercise: Configuring Multicast Routing

In this Configuration Exercise, you implement multicast routing.

Introduction to the Configuration Exercises

This book uses Configuration Exercises to help you practice configuring routers with the commands and topics presented. If you have access to real hardware, you can try these exercises on your routers. See Appendix B, "Configuration Exercise Equipment Requirements and Backbone Configurations," for a list of recommended equipment and initial configuration commands for the backbone routers. However, even if you do not have access to any routers, you can go through the exercises, and keep a log of your own running configurations, or just read through the solution. Commands used and solutions to the Configuration Exercises are provided within the exercises.

In the Configuration Exercises, the network is assumed to consist of two pods, each with four routers. The pods are interconnected to a backbone. You configure pod 1. No interaction between the two pods is required, but you might see some routes from the other pod in your routing tables in some exercises if you have it configured. In most of the exercises, the backbone has only one router; in some cases, another router is added to the backbone. Each Configuration Exercise assumes that you have completed the previous chapters' Configuration Exercises on your pod.

NOTE Throughout this exercise, the pod number is referred to as *x*, and the router number is referred to as *y*. Substitute the appropriate numbers as needed.

Objectives

The objectives of this exercise are to implement multicast routing, configure PIM sparse-dense mode, analyze a multicast group, configure auto-RP, and enable a router to join a multicast group.

Visual Objective

Figure 9-21 illustrates the topology used and what you will accomplish in this exercise.

Figure 9-21 *Multicast Routing Configuration Exercise Topology*

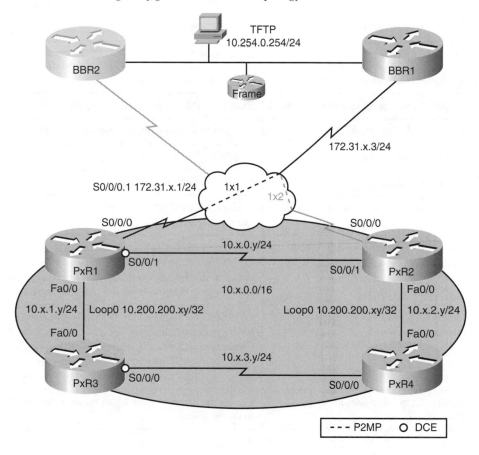

> **NOTE**   This exercise assumes that multicast traffic is coming from the backbone, using both of the 224.*x.x.x* addresses (where *x* is the pod number). During our testing, we used a Cisco proprietary traffic generator running on the router that is configured as the Frame Relay switch. Any traffic generator that is able to generate packets to the 224.*x.x.x* addresses will suffice.

Command List

In this exercise, you use the commands in Table 9-3, listed in logical order. Refer to this list if you need configuration command assistance during the exercise.

> **CAUTION**   Although the command syntax is shown in this table, the addresses shown are typically for the PxR1 and PxR3 routers. Be careful when addressing your routers! Refer to the exercise instructions and the appropriate visual objective diagram for addressing details.

Table 9-3 *Multicast Routing Configuration Exercise Commands*

Command	Description
(config)#**ip multicast-routing**	Enables IP multicast routing.
(config-if)#**ip pim sparse-dense-mode**	Enables IP PIM sparse-dense mode on an interface.
#**show ip pim interface**	Displays PIM information about each interface.
#**show ip pim neighbor**	Displays a list of PIM neighbors.
#**show ip mroute**	Displays the multicast routing table.
(config)#**access-list 50 permit 224.**x.x.x **0.0.0.0**	Creates an access list that permits only addresses that match exactly 224.x.x.x.
(config)#**ip pim send-rp-announce loopback 0 scope 3 group-list 50**	Announces the availability of the router to be an RP, using the address of the loopback 0 interface as the RP address, only within a hop radius dictated by the scope value 3, and only for groups in the range described by access list 50.
(config)#**ip pim send-rp-discovery loopback 0 scope 3**	Configures the router as an RP mapping agent that sends RP-to-group mappings so that other routers in the multicast domain can dynamically discover an RP, using the address of the loopback 0 interface as the RP mapping agent address and only within a hop radius dictated by the scope value 3.
(config-if)#**ip igmp join-group 224.**x.x.x	Causes the router to issue a join message for the 224.x.x.x multicast group.

Task 1: Cleaning Up

In this task, you prepare your pod routers before configuring multicast routing.

Follow these steps:

Step 1   The only connection to the backbone routers in this activity is the PxR1 connection to the BBR1 router. Therefore, on PxR1, shut down the S0/0/0.2 subinterface to BBR2, and on PxR2 shut down the S0/0/0 interface.

Step 2   On all routers in your pod, disable all routing protocols currently running (RIPv2 and Border Gateway Protocol [BGP]) and configure EIGRP with autonomous system number 1 and with autosummarization disabled.

Solution:

The following shows how to do the required steps on the P1R1, P1R2, and P1R3 routers:

```
P1R1(config)#interface s0/0/0.2
P1R1(config-subif)#shutdown
P1R1(config-subif)#exit
P1R1(config)#no router rip
P1R1(config)#no router bgp 65001
P1R1(config)#router eigrp 1
P1R1(config-router)#network 10.0.0.0
P1R1(config-router)#network 172.31.0.0
P1R1(config-router)#no auto-summary

P1R2(config)#interface s0/0/0
P1R2(config-if)#shutdown
P1R2(config-if)#exit
P1R2(config)#no router rip
P1R2(config)#no router bgp 65001
P1R2(config)#router eigrp 1
P1R2(config-router)#network 10.0.0.0
P1R2(config-router)#no auto-summary

P1R3(config)#no router rip
P1R3(config)#no router bgp 65001
P1R3(config)#router eigrp 1
P1R3(config-router)#network 10.0.0.0
P1R3(config-router)#no auto-summary
```

Task 2: Enable IP Multicast Routing

In this task, you enable multicast routing before configuring IP multicast specific options.

Follow these steps:

Step 1   Verify that there is a loopback 0 interface with the appropriate address (10.200.200.xy/32) on each router in your pod.

Step 2   Enable multicast routing on all four routers in your pod.

Solution:

The following shows how to do the required steps on the P1R1 router:

```
P1R1#sh run | begin inter
interface Loopback0
 ip address 10.200.200.11 255.255.255.255
!
<output omitted>
P1R1(config)#ip multicast-routing
```

Task 3: Configure PIM Sparse-Dense Mode on All Interfaces

In this task, you enable PIM sparse-dense mode on all interfaces, including loopbacks.

Follow these steps:

Step 1   Enable PIM sparse-dense mode on all interfaces (including the loopback interfaces) on all four routers in your pod. For the P*x*R1 router, enable PIM sparse-dense mode on the s0/0/0.1 subinterface, not on the main interface.

Solution:

The following shows how to do the required steps on the P1R1 router:

```
P1R1(config)#interface loop 0
P1R1(config-if)#ip pim sparse-dense-mode
P1R1(config-if)#interface fa0/0
P1R1(config-if)#ip pim sparse-dense-mode
P1R1(config-if)#interface s0/0/0.1
P1R1(config-subif)#ip pim sparse-dense-mode
P1R1(config-if)#interface s0/0/1
P1R1(config-if)#ip pim sparse-dense-mode
```

Step 2   From privileged EXEC mode on each of your pod routers, enter the **show** command that will list all interfaces configured for PIM and associated information. Are all of your required interfaces configured for PIM?

Solution:

The following shows sample output on the P1R1 and P1R3 routers. All of the required interfaces are configured for PIM:

```
P1R1#show ip pim interface

Address           Interface        Ver/  Nbr    Query  DR    DR
                                   Mode  Count  Intvl  Prior
10.200.200.11     Loopback0        v2/SD 0      30     1     10.200.200.11
10.1.1.1          FastEthernet0/0  v2/SD 1      30     1     10.1.1.3
172.31.1.1        Serial0/0/0.1    v2/SD 1      30     1     172.31.1.3
10.1.0.1          Serial0/0/1      v2/SD 1      30     1     0.0.0.0

P1R3#show ip pim interface

Address           Interface        Ver/  Nbr    Query  DR    DR
                                   Mode  Count  Intvl  Prior
10.200.200.13     Loopback0        v2/SD 0      30     1     10.200.200.13
10.1.1.3          FastEthernet0/0  v2/SD 1      30     1     10.1.1.3
10.1.3.3          Serial0/0/0      v2/SD 1      30     1     0.0.0.0
```

Step 3   On each of your pod routers, issue the **show** command to display all of your PIM neighbors. Do you have the correct number of neighbors?

Solution:

The following shows sample output on the P1R1 and P1R3 routers. Each router has the correct number of neighbors:

```
P1R1#show ip pim neighbor
PIM Neighbor Table
```

```
Neighbor          Interface          Uptime/Expires     Ver   DR
Address                                                       Prio/Mode
10.1.1.3          FastEthernet0/0    00:02:10/00:01:32  v2    1 / DR S
172.31.1.3        Serial0/0/0.1      00:05:12/00:01:27  v2    1 / DR S
10.1.0.2          Serial0/0/1        00:03:08/00:01:34  v2    1 / S

P1R3#show ip pim neighbor
PIM Neighbor Table
Neighbor          Interface          Uptime/Expires     Ver   DR
Address                                                       Prio/Mode
10.1.1.1          FastEthernet0/0    00:04:16/00:01:25  v2    1 / S
10.1.3.4          Serial0/0/0        00:03:14/00:01:27  v2    1 / S
```

Step 4   On each of your pod routers, issue the **show** command to display any known multicast routes. You should see a (*,G) and (S,G) for each of the multicast streams being generated, and you should see a (*,224.0.1.40). Where did the 224.0.1.40 address come from?

Solution:

The following shows sample output on the P1R1 and P1R3 routers. Each router has a (*,G) and (S,G) for each of the two multicast streams being generated, plus a (*,224.0.1.40). The routers listen to 224.0.1.40 to automatically discover the RP:

```
P1R1#show ip mroute
IP Multicast Routing Table
Flags: D - Dense, S - Sparse, B - Bidir Group, s - SSM Group, C - Connected,
       L - Local, P - Pruned, R - RP-bit set, F - Register flag,
       T - SPT-bit set, J - Join SPT, M - MSDP created entry,
       X - Proxy Join Timer Running, A - Candidate for MSDP Advertisement,
       U - URD, I - Received Source Specific Host Report,
       Z - Multicast Tunnel, z - MDT-data group sender,
       Y - Joined MDT-data group, y - Sending to MDT-data group
Outgoing interface flags: H - Hardware switched, A - Assert winner
 Timers: Uptime/Expires
 Interface state: Interface, Next-Hop or VCD, State/Mode

(*, 224.1.1.1), 00:05:15/stopped, RP 0.0.0.0, flags: D
  Incoming interface: Null, RPF nbr 0.0.0.0
  Outgoing interface list:
    FastEthernet0/0, Forward/Sparse-Dense, 00:02:13/00:00:00
    Serial0/0/1, Forward/Sparse-Dense, 00:03:12/00:00:00
    Serial0/0/0.1, Forward/Sparse-Dense, 00:05:15/00:00:00

(10.254.0.3, 224.1.1.1), 00:05:15/00:01:53, flags: PT
  Incoming interface: Serial0/0/0.1, RPF nbr 172.31.1.3
  Outgoing interface list:
    FastEthernet0/0, Prune/Sparse-Dense, 00:01:12/00:01:47
    Serial0/0/1, Prune/Sparse-Dense, 00:01:13/00:01:46

(*, 224.2.2.2), 00:05:16/stopped, RP 0.0.0.0, flags: D
  Incoming interface: Null, RPF nbr 0.0.0.0
  Outgoing interface list:
    FastEthernet0/0, Forward/Sparse-Dense, 00:02:15/00:00:00
    Serial0/0/1, Forward/Sparse-Dense, 00:03:13/00:00:00
    Serial0/0/0.1, Forward/Sparse-Dense, 00:05:16/00:00:00

(10.254.0.3, 224.2.2.2), 00:05:21/00:01:47, flags: PT
  Incoming interface: Serial0/0/0.1, RPF nbr 172.31.1.3
  Outgoing interface list:
    FastEthernet0/0, Prune/Sparse-Dense, 00:01:17/00:01:42
    Serial0/0/1, Prune/Sparse-Dense, 00:01:18/00:01:41
```

```
(*, 224.0.1.40), 00:05:44/00:02:21, RP 0.0.0.0, flags: DCL
  Incoming interface: Null, RPF nbr 0.0.0.0
  Outgoing interface list:
    FastEthernet0/0, Forward/Sparse-Dense, 00:02:28/00:00:00
    Serial0/0/1, Forward/Sparse-Dense, 00:03:26/00:00:00
    Serial0/0/0.1, Forward/Sparse-Dense, 00:05:30/00:00:00
    Loopback0, Forward/Sparse-Dense, 00:05:45/00:00:00

P1R3#sh ip mroute
IP Multicast Routing Table
Flags: D - Dense, S - Sparse, B - Bidir Group, s - SSM Group, C - Connected,
       L - Local, P - Pruned, R - RP-bit set, F - Register flag,
       T - SPT-bit set, J - Join SPT, M - MSDP created entry,
       X - Proxy Join Timer Running, A - Candidate for MSDP Advertisement,
       U - URD, I - Received Source Specific Host Report,
       Z - Multicast Tunnel, z - MDT-data group sender,
       Y - Joined MDT-data group, y - Sending to MDT-data group
Outgoing interface flags: H - Hardware switched, A - Assert winner
 Timers: Uptime/Expires
 Interface state: Interface, Next-Hop or VCD, State/Mode

(*, 224.1.1.1), 00:04:18/stopped, RP 0.0.0.0, flags: D
  Incoming interface: Null, RPF nbr 0.0.0.0
  Outgoing interface list:
    Serial0/0/0, Forward/Sparse-Dense, 00:03:17/00:00:00
    FastEthernet0/0, Forward/Sparse-Dense, 00:04:18/00:00:00

(10.254.0.3, 224.1.1.1), 00:04:18/00:02:51, flags: PT
  Incoming interface: FastEthernet0/0, RPF nbr 10.1.1.1
  Outgoing interface list:
    Serial0/0/0, Prune/Sparse-Dense, 00:00:17/00:02:42

(*, 224.2.2.2), 00:04:19/stopped, RP 0.0.0.0, flags: D
  Incoming interface: Null, RPF nbr 0.0.0.0
  Outgoing interface list:
    Serial0/0/0, Forward/Sparse-Dense, 00:03:18/00:00:00
    FastEthernet0/0, Forward/Sparse-Dense, 00:04:19/00:00:00

(10.254.0.3, 224.2.2.2), 00:04:19/00:02:50, flags: PT
  Incoming interface: FastEthernet0/0, RPF nbr 10.1.1.1
  Outgoing interface list:
    Serial0/0/0, Prune/Sparse-Dense, 00:00:18/00:02:41

(*, 224.0.1.40), 00:04:35/00:02:18, RP 0.0.0.0, flags: DCL
  Incoming interface: Null, RPF nbr 0.0.0.0
  Outgoing interface list:
    Serial0/0/0, Forward/Sparse-Dense, 00:03:23/00:00:00
    FastEthernet0/0, Forward/Sparse-Dense, 00:04:24/00:00:00
    Loopback0, Forward/Sparse-Dense, 00:04:35/00:00:00
```

Step 5   On PxR1 configure an access list to permit only the 224.*x.x.x* multicast
stream, where *x* is your pod number. Do not use this access list to filter
traffic; rather use this access list to configure P*x*R1 to announce itself as
available to be an RP for only the 224.*x.x.x* stream for your pod, using the
loopback 0 interface and the scope equal to 3.

Step 6   Configure P*x*R1 to send RP-to-group mappings so that other routers can
dynamically discover the RP.

Solution:

The following shows the required configuration on the P1R1 router:

```
P1R1(config)#access-list 50 permit 224.1.1.1 0.0.0.0
P1R1(config)#ip pim send-rp-announce loop 0 scope 3 group-list 50
P1R1(config)#ip pim send-rp-discovery loop 0 scope 3
```

Step 7   After a few minutes, the 224.*x.x.x* route for your pod should no longer be in the multicast table on the non-RP routers in your pod; it should still be in the multicast table on your P*x*R1, the RP. On each of your pod routers, again issue the **show** command to display any known multicast routes. Where did the 224.0.1.39 address come from?

Solution:

The following shows sample output on the P1R1 and P1R3 routers. (If your display differs from this, wait a few minutes and reissue the commands again.)

Your P*x*R1 is now the RP for your 224.*x.x.x* group; therefore, this group is now in sparse mode. The other routers in your pod have pruned this group since they have no members in it, so your 224.*x.x.x* routes are not in the non-RP routers in your pod. Notice, however, that the 224.*x.x.x* group for other pod does still appear in all the routers in your pod. This is because your P*x*R1 is not the RP for that other group (there is no RP for that group), so it is still in dense mode.

The RP (P1R1) sends an auto-RP message to the 224.0.1.39 address, announcing it as a candidate RP for the group specified by the access list:

```
P1R1#show ip mroute
IP Multicast Routing Table
Flags: D - Dense, S - Sparse, B - Bidir Group, s - SSM Group, C - Connected,
       L - Local, P - Pruned, R - RP-bit set, F - Register flag,
       T - SPT-bit set, J - Join SPT, M - MSDP created entry,
       X - Proxy Join Timer Running, A - Candidate for MSDP Advertisement,
       U - URD, I - Received Source Specific Host Report,
       Z - Multicast Tunnel, z - MDT-data group sender,
       Y - Joined MDT-data group, y - Sending to MDT-data group
Outgoing interface flags: H - Hardware switched, A - Assert winner
 Timers: Uptime/Expires
 Interface state: Interface, Next-Hop or VCD, State/Mode

(*, 224.1.1.1), 00:19:12/stopped, RP 10.200.200.11, flags: SP
  Incoming interface: Null, RPF nbr 0.0.0.0
  Outgoing interface list: Null

(10.254.0.3, 224.1.1.1), 00:02:27/00:00:32, flags: PT
  Incoming interface: Serial0/0/0.1, RPF nbr 172.31.1.3
  Outgoing interface list: Null

(*, 224.2.2.2), 00:19:12/stopped, RP 0.0.0.0, flags: D
  Incoming interface: Null, RPF nbr 0.0.0.0
  Outgoing interface list:
    FastEthernet0/0, Forward/Sparse-Dense, 00:16:12/00:00:00
    Serial0/0/1, Forward/Sparse-Dense, 00:17:10/00:00:00
    Serial0/0/0.1, Forward/Sparse-Dense, 00:19:14/00:00:00
```

```
  (10.254.0.3, 224.2.2.2), 00:19:14/00:02:54, flags: T
    Incoming interface: Serial0/0/0.1, RPF nbr 172.31.1.3
    Outgoing interface list:
      FastEthernet0/0, Prune/Sparse-Dense, 00:00:05/00:02:54
      Serial0/0/1, Forward/Sparse-Dense, 00:12:12/00:00:00

  (*, 224.0.1.39), 00:09:34/stopped, RP 0.0.0.0, flags: DCL
    Incoming interface: Null, RPF nbr 0.0.0.0
    Outgoing interface list:
      Loopback0, Forward/Sparse-Dense, 00:09:21/00:00:00
      Serial0/0/1, Forward/Sparse-Dense, 00:09:34/00:00:00
      Serial0/0/0.1, Forward/Sparse-Dense, 00:09:34/00:00:00
      FastEthernet0/0, Forward/Sparse-Dense, 00:09:34/00:00:00

  (10.200.200.11, 224.0.1.39), 00:09:35/00:02:24, flags: LT
    Incoming interface: Loopback0, RPF nbr 0.0.0.0
    Outgoing interface list:
      FastEthernet0/0, Forward/Sparse-Dense, 00:09:22/00:00:00
      Serial0/0/0.1, Forward/Sparse-Dense, 00:09:35/00:00:00
      Serial0/0/1, Forward/Sparse-Dense, 00:09:22/00:00:00

  (*, 224.0.1.40), 00:19:34/stopped, RP 0.0.0.0, flags: DCL
    Incoming interface: Null, RPF nbr 0.0.0.0
    Outgoing interface list:
      FastEthernet0/0, Forward/Sparse-Dense, 00:16:18/00:00:00
      Serial0/0/1, Forward/Sparse-Dense, 00:17:16/00:00:00
      Serial0/0/0.1, Forward/Sparse-Dense, 00:19:21/00:00:00
      Loopback0, Forward/Sparse-Dense, 00:19:34/00:00:00

  (10.200.200.11, 224.0.1.40), 00:08:35/00:02:19, flags: LT
    Incoming interface: Loopback0, RPF nbr 0.0.0.0
    Outgoing interface list:
      Serial0/0/0.1, Forward/Sparse-Dense, 00:08:35/00:00:00
      Serial0/0/1, Forward/Sparse-Dense, 00:08:35/00:00:00
      FastEthernet0/0, Forward/Sparse-Dense, 00:08:36/00:00:00

P1R1#

P1R3#show ip mroute
IP Multicast Routing Table
Flags: D - Dense, S - Sparse, B - Bidir Group, s - SSM Group, C - Connected,
       L - Local, P - Pruned, R - RP-bit set, F - Register flag,
       T - SPT-bit set, J - Join SPT, M - MSDP created entry,
       X - Proxy Join Timer Running, A - Candidate for MSDP Advertisement,
       U - URD, I - Received Source Specific Host Report,
       Z - Multicast Tunnel, z - MDT-data group sender,
       Y - Joined MDT-data group, y - Sending to MDT-data group
Outgoing interface flags: H - Hardware switched, A - Assert winner
 Timers: Uptime/Expires
 Interface state: Interface, Next-Hop or VCD, State/Mode

  (*, 224.2.2.2), 00:17:01/stopped, RP 0.0.0.0, flags: D
    Incoming interface: Null, RPF nbr 0.0.0.0
    Outgoing interface list:
      Serial0/0/0, Forward/Sparse-Dense, 00:16:00/00:00:00
      FastEthernet0/0, Forward/Sparse-Dense, 00:17:01/00:00:00

  (10.254.0.3, 224.2.2.2), 00:17:01/00:02:08, flags: PT
    Incoming interface: FastEthernet0/0, RPF nbr 10.1.1.1
    Outgoing interface list:
      Serial0/0/0, Prune/Sparse-Dense, 00:00:56/00:02:03

  (*, 224.0.1.39), 00:10:25/stopped, RP 0.0.0.0, flags: DC
    Incoming interface: Null, RPF nbr 0.0.0.0
    Outgoing interface list:
      Serial0/0/0, Forward/Sparse-Dense, 00:10:25/00:00:00
      FastEthernet0/0, Forward/Sparse-Dense, 00:10:25/00:00:00
```

```
(10.200.200.11, 224.0.1.39), 00:10:25/00:00:42, flags: PTX
  Incoming interface: FastEthernet0/0, RPF nbr 10.1.1.1
  Outgoing interface list:
    Serial0/0/0, Prune/Sparse-Dense, 00:02:25/00:00:34

(*, 224.0.1.40), 00:17:21/stopped, RP 0.0.0.0, flags: DCL
  Incoming interface: Null, RPF nbr 0.0.0.0
  Outgoing interface list:
    Serial0/0/0, Forward/Sparse-Dense, 00:16:08/00:00:00
    FastEthernet0/0, Forward/Sparse-Dense, 00:17:09/00:00:00
    Loopback0, Forward/Sparse-Dense, 00:17:21/00:00:00

(10.200.200.11, 224.0.1.40), 00:09:26/00:02:31, flags: LT
  Incoming interface: FastEthernet0/0, RPF nbr 10.1.1.1
  Outgoing interface list:
    Loopback0, Forward/Sparse-Dense, 00:09:26/00:00:00
    Serial0/0/0, Forward/Sparse-Dense, 00:09:26/00:00:00
```

Step 8   Configure the FastEthernet 0/0 interface on the P*x*R4 router to issue a join message for the 224.*x.x.x* multicast group, where *x* is your pod number.

Solution:

The following shows the required configuration on the P1R4 router:

```
P1R4(config)#interface fa0/0
P1R4(config-if)#ip igmp join-group 224.1.1.1
```

Step 9   Look at the multicast tables again. The 224.*x.x.x* multicast group should be back in the multicast tables on all of your pod routers. Why?

Solution:

The following shows sample output on the P1R1 and P1R3 routers. The 224.1.1.1 group is back in the multicast tables of all pod routers because the routers now require the traffic for that group and have therefore "unpruned" the group:

```
P1R1#show ip mroute
IP Multicast Routing Table
Flags: D - Dense, S - Sparse, B - Bidir Group, s - SSM Group, C - Connected,
       L - Local, P - Pruned, R - RP-bit set, F - Register flag,
       T - SPT-bit set, J - Join SPT, M - MSDP created entry,
       X - Proxy Join Timer Running, A - Candidate for MSDP Advertisement,
       U - URD, I - Received Source Specific Host Report,
       Z - Multicast Tunnel, z - MDT-data group sender,
       Y - Joined MDT-data group, y - Sending to MDT-data group
Outgoing interface flags: H - Hardware switched, A - Assert winner
 Timers: Uptime/Expires
 Interface state: Interface, Next-Hop or VCD, State/Mode

(*, 224.1.1.1), 00:23:11/00:02:35, RP 10.200.200.11, flags: S
  Incoming interface: Null, RPF nbr 0.0.0.0
  Outgoing interface list:
    FastEthernet0/0, Forward/Sparse-Dense, 00:00:54/00:02:35

(10.254.0.3, 224.1.1.1), 00:03:26/00:03:26, flags: T
  Incoming interface: Serial0/0/0.1, RPF nbr 172.31.1.3
  Outgoing interface list:
    FastEthernet0/0, Forward/Sparse-Dense, 00:00:54/00:02:36
```

```
(*, 224.2.2.2), 00:23:13/stopped, RP 0.0.0.0, flags: D
  Incoming interface: Null, RPF nbr 0.0.0.0
  Outgoing interface list:
    FastEthernet0/0, Forward/Sparse-Dense, 00:20:11/00:00:00
    Serial0/0/1, Forward/Sparse-Dense, 00:21:09/00:00:00
    Serial0/0/0.1, Forward/Sparse-Dense, 00:23:13/00:00:00

(10.254.0.3, 224.2.2.2), 00:23:13/00:02:55, flags: T
  Incoming interface: Serial0/0/0.1, RPF nbr 172.31.1.3
  Outgoing interface list:
    FastEthernet0/0, Prune/Sparse-Dense, 00:01:11/00:01:48
    Serial0/0/1, Forward/Sparse-Dense, 00:16:17/00:00:00

(*, 224.0.1.39), 00:13:41/stopped, RP 0.0.0.0, flags: DCL
  Incoming interface: Null, RPF nbr 0.0.0.0
  Outgoing interface list:
    Loopback0, Forward/Sparse-Dense, 00:13:28/00:00:00
    Serial0/0/1, Forward/Sparse-Dense, 00:13:41/00:00:00
    Serial0/0/0.1, Forward/Sparse-Dense, 00:13:41/00:00:00
    FastEthernet0/0, Forward/Sparse-Dense, 00:13:41/00:00:00

(10.200.200.11, 224.0.1.39), 00:13:41/00:02:18, flags: LT
  Incoming interface: Loopback0, RPF nbr 0.0.0.0
  Outgoing interface list:
    FastEthernet0/0, Forward/Sparse-Dense, 00:13:30/00:00:00
    Serial0/0/0.1, Forward/Sparse-Dense, 00:13:42/00:00:00
    Serial0/0/1, Forward/Sparse-Dense, 00:13:30/00:00:00

(*, 224.0.1.40), 00:23:41/stopped, RP 0.0.0.0, flags: DCL
  Incoming interface: Null, RPF nbr 0.0.0.0
  Outgoing interface list:
    FastEthernet0/0, Forward/Sparse-Dense, 00:20:25/00:00:00
    Serial0/0/1, Forward/Sparse-Dense, 00:21:23/00:00:00
    Serial0/0/0.1, Forward/Sparse-Dense, 00:23:28/00:00:00
    Loopback0, Forward/Sparse-Dense, 00:23:41/00:00:00

(10.200.200.11, 224.0.1.40), 00:12:42/00:02:11, flags: LT
  Incoming interface: Loopback0, RPF nbr 0.0.0.0
  Outgoing interface list:
    Serial0/0/0.1, Forward/Sparse-Dense, 00:12:42/00:00:00
    Serial0/0/1, Forward/Sparse-Dense, 00:12:42/00:00:00
    FastEthernet0/0, Forward/Sparse-Dense, 00:12:42/00:00:00

P1R1#

P1R3#show ip mroute
IP Multicast Routing Table
Flags: D - Dense, S - Sparse, B - Bidir Group, s - SSM Group, C - Connected,
       L - Local, P - Pruned, R - RP-bit set, F - Register flag,
       T - SPT-bit set, J - Join SPT, M - MSDP created entry,
       X - Proxy Join Timer Running, A - Candidate for MSDP Advertisement,
       U - URD, I - Received Source Specific Host Report,
       Z - Multicast Tunnel, z - MDT-data group sender,
       Y - Joined MDT-data group, y - Sending to MDT-data group
Outgoing interface flags: H - Hardware switched, A - Assert winner
 Timers: Uptime/Expires
 Interface state: Interface, Next-Hop or VCD, State/Mode

(*, 224.1.1.1), 00:01:40/00:02:48, RP 10.200.200.11, flags: S
  Incoming interface: FastEthernet0/0, RPF nbr 10.1.1.1
  Outgoing interface list:
    Serial0/0/0, Forward/Sparse-Dense, 00:01:40/00:02:48
```

```
(10.254.0.3, 224.1.1.1), 00:01:39/00:03:24, flags: T
  Incoming interface: FastEthernet0/0, RPF nbr 10.1.1.1
  Outgoing interface list:
    Serial0/0/0, Forward/Sparse-Dense, 00:01:39/00:02:49

(*, 224.2.2.2), 00:20:57/stopped, RP 0.0.0.0, flags: D
  Incoming interface: Null, RPF nbr 0.0.0.0
  Outgoing interface list:
    Serial0/0/0, Forward/Sparse-Dense, 00:19:56/00:00:00
    FastEthernet0/0, Forward/Sparse-Dense, 00:20:57/00:00:00

(10.254.0.3, 224.2.2.2), 00:20:57/00:01:13, flags: PT
  Incoming interface: FastEthernet0/0, RPF nbr 10.1.1.1
  Outgoing interface list:
    Serial0/0/0, Prune/Sparse-Dense, 00:01:59/00:00:59

(*, 224.0.1.39), 00:14:27/stopped, RP 0.0.0.0, flags: DC
  Incoming interface: Null, RPF nbr 0.0.0.0
  Outgoing interface list:
    Serial0/0/0, Forward/Sparse-Dense, 00:14:27/00:00:00
    FastEthernet0/0, Forward/Sparse-Dense, 00:14:27/00:00:00

(10.200.200.11, 224.0.1.39), 00:14:27/00:00:40, flags: PTX
  Incoming interface: FastEthernet0/0, RPF nbr 10.1.1.1
  Outgoing interface list:
    Serial0/0/0, Prune/Sparse-Dense, 00:02:27/00:00:32

(*, 224.0.1.40), 00:21:22/stopped, RP 0.0.0.0, flags: DCL
  Incoming interface: Null, RPF nbr 0.0.0.0
  Outgoing interface list:
    Serial0/0/0, Forward/Sparse-Dense, 00:20:10/00:00:00
    FastEthernet0/0, Forward/Sparse-Dense, 00:21:12/00:00:00
    Loopback0, Forward/Sparse-Dense, 00:21:23/00:00:00

(10.200.200.11, 224.0.1.40), 00:13:28/00:02:29, flags: LT
  Incoming interface: FastEthernet0/0, RPF nbr 10.1.1.1
  Outgoing interface list:
    Loopback0, Forward/Sparse-Dense, 00:13:28/00:00:00
    Serial0/0/0, Forward/Sparse-Dense, 00:13:28/00:00:00

P1R3#
```

Step 10   Save your configurations to NVRAM.

Solution:

The following shows the required step on the P1R1 router:

```
P1R1#copy run start
Destination filename [startup-config]?
Building configuration...
[OK]
```

Exercise Verification

You have successfully completed this exercise when you have configured multicast routing, configured PIM sparse-dense mode, analyzed a multicast group, configured auto-RP, and enabled a router to join a multicast group.

Review Questions

Answer the following questions, and then refer to Appendix A, "Answers to Review Questions," for the answers.

1. Why is IP multicast considered more efficient than unicast?

2. What are some disadvantages of using UDP-based multicast applications?

3. What is the range of multicast IP addresses?

4. Match the range of IP multicast addresses with its description:

Range of Addresses	Description
1—224.0.0.0 through 224.0.0.255	A—Globally scoped addresses
2—224.0.1.0 through 238.255.255.255	B—Organization local scope addresses
3—239.0.0.0 through 239.255.255.255	C—Local scope addresses
4—239.255.0.0/16 (and 239.252.0.0/16, 239.253.0.0/16, and 239.254.0.0/16)	D— Site-local scope addresses
5—239.192.0.0 to 239.251.255.255	E—Limited, or administratively, scoped addresses

5. In an Ethernet address, which bit indicates that the frame is a multicast frame?

6. How are IP multicast addresses translated to Layer 2 MAC multicast addresses?

7. How many IP multicast addresses map to a Layer 2 MAC multicast address?

8. Which two types of devices is IGMP used between? Which two types of devices is CGMP used between?

9. Describe the difference between how a host leaves a group when it is running IGMPv1 versus when it is running IGMPv2.

10. To which address does a host send a multicast report in IGMPv2? In IGMPv3?

11. What is IGMP snooping?

12. Which statement best describes the interaction between the PIM protocol and a unicast routing protocol running on a network?

    a. There is no interaction between the two protocols.

    b. Only PIM or a unicast routing protocol can be run in a network; they cannot be run simultaneously.

    c. PIM uses the routing table populated by the unicast routing protocol in its multicast routing calculations.

    d. The unicast routing protocol uses the routing table populated by PIM in its multicast routing calculations.

13. Select the two true statements.

   a. A shared tree is created for each source sending to each multicast group.

   b. A source tree is created for each source sending to each multicast group.

   c. A shared tree has a single common root, called an RP.

   d. A source tree has a single common root, called an RP.

14. Which type of distribution tree does PIM-SM use?

15. What does the notation (S, G) indicate?

16. What does the notation (*, G) indicate?

17. What is the recommended PIM mode on Cisco routers?

18. Which command enables IP multicasting on a Cisco router?

19. What are the multicast addresses 224.0.1.39 and 224.0.1.40 used for?

20. Which command is used to display the IP multicast routing table on a Cisco router?

21. Which command is used on a Cisco router to display information about multicast routers that are peering with the local router?

22. What does the **show ip igmp groups** command display?

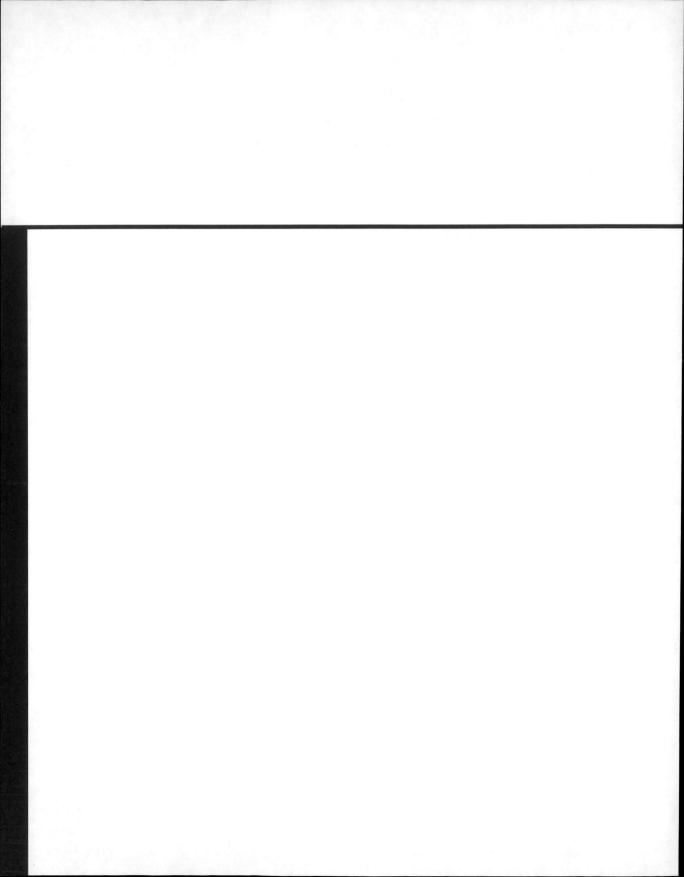

Part IV: IP Version 6

This chapter introduces IPv6 and covers the following topics:

- Introducing IPv6

- IPv6 Addressing

- IPv6 Configuration and Using OSPF and Other Routing Protocols for IPv6

- Transitioning IPv4 to IPv6

Implementing IPv6

IP Version 6 (IPv6) is a technology developed to overcome the limitations of the current standard, IP Version 4 (IPv4), which allows end systems to communicate and forms the foundation of the Internet as we know it today. One of the major shortcomings of IPv4 is its limited amount of address space. The explosion of new IP-enabled devices, the growth of undeveloped regions, and the rapid growth of other regions have fueled the need for more addresses. In the United States, the Department of Defense (DoD) is a primary driver for the adoption of IPv6 and has set a date of 2008 for all systems to be migrated to this new standard. Other potential IPv6 users include the National Research and Education Network (NREN), government agencies, enterprises, service providers, home networks, consumer appliances, distributed online gaming, and wireless services.

This chapter introduces IPv6 and the IPv6 addressing scheme. Routing protocols that support IPv6 are explored, and the details of Open Shortest Path First (OSPF) for IPv6 configuration are presented. The chapter concludes with a discussion of how IPv4 networks can be transitioned to IPv6.

Introducing IPv6

The ability to scale networks for future demands requires a limitless supply of IP addresses and improved mobility; IPv6 combines expanded addressing with a more efficient and feature-rich header to meet the demands. IPv6 satisfies the increasingly complex requirements of hierarchical addressing that IPv4 does not support.

> **NOTE** IPv6 is defined in Requests for Comments (RFC) 2460, *Internet Protocol, Version 6 (IPv6) Specification*.

This section introduces the key features and benefits of IPv6, and its addressing features. The Cisco IOS supports IPv6 in Release 12.2(2)T and later.

Features of IPv6

IPv6 is a powerful enhancement to IPv4 with features that better suit current and foreseeable network demands, including the following:

- **Larger address space**—IPv6 addresses are 128 bits, compared to IPv4's 32 bits. This larger address space provides several benefits, including: improved global reachability and flexibility; the ability to aggregate prefixes that are announced in routing tables; easier multihoming to several Internet service providers (ISPs); autoconfiguration that includes link-layer addresses in the IPv6 addresses for "plug and play" functionality and end-to-end communication without network address translation (NAT); and simplified mechanisms for address renumbering and modification.

- **Simplified header**—A simpler header provides several advantages over IPv4, including: better routing efficiency for performance and forwarding-rate scalability; no requirement for processing checksums; simpler and more efficient extension header mechanisms; and flow labels for per-flow processing with no need to examine the transport layer information to identify the various traffic flows.

- **Support for mobility and security**—Mobility and security help ensure compliance with mobile IP and IP security (IPsec) standards.

  Mobility enables people to move around in networks with mobile network devices, with many having wireless connectivity. Mobile IP is an Internet Engineering Task Force (IETF) standard available for both IPv4 and IPv6 that enables mobile devices to move without breaks in established network connections. Because IPv4 does not automatically provide this kind of mobility, supporting it requires additional configurations.

  In IPv6, mobility is built in, which means that any IPv6 node can use it when necessary. The routing headers of IPv6 make mobile IPv6 much more efficient for end nodes than mobile IPv4 does.

  IPsec is the IETF standard for IP network security, available for both IPv4 and IPv6. Although the functions are essentially identical in both environments, IPSec is mandatory in IPv6. IPSec is enabled and is available for use on every IPv6 node, making the IPv6 Internet more secure. IPSec also requires keys for each device, which implies global key deployment and distribution.

- **Transition richness**—There are a variety of ways to transition IPv4 to IPv6.

  One approach is to have a dual stack with both IPv4 and IPv6 configured on the interface of a network device.

  Another technique uses an IPv4 tunnel to carry IPv6 traffic. One implementation is IPv6-to-IPv4 (6-to-4) tunneling. This newer method (defined in RFC 3056, *Connection of IPv6 Domains via IPv4 Clouds*) replaces an older technique of

IPv4-compatible tunneling (first defined in RFC 2893, *Transition Mechanisms for IPv6 Hosts and Routers*, which has been made obsolete by RFC 4213, *Basic Transition Mechanisms for IPv6 Hosts and Routers*).

Cisco IOS Software Version 12.3(2)T (and later) also allows NAT protocol translation (NAT-PT) between IPv6 and IPv4, providing direct communication between hosts that are using the different protocol suites.

IPv6 Address Space

KEY POINT

IPv6 Addresses Are 128 bits

IPv6 increases the number of address bits by a factor of 4, from 32 to 128, providing a very large number of addressable nodes.

The increased number of address bits are illustrated in Figure 10-1. However, as in any addressing scheme, not all the addresses are used or available.

Figure 10-1 *IPv6 Provides Four Times as Many Address Bits as IPv4*

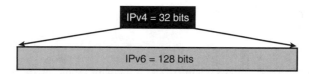

With 32 bits, IPv4 allows for approximately 4,200,000,000 possible addressable nodes, with some 2 billion usable addresses. Current IPv4 address use is extended by applying techniques such as private-to-public address space NAT and temporary address allocations (such as addresses leased by the Dynamic Host Control Protocol [DHCP]). However, the manipulation of the packet by intermediate devices complicates the advantages of peer-to-peer communication, end-to-end security, and quality of service (QoS).

In contrast, the 128 bits in an IPv6 address allow for approximately 3.4×10^{38} possible addressable nodes, which works out to approximately 5×10^{28} addresses for every person on our planet!

Thus, IPv6 has enough address space such that every user could have multiple global addresses that can be used for a wide variety of devices; these addresses would be reachable without using IP address translation, pooling, or temporary allocation techniques.

Note, however, that increasing the number of bits for the address also increases the IPv6 header size. Because each IP header contains a source address and a destination address, the size of the header fields that contains the addresses is 256 bits for IPv6 compared to 64 bits for IPv4.

> **NOTE**   For more information on IPv6 addressing details, refer to RFC 4291, *IP Version 6 Addressing Architecture*.

IPv6's larger address spaces allow for sizable address allocations to ISPs and organizations. As illustrated in Figure 10-2, an ISP can aggregate all the prefixes of its customers into a single prefix and announce the single prefix to the IPv6 Internet. The increased address space is also sufficient to allow organizations to define a single prefix for their entire network.

Figure 10-2   *IPv6 Enables Large Address Allocations*

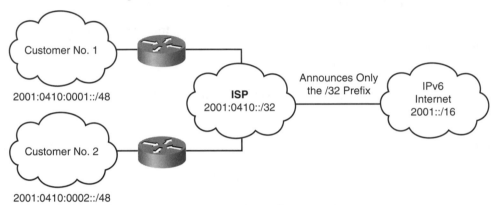

Aggregation of customer prefixes results in an efficient and scalable routing table. Scalable routing is necessary for broader adoption of network functions. Improved network bandwidth and functionality for user traffic will accommodate Internet usage such as the following:

■ A huge increase in the number of broadband consumers with high-speed, "always-on" connections

■ Users who spend more time online and are generally willing to spend more money on communication services and high-value searchable offerings

■ Home networks with expanded network applications such as wireless Voice over IP (VoIP), home surveillance, and advanced services such as real-time video on demand (VoD)

■ Massively scalable games with global participants

■ Media-rich e-learning, providing learners with features such as on-demand remote labs or lab simulations

The Need for Larger Address Space

The Internet, with approximately 973 million users as of November 2005, will be transformed after IPv6 fully replaces its less versatile parent years from now. Nevertheless, IPv4 is in no danger of disappearing overnight. Rather, it will coexist with and then gradually be replaced by IPv6. This change has already begun, particularly in Europe, Japan, and the Asia Pacific.

These areas of the world are exhausting their allotted IPv4 addresses, which makes IPv6 all the more attractive. As noted, in addition to its technical and business potential, IPv6 offers a virtually unlimited supply of IP addresses—enough to allocate more than the entire IPv4 Internet address space to everyone on the planet. These addresses could be used for a variety of devices, including the following:

■ Personal digital assistants (PDAs), pen-tablets, notepads, and so forth, of which there were approximately 20 million in 2004.

■ Mobile/cell phones, of which there are already over 1 billion in existence.

■ Transportation, including IP-enabled automobiles (1 billion automobiles are forecast in 2008) and Internet access in airplanes.

■ Consumer devices, including billions of home and industrial appliances that will be "always-on."

Consequently, some countries, such as Japan, are aggressively adopting IPv6 today. Others, such as those in the European Union, are moving toward IPv6, and China is considering building pure IPv6 networks from the ground up. As of October 1, 2003, even in North America where Internet addresses are abundant, the U.S. DoD mandated that all new equipment purchased be IPv6-capable. As noted earlier, DoD intends to migrate to IPv6 by 2008. As these examples illustrate, IPv6 enjoys strong momentum.

IPv6 Addressing

This section explores the IPv6 packet header, address representation, address types, interface identifiers, unicast addresses, anycast addresses, multicast addresses, stateless autoconfiguration, and mobility.

IPv6 Packet Header

As shown in Figure 10-3, the IPv6 header has 40 octets, in contrast to the 20 octets in the IPv4 header. IPv6 has fewer fields, and the header is 64-bit aligned to enable fast, efficient, hardware-based processing. The IPv6 address fields are four times larger than in IPv4.

The IPv4 header contains 12 basic header fields, followed by an options field and a data portion (which usually includes a transport layer segment). The basic IPv4 header has a fixed size of 20 octets; the variable-length options field increases the size of the total IP header. IPv6 contains fields similar to 7 of the 12 IPv4 basic header fields (five plus the source and destination address fields), but does not require the other fields.

Figure 10-3 *IPv4 and IPv6 Headers*

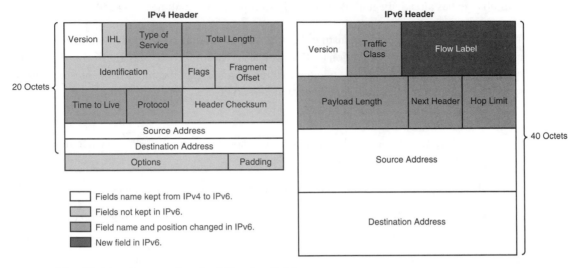

The IPv6 header contains the following fields:

- **Version**—A 4-bit field, the same as in IPv4. For IPv6, this field contains the number 6; for IPv4, this field contains the number 4.

- **Traffic class**—An 8-bit field similar to the type of service (ToS) field in IPv4. This field tags the packet with a traffic class that it uses in differentiated services (DiffServ) QoS. These functionalities are the same for IPv6 and IPv4.

- **Flow label**—This 20-bit field is new in IPv6. It can be used by the source of the packet to tag the packet as being part of a specific flow, allowing multilayer switches and routers to handle traffic on a per-flow basis rather than per-packet, for faster packet-switching performance. This field can also be used to provide QoS.

- **Payload length**—This 16-bit field is similar to the IPv4 total length field.

- **Next header**—The value of this 8-bit field determines the type of information that follows the basic IPv6 header. It can be a transport-layer packet, such as Transmission Control Protocol (TCP) or User Datagram Protocol (UDP), or it can be an extension header. The next header field is similar to the protocol field of IPv4.

- **Hop limit**—This 8-bit field specifies the maximum number of hops that an IP packet can traverse. Similar to the time to live (TTL) field in IPv4, each router decreases this field by one. Because there is no checksum in the IPv6 header, an IPv6 router can decrease the field without recomputing the checksum; in IPv4 routers the recomputation costs processing time. If this field ever reaches 0, a message is sent back to the source of the packet and the packet is discarded.

- **Source address**—This field has 16 octets or 128 bits. It identifies the source of the packet.

- **Destination address**—This field has 16 octets or 128 bits. It identifies the destination of the packet.

- **Extension headers**—The extension headers, if any, and the data portion of the packet follow the other eight fields. The number of extension headers is not fixed, so the total length of the extension header chain is variable.

Notice that the IPv6 header does not have a header checksum field. Because link-layer technologies perform checksum and error control and are considered relatively reliable, an IP header checksum is considered to be redundant. Without the IP header checksum, upper-layer checksums, such as within UDP, are mandatory with IPv6.

Extension Headers

IPv6 has extension headers that handle options more efficiently and enable a faster forwarding rate and faster processing by end-nodes. The next-header field points to the next header in the chain, as shown in Figure 10-4.

Figure 10-4 *IPv6 Extension Headers*

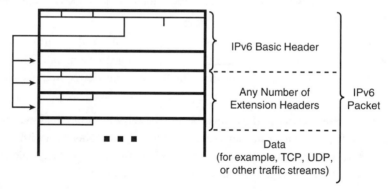

KEY POINT

Extension Headers

Generally, extension headers are not examined or processed by any node other than the node to which the packet is destined.

The destination node examines the first extension header (if there is one); the contents of an extension header determine whether or not the node should examine the next header. Therefore, extension headers must be processed in the order they appear in the packet.

There are many types of extension headers. Only a hop-by-hop options header, if it is present, must be examined by every node along the path. This hop-by-hop options header, if present, must immediately follow the IPv6 header, and is indicated by a value of 0 in the next-header field.

When multiple extension headers are used in the same packet, the order of the headers in the chain should be as follows:

1. **IPv6 header:** This is the basic IPv6 header.

2. **Hop-by-hop options header:** When this header is used, it is processed by all hops (routers) in the path of the packet. Example uses are for a Router Alert, including for Resource Reservation Protocol (RSVP) and Multicast Listener Discovery (MLD) messages (as defined in RFC 2711, *IPv6 Router Alert Option*), and for IPv6 Jumbograms (as defined in RFC 2147, *IPv6 Jumbograms*).

3. **Destination options header (when a routing header is used):** This header (with a next-header value = 60) follows any hop-by-hop options header, in which case the destination options header is processed at the final destination and also at each destination specified by a routing header. Alternatively, the destination options header can follow any Encapsulating Security Payload (ESP) header, in which case the destination options header is processed only at the final destination. Mobile IPv6 is an example of when this header is used.

4. **Routing header:** This header (with a next-header value = 43) is used for source routing and mobile IPv6. An IPv6 source lists one or more intermediate nodes that are to be visited on the way to a packet's destination in this header.

5. **Fragment header:** This header (with a next-header value = 44) is used when a source must fragment a packet that is larger than the maximum transmission unit (MTU) for the path between itself and a destination device. The fragment header is used in each fragmented packet.

6. **Authentication header and Encapsulating Security Payload header:** The authentication header (AH) (with a next-header value = 51) and the ESP header (with a next-header value = 50) are used within IPsec to provide authentication, integrity, and confidentiality of a packet. These headers are identical for both IPv4 and IPv6.

7. **Upper-layer header:** The upper-layer (transport) headers are the typical headers used inside a packet to transport the data. The two main transport protocols are TCP (with a next-header value = 6) and UDP (with a next-header value = 17).

MTU Discovery

In IPv4, routers handle fragmentation, causing a variety of processing issues.

IPv6 routers no longer perform fragmentation; instead, a discovery process is used to determine the optimum MTU to use during a given session. In this discovery process, the source IPv6 device attempts to send a packet at the size that is specified by the upper IP layers, for example, the transport and application layers. If the device receives an Internet Control Message Protocol (ICMP) "packet too big" message, it retransmits the MTU discover packet with a smaller MTU; this process is repeated until the device receives a response that the discover packet arrived intact. The device then sets the MTU for the session.

The ICMP "packet too big" message contains the proper MTU size for the path. Each source device tracks the MTU size for each session. Generally, the tracking is done by creating a cache based on the destination address; however, it can also be done by using the flow label. Alternatively, if source-based routing is performed, the tracking of the MTU size can be done by using the source address.

The discovery process is beneficial because, as routing paths change, a new MTU might be more appropriate. When a device receives an ICMP "packet too big" message, it decreases its MTU size if the ICMP message contains a recommended MTU that is less than the current MTU of the device. Devices perform an MTU discovery every five minutes to see whether the MTU has increased along the path. Application and transport layers for IPv6 accept MTU reduction notifications from the IPv6 layer. If for some reason these upper layers do not accept the notifications, IPv6 has a mechanism to fragment packets that are too large; however, upper layers are encouraged to avoid sending messages that require fragmentation.

IPv6 Address Representation

Rather than using dotted decimal format, IPv6 addresses are written as hexadecimal numbers with colons between each set of four hexadecimal digits (which is 16 bits); we like to call this the "coloned hex" format. The format is $x:x:x:x:x:x:x:x$, where x is a 16-bit hexadecimal field. An example address is as follows:

2035:0001:2BC5:0000:0000:087C:0000:000A

KEY POINT

IPv6 Address Format

Fortunately, you can shorten the written form of IPv6 addresses. Leading 0s within each set of four hexadecimal digits can be omitted, and a pair of colons ("::") can be used, once within an address, to represent any number of successive 0s.

For example, the previous address can be shortened to the following:

2035:1:2BC5::87C:0:A

An all-0s address can be written as **::**.

KEY POINT

Only One Pair of Colons Allowed

A pair of colons (::) can be used only once within an IPv6 address. This is because an address parser identifies the number of missing 0s by separating the two parts and entering 0 until the 128 bits are complete. If two :: notations were to be placed in the address, there would be no way to identify the size of each block of 0s.

Similar to how IPv4 subnet masks can be written as a prefix (for example, /24), IPv6 uses prefixes to indicate the number of bits of network or subnet.

> **NOTE** The hexadecimal digits A, B, C, D, E, and F in IPv6 addresses are not case-sensitive.

IPv6 Address Types

The following are the three main types of IPv6 addresses:

- **Unicast**—Similar to an IPv4 unicast address, an IPv6 unicast address is for a single interface. A packet that is sent to a unicast address goes to the interface identified by that address. The two currently defined types of unicast addresses are global aggregatable (which is also called global unicast) and link-local. As in IPv4, a subnet prefix in IPv6 is associated with one link. The IPv6 unicast address space encompasses the entire IPv6 address range, with the exception of the FF00::/8 range (addresses starting with binary 1111 1111), which is used for multicast addresses.

- **Anycast**—An IPv6 anycast address is a new type of address that is assigned to a *set* of interfaces on different devices; an anycast address identifies multiple interfaces. A packet that is sent to an anycast address goes to the *closest* interface (as determined by the routing protocol being used) identified by the anycast address. Thus, all nodes with the same anycast address should provide uniform service. Examples of when anycast addresses could be used are load balancing and content delivery services.

  Anycast addresses are syntactically indistinguishable from global unicast addresses because anycast addresses are allocated from the global unicast address space.

  Anycast addresses must not be used as the source address of an IPv6 packet.

- **Multicast**—An IPv6 multicast address identifies a set of interfaces on different devices. A packet sent to a multicast address is delivered to *all* the interfaces identified by the multicast address. The range of multicast addresses in IPv6 is larger than in IPv4, and for the foreseeable future, allocation of IPv6 multicast groups is not being limited.

In IPv4, broadcasting results in a number of problems, including generating interrupts in every computer on the network and, in some cases triggering malfunctions, known as *broadcast storms*, which can completely halt an entire network.

KEY POINT | **IPv6 Does Not Have Broadcast Addresses**
Broadcasting does not exist in IPv6; broadcasts are replaced by multicasts and anycasts.

Multicast enables efficient network operation by using a number of specific multicast groups to send requests to a limited number of computers on the network. The multicast groups prevent most of the problems related to broadcast storms in IPv4.

| **IPv6 Interfaces May Have Multiple Addresses**

A single interface may be assigned multiple IPv6 addresses of any type (unicast, anycast, and multicast).

Every IPv6-enabled interface must contain at least one loopback (::1/128) and one link-local address. Optionally, an interface may have multiple unique local and global addresses.

Interface Identifiers in IPv6 Addresses

In IPv6, a link is a network medium over which network nodes communicate using the link layer. Interface identifiers (IDs) in IPv6 addresses are used to identify a unique interface on a link. They may also be thought of as the "host portion" of an IPv6 address. Interface IDs are required to be unique on a link, and may also be unique over a broader scope. When the interface identifier is derived directly from the data link layer address of the interface, the scope of that identifier is assumed to be universal (global).

Interface identifiers are always 64 bits and are dynamically created based on Layer 2 media and encapsulation.

IPv6 is defined on most of the current data link layers, including those shown in Table 10-1.

Table 10-1   *Data-Link Layers Supported by IPv6*

Ethernet[1]
Point-to-Point Protocol (PPP)[1]
High-Level Data Link Control (HDLC)[1]
Fiber Distributed Data Interface (FDDI)
Token Ring
Attached Resource Computer Network (ARCNET)
Nonbroadcast multiaccess (NBMA)
Asynchronous Transfer Mode (ATM)[2]
Frame Relay[3]
IEEE 1394[4]

[1]Data-link layers supported by Cisco.
[2]Cisco supports only ATM permanent virtual circuit (PVC) and ATM LAN Emulation (LANE).
[3]Cisco supports only Frame Relay PVCs.
[4]A Standard for a High Performance Serial Bus, supporting data rates of up to 800 Mbps (in IEEE 1394b).

The data link layer defines how IPv6 interface identifiers are created and how neighbor discovery deals with data link layer address resolution. RFCs describe the behavior of IPv6 in each of these specific data link layers, but the Cisco IOS Software does not necessarily support all of them.

KEY POINT

Ethernet Interface Identifier

For Ethernet, the interface ID used is based on the Media Access Control (MAC) address of the interface and is in an extended universal identifier 64-bit (EUI-64) format. The EUI-64 format interface ID is derived from the 48-bit link-layer MAC address by inserting the hexadecimal number FFFE between the upper three bytes (the organizationally unique identifier [OUI] field) and the lower 3 bytes (the vendor code or serial number field) of the link-layer address. The seventh bit in the high-order byte is set to 1 (equivalent to the IEEE G/L bit) to indicate the uniqueness of the 48-bit address.

This process is illustrated in Figure 10-5.

Figure 10-5 *EUI-64 Format IPv6 Interface Identifier*

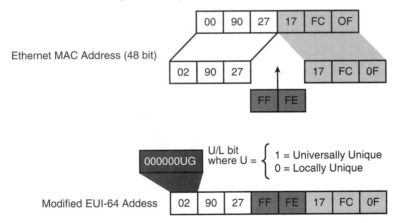

The seventh bit in an IPv6 interface identifier is referred to as the Universal/Local (U/L) bit. This bit identifies whether this interface identifier is locally unique on the link or whether it is universally unique. When the interface identifier is created from an Ethernet MAC address, it is assumed that the MAC address is universally unique and, therefore, that the interface identifier is universally unique. The purpose of the U/L bit is for future use by upper-layer protocols to uniquely identify a connection, even in the context of a change in the leftmost part of the address. However, this feature is not yet used.

The eighth bit in an IPv6 interface identifier, also known as the "G" bit, is the group/individual bit for managing groups.

Because of privacy and security concerns, hosts may create a random interface identifier using the MAC address as a base. This is considered a privacy extension because, without it, creating an interface identifier from a MAC address allows activity to be tracked to the point of connection. Microsoft Windows XP is currently the only known implementation of this capability and prefers to use this address for outgoing communication because the address has a short lifetime and will be regenerated periodically. This process is defined in RFC 3041, *Privacy Extensions for Stateless Address Autoconfiguration in IPv6*.

IPv6 Global Unicast Addresses

The IPv6 addressing architecture is defined in RFC 4291.

KEY POINT

> **IPv6 Global Aggregatable Unicast Address**
>
> The IPv6 global aggregatable unicast address, also known as the IPv6 global unicast address, is the equivalent of the IPv4 global unicast address.

A global unicast address is an IPv6 address from the global unicast prefix. The structure of global unicast addresses enables aggregation of routing prefixes so that the number of routing table entries in the global routing table can be reduced. Global unicast addresses used on links are aggregated upward through organizations and eventually to the ISPs, as illustrated in Figure 10-6. This provides for more efficient and scalable routing within the Internet, and improved bandwidth and functionality for user traffic.

Figure 10-6 *IPv6's Larger Address Space Enables Address Aggregation*

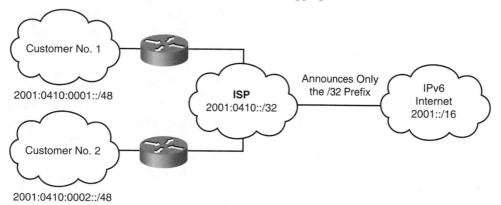

The global unicast address typically consists of a 48-bit global routing prefix, a 16-bit subnet ID, and a 64-bit interface ID (typically in EUI-64 bit format), as illustrated in the example in Figure 10-7.

The subnet ID can be used by individual organizations to identify subnets and create their own local addressing hierarchy. This field allows an organization to use up to 65,536 individual subnets.

Figure 10-7   *Example of an IPv6 Global Unicast Address*

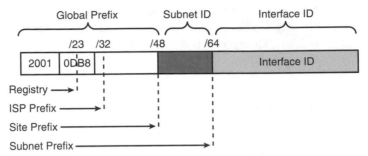

Addresses with a prefix of 2000::/3 [binary 001] through E000::/3 [binary 111], excluding the FF00::/8 [binary 1111 1111] multicast addresses, are required to have 64-bit interface identifiers in the EUI-64 format.

The current global unicast address assignment by the Internet Assigned Numbers Authority (IANA) uses the range of addresses that start with binary value 001 (2000::/3). This is one-eighth of the total IPv6 address space and is the largest block of assigned addresses.

The IANA is allocating the IPv6 address space in the ranges of 2001::/16 to the registries.

In the now obsoleted RFC 2374, *An IPv6 Aggregatable Global Unicast Address Format*, the global routing prefix included two other hierarchically structured fields called Top-Level Aggregator and Next-Level Aggregator. Because these fields were policy based, the IETF decided to remove the fields from the RFCs. However, some existing IPv6 networks deployed in the early days might still be using networks based on the older architecture. (RFC 2374 has now been replaced by RFC 3587, *IPv6 Aggregatable Global Unicast Address Format*.)

IPv6 Link-Local Unicast Addresses

Link-local addresses have a scope limited to the local link and are dynamically created on all IPv6 interfaces by using a specific link-local prefix FE80::/10 and a 64-bit interface identifier, as shown in Figure 10-8. Link-local addresses are used for automatic address configuration, neighbor discovery, router discovery, and by many routing protocols.

Figure 10-8   *IPv6 Link-Local Address Structure*

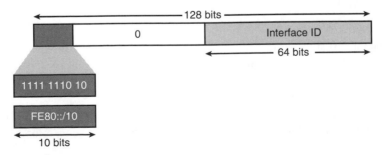

KEY
POINT | **Link-Local Unicast Addresses**

A link-local unicast address can serve as a method to connect devices on the same local network without requiring global addresses.

When communicating with a link-local address, the outgoing interface must be specified because every interface is connected to FE80::/10.

IPv6 Anycast Addresses

An IPv6 anycast address is a global unicast address that is assigned to more than one interface; the format is illustrated in Figure 10-9. For IPv6, anycast is defined as a way to send a packet to the nearest (or closest) interface that is a member of the anycast group, thus providing a discovery mechanism to the nearest point.

Figure 10-9 *IPv6 Anycast Address Structure*

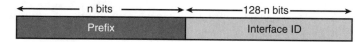

A sender creates a packet with an anycast address as the destination address and forwards the packet to its nearest router. The router routes the packet to the nearest anycast interface—the closest device or interface that shares that address. In a WAN scope, the nearest interface is found according to the measure of the metric of the routing protocol. In a LAN scope, the nearest interface is found according to the first neighbor that is learned about.

Anycast addresses are allocated from the unicast address space and have the same format as unicast addresses, so they are indistinguishable from unicast addresses. To devices that are not configured for anycast, these addresses appear as unicast addresses. When a unicast address is assigned to more than one interface—thus turning it into an anycast address—the nodes to which the address is assigned must be explicitly configured to use and know that the address is an anycast address.

The idea of anycast in IP was proposed in 1993; however, there is little experience with widespread anycast usage to date. Only a few anycast addresses are currently assigned, including the router-subnet anycast and the Mobile IPv6 home agent anycast.

A source can use anycast addresses to control the paths across which traffic flows. An example of anycast use in a Border Gateway Protocol (BGP) multihomed network is when a customer has multiple ISPs and multiple connections to each one. The customer can configure a different anycast address for each ISP, and configure the same anycast address for each router of a given ISP. The source device can choose which ISP to send the packet to; however, the routers along the path determine the closest router by which that ISP can be reached using the IPv6 anycast address.

Another use for an anycast address is when multiple routers are attached to a LAN. These routers can have the same IPv6 anycast address so that distant devices only need to identify the anycast address; intermediate devices choose the best path to reach the closest entry point to that LAN.

IPv6 Multicast Addresses

As described in Chapter 9, "Implementing IP Multicast," a multicast address identifies a group of interfaces; traffic sent to a multicast address travels to multiple destinations at the same time. An interface may belong to any number of multicast groups. Multicasting is extremely important to IPv6, because it is at the core of many IPv6 functions and it is a replacement for broadcast.

The format of an IPv6 multicast address is illustrated in Figure 10-10. IPv6 multicast addresses are defined by the prefix FF00::/8. The second octet of the address defines the lifetime (flag) and the scope of the multicast address, as follows:

- The flag parameter is equal to 0 for a permanent, or well-known, multicast address. The flag is equal to 1 for a temporary multicast address.

- The scope parameter is equal to 1 for the interface scope (loopback transmission), 2 for the link scope (similar to unicast link-local scope), 3 for the subnet-local scope where subnets may span multiple links, 4 for the admin-local scope (administratively configured), 5 for the site-local scope, 8 for the organizational scope (multiple sites), and E for the global scope.

Figure 10-10 *IPv6 Multicast Address Structure*

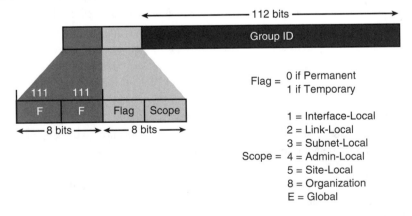

For example, a multicast address starting with FF02::/16 is a permanent multicast address with a link-local scope. There is no TTL field in IPv6 multicast packets because the scoping is defined inside the address.

The multicast group ID consists of the lower 112 bits of the multicast address.

The multicast addresses FF00:: to FF0F:: have the flag set to 0 and are reserved. Within that range, the following are some example assigned addresses (there are many more assignments made; assignments are tracked by IANA):

- **FF02::1**—"All nodes" on a link (link-local scope)

- **FF02::2**—"All routers" on a link

- **FF02::9**—"All routing information protocol (RIP) routers" on a link

- **FF02::1:FFXX:XXXX**—Solicited-node multicast on a link, where the XX:XXXX is the rightmost 24 bits of the corresponding unicast or anycast address of the node. Neighbor solicitation messages are sent on a local link when a node wants to determine the link-layer address of another node on the same local link, similar to the Address Resolution Protocol (ARP) in IPv4; this process is illustrated in the example following these bullets.

- **FF05::101**—"All Network Time Protocol (NTP) servers" in the site (site-local scope). (The site-local multicast scope has an administratively assigned radius and has no direct correlation to the now deprecated site-local unicast prefix of FEC0::/10.)

Solicited-node multicast addresses are used in IPv6 for address resolution of an IPv6 address to a MAC address on a LAN segment. In very rare cases, the rightmost 24 bits of the unicast address of the target will not be unique on a link, but this will not cause a problem, as illustrated by an example using the devices in Figure 10-11:

- Node A has IPv6 address 2001:DB8:200:300:400:500:1234:5678.

- Node B has IPv6 address 2001:DB8:200:300:400:500:AAAA:BBBB, and would therefore have solicited-node multicast address FF02:0:0:0:0:1:FFAA:BBBB, which can also be written as FF02::1:FFAA:BBBB.

- Node C has IPv6 address 2001:DB8:200:300:400:501:AAAA:BBBB, and would therefore have solicited-node multicast address FF02::1:FFAA:BBBB. Note that this is the same as node B's solicited-node multicast address.

Figure 10-11 *Network for IPv6 Solicited Node Multicast Address Example*

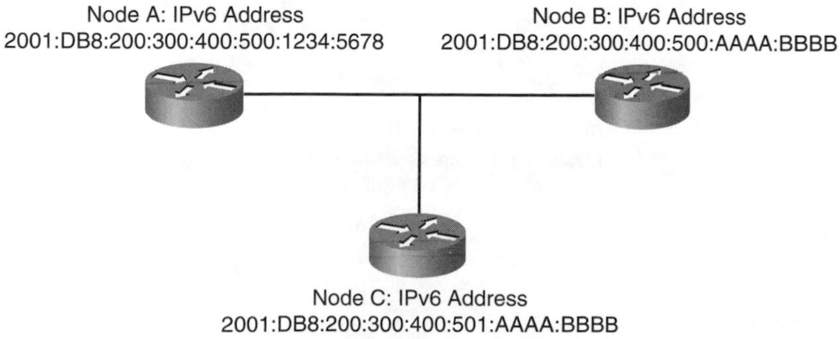

Node A: IPv6 Address
2001:DB8:200:300:400:500:1234:5678

Node B: IPv6 Address
2001:DB8:200:300:400:500:AAAA:BBBB

Node C: IPv6 Address
2001:DB8:200:300:400:501:AAAA:BBBB

When Node A desires to exchange packets with Node B, Node A sends a neighbor discovery (solicitation) packet to the solicited-node multicast address of B, FF02::1:FFAA:BBBB. The packet contains, in addition to other data, the full IPv6 address that Node A is looking for, 2001:DB8:200:300:400:500:AAAA:BBBB; this is called the target address.

Both node B and node C are listening to the same solicited-node multicast address, so they both receive and process the packet. Node B sees that the target address inside the packet is its own and responds with a neighbor advertisement that includes its MAC address. Meanwhile, Node C sees that the target address inside the packet is not its own and does not respond.

In this manner, nodes can have the same solicited-node multicast address on-link, but not cause neighbor discovery or solicitation process to malfunction.

Stateless Autoconfiguration

KEY POINT

> **Stateless Autoconfiguration**
>
> A router on a local link can send (either periodically or upon a host's request) network information, such as the 64-bit prefix of the local link network and the default route, to all the nodes on the local link. Hosts can autoconfigure themselves by appending their IPv6 interface identifier (in EUI-64 format) to the local link 64-bit prefix.

This process is illustrated in Figures 10-12, 10-13, and 10-14, and results in a full 128-bit address that is usable and guaranteed to be globally unique.

Figure 10-12 *A PC Solicits a Router for Network Information*

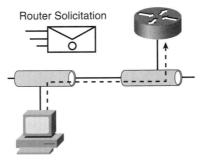

Router Solicitation

Source address = ::
Destination address = FF02::2, the
all routers multicast address

Figure 10-13 *A Router Advertises Network Information*

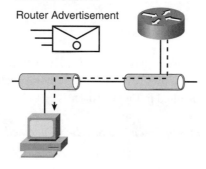

Source address = Router's link-local address
Destination address = FF02::1, the all nodes
multicast address

Router Advertisement

Figure 10-14 *A PC Configures Itself Based on the Router Advertisement*

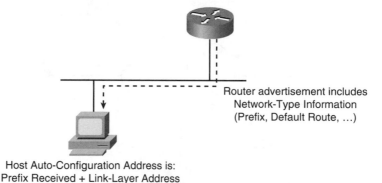

Router advertisement includes
Network-Type Information
(Prefix, Default Route, ...)

Host Auto-Configuration Address is:
Prefix Received + Link-Layer Address

In Figure 10-12, a PC sends a router solicitation, with a source address of :: and a destination address of FF02::2, the all routers multicast address, to request a prefix for stateless autoconfiguration. In Figure 10-13, the router replies with a router advertisement, with a source address of the router's link-local address and a destination address of FF02::1, the all nodes multicast address. In Figure 10-14, the PC configures itself. A process called duplicate address detection (DAD) detects and avoids duplicate addresses.

Stateless autoconfiguration allows devices to "plug-and-play," to connect themselves to the network without any configuration and without any servers (such as DHCP servers). This key IPv6 feature enables deployment of new devices on the IPv6 Internet, such as cellular phones, wireless devices, home appliances, and home networks.

DHCP Version 6 (DHCPv6), an updated version of DHCP for IPv4, can also be used to provide IPv6 addresses to devices. Stateless DHCPv6 is a concept (introduced in February 2004) that strikes a middle ground between stateless autoconfiguration and the thick-client approach of the stateful DHCPv6. Stateless DHCPv6 is also called DHCP-lite. For more details of stateless DHCPv6, refer to RFC 3736, *Stateless Dynamic Host Configuration Protocol (DHCP) Service for IPv6.*

IPv6 Mobility

Mobility is a very important feature in networks today. The Mobile IPv6 protocol, defined in RFC 3775, *Mobility Support in IPv6,* allows IPv6 nodes to remain reachable while they are moving about the IPv6 Internet, as illustrated in Figure 10-15.

Figure 10-15 *IPv6 Mobility Allows Nodes to Roam and Still Be Connected*

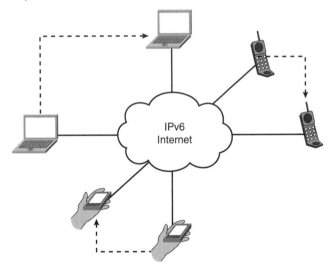

KEY POINT

IPv6 Mobility Ensures Mobile Nodes Remain Connected

Each IPv6 mobile node is always identified by its *home address*, regardless of where it is. When it is away from its home, a mobile node is also associated with a *care-of address*, which provides information about the mobile node's current location. IPv6 packets addressed to a mobile node's home address are transparently routed to its care-of address. All IPv6 nodes, whether mobile or stationary, can communicate with mobile nodes.

In IPv6, mobility is built in, which means that any IPv6 node can use it as needed. In IPv4, however, mobility is a new function that must be added as nodes require it.

IPv6's routing headers make Mobile IPv6 much more efficient for end nodes than Mobile IPv4; a new "mobility" extension header has been created. Mobility takes advantage of IPv6's flexibility. For example, the binding of the home address of a mobile node with a care-of address for that mobile node uses the destination options header, support of which is mandatory for every IPv6 device.

IPv6 mobility is different from IPv4 mobility in several ways, including the following:

- The IPv6 address space enables Mobile IPv6 deployment in any environment.

- Because of the vast IPv6 address space, foreign agents (routers on the networks other than the node's home network) are no longer required.

- The network infrastructure does not need to be upgraded to allow Mobile IPv6 nodes. The care-of address can be a global IPv6 routable address for all mobile nodes.

- The Mobile IPv6 model takes advantage of some of the benefits of the IPv6 protocol itself. Examples include option headers, neighbor discovery, and autoconfiguration.

- In many cases, triangle routing is eliminated, because Mobile IPv6 route optimization allows mobile nodes to communicate directly with other nodes. Support for route optimization is a fundamental part of the protocol, rather than a nonstandard set of extensions. Support is also integrated into Mobile IPv6 for allowing route optimization to coexist efficiently with routers that perform ingress filtering. Mobile IPv6 route optimization can operate securely even without prearranged security associations. It is expected that route optimization can be deployed on a global scale between all mobile nodes and correspondent nodes.

- Mobile nodes work transparently even with other nodes that do not support mobility (as is done in IPv4 mobility).

- The dynamic home agent address discovery mechanism in Mobile IPv6 returns a single reply to the mobile node. The directed broadcast approach used in IPv4 returns separate replies from each home agent.

- Most packets sent to a mobile node while it is away from home in Mobile IPv6 are sent using an IPv6 routing header rather than IP encapsulation, reducing the amount of overhead compared to Mobile IPv4.

IPv6 Configuration and Using OSPF and Other Routing Protocols for IPv6

This section describes the routing protocols available for IPv6, and focuses on the concepts and tasks needed to implement OSPF for IPv6. Enabling IPv6 and configuring IPv6 addresses are also covered in this section.

IPv6 Routing Protocols

IPv6 uses the same "longest-prefix match" routing that IPv4 classless interdomain routing (CIDR) uses. Updates to the existing IPv4 routing protocols were necessary for handling the longer IPv6 addresses and different header structures. Currently, the following updated routing protocols are available:

- Static routes

- RIP new generation (RIPng) (defined in RFC 2080, *RIPng for IPv6*)

- OSPF Version 3 (OSPFv3) (defined in RFC 2740, *OSPF for IPv6*)

- Intermediate System-Intermediate System (IS-IS) for IPv6

- Enhanced Interior Gateway Routing Protocol (EIGRP) for IPv6

- Multiprotocol Border Gateway Protocol Version 4 (MP-BGP4) (defined in RFC 2545, *Use of BGP-4 Multiprotocol Extensions for IPv6 Inter-Domain Routing,* and RFC 2858, *Multiprotocol Extensions for BGP-4*)

These protocols are described in the following sections.

<table>
<tr><td>**KEY POINT**</td><td>**Enabling IPv6 Routing**

The Cisco IOS **ipv6 unicast-routing** global configuration command for IPv6 enables IPv6 routing, and is required before any IPv6 routing protocol is configured.</td></tr>
</table>

Static Routing

Static routing in IPv6 is used and configured in the same way as in IPv4. There is an IPv6 specific requirement per RFC 2461, *Neighbor Discovery for IP Version 6 (IPv6)*, that a router must be able to determine the link-local address of each of its neighboring routers to ensure that the target address of a redirect message identifies the neighbor router by its link-local address. For static routing this requirement means that the next-hop router's address should be specified using the link-local address of the router, not a global unicast address.

IPv6 static routes can be configured with the **ipv6 route** *ipv6-prefix/prefix-length interface-type interface-number* [*administrative-distance*] global configuration command, similar to IPv4 static routes.

RIPng

Similar to IPv4's RIP, RIPng is a distance vector routing protocol with a metric limit of 15 hops that uses split-horizon and poison reverse to prevent routing loops. IPv6 features include the following:

- RIPng is based on IPv4 RIP Version 2 (RIPv2).

- RIPng uses IPv6 for transport.

- RIPng uses link-local addresses as source addresses.

- RIPng uses an IPv6 prefix and a next-hop IPv6 address.

- RIPng uses the multicast address FF02::9, the all RIP routers multicast address, as the destination address for RIP updates.

- RIPng updates are sent on UDP port 521.

OSPFv3

OSPFv3 is a new protocol implementation for IPv6. It uses the same mechanisms as OSPF Version 2 (OSPFv2), but is a major rewrite of the internals of the protocol.

OSPFv3 distributes (transports) IPv6 prefixes and runs directly over IPv6.

If both OSPFv2 and OSPFv3 are configured on a router, they run completely separate from each other and run a separate shortest path first (SPF) instance. In other words, the two protocols are like "ships in the night," passing without knowing of the other's existence.

OSPFv3 includes the following IPv6-specific features:

- Every OSPFv2 IPv4-specific semantic is removed.

- Uses 128-bit IPv6 addresses.

- Uses link-local addresses as source addresses.

- Multiple addresses and OSPF instances per interface are permitted.

- Supports authentication (using IPsec).

- Runs over a link rather than a subnet.

OSPF for IPv6 is currently an IETF proposed standard.

The configuration of OSPFv3 is described in the "OSPFv3 Configuration" section later in this chapter.

IS-IS for IPv6

The large address support in IS-IS facilitates the IPv6 address family. IS-IS for IPv6 is the same as IS-IS for IPv4, with the following extensions added:

- Two new Types, Lengths, Values (TLVs):

    — IPv6 reachability

    — IPv6 interface address

- A new protocol identifier

IS-IS for IPv6 is not yet an IETF standard.

EIGRP for IPv6

EIGRP for IPv6 is available in Cisco IOS Release 12.4(6)T and later. EIGRP for IPv4 and EIGRP for IPv6 are configured and managed separately; however, the configuration and operation of EIGRP for IPv4 and IPv6 is similar. For more information on this protocol, refer to "Implementing EIGRP for IPv6," available at http://www.cisco.com.

MP-BGP4

To make Border Gateway Protocol Version 4 (BGP-4) available for other network layer protocols, including Multiprotocol Label Switching (MPLS) and IPv6, RFC 2858 defines multiprotocol extensions for BGP-4. RFC 2545 defines how these extensions are used for IPv6.

NOTE   RFC 2858 replaces the now obsolete RFC 2283, also named *Multiprotocol Extensions for BGP-4.*

IPv6-specific extensions incorporated into MP-BGP4 include the following:

■ A new identifier for the IPv6 address family.

■ Scoped addresses: The NEXT_HOP attribute contains a global IPv6 address and potentially a link-local address (only when there is link-local reachability with the peer).

■ The NEXT_HOP and Network Layer Reachability Information (NLRI) attributes are expressed as IPv6 addresses and prefixes. (The NLRI field in a BGP update message lists the networks reachable on the BGP path described by the update message.)

OSPFv3 Compared to OSPFv2

Recall that OSPF is an IP link-state routing protocol. A link is an interface on a networking device, and a link-state protocol makes its routing decisions based on the states of the links that connect source and destination devices. The state of a link is a description of the interface and its relationship to its neighboring networking devices.

For OSPFv3, the interface information includes the IPv6 prefix of the interface, the network mask, the type of network it is connected to, the routers connected to the network, and so forth. This information is propagated in various types of link-state advertisements (LSAs). A router's collection of LSA data is stored in a link-state database (LSDB). The contents of the database, when subjected to Dijkstra's algorithm, result in the creation of the OSPF routing table.

Similarities Between OSPFv2 and OSPFv3

Although most of the algorithms of OSPFv2 are the same as those of OSPFv3, some changes have been made in OSPFv3, particularly to handle the increased address size in IPv6 and the fact that OSPFv3 runs directly over IPv6. The similarities between OSPFv3 and OSPFv2 include the following:

- OSPFv3 uses the same basic packet types as OSPFv2, as shown in Table 10-2: hello, database description (DBD) (also called database description packets [DDP]), link-state request (LSR), link-state update (LSU), and link-state acknowledgment (LSAck). Some of the fields within the packets have changed.

- The mechanisms for neighbor discovery and adjacency formation are identical.

- OSPFv3 operation over nonbroadcast multiaccess (NBMA) topologies is the same. The RFC-compliant nonbroadcast and point-to-multipoint modes are supported, and OSPFv3 also supports the Cisco modes such as point-to-point and broadcast.

- LSA flooding and aging are the same.

Table 10-2   *OSPFv3 Packet Types*

Packet Type	Description
1	Hello
2	DBD
3	LSR
4	LSU
5	LSAck

All of the optional capabilities of OSPF for IPv4, including on-demand circuit support, not-so-stubby areas (NSSAs), and the extensions to Multicast OSPF (MOSPF), are also supported in OSPF for IPv6.

Differences Between OSPFv2 and OSPFv3

Because OSPFv2 is heavily dependent on the IPv4 address for its operation, changes were necessary in the OSPFv3 protocol to support IPv6, as outlined in RFC 2740. Some of the notable changes include platform-independent implementation, protocol processing per-link rather than per-node, explicit support for multiple instances per link, and changes in authentication and packet format.

Like RIPng, OSPFv3 uses IPv6 for transport and uses link-local addresses as source address.

All OSPFv3 packets have a 16-byte header, in comparison to OSPFv2's 24-byte header. The two headers are illustrated in Figure 10-16.

Figure 10-16   *OSPFv2 and OSPFv3 Packet Headers*

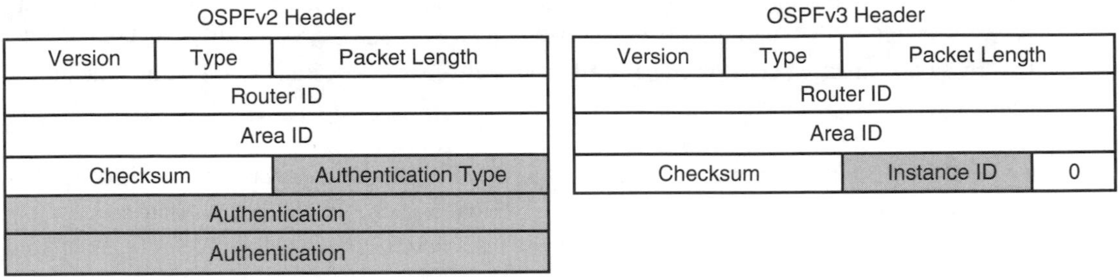

OSPFv2 Header		
Version	Type	Packet Length
Router ID		
Area ID		
Checksum		Authentication Type
Authentication		
Authentication		

OSPFv3 Header			
Version	Type	Packet Length	
Router ID			
Area ID			
Checksum		Instance ID	0

OSPFv2 does not define or allow for multiple instances per link, although similar functionality can be implemented by using other mechanisms such as subinterfaces. In contrast, OSPFv3 has explicit support for multiple instances per link through the instance ID field in the packet header. This feature allows separate autonomous systems, each running OSPF, to use a common link. A single link could belong to multiple areas. Two instances need to have the same instance ID to communicate with each other. By default, the instance ID is 0, and it is increased for any additional instances.

Authentication is no longer part of OSPF; it is now the job of IPv6 to make sure the right level of authentication is in use.

OSPFv2 is primarily concerned with the *subnet* on which it is operating, whereas OSPFv3 is concerned with the *links* to which the router is connected. As discussed, IPv6 uses the term *link* to indicate a communication facility or medium over which nodes can communicate at the link layer; OSPF interfaces connect to links instead of to IP subnets. Multiple IPv6 subnets can be assigned to a single link, and two nodes can talk directly over a single link, even if they do not share a common IPv6 subnet (IPv6 prefix). OSPF for IPv6 therefore runs per-link instead of the IPv4 behavior of per-IP-subnet, and the terms *network* and *subnet* are generally replaced by the term *link*. This change affects the receiving of OSPF protocol packets, and the contents of hello packets and network LSAs.

OSPFv3 uses IPv6 link-local addresses to identify the OSPFv3 adjacency neighbors.

The multicast addresses used by OSPFv3 are as follows:

■ **FF02::5**—This address represents all SPF routers on the link-local scope; it is equivalent to 224.0.0.5 in OSPFv2.

■ **FF02::6**—This address represents all designated routers (DRs) on the link-local scope; it is equivalent to 224.0.0.6 in OSPFv2.

Address semantics that were in OSPFv2 have been removed in OSPFv3, as follows:

- IPv6 addresses are not present in the OSPF packet header (rather they are part of payload information).

- Router LSAs and network LSAs do not carry IPv6 addresses.

- The router ID, area ID, and link-state ID remain at 32 bits and are written in an IPv4-address format (dotted decimal).

- The DR and backup designated router (BDR) are now identified by their router ID, not by their IP address.

For security, OSPFv3 uses IPv6 AH and ESP extension headers instead of the variety of mechanisms defined in OSPFv2.

OSPF LSA Types for IPv6

Table 10-3 shows the OSPFv3 LSAs. The link-state (LS) type field indicates the function performed by the LSA: The high-order three bits of the LS type indicate generic properties of the LSA, while the remaining bits, called the LSA function code, indicate the LSA's specific functions.

Table 10-3   *OSPFv3 LSAs*

Description	LSA Function Code	LS Type
Router-LSA	1	0x2001
Network-LSA	2	0x2002
Inter-Area-Prefix-LSA	3	0x2003
Inter-Area-Router-LSA	4	0x2004
Autonomous System-External-LSA	5	0x2005
Group-Membership-LSA	6	0x2006
Type-7-LSA	7	0x2007
Link-LSA	8	0x2008
Intra-Area-Prefix-LSA	9	0x2009

LSA characteristics include the following:

- An LSA contains a router ID, area ID, and link-state ID. Each of these IDs is 32 bits long; the IDs are not derived from an IPv4 or IPv6 address. (Note, however, that these IDs are written in an IPv4-address dotted decimal format.)

- Router LSAs and network LSAs contain only 32-bit IDs; they do not contain addresses.

- LSAs have flooding scopes that define a diameter to which they should be flooded, as follows:

    — Link-local (flood to all routers on the link)

    — Area (flood to all routers within an OSPF area)

    — Autonomous System (flood to all routers within the entire OSPF autonomous system)

- OSPFv3 supports the forwarding of unknown LSAs based on the flooding scope. This can be useful in an NSSA.

- OSPFv3 takes advantage of IPv6 multicasting, using FF02::5 for all OSPF routers and FF02::6 for the OSPF DR and BDR.

The two renamed LSAs in OSPFv3 are as follows:

- **Interarea prefix LSAs for area border routers (ABRs) (type 3)**—Type 3 LSAs advertise internal networks to routers in other areas (interarea routes). Type 3 LSAs may represent a single network or a set of networks summarized into one advertisement. Only ABRs generate type 3 LSAs. In OSPF for IPv6, addresses for these LSAs are expressed as *prefix, prefix length* instead of *address, mask*. The default route is expressed as a prefix with length 0.

- **Interarea router LSAs for Autonomous System Boundary Routers (ASBRs) (type 4)**— Type 4 LSAs advertise the location of an ASBR. Routers that are trying to reach an external network use these advertisements to determine the best path to the next hop. ASBRs generate type 4 LSAs.

The two new LSAs in OSPFv3 are as follows:

- **Link LSAs (type 8)**—Type 8 LSAs have link-local flooding scope and are never flooded beyond the link with which they are associated. Link LSAs provide the link-local address of the router to all other routers attached to the link, inform other routers attached to the link of a list of IPv6 prefixes to associate with the link, and allow the router to assert a collection of options bits to associate with the network LSA that will be originated for the link.

- **Intra-area prefix LSAs (type 9)**—A router can originate multiple intra-area prefix LSAs for each router or transit network, each with a unique link-state ID. The link-state ID for each intra-area prefix LSA describes its association to either the router LSA or the network LSA. The link-state ID also contains prefixes for stub and transit networks.

> **NOTE** The **show ipv6 ospf** [*process-id*] **database link** and **show ipv6 ospf** [*process-id*] **database prefix** commands display the new type 8 and type 9 LSAs.

An address prefix is represented by three fields: prefix length, prefix options, and address prefix. As discussed, in OSPFv3, addresses for these LSAs are expressed as *prefix, prefix length* instead of *address, mask*. Type 3 and type 9 LSAs carry all IPv6 prefix information, which, in IPv4, is included in router LSAs and network LSAs.

> **NOTE**   For more information on address prefixes, refer to RFC 2740, section 3.4.3.7, Intra-Area-Prefix-LSAs.

IPv6 Configuration

Before configuring OSPFv3, IPv6 must be enabled with the **ipv6 unicast-routing** global configuration command.

Use the **ipv6 cef** global configuration command to enable Cisco Express Forwarding (CEF) for IPv6 (CEFv6). CEFv6 is advanced, Layer 3 IP switching technology for the forwarding of IPv6 packets. When CEFv6 is enabled, network entries that are added, removed, or modified in the IPv6 Routing Information Base (RIB), as dictated by the routing protocol in use, are reflected in the Forwarding Information Bases (FIBs), and the IPv6 adjacency tables maintain Layer 2 next-hop addresses for all entries that are in each FIB.

Use the **ipv6 address** *address/prefix-length* [**eui-64**] interface configuration command to configure an IPv6 address for an interface and enable IPv6 processing on the interface. The **eui-64** parameter forces the router to complete the addresses' low-order 64-bits using an EUI-64 format interface ID.

OSPFv3 Configuration

When configuring and verifying OSPFv3 within the Cisco IOS, many interface and EXEC mode commands are similar to those for OSPFv2, with only the **ipv6** keyword added.

One difference between OSPFv2 and OSPFv3 configuration is the way that IPv6 networks that are part of the OSPFv3 network are identified. The **network area** command used in OSPFv2 is not used in OSPFv3. Rather, in OSPFv3, interfaces are directly configured to specify which IPv6 networks are part of the OSPFv3 network.

There is also a separate native IPv6 router mode under which OSPFv3 parameters are defined. To enable an OSPFv3 process on a router, use the **ipv6 router ospf** *process-id* global configuration command. The *process-id* parameter identifies a unique OSPFv3 process.

> **NOTE**   The **ipv6 router ospf** *process-id* global configuration command also places you in router configuration mode, which for OSPFv3 is identified by the Router(config-rtr)# prompt, not the Router(config-router)# prompt that is used by OSPFv2 and other IPv4 routing protocols.

A router ID must be configured, using the **router-id** *router-id* router configuration command. The *router-id* parameter can be any arbitrary 32-bit value, in an IPv4 address format (dotted decimal), but it must be unique on each router.

Use the **ipv6 ospf** *process-id* **area** *area-id* [**instance** *instance-id*] interface configuration command to enable OSPF for IPv6 on an interface. Table 10-4 explains the parameters of this command. In OSPF for IPv6, all addresses on an interface are included by default. There is no limit to the number of **ipv6 ospf area** commands you can use on the router.

Table 10-4 **ipv6 ospf area** *Command Description*

Parameter	Description
process-id	Used for internal identification. The process-id is locally assigned and can be any positive integer. This is the same number used when enabling the OSPF routing process.
area-id	Specifies the area that is to be associated with the OSPF interface.
instance-id	(Optional) Instance identifier. An OSPF instance (also known as an OSPF process) can be considered a logical router running OSPF in a physical router. Use the *instance-id* to control selection of other routers as neighboring routers; the router becomes neighbors only with routers that have the same instance ID.

The OSPF priority, used in DR election, can be changed using the **ipv6 ospf priority** *number-value* interface configuration command. The *number-value* can range from 0 to 255; the default is 1. The router with the higher router priority takes precedence in an election. If there is a tie, the router with the higher router ID takes precedence. A router with a router priority set to zero is ineligible to become the DR or BDR.

The OSPF cost of sending a packet on an interface can be specified using the **ipv6 ospf cost** *interface-cost* interface configuration command. The *interface-cost* can be a value in the range from 1 to 65535. The default cost is related to the bandwidth of the interface, the same as it is for OSPF for IPv4.

Example 10-1 illustrates a basic OSPFv3 configuration example.

Example 10-1 *Basic OSPFv3 Configuration*

```
ipv6 unicast-routing
!
ipv6 router ospf 1
 router-id 10.2.2.2
!
interface FastEthernet0/0
 ipv6 address 3FFE:FFFF:1::1/64
```

Example 10-1 *Basic OSPFv3 Configuration (Continued)*

```
ipv6 ospf 1 area 0
ipv6 ospf priority 20
ipv6 ospf cost 20
```

To consolidate and summarize routes at an area boundary use the **area** *area-id* **range** *ipv6-prefix/prefix-length* [**advertise** | **not-advertise**] [**cost** *cost*] IPv6 OSPF router configuration command. Table 10-5 explains the parameters of this command.

Table 10-5 **area range** *Command Description*

Parameter	Description
area-id	Identifies the area subject to route summarization.
ipv6-prefix/prefix-length	The IPv6 address and prefix length for the range of addresses in the summary route.
advertise	(Optional) Sets the address range status to advertise and generates a type 3 summary LSA.
not-advertise	(Optional) Sets the address range status to DoNotAdvertise. The type 3 summary LSA is suppressed, and the component networks remain hidden from other networks.
cost	(Optional) Metric or cost for this summary route, which is used during OSPF SPF calculation to determine the shortest paths to the destination. The value can be 0 to 16777215.

The cost of the summarized routes is the *highest* cost of the routes being summarized. For example, consider the following routes:

```
OI 2001:0DB8:0:0:7::/64 [110/20]
  via FE80::A8BB:CCFF:FE00:6F00, FastEthernet0/0
OI 2001:0DB8:0:0:8::/64 [110/100]
  via FE80::A8BB:CCFF:FE00:6F00, FastEthernet0/0
OI 2001:0DB8:0:0:9::/64 [110/20]
  via FE80::A8BB:CCFF:FE00:6F00, FastEthernet0/0
```

If they are summarized, they become one route, as follows:

```
OI 2001:0DB8::/48 [110/100]
  via FE80::A8BB:CCFF:FE00:6F00, FastEthernet0/0
```

Figure 10-17 shows an OSPF network of two routers and two areas, area 0 and area 1. The configuration of Router 1 is shown in Example 10-2, and the configuration of Router 2 is shown in Example 10-3. The interface-specific commands **ipv6 ospf 100 area 0** and **ipv6 ospf 100 area 1** create the "ipv6 router ospf 100" process dynamically. The **area 0 range 2001:410::/32** command in Router 1 summarizes area 0's routes to the 2001:410::/32 route.

Figure 10-17 *OSPFv3 Configuration Example*

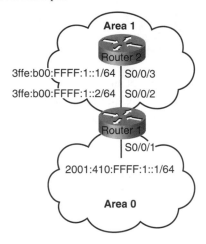

Example 10-2 *Configuration of Router 1 in Figure 10-17*

```
interface Serial0/0/1
 ipv6 address 2001:410:FFFF:1::1/64
 ipv6 ospf 100 area 0
!
interface Serial0/0/2
 ipv6 address 3FFE:B00:FFFF:1::2/64
 ipv6 ospf 100 area 1
!
ipv6 router ospf 100
 router-id 10.1.1.3
 area 0 range 2001:410::/32
```

Example 10-3 *Configuration of Router 2 in Figure 10-17*

```
interface Serial0/0/3
 ipv6 address 3FFE:B00:FFFF:1::1/64
 ipv6 ospf 100 area 1
!
ipv6 router ospf 100
 router-id 10.1.1.4
```

Verifying IPv6 and OSPFv3

This section explores some of the commands used to verify IPv6 and OSPFv3.

clear ipv6 ospf Command

The **clear ipv6 ospf** [*process-id*] {**process** | **force-spf** | **redistribution** | **counters** [**neighbor** [*neighbor-interface* | *neighbor-id*]]]} command triggers SPF recalculation and repopulation of the RIB.

show ipv6 route Command

The **show ipv6 route** [*ipv6-address* | *ipv6-prefix/prefix-length* | *protocol* | *interface-type interface-number*] command displays the IPv6 routing table, as illustrated in Example 10-4.

Example 10-4 **show ipv6 route** *Command Output*

```
Router1#show ipv6 route
IPv6 Routing Table - 8 entries
Codes: C - Connected, L - Local, S - Static, R - RIP, B - BGP
       U - Per-user Static route
       I1 - ISIS L1, I2 - ISIS L2, IA - ISIS interarea, IS - ISIS summary
       O - OSPF intra, OI - OSPF inter, OE1 - OSPF ext 1, OE2 - OSPF ext 2
       ON1 - OSPF NSSA ext 1, ON2 - OSPF NSSA ext 2
C    2001:410:1:1::/64 [0/0]
      via ::, FastEthernet0/0
L    2001:410:1:1:216:46FF:FE50:C470/128 [0/0]
      via ::, FastEthernet0/0
O    2001:410:1:2::/64 [110/782]
      via FE80::216:46FF:FE10:FC00, Serial0/0/1
C    2001:410:1:3::/64 [0/0]
      via ::, Serial0/0/1
L    2001:410:1:3:216:46FF:FE50:C470/128 [0/0]
      via ::, Serial0/0/1
O    2001:410:1:4::/64 [110/782]
      via FE80::216:46FF:FE10:FDB0, FastEthernet0/0
L    FE80::/10 [0/0]
      via ::, Null0
L    FF00::/8 [0/0]
      via ::, Null0
```

show ipv6 interface Command

The **show ipv6 interface** [**brief**] [*interface-type interface-number*] [**prefix**] command displays IPv6 information about an interface, as displayed in Example 10-5.

Example 10-5 **show ipv6 interface** *Command Output*

```
Router1#show ipv6 interface
FastEthernet0/0 is up, line protocol is up
  IPv6 is enabled, link-local address is FE80::216:46FF:FE50:C470
  No Virtual link-local address(es):
  Global unicast address(es):
    2001:410:1:1:216:46FF:FE50:C470, subnet is 2001:410:1:1::/64 [EUI]
  Joined group address(es):
    FF02::1
    FF02::2
    FF02::1:FF50:C470
```

continues

Example 10-5 **show ipv6 interface** *Command Output (Continued)*

```
   MTU is 1500 bytes
   ICMP error messages limited to one every 100 milliseconds
   ICMP redirects are enabled
   ICMP unreachables are sent
   ND DAD is enabled, number of DAD attempts: 1
   ND reachable time is 30000 milliseconds
   ND advertised reachable time is 0 milliseconds
   ND advertised retransmit interval is 0 milliseconds
   ND router advertisements are sent every 200 seconds
   ND router advertisements live for 1800 seconds
   ND advertised default router preference is Medium
   Hosts use stateless autoconfig for addresses.
Serial0/0/1 is up, line protocol is up
  IPv6 is enabled, link-local address is FE80::216:46FF:FE50:C470
  No Virtual link-local address(es):
  Global unicast address(es):
    2001:410:1:3:216:46FF:FE50:C470, subnet is 2001:410:1:3::/64 [EUI]
  Joined group address(es):
    FF02::1
    FF02::2
    FF02::1:FF50:C470
  MTU is 1500 bytes
  ICMP error messages limited to one every 100 milliseconds
  ICMP redirects are enabled
  ICMP unreachables are sent
  ND DAD is enabled, number of DAD attempts: 1
  ND reachable time is 30000 milliseconds
  Hosts use stateless autoconfig for addresses.
```

Example 10-6 illustrates an example of the output of this command with the **brief** parameter.

Example 10-6 **show ipv6 interface brief** *Command Output*

```
Router3#show ipv6 interface brief
FastEthernet0/0            [up/up]
    FE80::216:46FF:FE10:FC00
    2001:410:1:2:216:46FF:FE10:FC00
FastEthernet0/1            [administratively down/down]
    unassigned
Serial0/0/0                [administratively down/down]
    unassigned
Serial0/0/0.1              [administratively down/down]
    unassigned
Serial0/0/0.2              [administratively down/down]
    unassigned
```

Example 10-6   **show ipv6 interface brief** *Command Output (Continued)*

```
Serial0/0/1                    [up/up]
    FE80::216:46FF:FE10:FC00
    2001:410:1:3:216:46FF:FE10:FC00
Loopback0                      [up/up]
    unassigned
```

show ipv6 ospf interface Command

The **show ipv6 ospf** [*process-id*] [*area-id*] **interface** [*interface*] command displays OSPF for IPv6-related interface information, as displayed in Example 10-7.

Example 10-7   **show ipv6 ospf interface** *Command Output*

```
Router1#show ipv6 ospf interface s0/0/1
Serial0/0/1 is up, line protocol is up
  Link Local Address FE80::213:C3FF:FEDF:5658, Interface ID 7
  Area 0, Process ID 100, Instance ID 0, Router ID 10.200.200.11
  Network Type POINT_TO_POINT, Cost: 781
  Transmit Delay is 1 sec, State POINT_TO_POINT,
  Timer intervals configured, Hello 10, Dead 40, Wait 40, Retransmit 5
    Hello due in 00:00:05
  Index 1/2/2, flood queue length 0
  Next 0x0(0)/0x0(0)/0x0(0)
  Last flood scan length is 1, maximum is 4
  Last flood scan time is 0 msec, maximum is 0 msec
  Neighbor Count is 1, Adjacent neighbor count is 1
    Adjacent with neighbor 10.200.200.12
  Suppress hello for 0 neighbor(s)
```

show ipv6 ospf Command

The **show ipv6 ospf** [*process-id*] [*area-id*] command displays general information about the IPv6 OSPF processes. Example 10-8 illustrates example output from this command.

Example 10-8   **show ipv6 ospf** *Command Output*

```
Router7#show ipv6 ospf
Routing Process "ospfv3 1" with ID 172.16.3.3
It is an area border and autonomous system boundary router
Redistributing External Routes from, connected
SPF schedule delay 5 secs, Hold time between two SPFs 10 secs
Minimum LSA interval 5 secs. Minimum LSA arrival 1 secs
LSA group pacing timer 240 secs
Interface flood pacing timer 33 msecs
Retransmission pacing timer 33 msecs
```

continues

Example 10-8 **show ipv6 ospf** *Command Output (Continued)*

```
Number of external LSA 3. Checksum Sum 0x12B75
Number of areas in this router is 2. 1 normal 0 stub 1 nssa
    Area BACKBONE(0)
        Number of interfaces in this area is 1
        SPF algorithm executed 23 times
        Number of LSA 14. Checksum Sum 0x760AA
        Number of DCbitless LSA 0
        Number of Indication LSA 0
        Number of DoNotAge LSA 0
        Flood list length 0
    Area 2
        Number of interfaces in this area is 1
        It is a NSSA area
        Perform type-7/type-5 LSA translation
        SPF algorithm executed 17 times
        Number of LSA 25. Checksum Sum 0xE3BF0
        Number of DCbitless LSA 0
        Number of Indication LSA 0
        Number of DoNotAge LSA 0
        Flood list length 0
```

Table 10-6 provides a description of some of the fields in the output of the **show ipv6 ospf** command in Example 10-8.

Table 10-6 *Description of* **show ipv6 ospf** *Command Output in Example 10-8*

Field	Description
Routing process "ospfv3 1" with ID 172.16.3.3	Process ID and OSPF router ID
LSA group pacing timer	Configured LSA group pacing timer (in seconds)
Interface flood pacing timer	Configured LSA flood pacing timer (in milliseconds [ms])
Retransmission pacing timer	Configured LSA retransmission pacing timer (in ms)
Number of areas	Number of areas to which the router is attached

show ipv6 ospf neighbor Command

The **show ipv6 ospf neighbor** [**detail**] command provides information about IPv6 OSPF neighbors. With the **detail** parameter, detailed information about IPv6 OSPF neighbors is displayed, as illustrated in Example 10-9.

Example 10-9   **show ipv6 ospf neighbor detail** *Command Output*

```
Router1#show ipv6 ospf neighbor detail
 Neighbor 10.200.200.12
    In the area 0 via interface Serial0/0/1
    Neighbor: interface-id 7, link-local address FE80::217:95FF:FE42:C330
    Neighbor priority is 1, State is FULL, 6 state changes
    Options is 0x46EAC429
    Dead timer due in 00:00:33
    Neighbor is up for 00:31:57
    Index 1/1/1, retransmission queue length 0, number of retransmission 1
    First 0x0(0)/0x0(0)/0x0(0) Next 0x0(0)/0x0(0)/0x0(0)
    Last retransmission scan length is 1, maximum is 1
    Last retransmission scan time is 0 msec, maximum is 0 msec
```

Table 10-7 provides a description of some of the fields in the output of the **show ipv6 ospf neighbor detail** command in Example 10-9.

Table 10-7   *Description of* **show ipv6 ospf neighbor detail** *Command Output in Example 10-9*

Field	Description
Neighbor	Neighbor router ID
In the area	Area and interface through which the OSPF neighbor is known
Neighbor priority	OSPF priority of the neighbor
State	OSPF neighbor relationship state
State changes	Number of state changes since the neighbor relationship was established
Options	Hello packet options field contents (Possible values of the external bit [e-bit] are 0 and 2; 2 indicates that the area is not a stub, and 0 indicates that the area is a stub.)
Dead timer due in	Amount of time before the neighbor is declared dead
Neighbor is up for	Time, in hours:minutes:seconds, since the neighbor went into two-way state
Index	Neighbor location in the area-wide and autonomous system-wide retransmission queue
retransmission queue length	Number of elements in the retransmission queue
number of retransmission	Number of times update packets have been resent during flooding
First	Memory location of the flooding details
Next	Memory location of the flooding details

continues

Table 10-7 *Description of* **show ipv6 ospf neighbor detail** *Command Output in Example 10-9 (Continued)*

Field	Description
Last retransmission scan length	Number of LSAs in the last retransmission packet
maximum	Maximum number of LSAs sent in any retransmission packet
Last retransmission scan time	Time taken to build the last retransmission packet
maximum	Maximum time taken to build any retransmission packet

show ipv6 ospf database Command

The **show ipv6 ospf database** command displays the OSPF for IPv6 database, as illustrated in Example 10-10.

Example 10-10 **show ipv6 ospf database** *Command Output*

```
RouterA#show ipv6 ospf database

            OSPFv3 Router with ID (1.1.1.1) (Process ID 1)

            Router Link States (Area 0)

ADV Router      Age         Seq#          Fragment ID  Link count  Bits
1.1.1.1         485         0x80000005    0            1           B
3.3.3.3         485         0x80000002    0            1           None

            Net Link States (Area 0)

ADV Router      Age         Seq#          Link ID    Rtr count
1.1.1.1         494         0x80000001    4          2

            Inter Area Prefix Link States (Area 0)

ADV Router      Age         Seq#          Prefix
1.1.1.1         1360        0x80000001    3FEE:FFEF:1::/64

            Link (Type-8) Link States (Area 0)

ADV Router      Age         Seq#          Link ID    Interface
1.1.1.1         1504        0x80000001    4          Fa0/0
3.3.3.3         496         0x80000001    4          Fa0/0

            Intra Area Prefix Link States (Area 0)

ADV Router      Age         Seq#          Link ID    Ref-lstype   Ref-LSID
1.1.1.1         561         0x80000001    1004       0x2002       4
```

Example 10-10   **show ipv6 ospf database** *Command Output (Continued)*

```
                Router Link States (Area 1)

ADV Router      Age       Seq#        Fragment ID  Link count  Bits
1.1.1.1         1316      0x80000002  0            0           B

                Inter Area Prefix Link States (Area 1)

ADV Router      Age       Seq#        Prefix
1.1.1.1         1436      0x80000001  3FEE:FFFF:1::/64

                Link (Type-8) Link States (Area 1)

ADV Router      Age       Seq#        Link ID   Interface
1.1.1.1         1436      0x80000001  6         Se0/0/0

                Intra Area Prefix Link States (Area 1)

ADV Router      Age       Seq#        Link ID   Ref-lstype  Ref-LSID
1.1.1.1         1436      0x80000001  0         0x2001      0
```

Table 10-8 provides a description of some of the fields in the output of the **show ipv6 ospf database** command in Example 10-10.

Table 10-8   *Description of* **show ipv6 ospf database** *Command Output in Example 10-10*

Field	Description
ADV Router	Advertising router ID
Age	Link-state age
Seq#	Link-state sequence number (detects old or duplicate LSAs)
Link ID	Interface ID number
Ref-lstype	Referenced link-state type (as described in Table 10-3)

The **show ipv6 ospf database database-summary** command displays a summary of the OSPF for IPv6 database, as illustrated in Example 10-11.

Example 10-11   **show ipv6 ospf database database-summary** *Command Output*

```
RouterA#show ipv6 ospf database database-summary

            OSPFv3 Router with ID (1.1.1.1) (Process ID 1)

Area 0 database summary
```

continues

Example 10-11   **show ipv6 ospf database database-summary** *Command Output (Continued)*

```
    LSA Type            Count    Delete   Maxage
    Router              2        0        0
    Network             1        0        0
    Link                2        0        0
    Prefix              1        0        0
    Inter-area Prefix   1        0        0
    Inter-area Router   0        0        0
    Type-7 External     0        0        0
    Unknown             0        0        0
    Subtotal            7        0        0

Area 1 database summary
    LSA Type            Count    Delete   Maxage
    Router              1        0        0
    Network             0        0        0
    Link                1        0        0
    Prefix              1        0        0
    Inter-area Prefix   1        0        0
    Inter-area Router   0        0        0
    Type-7 External     0        0        0
    Unknown             0        0        0
    Subtotal            4        0        0

Process 1 database summary
    LSA Type            Count    Delete   Maxage
    Router              3        0        0
    Network             1        0        0
    Link                3        0        0
    Prefix              2        0        0
    Inter-area Prefix   2        0        0
    Inter-area Router   0        0        0
    Type-7 External     0        0        0
    Unknown             0        0        0
    Type-5 Ext          0        0        0
    Unknown AS          0        0        0
    Total               11       0        0
```

Transitioning IPv4 to IPv6

The successful market adoption of any new technology depends on its easy integration with the existing infrastructure without significant disruption of services. The Internet consists of hundreds of thousands of IPv4 networks and millions of IPv4 nodes. The challenge for IPv6 lies in making the integration of IPv4 and IPv6 nodes and the transition to IPv6 as transparent as possible to end users.

The transition from IPv4 to IPv6 does not require upgrades on all nodes at the same time; IPv4 and IPv6 will coexist for some time.

The two most common techniques to transition from IPv4 to IPv6 are dual stack and tunneling. Alternatively, mechanisms that allow communication between IPv4 and IPv6 nodes can be used. These techniques and mechanisms are described in the following sections.

Dual Stack

Dual stack is an integration method where a node has connectivity to both an IPv4 and IPv6 network; thus the node has two protocol stacks, as illustrated in Figure 10-18. The two stacks can be on the same interface or on multiple interfaces.

Figure 10-18 *Devices Can Be Dual-Stacked to Communicate with Both IPv4 and IPv6*

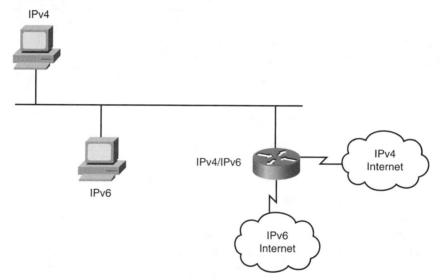

A dual-stack node chooses which stack to use based on destination address; the node should prefer IPv6 when available. The dual-stack approach to IPv6 integration will be one of the most commonly used methods. Old IPv4-only applications will continue to work as before, while new and modified applications take advantage of both IP layers.

A new application programming interface (API) supports both IPv4 and IPv6 addresses and Domain Name System (DNS) requests and replaces the "gethostbyname" and "gethostbyaddr" calls. A converted application will be able to make use of both IPv4 and IPv6. An application can be converted to the new API while still using only IPv4.

Past experience in porting IPv4 applications to IPv6 suggests that, for most applications, it is a minimal change in some localized places inside the source code. This technique is well-known and has been applied in the past for other protocol transitions, enabling gradual application upgrades one-by-one to IPv6.

Cisco IOS Software is IPv6-ready: As soon as IPv4 and IPv6 configurations are complete on an interface, the interface is dual-stacked and it forwards both IPv4 and IPv6 traffic.

As discussed earlier, using IPv6 on a Cisco IOS router requires that you use the **ipv6 unicast-routing** global configuration command to enable the forwarding of IPv6 datagrams. All interfaces that forward IPv6 traffic must have an IPv6 address, which is configured with the **ipv6 address** *address/prefix-length* [**eui-64**] interface configuration command. This command specifies the IPv6 network assigned to the interface and enables IPv6 processing on the interface.

Figure 10-19 illustrates an example of a router with both IPv4 and IPv6 addresses connected to a network that is running both protocols.

Figure 10-19 *When Both IPv4 and IPv6 Addresses Are Configured, the Interface Is Dual-Stacked*

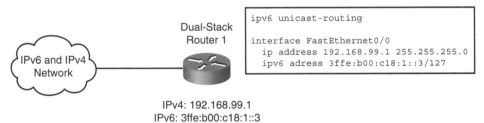

Tunneling

Tunnels are often used in networking to overlay incompatible functions over an existing network. For IPv6, tunneling is an integration method in which an IPv6 packet is encapsulated within another protocol, such as IPv4. Tunneling IPv6 inside of IPv4 uses IPv4 protocol 41. When tunneling IPv6 traffic over an IPv4 network, one edge router encapsulates the IPv6 packet inside an IPv4 packet and the router at the other edge decapsulates it, and vice versa. This enables the connection of IPv6 islands without the need to convert the intermediary network to IPv6.

As illustrated in Figure 10-20, a 20-byte IPv4 header (if there are not any options in the header) is included before the IPv6 header and payload (data). The routers involved are dual stacking.

Figure 10-20 *Tunneling IPv6 Inside IPv4 Packets*

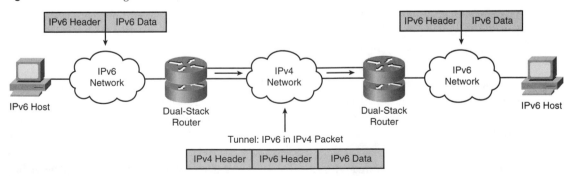

When tunneling, the MTU is effectively decreased by 20 octets (or more if the IPv4 header contains any optional fields). Because of this restriction and the fact that a tunneled network is often difficult to troubleshoot, tunneling is an intermediate integration/transition technique that should not be considered a final solution. A native IPv6 network should be the ultimate goal.

Tunneling can be done by edge routers either between hosts as shown in Figure 10-20, or between a host and a router, as shown in Figure 10-21. In Figure 10-21, an isolated dual-stack host uses an encapsulated tunnel to connect to the edge router of the IPv6 network.

Figure 10-21 *Isolated Dual-Stack Host*

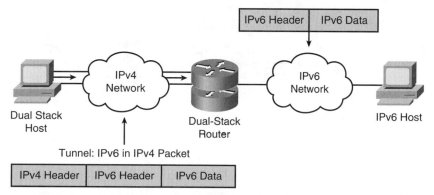

Note that tunneling will not work if an intermediary node between the two end points of the tunnel, such as a firewall, filters out IPv4 protocol 41, the IPv6 in IPv4 encapsulation protocol.

Configured tunnels require dual-stack end points and IPv4 and IPv6 addresses configured at each end, as illustrated in Figure 10-22.

Figure 10-22 *Tunneling Requires IPv6 and IPv4 Configured at Each End*

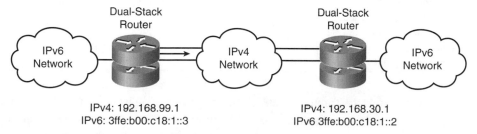

Tunnels can be either manually or automatically configured.

Manually Configured Tunnels

For a manually configured tunnel, you configure both the IPv4 and IPv6 addresses statically on the routers at each end of the tunnel.

The end routers must be dual-stacked, and the configuration will not change dynamically as network and routing needs change. IPv4 routing must be set up properly to forward a packet between the two IPv6 networks.

The interfaces used as tunnel end points can be unnumbered, but unnumbered interfaces make troubleshooting more difficult. The IPv4 practice of using unnumbered interfaces to save address space is no longer an issue.

Figure 10-23 shows two routers connecting IPv6 networks through IPv4 encapsulation. Example 10-12 and Example 10-13 provide the configurations for the two routers.

Figure 10-23 *Network Used to Illustrate Tunnel Configuration*

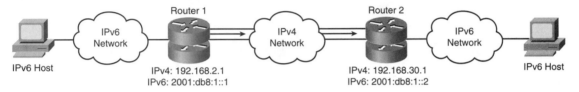

Example 10-12 *Configuration of Router 1 in Figure 10-23*

```
interface Tunnel0
 ipv6 address 2001:db8:1::1/64
 tunnel source 192.168.2.1
 tunnel destination 192.168.30.1
 tunnel mode ipv6ip
```

Example 10-13 *Configuration of Router 2 in Figure 10-23*

```
interface Tunnel0
 ipv6 address 2001:db8:1::2/64
 tunnel source 192.168.30.1
 tunnel destination 192.168.2.1
 tunnel mode ipv6ip
```

The command **interface Tunnel0** creates the tunnel interface, on which a static IPv6 address is configured with the **ipv6 address** command. The **tunnel source** and **tunnel destination** commands specify the IPv4 source and destination addresses of the tunnel, respectively. These are addresses in the underlying IPv4 network. The **tunnel mode ipv6ip** command specifies a manual IPv6 tunnel with IPv6 as the passenger protocol, and IPv4 as both the encapsulation and transport protocol.

The **clear counters tunnel** *interface-number* command clears the counters displayed in the **show interface tunnel** command.

Other Tunneling Mechanisms

Several automatic tunneling transition mechanisms exist, including the following:

- **6-to-4**—This mechanism uses the reserved prefix 2002::/16 to allow an IPv4-connected site to create and use a /48 IPv6 prefix based on a single globally routable/reachable IPv4 address. 6-to-4 tunneling is described further in the next section, "6-to-4 Tunneling."

- **Intra-Site Automatic Tunnel Addressing Protocol (ISATAP)**—ISATAP allows an IPv4 private intranet (that may or may not be using RFC 1918 addresses) to incrementally implement IPv6 nodes without upgrading the network.

- **Teredo (formerly known as shipworm)**—This mechanism tunnels IPv6 datagrams within IPv4 UDP datagrams, allowing private IPv4 address and IPv4 NAT traversal to be used.

6-to-4 Tunneling

The 6-to-4 tunneling method automatically connects IPv6 islands through an IPv4 network, as illustrated in Figure 10-24.

Figure 10-24 *6-to-4 Tunnels Are Built Automatically by the Edge Routers*

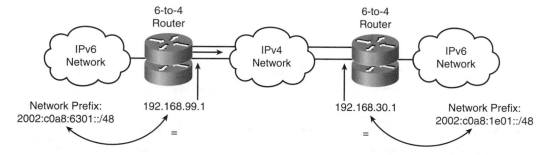

Each 6-to-4 edge router has an IPv6 address with a /48 prefix, which is the concatenation of 2002::/16 and the hexadecimal representation of the IPv4 address of the edge router; 2002::/16 is a specially assigned address range for the purpose of 6-to-4 tunneling. The edge routers automatically build the tunnel using the IPv4 addresses that are embedded in the IPv6 addresses. For example, if the IPv4 address of an edge router is 192.168.99.1, the prefix of its IPv6 address is 2002:c0a8:6301::/48, because 0xc0a86301 is the hexadecimal representation of 192.168.99.1.

6-to-4 tunnels enable the fast deployment of IPv6 in a corporate network without the need for addresses from ISPs or registries. The 6-to-4 tunneling method requires special code on the edge routers, but the IPv6 hosts and routers inside of the 6-to-4 site do not require new features.

When the edge router receives an IPv6 packet with a destination address in the range of 2002::/16, it determines from its routing table that the packet must traverse the tunnel. The router extracts the IPv4 address embedded in the third to sixth octets, inclusively, in the IPv6 next-hop address. This

IPv4 address is the IPv4 address of the 6-to-4 router at the destination site—the router at the other end of the tunnel. The router encapsulates the IPv6 packet in an IPv4 packet with the destination edge router's extracted IPv4 address.

The packet passes through the IPv4 network. The destination edge router decapsulates the IPv6 packet from the received IPv4 packet and forwards the IPv6 packet to its final destination. (A 6-to-4 relay router, which offers traffic forwarding to the IPv6 Internet, is required for reaching a native IPv6 Internet.)

Translation Mechanisms

Dual stack and tunneling techniques manage the interconnection of IPv6 domains. For legacy equipment that will not be upgraded to IPv6 and for some deployment scenarios, techniques are available for connecting IPv4-only nodes to IPv6-only nodes using translation, an extension of NAT techniques.

As shown in Figure 10-25, NAT-PT is a translation mechanism that sits between an IPv6 network and an IPv4 network. The job of the translator is to translate IPv6 packets into IPv4 packets and vice versa.

Figure 10-25 *IPv4 - IPv6 Translation Mechanism*

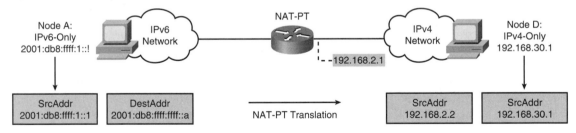

The Stateless IP/ICMP Translation (SIIT) algorithm translates the IP header fields, while NAT handles the IP address translation. Figure 10-25 shows static NAT-PT translations; NAT-PT translations may also be mapped dynamically based on DNS queries using a DNS-application layer gateway (DNS-ALG). ALGs use a dual-stack approach and enable a host in an IPv6-only domain to send data to another host in an IPv4-only domain. This method requires that all application servers run IPv6.

The example in Figure 10-25 illustrates the translation of an IPv6 datagram sent from node A to node D. From the perspective of node A, it is establishing a communication to another IPv6 node. One advantage of NAT-PT is that no modifications are required on IPv6 node A; all it needs to know is the IPv6 address mapping of the IPv4 address of node D. This mapping can be obtained dynamically from the DNS server. IPv4 node D can also send a datagram to node A by using the IPv4 address mapped to the IPv6 address of node A. Again, from the perspective of node D, it is establishing IPv4 communication with node A; node D does not require modification.

APIs can be installed in a host's TCP/IP stack to intercept IP traffic through the API and convert it for the IPv6 counterpart.

Bump-in-the-API (BIA) and Bump-in-the-Stack (BIS) are localized implementations of NAT-PT. They provide support for translation from upper layers that are IPv4-only down through the Open Systems Interconnection (OSI) layers. These implementations intercept either API calls or packets in the stack and translate them on the fly. Only IPv6 packets will travel out on the network. Not all applications will work with BIA or BIS solutions though. For example, file transfer protocol (FTP), which embeds IP addresses in the packet payload, would not work because the outer IP addresses and packets would be translated by BIA or BIS, but the embedded IPv6 addresses would not be translated when going back up the stack.

Summary

In this chapter, you learned the basics of IPv6; the following topics were presented:

- The need for IPv6's larger address space as IPv4 addresses are exhausted

- IPv6 packet structure, including the use of extension headers

- IPv6 address representation, including the three types of addresses: unicast, anycast, and multicast

- The EUI-64 format for representing interface identifiers

- How IPv6's stateless autoconfiguration feature works

- IPv6 support for IP mobility

- The routing protocols available for IPv6, including RIPng, OSPFv3, IS-IS for IPv6, EIGRP for IPv6, and MP-BGP4

- How to enable IPv6 and how to configure IPv6 interface addresses

- The features of and how to configure and verify OSPF for IPv6

- The mechanisms available for the transition from IPv4 to IPv6, including dual stack, tunneling, and translation

References

For additional information, refer to the following resources:

- The Cisco IOS IPv6 Configuration Guide, Release 12.4, available at http://www.cisco.com/en/US/products/ps6350/products_configuration_guide_book09186a0080435e8c.html

- IPv6 Multicast at-a-glance, available at http://www.cisco.com/application/pdf/en/us/guest/tech/tk872/c1482/cdccont_0900aecd80260049.pdf

Configuration Exercise 10-1: Configuring IPv6 Addresses and OSPF for IPv6 Routing

In this Configuration Exercise, you enable IPv6 routing globally, configure IPv6 addresses on your pod routers, and enable IPv6 OSPF routing.

Introduction to the Configuration Exercises

This book uses Configuration Exercises to help you practice configuring routers with the commands and topics presented. If you have access to real hardware, you can try these exercises on your routers. See Appendix B, "Configuration Exercise Equipment Requirements and Backbone Configurations," for a list of recommended equipment and initial configuration commands for the backbone routers. However, even if you do not have access to any routers, you can go through the exercises, and keep a log of your own running configurations, or just read through the solution. Commands used and solutions to the Configuration Exercises are provided within the exercises.

In the Configuration Exercises, the network is assumed to consist of two pods, each with four routers. The pods are interconnected to a backbone. You configure pod 1. No interaction between the two pods is required, but you might see some routes from the other pod in your routing tables in some exercises if you have it configured. In most of the exercises, the backbone has only one router; in some cases, another router is added to the backbone. Each Configuration Exercise assumes that you have completed the previous chapters' Configuration Exercises on your pod.

NOTE   Throughout this exercise, the pod number is referred to as x, and the router number is referred to as y. Substitute the appropriate numbers as needed.

Objectives

The objectives of this exercise are to enable IPv6 globally and on an interface, and to enable IPv6 OSPF routing.

Visual Objective

Figure 10-26 illustrates the topology used in this exercise. The format for the IPv6 addresses used in this exercise is 2001:0410:000x:z::/64 eui-64, where

- x = pod number

- z = 1 for the FastEthernet 0/0 interfaces between PxR1 and PxR3

- z = 2 for the FastEthernet 0/0 interfaces between PxR2 and PxR4

- z = 3 for the Serial 0/0/1 interfaces between PxR1 and PxR2

- z = 4 for the Serial 0/0/0 interfaces between PxR3 and PxR4

The IPv4 addresses remain in place.

Figure 10-26   *IPv6 Addressing Configuration Exercise Topology*

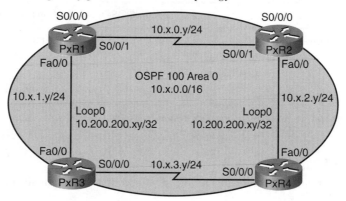

Command List

In this exercise, you use the commands in Table 10-9, listed in logical order. Refer to this list if you need configuration command assistance during the exercise.

> **CAUTION**   Although the command syntax is shown in this table, the addresses shown are typically for the P*x*R1 and P*x*R3 routers. Be careful when addressing your routers! Refer to the exercise instructions and the appropriate visual objective diagram for addressing details.

Table 10-9   *IPv6 Addressing Configuration Exercise Commands*

Command	Description
(config)#**ipv6 unicast-routing**	Enables IPv6 traffic forwarding.
(config)#**ipv6 cef**	Enables CEFv6.
(config-if)# **ipv6 address 2001:0410:000***x***:***z***::/64 eui-64**	Enables an IPv6 address on an interface (with the format specified earlier in this exercise) and forces the router to complete the addresses' low-order 64-bit by using the interface's link-layer address (MAC address) in EUI-64 format.
#show ipv6 interface	Displays IPv6 information about an interface.
(config)#**ipv6 router ospf 100**	Enables the OSPFv3 process 100 on the router.
(config-rtr)#**router-id 10.200.200.***xy*	Defines the OSPF router-id.
(config-if)#**ipv6 ospf 100 area 0**	Identifies the IPv6 prefix assigned to this interface as part of the OSPFv3 network for process-id 100 in area 0.

continues

Table 10-9 *IPv6 Addressing Configuration Exercise Commands (Continued)*

Command	Description
#show ipv6 ospf interface	Displays IPv6 OSPF information about an interface.
#show ipv6 ospf neighbor	Displays IPv6 OSPF neighbor information.
#show ipv6 route	Displays the IPv6 routing table.
#show cdp neighbor detail	Displays detailed CDP neighbor information.
#show ipv6 interface brief	Displays a brief list of IPv6 interface information.

Task 1: Cleaning Up

In this task, you remove the multicast routing configuration and isolate the pod from the backbone routers.

Follow these steps:

Step 1 Remove the multicast configuration from all the pod routers using the **no ip multicast-routing** global configuration command. Remove the multicast configuration from all interfaces it was enabled on using the **no ip pim sparse-dense-mode** command.

Step 2 On PxR1, remove the auto-rp configuration with the **no ip pim send-rp-announce loopback0 scope 3** command and the **no ip pim send-rp-discovery loopback0 scope 3** command.

Step 3 On the FastEthernet 0/0 interface on PxR4, disable join messages with the **no ip igmp join-group 224.x.x.x** command, where *x* is your pod number.

Step 4 On the edge routers, shut down Serial 0/0/0; IPv6 will not be used to the core.

Solution:

The following shows how to do the required steps on the P1R1 and P1R4 routers:

```
P1R1(config)#no ip multicast-routing
P1R1(config)#int loopback0
P1R1(config-if)#no ip pim sparse-dense-mode
P1R1(config-if)#int fa0/0
P1R1(config-if)#no ip pim sparse-dense-mode
P1R1(config-if)#int s0/0/0.1
P1R1(config-subif)#no ip pim sparse-dense-mode
P1R1(config-subif)#int s0/0/1
P1R1(config-if)#no ip pim sparse-dense-mode
```

```
P1R1(config-if)#exit
P1R1(config)#no ip pim send-rp-announce Loopback0 scope 3
P1R1(config)#no ip pim send-rp-discovery Loopback0 scope 3
P1R1(config)#int s0/0/0
P1R1(config-if)#shutdown

P1R4(config)#no ip multicast-routing
P1R4(config)#int loopback0
P1R4(config-if)#no ip pim sparse-dense-mode
P1R4(config-if)#int fa0/0
P1R4(config-if)#no ip pim sparse-dense-mode
P1R4(config-if)#int s0/0/0
P1R4(config-if)#no ip pim sparse-dense-mode
P1R4(config-if)#int fa0/0
P1R4(config-if)#no ip igmp join-group 224.1.1.1
```

Task 2: Configuring IPv6

In this task, you enable IPv6 globally on your router and configure IPv6 addresses on all interfaces that are not shut down.

In this task, the FastEthernet interfaces will use the following address format: 2001:0410:000x:1::/ 64 eui-64 or 2001:0410:000x:2::/64 eui-64, where

■   x = pod number

■   :1 is for odd router numbers (PxR1 and PxR3)

■   :2 is for even router numbers (PxR2 and PxR4)

For example, on P1R4, the Fa0/0 IPv6 address would be: 2001:0410:0001:2::/64. The :1 or :2 is the subnet portion of your IPv6 address, so it is important, for example, that PxR1 and PxR3's Fa0/ 0 interfaces are in the same subnet.

The Serial 0/0/1 interfaces for the *edge* routers and the Serial 0/0/0 for the *internal* routers will use the following address format: 2001:0410:000x:3::/64 eui-64 or 2001:0410:000x:4::/64 eui-64, where

■   x = pod number

■   :3 is for the edge routers (PxR1 and PxR2)

■   :4 is for the internal routers (PxR3 and PxR4)

For example, on P1R1, the S0/0/1 IPv6 address would be: 2001:0410:0001:3::/64. The :3 or :4 is the subnet portion of your IPv6 address on the serial interface.

Write down the IPv6 addresses for each of your routers in Table 10-10.

Table 10-10 *IPv6 Addresses*

Router	Fa0/0 Address	S0/0/0 or S0/0/1 Address
PxR1		
PxR2		
PxR3		
PxR4		

Follow these steps:

Step 1   Configure the edge and internal routers as follows:

- Enable IPv6 and CEFv6 on all routers in each pod.

- Configure an IPv6 global address on all Fa0/0 interfaces.

- Configure an IPv6 global address on the S0/0/1 interfaces on edge
  routers and the S0/0/0 interfaces on internal routers.

Solution:

The following shows the required steps on the P1R1 router:

```
P1R1(config)#ipv6 unicast-routing
P1R1(config)#ipv6 cef
P1R1(config)#int fa0/0
P1R1(config-if)#ipv6 address 2001:0410:0001:1::/64 eui-64
P1R1(config-if)#int s0/0/1
P1R1(config-if)#ipv6 address 2001:0410:0001:3::/64 eui-64
```

Step 2   Display the IPv6 interface information to verify that the appropriate
interfaces on all routers are configured with an IPv6 address.

On the interfaces, do you see an IPv6 address that you have not configured?
If so, what is that address?

Solution:

The following shows sample output on the P1R1 router. IPv6 addresses have been configured, with
the specified prefix and the interface ID in EUI-64 format. A link-local address has also been
configured on the interfaces; for example on P1R1 Fa0/0, the link-local address is
FE80::216:46FF:FE50:C470.

```
P1R1#show ipv6 interface
FastEthernet0/0 is up, line protocol is up
  IPv6 is enabled, link-local address is FE80::216:46FF:FE50:C470
  No Virtual link-local address(es):
  Global unicast address(es):
    2001:410:1:1:216:46FF:FE50:C470, subnet is 2001:410:1:1::/64 [EUI]
```

```
    Joined group address(es):
      FF02::1
      FF02::2
      FF02::1:FF50:C470
    MTU is 1500 bytes
    ICMP error messages limited to one every 100 milliseconds
    ICMP redirects are enabled
    ICMP unreachables are sent
    ND DAD is enabled, number of DAD attempts: 1
    ND reachable time is 30000 milliseconds
    ND advertised reachable time is 0 milliseconds
    ND advertised retransmit interval is 0 milliseconds
    ND router advertisements are sent every 200 seconds
    ND router advertisements live for 1800 seconds
    ND advertised default router preference is Medium
    Hosts use stateless autoconfig for addresses.
  Serial0/0/1 is up, line protocol is up
    IPv6 is enabled, link-local address is FE80::216:46FF:FE50:C470
    No Virtual link-local address(es):
    Global unicast address(es):
      2001:410:1:3:216:46FF:FE50:C470, subnet is 2001:410:1:3::/64 [EUI]
    Joined group address(es):
      FF02::1
      FF02::2
      FF02::1:FF50:C470
    MTU is 1500 bytes
    ICMP error messages limited to one every 100 milliseconds
    ICMP redirects are enabled
    ICMP unreachables are sent
    ND DAD is enabled, number of DAD attempts: 1
    ND reachable time is 30000 milliseconds
    Hosts use stateless autoconfig for addresses.
  P1R1#
```

Task 3: Enable IPv6 OSPF

In this task, you enable IPv6 OSPF on all pod routers.

Follow these steps:

Step 1   On each router in your pod, globally enable OSPF for IPv6 and configure
the router ID to be the same value as the loopback 0 interface's IPv4
address.

Step 2   Enable IPv6 OSPF in area 0 on all enabled FastEthernet and Serial
interfaces (those that are not shut down).

Solution:

The following shows the required steps on the P1R1 router:

```
P1R1(config)#ipv6 router ospf 100
P1R1(config-rtr)#router-id 10.200.200.11
P1R1(config-rtr)#int fa0/0
P1R1(config-if)#ipv6 ospf 100 area 0
P1R1(config-if)#int s0/0/1
P1R1(config-if)#ipv6 ospf 100 area 0
```

Step 3   Display the IPv6 OSPF interface information to confirm that you have enabled OSPF for IPv6 on your routers.

Solution:

The following shows sample output on the P1R1 router; OSPF for IPv6 is enabled on all interfaces, with process ID 100 in area0.

```
P1R1#show ipv6 ospf interface
Serial0/0/1 is up, line protocol is up
  Link Local Address FE80::216:46FF:FE50:C470, Interface ID 7
  Area 0, Process ID 100, Instance ID 0, Router ID 10.200.200.11
  Network Type POINT_TO_POINT, Cost: 781
  Transmit Delay is 1 sec, State POINT_TO_POINT,
  Timer intervals configured, Hello 10, Dead 40, Wait 40, Retransmit 5
    Hello due in 00:00:09
  Index 1/2/2, flood queue length 0
  Next 0x0(0)/0x0(0)/0x0(0)
  Last flood scan length is 1, maximum is 4
  Last flood scan time is 0 msec, maximum is 0 msec
  Neighbor Count is 1, Adjacent neighbor count is 1
    Adjacent with neighbor 10.200.200.12
  Suppress hello for 0 neighbor(s)
FastEthernet0/0 is up, line protocol is up
  Link Local Address FE80::216:46FF:FE50:C470, Interface ID 4
  Area 0, Process ID 100, Instance ID 0, Router ID 10.200.200.11
  Network Type BROADCAST, Cost: 1
  Transmit Delay is 1 sec, State DR, Priority 1
  Designated Router (ID) 10.200.200.11, local address FE80::216:46FF:FE50:C470
  Backup Designated router (ID) 10.200.200.13, local address FE80::216:46FF:FE10
:FDB0
  Timer intervals configured, Hello 10, Dead 40, Wait 40, Retransmit 5
    Hello due in 00:00:03
  Index 1/1/1, flood queue length 0
  Next 0x0(0)/0x0(0)/0x0(0)
  Last flood scan length is 1, maximum is 4
  Last flood scan time is 0 msec, maximum is 0 msec
  Neighbor Count is 1, Adjacent neighbor count is 1
    Adjacent with neighbor 10.200.200.13  (Backup Designated Router)
  Suppress hello for 0 neighbor(s)
```

Step 4   Verify that you see your OSPFv3 neighbors.

Solution:

The following shows sample output on the P1R1 router; both neighbors are displayed.

```
P1R1#show ipv6 ospf neighbor

Neighbor ID     Pri   State         Dead Time   Interface ID   Interface
10.200.200.12    1    FULL/  -      00:00:30    7              Serial0/0/1
10.200.200.13    1    FULL/BDR      00:00:36    4              FastEthernet0/0
P1R1#
```

Step 5   View the IPv6 routing table on your routers.

Solution:

The following shows sample output on the P1R1 router.

```
P1R1#show ipv6 route
IPv6 Routing Table - 8 entries
```

```
Codes: C - Connected, L - Local, S - Static, R - RIP, B - BGP
       U - Per-user Static route
       I1 - ISIS L1, I2 - ISIS L2, IA - ISIS interarea, IS - ISIS summary
       O - OSPF intra, OI - OSPF inter, OE1 - OSPF ext 1, OE2 - OSPF ext 2
       ON1 - OSPF NSSA ext 1, ON2 - OSPF NSSA ext 2
C   2001:410:1:1::/64 [0/0]
     via ::, FastEthernet0/0
L   2001:410:1:1:216:46FF:FE50:C470/128 [0/0]
     via ::, FastEthernet0/0
O   2001:410:1:2::/64 [110/782]
     via FE80::216:46FF:FE10:FC00, Serial0/0/1
C   2001:410:1:3::/64 [0/0]
     via ::, Serial0/0/1
L   2001:410:1:3:216:46FF:FE50:C470/128 [0/0]
     via ::, Serial0/0/1
O   2001:410:1:4::/64 [110/782]
     via FE80::216:46FF:FE10:FDB0, FastEthernet0/0
L   FE80::/10 [0/0]
     via ::, Null0
L   FF00::/8 [0/0]
     via ::, Null0
P1R1#
```

Step 6   If you can see the neighboring router's IPv6 networks in the routing table, you should be able to ping their IPv6 addresses. To make pinging of IPv6 addresses simpler, find the IPv6 addresses of each of the enabled interfaces on all the routers in your pod and copy and paste them into Notepad. Use the **show cdp neighbor detail** command to display the IPv6 addresses of your immediate neighbors or the **show ipv6 interface brief** command to display the IPv6 address of the router you are on.

After you have documented the IPv6 addresses, you can simply copy and paste the address into your terminal program when you want to ping one of your neighboring routers' IPv6 interfaces. Ping all the IPv6 addresses in your pod.

Solution:

The following shows an example of the display of the IPv6 addresses on the P1R2 router, and pings to those addresses from the P1R1 router. The pings are successful.

```
P1R2#show ipv6 interface brief
FastEthernet0/0            [up/up]
    FE80::216:46FF:FE10:FC00
    2001:410:1:2:216:46FF:FE10:FC00
FastEthernet0/1            [administratively down/down]
    unassigned
Serial0/0/0                [administratively down/down]
    unassigned
Serial0/0/0.1              [administratively down/down]
    unassigned
Serial0/0/0.2              [administratively down/down]
    unassigned
Serial0/0/1                [up/up]
    FE80::216:46FF:FE10:FC00
    2001:410:1:3:216:46FF:FE10:FC00
Loopback0                  [up/up]
    unassigned
```

```
P1R2#

P1R1#ping 2001:410:1:2:216:46FF:FE10:FC00

Type escape sequence to abort.
Sending 5, 100-byte ICMP Echos to 2001:410:1:2:216:46FF:FE10:FC00, timeout is 2
seconds:
!!!!!
Success rate is 100 percent (5/5), round-trip min/avg/max = 28/28/28 ms
P1R1#ping 2001:410:1:3:216:46FF:FE10:FC00

Type escape sequence to abort.
Sending 5, 100-byte ICMP Echos to 2001:410:1:3:216:46FF:FE10:FC00, timeout is 2
seconds:
!!!!!
Success rate is 100 percent (5/5), round-trip min/avg/max = 28/28/28 ms
P1R1#
```

Step 7   Save your configurations to NVRAM.

Solution:

The following shows the required step on the P1R1 router.

```
P1R1#copy run start
Destination filename [startup-config]?
Building configuration...
[OK]
```

Exercise Verification

You have successfully completed this exercise when you have enabled IPv6 routing globally, configured IPv6 addresses on your pod routers, and enabled and verified IPv6 OSPF routing.

Configuration Exercise 10-2: Configuring an IPv6 Tunnel

In this Configuration Exercise, you configure a manual IPv6 tunnel.

> **NOTE**   Throughout this exercise, the pod number is referred to as *x*, and the router number is referred to as *y*. Substitute the appropriate numbers as needed.

Objectives

The objectives of this exercise are to configure a manual IPv6 tunnel.

Visual Objective

Figure 10-27 illustrates the topology used and what you will accomplish in this exercise.

Figure 10-27 *IPv6 Tunnel Configuration Exercise Topology*

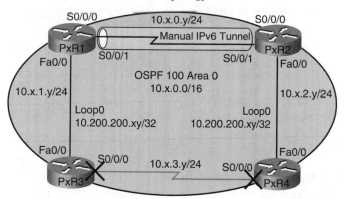

Command List

In this exercise, you use the commands in Table 10-11, listed in logical order. Refer to this list if you need configuration command assistance during the exercise.

> **CAUTION**   Although the command syntax is shown in this table, the addresses shown are typically for the P*x*R1 and P*x*R3 routers. Be careful when addressing your routers! Refer to the exercise instructions and the appropriate visual objective diagram for addressing details.

Table 10-11 *IPv6 Tunnel Configuration Exercise Commands*

Command	Description
(config)#**interface tunnel 0**	Specifies a tunnel interface number (0) on which to enable a configured tunnel.
(config-if)#**ipv6 address 2001:410:*x*:A::*y*/64**	Statically assigns an IPv6 address and a prefix length to the tunnel interface.
(config-if)#**tunnel source 10.*x*.0.*y***	Defines the local IPv4 address used as the source address for the tunnel interface.
(config-if)#**tunnel destination 10.*x*.0.*y***	Defines the tunnel endpoint's destination IPv4 address; in other words, the address of the remote end of the tunnel.
(config-if)#**tunnel mode ipv6ip**	Specifies a manual IPv6 tunnel.
(config-if)#**ipv6 ospf 100 area 0**	Identifies the IPv6 prefix assigned to this interface as part of the OSPFv3 network for process 100 in area 0.
#**show interface tunnel 0**	Displays information about the tunnel 0 interface.

continues

Table 10-11   *IPv6 Tunnel Configuration Exercise Commands (Continued)*

Command	Description
**#show run	begin interface Tunnel**	Displays the running configuration, starting at the words "interface Tunnel."
#show ipv6 route	Displays the IPv6 routing table.
#clear counters tunnel 0	Clears the counters displayed in the **show interface tunnel 0** command.

Task: Configuring the Tunnel Interface

In this task, you prepare the IPv4 tunnel interface to carry IPv6 packets.

Follow these steps:

Step 1   On the internal routers disable your serial 0/0/0 interfaces. Only the edge routers will be configured with the manual tunnel on their serial 0/0/1 interfaces.

Step 2   Remove the IPv6 address from the S0/0/1 interfaces on the edge routers.

Step 3   Create a tunnel and put both ends of the tunnel (PxR1 and PxR2) in the same IPv6 subnet, 2001:410:x:A::y/64, where x is your pod number and y is your router number. Configure the tunnel source and tunnel destination at both ends of the tunnel; for example, PxR1 points to PxR2's serial interface for the tunnel destination and its own serial interface for the tunnel source. Configure the tunnel mode for a manual IPv6 tunnel. Enable IPv6 OSPF routing on the tunnel interface.

Solution:

The following shows how to configure the required steps on the P1R1, P1R2, and P1R3 routers.

```
P1R1(config)#int s0/0/1
P1R1(config-if)#no ipv6 address
P1R1(config-if)#int tunnel0
P1R1(config-if)#ipv6 address 2001:410:1:A::1/64
P1R1(config-if)#tunnel source 10.1.0.1
P1R1(config-if)#tunnel destination 10.1.0.2
P1R1(config-if)#tunnel mode ipv6ip
P1R1(config-if)#ipv6 ospf 100 area 0

P1R2(config)#int s0/0/1
P1R2(config-if)#no ipv6 address
P1R2(config)#int tunnel 5
P1R2(config-if)#ipv6 address 2001:410:1:A::2/64
```

```
P1R2(config-if)#tunnel source 10.1.0.2
P1R2(config-if)#tunnel destination 10.1.0.1
P1R2(config-if)#tunnel mode ipv6ip
P1R2(config-if)#ipv6 ospf 100 area 0

P1R3(config)#int s0/0/0
P1R3(config-if)#shutdown
```

Step 4   Confirm your configuration by displaying information about the tunnel interface on your edge routers.

Solution:

The following shows sample output on the P1R1 router. The tunnel is up.

```
P1R1#show int tunnel 0
Tunnel0 is up, line protocol is up
  Hardware is Tunnel
  MTU 1514 bytes, BW 9 Kbit, DLY 500000 usec,
     reliability 255/255, txload 1/255, rxload 1/255
  Encapsulation TUNNEL, loopback not set
  Keepalive not set
  Tunnel source 10.1.0.1, destination 10.1.0.2
  Tunnel protocol/transport IPv6/IP
  Tunnel TTL 255
  Fast tunneling enabled
  Tunnel transmit bandwidth 8000 (kbps)
  Tunnel receive bandwidth 8000 (kbps)
  Last input 00:00:06, output 00:00:00, output hang never
  Last clearing of "show interface" counters never
  Input queue: 0/75/0/0 (size/max/drops/flushes); Total output drops: 0
  Queueing strategy: fifo
  Output queue: 0/0 (size/max)
  5 minute input rate 0 bits/sec, 0 packets/sec
  5 minute output rate 0 bits/sec, 0 packets/sec
     26 packets input, 3500 bytes, 0 no buffer
     Received 0 broadcasts, 0 runts, 0 giants, 0 throttles
     0 input errors, 0 CRC, 0 frame, 0 overrun, 0 ignored, 0 abort
     47 packets output, 4972 bytes, 0 underruns
     0 output errors, 0 collisions, 0 interface resets
     0 output buffer failures, 0 output buffers swapped out
P1R1#
```

Step 5   Use the **show run | begin interface Tunnel** command to see your tunnel configuration

Solution:

The following shows sample output on the P1R1 router.

```
P1R1# show run | begin interface Tunnel
interface Tunnel0
 no ip address
 ipv6 address 2001:410:1:A::1/64
 ipv6 ospf 100 area 0
 tunnel source 10.1.0.1
 tunnel destination 10.1.0.2
 tunnel mode ipv6ip
!
<output omitted>
```

Step 6   Look at your IPv6 routing table. Are you learning an OSPF route over the tunnel?

Solution:

The following shows sample output on the P1R1 router. An OSPF route is being learned over the tunnel.

```
P1R1#show ipv6 route
IPv6 Routing Table - 7 entries
Codes: C - Connected, L - Local, S - Static, R - RIP, B - BGP
       U - Per-user Static route
       I1 - ISIS L1, I2 - ISIS L2, IA - ISIS interarea, IS - ISIS summary
       O - OSPF intra, OI - OSPF inter, OE1 - OSPF ext 1, OE2 - OSPF ext 2
       ON1 - OSPF NSSA ext 1, ON2 - OSPF NSSA ext 2
C   2001:410:1:1::/64 [0/0]
     via ::, FastEthernet0/0
L   2001:410:1:1:216:46FF:FE50:C470/128 [0/0]
     via ::, FastEthernet0/0
O   2001:410:1:2::/64 [110/11112]
     via FE80::A01:2, Tunnel0
C   2001:410:1:A::/64 [0/0]
     via ::, Tunnel0
L   2001:410:1:A::1/128 [0/0]
     via ::, Tunnel0
L   FE80::/10 [0/0]
     via ::, Null0
L   FF00::/8 [0/0]
     via ::, Null0
P1R1#
```

Step 7   At this point, you should be able to ping across your tunnel. Use the IPv6 addresses that you copied in the previous configuration exercise to see whether packets can go across the tunnel. For example, on PxR1 ping the Fa0/0 interface of PxR2, and on PxR2, ping the Fa0/0 of PXR1.

Solution:

The following shows sample output on the P1R1 and P1R2 routers. In the first sample, P1R1 is pinging P1R2's Fa0/0 interface. In the second sample, P1R2 is pinging P1R1's Fa0/0 interface. Both pings are successful.

```
P1R1#ping 2001:410:1:2:216:46FF:FE10:FC00

Type escape sequence to abort.
Sending 5, 100-byte ICMP Echos to 2001:410:1:2:216:46FF:FE10:FC00, timeout is 2
seconds:
!!!!!
Success rate is 100 percent (5/5), round-trip min/avg/max = 32/33/36 ms
P1R1#

P1R2#ping 2001:410:1:1:216:46FF:FE50:C470

Type escape sequence to abort.
Sending 5, 100-byte ICMP Echos to 2001:410:1:1:216:46FF:FE50:C470, timeout is 2
seconds:
!!!!!
Success rate is 100 percent (5/5), round-trip min/avg/max = 32/34/36 ms
P1R2#
```

Step 8   To confirm that the traffic is going through the tunnel, clear the counters on the tunnel interface. Display information about the tunnel again, then ping the IPv6 address again, and then display information about the tunnel once more. Did you notice a difference in the displayed information? If so, what?

Solution:

The following shows sample output on the P1R1 router. The counters on the interface increased after the ping.

```
P1R1#clear counters tunnel 0
Clear "show interface" counters on this interface [confirm]
P1R1#
*Jul 10 01:58:18.295: %CLEAR-5-COUNTERS: Clear counter on interface Tunnel0 by console

P1R1#show int tunnel 0
Tunnel0 is up, line protocol is up
  Hardware is Tunnel
  MTU 1514 bytes, BW 9 Kbit, DLY 500000 usec,
     reliability 255/255, txload 1/255, rxload 1/255
  Encapsulation TUNNEL, loopback not set
  Keepalive not set
  Tunnel source 10.1.0.1, destination 10.1.0.2
  Tunnel protocol/transport IPv6/IP
  Tunnel TTL 255
  Fast tunneling enabled
  Tunnel transmit bandwidth 8000 (kbps)
  Tunnel receive bandwidth 8000 (kbps)
  Last input 00:00:01, output 00:00:05, output hang never
  Last clearing of "show interface" counters 00:00:05
  Input queue: 0/75/0/0 (size/max/drops/flushes); Total output drops: 0
  Queueing strategy: fifo
  Output queue: 0/0 (size/max)
  5 minute input rate 0 bits/sec, 0 packets/sec
  5 minute output rate 0 bits/sec, 0 packets/sec
     1 packets input, 120 bytes, 0 no buffer
     Received 0 broadcasts, 0 runts, 0 giants, 0 throttles
     0 input errors, 0 CRC, 0 frame, 0 overrun, 0 ignored, 0 abort
     0 packets output, 0 bytes, 0 underruns
     0 output errors, 0 collisions, 0 interface resets
     0 output buffer failures, 0 output buffers swapped out

P1R1#ping 2001:410:1:2:216:46FF:FE10:FC00

Type escape sequence to abort.
Sending 5, 100-byte ICMP Echos to 2001:410:1:2:216:46FF:FE10:FC00, timeout is 2
seconds:
!!!!!
Success rate is 100 percent (5/5), round-trip min/avg/max = 32/34/36 ms

P1R1#show int tunnel 0
Tunnel0 is up, line protocol is up
  Hardware is Tunnel
  MTU 1514 bytes, BW 9 Kbit, DLY 500000 usec,
     reliability 255/255, txload 1/255, rxload 28/255
  Encapsulation TUNNEL, loopback not set
  Keepalive not set
  Tunnel source 10.1.0.1, destination 10.1.0.2
  Tunnel protocol/transport IPv6/IP
  Tunnel TTL 255
  Fast tunneling enabled
  Tunnel transmit bandwidth 8000 (kbps)
  Tunnel receive bandwidth 8000 (kbps)
  Last input 00:00:04, output 00:00:04, output hang never
  Last clearing of "show interface" counters 00:00:28
```

```
      Input queue: 0/75/0/0 (size/max/drops/flushes); Total output drops: 0
      Queueing strategy: fifo
      Output queue: 0/0 (size/max)
      5 minute input rate 1000 bits/sec, 1 packets/sec
      5 minute output rate 0 bits/sec, 1 packets/sec
         8 packets input, 1060 bytes, 0 no buffer
         Received 0 broadcasts, 0 runts, 0 giants, 0 throttles
         0 input errors, 0 CRC, 0 frame, 0 overrun, 0 ignored, 0 abort
         7 packets output, 800 bytes, 0 underruns
         0 output errors, 0 collisions, 0 interface resets
         0 output buffer failures, 0 output buffers swapped out
   P1R1#
```

Step 9   Save your configurations to NVRAM.

Solution:

The following shows the required step on the P1R1 router.

```
   P1R1#copy run start
   Destination filename [startup-config]?
   Building configuration...
   [OK]
```

Exercise Verification

You have successfully completed this exercise when you have created a manual IPv6 to IPv4 tunnel and pinged across it.

Review Questions

Answer the following questions, and then refer to Appendix A, "Answers to Review Questions," for the answers.

1. What are some of the features of IPv6?

2. How many bits are in an IPv6 address?

3. How long is the basic IPv6 packet header?

4. What is the flow label in the IPv6 packet header used for?

5. Does the IPv6 packet header have a checksum field?

6. In general which node processes IPv6 extension headers?

7. In what format are IPv6 addresses written?

8. Which of the following are valid representations of the IPv6 address 2035:0001:2BC5:0000:0000:087C:0000:000A?

    a. 2035:0001:2BC5::087C::000A

    b. 2035:1:2BC5::87C:0:A

    c. 2035:0001:2BC5::087C:0000:000A

    d. 2035:1:2BC5:0:0:87C::A

    e. 2035:1:2BC5::087C:A

9. What is the format of an IPv6 broadcast address?

10. Which of the following are the true statements?

    a. A packet that is sent to an IPv6 anycast address goes to the closest interface identified by that address.

    b. A packet that is sent to an IPv6 anycast address goes to all interfaces identified by that address.

    c. A packet that is sent to an IPv6 multicast address goes to the closest interface identified by that address.

    d. A packet that is sent to an IPv6 multicast address goes to all interfaces identified by that address.

11. How is an IPv6 interface identifier created for Ethernet interfaces?

12. What is the IPv6 unicast address space?

13. What is the IPv6 link-local prefix?

14. What is the IPv6 multicast prefix?

15. What is an IPv6 solicited-node multicast address used for?

16. How does IPv6's stateless autoconfiguration work?

17. How does IPv6 mobility work?

18. What are some of the similarities between OSPFv2 and OSPFv3?

19. Fill in the following table to indicate the OSPFv3 packet types.

Packet Type	Description
1	
2	
3	
4	
5	

20. Which IPv6 multicast addresses does OSPFv3 use?

21. How many bits is an OSPFv3 router ID?

22. What are the two new LSAs introduced in OSPFv3?

23. What is the OSPFv3 instance ID used for?

24. Which command is used to summarize IPv6 OSPF routes?

25. What are some of the techniques available to transition from IPv4 to IPv6?

26. What addresses do the routers involved in 6-to-4 tunneling use?

Part V: Appendixes

Acronyms and Abbreviations

This appendix identifies abbreviations, acronyms, and initialisms used in this book and in the internetworking industry.

Many of these acronyms and other terms are also described in the Cisco Internetworking Terms and Acronyms resource, available at http://www.cisco.com/univercd/cc/td/doc/cisintwk/ita/.

Acronym	Expanded Term
6-to-4	IPv6-to-IPv4
ABR	Area Border Router
ACK	1. acknowledge
	2. acknowledgment
	3. acknowledgment bit in a TCP segment
ACL	access control list
AD	advertised distance
AFI	authority and format identifier
AfriNIC	African Network Information Centre
AH	Authentication Header
ALG	application layer gateway
ANSI	American National Standards Institute
AON	Application-Oriented Networking
API	application programming interface
APNIC	Asia Pacific Network Information Center
ARCnet	Attached Resource Computer Network

continues

(Continued)

Acronym	Expanded Term
ARIN	American Registry for Internet Numbers
ARP	Address Resolution Protocol
AS	autonomous system
ASBR	Autonomous System Boundary Router
ASIC	application-specific integrated circuit
ATM	Asynchronous Transfer Mode
BDR	Backup Designated Router
BGP	Border Gateway Protocol
BGP4	BGP Version 4
BIA	1. Burned-In Address
	2. Bump-in-the-API
BIS	Bump-in-the-Stack
BOOTP	Bootstrap Protocol
BOOTPS	Bootstrap Protocol Server
BPDU	bridge protocol data unit
bps	bits per second
BRI	Basic Rate Interface
BSCI	Building Scalable Cisco Internetworks
BSR	bootstrap router
CCDP	Cisco Certified Design Professional
CCNA	Cisco Certified Network Associate
CCNP	Cisco Certified Network Professional
CCSI	Cisco Certified Systems Instructor
CCSP	Cisco Certified Security Professional
CDP	Cisco Discovery Protocol
CEF	Cisco Express Forwarding

(Continued)

Acronym	Expanded Term
CEFv6	Cisco Express Forwarding for IPv6
CGMP	Cisco Group Management Protocol
CIDR	classless interdomain routing
CIR	committed information rate
CLNP	Connectionless Network Protocol
CLNS	Connectionless Network Service
CLV	Code, Length, Value
CMIP	Common Management Information Protocol
CoS	class of service
CPU	central processing unit
CRC	cyclic redundancy check
CSMA/CD	carrier sense multiple access collision detect
CSNP	complete sequence number PDU
DBD	database description packets
DCC	Data Country Code
DCE	data circuit-terminating equipment
DDP	database description packets
DEC	Digital Equipment Corporation
DESGN	Designing for Cisco Internetwork Solutions
DHCP	Dynamic Host Configuration Protocol
DHCPv6	DHCP for IPv6
DiffServ	Differentiated Services
DIS	designated intermediate system
DLCI	data-link connection identifier
DNA	DoNotAge
DNS	Domain Name Service or Domain Name System

continues

(Continued)

Acronym	Expanded Term
DoD	Department of Defense
DR	designated router
DSL	digital subscriber line
DSP	domain-specific part
DTE	data terminal equipment
DUAL	Diffusing Update Algorithm
DVMRP	Distance Vector Multicast Routing Protocol
E1	External Type 1
E2	External Type 2
EAP	Extensible Authentication Protocol
EBGP	External BGP
e-bit	external bit
EGP	Exterior Gateway Protocol
EIGRP	Enhanced Interior Gateway Routing Protocol
ES	end system
ESH	End System Hello
ES-IS	End System-to-Intermediate System
ESP	Encapsulating Security Payload
EUI-64	extended universal identifier 64-bit
FD	feasible distance
FDDI	Fiber Distributed Data Interface
FIB	Forwarding Information Base
FLSM	fixed-length subnet mask
FS	feasible successor
FTAM	File Transfer, Access, and Management
FTP	File Transfer Protocol
Gbps	gigabits per second

(Continued)

Acronym	Expanded Term
GDA	group destination address
GIF	Graphics Interchange Format
GOSIP	Government OSI Profile
HDLC	High-Level Data Link Control
HODSP	high-order domain-specific part
HSRP	Hot Standby Router Protocol
HTTP	Hypertext Transfer Protocol
Hz	hertz
IANA	Internet Assigned Numbers Authority
IBGP	Internal BGP
ICD	International Code Designation
ICMP	Internet Control Message Protocol
ICND	Interconnecting Cisco Network Devices
ID	identifier
IDI	initial domain identifier
IDP	initial domain part
IDRP	Interdomain Routing Protocol
IEEE	Institute of Electrical and Electronics Engineers
IETF	Internet Engineering Task Force
IGMP	Internet Group Management Protocol
IGMPv1	IGMP Version 1
IGMPv2	IGMP Version 2
IGMPv3	IGMP Version 3
IGP	Interior Gateway Protocol
IGRP	Interior Gateway Routing Protocol
IIH	IS-IS Hello

continues

(Continued)

Acronym	Expanded Term
IIN	Intelligent Information Network
INTRO	Introduction to Cisco Networking Technologies
IntServ	Integrated Services
IOS	Internet Operating System
IP	Internet Protocol
IPsec	IP security
IP/TV	Internet Protocol Television
IPv4	IP Version 4
IPv6	IP Version 6
IPX	Internetwork Packet Exchange
IS	1. information systems
	2. intermediate system
ISATAP	Intra-Site Automatic Tunnel Addressing
ISH	Intermediate System Hello
IS-IS	Intermediate System-to-Intermediate System
IS-ISv6	IS-IS for IPv6
ISDN	Integrated Services Digital Network
ISO	International Organization for Standardization
ISP	Internet service provider
ISR	integrated services router
ITU-T	International Telecommunication Union Telecommunication Standardization Sector
JPEG	Joint Photographic Experts Group
kbps	kilobits per second
L1	Level 1
L1/L2	Level 1/Level 2
L2	Level 2
L3	Level 3

(Continued)

Acronym	Expanded Term
LACNIC	Latin American and Caribbean IP Address Regional Registry
LAN	local-area network
LANE	LAN Emulation
LLC	Logical Link Control
LS	link state
LSA	link-state advertisement
LSAck	link-state acknowledgment
LSDB	link-state database
LSP	link-state packet
LSR	link-state request
LSU	link-state update
MAC	Media Access Control
MAN	metropolitan-area network
MB	megabyte
MBGP	Multiprotocol BGP
Mbps	megabits per second
MD5	message digest algorithm 5
MDSP	Multicast Source Discovery Protocol
MED	Multi-Exit-Discriminator
MIME	Multipurpose Internet Mail Extensions
MLD	Multicast Listener Discovery
MLS	multilayer switching
MOSPF	Multicast OSPF
MP-BGP4	Multiprotocol Border Gateway Protocol Version 4
MPEG	Motion Picture Experts Group
MPLS	Multiprotocol Label Switching
ms	millisecond

continues

(Continued)

Acronym	Expanded Term
MTU	maximum transmission unit
NAT	Network Address Translation
NAT-PT	NAT-Protocol Translation
NBMA	nonbroadcast multiaccess
NET	network-entity title
NetBIOS	Network Basic Input/Output System
NIC	1. network interface card
	2. Network Information Center
NLRI	Network Layer Reachability Information
NREN	National Research and Education Network
NSAP	network service access point
NSEL	NSAP-selector
NSFnet	National Science Foundation Network
NSSA	not-so-stubby area
NTP	Network Time Protocol
NVRAM	nonvolatile random-access memory
ODR	on-demand routing
OS	operating system
OSI	Open System Interconnection
OSPF	Open Shortest Path First
OSPFv1	OSPF Version 1
OSPFv2	OSPF Version 2
OSPFv3	OSPF Version 3
OUI	organizationally unique identifier
PBR	policy-based routing
PDA	personal digital assistant
PDM	protocol-dependent module

(Continued)

Acronym	Expanded Term
PDU	protocol data unit
PIM	Protocol Independent Multicast
PIM DM	Protocol Independent Multicast dense mode
PIM SM	Protocol Independent Multicast sparse mode
PIMv1	PIM Version 1
PPP	Point-to-Point Protocol
pps	packets per second
PRI	Primary Rate Interface
PRC	partial route calculation
PSNP	partial sequence number PDU
PSTN	public switched telephone network
PVC	permanent virtual circuit
QoS	quality of service
RAM	random-access memory
RCP	Remote Copy Protocol
RFC	Request For Comments
RIB	Routing Information Base
RID	router ID
RIP	Routing Information Protocol
RIPE-NCC	Réseaux IP Européens-Network Cooordination Center
RIPng	Routing Information Protocol new generation
RIPv1	Routing Information Protocol Version 1
RIPv2	Routing Information Protocol Version 2
RP	rendezvous point
RPF	Reverse Path Forwarding
RR	route reflector
RSVP	Resource Reservation Protocol

continues

(Continued)

Acronym	Expanded Term
RTO	retransmit timeout
RTP	Reliable Transport Protocol
RTSP	Real Time Streaming Protocol
SAP	1. Session Announcement Protocol
	2. service access point
SCP	Session Control Protocol
sd	Session Directory
SDP	Session Description Protocol
sdr or SDR	1. session directory application
	2. Session Description Protocol
SDU	service data unit
SIA	stuck in active
SIIT	Stateless IP/ICMP Translation
SIN	ships in the night
SIP	Session Initiation Protocol
SMTP	Simple Mail Transfer Protocol
SNAP	Subnetwork Access Protocol
SNMP	Simple Network Management Protocol
SNP	sequence number PDU
SNPA	subnetwork point of attachment
SONA	Service-Oriented Network Architecture
SPF	shortest path first
SPT	shortest path tree
SPX	Sequenced Packet Exchange
SRTT	smooth round-trip time
SSM	Source Specific Multicast
STP	1. shielded twisted-pair
	2. Spanning Tree Protocol

(Continued)

Acronym	Expanded Term
SVC	switched virtual circuit
SYN	Synchronize
TCP	Transmission Control Protocol
TCP/IP	Transmission Control Protocol/Internet Protocol
TFTP	Trivial File Transfer Protocol
TLV	Type, Length, Value
ToS	type of service
TTL	Time To Live
UDP	User Datagram Protocol
U/L	Universal/Local
URL	Uniform Resource Locator
UTP	unshielded twisted-pair
VC	virtual circuit
VLAN	virtual LAN
VLSM	variable-length subnet mask
VoD	video on demand
VoIP	Voice over IP
VPN	virtual private network
VRF	VPN routing and forwarding
VTP	1. Virtual Terminal Protocol
	2. VLAN Trunking Protocol
vty	virtual terminal
WAN	wide-area network
WFQ	weighted fair queuing
WLAN	wireless LAN
WRED	weighted random early detection
WWW	World Wide Web
ZIP	Zone Information Protocol

Answers to Review Questions

Chapter 1

1. What is a converged network?

   Answer: A converged network is one in which data, voice, and video traffic coexists on a single network.

2. What are the three phases of the IIN?

   Answer: Integrated transport, integrated services, and integrated applications

3. Which are layers within the SONA framework?

   a. Access

   b. Network Infrastructure

   c. Interactive Services

   d. Enterprise Edge

   e. Application

   f. Edge Distribution

   Answer: b, c, e

4. What are the components of the Cisco Enterprise Architecture?

   Answer: Campus, data center, branches, teleworkers, and WAN

5. Which are the layers within the hierarchical network model?

   a. Access

   b. Network Infrastructure

   c. Core

   d. Distribution

    e. Application

    f. Edge Distribution

    g. Network Management

    Answer: a, c, d

6. Describe each of the functional areas of the Enterprise Composite Network Model.

    Answer: The Enterprise Composite Network Model first divides the network into three functional areas, as follows:

    — **Enterprise Campus**—This functional area contains the modules required to build a hierarchical, highly robust campus network.

    — **Enterprise Edge**—This functional area aggregates connectivity from the various elements at the edge of the enterprise network, including to remote locations, the Internet, and remote users.

    — **Service Provider Edge**—This area is not implemented by the organization; instead, it is included to represent connectivity to service providers.

7. Which modules are within the Enterprise Campus functional area?

    Answer: The Enterprise Campus functional area comprises the following modules: Building, Building Distribution, Core (also called the backbone), Edge Distribution, Server, and Management.

8. Why might a network need to have more than one routing protocol running?

    Answer: Each part of the network might have different routing protocol requirements. For example, BGP might be required in the Corporate Internet module, whereas static routes are often used for remote-access and VPN users. Therefore, enterprises might have to run multiple routing protocols.

Chapter 2

1. Which of the following is not a scenario in which static routes would be used?

    a. When the administrator needs total control over the routes used by the router

    b. When a backup to a dynamically recognized route is necessary

    c. When rapid convergence is needed

    d. When a route should appear to the router as a directly connected network

Answer: c. Note that Answer d refers to the situation when a static route is configured and the *interface* parameter is used, specifying the local router outbound interface to use to reach the destination network. The router considers this a directly connected route, and the default administrative distance is 0.

2. What are two drawbacks of static routes?

    a. Reconfiguring to reflect topology changes

    b. Complex metrics

    c. Involved convergence

    d. Absence of dynamic route discovery

    Answer: a, d

3. What is used by traffic for which the destination network is not specifically listed in the routing table?

    a. Dynamic area

    b. Default route

    c. Border gateway

    d. Black hole

    Answer: b

4. The **show ip route** command usually provides information on which of the following two items?

    a. Next hop

    b. Metric

    c. CDP

    d. Hostname

    Answer: a, b

5. When using dynamic routing protocols, what does the administrator configure the routing protocol on?

    a. Each area

    b. Each intermediate system

    c. Each router

    d. Each gateway of last resort

    Answer: c

6.   Which of the following is not a dynamic routing protocol?

   a.   IS-IS

   b.   CDP

   c.   EIGRP

   d.   BGP

   e.   RIPv2

   Answer: b

7.   What is a metric?

   a.   A standard of measurement used by routing algorithms

   b.   The set of techniques used to manage network resources

   c.   Interdomain routing in TCP/IP networks

   d.   Services limiting the input or output transmission rate

   Answer: a

8.   Which routing protocol uses only major classful networks to determine the interfaces participating in the protocol?

   a.   EIGRP

   b.   RIPv1

   c.   IS-IS

   d.   BGP

   e.   OSPF

   Answer: b

9.   ODR uses what to carry network information between spoke (stub) routers and the hub?

   a.   Metric

   b.   BGP

   c.   Convergence

   d.   CDP

   Answer: d

10. Which of the following is not a classification of routing protocols?

   a. Link-state

   b. Default

   c. Hybrid

   d. Distance vector

   Answer: b

11. What do you call the process when a router, using a classful routing protocol, sends an update about a subnet of a classful network across an interface belonging to a different classful network and assumes that the remote router will use the default subnet mask for that class of IP address?

   a. Autosummarization

   b. Default routing

   c. Classful switching

   d. Tunneling

   Answer: a

12. True or false: Discontiguous subnets are subnets of the same major network that are separated by a different major network.

   Answer: True

13. Classless routing protocols allow _____.

   a. QoS

   b. VLSM

   c. VPN

   d. RIP

   Answer: b

14. What is the command to turn off autosummarization?

   a. **no auto-summarization**

   b. **enable classless**

   c. **ip route**

   d. **no auto-summary**

   Answer: d

15. What is the OSPF default administrative distance value?

   a. 90

   b. 100

   c. 110

   d. 120

Answer: c

16. When a static route's administrative distance is manually configured to be higher than the default administrative distance of dynamic routing protocols, that static route is called what?

   a. Semistatic route

   b. Floating static route

   c. Semidynamic route

   d. Manual route

Answer: b

17. Which variables can be used to calculate metrics?

   a. Hops

   b. Convergence time

   c. Administrative distance

   d. Path attributes

   e. Cost

Answer: a, d, e

Chapter 3

1. What are some features of EIGRP?

Answer: Features of EIGRP include fast convergence, VLSM support, partial updates, multiple network layer support, seamless connectivity across all data-link protocols and topologies, sophisticated metric, and use of multicast and unicast.

2. Is EIGRP operational traffic multicast or broadcast?

Answer: EIGRP operational traffic is multicast (and unicast).

3. What are the four key technologies employed by EIGRP?

Answer: The four key technologies are: neighbor discovery/recovery mechanism, Reliable Transport Protocol (RTP), Diffusing Update Algorithm (DUAL) finite state machine, and protocol-dependent modules.

4. How do IGRP and EIGRP differ in their metric calculation?

Answer: IGRP and EIGRP use the same algorithm for metric calculation, but EIGRP's metric value is multiplied by 256 to provide it more granular decision-making. EIGRP represents its metrics in 32-bit format instead of the 24-bit representation used by IGRP.

5. Which of the following best describes the EIGRP topology table?

   a. It is populated as a result of receiving hello packets.

   b. It contains all learned routes to a destination.

   c. It contains only the best routes to a destination.

Answer: b

6. Describe the five types of EIGRP packets.

Answer: EIGRP uses the following five types of packets:

- Hello—Hello packets are used for neighbor discovery. They are sent as multicasts and carry an acknowledgment number of 0.

- Update— Update packets contain route change information. An update is sent to communicate the routes a particular router has used to converge; an update is sent only to affected routers. These updates are sent as multicasts when a new route is discovered and when convergence is completed (when the route becomes passive). To synchronize topology tables, updates are sent as unicasts to neighbors during their EIGRP startup sequence. Updates are sent reliably.

- Query—When a router is performing route computation and does not find a feasible successor, it sends a query packet to its neighbors, asking if they have a successor to the destination. Queries are normally multicast but can be retransmitted as unicast packets in certain cases; they are sent reliably.

- Reply—A reply packet is sent in response to a query packet. Replies are unicast to the originator of the query and are sent reliably.

- Acknowledge (ACK)—The ACK is used to acknowledge updates, queries, and replies. ACK packets are unicast hello packets and contain a nonzero acknowledgment number. (Note that hello and ACK packets do not require acknowledgment.)

7. True or false: EIGRP hello packets are sent every 5 seconds on LAN links.

Answer: True.

8. What is the difference between the hold time and the hello interval?

Answer:

The hello interval determines how often hello packets are sent. It is 5 or 60 seconds by default, depending on the media type.

The hold time is the amount of time a router considers a neighbor up without receiving a hello or some other EIGRP packet from that neighbor. Hello packets include the hold time. The hold time interval is set by default to 3 times the hello interval.

9. Which of the following statements are true?

   a. A route is considered passive when the router is not performing recomputation on that route.

   b. A route is passive when it is undergoing recomputation.

   c. A route is active when it is undergoing recomputation.

   d. A route is considered active when the router is not performing recomputation on that route.

   e. Passive is the operational state for a route.

   f. Active is the operational state for a route.

   Answer: a, c, e

10. Which command is used to see the RTO and hold time?

   a. **show ip eigrp traffic**

   b. **show ip eigrp timers**

   c. **show ip eigrp route**

   d. **show ip eigrp neighbors**

   Answer: d

11. Why are EIGRP routing updates described as reliable?

   Answer: EIGRP update packets are generated by the Reliable Transport Protocol (RTP) within EIGRP. Reliable packets have a sequence number assigned to them, and the receiving device must acknowledge them.

12. What units are the bandwidth and delay parameters in the EIGRP metric calculation?

Answer:

The default formula for the EIGRP metric is metric = bandwidth + delay.

In this formula, the EIGRP delay value is the sum of the delays in the path, in tens of microseconds, multiplied by 256.

The bandwidth is calculated using the minimum bandwidth link along the path, represented in kbps. 10^7 is divided by this value, and then the result is multiplied by 256.

13. Which of the following statements are true regarding AD and FD?

   a. The AD is the EIGRP metric for a *neighbor router* to reach a particular network.

   b. The AD is the EIGRP metric for *this router* to reach a particular network.

   c. The FD is the EIGRP metric for *this router* to reach a particular network.

   d. The FD is the EIGRP metric for *the neighbor router* to reach a particular network.

   Answer: a, c

14. What does it mean when a route is marked as an FS?

   Answer: A feasible successor (FS) is a router providing a backup route. The route through the feasible successor must be loop free; in other words, it must not loop back to the current successor. To qualify as an FS, a next-hop router must have an advertised distance less than the feasible distance of the current successor route for the particular network.

15. In the following table, place the letter of the description next to the term the description describes. The descriptions may be used more than once.

   Descriptions:

   a. A network protocol that EIGRP supports.

   b. A table that contains FS information.

   c. The administrative distance determines routing information that is included in this table.

   d. A neighbor router that has the best path to a destination.

   e. A neighbor router that has a loop-free alternative path to a destination.

   f. An algorithm used by EIGRP that ensures fast convergence.

   g. A multicast packet used to discover neighbors.

   h. A packet sent by EIGRP routers when a new neighbor is discovered and when a change occurs.

Answer:

Term	Description Letter
Successor	d
Feasible successor	e
Hello	g
Topology table	b
IP	a
Update	h
AppleTalk	a
Routing table	c
DUAL	f
IPX	a

16. Answer true or false to the following statements.

    Answer:

    EIGRP performs autosummarization. True

    EIGRP autosummarization cannot be turned off. False

    EIGRP supports VLSM. True

    EIGRP can maintain three independent routing tables. True

    The EIGRP hello interval is an unchangeable fixed value. False

17. Which of the following are true?

    a. For Frame Relay point-to-point interfaces, set the **bandwidth** to the CIR.

    b. For Frame Relay point-to-point interfaces set the **bandwidth** to the sum of all CIRs.

    c. For Frame Relay multipoint connections, set the **bandwidth** to the sum of all CIRs.

    d. For generic serial interfaces such as PPP and HDLC, set the **bandwidth** to match the line speed.

    e. For Frame Relay multipoint connections, set the **bandwidth** to the CIR.

    Answer: a, c, d

18. Router A has three interfaces with IP addresses 172.16.1.1/24, 172.16.2.3/24, and 172.16.5.1/24. What commands would be used to configure EIGRP to run in autonomous system 100 on only the interfaces with addresses 172.16.2.3/24 and 172.16.5.1/24?

Answer: One EIGRP configuration for Router A is as follows:

```
RouterA(config)#router eigrp 100
RouterA(config-router)#network 172.16.2.0 0.0.0.255
RouterA(config-router)#network 172.16.5.0 0.0.0.255
```

19. Routers A and B are connected and are running EIGRP on all their interfaces. Router A has four interfaces, with IP addresses 172.16.1.1/24, 172.16.2.3/24, 172.16.5.1/24, and 10.1.1.1/24. Router B has two interfaces, with IP addresses 172.16.1.2/24 and 192.168.1.1/24. There are other routers in the network that are connected on each of the interfaces of these two routers that are also running EIGRP. Which summary routes does Router A generate automatically?

   a. 172.16.0.0/16

   b. 192.168.1.0/24

   c. 10.0.0.0/8

   d. 172.16.1.0/22

   e. 10.1.1.0/24

Answer: a, c

20. Router A has four EIGRP paths to a destination with the following EIGRP metrics. Assuming no potential routing loops exist and the command **variance 3** is configured on Router A, which paths are included for load balancing?

   a. Path 1: 1100

   b. Path 2: 1200

   c. Path 3: 2000

   d. Path 4: 4000

Answer: a, b, c

21. Router A has the following configuration:

```
interface s0
  ip bandwidth-percent eigrp 100 40
  bandwidth 256
router eigrp 100
  network 10.0.0.0
```

What is the maximum bandwidth that EIGRP uses on the S0 interface?

a. 100

b. 40

c. 256

d. 102

e. 10

f. 47

Answer: d

22. What is the default EIGRP authentication?

a. Simple password

b. MD5

c. None

d. IPsec

Answer: c

23. True or false: When configuring EIGRP authentication, each router must have a unique password configured.

Answer: False

24. What does the **accept-lifetime** command do for EIGRP authentication?

Answer: This command specifies the time period during which the key will be accepted for use on received packets.

25. What command is used to troubleshoot EIGRP authentication?

a. **debug eigrp authentication**

b. **debug ip eigrp packets**

c. **debug eigrp packets**

d. **debug ip eigrp authentication**

Answer: c

26. What is the default EIGRP stuck-in-active timer?

Answer: The default EIGRP stuck-in-active timer is 3 minutes. If the router does not receive a reply to all the outstanding queries within this time, the route goes to the stuck-in-active state, and the router resets the neighbor relationships for the neighbors that failed to reply.

27. With the EIGRP active process enhancement, when does the SIA-Query get sent?

    Answer: The SIA-Query is sent at the midway point of the active timer (one and a half minutes by default).

28. How does EIGRP summarization limit the query range?

    Answer: Summarization limits the query range because a remote router extends the query about a network only if it has an exact match in the routing table.

29. How does the EIGRP stub feature limit the query range?

    Answer: Stub routers are not queried. Instead, hub routers connected to the stub router answer the query on behalf of the stub router.

30. What does the **eigrp stub receive-only** command do?

    Answer: This command makes the router an EIGRP stub; the **receive-only** keyword restricts the router from sharing any of its routes with any other router within the EIGRP autonomous system.

31. True or false: Goodbye messages are sent in hello packets.

    Answer: True.

32. The following is part of the output of the **show ip eigrp topology** command:

    ```
    P 10.1.3.0/24, 1 successors, FD is 10514432
            via 10.1.2.2 (10514432/28160), Serial0/0/0
    ```

    What are the two numbers in parentheses?

    Answer: The first number is the feasible distance for the network through the next-hop router, and the second number is the advertised distance from the next-hop router to the destination network.

Chapter 4

1. Which of the following is not a characteristic of link-state routing protocols?

    a. They respond quickly to network changes.

    b. They broadcast every 30 minutes.

    c. They send triggered updates when a network change occurs.

    d. They may send periodic updates, known as link-state refresh, at long time intervals, such as every 30 minutes.

    Answer: b

2. For all the routers in the network to make consistent routing decisions, each link-state router must keep a record of all the following items except which one?

   a. Its immediate neighbor routers

   b. All of the other routers in the network, or in its area of the network, and their attached networks

   c. The best paths to each destination

   d. The version of the routing protocol used

   Answer: d

3. Link-state routing protocols use a two-layer area hierarchy composed of which two areas?

   a. Transit area

   b. Transmit area

   c. Regular area

   d. Linking area

   Answer: a, c

4. Which of the following is not a characteristic of an OSPF area?

   a. It may minimize routing table entries.

   b. It requires a flat network design.

   c. It may localize the impact of a topology change within an area.

   d. It may stop detailed LSA flooding at the area boundary.

   Answer: b

5. True or false: An ABR connects area 0 to the nonbackbone areas.

   Answer: True

6. When a router receives an LSA (within an LSU), it does not do which of the following?

   a. If the LSA entry does not already exist, the router adds the entry to its LSDB, sends back an LSAck, floods the information to other routers, runs SPF, and updates its routing table.

   b. If the entry already exists and the received LSA has the same sequence number, the router overwrites the information in the LSDB with the new LSA entry.

c. If the entry already exists but the LSA includes newer information (it has a higher sequence number), the router adds the entry to its LSDB, sends back an LSAck, floods the information to other routers, runs SPF, and updates its routing table.

d. If the entry already exists but the LSA includes older information, it sends an LSU to the sender with its newer information.

Answer: b

7. What is an OSPF type 2 packet?

a. Database description (DBD), which checks for database synchronization between routers

b. Link-state request (LSR), which requests specific link-state records from router to router

c. Link-state update (LSU), which sends specifically requested link-state records

d. Link-state acknowledgment (LSAck), which acknowledges the other packet types

Answer: a

8. Which of the following is true of hellos and dead intervals?

a. They do not need to be the same on neighboring routers, because the lowest common denominator is adopted.

b. They do not need to be the same on neighboring routers, because the highest common denominator is adopted.

c. They do not need to be the same on neighboring routers, because it is a negotiated interval between neighboring routers.

d. They need to be the same on neighboring routers.

Answer: d

9. Which IP address is used to send an updated LSA entry to OSPF DRs and BDRs?

a. Unicast 224.0.0.5

b. Unicast 224.0.0.6

c. Multicast 224.0.0.5

d. Multicast 224.0.0.6

Answer: d

10. To ensure an accurate database, how often does OSPF flood (refresh) each LSA record?

   a. Every 60 minutes.

   b. Every 30 minutes.

   c. Every 60 seconds.

   d. Every 30 seconds.

   e. Flooding each LSA record would defeat the purpose of a link-state routing protocol, which strives to reduce the amount of routing traffic it generates.

Answer: b

11. What command is used to display the router ID, timers, and statistics?

   a. **show ip ospf**

   b. **show ip ospf neighbors**

   c. **show ip ospf stats**

   d. **show ip ospf neighborship**

Answer: a

12. Which of the following is not a way in which the OSPF router ID (a unique IP address) can be assigned?

   a. The highest IP address of any physical interface

   b. The lowest IP address of any physical interface

   c. The IP address of a loopback interface

   d. The **router-id** command

Answer: b

13. True or false: On point-to-point networks, the router dynamically detects its neighboring routers by multicasting its hello packets to all SPF routers using the address 224.0.0.6.

Answer: False

14. An adjacency is the relationship that exists where?

   a. Between routers located on the same physical network

   b. Between routers in different OSPF areas

   c. Between a router and its DR and BDR on different networks

   d. Between a backbone DR and a transit BDR

Answer: a

15. Which of the following is not true regarding the OSPF DR/BDR election?

   a. The router with the highest priority value is the DR.

   b. The router with the second-highest priority value is the BDR.

   c. If all routers have the default priority, the router with the lowest router ID becomes the DR.

   d. The router with a priority set to 0 cannot become the DR or BDR.

   Answer: c

16. Which of the following is not true of OSPF point-to-multipoint mode?

   a. It does not require a full-mesh network.

   b. It does not require a static neighbor configuration.

   c. It uses multiple IP subnets.

   d. It duplicates LSA packets.

   Answer: c

17. What is the default OSPF mode on a point-to-point Frame Relay subinterface?

   a. Point-to-point mode

   b. Multipoint mode

   c. Nonbroadcast mode

   d. Broadcast mode

   Answer: a

18. What is the default OSPF mode on a Frame Relay multipoint subinterface?

   a. Point-to-point mode

   b. Multipoint mode

   c. Nonbroadcast mode

   d. Broadcast mode

   Answer: c

19. What is the default OSPF mode on a main Frame Relay interface?

   a. Point-to-point mode

   b. Multipoint mode

   c. Nonbroadcast mode

   d. Broadcast mode

   Answer: c

Chapter 5

1. True or false: OSPF performs route summarization by default.

   Answer: False

2. True or false: In a large network where topological changes are frequent, routers spend many CPU cycles recalculating the SPF algorithm and updating the routing table.

   Answer: True

3. Match the type of router with its description:

Type of Router	Description
1—Internal router	**A**—A router that sits in the perimeter of the backbone area and that has at least one interface connected to area 0. It maintains OSPF routing information using the same procedures and algorithms as an internal router.
2—Backbone router	**B**—A router that has interfaces attached to multiple areas, maintains separate LSDBs for each area to which it connects, and routes traffic destined for or arriving from other areas. This router is an exit point for the area, which means that routing information destined for another area can get there only via the local area's router of this type. This kind of router can be configured to summarize the routing information from the LSDBs of its attached areas. This router distributes the routing information into the backbone.
3—ABR	**C**—A router that has all its interfaces in the same area.
4—ASBR	**D**—A router that has at least one interface attached to an external internetwork (another AS), such as a non-OSPF network. This router can import non-OSPF network information to the OSPF network and vice versa; this process is called route redistribution.

Answer:

1—C

2—A

3—B

4—D

4. How many different types of LSAs are there?

    a. 5

    b. 9

    c. 10

    d. 11

Answer: d

5. What kind of router generates LSA type 5?

    a. DR

    b. ABR

    c. ASBR

    d. ADR

Answer: c

6. True or false: By default, OSPF does not automatically summarize groups of contiguous subnets.

Answer: True

7. Where does a type 1 LSA flood to?

    a. To immediate peers

    b. To all other routers in the area where it originated

    c. To routers located in other areas

    d. To all areas

Answer: b

8. How does a routing table reflect the link-state information of an intra-area route?

    a. The route is marked with O.

    b. The route is marked with I.

    c. The route is marked with IO.

    d. The route is marked with EA.

    e. The route is marked with O IA.

Answer: a

9. Which type of external route is the default?

   a. E1.

   b. E2.

   c. E5.

   d. There is no default external route. OSPF adapts and chooses the most accurate one.

   Answer: b

10. E1 external routes calculate the cost by adding what?

   a. The internal cost of each link the packet crosses

   b. The external cost to the internal cost of each link the packet crosses

   c. The external cost only

   d. All area costs, even those that are not used

   Answer: b

11. What does the OSPF **max-lsa** command do?

   a. Defines the maximum number of LSAs that the router can generate

   b. Protects the router from an excessive number of received (non-self-generated) LSAs in its LSDB

   c. Defines the maximum size of the LSAs that the router generates

   d. Protects the router from excessively large received (non-self-generated) LSAs in its LSDB

   Answer: b

12. How is the OSPF metric calculated, by default?

   a. OSPF calculates the OSPF metric for a router according to the bandwidth of all its interfaces.

   b. OSPF calculates the OSPF metric by referencing the DR.

   c. OSPF calculates the OSPF metric for an interface according to the interface's inverse bandwidth.

   d. OSPF calculates the OSPF metric by using the lowest bandwidth value among all of its interfaces.

   Answer: c

13. Why is configuring a stub area advantageous?

    a. It reduces the size of the LSDB inside an area.

    b. It increases the memory requirements for routers in that area.

    c. It further segments the hierarchy.

    d. It starts to behave like a distance vector routing protocol, thus speeding up convergence.

Answer: a

14. A stub area is typically created using what kind of topology?

    a. Point to point

    b. Broadcast

    c. Hub and spoke

    d. Full mesh

Answer: c

15. True or false: By default, in standard areas, routers generate default routes.

Answer: False

16. What command makes an OSPF router generate a default route?

    a. **ospf default-initiate**

    b. **default-information originate**

    c. **default information-initiate**

    d. **ospf information-originate**

Answer: b

17. If your router has an interface faster than 100 Mbps that is used with OSPF, consider using the _____ command under the _____ process.

    a. **auto-cost reference-bandwidth**, OSPF

    b. **auto-cost reference-bandwidth**, interface

    c. **autocost reference-speed**, OSPF

    d. **autocost reference-speed**, interface

Answer: a

18. True or false: OSPF design requires that all areas be directly connect to the backbone.

Answer: True

19. True or false: Virtual links are very useful, and you should include them in your network architecture when designing a completely new OSPF network.

Answer: False

20. Which of the following would result in the smallest routing tables on OSPF internal routers?

   a. Stub area

   b. Totally stubby area

   c. Standard area

   d. Transit area

Answer: b

21. What is the default OSPF authentication?

   a. Simple password

   b. MD5

   c. Null

   d. IPsec

Answer: c

22. True or false: When configuring OSPF authentication, each router must have a unique password configured.

Answer: False

23. What command is used to troubleshoot OSPF authentication?

   a. debug ip ospf adj

   b. debug ip ospf auth

   c. debug ip ospf md5

   d. debug ip ospf packet

Answer: a

24. True or false: Only one MD5 OSPF authentication key can be configured at a time on a Cisco router.

Answer: False

Chapter 6

1. Which of the following does Integrated IS-IS support?

    a. BGP

    b. IP

    c. OSPF

    d. IPX

Answer: b

2. What is an IS? What is an ES?

Answer: An IS is a router. An ES is a host.

3. Because IS-IS is protocol independent, it can support which of the following?

    a. IPv4

    b. IPv6

    c. OSI CLNS

    d. All of the above

Answer: d

4. IS-IS routers use what to establish and maintain neighbor relationships?

    a. OSHs

    b. IIHs

    c. ISKs

    d. CLHs

Answer: b

5. As soon as neighbor adjacency is established, IS-IS routers exchange link-state information using what?

    a. Link-state packets

    b. Logical state packets

    c. Adjacency state packets

    d. Reachability state packets

Answer: a

6. Describe the four OSI routing levels.

Answer: The following are the OSI routing levels:

— Level 0 routing is conducted by ES-IS.

— Level 1 and Level 2 routing are functions of IS-IS.

— The Interdomain Routing Protocol (IDRP) conducts Level 3 routing; Cisco routers do not support IDRP.

7. What are some of the similarities between OSPF and IS-IS?

Answer: The OSPF and IS-IS routing protocols have the following characteristics:

— They are open standard link-state routing protocols.

— They support VLSM.

— They use similar mechanisms (link-state advertisements [LSAs], link-state aging timers, and link-state database synchronization) to maintain the health of the LSDB.

— They use the shortest path first (SPF) algorithm, with similar update, decision, and flooding processes.

— They are successful in the largest and most demanding deployments (Internet Service Provider [ISP] networks).

— They converge quickly after network changes.

8. What are CLNS addresses used by routers called?

  a. DSAPs

  b. NOTs

  c. MSAPs

  d. NETs

Answer: d

9. What are NSAP addresses equivalent to?

  a. A combination of the IP address and upper-layer protocol in an IP header

  b. Layer 2 addresses

  c. A combination of the transport layer address and data link address

  d. Layer 4 addresses

Answer: a

10. The Cisco implementation of Integrated IS-IS divides the NSAP address into what three fields?

   a. The data-link address, the logical address, and the upper-layer address

   b. The PDU address, the NSAP selector, and the cluster ID

   c. The area address, the system ID, and the NSAP selector

   d. The transport layer address, the CPU ID, and the NSAP selector

   Answer: c

11. True or false: Cisco routers routing CLNS data do not use addressing that conforms to the ISO 10589 standard.

   Answer: False

12. What is the first part of a NET?

   a. Zone address

   b. Area address

   c. Cluster address

   d. ISO address

   Answer: b

13. How does an IS-IS L1/L2 router route a packet?

   Answer: An L1 IS sends a packet to the nearest L1/L2 IS. The L1/L2 IS routes by area address to other L1/L2 or L2 ISs. Forwarding through L1/L2 or L2 ISs, by area address, continues until the packet reaches an L1/L2 or L2 IS in the destination area. Within the destination area, ISs forward the packet along the best path, routing by system ID, until the destination ES is reached.

14. What kind of IS-IS router is aware of only the local area topology?

   a. External

   b. Level 2

   c. Internal

   d. Level 1

   Answer: d

15. Routing between IS-IS areas is based on what?

    a. Area address

    b. IP address

    c. Level 2

    d. Level 1/Level 2

Answer: a

16. True or false: In IS-IS, area boundaries fall on the links.

Answer: True

17. True or false: Symmetrical routing is a feature of IS-IS.

Answer: False

18. What does the IS-IS route leaking feature do?

Answer: Route leaking helps reduce sub-optimal routing by providing a mechanism for leaking, or redistributing, L2 information into L1 areas. By having more detail about interarea routes, a L1 router is able to make a better choice with regard to which L1/L2 router to forward the packet.

19. In IS-IS, PDUs are encapsulated directly into an OSI data-link frame, so there is no what?

    a. ISO or area address header

    b. CLNP or IP header

    c. ES or IP header

    d. CLNS or area address header

Answer: b

20. Cisco IOS Software automatically uses IS-IS broadcast mode for which two of the following?

    a. Dialer interfaces

    b. LAN interfaces

    c. Multipoint WAN interfaces

    d. Point-to-point subinterfaces

Answer: b, c

21. True or false: IS-IS offers support specifically for NBMA networks.

Answer: False

22. In IS-IS, rather than having each router connected to a LAN advertise an adjacency with every other router on the LAN, each router just advertises a single adjacency to what?

   a. Area

   b. Cluster

   c. LSDB

   d. Pseudo-node

Answer: d

23. True or false: IS-IS maintains the L1 and L2 LSPs in different LSDBs.

Answer: True

24. True or false: CSNPs are periodically sent on point-to-point links.

Answer: False

25. When configuring Integrated IS-IS for IP, which command is required to be configured on an interface?

   a. **ip router net**

   b. **router isis net**

   c. **ip router isis**

   d. **ip isis router**

Answer: c

26. What is the default IS-IS metric on an interface of a Cisco router? How can this be changed?

Answer: The default IS-IS interface metric is 10. To change the metric value, use the **isis metric** *metric* [*delay-metric* [*expense-metric* [*error-metric*]]] {**level-1** | **level-2**} interface configuration command. Alternately, the **metric** *default-value* {**level-1** | **level-2**} router configuration command can be used to change the metric value for all IS-IS interfaces.

27. What does "i L2" indicate in the output of the **show ip route isis** command?

Answer: The **show ip route isis** command displays the IS-IS routes in the IP routing table. The i L2 tag indicates that the route was learned by IS-IS and it is from Level 2.

28. What is a subnetwork point of attachment (SNPA)?

Answer: The SNPA is the point that provides subnetwork services. SNPA is the equivalent of the Layer 2 address corresponding to the NET or NSAP address. The SNPA is assigned by using one of the following:

— The MAC address on a LAN interface.

— The virtual circuit ID from X.25 or ATM connections, or the data-link connection identifier (DLCI) from Frame Relay connections.

— For High-Level Data Link Control (HDLC) interfaces, the SNPA is simply set to "HDLC."

Chapter 7

1. What are some of the things you need to consider when migrating to another routing protocol?

Answer:

An accurate topology map of the network and an inventory of all network devices

A hierarchical network structure

A redistribution strategy

A new addressing scheme and address summarization

2. List some things you may need to consider when transitioning to a new IP addressing plan.

Answer:

Host addressing

Access lists and other filters

NAT

DNS

Timing and transition strategy

3. A router is configured with a primary and secondary address on its FastEthernet 0/0 interface. It is also configured to run EIGRP on this interface. How will the secondary address interact with EIGRP?

Answer: EIGRP uses an interface's primary IP address as the source of its updates, and it expects the routers on both sides of a link to belong to the same subnet. Therefore, EIGRP will not use the secondary address on the interface.

4. What steps are involved when migrating to a new routing protocol?

    Answer:

    Step 1   Create a clear and comprehensive timeline for all the steps in the migration, including implementing and testing the new router configurations.

    Step 2   Determine which routing protocol is the core and which is the edge.

    Step 3   Identify the boundary routers where the multiple routing protocols will run.

    Step 4   Determine how you want to redistribute information between the core and edge routing protocols.

    Step 5   Verify that all devices support the new routing protocol.

    Step 6   Implement and test the routing solution in a lab environment.

5. List some reasons why you might use multiple routing protocols in a network.

    Answer:

    When you are migrating from an older IGP to a new IGP, multiple redistribution boundaries might exist until the new protocol has displaced the old protocol completely.

    You want to use another protocol, but you need to keep the old protocol because of the host systems' needs.

    Different departments might not want to upgrade their routers to support a new routing protocol.

    If you have a mixed-router vendor environment, you can use a Cisco-specific protocol in the Cisco portion of the network and use a common standards-based routing protocol to communicate with non-Cisco devices.

6. What is redistribution?

    Answer: Cisco routers allow internetworks using different routing protocols (referred to as routing domains or autonomous systems) to exchange routing information through a feature called route redistribution. Redistribution is defined as the capability of boundary routers connecting different routing domains to exchange and advertise routing information between those routing domains (autonomous systems).

7. Does redistributing between two routing protocols change the routing table on the router that is doing the redistribution?

    Answer: No. Redistribution is always performed outbound. The router doing the redistribution does not change its routing table.

8.   What are some issues that arise with redistribution?

Answer: The key issues that may arise with redistribution are routing loops, incompatible routing information, and inconsistent convergence times.

9.   What may be the cause of a routing loop in a network that has redundant paths between two routing processes?

Answer: Depending on how you employ redistribution, routers might send routing information received from one autonomous system back into that same autonomous system. The feedback is similar to the routing loop problem that occurs with distance vector protocols.

10.   What two parameters do routers use to select the best path when they learn two or more routes to the same destination from different routing protocols?

Answer:

Each routing protocol is prioritized in order from most to least believable (reliable) using a value called administrative distance. This criterion is the first thing a router uses to determine which routing protocol to believe if more than one protocol provides route information for the same destination.

The routing metric is a value representing the path between the local router and the destination network, according to the routing protocol being used. The metric is used to determine the routing protocol's "best" path to the destination.

11.   Fill in the default administrative distances for the following routing protocols.

Answer:

Routing Protocols	Default Administrative Distance Value
Connected interface	0
Static route out an interface	0
Static route to a next-hop address	1
EIGRP summary route	5
External BGP	20
Internal EIGRP	90
IGRP	100
OSPF	110
IS-IS	115

(Continued)

Routing Protocols	Default Administrative Distance Value
RIPv1 and RIPv2	120
EGP	140
ODR	160
External EIGRP	170
Internal BGP	200
Unknown	255

12. When configuring a default metric for redistributed routes, should the metric be set to a value *larger* or *smaller* than the largest metric within the receiving autonomous system?

    Answer: When configuring a default metric for redistributed routes, set the metric to a value larger than the largest metric within the receiving autonomous system.

13. Fill in the default seed metrics for the following protocols.

    Answer:

Protocol That the Route Is Redistributed Into	Default Seed Metric
RIP	0, which is interpreted as infinity
IGRP/EIGRP	0, which is interpreted as infinity
OSPF	20 for all except BGP routes, which have a default seed metric of 1
IS-IS	0
BGP	BGP metric is set to IGP metric value

14. What is the safest way to perform redistribution between two routing protocols?

    Answer: The safest way to perform redistribution is to redistribute routes in only one direction, on only one boundary router within the network.

15. Can redistribution be configured between IPX RIP and IP RIP? Between IPX EIGRP and IP EIGRP? Between IP EIGRP and OSPF?

    Answer: You can redistribute only protocols that support the same protocol stack. Therefore, redistribution cannot be configured between IPX RIP and IP RIP or between IPX EIGRP and IP EIGRP. Redistribution can be configured between IP EIGRP and OSPF.

16. When configuring redistribution into RIP, what is the *metric-value* parameter?

    Answer: The *metric-value* parameter in the **redistribute** command for RIP is an optional parameter used to specify the RIP seed metric for the redistributed route. The default seed metric for RIP is 0, which is interpreted as infinity. The metric for RIP is hop count.

17. Router A is running RIPv2 and OSPF. In the RIPv2 domain, it learns about the 10.1.0.0/16 and 10.3.0.0/16 routes. In the OSPF domain, it learns about the 10.5.0.0/16 and 172.16.1.0/24 routes. What is the result of the following configuration on Router A?

    ```
    router ospf 1
      redistribute rip metric 20
    ```

    Answer: The **subnets** keyword is not configured on this **redistribute** command. As a result, the 10.1.0.0/16 and 10.3.0.0/16 routes are *not* redistributed into the OSPF domain.

18. What are the five components of the EIGRP routing metric?

    Answer:

    Bandwidth—The route's minimum bandwidth in kbps

    Delay—Route delay in tens of microseconds

    Reliability—The likelihood of successful packet transmission expressed as a number from 0 to 255, where 255 means that the route is 100 percent reliable

    Loading—The route's effective loading, expressed as a number from 1 to 255, where 255 means that the route is 100 percent loaded

    MTU—Maximum transmission unit, the maximum packet size along the route in bytes. An integer greater than or equal to 1

19. When redistributing routes into IS-IS, what is the default *level-value* parameter?

    Answer: The default for *level-value* is **level-2**.

20. What happens if you use the **metric** parameter in a **redistribute** command and you use the **default-metric** command?

    Answer: If you use the **metric** parameter in a **redistribute** command, you can set a different default metric for each protocol being redistributed. A metric configured in a **redistribute** command overrides the value in the **default-metric** command for that one protocol.

21. What does the **passive-interface default** command do?

    Answer: The **passive-interface** command prevents routing updates for a routing protocol from being sent through a router interface. The **passive-interface default** command sets all router interfaces to passive.

22. Suppose you have a dialup WAN connection between site A and site B. What can you do to prevent excess routing update traffic from crossing the link but still have the boundary routers know the networks that are at the remote sites?

Answer: Use static routes, possibly in combination with passive interfaces.

23. A distribute list allows routing updates to be filtered based on what?

Answer: Options in the **distribute-list** command allow updates to be filtered based on factors including the following:

- Incoming interface
- Outgoing interface
- Redistribution from another routing protocol

24. What is the difference between the **distribute-list out** and **distribute-list in** commands?

Answer:

The **distribute-list out** command filters updates going *out of* the interface or routing protocol specified in the command, *into* the routing process under which it is configured.

The **distribute-list in** command filters updates going *into* the interface specified in the command, *into* the routing process under which it is configured.

25. What command is used to configure filtering of the routing update traffic from an interface? At what prompt is this command entered?

Answer: To assign an access list to filter outgoing routing updates, use the **distribute-list** {*access-list-number* | *name*} **out** [*interface-name* | *routing-process* [*routing-process parameter*]] command. This command is entered at the Router(config-router)# prompt.

26. True or false: In a route map statement with multiple **match** commands, all **match** statements in the route map statement must be considered true for the route map statement to be considered matched.

Answer: True

27. True or false: In a **match** statement with multiple conditions, all conditions in the **match** statement must be true for that **match** statement to be considered a match.

Answer: False. In a single match statement that contains multiple conditions, at least one condition in the match statement must be true for that match statement to be considered a match.

28. What are some applications of route maps?

Answer:

Route filtering during redistribution

PBR

NAT

BGP

29. What is the *map-tag* parameter in a **route-map** command?

Answer: *map-tag* is the name of the route map.

30. What commands would be used to configure the use of a route map called TESTING when redistributing OSPF 10 traffic into RIP?

Answer:

```
router rip
   redistribute ospf 10 route-map TESTING
```

31. What does the following command do?

```
distance 150 0.0.0.0 255.255.255.255 3
```

Answer: The **distance** command is used to change the default administrative distance of routes from specific source addresses that are permitted by an access list. The parameters in this command are as follows:

Parameter	Description
150	Defines the administrative distance that specified routes are assigned
0.0.0.0 255.255.255.255	Defines the source address of the router supplying the routing information—in this case, any router
3	Defines the access list to be used to filter incoming routing updates to determine which will have their administrative distance changed

Thus, routes matching access list 3 from any router are assigned an administrative distance of 150.

32. What command can be used to discover the path that a packet takes through a network?

Answer: The **traceroute** privileged EXEC command.

33. What are the three DHCP roles that a Cisco IOS device can perform?

Answer: Cisco IOS devices can be DHCP servers, DHCP relay agents, and DHCP clients.

34.   In what ways can DHCP addresses be allocated?

Answer: DHCP supports three possible address allocation mechanisms:

- Manual—The network administrator assigns an IP address to a specific MAC address. DHCP is used to dispatch the assigned address to the host.

- Automatic—The IP address is permanently assigned to a host.

- Dynamic—The IP address is assigned to a host for a limited time or until the host explicitly releases the address. This mechanism supports automatic address reuse when the host to which the address has been assigned no longer needs the address.

35.   What does the **service dhcp** command do?

Answer: The Router(config)#**service dhcp** command enables DHCP features on router; it is on by default.

36.   What must be enabled on an interface for the IOS DHCP relay agent to be enabled?

Answer: The Cisco IOS DHCP server and relay agent are enabled by default. However, the Cisco IOS DHCP relay agent will be enabled on an interface only when a helper address is configured to enable the DHCP broadcast to be forwarded to the configured DHCP server.

37.   Packets sent to which ports are forwarded by default when the **ip helper-address** command is configured on an interface?

Answer: By default, the **ip helper-address** command enables forwarding of packets sent to all the well-known UDP ports that may be included in a UDP broadcast message, which are the following:

- Time: 37

- TACACS: 49

- DNS: 53

- BOOTP/DHCP server: 67

- BOOTP/DHCP client: 68

- TFTP: 69

- NetBIOS name service: 137

- NetBIOS datagram service: 138

Chapter 8

1. What is the difference between an IGP and an EGP?

   Answer: An IGP is a routing protocol used to exchange routing information within an AS. An EGP is a routing protocol used to connect between autonomous systems.

2. What type of routing protocol is BGP?

   Answer: BGP is an exterior path vector routing protocol.

3. What is BGP multihoming?

   Answer: Multihoming describes when an AS is connected to more than one ISP. This is usually done for one of the following reasons:

   ■ To increase the reliability of the Internet connection so that if one connection fails, another is still available

   ■ To increase performance so that better paths to certain destinations can be used

4. What are three common design options for BGP multihoming?

   Answer:

   All ISPs pass only default routes to the AS.

   All ISPs pass default routes and provider-owned specific routes to the AS.

   All ISPs pass all routes to the AS.

5. What are some advantages of getting default routes and selected specific routes from your ISPs?

   Answer: Acquiring a partial BGP table from each ISP is beneficial because path selection will be more predictable than when using a default route. For example, the ISP that a specific router within the AS uses to reach the networks that are passed into the AS will be based on the BGP path attributes; it usually is the shortest AS-path. If instead only default routes are passed into the AS, the ISP that a specific router within the AS uses to reach any external address is decided by the IGP metric used to reach the default route within the AS.

6. What is a disadvantage of having all ISPs pass all BGP routes into your AS?

   Answer: This configuration requires a lot of resources within the AS, because it must process all the external routes.

7. A BGP router knows of three paths to a network and has chosen the best path. Can this BGP router advertise to its peer routers a route to that network other than the best path?

    Answer: No. BGP specifies that a BGP router can advertise to its peers in neighboring autonomous systems only those routes that it itself uses—in other words, its best path.

8. When is it appropriate to use BGP to connect to other autonomous systems?

    Answer: BGP use in an AS is most appropriate when the effects of BGP are well-understood and at least one of the following conditions exists:

    - The AS allows packets to transit through it to reach other autonomous systems (for example, it is a service provider).

    - The AS has multiple connections to other autonomous systems.

    - Routing policy and route selection for traffic entering and leaving the AS must be manipulated.

9. When is it appropriate to use static routes rather than BGP to interconnect autonomous systems?

    Answer: It is appropriate to use static routes rather than BGP if at least one of the following conditions exists:

    - A single connection to the Internet or another AS

    - Lack of memory or processor power on routers to handle constant BGP updates

    - You have limited understanding of route filtering and the BGP path-selection process

10. What protocol does BGP use as its transport protocol? What port number does BGP use?

    Answer: BGP uses TCP as its transport protocol; port 179 has been assigned to BGP.

11. How does BGP guarantee a loop-free AS path?

    Answer: The BGP AS path is guaranteed to always be loop-free, because a router running BGP does not accept a routing update that already includes its AS number in the path list. Because the update has already passed through its AS, accepting it again would result in a routing loop.

12. Any two routers that have formed a BGP connection can be referred to by what two terms?

    Answer: Any two routers that have formed a BGP connection are called BGP peer routers or BGP neighbors.

13. Write a brief definition for each of the following:

— IBGP

— EBGP

— Well-known attribute

— Transitive attribute

— BGP synchronization

Answer:

IBGP—When BGP is running between routers within one AS, it is called IBGP.

EBGP—When BGP is running between routers in different autonomous systems, it is called EBGP.

Well-known attribute—A well-known attribute is one that all BGP implementations must recognize. Well-known attributes are propagated to BGP neighbors.

Transitive attribute—A transitive attribute that is not implemented in a router can be passed to other BGP routers untouched.

BGP synchronization—The BGP synchronization rule states that a BGP router should not use or advertise to an external neighbor a route learned by IBGP unless that route is local or is learned from an IGP. BGP synchronization is disabled by default in Cisco IOS Software Release 12.2(8)T and later; it was on by default in earlier Cisco IOS Software releases.

14. What tables are used by BGP?

Answer: A router running BGP keeps its own table for storing BGP information received from and sent to other routers. This table is separate from the IP routing table in the router. The router can be configured to share information between the BGP table and the IP routing table. BGP also keeps a neighbor table containing a list of neighbors that it has a BGP connection with.

15. What are the four BGP message types?

Answer: The four BGP message types are open, keepalive, update, and notification.

16. How is the BGP router ID selected?

Answer: The BGP router ID is an IP address assigned to that router and is determined on startup. The BGP router ID is chosen the same way that the OSPF router ID is chosen—it is the highest active IP address on the router, unless a loopback interface with an IP address exists, in which case it is the highest such loopback IP address. Alternatively, the router ID can be statically configured, overriding the automatic selection.

17. What are the BGP states a router can be in with its neighbors?

Answer: BGP is a state machine that takes a router through the following states with its neighbors:

- Idle

- Connect

- Active

- Open sent

- Open confirm

- Established

Only when the connection is in the established state are update, keepalive, and notification messages exchanged.

18. What type of BGP attributes are the following?

— AS-path

— Next-hop

— Origin

— Local preference

— Atomic aggregate

— Aggregator

— Community

— Multi-exit-discriminator

Answer:

The following are well-known mandatory attributes:

- AS-path

- Next-hop

- Origin

The following are well-known discretionary attributes:

- Local preference

- Atomic aggregate

The following are optional transitive attributes:

- Aggregator
- Community
- The multi-exit-discriminator (MED) is an optional nontransitive attribute.

19. When IBGP advertises an external update, where does the value for the next-hop attribute of an update come from?

   Answer: When IBGP advertises an external update, the value of the next-hop attribute is carried from the EBGP update, by default.

20. Describe the complication that an NBMA network can cause for an update's next-hop attribute.

   Answer: When running BGP over a multiaccess network, a BGP router uses the appropriate address as the next-hop address to avoid inserting additional hops into the path. The address used is of the router on the multiaccess network that sent the advertisement. On Ethernet networks, that router is accessible to all other routers on the Ethernet. On NBMA media, however, all routers on the network might not be accessible to each other, so the next-hop address used might be unreachable. This behavior can be overridden by configuring a router to advertise itself as the next-hop address for routes sent to other routers on the NBMA network.

21. Complete the following table to answer these questions about three BGP attributes:

   — In which order are the attributes preferred (1, 2, or 3)?

   — For the attribute, is the highest or lowest value preferred?

   — Which other routers, if any, is the attribute sent to?

   Answer:

Attribute	Order Preferred In	Highest or Lowest Value Preferred?	Sent to Which Other Routers?
Local preference	2	Highest	Internal BGP neighbors only.
MED	3	Lowest	External BGP neighbors; those routers propagate the MED within their AS, and the routers within the AS use the MED, but do not pass it on to the next AS.
Weight	1	Highest	Not sent to any BGP neighbors; local to the router only.

22. When is it safe to have BGP synchronization disabled?

Answer: It is safe to have BGP synchronization disabled only if all routers in the transit path in the AS (in other words, in the path between the BGP border routers) are running BGP.

23. What does the **neighbor 10.1.1.1 ebgp-multihop** command do?

Answer: The **neighbor 10.1.1.1 ebgp-multihop** command sets the Time to Live (TTL) value for the EBGP connection to 10.1.1.1 to 255 (by default). This command is necessary if the EBGP neighbor address 10.1.1.1 is not directly connected to this router. An additional parameter for this command allows you to set the TTL to another value.

24. Which commands are used to configure Routers A and B if Router A is to run BGP in AS 65000 and establish a neighbor relationship with Router B in AS 65001? The two routers are directly connected but should use their loopback 0 addresses to establish the BGP connection; Router A has loopback 0 address 10.1.1.1/24, and Router B has loopback 0 address 10.2.2.2/24.

Answer: The BGP configuration for Router A is as follows:

```
RouterA(config)#router bgp 65000
RouterA(config-router)#neighbor 10.2.2.2 remote-as 65001
RouterA(config-router)#neighbor 10.2.2.2 update-source loopback 0
RouterA(config-router)#neighbor 10.2.2.2 ebgp-multihop 2
```

The BGP configuration for Router B is as follows:

```
RouterB(config)#router bgp 65001
RouterB(config-router)#neighbor 10.1.1.1 remote-as 65000
RouterB(config-router)#neighbor 10.1.1.1 update-source loopback 0
RouterB(config-router)#neighbor 10.1.1.1 ebgp-multihop 2
```

25. What command disables BGP synchronization if it is enabled?

Answer: Use the **no synchronization** router configuration command to disable BGP synchronization; in current IOS releases it is disabled by default.

26. Which command would Router A in AS 65000 use to activate an IBGP session with Router B, 10.1.1.1, also in AS 65000?

Answer: The **neighbor 10.1.1.1 remote-as 65000** router configuration command would be used.

27. What is the difference between the BGP **neighbor** command and the BGP **network** command?

Answer: The **neighbor** command tells BGP *where* to advertise. The **network** command tells BGP *what* to advertise.

28. What does the BGP **network 192.168.1.1 mask 255.255.255.0** command do?

Answer: If you configure **network 192.168.1.1 mask 255.255.255.0**, BGP looks for exactly 192.168.1.1/24 in the routing table. It might find 192.168.1.0/24 or 192.168.1.1/32, but it will never find 192.168.1.1/24. Because the routing table does not contain a specific match to the network, BGP does not announce the 192.168.1.1/24 network to any neighbors.

29. What does the **clear ip bgp 10.1.1.1 soft out** command do?

Answer: The **soft out** option of the **clear ip bgp** command allows BGP to do a soft reset for outbound updates. The router issuing the **soft out** command does not reset the BGP session; instead, the router creates a new update and sends the whole table to the specified neighbors. This update includes withdrawal commands for networks that the other neighbor will not see anymore based on the new outbound policy. (Note that the **soft** keyword of this command is optional; **clear ip bgp 10.1.1.1 out** does a soft reset for outbound updates.)

30. Which command is used to display detailed information about BGP connections to neighbors?

Answer: The **show ip bgp neighbors** command is used to display detailed information about BGP connections to neighbors.

31. What does a > in the output of the **show ip bgp** command mean?

Answer: The > indicates the best path for a route selected by BGP; this route is offered to the IP routing table.

32. What column in the **show ip bgp** command output displays the MED?

Answer: The metric column displays the MED.

33. How is the *established* neighbor state represented in the output of the **show ip bgp summary** command?

Answer: If the neighbor state is *established*, the State/PfxRcd column either is blank or has a number in it. The number represents how many BGP network entries have been received from this neighbor.

34. What type of authentication does BGP support?

Answer: BGP supports Message Digest 5 (MD5) neighbor authentication. MD5 sends a "message digest" (also called a "hash"), which is created using the key and a message. The message digest is then sent instead of the key. The key itself is not sent, preventing it from being read while it is being transmitted. This ensures that nobody can eavesdrop on the line and learn keys during transmission.

35. How can BGP path manipulation affect the relative bandwidth used between two connections to the Internet?

Answer: BGP path manipulation can affect which traffic uses which Internet connection. For example, all traffic going to a particular IP address or AS can be forced to go out one connection to the Internet, and all other traffic can be routed out the other connection. Depending on the volume of Internet traffic, the bandwidth of these connections is affected.

36. Describe what the following configuration on Router A does:

```
route-map local_pref permit 10
 match ip address 65
 set local-preference 300
route-map local_pref permit 20
router bgp 65001
 neighbor 192.168.5.3 remote-as 65002
 neighbor 192.168.5.3 route-map local_pref in
```

Answer: The first line of the route map called local_pref is a **permit** statement with a sequence number of 10; this defines the first **route-map** statement. The **match** condition for this statement checks all networks to see which are permitted by access list 65. The route map sets these networks to a local preference of 300.

The second statement in the route map called local_pref is a **permit** statement with a sequence number of 20, but it does not have any **match** or **set** statements. Because there are no match conditions for the remaining networks, they are all permitted with their current settings. In this case, the local preference for the remaining networks stays set at the default of 100. This route map is linked to neighbor 192.168.5.3 as an inbound route map. Therefore, as Router A receives updates from 192.168.5.3, it processes them through the local_pref route map and sets the local preference accordingly as the networks are placed into Router A's BGP forwarding table.

37. Place the BGP route selection criteria in order from the first step to the last step evaluated by placing a number in the blank provided.

Answer:

   10   Prefer the path with the lowest neighbor BGP router ID

   6   Prefer the lowest MED

   4   Prefer the shortest AS-path

   9   Prefer the oldest route for EBGP paths

   5   Prefer the lowest origin code

   1   Prefer the highest weight

   8   Prefer the path through the closest IGP neighbor

   2   Prefer the highest local preference

   3   Prefer the route originated by the local router

   11   Prefer the route with the lowest neighbor IP address

   7   Prefer the EBGP path over the IBGP path

38. What command is used to assign a weight to updates from a BGP neighbor connection?

Answer: The **neighbor** {*ip-address* | *peer-group-name*} **weight** *weight* router configuration command is used to assign a weight to updates from a neighbor connection.

Chapter 9

1. Why is IP multicast considered more efficient than unicast?

Answer: Multicast data is sent from the source as one stream; this single data stream travels as far as it can in the network. Devices only replicate the data if they need to send it out on multiple interfaces to reach all members of the destination multicast group.

2. What are some disadvantages of using UDP-based multicast applications?

Answer: Some disadvantages are as follows:

■ UDP's best-effort delivery results in occasional packet drops.

■ UDP's lack of congestion control may result in network congestion and overall network degradation.

- Duplicate packets may occasionally be generated as multicast network topologies change.

- Out-of-sequence delivery of packets to the application may result during network topology changes or other network events.

3. What is the range of multicast IP addresses?

Answer: The Class D multicast address range is 224.0.0.0 through 239.255.255.255.

4. Match the range of IP multicast addresses with its description:

Range of Addresses	Description
1—224.0.0.0 through 224.0.0.255	A—Globally scoped addresses
2—224.0.1.0 through 238.255.255.255	B—Organization local scope addresses
3—239.0.0.0 through 239.255.255.255	C—Local scope addresses
4—239.255.0.0/16 (and 239.252.0.0/16, 239.253.0.0/16, and 239.254.0.0/16)	D— Site-local scope addresses
5—239.192.0.0 to 239.251.255.255	E—Limited, or administratively, scoped addresses

Answer:

1—C

2—A

3—E

4—D

5—B

5. In an Ethernet address, which bit indicates that the frame is a multicast frame?

Answer: In the 802.3 standard, bit 0 of the first octet is used to indicate a broadcast or multicast frame.

6. How are IP multicast addresses translated to Layer 2 MAC multicast addresses?

Answer: The translation between IP multicast and layer 2 multicast MAC address is achieved by the mapping of the low-order 23 bits of the IP (Layer 3) multicast address into the low-order 23 bits of the MAC (Layer 2) address.

7. How many IP multicast addresses map to a Layer 2 MAC multicast address?

Answer: Because there are 28 bits of unique address space for an IP multicast address (32 minus the first 4 bits containing the 1110 Class D prefix), and there are only 23 bits mapped into the MAC address, there are five (28 − 23 = 5) bits of overlap. These 5 bits represent $2^5 = 32$ addresses. Thus, there is a 32:1 overlap of IP addresses to MAC addresses, so 32 IP multicast addresses map to the same MAC multicast address.

8. Which two types of devices is IGMP used between? Which two types of devices is CGMP used between?

Answer: IGMP is used between a host and its local router. CGMP is used between routers and switches.

9. Describe the difference between how a host leaves a group when it is running IGMPv1 versus when it is running IGMPv2.

Answer: IGMPv1 does not have a mechanism defined for hosts to leave a multicast group. IGMPv1 hosts therefore leave a group silently at any time, without any notification to the router. An IGMPv2 Leave Group message allows hosts to tell the router they are leaving the group.

10. To which address does a host send a multicast report in IGMPv2? In IGMPv3?

Answer: In IGMPv2, reports are sent to 224.0.0.2 (all multicast routers). In IGMPv3, reports are sent to 224.0.0.22 rather than 224.0.0.2.

11. What is IGMP snooping?

Answer: With IGMP snooping, a switch eavesdrops on the IGMP messages sent between routers and hosts, and updates its MAC address table accordingly. The switch must be IGMP aware to listen in on the IGMP conversations between hosts and routers.

12. Which statement best describes the interaction between the PIM protocol and a unicast routing protocol running on a network?

  a. There is no interaction between the two protocols.

  b. Only PIM or a unicast routing protocol can be run in a network; they cannot be run simultaneously.

c. PIM uses the routing table populated by the unicast routing protocol in its multicast routing calculations.

d. The unicast routing protocol uses the routing table populated by PIM in its multicast routing calculations.

Answer: c

13. Select the two true statements.

a. A shared tree is created for each source sending to each multicast group.

b. A source tree is created for each source sending to each multicast group.

c. A shared tree has a single common root, called an RP.

d. A source tree has a single common root, called an RP.

Answer: b, c

14. Which type of distribution tree does PIM-SM use?

Answer: PIM-SM uses a shared tree and therefore requires an RP to be defined.

15. What does the notation (S, G) indicate?

Answer: The notation (S, G) (pronounced "S comma G") is the forwarding state associated with a source tree, where S is the IP address of the source and G is the multicast group address.

16. What does the notation (*, G) indicate?

Answer: The notation (*, G) (pronounced "star comma G") is the default forwarding state for a shared tree, where * is a wildcard entry, meaning any source, and G is the multicast group address.

17. What is the recommended PIM mode on Cisco routers?

Answer: Cisco recommends PIM sparse-dense mode for IP multicast, because PIM-DM does not scale well and requires a lot of router resources, and PIM-SM has limited RP configuration options.

18. Which command enables IP multicasting on a Cisco router?

Answer: The **ip multicast-routing** global configuration command enables IP multicast on a Cisco router.

19. What are the multicast addresses 224.0.1.39 and 224.0.1.40 used for?

    Answer: An RP router sends an auto-RP message to 224.0.1.39, announcing itself as a candidate RP. An RP-mapping agent router listens to the 224.0.1.39 address and sends a RP-to-group mapping message to 224.0.1.40. Other PIM routers listen to 224.0.1.40 to automatically discover the RP.

20. Which command is used to display the IP multicast routing table on a Cisco router?

    Answer: The **show ip mroute** [*group-address*] [**summary**] [**count**] [**active** *kbps*] command displays the IP multicast routing table.

21. Which command is used on a Cisco router to display information about multicast routers that are peering with the local router?

    Answer: The **mrinfo** [*hostname | address*] command displays information about multicast routers that are peering with the local router (if no address is specified) or with the specified router.

22. What does the **show ip igmp groups** command display?

    Answer: The **show ip igmp groups** [*group-address | type number*] command lists the multicast groups known to the router—both local groups (directly connected) and those that were learned via IGMP.

Chapter 10

1. What are some of the features of IPv6?

    Answer: IPv6 features include a larger address space, a simplified header, support for mobility and security, and a richness of transition solutions.

2. How many bits are in an IPv6 address?

    Answer: There are 128 bits in an IPv6 address.

3. How long is the basic IPv6 packet header?

    Answer: The IPv6 packet header is 40 octets.

4. What is the flow label in the IPv6 packet header used for?

Answer: The 20-bit flow label field is new in IPv6. It can be used by the source of the packet to tag the packet as being part of a specific flow, allowing multilayer switches and routers to handle traffic on a per-flow basis rather than per-packet, for faster packet-switching performance. This field can also be used to provide QoS.

5. Does the IPv6 packet header have a checksum field?

Answer: The IPv6 header does not have a header checksum field. Because link-layer technologies perform checksum and error control and are considered relatively reliable, an IP header checksum is considered to be redundant. Without the IP header checksum, upper-layer checksums, such as within UDP, are now mandatory.

6. In general which node processes IPv6 extension headers?

Answer: Generally, extension headers are not examined or processed by any node other than the node to which the packet is destined. The destination node examines the first extension header (if there is one); the contents of an extension header determine whether or not the node should examine the next header. Therefore, extension headers must be processed in the order they appear in the packet.

7. In what format are IPv6 addresses written?

Answer: IPv6 addresses are written as hexadecimal numbers with colons between each set of four hexadecimal digits (which is 16 bits). The format is $x:x:x:x:x:x:x:x$, where x is a 16-bit hexadecimal field.

8. Which of the following are valid representations of the IPv6 address 2035:0001:2BC5:0000:0000:087C:0000:000A?

   a. 2035:0001:2BC5::087C::000A

   b. 2035:1:2BC5::87C:0:A

   c. 2035:0001:2BC5::087C:0000:000A

   d. 2035:1:2BC5:0:0:87C::A

   e. 2035:1:2BC5::087C:A

   Answer: b, c, d

9. What is the format of an IPv6 broadcast address?

   Answer: IPv6 does not have broadcast addresses.

10.   Which of the following are the true statements?

   a.   A packet that is sent to an IPv6 anycast address goes to the closest interface identified by that address.

   b.   A packet that is sent to an IPv6 anycast address goes to all interfaces identified by that address.

   c.   A packet that is sent to an IPv6 multicast address goes to the closest interface identified by that address.

   d.   A packet that is sent to an IPv6 multicast address goes to all interfaces identified by that address.

   Answer: a, d

11.   How is an IPv6 interface identifier created for Ethernet interfaces?

   Answer: The interface identifier used for Ethernet is based on the MAC address of the interface and is in an extended universal identifier 64-bit (EUI-64) format. The EUI-64 format interface ID is derived from the 48-bit link-layer MAC address by inserting the hexadecimal number FFFE between the upper 3 bytes (the organizationally unique identifier [OUI] field) and the lower 3 bytes (the vendor code or serial number) of the link-layer address. The seventh bit in the high-order byte is set to 1 (equivalent to the IEEE G/L bit) to indicate the uniqueness of the 48-bit address.

12.   What is the IPv6 unicast address space?

   Answer: The IPv6 unicast address space encompasses the entire IPv6 address range, with the exception of the FF00::/8 range (addresses starting with binary 1111 1111), which is used for multicast addresses.

13.   What is the IPv6 link-local prefix?

   Answer: The IPv6 link-local prefix is FE80::/10.

14.   What is the IPv6 multicast prefix?

   Answer: The IPv6 multicast addresses are defined by the prefix FF00::/8.

15.   What is an IPv6 solicited-node multicast address used for?

   Answer: Solicited-node multicast addresses on a link have addresses FF02::1:FFXX:XXXX, where the XX:XXXX is the rightmost 24 bits of the corresponding unicast or anycast address of the node. Neighbor solicitation messages are sent on a local link when a node wants to determine the link-layer address of another node on the same local link, similar to ARP in IPv4.

16. How does IPv6's stateless autoconfiguration work?

Answer: An IPv6 router on a local link can send (either periodically or upon a host's request) network information, such as the 64-bit prefix of the local link network and the default route, to all the nodes on the local link. Hosts can autoconfigure themselves by appending their IPv6 interface identifier (in EUI-64 format) to the local link prefix (64 bits).

17. How does IPv6 mobility work?

Answer: Each IPv6 mobile node is always identified by its *home address*, regardless of where it is. When it is away from its home, a mobile node is also associated with a *care-of address*, which provides information about the mobile node's current location. IPv6 packets addressed to a mobile node's home address are transparently routed to its care-of address. All IPv6 nodes, whether mobile or stationary, can communicate with mobile nodes.

18. What are some of the similarities between OSPFv2 and OSPFv3?

Answer: The similarities between OSPFv3 and OSPFv2 include the following:

- OSPFv3 uses the same basic packet types as OSPFv2: hello, DBD (also called DDP), LSR, LSU, and LSAck. Some of the fields within the packets have changed.

- The mechanisms for neighbor discovery and adjacency formation are identical.

- OSPFv3 operations over NBMA topologies are the same. The RFC-compliant nonbroadcast and point-to-multipoint modes are supported. OSPFv3 also supports the other modes from Cisco such as point-to-point and broadcast.

- LSA flooding and aging are the same.

19. Fill in the following table to indicate the OSPFv3 packet types.

Answer:

Packet Type	Description
1	Hello
2	DBD
3	LSR
4	LSU
5	LSAck

20. Which IPv6 multicast addresses does OSPFv3 use?

    Answer: The multicast addresses used by OSPFv3 are as follows:

    - **FF02::5**—This address represents all SPF routers on the link-local scope; it is equivalent to 224.0.0.5 in OSPFv2.

    - **FF02::6**—This address represents all DRs on the link-local scope; it is equivalent to 224.0.0.6 in OSPFv2.

21. How many bits is an OSPFv3 router ID?

    Answer: The OSPFv3 router ID remains at 32 bits.

22. What are the two new LSAs introduced in OSPFv3?

    Answer: The two new LSAs in OSPFv3 are as follows:

    - Link LSAs (type 8)—Type 8 LSAs have link-local flooding scope and are never flooded beyond the link with which they are associated. Link LSAs provide the link-local address of the router to all other routers attached to the link, inform other routers attached to the link of a list of IPv6 prefixes to associate with the link, and allow the router to assert a collection of options bits to associate with the network LSA that will be originated for the link.

    - Intra-area prefix LSAs (type 9)—A router can originate multiple intra-area prefix LSAs for each router or transit network, each with a unique link-state ID. The link-state ID for each intra-area prefix LSA describes its association to either the router LSA or the network LSA. The link-state ID also contains prefixes for stub and transit networks.

23. What is the OSPFv3 instance ID used for?

    Answer: An OSPF instance (also known as an OSPF process) can be considered a logical router running OSPF in a physical router. The instance ID controls selection of other routers as neighboring routers; the router becomes neighbors only with routers that have the same instance ID.

24. Which command is used to summarize IPv6 OSPF routes?

    Answer: To consolidate and summarize routes at an area boundary use the **area** *area-id* **range** *ipv6-prefix/prefix-length* [**advertise** | **not-advertise**] [**cost** *cost*] IPv6 OSPF router configuration command.

25.   What are some of the techniques available to transition from IPv4 to IPv6?

Answer: The two most common techniques to transition from IPv4 to IPv6 are dual stack and tunneling. Alternatively, mechanisms that allow communication between IPv4 and IPv6 nodes can be used.

26.   What addresses do the routers involved in 6-to-4 tunneling use?

Answer: Each 6-to-4 edge router has an IPv6 address with a /48 prefix, which is the concatenation of 2002::/16 and the hexadecimal representation of the IPv4 address of the edge router; 2002::/16 is a specially assigned address range for the purpose of 6-to-4 tunneling. The edge routers automatically build the tunnel using the IPv4 addresses that are embedded in the IPv6 addresses. For example, if the IPv4 address of an edge router is 192.168.99.1, the prefix of its IPv6 address is 2002:c0a8:6301::/48, because 0xc0a86301 is the hexadecimal representation of 192.168.99.1.

This appendix contains information about the equipment requirements for the Configuration Exercises in this book, along with the configuration commands for the backbone routers. This appendix is organized into the following sections:

- Configuration Exercise Equipment Requirements

- TFTP Server Setup

- Multicast Traffic Generator

- Configuration Exercise Setup Diagram

- Configuration Exercise Equipment Wiring

- Backbone Router Configurations

Configuration Exercise Equipment Requirements and Backbone Configurations

This book provides Configuration Exercises to give you practice in configuring routers. If you have access to real hardware, you can try these exercises on your routers; this appendix provides a list of recommended equipment and configuration commands for the backbone routers. However, even if you do not have access to any routers, you can go through the exercises and keep a log of your own running configurations or just read through the solutions. Commands used and solutions to the Configuration Exercises are provided within the exercises in each chapter.

Configuration Exercise Equipment Requirements

In the Configuration Exercises in this book, the network is assumed to consist of two pods, each with four routers. The pods are interconnected to a backbone. You configure one of the pods, pod 1. No interaction between the two pods is required, although you might see some routes from the other pod in your routing tables in some exercises if you have it configured. In most of the exercises, the backbone has only one router; in some cases, another router is added to the backbone. Each of the Configuration Exercises in this book assumes that you have completed the previous chapters' Configuration Exercises on your pod.

The equipment listed in Table B-1 is for two pods (each with four routers) and the backbone (with three routers).

Table B-1   *Configuration Exercise Equipment Requirements for Two Pods and the Backbone*

Quantity	Required Product Description	Recommended Product Number
3	PC, with one COM port, running Hyperterminal. One per pod and one for the backbone. The backbone PC must also have a 10/100 Ethernet interface; it may also function as a Trivial File Transfer Protocol (TFTP) server and would therefore also have TFTP server software installed. (Refer to the "TFTP Server Setup" section for more information.)	—
3	A/B/C/D switch to connect the pod or backbone PC to the router's console port.	—
1	4-port 10/100 switch to interconnect the backbone routers and the backbone PC.	Any switch with 410/100 ports
4	Router with 1 FastEthernet port and 1 serial port (2 per pod).	Cisco 2811 (with 1 WIC 2 A/S installed)
4	Router with 2 serial ports and 1 FastEthernet port (2 per pod).	Cisco 2811 (with 1 WIC 2 A/S installed)
2	Router with 1 FastEthernet port and 1 serial port (for the backbone BBR1 and BBR2 routers).	Cisco 2811 (with 1 WIC 2 A/S installed)
10	2-port async/sync serial WAN interface card for 2811 routers.	WIC 2 A/S
10	Version 12.4(4)T1 Cisco IOS advanced IP services software for the pod and backbone BBR1 and BBR2 routers (refer to your router's documentation for Flash and RAM memory requirements).	c2800nm-advipservicesk9-mz.124-4.T1
1	Router with 1 Ethernet port and 6 serial ports (for the Frame_Switch Frame Relay backbone).	Cisco 3620 (with NM-1E module installed in slot 0 [on the right] and NM-8A/S module installed in slot 1 [on the left])
1	Version 12.1(15) or later Cisco IOS Enterprise Plus software for the Frame_Switch Frame Relay backbone router (refer to your router's documentation for Flash and RAM memory requirements).	c3620-js-mz.121-15

Table B-1   *Configuration Exercise Equipment Requirements for Two Pods and the Backbone (Continued)*

Quantity	Required Product Description	Recommended Product Number
1	8-port asynchronous/synchronous serial network module (for the Frame_Switch Frame Relay backbone router; 6 serial ports required).	NM-8A/S
1	1-port Ethernet Network Module (for the Frame_Switch Frame Relay backbone router).	NM-1E
11	Power cord, 110V.	CAB-AC
10	V.35 Female data terminal equipment/data circuit-terminating equipment (DTE/DCE) crossover cable	CAB SS 2660x
4	Ethernet crossover CAT5 cable.	—
3	Ethernet straight-through CAT5 cable.	—

KEY POINT

Configuration Exercise Equipment

The Configuration Exercise diagrams and configurations provided in this book assume that the equipment stated in Table B-1 is used. If you use different routers or modules, you must adjust the connections and configurations accordingly.

TFTP Server Setup

KEY POINT

TFTP Functionality Not Required

The backbone PC is referred to as the *TFTP server* in this appendix and throughout the Configuration Exercises in the rest of the book. However, the Configuration Exercises do not actually use the TFTP functionality; the backbone PC's IP address is only used as a destination for pings, during connectivity testing in some of the exercises.

If you want to save your configurations to a TFTP server, you should install TFTP server software on the backbone PC.

The TFTP server should be configured with the static IP address 10.254.0.254 255.255.255.0. The default gateway on the TFTP server should be set to its own address, 10.254.0.254. (If you set the default gateway to be one of the core routers, you must change this setting during the Configuration Exercises, because not all core routers can be reached at all times.)

Multicast Traffic Generator

Chapter 9, "Implementing IP Multicast," includes an IP multicast Configuration Exercise. This exercise assumes that multicast traffic is coming from the backbone, using the 224.*x.x.x* addresses (where *x* is the pod number). During our testing, we used a Cisco proprietary traffic generator running on the router that is configured as the Frame Relay switch. Any traffic generator that can generate packets to the 224.*x.x.x* addresses will suffice.

Configuration Exercise Setup Diagram

The network consists of the following:

■ Two pods, each with four routers named P*x*R1, P*x*R2, P*x*R3, and P*x*R4, where *x* = the pod number

■ Two backbone routers, named BBR1 and BBR2

■ A third backbone router used as a Frame Relay switch, named Frame_Switch

Figure B-1 shows the Configuration Exercise setup diagram.

Figure B-1   *Configuration Exercise Setup Diagram*

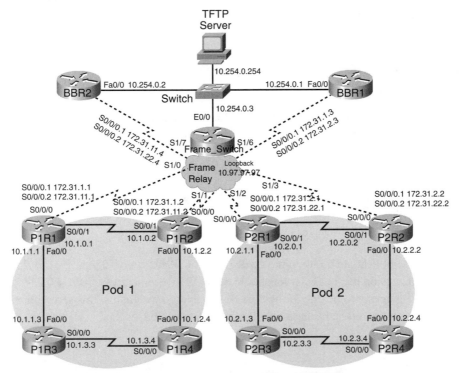

On All Pod Routers Loopback 0: 10.200.200.xy/32

NOTE   Figure B-1 is also posted on the Cisco Press website so that you can print it and copy it when you are doing the Configuration Exercises. See the section "Online Material" in the introduction for details.

The backbone router addresses shown in Figure B-1 are in the configurations provided in the "Backbone Router Configurations" section later in this appendix. The addresses shown for the pod routers will be configured in the Configuration Exercises.

NOTE   The backbone switch shown between the backbone devices in Figure B-1 is not shown in subsequent Configuration Exercise network diagrams.

Configuration Exercise Equipment Wiring

The Frame Relay backbone 3620 router requires six serial ports. All interfaces on the 3620 router are DCE. The Serial 0/0/1 interfaces on the P*x*R1 routers are DCE. The Serial 0/0/0 interfaces on the P*x*R3 routers are DCE. All other serial interfaces are DTE.

The Frame_Switch Frame Relay backbone router interfaces should be cabled as shown in Table B-2. (Note that interfaces S1/4 and S1/5 on Frame_Switch are unused.)

Table B-2   *Frame_Switch Cabling*

Frame_Switch Interface	Pod Router and Interface
S1/0 DCE	P1R1 S0/0/0 DTE
S1/1 DCE	P1R2 S0/0/0 DTE
S1/2 DCE	P2R1 S0/0/0 DTE
S1/3 DCE	P2R2 S0/0/0 DTE
S1/6 DCE	BBR1 S0/0/0 DTE
S1/7 DCE	BBR2 S0/0/0 DTE
E0/0	Backbone switch

The BBR1 and BBR2 Fa0/0 router interfaces and the TFTP server (backbone PC) should be connected to the backbone switch.

The remaining pod router interfaces should be cabled as shown in Table B-3.

Table B-3 *Other Pod Interface Cabling*

This Interface	Goes to This Interface
P*x*R1 S0/0/1 (DCE)	P*x*R2 S0/0/1 (DTE)
P*x*R3 S0/0/0 (DCE)	P*x*R4 S0/0/0 (DTE)
P*x*R1 Fa0/0	P*x*R3 Fa0/0
P*x*R2 Fa0/0	P*x*R4 Fa0/0

Backbone Router Configurations

The backbone routers need to be configured only one time, before the first Configuration Exercise. The text of the configurations is provided in the following sections. To use the configurations, create text files from the information provided. These configurations are written to be sent using the Transfer, Send Text File menu command in Hyperterminal into the devices' console port. Each configuration assumes that the router has no configuration. In other words, it assumes that the startup configuration has been erased and that the router has been reloaded.

> **NOTE**   The backbone router configurations are also posted as text files on the Cisco Press website. See the section "Online Material" in the introduction for details.

> **NOTE**   You might need to modify the configurations provided so that they work with the specific routers you are using. For example, if you have routers with fixed interfaces where we used routers with modular interfaces, you have to change how the interfaces are referenced.

Before sending a configuration file, go into privileged EXEC mode on the router. The configurations have **config t** commands at the beginning, followed by the necessary configuration commands, and then commands to save the configuration into nonvolatile random-access memory (NVRAM).

> **NOTE**   In each of the configurations provided, the enable secret password is set to *sanfran*, and the vty password is set to *cisco*; you might want to change these passwords.
>
> The last command in each configuration is **copy run start**. If you create your own text files, enter a carriage return after this command and then another carriage return. This ensures that the configuration is saved and that the router returns to the privileged EXEC prompt.

When testing similar configurations, we ran into a problem on some 3640 routers. Loading the files from Hyperterminal was too fast for the 3640. It would lose some of the commands, and then the rest of the file would get mixed up. To fix this problem in Hyperterminal, do the following:

1. Select File, Properties.

2. Click the **Settings** tab.

3. Click the **ASCII Settings** button.

4. Set the Line Delay to 200 milliseconds. (You might have to increase the line delay further if you get errors.)

BBR1 Configuration

Example B-1 provides the text of the configuration file for the BBR1 router.

Example B-1 *BBR1 Configuration*

```
!
!BBR1 configuration exercise configuration
!
! This file is designed to be copied and pasted into an erased router, at
! the # prompt.
!
! This configuration was tested with the c2800nm-advipservicesk9-mz.124-4.T1 IOS image
!
conf t
service timestamps debug datetime
service timestamps log datetime
no service password-encryption
!
hostname BBR1
!
enable secret sanfran
!
resource policy
!
ip subnet-zero
!
ip cef
!
no ip domain lookup
ip multicast-routing
!
voice-card 0
 no dspfarm
```

continues

Example B-1 *BBR1 Configuration (Continued)*

```
!
ip host bbr1 10.254.0.1 172.31.1.3 172.31.2.3
ip host bbr2 10.254.0.2 172.31.11.4 172.31.22.4
ip host Frame_Switch 10.254.0.3
ip host tftp 10.254.0.254
!
ip host P2R4 10.2.3.4 10.2.2.4
ip host P2R3 10.2.1.3 10.2.3.3
ip host P2R2 10.2.2.2 10.2.0.2 172.31.2.2 172.31.22.2
ip host P2R1 10.2.1.1 10.2.0.1 172.31.2.1 172.31.22.1
!
ip host P1R4 10.1.3.4 10.1.2.4
ip host P1R3 10.1.1.3 10.1.3.3
ip host P1R2 10.1.2.2 10.1.0.2 172.31.1.2 172.31.11.2
ip host P1R1 10.1.1.1 10.1.0.1 172.31.1.1 172.31.11.1
!
interface FastEthernet0/0
 description Backbone LAN Connection
 ip address 10.254.0.1 255.255.255.0
 ip pim sparse-dense-mode
 duplex half
 speed auto
 no shutdown
!
interface Serial0/0/0
 description Interface for Frame Relay Multipoint
 bandwidth 128
 no ip address
 ip pim sparse-dense-mode
 encapsulation frame-relay
 no fair-queue
 cdp enable
 no frame-relay inverse-arp
 frame-relay lmi-type cisco
 no shutdown
!
interface Serial0/0/0.1 multipoint
 description Frame Relay DLCI 111 and 112 for Pod 1
 ip address 172.31.1.3 255.255.255.0
 ip pim sparse-dense-mode
 ip rip send version 1 2
 ip rip receive version 1 2
 ip ospf network non-broadcast
 ip ospf priority 50
 cdp enable
```

Example B-1 *BBR1 Configuration (Continued)*

```
 frame-relay map ip 172.31.1.1 111 broadcast
 frame-relay map ip 172.31.1.2 112 broadcast
!
interface Serial0/0/0.2 multipoint
 description Frame Relay DLCI 121 and 122 for Pod 2
 ip address 172.31.2.3 255.255.255.0
 ip pim sparse-dense-mode
 ip rip send version 1 2
 ip rip receive version 1 2
 ip ospf network non-broadcast
 ip ospf priority 50
 cdp enable
 frame-relay map ip 172.31.2.1 121 broadcast
 frame-relay map ip 172.31.2.2 122 broadcast
!
!
router eigrp 1
 network 10.254.0.0 0.0.0.255
 network 172.31.0.0
 distribute-list 1 in
 no auto-summary
 no eigrp log-neighbor-changes
!
router ospf 1
 router-id 100.100.100.100
 log-adjacency-changes
 redistribute connected metric 50 subnets
 network 172.31.0.0 0.0.255.255 area 0
 neighbor 172.31.2.1
 neighbor 172.31.2.2
 neighbor 172.31.1.1
 neighbor 172.31.1.2
!
router rip
 version 2
 passive-interface FastEthernet0/0
 network 10.0.0.0
 network 172.31.0.0
 distribute-list 1 in
 no auto-summary
!
router bgp 64998
 no synchronization
 bgp log-neighbor-changes
 network 10.254.0.0 mask 255.255.255.0
```

continues

Example B-1 *BBR1 Configuration (Continued)*

```
 network 172.31.1.0 mask 255.255.255.0
 network 172.31.2.0 mask 255.255.255.0
 neighbor 10.254.0.2 remote-as 64999
 neighbor 10.254.0.3 remote-as 64997
 neighbor 172.31.1.1 remote-as 65001
 neighbor 172.31.1.2 remote-as 65001
 neighbor 172.31.2.1 remote-as 65002
 neighbor 172.31.2.2 remote-as 65002
 no auto-summary
!
ip classless
ip route 192.168.1.0 255.255.255.0 172.31.1.1
ip route 192.168.2.0 255.255.255.0 172.31.2.1
ip route 192.168.11.0 255.255.255.0 172.31.1.2
ip route 192.168.22.0 255.255.255.0 172.31.2.2
!
ip http server
no ip http secure-server
!
access-list 1 deny   0.0.0.0
access-list 1 permit any
!
control-plane
!
line con 0
 exec-timeout 60 0
 privilege level 15
 logging synchronous
line aux 0
line vty 0 4
 exec-timeout 5 0
 password cisco
 logging synchronous
 login
!
ntp server 10.254.0.2
end
copy run start
```

BBR2 Configuration

Example B-2 provides the text of the configuration file for the BBR2 router.

Example B-2   *BBR2 Configuration*

```
!
!BBR2 configuration exercise configuration
!
! This file is designed to be copied and pasted into an erased router, at
! the # prompt.
!
! This configuration was tested with the c2800nm-advipservicesk9-mz.124-4.T1 IOS image
!
conf t
service timestamps debug datetime
service timestamps log datetime
no service password-encryption
!
hostname BBR2
!
enable secret sanfran
!
resource policy
!
ip subnet-zero
!
ip cef
!
no ip domain lookup
ip multicast-routing
!
voice-card 0
 no dspfarm
!
ip host bbr1 10.254.0.1 172.31.1.3 172.31.2.3
ip host bbr2 10.254.0.2 172.31.11.4 172.31.22.4
ip host Frame_Switch 10.254.0.3
ip host tftp 10.254.0.254
!
ip host P2R4 10.2.3.4 10.2.2.4
ip host P2R3 10.2.1.3 10.2.3.3
ip host P2R2 10.2.2.2 10.2.0.2 172.31.2.2 172.31.22.2
ip host P2R1 10.2.1.1 10.2.0.1 172.31.2.1 172.31.22.1
!
ip host P1R4 10.1.3.4 10.1.2.4
ip host P1R3 10.1.1.3 10.1.3.3
```

continues

Example B-2 *BBR2 Configuration (Continued)*

```
ip host P1R2 10.1.2.2 10.1.0.2 172.31.1.2 172.31.11.2
ip host P1R1 10.1.1.1 10.1.0.1 172.31.1.1 172.31.11.1
!
interface FastEthernet0/0
 description Backbone LAN Connection
 ip address 10.254.0.2 255.255.255.0
 ip pim sparse-dense-mode
 duplex half
 speed auto
 no shutdown
!
interface Serial0/0/0
 description Interface for Frame Relay Multipoint
 bandwidth 128
 no ip address
 ip pim sparse-dense-mode
 encapsulation frame-relay
 no fair-queue
 no frame-relay inverse-arp
 frame-relay lmi-type cisco
 no shutdown
!
interface Serial0/0/0.1 multipoint
 description Frame Relay DLCI 211 and 212 for Pod 1
 ip address 172.31.11.4 255.255.255.0
 ip pim sparse-dense-mode
 ip ospf network point-to-multipoint
 cdp enable
 frame-relay map ip 172.31.11.1 211 broadcast
 frame-relay map ip 172.31.11.2 212 broadcast
 no frame-relay inverse-arp
!
interface Serial0/0/0.2 multipoint
 description Frame Relay DLCI 221 and 222 for Pod 2
 ip address 172.31.22.4 255.255.255.0
 ip pim sparse-dense-mode
 ip ospf network point-to-multipoint
 cdp enable
 frame-relay map ip 172.31.22.1 221 broadcast
 frame-relay map ip 172.31.22.2 222 broadcast
!
!
router eigrp 1
 network 10.0.0.0
 distribute-list 1 in
 no auto-summary
 no eigrp log-neighbor-changes
```

Example B-2 *BBR2 Configuration (Continued)*

```
!
router ospf 1
 router-id 200.200.200.200
 log-adjacency-changes
 redistribute connected metric 50 subnets
 network 172.31.0.0 0.0.255.255 area 0
!
router bgp 64999
 no synchronization
 bgp log-neighbor-changes
 network 10.254.0.0 mask 255.255.255.0
 network 172.31.11.0 mask 255.255.255.0
 network 172.31.22.0 mask 255.255.255.0
 neighbor 10.254.0.1 remote-as 64998
 neighbor 10.254.0.3 remote-as 64997
 neighbor 172.31.11.1 remote-as 65001
 neighbor 172.31.11.2 remote-as 65001
 neighbor 172.31.22.1 remote-as 65002
 neighbor 172.31.22.2 remote-as 65002
 no auto-summary
!
ip classless
!
ip http server
no ip http secure-server
!
access-list 1 deny   0.0.0.0
access-list 1 permit any
!
control-plane
!
line con 0
 exec-timeout 60 0
 privilege level 15
 logging synchronous
line aux 0
line vty 0 4
 exec-timeout 5 0
 password cisco
 logging synchronous
 login
!
ntp master 2
!
end
copy run start
```

Frame_Switch Configuration

Example B-3 provides the text of the configuration file for the Frame_Switch Frame Relay backbone router.

Example B-3 *Frame_Switch Configuration*

```
!
!Frame_Switch configuration exercise configuration
!
! This file is designed to be copied and pasted into an erased router, at
! the # prompt. The configuration is based on 3620 Router with Ethernet
! in slot 0 and an 8-port Serial Module in slot 1.
!
! This configuration was tested with the c3620-js-mz.121-15 IOS image
!
conf t
service timestamps debug uptime
service timestamps log uptime
service password-encryption
!
hostname Frame_Switch
!
enable secret sanfran
!
ip subnet-zero
ip cef
!
no ip domain-lookup
!
ip host bbr1 10.254.0.1
ip host bbr2 10.254.0.2
ip host Frame_Switch 10.254.0.3
ip host tftp 10.254.0.254
!
frame-relay switching
!
interface Loopback0
 ip address 10.97.97.97 255.255.255.0
!
interface Ethernet0/0
 description Backbone LAN Connection
 ip address 10.254.0.3 255.255.255.0
 no shutdown
!
interface Serial1/0
 description to P1R1 Serial 0/0/0
 no ip address
 encapsulation frame-relay
```

Example B-3   *Frame_Switch Configuration (Continued)*

```
 clockrate 115200
 frame-relay intf-type dce
 frame-relay route 111 interface Serial1/6 111
 frame-relay route 122 interface Serial1/1 221
 frame-relay route 211 interface Serial1/7 211
 no shutdown
!
interface Serial1/1
 description to P1R2 Serial 0/0/0
 no ip address
 encapsulation frame-relay
 clockrate 115200
 frame-relay intf-type dce
 frame-relay route 112 interface Serial1/6 112
 frame-relay route 212 interface Serial1/7 212
 frame-relay route 221 interface Serial1/0 122
 no shutdown
!
interface Serial1/2
 description to P2R1 Serial 0/0/0
 no ip address
 encapsulation frame-relay
 clockrate 115200
 frame-relay intf-type dce
 frame-relay route 121 interface Serial1/6 121
 frame-relay route 122 interface Serial1/3 221
 frame-relay route 221 interface Serial1/7 221
 no shutdown
!
interface Serial1/3
 description to P2R2 Serial 0/0/0
 no ip address
 encapsulation frame-relay
 clockrate 115200
 frame-relay intf-type dce
 frame-relay route 122 interface Serial1/6 122
 frame-relay route 221 interface Serial1/2 122
 frame-relay route 222 interface Serial1/7 222
 no shutdown
!
interface Serial 1/4
 no ip address
 shutdown
!
interface Serial 1/5
 no ip address
 shutdown
```

continues

Example B-3   *Frame_Switch Configuration (Continued)*

```
!
interface Serial 1/6
 description to BBR1 Serial 0/0/0
 no ip address
 encapsulation frame-relay
 clockrate 115200
 frame-relay intf-type dce
 frame-relay route 111 interface Serial1/0 111
 frame-relay route 112 interface Serial1/1 112
 frame-relay route 121 interface Serial1/2 121
 frame-relay route 122 interface Serial1/3 122
 no shutdown
!
interface Serial 1/7
 description to BBR2 Serial 0/0/0
 no ip address
 encapsulation frame-relay
 clockrate 115200
 frame-relay intf-type dce
 frame-relay route 211 interface Serial1/0 211
 frame-relay route 212 interface Serial1/1 212
 frame-relay route 221 interface Serial1/2 221
 frame-relay route 222 interface Serial1/3 222
 no shutdown
!
router eigrp 1
 network 10.0.0.0
 auto-summary
 no eigrp log-neighbor-changes
!
router bgp 64997
 no synchronization
 bgp log-neighbor-changes
 network 10.97.97.0 mask 255.255.255.0
 neighbor 10.254.0.1 remote-as 64998
 neighbor 10.254.0.2 remote-as 64999
 no auto-summary
!
ip classless
!
ip http server
!
control-plane
!
line con 0
 exec-timeout 60 0
```

Example B-3 *Frame_Switch Configuration (Continued)*

```
 privilege level 15
 logging synchronous
line aux 0
line vty 0 4
 exec-timeout 5 0
 password cisco
 logging synchronous
 login
!
ntp server 10.254.0.2
!
end
copy run start
```

Index

Symbols

(*, G), 614
(S, G), 612–614

Numerics

6-to-4 tunnels, migration to IPv6, 693–694
802.3 MAC address format, 599

A

ABRs (area border routers), 165–166, 227
    summarization, configuring, 242–244
access layer (hierarchical network model), 11
ACK packets, suppressing, 107
active IGMP version, displaying, 607
Active Process Enhancement feature
    (EIGRP), 120
active routes (EIGRP), 73
active state (BGP), troubleshooting, 540
AD (advertised distance), 71, 83–84
address bindings, 433–434
address format, IPv6, 657–658
address space (IPv6), 651–652
    need for increase in, 652–653
adjacencies (OSPF), 166
    displaying, 203–205
    in broadcast networks, 190–191
    in NBMA networks, 192
    in point-to-point networks, 189–190
adjacency database, 163
adjusting
    EIGRP hello interval, 75
    EIGRP link utilization, 103

administrative distance, 42–43, 383–384
    best path selection, influencing, 420–422
    modifying, 423–424
    redistribution, example of, 425–430
advanced distance vector protocols, 484
    EIGRP. *See* EIGRP
advantages of multicast, 596
AfriNIC (African Network Information
    Centre), 471
ALGs (application-layer gateways), 694
allocating IP addresses in multiple routing
    protocol environments, 374–377
ANSI (American National Standards
    Institute), 319
anycast addresses (IPv6), 663–664
anycast IPv6 addresses, 658
APNIC (Asia Pacific Network Information
    Centre), 471
application layer, Cisco SONA, 9
architectural frameworks for integrated
    networks, Cisco SONA, 7–9
area addresses, 326
area authentication command, 268
area virtual-link command, 263
areas, 164, 248–249
    NSSAs, configuring, 257–259
    standard areas
        default routes, injecting, 260
        routing table, interpreting, 255
    stub areas
        configuring, 250–252
        routing table, interpreting, 255–256
    totally stubby areas
        configuring, 252–254
        routing table, interpreting, 256–257
    verifying configuration, 260
    virtual links, configuring, 261–266

ISPs, 471
    BGP, multihoming, 476–477
        with default routes and partial table
            from all providers, 478–479
        with default routes from all providers,
            477–478
        with full routes from all providers, 480
ISs (intermediate systems), 312
is-type command, 349

K-L

keepalive messages (BGP), 497–498
key chains, 109

L0 routing, 313, 318
L1 routing, 318, 329
L1/L2 routing, 313, 329
L2 routing, 313, 319, 329
L3 routing, 319
LACNIC (Latin American and Caribbean IP
    Address Regional Registry), 471
LAN adjacencies, 343
Layer 2 multicast addresses, 598–600
Layer 2 switches, 608
    multicast switching
        CGMP, 608–609
        IGMP snooping, 609
Layer 3 protocols, IGMP, 608
Leave Group message (IGMPv2), 604
limiting EIGRP query range, 124–130
link utilization, EIGRP, 103–104
link-state routing protocols, 31, 162, 474
    IS-IS, 312–313
        comparing with OSPF, 319
        differences with OSPF, 321–323
        history of, 319–320
        LAN adjacencies, 343
        LSDB synchronization, 341–342
        LSP flooding, 340–341
        LSPs, 335–336
        PDUs, 334
        routing examples, 331–333
        routing levels, 312–313
        similarities to OSPF, 320
        WAN adjacencies, 343–344
    LSAs, 161

OSPFv3
    comparing with OSPFv2, 672–675
    configuring, 677–679
    LSAs, 675–676
    verifying configuration, 680–688
    shopping mall map analogy, 162
link-state sequence numbers field, 177–179
load balancing, EIGRP, 100–103
loading state, 175
local network control block, 597
local preference (BGP), configuring, 545–548
local preference attribute (BGP), 506
local scope IP multicast addresses, 597
loopback interfaces, configuring router ID on
    OSPF, 186
LSAs, 161, 228–229
    flooding process, 176
    for OSPFv3, 675–676
    link-state sequence number field, 177–179
    Type 1, 230–231
    Type 2, 231
    Type 3, 231–232
    Type 4, 232–233
    Type 5, 233
LSDB (link-state database), 161, 227, 234
    information, displaying, 235–236
    synchronization on IS-IS, 341–342
LSPs, IS-IS, 335–336
    flooding, 340–341
LSRefreshTime, 177
LSUs (link-state updates), 168

M

MAC addresses, 598
managing routing protocol migration,
    373–374, 378–379
manual binding, 433–434
manual summarization
    EIGRP, configuring, 98–100
    RIP, configuring, 40–41
manually configured tunnels, migration to
    IPv6, 691–692
many-to-many multicast applications, 595
maximum-paths command, 511
max-lsa command, 239
MBone (Multicast Backbone), 598

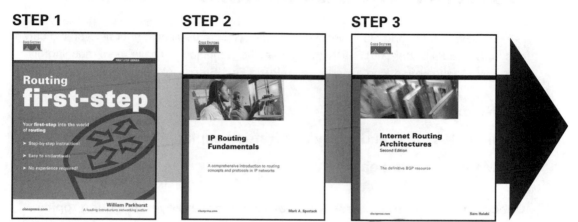

CISCO SYSTEMS

Cisco Press

CISCO SYSTEMS

Cisco Press

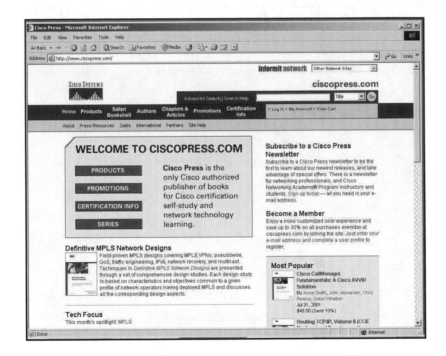

THIS BOOK IS SAFARI ENABLED

INCLUDES FREE 45-DAY ACCESS TO THE ONLINE EDITION

The Safari® Enabled icon on the cover of your favorite technology book means the book is available through Safari Bookshelf. When you buy this book, you get free access to the online edition for 45 days.

Safari Bookshelf is an electronic reference library that lets you easily search thousands of technical books, find code samples, download chapters, and access technical information whenever and wherever you need it.

TO GAIN 45-DAY SAFARI ENABLED ACCESS TO THIS BOOK:

- Go to **http://www.ciscopress.com/safarienabled**

- Complete the brief registration form

- Enter the coupon code found in the front of this book before the "Contents at a Glance" page

If you have difficulty registering on Safari Bookshelf or accessing the online edition, please e-mail customer-service@safaribooksonline.com.

CCNP Prep Center

CCNP Preparation Support from Cisco

Visit the **Cisco® CCNP® Prep Center** for tools that will help with your CCNP certification studies. Site features include:

- CCNP TV broadcasts, with experts discussing CCNP topics and answering your questions

- Study tips

- Practice questions

- Quizzes

- Discussion forums

- Job market information

- Quick learning modules

The site is free to anyone with a Cisco.com login.

Visit the **CCNP Prep Center** at **http://www.cisco.com/go/prep-ccnp** and get started on your CCNP today!